World Religions

From Ancient History
to the Present

World Religions

From Ancient History to the Present

Editor: Geoffrey Parrinder

Facts On File Publications
New York, New York ● Bicester, England

World Religions
From Ancient History to the Present

Copyright © 1971 by The Hamlyn Publishing Group Limited, Newnes Books
1983, a division of The Hamlyn Publishing Group Limited.

World Religions is a revised and updated edition of the book first published in
1971 as *Man and His Gods* in the United Kingdom and as *Religions of the
World* in the U.S.

Published in North America by Facts On File, 460 Park Avenue
South, New York, N.Y. 10016

Library of Congress Cataloging in Publication Data
Main entry under title:

World religions.

  Bibliography: p.
  Includes index.
  1. Religions. I. Parrinder, Edward Geoffrey.
BL80.2.W67 1984   291   83-1510
ISBN 0-87196-129-6

10 9 8 7 6 5 4 3 2 1

Printed in the United States

Contents

Foreword

The religions of the world provide a great record of human thought and artistic expression. From the earliest times of prehistory down to the present day people have expressed their deepest convictions about the universe and mortal life in worship and symbol. All the arts have been brought into the service of religion: architecture and sculpture, painting and writing, music and costume.

This book brings together studies of religions past and present. It seeks to present not only a study of religion in a narrow sense, but a picture of history, geography, social life, current affairs and international relationships.

An encyclopedia can be arranged alphabetically, with many long or short articles, on major items and trivial details. But such a book tends to become merely a work of reference, to be put aside and rarely consulted. The method adopted here is to provide articles on all the major religions, with reference to minor ones, and a comprehensive alphabetical index which refers back to the great and small topics discussed in the body of the work. This makes for a much more attractive and interesting display of the great variety of religious life in all countries of the world. The chapters can be read consecutively or at random, as each is complete in itself though often themes are continued in other chapters.

The different religions described in this encyclopedia are expounded by experts, all of them specialists on the particular religions which they study. It will be of interest to the average person, and it also provides reliable and scholarly work for the student. The illustrations help to explain beliefs and practices. Those who wish to continue with further study will find references and lists of authoritative books in the various fields described.

The arrangement of chapters must be arbitrary to some extent, but the one that is adopted here aims both at showing something of the development and historical position of the religions, and at including a wider range of religions than is generally found in such a comprehensive work. It is sometimes said that there are eleven living religions, and these can be noted in the list of contents, running from Ancient Iran to Islam, with China including Confucianism and Taoism as well as Buddhism. But such a division of living and dead, though excluding the virtually extinct religions of ancient Europe and the Near East, ignores those still living faiths of other continents which chiefly remain outside the scope of the historical religions.

Many pre-literate peoples, in Africa, Asia, Australasia and America, have been studied in recent times and more is now known of them than before. These continents have many tribes, and it is not possible to give accounts of all the tribal religions of Asia and Africa, so that a representative selection has been given. But in America the problem is even more acute, for before Columbus there were great cultures and religions in America which perhaps had no literature, in the strictest sense of scriptures, but they had complex calendars and symbolism. Pre-Columbian America has been placed therefore between the pre-literate African world and Northern Europe, to be followed by the literate cultures of Mesopotamia, Egypt, Greece and Rome.

There are many common themes in religion: 'human being, eternity, and God', as Wordsworth said. But there is also great diversity. As well as an underlying search for reality, there is an infinite variety of doctrine and mythology, of symbolism and ritual. This encyclopedia seeks to illustrate and explain these things.

Introduction

Religion has been present at every level of human society from the earliest times. But what exactly is it? The Oxford English Dictionary defines religion as 'the recognition of superhuman controlling power, and especially of a personal god, entitled to obedience'. Belief in a god or gods is found in most religions, but different superhuman powers are often revered, particularly those connected with the dead. There are many other elements of religious life which cannot be included in a short definition, but which appear in this encyclopedia.

The remains of prehistoric peoples reveal some aspects of their religious belief, which will be discussed in the next chapter, but there may have been much more which by its ephemeral nature could not leave physical traces for archaeologists to dig up thousands of years later. Many historical peoples have believed in a supreme god or providence, but often they built no temples and made few sacrifices, and so nothing tangible remains. There may have been further complicated systems of belief and worship in prehistory, which expressed the reactions of thinking men and women to the universe, but which have left no clues for later ages to piece together.

That religion has been universal, at all stages of history and human geography, does not necessarily mean that all individuals are religious, or religious to the same degree. Today some people claim to be irreligious, doubtful about or even hostile to all forms of religion, and they are called atheists if they deny the existence of any superhuman power, or agnostic if they hold that this cannot be known or established with certainty. It is likely that this was so to a lesser degree in the past, though such people probably appeared more among literate and individualistic peoples than in closely-knit societies. Socrates was condemned to death at Athens for teaching atheism to the young men, but in fact he had only criticized the myths about the Greek gods for being immoral. He believed in the immortality of the soul and in a divine genius which, he believed, guided him.

Psychologists tend nowadays to deny that there is a religious instinct, because it seems to be absent in animals with whom we share many physical instincts. But at the same time the capacity for religious response may be found in all people, though its quality varies considerably from individual to individual. Both social environment and upbringing are very important in the development of religious life, but differences between individuals, when they are allowed scope, produce various religious types.

Some people have supernormal experiences, while others are introspective thinkers, and both of these may be specially or persistently religious. Some others show an interest in religion only occasionally, in times of great need or when taking part in a social ritual. Even in apparently atheistic countries there are not only state rituals which resemble religious ceremonies but also special personalities who either lead the social pattern or break through it and seem to have a significance akin to the religious.

The study of religion reveals that an important feature of it is a longing for value in life, a belief that life is not accidental and meaningless. The search for meaning leads to faith in a power greater than the human, and finally to a universal or superhuman mind which has the intention and will to maintain the highest values for human life. There is an intellectual element in religion's search for purpose and value, and an emotional element in the dependence upon the power which creates or guarantees those values.

Religion and Morality

The intellectual and emotional sides of religion affect behaviour. Religion has always been linked with morality, though moral systems differ greatly from place to place. Whether morals can exist without religion or some supernatural belief has been debated, but at least all religions have important moral commandments. The famous laws of Hammurapi of Babylon, which date from about the eighteenth century BC, gave royal, feudal, legal and social prescriptions, but were said to have been received from the god of justice.

The philosopher A.N. Whitehead defined religion as what 'the individual does with his own solitariness', but religion always has a social side and it is expressed in patterns of behaviour. Sometimes there is a strong organization, such as a church, while at other times the model of religious life may be that of a lonely ascetic in a forest. But even the latter depends upon society for support: giving food is regarded as an act of religious merit and in return he or she blesses those who offer charity. The rules of moral behaviour in most societies have a strong religious basis, and they are supported by the teachings of scriptures and the actions of religious officials.

The study of religions depends upon many elements. Archaeology is particularly important for a knowledge of the prehistoric and ancient historic periods of human life. Anthropology and sociology consider the role of religion in the lives of individuals and societies, especially among modern illiterate peoples. The psychology of religion studies both the role of individuals and the effect of social activities upon their participants. The comparative study of religions takes account of both similarities and differences between religions, traces their history and examines similar patterns of behaviour. In addition to these, folklore, mythology, philosophy and theology, linguistics, music, art and almost any human activity can be important for understanding religious life.

The Origins of Religion

In his *Theogony* Hesiod made one of the first attempts to shape the stories of the Greek gods into a consistent whole, and Herodotus claimed that 'all men know equally about divine things'. But neither of these great writers can be reckoned as a critical historian of religion nor, despite their antiquity, did they discover its origin.

Speculations as to how, when and why religion began have flourished only in the last hundred years. Previously, in medieval and modern Europe, it was assumed that the first human beings, or Adam and Eve, in the creation myth of *Genesis*, had received a perfect revelation from a divine being, or that they had worked out a pure religion based upon the principles of reason. Theologians held that this early religion was corrupted by sin and the fall from grace, and rationalists declared that priests and ignorance had produced the idolatry and diversity of religion now found all over the world. In the nineteenth century the theory of evolution and the growth of a critical science of history forced people to consider the evolution of religion and speculate upon its possible origins.

In 1871 Edward B. Tylor coined the word 'animism' to describe his theory of religion. Derived from *anima,* the Latin word for the soul, the theory of animism suggested that primitive people had deduced from dreams, visions, delirium and the fact of death that they were inhabited by an immaterial soul. Since the dead appeared in dreams it was assumed that their spirits continued to exist after death, that they might dwell in various objects, and it was suggested that the dead gradually came to be regarded as gods. About the same time the sociologist and philosopher Herbert Spencer suggested that religion had its origins in visions or the appearance of the ghosts of the dead, and these ancestors were worshipped as gods. But Tylor, Spencer, and others who expounded such theories could not prove that really primitive people, in prehistoric times, had thought in this way, and the jump from ghosts or souls to divine spirits and gods was based upon conjecture. Even if it had happened sometimes there is no certainty that it was universal. Animism in this form is virtually abandoned as a scientific explanation of religion today.

A refinement of the theory of animism was suggested by R.R. Marett in 1899, who said that primitive humans did not at first conceive of personal souls, but believed in an impersonal force or forces which animated the world; this he called 'animatism'. His hypothesis was linked, rather unfortunately, with the word *mana* used by the Melanesians of the Pacific to express the idea of a spiritual power. It was assumed that all peoples had such a notion and that belief in this impersonal power was the origin of religion. Moreover, Marett considered that early peoples were actors rather than thinkers, saying that their religion was 'not so much thought out as danced out', and so it was very little different from magic in its early stages.

But later investigation showed that by *mana* the Melanesians did not mean an impersonal force animating the universe such as Marett and others supposed, but rather a quality in spirits and people which gave them distinction.

The Golden Bough

In 1890 James Frazer began publication of a long series of books, the chief of which was *The Golden Bough*. This opened with the story of a sacred tree guarded by a priest of Diana at Aricia in ancient Italy. Frazer thought that the view of the world as pervaded by spiritual forces was the idea behind the practice of magic, used by priests who were seeking to control nature.

He held that magic was the first stage of human intellectual development, a sort of primitive science, in which people imagined that they could influence their own lives and those of others by means of magical objects or incantations. Some magic could be described as sympathetic, because it had a resemblance or contact with its object by a 'law of similarity' or a 'law of contagion'. An example of the law of similarity was that many magicians made images of their enemies and stuck thorns into the places where they wished to produce pain. Following the law of contagion they used the hair or nails of the victim, or some object close to the person, in a ceremony designed to cause harm.

This description is generally accurate, but Frazer's further theories were severely criticized. He supposed that after the first magical phase had produced failures people imagined that there were supernatural beings which could help them, and so they turned to religion. This also turned out to be an illusion however, and eventually there came the knowledge of science and humans became logical and experimental. This hypothesis was attractive for a time because it seemed to fit in with the theory of evolutionary progress. But it was soon pointed out that there is no evidence for the assumption that magic came before religion – they have existed together at many levels of culture. The notion of a progress from magic to religion to science is unhistorical and many advanced and highly civilized peoples have been profoundly religious. Frazer's theories on the origins and development of religion are now abandoned, though some of his distinctions between the different kinds of magic are useful.

In 1922 Lucien Lévy-Bruhl advanced the theory of primitive mentality, in which he suggested that 'savages' used a 'pre-logical thinking' which was different from our own. He criticized the assumptions of other writers who stressed the similarities between all humans and imagined how they would act and think under primitive conditions. Lévy-Bruhl emphasized the different conditions and mental processes of civilized and primitive people. For example, he said that all 'uncivilized' races explain death by other than natural causes, as being due not simply to disease or the weakness of old age, but rather to the agency of a mystical force. He thought this a kind of socially accepted reasoning upon which experience had no effect.

But Lévy-Bruhl, like so many other writers on the origins of religion in the last hundred years, was an armchair theorist who had no experience of modern primitive peoples, and of course he had little knowledge of how prehistoric men and women thought. He made primitive people out to be much more superstitious than they are, since they do not live simply in an imaginary world but are close to nature and can only survive if they direct their lives by reason and experiment. Primitive people understand well how death is caused physically, though generally they also add a spiritual explanation.

The Social Importance of Religion

Another Frenchman, Émile Durkheim, had in 1912 already published his book on the elementary forms of religious life. He emphasized religion as a social fact and not simply the product of the psychology of certain individuals. It could not be an illusion, for religion was universal and had appeared in every age, producing great cultures and systems of morality and law. For Durkheim, however, religion is the worship of society itself, though it may be disguised by myths and symbols. Society is an abiding reality: it has full control over people and they depend upon it and pay it their reverence.

Illustration page 17

Durkheim tried to support his case from the example of some of the aborigines of Australia, an unhappy choice because he never went there, based his theory upon the incomplete researches of others, and then deduced that all primitive peoples have behaved like the aborigines. These aborigines belong to clans which hold certain plants or animals sacred and do not harm or eat them. Their sacred objects and pictures made of them were described as totems, because of their similarity to the totems of the North American Indians. Durkheim saw the totems as embodying the ideals of the clan, so that in fact people worshipped society itself. But the meaning of the Australian totems is still being debated: it differs from place to place, and the assumption that this was the earliest form of religion is unwarranted. Moreover, people do not usually worship society but claim to revere something greater and more abiding, often in opposition to the dominant organization of society.

An even less likely account of the origins of religion was put forward by the Austrian psychologist Sigmund Freud in 1913, in his book *Totem and Taboo*. Freud produced a theory based upon information about the behaviour of some Pacific tribes, and also of wild horses and cattle, that in ancient times the powerful father of the horde kept all the females to himself and drove away his growing sons. But the latter eventually became strong and 'one day' they joined forces, killed the father, and shared out the females among themselves. 'Of course these cannibalistic savages ate their victim,' said Freud, and by this meant that they identified themselves with the father whom they had feared, both acquiring his strength and giving him honour in repeated totemic feasts. They made totems of animals which were symbols of the power of the father. So, the totem feast would be the commemoration of this criminal act with which, he argued, social organization, morality, art and religion began.

There is no historical evidence for this astonishing theory. Freud was mistaken in thinking that primitive peoples ate their totems, for there is only one instance in the world where this has been noted, in Australia, and even there the evidence is confused. There is no historical, archaeological or other evidence for the supposition that religion began with a murderous attack on a father by jealous sons, or that religion spread from one place to all other lands, or that it began in such a manner all over the world. Great psychologist as he was, Freud went as wildly astray in his hypothesis of religious origins as he did in his speculations on Hebrew history in *Moses and Monotheism*.

One Supreme Being

In opposition to psychological or sociological theories of religious origins, some writers have put forward the claim that the earliest religious belief was in one supreme being. Andrew Lang in *The Making of Religion* in 1898, and Wilhelm Schmidt in *The Origin of the Idea of God* (1912–55), were two leading exponents of this view. Australia again was called upon to provide information for Lang, since it was said that some tribes there did not worship souls or spirits but all of them had an idea of a supreme god. And Wilhelm Schmidt, probably influenced by the story of Adam's knowledge of God in *Genesis*, followed by the Fall, spent many years accumulating evidence from all over the world to show that belief in god existed among the most primitive peoples and might be called the earliest form of religion. Later writers, while agreeing that many peoples have a belief in a heavenly god, who by location is high and lofty and often supreme over others, try to show that this belief has existed alongside faith in many other spiritual beings and gods, so that this is not a primitive monotheism, belief in one god, but an aspect of polytheism, belief in many gods.

In recent times the errors in speculations about the origins of religion have made scholars cautious. If religion is as old as thinking human beings, as seems likely, then its origins are so remote that it is improbable much evidence will appear to explain its beginnings. In any case religion is a complex phenomenon and may be the result of many causes. The great Rumanian authority, Mircea Eliade, says that the modern historian of religions knows that it is impossible to reach the origins of religion, and this is a problem that need no longer cause concern. The important task today is to study the different phases and aspects of religious life, and to discover from these the role of religion for humankind.

Some scholars have stressed the importance of the scientific study of the religious beliefs and practices of specific peoples, at different levels of material culture. Beliefs and rites must be studied as facts, whether or not they are appealing to the investigator. In the past too many theorists were concerned not simply to describe or explain religion but to explain it away, feeling that if the early forms were shown to be based upon illusions then the later and higher religions might be undermined. But in studying religion the believer may have a better chance of understanding other faiths than the sceptic, for the unbeliever often seeks to explain religion away, as psychological or sociological illusion. E. Evans-Pritchard says that 'the believer seeks rather to understand the manner in which a people conceives of a reality and their relations to it.'

The theory of evolution propounded by Charles Darwin in 1859 has been one of the most influential ideas of modern times and has affected many studies. It was applied to the development of religion by Herbert Spencer and others though some assumptions were made which later had to be discarded. It was assumed that evolutionary growth proceeded everywhere in the same manner, that all peoples passed through the same stages and that progress was inevitable. Those who now seem to be at a low stage of material culture were thought to have remained there from prehistoric times, while other peoples had progressed beyond them. Little attention was given to the fact of degeneration as well as progress. Thus those who are 'primitive' today were believed to show what religion was like in its earliest forms. On the other hand, the 'higher religions' were supposed to represent the supreme peak of religious development. Clearly many of these assumptions were unfounded, biased, or incapable of proof. There is no reason why all peoples should pass through the same stages of religious growth, and there are great differences that cannot be explained simply by inevitable development. Some quite 'primitive' people believe in a supreme god, while many advanced Buddhists do not.

Developing Beliefs

At the same time there is clearly development in many religions. The Buddhism of Tibet is widely different from that of Burma, and some forms of Christianity in Europe or America have travelled far in ritual and faith from those of the ancient Holy Land. There are many similarities of religion, but the differences are also numerous and need proper attention. Some religions have influenced each other historically, such as Judaism and Christianity, or Hinduism and Buddhism, but they also have their own internal dynamism and particularity. The decision as to which religions are 'higher' or more true than others is an act of personal assessment and faith, belonging to apologetic and mission, and it is beyond the purpose of this encyclopedia.

Belief in a god is a natural feature of most religions and is included under the general term 'theism'. Belief in one god alone is 'monotheism', and is seen in Judaism, Christianity and Islam, and in some of the most important religious groups in Hinduism and elsewhere.

Belief in many gods is 'polytheism' and these gods together are said to form a pantheon. However, within a pantheon one god may be supreme, a 'president of the immortals', like Zeus in ancient Greek mythology, who in theory dominates all others. 'Monolatry' appears when one group worships a single god yet recognizes that other people worship different beings, as when in the Bible the judge Jephthah professed to follow Yahweh but told the Moabites to possess the land which Chemosh their god gave them. Rather different is 'henotheism', concentration upon one god at a time while recognizing that other gods have a claim upon one at different times. Or one god may be recognized under different names, as when the vedic Indians said that 'they call it Indra, Mitra, Varuna, Fire, or the heavenly sun-bird. That which is One the sages speak of in various terms.'

Henotheism seems to prepare the way for monotheism, or it may develop into 'pantheism'. When people began to reflect upon the universe and its gods they sought some unifying principle to explain it. A famous dialogue in the Indian Upanishads reduces the gods from 3,306 to one, and that one is Brahman, the holy power. From this unification came pantheism, the idea that everything is god and god is everything. Perhaps this is more accurately termed 'monism', the doctrine that only one reality exists. Hindu thinkers called it 'non-dualism', meaning that there is no duality or difference between the human and the divine. In another direction 'dualism' was illustrated in the ancient Zoroastrianism of Iran, which postulated two principal spirits, one good and one evil. The term is also used of other forms of belief in which the eternal dualism or difference between god and human is taught.

Fetish and Totem

The word 'fetish' was introduced by the Portuguese to describe the 'made' (factitious) charms worn and revered by Africans with whom they traded, and by extension 'fetishism' has been applied to many forms of 'primitive' religion. Tylor tried to confine the use of the word to belief in influence passing through 'certain material objects'. But this belief is found in many religions, even the highest in sacramental doctrine, and the word 'fetish' is best abandoned altogether, even for magical charms in Africa, since these are found all over the world.

The word 'totem' came from the Ojibway Indians of North America, who used it of clan relationships and of the kinship of humans and animals, represented by carvings. The totem animal must not be hurt or killed. The role of totemism in the social system appeared often also in the prohibition of a member of the totemic group marrying another member, and this involved marriage outside the group, called 'exogamy'. 'Taboo' (*tapu*) was a Polynesian word meaning 'marked' or 'prohibited', used of persons, objects, animals, foods and so on. Taboo is not necessarily connected with totems, and there are prohibitions of people or foods in many places which have no totemic origin.

Reverence for or worship of the dead is found in all societies, because belief in life after death is universal. This was one of the earliest forms of religious belief, at least as far as is shown by traces which still remain. In central Europe about 100,000 years ago Neanderthal peoples buried their dead with food for travel in afterlife.

Right A tenth-century sculpture of Shiva and Parvati, Hindu personifications of the male and female elements in the universe. British Museum, London.

Far right Decorating the church for the annual harvest festival at Burton Bradstock, Dorset, in England.

Right The ultimate austerity of the yogi's life, depicted in an eighteenth-century gouache from Mankot. Private collection.

Earlier remains in China and elsewhere suggest similar beliefs. The Greek writer Euhemerus said that the gods had originally been great kings on earth, and 'euhemerism' was the term later applied to the notion that gods were once human heroes. Some of them may have been, but the study of religions shows that many gods arose rather from fear or worship of natural forms, or from search for a unifying divine principle within them. Ancestor worship is often conducted differently from the worship of divinities.

Religion is a social as well as a personal activity. It may be identified with the whole life of a tribe in illiterate societies, and develop into a state church in more advanced lands. Religions rarely have a name for themselves: they are the ideals and the way of life of the people, and provide the sanctions for moral laws passed down by tradition and worked out by philosophers. The head of a society may be a sacred king, who represents the people in life and rituals. In other societies a sacred priesthood may rule, forming a theocracy in which it is said that people are ruled by god through priests or prophets.

Order and Worship

The organization of religion in churches is especially characteristic of Christianity, and it may owe much to the organizing ability of Greek, Roman and later rulers. Many eastern religions have little organization. There are priests in Hinduism and special religious communities, but no overall organization. In Buddhism there is a monastic order, but little in the way of societies for lay people. This has an effect upon worship. Christian churches stress the value of communal worship and social service, but there is no obligation for a Buddhist or Hindu to visit a temple. That many people go there is due to the noise and lack of privacy in many eastern towns, where the temple, pagoda or mosque affords a quiet sanctuary for private prayer and meditation. There are great annual festivals at which temples are crowded and processions enliven the streets, but much religion is centred on the home and the sacraments of family life: naming of babies, initiation rites in adolescence, marriage and burial.

The simplest form of worship is prayer, which can be a personal wish or invocation, offered to the deity without ritual or priestly intermediary. Prayer can also be formal, communal, and led by priests or laymen. Sacrifice develops from prayer, as with the offering of gifts to the deity. A simple gift may be a thanksgiving, or one that expects a gift in return. Offerings are made when planting seeds in the spring-time, so that the harvest may prosper, and when the first fruits are gathered they are offered to god in recognition of blessing. Harvest festivals still express this acknowledgement. The sacrifice *Illustration page 18* may be offered to the deity and eaten by a human, and so it forms a bond of communion between them. A libation is a liquid poured out on an altar or on the ground. It is probably not thought that the deity consumes the physical offering, since worshippers observe that it stays on the altar or is absorbed into the soil, but they believe that the essence or soul of the gift is taken by the god.

Sacrifice may be composed of vegetable matter, drink, or blood. Animal sacrifice also has been very widely practised, though in the development of religion it often came to be banned, as it was by Jains and Buddhists. Human sacrifice has also been practised on momentous occasions, as the greatest gift that could be offered. Terrible holocausts were made in the later days of the Aztec empire, but the Hebrews, Hindus and Chinese all came to oppose such sacrifices and demanded a spiritual worship. The sacrificial object might have been thought to appease the divine anger or to provide a scapegoat for the rest of the community.

The various acts of worship may be made formal in ritual, in which words and actions express the needs and aspirations of the society. Music and dance, costume and procession help to intensify the effect of ritual. The ritual may be performed in exactly the same way each time, according to traditional or written texts, but this brings the danger of vain repetitions and it arouses the feeling that if the correct ritual is performed the deity will be obliged to respond. Hindu think-

Illustration page 18

ers sought communion with the divine directly by wisdom or loving devotion, as opposed to the meticulous rituals of the ancient Brahmin priests. Many rituals among illiterate peoples seem to proceed almost casually and with unprepared phrases, but it is the offering and the festival that are most important.

Myth and Ritual

The elaborate rituals of many religions form sacred dramas, and there is a close association between religion and many forms of dramatic and other arts. The dramas of ritual express the myth or sacred story which is celebrated at intervals. There are myths of many kinds: of creation, divine example, renewal, construction, initiation and eternal life. Myths of the creation of the world or the renewal of vegetation are enacted at the new year and at harvest. Other myths tell of the activities of the gods and supernatural beings, the marriage of the divine principles of male and female, or the wars of light against

Illustration page 18

darkness. These are illustrated in Indian myths of Shiva and Parvati, or Greek tales of the gods on Mount Olympus, or Japanese stories of sun and storm gods. Myths are not mere fairy tales, and modern psychological study has revealed their profound importance in human thought.

It is better to confine the term 'myth' to supernatural beings and stories, and to speak of legends when referring to historical people and past heroes. But often the two overlap: St George fighting the dragon or Krishna helping the Pandu brothers in their war may have had some historical foundation. Snakes are natural beings, but circular or two-headed snakes occur in countless myths as symbols of life, power, wisdom and eternity.

Ritual cults come to be located in sacred places, or are held there because the site is believed to be invested with holy power. The place is sacred, separate from the profane and the ordinary, and it may be seen as the centre of the world where the sacred drama is played out.

Worship may be performed in the open air at places marked by sacred stones like Stonehenge, and in many tropical countries even great temples and mosques consist largely of courtyards open to the sky, with quite small shrines for images or holy books and rites. Temples are constructed in symbolical shapes, perhaps in the form of a cross or a stepped pyramid. They enclose sacred objects or relics, and there are focal shrines with altars for gifts or rituals. Around the shrine there are usually passages to allow for circumambulation, normally keeping the shrine on the right hand, though at Mecca Mohammed ordered processions to go in an anti-clockwise direction round the sacred Kaaba so as to break with ancient pagan rites.

INTRODUCTION
Illustration page 30

Many of the great temples of the world are among the finest architectural treasures of mankind, and care and skill have been lavished on them by countless generations of devotees and craftsmen. The riotous abundance of sculpture on South Indian temples surpasses even that of the Gothic cathedrals of Europe, while the classic perfection of the Taj Mahal matches that of the Parthenon or St Peter's.

Illustration page 17

Rituals in temples are performed by specially selected and trained sacred persons called priests, although in family rites and the commemoration of ancestors the head of the family may officiate. Priests are married in most religions, but monks and nuns live in enclosed communities and are celibate. Preachers who are regarded as inspired by a divine being or coming with a sacred message are designated as prophets. The word 'shaman' originated in Siberia and is used of a religious leader who goes into a state of trance, seeing visions and giving oracles. A shaman may also be a priest or a magician, but there are other magicians whose chief task is the manipulation of magical materials. Such magicians may also be called 'medicine-men', but while many medicines are believed to have spiritual as well as material effects, there are more ordinary herbalists who know the properties of plants and apply them to patients. These are also called doctors, and a variety of them are 'witch-doctors', who seek to cure people who are thought to have been bewitched. Magicians may also be called 'sorcerers' if they practise 'black magic' or harmful magic, but most magicians are regarded as working for the good of individuals and society.

Illustration page 17

Magic functions on the lower levels of belief, though it is universally practised and it lingers in sophisticated societies in astrology and the use of lucky charms. Religious belief and practices are found at all levels of civilization, though reforms and changes come with growing knowledge. Wise people may not practise the same cults as their brothers and sisters, but they can regard them tolerantly as helpful at their level, while they themselves seek the truth about human life and the universe according to the best knowledge and insight available.

Chapter One

Prehistoric Religion

It would appear that religion in some form or other has been an essential element in the life and culture of humankind throughout the ages, going back far beyond the threshold of history. Moreover, many of the beliefs and practices of the later and higher religions, both ancient and modern, are rooted in their prehistoric prototypes of the Old Stone Age, a period lasting roughly from about 500,000 BC to 10,000 BC. This phase therefore has its place and significance in any study of the religions of the world, past or present. The difficulty, however, about such an inquiry is that nearly all the available data are confined to those concrete survivals like graves, sacred places and their contents, sculptures, bas-reliefs, engravings and paintings that have escaped the ravages of time. Their interpretation must be to some extent conjectural, but much of the material has survived, little changed, in everyday occurrence among the peoples who live today under conditions very similar to those of early humans. If employed with proper caution such evidence can afford useful and illuminating clues to the purpose and meaning of prehistoric religion.

Since of all mysterious events the most prominent, puzzling, disturbing and arresting is that of death, it is not surprising that the earliest traces of religious belief and practice have clustered round the burial of the dead, centred on what was to become a highly developed cult. Various forms of this seem to go back in China to a very early period in the Old Stone Age, estimated by Professor Zeuner as being in the region of 500,000 years ago. Thus, in the caves near Peking, indications have been found of the cutting off and preserving of the heads of some of those interred, either to keep them as trophies or to abstract their contents to be eaten in order to obtain the vitality of the deceased. And this is by no means an isolated instance, skulls having been treated in a similar way in Europe before the arrival of the species *homo sapiens,* towards the end of the fourth phase of the Pleistocene Ice Age, about 70,000 BC.

Skulls found in the Placard cave in Charente in France had been made into drinking cups, which suggests that they were used for sacramental purposes. Similar vessels have been found in the Dordogne, near the village of Les Eyzies, now well known as a centre for decorated caves, and again at Puente Viesgo not far from Santander in Spain, in a cave called Castillo, full of paintings.

In this phase of the Old Stone Age the corpse was often laid in a grave containing red ochreous powder, sometimes with quantities of shells and other objects in bone and ivory. The ochre represented blood, the life-giving agent, and there were often shells, like cowries, in the grave, shaped in the form of the portal through which the child enters the world. These emblems were associated with the female principle, and were widely used as fertility charms and givers of life. Therefore, if the dead were to live again in their own bodies, to colour the bodies red was an attempt to revivify them and make them serviceable to their occupants in the hereafter.

Near Nördlingen in Bavaria, nests of skulls have been found, twenty-seven in each of two caves, and six in another. The heads had been intentionally cut off the trunk with flint knives after death, and then dried and ceremonially preserved in the nest with the faces looking westward. Some were crushed, and had apparently been added later.

It was not only the skull which received this ritual mortuary treatment however. A number of skeletons have been discovered, ceremonially interred with very great care and supplied with grave goods. At Le Moustier in the Dordogne, a great centre of mid-Palaeolithic culture, the skeleton of a youth was laid to rest on its right side with the forearm under the head and the cranium resting on a pillow of flint chips. Near the left hand was a fine oval axe, and a scraper was placed not far away with the burnt bones of a prehistoric ox above the skull, suggesting a funeral feast.

In a low-roofed cave close to the village of La Chapelle-aux-Saints in the Department of Corrèze, a well-preserved Neanderthal skeleton was deposited with its face to the west in a pit dug in the middle of the marly floor, and wedged into position by several stones. The legs were folded, and near the hand was the foot of an ox, with the vertebral column of a reindeer at the back. Surrounding it were quantities of flint implements; remains of the broken bones of contemporary animals, including the bison and the woolly rhinoceros, were nearby.

It is hardly likely that early people would have gone to all this trouble in the disposal of the dead, which often involved reburial, providing them with what they were thought to need after death, unless survival, whether temporary or permanent, was the intention.

Forms of Burial

The prevalent practice of interment in the contracted position, with the limbs drawn up in the attitude of sleep and sometimes tightly flexed before *rigor mortis* had set in, has been regarded as typifying the foetus in the womb of its mother, indicating the hope of rebirth after death. But this conjecture presupposes a knowledge of embryology and powers of symbolic representation, quite beyond the information and capacity of Neanderthal peoples, or even of their immediate *homo sapiens* successors. Apart from the motive being that of economy of space in the grave, the practice may have been adopted sometimes as an attempt to prevent the deceased returning to molest the living by paying off old scores, or avenging any neglect in the performance of the funeral ritual. This is more likely in the case of the firm trussing of the corpse in an unnatural posture immediately after death, as, for instance, in that of a woman, thought possibly to have negroid features, in the cave named Grottes des Enfants at Grimaldi on the Italian Riviera. The same treatment was found in a flexed burial at Chancelade in the Dordogne.

Illustration page 27

On the other hand, bodies preserved as trophies may have been more in the nature of a cenotaph commemorating outstanding members of the group. This is suggested by a skull found in a grotto at Monte Circeo in the Tyrrhenian Pontine marshes in Italy. The skull was placed in a small chamber within a circle of stones; the brain had apparently been extracted from it, doubtless for sacramental purposes, and it had then been erected in a position suggestive of veneration, probably to promote and conserve life.

Throughout the ages the deepest emotions, wants, hopes and fears of a preliterate society have always arisen chiefly from the corporate life of the community, and centred on propagation, nutrition and survival while living and after death. As J.G. Frazer said in *The Golden Bough:* 'To live and to cause to live, to eat food and to beget children, these were the primary wants of man in the past, and they will be the primary wants in the future so long as the world lasts' (vol. IV pt i p5). Under the precarious conditions in which the human species emerged, food, children and an orderly corporate life were essential for survival. Therefore, it was around these basic needs that prehistoric religion grew and developed, concentrating upon the mysterious life-giving forces.

Illustration page 27

Stone Age Artists

This is clear in the cave art, sculptures, paintings and engravings of the Upper Palaeolithic Age, from about 40,000 to 12,000 BC, especially in the decorated caves in France and Spain. These were executed by the earlier representatives of *homo sapiens,* and not infrequently they occur on the walls of deep and tortuous limestone caverns, often in nooks and crannies and obscure positions none too easy to reach.

To make a first-hand study of this very important aspect of prehistoric religion the best centre is Les Eyzies on the banks of the Vézère in the Dordogne, within easy reach of which are a number of the principal examples, such as that known as Font-de-Gaume, less than a kilometre and a half from the village. A little further along the Sarlat road in the valley of the Beune is a long subterranean tunnel called Les Combarelles with a number of engravings. Not far away at Laussel a rock-shelter contained a frieze depicting an obese nude female carved on a block of stone, apparently in an advanced stage of pregnancy and holding in her right hand what seems to be the horn of a bison. The figure had been covered with red ochre to increase its life-giving properties and female potency. Some 48 kilometres (30 miles) up-stream from Les Eyzies is the recently discovered

Illustration page 29

cave at Lascaux near Montignac, about which more will be said later.
Also important are the regions of Ariège in the Pyrénées and Santander in northern Spain.

In several of the more popular decorated caves the installation of electric lighting has made it possible to get a better view of the remarkable polychrome paintings and the less accessible figures than ever before, but with disastrous effects upon them at Lascaux. Moreover, it has destroyed the numinous atmosphere, the aura of awe and wonder, and the conditions in which they were originally fashioned, obscuring their purpose and significance. Thus, at Font-de-Gaume in a sacred chamber beyond a stalactite barrier at the end of the cave there is the figure of a woolly rhinoceros in red ochre high up on a narrow crevice, together with engravings of a lion and horses. It would appear that the prehistoric artist could only have done these while standing on the shoulders of an assistant, having only a flickering lamp burning marrow or fat with a wick of moss. It is inconceivable that this was done merely for aesthetic reasons as 'art for art's sake' on an almost vertical wall 3 metres (10 feet) above the floor.

Magic for Good Hunting

Or, again, in the vast Pyrenean cavern of Niaux near Tarascon-sur-Ariège south of Toulouse, the paintings are 5.4–6.4 metres (6–7 yards) from the entrance, and separated from it by a depression full of water. Among them are three small cup-like hollows under an overhanging wall skilfully included in the design to depict wounds in red ochre on the flank of a bison, by drawing round them its outline with its legs in the contracted position. In front of the expiring bison are club-shaped designs to indicate missiles. Similar spear-markings have frequently been placed near the heart in a number of paintings, as, for instance, in those in the gallery of a cavern at Montespan in Haute Garonne near the château of the celebrated marquise, mistress of Louis XIV.

Illustration page 28

This was so inaccessible that M. Casteret could only re-enter it in 1923 by swimming for a kilometre and a half through a subterranean stream. There, in addition to animals engraved on the walls, a number of clay models of wounded felines have been brought to light. On a platform in the centre there is the figure of a small headless bear in a crouching posture covered with javelin wounds. Against the walls three clay statues had been broken in pieces, apparently in a magical ceremony. On the floor is the figure of a horse with the marks of spear thrusts on its neck. At Marsoulas, also in the Haute Garonne, a series of polychrome paintings have spear designs painted one over the other which shows that it was constantly renewed for magico-religious purposes to effect a kill in the chase.

Scenes of this kind could be multiplied almost indefinitely, showing that the ritual experts of the Stone Age penetrated into the inner depths of these sacred caverns (which incidentally were never lived in) to control the chase by casting spells on the animals hunted.

This, however, was not the only intention of the cult practised in them. The food supply had to be maintained as well as procured. Therefore the species on which early man depended for his subsistence had to be made prolific. An important find was made in a very inaccessible chamber in a cave known as the Tuc d'Audoubert in the foot-hills of the Pyrénées. When it was first re-entered in 1912, a boat had to be rowed up the subterranean River Volp, and the explorers had to scramble through stalactites. The skilfully modelled figures of a male bison followed by a female were discovered leaning against a boulder. In front of a small clay hillock nearby were heel-marks, thought to have been made during a fertility dance to make the species increase and multiply, the scene portraying propagation. It would seem then that in the rituals at Niaux the animals required for food were symbolically captured and killed, whereas at Tuc d'Audoubert they were rendered more prolific.

Illustration page 28

'The Sorcerer'

The three dauntless sons of the Count Bégouen first brought to light these clay bison, now realistically displayed in a tableau in the Natural History Museum at Toulouse. Two years later they crawled through a small vertical shaft, not much bigger than a rabbit-hole, at the end of a little cave called Enlène near the entrance of the Tuc d'Audoubert. There was a small chamber within the cave, now aptly named Les Trois Frères. On a wall beside a sort of window they found the partly painted, partly engraved figure of a man known as 'the Sorcerer', with a human face and long beard, the eyes of an owl, the claws of a lion and the tail of a horse.

Illustration page 30

It would seem, in fact, to have been the representation of a sorcerer or 'shaman', engaged in a sacred dance, portrayed in an aperture serving the purpose of a window at which the ritual expert stood to perform his rites in the presence of the cult-image. Whether or not he was an arch-sorcerer embodying the attributes and exercising the functions of all the creatures he depicted, or, as the Abbé Breuil conjectured, an embryonic deity controlling the multiplying of the animals embraced in the figure, a ceremony is indicated that brought together men and animals in a mystic fellowship in a joint effort to conserve and promote the food supply.

Illustration page 30

This motive recurs in the scene of a ritual dance in a rock-shelter at Cogul near Lérida in Catalonia, on the eastern side of the Spanish Pyrénées. There a group of nine narrow-waisted women, wearing skirts reaching to the knees in present-day fashion but devoid of facial features, are represented dancing round a small naked male figure. He may have been a later addition to the scene, which appears to have been employed by a succession of ritual experts for fertility purposes.

It was this aspect of prehistoric religion in and after Palaeolithic times which found expression in a number of female figurines commonly called 'Venuses', with the maternal attributes strongly emphasized. They were introduced into Europe about 30,000 BC from

Left An interment in the Grotte des Enfants at Grimaldi, Italy, of a skeleton thought to have negroid features. The body was buried with legs folded, and care has obviously been taken over the burial.

Left A chamber in a megalithic passage-grave at New Grange on the River Boyne in County Meath, Eire. Cut into a large circular mound, it was built by the Boyne farmers for their cremated dead.

Above The figure of a wounded bison in the cave of Niaux, south of Toulouse, France, showing spear marks near the heart designed to have reciprocal magical effects on the animals hunted in the chase.

Above right The 'problem painting' from the caves at Lascaux, France, depicting a figure of a man killed by a bison which has had its flank ripped by a rhinoceros, exposing the entrails. In front is a bird on a pole.

Right Two clay figures of bison, apparently arranged to look as if they are mating, from the Grotte du Tuc d'Audoubert in Ariège, France.

Opposite A bas-relief on a block of limestone from Laussel, France, of a woman holding the horn of a bison. Commonly called the 'Venus' figurine, it was probably carved to promote fertility. Musée de l'Homme, Paris.

Right A very dark part of the cave of Niaux is illuminated so that visitors may see the paintings. They suggest that this area was once a sanctuary in which sacred rites were performed.

29

the Don in the middle of Russia and from Siberia, where it would seem the worship of the mother-goddess arose.

Whether or not this was the earliest manifestation of the concept of deity, as has been suggested, the symbolism was a very early, prominent and persistent feature in the archaeological evidence. It was not, however, until agriculture and herding were adopted in the Middle East that the female principle was personified as the Great Mother. In the Old Stone Age its life-giving powers and functions were symbolized by these feminine statuettes, endowed with pro-creative attributes. As the mother of the race, woman was regarded essentially as the life-producer before her male partner was recognized as the begetter. This deeply laid belief was demonstrated in the Palaeolithic sculptures, reliefs, engravings, cowrie shells and fertility scenes and dances extended to the renewal of life beyond the grave.

The Bison of Lascaux

As long as primitive man led a precarious existence eked out by hunting, fishing and finding edible berries and fruit, fertility and the propagation of the animal and vegetable species which formed the staple diet maintained a sacred character and significance. This involved a variety of rites and motives and recourse to the cavern sanctuaries and the ritual techniques, ranging from hunting magic and rites of increase to the hazards of the chase. Thus, the great sanctuary of Lascaux, accidentally discovered by some boys in 1940, must have been a cult-centre for several thousand years as every form of the Palaeolithic art of Périgord is represented in it.

In Lascaux, in addition to the numerous representations of mythical animals, there is, in the most secluded recess, a sort of crypt entered by a drop of some 7.5 metres (25 feet) below the level of the floor, a scene portraying a man killed by a bison with its flank transfixed by a spear exposing its entrails. To the left is a woolly rhinoceros painted in a different style, which seems to be slowly moving away after having ripped up the bison. In front of the man is a bird on a pole.

Breuil interprets this problematical scene as a votive painting to a deceased hunter whom he thinks may have been buried in the cave. Another possible explanation would be that it had a more sinister motive, having been executed with malicious intent to bring about the destruction of the hunter. In any case, in view of its position it must have been regarded as having great potency for good or evil by those who painted it in this very difficult and dangerous part of the cave. More accessible is a mythical animal of a unicorn type, unless it is a masked sorcerer in a spotted skin rather like that in Les Trois Frères, impersonating perhaps some ancestral spirit believed to be responsible for fertility and success in hunting.

The Mystery of the Caves

While the motives underlying Palaeolithic art were many and various, no one who, like myself, has visited a great many of the decorated caves over a number of years, especially before the more famous of

Opposite above left 'The Sorcerer', from Les Trois Frères, in the foothills of the Pyrénées in France. This is a controversial figure, but most experts believe it to be a man dressed in the skin of a horse or wolf and the antlers of a red deer. A reconstruction is used to show the features more clearly.

Opposite above right A reconstruction of a wall painting in red and black of two groups of women, with a little man in the midst, engaged in a fertility dance, from the rock shelter of Cogul, in Lérida, Spain. Musée de l'Homme, Paris.

Opposite below The massive stone arches of Stonehenge, on Salisbury Plain, England. This remarkable site was probably a temple for sun worship.

Illustration page 28

Illustration page 28

them became commercialized and illuminated by electricity, can be in doubt that primarily they were prehistoric sanctuaries with an intensely awe-inspiring atmosphere. In them rites and sometimes sacred dances were held by ritual experts to control and maintain the always precarious food supply on which subsistence depended, arousing the deepest emotions because upon them their hopes and fears were concentrated.

They are, therefore, the outward expression of one of the most vital aspects of prehistoric religion. Having little understanding of natural processes and their laws beyond their own observations, early people felt the need of establishing friendly and beneficial relations with the ultimate reality behind the mysterious phenomena around them, however this may have been interpreted. In all probability it constituted their conception of divine providence, the transcendent universal good, greater than themselves and the source of all bounty and beneficence, controlling their destiny. This concept of deity at once above and within the world was not very far removed from what in our idiom could be described as both transcendent and immanent.

Whether it involved any idea of a theistic supreme being, as has been conjectured, is very difficult to determine. It is true that among preliterate primitive peoples today there is a widespread belief in a high god in association with lesser spiritual beings such as totems, culture heroes, ancestors and localized gods. He stands head and shoulders above them as a shadowy otiose figure, but as he is not intimately concerned with everyday affairs it is mainly from the lesser divinities that supernatural aid is sought.

It has to be remembered, moreover, that the primitive mind had a very limited capacity, and could hardly conceive of the higher attributes of gods and spirits. Natural processes could not have been personified and interpreted in theistic and animistic terms, until conceptual thought emerged in the way that Tylor and Frazer, and the evolutionary school, contended when they declared that in their judgement the 'minimum definition of religion' was 'the belief in spiritual beings'.

For an explanation of the theory of animism, see pages 11–12.

From this beginning animism was alleged to have developed into polytheism when, as Frazer affirmed, the innumerable spirits in 'every tree and flower, every brook and river, every breeze that blew and every cloud that flecked with silvery white the blue expanse of heaven' were conceived of as departmental gods. Then the spirits in all the trees were personified as a Silvanus, or god of the woods in general, or an Aeolus, the single god of the winds. By a further generalization and abstraction 'the instinctive craving of the mind after simplification and unification of its ideas' caused the many localized and departmentalized gods to be deposed in favour of one supreme creator and controller of all things. In this way polytheism evolved into monotheism with a single sovereign lord of heaven and earth (Frazer, *The Worship of Nature*, 1926, p.9f).

This speculation was in line with the evolutionary thought of the period in which it arose, but it has now become apparent that it was too neat and tidy, too specialized and intellectualized an approach to explain accurately the origin and development of religion and of the concept of deity.

The starting point of religion must be sought in something more comprehensive: in a belief in a sacred power which transcends the universe, and is its ground and support. This may not have been personified, and so it would seem to have been a vague conception of providence as a creative and recreative power operating in the food quest, sex, fertility, birth, death and the sequence of the seasons. When the idea of this potency acquired an independent life of its own in its various aspects and functions, it found expression in spiritual beings, ghosts of the dead and departmentalized divinities. These had many different shapes and forms, and characteristic features and functions of their own, emerging from a common providential source, incalculable, strong and good, determining the operations of nature and the destinies of humanity, at once above and within the world of time and space.

The recurrence of this conception of deity in all states of culture and phases of religious development from prehistoric times onwards suggests that it arose spontaneously.

It was the expression of some inborn thought and feeling, rather than a developed kind of knowledge about the universe and natural phenomena. Its highest expression undoubtedly has been in its monotheistic idea of god as the sole creator and sustainer of all things. So far from polytheism passing into monotheism, speculation about the cosmos and its processes led to the peopling of the natural order with a multitude of spirits and gods, making the supreme being a very vague and inoperative figure obscured in the mist of animism and polytheism, unless it became a pantheistic impersonal absolute as in Hinduism in India and elsewhere in the Far East. In the other higher religions, to be considered later in this volume, a genuine monotheism was firmly established, notably in Zoroastrianism, Judaism, Christianity and Islam. Under Palaeolithic conditions the notion of providence was much more within the capacity of this stage of prehistoric mentality than speculation about the animation of nature in relation to spiritual beings and departmentalized divinities organized on a personalized hierarchal basis, or of one wholly exclusive living god like the Aten in Egypt, Ahura Mazdah in Iran, Yahweh in Israel and Allah in the Islamic world, or the Trinity in unity in Christendom.

Early Mother-Goddesses

Whether or not the mother-goddess was actually the earliest attempt to give expression to the concept of deity, as we have seen, her symbolism was the most prominent feature in this aspect of prehistoric religion in the Upper Palaeolithic Age with its sculptured 'Venuses' and other emblems in the decorated caves. Subsequently, this

For the Great Mother cult in the Aegean, see pages 146–7; in India, see pages 213–4 and 220–1.

life-symbol became the central feature in the cult of the Great Mother in the Ancient Near East, the Aegean, Crete and Western Asia, and when the king was identified with the sky as the source of transcendental vitality and beneficence, the queen was equated with the earth as the immanent principle essential to the bestowal of providential bounty. Therefore, as he was reborn as the gods he embodied by his consecration, so his consort became the mother-goddess in one or other of her several capacities as the creatrix, having been the dominant figure in the earlier cult.

As the Great Mother became more clearly defined, and consciousness of the duality of male and female in procreation was recognized increasingly, from being the Unmarried Mother personifying the divine principle in maternity she became associated with the young god as her son and consort. Then, while she remained the crucial figure, the goddess cult assumed a twofold aspect in the ancient seasonal drama in which both the partners in generation played their respective roles of creative energy, the one female and receptive, the other male and active. From Neolithic times onward phallic emblems were increasingly prevalent, though maternal imagery was predominant in Western Asia and the eastern Mediterranean, where in the first instance the male god was subordinate to the goddess.

The Struggle for Life

In the primeval and perennial struggle between the two opposed forces in the seasonal sequence, manifest in the creative powers of spring and the autumnal decline, the goddess was always supreme because she was the source of life, and her male partner was only secondarily her spouse. In short, the creative powers were secondary and dependent upon forces over which man had but a limited measure of control. All life was born unto death, and even the Great Mother became a tragic figure, as many myths portray her pursuing her search for her lover-son amid lamentation and woe.

But behind this pessimistic view of the world and the natural order lay the earlier conception, going back to the Old Stone Age, of the control of the cosmic forces by a transcendent providence which sustained the universe and its operations, as these were observed and understood, and was felt to be responsive to human needs by means of religion or magic. It was not, however, only to secure the means of subsistence and to advance with hope and confidence on life's journey that supernatural aid was sought by prehistoric people. Already they had begun to look forward to a continuous existence beyond the grave, and to make provision for the requirements of the afterlife.

Chapter Two

Tribal Religions in Asia

Throughout the greater part of history people have led the nomadic life of hunter and foodgatherer, and the earliest religious ideas must have developed among small bands of men and women roaming over a world still sparsely inhabited and untamed by civilizing efforts. Only in the past 10,000 years did people begin to transform their environment and create conditions of living which allowed for complex social structures and the associated development and diversification of ideologies. Archaeological evidence tells us little about the religious concepts of Palaeolithic men and women, but anthropological observation among those living primitive peoples who have never progressed beyond the hunting and gathering stage throws some light on the kind of religious ideas and practices which are compatible with the style of life of nomadic foodgatherers.

It has become evident that there exists no human group, however primitive, which lacks all ideas of supernatural beings or entities. We can reasonably assume therefore that in prehistoric times too, the hunting and foodgathering people of Asia had the necessary mental ability to conceive ideas which can be described as religious. There is no possibility of discovering to what extent they resemble beliefs held by present-day foodgathering tribes, but it is not unlikely that the concepts and practices found among such tribes preserve some of the features of archaic religious systems which crystallized at a time when humankind's whole economy was based on hunting and gathering.

For this reason tribal groups representing an infinitesimally small fraction of the present population of Asia are of sufficient interest to warrant a description of their religious ideas. Primitive tribes of forest nomads are found in peninsular India, the Andaman Islands, in Malaya, in Sumatra, and in the Philippines, and in all these regions they are still maintaining their ethnic and cultural identity.

The Deities of Indian Forest Nomads

To demonstrate the religious ideas and practices associated with an extremely primitive economic system we may turn to the Chenchus, a Dravidian-speaking tribe of jungle nomads in the Indian state of Andhra Pradesh. The Chenchus, though familiar with the style of life of settled farmers, have chosen to remain in the forest and subsist on wild roots, tubers and berries and the occasional game killed with bow and arrow. The principal social unit is a group of families possessing hereditary rights to a tract of land within whose boundaries its members are free to hunt and collect edible plants.

Fundamental to the Chenchu view of the world is the feeling of human dependence on invisible beings conceived of in anthropomorphic terms. The Chenchus regard the world of humans and gods as an entity and accept the existence of invisible beings affecting human fates as part of the natural order. They do not reflect about the origin of these beings, and their attitude to the gods is sober and free of emotional involvement.

In the forefront of the Chenchus' religious thinking stands a female deity called Garelamaisama, who is closely linked with the chase and the collection of edible plants. She is credited with power over the wild animals of the forests and hence with the luck of the chase. When a hunter sets out in the morning, he murmurs a prayer, asking Garelamaisama to give him success and promising her a part of the kill. If he brings down any animal, he roasts a small piece of the flesh on the spot and offers it to Garelamaisama with a prayer of thanks. The Chenchus believe that in the old times only male animals were killed, because the shooting of female animals arouses the wrath of Garelamaisama. If by chance a man killed a female animal, he prayed to the goddess for forgiveness lest she withhold food.

Garelamaisama is believed to influence human behaviour, and she is invoked to prevent people from quarrelling when they get drunk. The care the benevolent deity extends to those who trust in her protection is reflected by myths and legends which relate how, in the guise of an old woman, Garelamaisama appeared to men and women in need, and saved them from peril or death. Although the Chenchus have a fairly clear idea of her nature, they know nothing about her origin or the beginning of her involvement with humankind.

The God of Thunder and Rain

Another deity prominent in Chenchu belief is Bhagavantaru. He is thought to dwell in the sky and to control thunder and rain. Though the name is clearly derived from the Hindu term for the concept of an impersonal godhead, Bhagavantaru is imagined no less anthropomorphically than the forest-goddess Garelamaisama.

Neither of these deities is credited with an interest in human morality. Divine injunctions do not refer to social relations. The gods are not thought to concern themselves with such actions as adultery, violence or even murder, and there is little to suggest that moral lapses are subject to supernatural sanctions. The Chenchus' ideas of people's fate after death are vague. There is no definite belief that a person's fate after death depends on deeds in this life.

Besides Garelamaisama and Bhagavantaru, the Chenchus worship a number of minor deities associated with specific localities or clans. They are propitiated by offerings, but the Chenchus look upon such acts of worship as necessary but emotionally neutral appeals to supernatural powers. Unlike many of the more advanced Indian tribes, the

Illustration page 39

Chenchus are not haunted by a fear of evil spirits or anxious about the effects of black magic.

Their approaches to the deities are spontaneous and devoid of complicated ritual. There are no priests or other religious experts, for the hand-to-mouth existence of a tribe of foodgatherers leaves no scope for specialization, and ritual acts such as the offerings of the first fruits to Garelamaisama can be undertaken by any adult man. The structure of Chenchu religion is thus one of extreme simplicity. Humans and gods are believed to operate within a single sphere, and every individual has direct and immediate access to deities who, though invisible, appear to the Chenchus as part of the natural world.

The Religion of a Peasant Tribe

While the religious ideas of such hunters and foodgatherers as the Chenchus are simple and their ritual practices are straightforward, the economically more advanced Indian tribes have developed religious patterns of great complexity and their relations with the supernatural world are channelled into elaborate ceremonies conducted by ritual specialists. A wealth of myths and sacred texts, transmitted from generation to generation by oral tradition, form a firm framework for religious beliefs and the performance of cult acts. Such a situation is exemplified by the Gond tribes, a population some three million strong extending over the hill regions of Madhya Pradesh and northern Andhra Pradesh.

The myths telling of the origin of the Gond race and the feats of culture-heroes and clan-ancestors provide the pragmatic sanction for institutions which determine the behaviour of every Gond towards fellow-tribespeople, and they define and authorize relations with the divine powers on whom human welfare depends. A mutually enlivening relationship links myths and ritual; as the myths lend significance and power to ritual acts, so the symbolic re-enactment of myths during the cardinal clan-rites endows the myths with reality. To the Gonds the myths are of never-fading actuality: they sanction human conduct, and in their dramatization religious urges find expression and people feel themselves one with untold generations of predecessors and with the divine ancestors. Hereditary bards are guardians of the sacred lore. At each of the major annual feasts they recite the appropriate myths or legends, and thereby keep the tradition alive.

Illustration page 40

The deity who resides over the world is Bhagavan, often identified with the Hindu god Shiva and hence addressed as Shri Shembu Mahadeo. His court, populated by numerous deities, resembles that of a human ruler. Gods and people turn to him for advice and assistance in difficulties, but usually he communicates with mortals only indirectly, such as through his messenger Yama, the god of death. Though Bhagavan occupies an important place in myths and legends, his role in the system of worship is relatively insignificant. Only two or three times a year do the Gonds give offerings to Bhagavan, and the ritual accompanying these acts of worship takes only a few minutes.

Guardians of the Clan

Far more elaborate are the rites connected with the worship of the clan-deities. The cult of these deities is central to Gond religion, and the sacrifice of cows, goats and sheep constitutes an important part of their worship. The origin of the cult of the clan-deities is explained in two different ways. One cycle of myths describes how the primordial ancestors of the Gonds learnt of these deities and secured their protection by the promise of regular sacrifices. Another cycle of myths deals in detail with the deification of legendary figures, who in their terrestial life were members of Gond clans. In a miraculous manner they were transformed into tangible symbols of clan-deities, and henceforth they were worshipped as the divine guardians of their original clans. The nature of these deities is complex. Most of them represent an amalgam of a female and a male figure, conceived of as mother and son yet afterwards often referred to as a single deity. The sacred objects symbolizing the clan-deities are an iron spearpoint and a fly-whisk made of a yak's tail such as Hindus use in temple ritual.

Illustration page 39

While the origin and nature of the clan-deities is obscure, their cult conforms to a clear and rigid pattern observed by all Gond clans. Three ritual functionaries are responsible for the worship of each set of clan-deities, and the sacred symbols remain in their care. Twice a year the clan-members gather at the clan-shrine, a simple structure of wood and thatch, and spend several days in worship and feasting. On the occasion of one of these annual rites the souls of all clan-members deceased during the past year are formally introduced into the company of the clan-deity and all departed clan-members.

Illustration page 39

The cult of the clan-deities represents one side of the Gonds' religious system; another relates to the worship of local and village-deities. In every village there is a shrine of the village mother and a sanctuary of the village guardian represented by a pointed wooden post. The village mother is one of numerous goddesses whose sanctuaries are scattered over the land of the Gonds. A special position among them is occupied by the earth mother, worshipped by the Gond farmers before sowing and at the time of harvest. The female deities are not regarded as invariably benevolent. Among them are the deities who threaten the villagers with cholera and smallpox and who have to be placated with animal sacrifices.

Illustration page 42

Priests and Seers

On many occasions the Gonds do not limit themselves to the invocation of a single deity but direct their prayers to several of the supernatural powers believed to affect their fate. Clan-gods, earth-mother, village-deities, mountain-gods, and ancestor-spirits are invoked in one breath, and no Gond thinks of them as arranged in a hierarchical order. Only Bhagavan stands above all the other deities. In their relations with the invisible powers the Gonds depend on the charisma of hereditary priests. No one except a member of the lineage of clan-priests may function at the rites in honour of the clan-deities, and the cult of village mother and village guardian is a prerogative

Left A Chenchu making an offering of cooked millet at the stone altar of a local deity in Andhra Pradesh, India.

Left A Raj Gond woman bows before a cow to be sacrificed at a funeral feast in Andhra Pradesh.

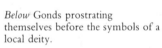

Below Gonds prostrating themselves before the symbols of a local deity.

Above Ifugao priests perform a curing ritual in northern Luzon, in the Philippines. The rice beer contained in the wooden bowls is offered to the spirits suspected of having caused the illness.

Rignt Raj Gond masked dancers of Andhra Pradesh with peacock-feather crowns and clubs. They represent mythical figures and are a traditional feature of the dance festival after harvest.

Left A Bondo shaman performs a ritual to cleanse the village from disease in Orissa, India.

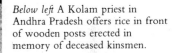

Below left A Kolam priest in Andhra Pradesh offers rice in front of wooden posts erected in memory of deceased kinsmen.

Below A carved memorial pillar erected near a village in Bastar province, Madhya Pradesh.

Above A Gond tribesman offers a chicken to Mother Earth before the sowing of the crops.

Right An Apa Tani seer in ritual dress.

Far right A Konda Reddi drumming and dancing during a festival held to celebrate the first ritual eating of the newly ripened wild mangoes in Andhra Pradesh.

which belongs exclusively to the lineage of the village founder.

Apart from these hereditary priests, there are seers capable of falling into a trance and acting as oracles and mediums. Through their mouths the gods speak directly to people, and the frequent experience of such divine manifestations invests the relations to supernatural beings with an immediacy absent in religions lacking the ecstatic aspect.

The soul-concepts of the Gonds and many other Middle Indian tribes are based on the belief that the impersonal life-substance (*jiv*), which animates a person from birth to death, is different from the personality which continues to exist after death and joins the ancestors in the land of the dead. The life-substance enlivening a child while it is still in the mother's womb is believed to emanate from Bhagavan. Little attention is paid to this life-substance throughout a Gond's life-time, for it is unrelated to consciousness and the emotions. But when a Gond's span of life draws to its end, Bhagavan recalls the life-substance and thereby causes death. When the life-substance has returned to Bhagavan it is added to a pool of such substances available for reincarnation, but the link between the personality of the deceased and the life-substance comes to an end.

The personality of the deceased survives after death in the form of a spirit referred to as *sanal,* which in Gondi means literally 'the departed'. Most of the rites and ceremonies of the funeral and the memorial feast relate to the *sanal* in whom the personality of the departed is perpetuated. The departed are believed to live in a sphere of their own, which they share with the clan-deities, but they also come to the habitations of the living and partake of the food offerings of their kinsmen. Together with the clan-deities, they bestow substantial benefits on the living, and the Gonds consider it desirable for a village to have on its land a shrine that contains the sacred symbols of prominent clan-ancestors.

There is no connection between people's moral conduct in this life and their fate in the land of the dead, nor do the Gonds believe that the gods concern themselves with human morality. To the Gond, religion is not so much a personal relationship to individual invisible beings as a system of rites and sacrifices by means of which a community achieves the integration of human actions with the influence of the gods and spirits sharing its environment. Many of these invisible beings are considered as neutral *vis-à-vis* humans; they can be propitiated by offerings and offended or irritated by an attitude of disrespect. Fundamentally hostile spirits do not figure prominently in Gond ideology, and the idea of a battle between good and evil forces is foreign to the Gond's view of the world.

Hosts of Ifugao Gods

A religious system of a very different order prevails among the Ifugaos, a hill-tribe of the Philippine island of Luzon. About 80,000 Ifugaos inhabit a mountainous region which until the beginning of the century was not easily accessible from the lowlands and hence isolated from the mainstream of Philippine civilization. The Ifugaos are subsistence cultivators, famous for the ingeniously engineered terrace-fields on which they grow irrigated rice. Until recently they were feared as war-like headhunters and maintained few relations with neighbouring tribes. Their internal social structure is characterized by the absence of any institutionalized community organization. The individual, supported only by a bilateral kin-group extending to third cousins, neither recognizes nor enjoys the protection of any village or tribal authority, and in an atmosphere of feuds and vengeance killing there is little sense of personal security. Yet while lacking political organization, the Ifugaos have developed one of the most pervasive religious systems reported in ethnographic literature.

Even today, when about half the Ifugaos have embraced Christianity, the pagan religion still flourishes and innumerable rituals are being performed with undiminished elaboration and the expenditure of large resources. The performance of any rite has to be conducted by a trained priest capable of reciting lengthy incantations and myths. For the more complex rites at least two priests are required, and as many as fifteen priests may officiate at an important ritual. If the rite is a purely domestic affair, as most rituals are, only priests drawn from the husband's and the wife's kin-groups participate.

There is no organized priesthood recruited from a special social class. Any Ifugao possessing intellectual ability and a good memory may attach himself as apprentice to an experienced priest of his kingroup or locality, but in many cases sons follow in the footsteps of fathers enjoying a reputation as knowledgeable and successful priests. Ifugao priests act also as chroniclers and genealogists, for the frequently repeated incantations of ancestors give them an unrivalled knowledge of genealogies.

Five Regions of the Universe

The basic framework of Ifugao religion is provided by a cosmology which divides the universe into five regions. In the centre lies the known earth, the habitat of the Ifugaos. Above is the skyworld and below is the underworld. Down the river beyond the known earth lies the downstream region, and up the river is a similar remote region, the upstream region. The latter two, like skyworld and underworld, are imaginary regions and not accessible to ordinary men and women. An enormous host of deities and spirits is believed to inhabit these five regions. As many as 1240 separate named deities have been counted, but according to R. F. Barton's estimate the best priests of any locality in Central Ifugao know the names of at least 1500 deities. There is little in the Ifugao universe which has not been deified, and despite the great number of deities no two are conceived of as exactly the same in nature and powers.

The Ifugaos think of their deities as grouped in about forty main classes, which are given separate designations appropriate to the deities' general nature and roles. There are certain gods of the skyworld who are believed to have taught the Ifugaos ritual and given them their technological equipment and all their domestic animals. In all general feasts the principal offerings are due to those deities. Among the other classes there are the gods of deception concerned with war and sorcery, the omen-deities, the gods of reproduction, the guardians of property, the messenger-deities, the gods of the winds, and the deities of disease.

In each of these classes there are numerous individual deities, mostly named according to the function they are believed to fulfil. A god known as 'Deceiver', for instance, leads people into danger from enemies and accident, and into all kinds of violent or insidious death. He also coaxes away their souls and carries them off into the sky-world. To recover such souls special rites have to be performed and a priest in a state of trance must follow the soul and bring it back into the body which it has deserted. If he does not succeed in bringing the soul back, the afflicted person will die and the soul remain with the gods of deception in the skyworld. The victims of headhunting and even people killed in quarrels share the same fate, whereas all other departed go to the land of the dead.

Sacrificial Rites

Ifugaos spend a great deal of time and wealth on the performance of rituals, and it is not unusual for six or seven pigs, one buffalo and innumerable chickens to be sacrificed in the course of a single cere-mony. The procedure, though varying in detail, follows generally a standard pattern and comprises the following phases: the invocation of the ancestors, during which the priest invokes the ancestors of his own kin-group; the possession of the priest by the ancestors, who drink rice-beer and speak through the mouth of the priest; one of the priests assumes the leadership of the rite and allocates the classes of deities to be worshipped among the assembled priests; each priest invokes the messenger deities and sends them to summon the classes of deities he has been allotted; each priest, simultaneously with the other priests, invokes the classes of deities assigned to him; the priest is possessed by the deities invoked and they drink through his mouth of the rice-beer offered; the performance of special chants or rites concerned with the particular occasion; the slaughter of the sacrificial animals and invocation of the deities to whom they are offered; the recitation of myths by the officiating priests.

Illustration page 40

The myths to be recited during a rite are also allocated among the priests, and they recite them simultaneously, producing a hum of voices in which the words are usually not distinguishable. Most myths have the character of sympathetic magic and tell about ances-tors or gods who in the past resolved problems similar to those with which the present-day Ifugaos are confronted.

Ifugao rituals can be described as worship only in the sense that through them people establish contact with supernatural beings in order to obtain their support. There is no element of reverence or devotion in this ritual, and the relation between human and deities is considered as one of bargaining and give and take. But the Ifugao undoubtedly feels dependent on a host of invisible beings, and believes that happiness, prosperity and health can be visually influenced by their actions. At the same time the Ifugao thinks that priests knowledgeable in the appropriate ritual can manipulate the deities and coax them to aid human endeavour. Ifugao gods are considered morally neutral and unconcerned with the ethical conduct of humans. Hence religion does not provide sanctions for a moral code, but has the major function of inspiring people with confidence in their own ability to temper the blows of fate by recourse to the power of ritual.

The World-View of Central Asian Pastoral Tribes

The fourth and last example of religious systems developed outside the compass of the literate Asian civilizations is the world-view of the pastoral peoples of Central Asia.

The religions of such Central Asian peoples as Altaians, Tatars, Burjats and Yakuts, though differing in many details, conform to a general pattern characteristic of a part of the world where as late as the nineteenth century indigenous ethnic groups persisted in their traditional ideology. Their world-view is based on the division of the world into three spheres: the upperworld or sky, the middleworld or earth, and the underworld or hell. Within that major division, there are numerous specific layers and in particular the skyworld is conceived as subdivided into either seven or nine separate layers. These layers correspond to a hierarchy of divine beings allocated to higher or lower layers according to their rank in the pantheon of gods. A supreme being occupying a dominant place in the religious system of all Central Asian peoples is invariably associated with the sky, whereas a mythical figure personifying the principle of evil is generally, but not exclusively, located in the underworld.

The supreme deity, sometimes simply referred to as 'sky', but occasionally also as 'creator', is credited with the qualities of unlimited authority, creative power, wisdom bordering on omniscience, and usually benevolence towards humanity. This celestial god, who dwells in the highest sky, has several sons or messengers who are subordinate to him and who occupy lower heavens. Their number varies from tribe to tribe, and they are charged with watching over and helping human beings.

In the mythology of many of the Central Asian peoples the supreme deity is confronted by an adversary representing the powers of darkness and evil. This figure attempts to counter the plans of the celestial good being and aims at gaining dominance over the world and at establishing a realm of his own in which he would rule over humanity. The forces of good and evil are not equally balanced, however, and there is never any real doubt about the final supremacy of the sky-god. Yet according to some myths the representative of evil and darkness succeeded in leading people astray and bringing about a Fall similar to that of Adam and Eve.

Both the sky-god and his opponent figure in many of the creation-myths which play an important role in the thinking of the peoples of Central Asia and Siberia. Most of these myths relate how in the beginning the world was filled by an immense ocean and how the sky-god obtained by various means a small lump of earth from the bottom of that ocean, and out of this created the entire earth which was soon to be inhabited by people and animals.

The Shaman

The most distinctive phenomenon of the religion of Central Asia as well as of Siberia is known as 'shamanism'. Throughout Central and North Asia the magico-religious life of the indigenous population traditionally centres on the shaman. Though in many tribes there are also priests concerned with the performance of animal sacrifices and every head of a family is also the head of the domestic cult, the shaman is the dominating figure.

Illustration page 41

The ecstatic state is considered the religious experience par excellence, and the shaman is the great master of ecstasy. Unlike persons possessed by spirits and temporarily in their power, the shaman controls the spirits, in the sense that he or she is able to communicate with the dead, demons and nature spirits without becoming their instrument. Shamans are separated from the rest of society by the intensity of their religious experience, and in this sense they resemble the mystics of religions with a written history.

Shamanism always represents an ecstatic technique at the disposal of a particular élite, and it is the shamans who act for the peoples of Central Asia as mediators between them and their gods, celestial or infernal. The shaman, moreover, is the great specialist in human souls, for he or she alone sees a soul, and knows its form and destiny. The powers of a shaman are obtained either by hereditary transmission or by spontaneous vocation, through the call of gods and spirits. In either case introduction is given by an old master shaman as well as directly by the spirits. The initiation can be by public ritual or by dreams and ecstatic experiences. Usually the vocation involves the traditional scheme of an initiation ceremony: suffering, death and resurrection. A shaman may be chosen by a tutelary spirit, and there are cases of a female spirit marrying the shaman and becoming his wife and giving him secret instruction or helping him in his ecstatic experiences.

The Disembodied Soul

The shaman acts primarily as a healer and is indispensable in any ceremony that concerns a human soul. There is a widespread belief that the soul can forsake the body even while a person is still alive and while straying into other spheres easily falls prey to demons and sorcerers. The shaman diagnoses the trouble, goes in search of the patient's fugitive soul, captures it, and makes it return to the body.

While the shaman is in a state of ecstasy, his or her own soul can safely abandon the body, roam through distant regions, and rise to the sky or penetrate the underworld. The ascent to the sky is enacted in elaborate rites which include the climbing of a ladder or a pole. Among the Altaians, shamans used to sacrifice horses to the celestial being because they alone could conduct the sacrificed animal to heaven. The counterpart to the ascent to the sky is the descent to the underworld down seven successive levels, a far more dangerous enterprise which brings the shaman to the palace of the ruler of the subterranean regions. Such descents to the underworld are undertaken especially to find and bring back a sick person's soul, or conversely, to escort the soul of a deceased person to the realm of shadows. Only shamans can undertake such tasks, for they alone see spirits and disembodied souls and know how to deal with them.

The passage from one cosmic region to another is the pre-eminent shamanistic technique. The shamanistic ecstasy can be regarded as a reactualization of the mythical time when people could communicate directly with the sky. Because of their ecstatic experience, which enables them to relive a state inaccessible to the rest of humanity, the shaman is regarded as a privileged being, and the myths refer to intimate relations between the supreme beings and shamans. Hence Asiatic shamanism appears as an archaic technique of ecstasy whose underlying ideology implies the belief in a celestial deity with whom it is possible to have direct relations by ascending into the sky. The shaman's role in the defence of a community's psychic integrity rests on the conviction that human beings are not alone in a hostile world surrounded by demons and the forces of evil, but that there are men and women specially qualified to approach the gods and spirits, and to bring back reliable information from the supernatural spheres.

Pattern and Diversity

The four types of tribal religion here discussed represent only a small sample of the enormous diversity of religious phenomena encountered among the preliterate societies of Asia. Within this diversity certain patterns are discernible and there can be no doubt that in the same way as the great historic religions such as Buddhism, Christianity and Islam extended their sway over large parts of the world, primitive ideologies also spread across ethnic boundaries. Consequently, similar concepts, attitudes and practices occur in widely separated areas and among peoples of different social structure.

Thus the idea of a powerful and basically benevolent sky-god and of an adversary inimical to humanity prevails among a large number of the peoples of Central and Northern Asia, and the same mythical elements appear in different permutations throughout this large region. Similarly the concept of the fugitive soul separated from the body of an ailing person and held captive by spirits of an extraterrestial sphere extends from Northern Asia to Southeast Asia and as far as the Philippines, and so do the practices of shamans who alone can follow such a truant soul and bring it back to earth.

This wide spread of similar religious phenomena and concepts throughout societies of different structure and economic background suggests that ideas about the supernatural are not neccessarily linked with specific material and social circumstances, but that on occasions they have an impetus of their own.

Chapter Three

Early Australasia

The pre-European religious patterns in Australasia were not well described before they began to change, and the traditional pictures are still being reconstructed. A primary difficulty has been the inappropriateness of Western religious categories when applied to either Australian Aborigines or New Zealand Maoris. The early accounts of Maori religion were by Christian missionaries, preoccupied it now seems with showing that the religion of the Maoris was at least compatible with Christianity, if not parallel to that of the Hebrews in the old Testament. The observations made by Thomas Kendall, from 1815, show this characteristic clearly, although his is 'the only known description taken from conversation with men who had not been converted to Christianity'. It is therefore on these early missionaries that we must rely for an account of the early religious forms, since the Maoris then had only an oral tradition.

A further difficulty is the esoteric or secret nature of many aspects of sacred knowledge. This may be an explanation for the late description (by Te Matorohanga in the late 1850s) of a Maori belief in a high god, Io, since his name may have been too sacred to mention. Alternatively the cult of Io may be a post-European phenomenon, derived from Christian teaching. Religious beliefs are too often ambiguous, and it is difficult to know how they were accepted and whether they were only half believed.

The gods of the Maoris are to be found in other parts of Polynesia, and in contrast to their polytheism the religion of the Autralian Aborigines is totemic. Early accounts of Aboriginal religion are confused, particularly since theorists like Tylor, Durkheim and Freud used the inadequate information available as a basis for argument about the role of religion in primitive society. In doing so, it is now agreed, they misinterpreted the nature of Aboriginal religion, because they could not gain an 'inside' view. This has been corrected in the work of later scholars who have based their accounts on careful fieldwork.

For a summary of the theories of Tylor, Durkheim and Freud, see pages 11 and 13–14.

The two broad cultures have quite different religious beliefs and forms, and yet they agree on a close inter-relationship between the natural and the supernatural orders, and religion has been a stabilizing force for them. There is still dispute about the origins of these people, which need not concern us except to note that the nature of their religions has been used as an argument for the independence of their origins. It must be realized that, despite broad similarities in each place, there are great regional differences in particular forms of religion, both in Polynesia and Australia.

The Maoris of New Zealand

As E. Best says in *The Maori* (1924), 'There is much to learn from a study of pre-European Maori beliefs, much food for thought in the varied phases of Maori religion, from its grossest shamanism to its cult of the Supreme Being.' Much of the early Maori religion was concerned with securing supernatural help with food supplies and materials, and the potency of post-European Maori religion declined progressively because of the new ways introduced by missionaries.

The Maori world order was genealogically connected, and in one chant (in which histories were retained and transmitted) the beginning is Nothing (Te Kore) and leads through Night, Dawn, and Light of Day, to the Sky (a male, Rangi) and Earth (a female, Papa). The Earth and the Sky were closely bound, and their children were confined between the bodies of their parents. The number of these children varies with the location of the myth, from seventy to about six, but the children finally separated their parents. These children are the gods (or *atua*) that relate to the important areas of nature, and include Tu the war-god, Rongo the god of peace and agriculture, and Tangaroa the god of the ocean. The most important is Tane. He defeated and banished the powers of darkness, was the author of all vegetation, and created the first woman. His trees are rooted in the ground and stretch towards Rangi, the sky, and they forced Rangi upwards while the other sons held up the sky with poles. Continuing rain and mist express the sorrow of Earth and Sky, and their great longing for each other. These 'departmental' gods occur throughout Polynesia.

All elements in nature, including human beings, are linked together in kinship, and may therefore be called upon when help is needed, although there is also conflict, since the environment is full of spirits. The main Maori gods were male, and the needed female was fashioned out of earth. Tane breathed life into her. There are several variants in this myth (none being biologically satisfactory) but the basic opposition between earth and sky is preserved in male and female. In another form, Tane asked his father for a female, but was refused because the female element is on earth, and the sky is the realm of life. The earth is therefore for transitory beings while the sky is permanent. There is a similar duality between spirit and substance, or between life and fate, but there is no opposition between good and evil. The first woman was the earth-formed Maiden and her first child was a daughter, called the Dawn Maiden, who eventually became Tane's wife.

Idea of the Holy

The Maori view of the world was strongly influenced by a respect for things *tapu,* or holy. Almost any object could become *tapu* if it had been in contact with the supernatural order, while offences against

Above Maui pulling up North Island, New Zealand, symbolized by a fish. Maui is credited with having pulled up the land from the ocean for men to live on, with championing them against the gods, and with stealing fire for them from the keeper of the underworld. Woodcarving from a house at Whakewerawera, Rotorua, New Zealand. Dominion Museum, Wellington.

Above left Tribal ancestors are carved on this massive central post supporting the long ridge-pole of a Maori meeting-house. Dominion Museum, Wellington.

Left Modern Maoris demonstrating the ancient ritual of feeding a high priest. He was fed by a servant specially appointed for the purpose, who used a long instrument so that the priest was not touched and thus his *tapu* remained unbroken.

Right Three Maori god-sticks. They have a flax binding of the original criss-cross pattern and traces of red ochre appear on the right-hand one. From left to right: Te Maru, who was invoked before battle; Tangaroa (sea god) or Turanga (river god), invoked for fishing expeditions; and Rongo, whose aid was invoked during the planting season. Dominion Museum, Wellington.

Below right An early print of a Maori pulling on the string of a god-stick to gain the attention of a god.

Opposite above Carved and painted Aborigine grave posts from Snake Bay on Melville Island, Northern Territory. Art Gallery of New South Wales, Sydney.

Opposite below A *tjurunga* or sacred emblem of the Aranda people of Central Australia. In the Dreamtime each *tjurunga* was associated with a particular totemic ancestor and its spirit lived within it. When the spirit entered a woman, it was reincarnated as a child. So each person had his or her own *tjurunga*.

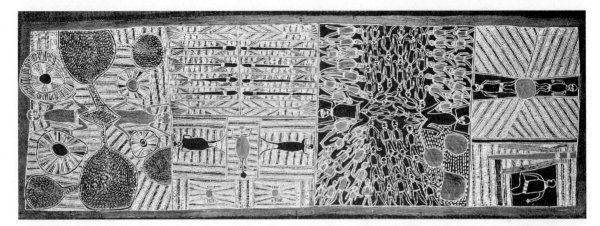

Right and below Ground paintings made to re-enact the activities of the great snake Wollonqua. The Warramunga people say he rose out of a waterhole in the Murchinson Range (in the Northern Territory) and was so enormous that though he travelled far his tail remained in the waterhole. The raised mound (*right*) represents the sandhill where he stood up and looked around, and the ground painting (*below*) the place where he ended his wanderings.

tapu could result in death. Thus fire might become *tapu* if lit by priests for their ceremonies, since the god might be brought to live in the fire. When the sweet potatoes (*kumara*) were planted, the god of the *kumara*, Rongo, might be brought to a fire to ensure a good harvest. Water could become sacred, particularly when a stream was used for religious rites. The sun, moon and stars were also invested with power. The moon was appealed to by women in childbirth, because, as Best suggests, the cyclic nature of the moon was similar to that of the women. Sources of food were carefully covered by religious rites aimed at preserving their supply, and priests performed rites for opening and closing the fishing and bird-snaring seasons.

Important *tapu* related to people, both during their lives and in death, although it was stronger for men than for women, who had it particularly if they were of high status, were menstruating, or giving birth. Men who were not slaves had *tapu* in their blood and in their heads, and any man who was captured thereby lost his *tapu* and became *noa*. Priests had *tapu* so strongly that even their shadows had to be avoided, and anything they touched immediately became *tapu,* so that special arrangements were needed for their feeding. Chiefs had *tapu*. They and priests were frequently fed by another person and even their mouths did not touch the eating utensils. It was customary to pour water into the mouths of important males, and as Best observes, this must have been very inconvenient. To violate a *tapu* not only endangered the violator but also took something from the *tapu* person.

A dead body was more *tapu* than a living person. The dwellings of supernatural beings were also *tapu,* although there were procedures for removing *tapu* in appropriate circumstances. A meeting house was *tapu* during its construction, as were the workers, and its opening on completion involved removing the *tapu*. There was an established duality between *tapu* and *noa*.

Power over Fate

A person with *tapu* had some *mana,* or power, by which he or she could prevail over fate. This was needed whenever he faced the unpredictable. Those who were successful had *mana,* and this resided particularly in chiefs and priests. When *mana* failed, it was because *tapu* had been broken, although certain things were impossible. The Sky cannot conquer the Earth, nor the spirit conquer the body. On those occasions when it was essential for the male spirit to remain unbroken, as in warfare or when building a meeting house or canoe, the men kept away from the women until the *tapu* had been removed by a priest.

A training in the knowledge of things *tapu* was achieved by stories about such cultural heroes as Maui. Carved figures on buildings, particularly the meeting house, represented important ancestors and events in mythology. Each tribal group had its own supernatural forces, or *atua,* which spanned both the common people, the priests and the chiefs. The *atua* were present if kept alive by the priests, and

Opposite top This fine painting on bark by the Aborigine artist Mawalan of Yirrkalla in eastern Arnhem Land illustrates the Djanggawul myth. The Djanggawul sisters giving birth to the first Aborigines are illustrated realistically in the second section from the right, and the same theme is represented semi-abstractly in the lefthand section. Between these panels are the special tree *rangga* used to make the first trees. Alongside are the Djanggawul and two symbols of the sun. In the bottom righthand panel is the artist.

Illustration page 51

Illustrations page 51

their activities explained many events. Local gods had both good and bad characteristics, and were given a place in the genealogy of the tribe. They had their own hierarchy, and their effects were channelled through personal possessions and hair, water and fire.

The Priests

A Maori village consisted of those of chiefly rank (*rangatira*), the main chief (*ariki*), the main body of the village and a small group of slaves. One *rangatira* was also the priest or *tohunga*, who guarded the *mana* of the group and himself had a special *mana*. There were several classes of *tohunga*, as specialists in art, magic, knowledge, or healing, and their power might outweigh that of a chief. The slaves, who had usually been captured, were important workers and could be used as human sacrifices, by being buried beneath the centre pole of a meeting house for example. Certain tasks automatically put the people involved under *tapu*.

One role of the priest was to diagnose the causes of adverse happenings, which were usually from witchcraft or by breaking a *tapu*. Priests also acted as healers. They were the mediums of their *atua*, or local gods, and were in constant contact with them. As shamans they relayed messages from the gods who typically communicated by whistling. The priest was therefore a central and indispensable person, since he guided and prepared for most of the important activities, including agriculture, hunting, building, war and sickness. A village might have several priests of different status, depending upon both their power and their skill in the spiritual world. The possession of power had to be established, and success increased a priest's *mana*, although he became *tapu* in proportion to his *mana*, and that could be easily infringed.

Rites and Worship

There was no worship in a European sense, and the crucial religious events were associated with *tapu* and with death. The practice at death was to place the corpse before burial on the *marae*, which was the area in front of the meeting house, and visiting parties from other villages joined the *tangi*, an occasion for a large and usually long meeting. The ritual function of the *tangi* was to speed the soul to the spirit land (Te Reinga) and to ensure that it properly left the body. Death was thought to be incomplete and so burial was temporary, until the flesh had decomposed, when the bones were moved to a permanent burial place.

Although the gods were not worshipped, there was contact with them for communication and control. Sacrifices to secure supernatural help with food supplies and materials were meals to which the appropriate god was invited. Alternatively, ritual formulae with power to influence spiritual beings were recited. The only images used for specifically religious purposes were 'god-sticks', a carved head on a stem bound with flax. These were not worshipped, but were used by a priest to command the attention of the relevant god, frequently by pulling at a string attached to the stick. Reverence was mainly for

Illustrations page 52

human ancestors, for the laws of *tapu,* and for some sacred places.

Maori Religious Life Now

The response of the Maoris to the Christianity of the colonists in the eighteen-twenties was one of confusion, while the fragmentation of their land destroyed their social structure and *mana.* Several syncretistic religious solutions resulted. Maoris have been recognized by many observers to have a 'religious' attitude to the natural world, and although they now belong to most of the common Christian denominations they are not considered to be much involved with formal church-going. The potent religious groups are still related to kinship. Schwimmer notes that what Christian 'denominations have done is not so much to set up specifically religious groups (though this was often their ambition) as to introduce new symbols which have transformed Maori religious thought'.

There are now two specifically Maori sects. Ratana, which was established during the nineteen-twenties, had 25,853 Maoris adhering in 1966, and Ringatu, established in the eighteen-sixties by Te Kooti, had 5,507 adherents. The Latter Day Saints (Mormons) also had a following, with 16,350 Maori (and 9,214 European) adherents. These groups may have an appeal because of their millenarian emphasis and their ability to adjust to new environments.

The founder of the Ratana Church effected miraculous cures and claimed to be God's direct mouth-piece for the Maoris. This Church became a significant social and political movement, gaining the four Maori seats in Parliament in 1943.

The most numerous groups are the Church of England, with 60,107 of the 201,159 Maoris in the 1966 census, and Roman Catholic with 36,358 Maoris. There were 15,877 Maori Methodists in 1966. All these groups have Maori clergy and a separate organization for Maori work, although there have been arguments about this. Religious observances tend to include Maoris from several denominations and conventional barriers are only loosely observed. Funerals conducted by Christian ministers still exhibit vestiges of Maori beliefs, and a Christian minister may be called to remove a *tapu* or to open a meeting house.

The Australian Aborigines

The Aborigines have no sharp differentiation between what we might call the sacred and the secular, as their ordinary world was filled with signs of the operation of spirit beings, with whom these nomadic people had a mythological relationship in their own regions. The natural species and objects in the environment had similar relationships to the spirit beings. The social groups into which people were born included their totemic ancestors and the design of life was fixed by a founding drama, which gave life mysterious properties, and defined a formal relationship between people and environment.

In one common form of the creation myth the earth was at first uncreated, a bare plain without physical features. Then in the mythical past or Eternal Dreamtime, the many supernatural beings or 'totemic ancestors' emerged from their sleep under the surface of the plain and instituted things in an enduring form. The sites where they emerged turned into such sacred features of the landscape as water holes and caves. The supernatural beings were linked with particular animals and plants, and so a rainbow snake ancestor usually moved about in human form, but could turn himself at will into a rainbow snake. From him the rainbow snakes of his original district were believed to have descended, as well as the human beings conceived in that district who were regarded as reincarnations of this ancestor and of his supernatural children. Totems were therefore ancestors in the form of local animals from whom the people in a tribe or region were descended, and a man shared the same life with his animal or plant totem.

For another creation myth, see illustration page 54.

After the processes of creation, the supernatural beings either returned to the earth or changed into sacred rocks or trees and went back to their eternal sleep. They retained the power to send rain or produce plants or animals of their own totems when summoned by the magic rites in which their human forms recited the secret verses that they themselves had first sung during the creation process.

Totemism is the key to understanding the Aboriginal philosophy, which regards man and nature as a corporate whole for social and religious purposes.

Illustration page 53

The Initiated

Those people fully initiated are the participants in religious rituals. There is not a special occupational class involved, since those who might be initiated are carefully specified by tribal rules. There are, however, specialized medicine men who produced cures by a variety of means. Rituals associated with death are directed to ensure that the spirit of the one who has died has a safe passage on its return to the spirit world, and does not return to trouble the living. A few groups erect graveposts of a stylized image of the dead person or as a representation of a spirit associated with that person's origins. There is thus a pervasive belief in a persistence of life in a different form, and of death as merely a transition, while wellbeing in the afterlife is not influenced by the quality of the person's previous life.

Illustration page 53

Illustrations page 54

Religious rituals are designed to honour the supernatural beings, to present them and their cult objects visually before those who are entitled to see them, to initiate tribal members, or to ensure an increase in food. The myths, songs and rituals are inherited, and so owned by direct blood descent.

Initiation marks full acceptance into the realm of the sacred. Men linked with other sacred rites can be invited to witness parts of a cycle, and to take part in the preparation of the cult objects used in them and with the decoration of the actors. Others might be invited as assistants. Religious life is revealed progressively by the elders, but appropriate initiation is a prerequisite for participation, and the proceedings are most secret. Women have their own sacred traditions, although some older women assist the men in parts of their secret rites. The form of decoration of the participants, the objects, totem poles and ground paintings, as well as the ritual and the chanted verses, are all believed to have been composed by the supernatural beings to whom they relate. There are therefore many restraints imposed on the participants during the long preparation for the ceremonies, which used to be performed only occasionally and are now very infrequent indeed. For this reason they are being lost.

Aboriginal Religious Life Now

The history of European contact with the Aborigines is an unhappy one, characterized by exploitation and the destruction of both their way of life and their sacred sites and cult-objects. Most Aborigines are now largely detribalized, and only a few very isolated groups remain in which there has not been a substantial European influence of one form or another. This influence has led to a forgetting of both the old ways and the rituals, which were of course orally transmitted. On the other hand it is only recently that full citizenship rights have been extended to the Aborigines, of whom 80,207 were enumerated in the 1966 Census. Of these, 26,459 are listed as giving 'no reply', 2,290 have 'no religion', 778 are 'indefinite' and 560 are 'non-Christian'. The Church of England (17,959) and the Roman Catholic Church (13,232) account for most of the 50,120 Christians. Christian missions have been extremely active in providing welfare, the price of this support often being the discard of the indigenous beliefs and practices of the Aborigines.

Chapter Four

Traditional Africa

For current Islamic expansion in Africa, see page 481.

Africa is a vast continent, with many races, but in religion as in other matters it is helpful for study to divide the continent at the Sahara Desert. For centuries the barriers of desert, tropical forest, and sea prevented religions from spreading south. North Africa belongs to the Mediterranean world and the religion of Islam was established there from the seventh century AD. Islam spread only slowly down the eastern and western coasts, and it did not enter the tropical forests and the East African interior until modern times. Christianity held the ancient Coptic churches in Egypt, flourished for a long time in the Sudan, and still survives in Ethiopia as the only African kingdom with a Christian state church. In the last hundred years Christian missions have spread to most African countries in the tropical and southern regions, and Islam has also made great advances in East and West Africa.

South of the Sahara, in the savannah regions and in the dense tropical forests, old traditional religious beliefs survive. These have often unhappily been called fetishist or animist (see Introduction), but they nearly always combine belief in a supreme being with the worship of other gods, cults of ancestors, and magical practices. Unfortunately there was no knowledge of writing in these areas before modern times, except among some peoples of the Sudan, and knowledge of the polytheistic traditional religions depends upon the records of observers, mostly foreign, and accounts dictated to them by Africans.

The races of tropical Africa are mostly Negro, divided by their languages roughly into Sudanese and Bantu groups. There are also small groups of Pygmies and Bushmen, and in Madagascar the population is chiefly Malaysian in origin, with some Indian and African strains. Over this vast area religious beliefs and practices vary considerably, owing not only to the absence of literature but also to the lack of central organization or missionary enterprise. Negro peoples have important religious beliefs which are comparable in their main themes, but there are many differences between particular places.

Pygmies, Bushmen and Hottentots

The Pygmies or Negritos live in the forest regions of the River Congo, and little is known of their languages or social organization since many of them are wandering hunters. They trade with the surrounding Bantu Negroes and many adopt some of their religious beliefs or myths. The Mbuti Pygmies believe in a great being of the sky, lord of storms and rainbows, sometimes called Creator, and envisaged as an old man with a long beard. He is named Tore and not only did he make everything but all belongs to him, so that before hunting he is invoked for food. The Pygmies also revere the moon, and some of them say that it was the moon who moulded the first man, covered him with skin and poured blood inside. Another story associates the first couple with the chameleon, a reptile that figures in many African tales.

The dominant Pygmy belief is in the god of the forest, who is benevolent, and to whom men pay as much respect as they do to their own parents. There are popular songs of joy and praise which have as motif the simple theme that the forest is good. The forest-god is in the trees or the river or waiting silently near his worshipper, and a basket of food is the sign that he has been invoked. There are religious societies, particularly male, which function in celebration of the forest-god and are active at festivals of puberty for boys and girls, with ritual dancing and feasting.

The Bushmen and Hottentots (the latter coming from the mixture of Bushmen with other races) live in southern Africa and were the original inhabitants of the land when the first Europeans arrived at the Cape. The Bushmen came from the north thousands of years ago, passing down through East and Central Africa, where their former presence is attested by rock-paintings in Tanzania, Zimbabwe and elsewhere. Today the true Bushmen (Khoisan) are restricted to the Kalahari Desert and Namibia.

The ancient Bushmen were great painters and engravers on flat rock surfaces, using black, white, red, brown and yellow colours in their pictures. The subjects of those paintings which have survived are largely of animals. They are clearly hunting scenes, which probably had the magical purpose of helping men to kill animals in the chase, as in the ancient European rock-paintings (see chapter on prehistoric religion). Human figures were generally more realistically drawn by the Bushmen than by the Lascaux artists in ancient southern France; sexual differences, ornaments, weapons and hair styles are clearly visible. But, apart from the hunting magic, the paintings reveal little of ancient Bushman religion, and Bushmen have now forgotten both how to paint and how to interpret the ancient patterns.

Modern Bushmen pray to celestial spirits and tell myths and legends about them. They pay special attention to the moon, which comes into their speculations about the origins of death, a common African preoccupation. Other natural forces are personified, and past heroes are glorified, and both are invoked at times, especially when there is need of rain. There are initiation ceremonies for girls, but not so many for boys and circumcision was not an ancient Bushman practice.

The Hottentots have largely become Christian and most of their ancient religious beliefs have disappeared, so much so that it was once thought that they had no former religion. Their ancient gods appear to have been a mingling of natural forces and ancestral spirits. The great tribal hero was Tsui 'goab, and to him the Hottentots prayed for rain and food, telling legends of his great exploits.

God Omnipotent

In the sub-Saharan and forest areas there are small groups of Hamites (Caucasians, related to Europeans) such as the Fulani of Nigeria, but they are Muslims like the major Hamite groups of North Africa and the Tuaregs of the Sahara. The vast majority of Africans south of the Sahara are Negroes, and they generally have a belief in a supreme being, though their conception of his role in daily life differs according to localities.

In East Africa a common name for the supreme being is Mulungu, a word of unknown origin but indicating the almighty and ever-present creator. The thunder is said to be his voice and the lightning his power; he rewards the good and punishes the wicked. From the northern Kalahari through the Congo to Tanzania the name Leza is used, perhaps from a root meaning 'to cherish', since he is the one who watches over people, providing for the needy and besetting the wayward. Leza is said to live in heaven, to which humans pray for rain, but finally he is transcendent and incomprehensible. Another divine name is Nyambe, perhaps from a root indicating power, and used from Botswana to Cameroun. A similar name, Nyame, is used in West Africa alongside other divine names, such as Ngewo the god of the Mende people of Sierra Leone, Amma of the Dogon of Mali, Mawu of the Ewe of Abomey, Olorun of the Yoruba and Chukwu of the Ibo and Soko of the Nupe, all of Nigeria.

Despite the universality of belief in a supreme being in Africa regular worship is not generally given to him. There are no great temples or organized cults for him in most places, though there are a few exceptions. There are low mud altars for Amma among the Dogon, a number of small temples and pots on forked sticks for Nyame in Ashanti, groves and sacred places among the Kikuyu of Kenya and the Shona of Zimbabwe.

Yet despite this absence of formal worship and temples over most of Africa, the supreme being (or God) is a reality to many people. He is transcendent and there is a popular myth, told from West African to the Upper Nile, which says that he or the sky his dwelling place was once much nearer to the earth. Owing to undue human familiarity, usually blamed on a woman, he withdrew to the distance where he now is. Despite his distance he supervises all the affairs of earth; proverbs tell of his providential care, and he is thought to send rewards and punishments. Where there are no temples or priests, ordinary people pray to him in time of need without any intermediary; he is the resort of those who find that all else has failed and the final court of appeal. The name of God comes in daily salutations, common proverbs, oaths and riddles. Many myths are told about him, in which he may have a wife and children, yet he lives in heaven

Above Olokun, the Benin (Nigeria) spirit of the sea. This bronze statue has mudfish legs and a lizard in each hand. Rijksmuseum voor Volkenkunde, Leiden.

Above left Painted clay sculptures of the Ibo, Nigeria. The central female figure is the great Earth Mother, Ala. Next to her is a European, wearing a sun helmet and riding a motorcycle.

Left A priest of Shango, thunder-god of the Yoruba of Nigeria, holding a carved, double-headed, wooden axe, symbolical of the thunderbolt.

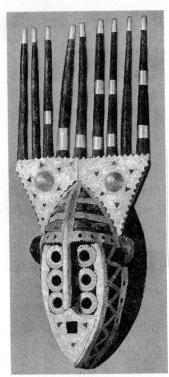

and is supreme. The Nuer of the Sudan have neither prophets nor sanctuaries of God, and make no material images of him, but he is present in the very atmosphere, in daily life and the social order. God is spoken of as spirit, invisible like wind and air, yet though he is in these things he is different from them. He is associated with the sky, as high up, yet he is different from the heavens, storm and rain, since he is everywhere.

Africans believe in many other spiritual beings, roughly divisible into nature spirits and ancestors, some of them having both human and natural origins. They are often called children of God, but most receive much more formal worship than he does. Yet it is said that in sacrifices offered to other deities the essence of the gift goes to the supreme being.

There are countless gods, and their cults are particularly well developed in West Africa, and rather less in eastern and southern Africa where the ancestral rituals tend to dominate. Many of these cults of the gods are declining nowadays but in some places, as among the Ewe of Abomey, they are highly organized and are as yet little affected by Islam or Christianity.

The gods may be distinguished according to their location in the regions of sky, earth, water and forest. There are very few references made to the sun, because in the tropics the sun is always present and oppressive and does not need to be induced to shine. There are a few moon cults, particularly in connection with ceremonies for babies, which are shown to the moon as a sign of blessing. The great gods of the sky are the storms, because of the fierce tornadoes which sweep across the tropical regions. One of the most notable deities is Shango of the Yoruba of Nigeria, who was the fourth king of the capital town of Oyo. He ascended to heaven by a chain, and became identified with the storm. This double function assured his popularity both as national- and storm-god, and many towns still have temples dedicated to Shango, with priests who impersonate the god at festivals and carry imitation axes to symbolize thunderbolts and lightning.

Spirits of the Earth

The spirits of the earth are associated with agriculture and many other sides of life. Asase Yaa, Mother Thursday, of the Ashanti, has no temple or regular worship, but work on the land is taboo on Thursday and at ploughing and harvest times libations and first-fruits are offered to her as the Earth Mother. Among the Ibo the earth-spirit Ala is the most popular deity of all and the greatest power in social life. There are countless temples, with life-size images of Ala with a child in her arms like a madonna, and regular sacrifices are offered. On special occasions new houses are erected for Ala, with clay images of many other creatures, divine, human and animal, brightly painted, but the Earth Mother is always the central figure. Ala is guardian of morality, and is particularly important as custodian of the dead since they are buried in the earth as in her womb. Other earth-spirits are associated with hills, rocks and special places of power, like Mount Kenya, the

Opposite above right Dancers of the Barotse (Rozi) people of Zambia, representing tribal spirits.

Opposite above left An initiation mask of the Bambara people of the Republic of Mali, made of wood, copper and aluminium. Initiation rites introduce youths into adult life, and masks represent ancestral figures. Walker Art Center, Minneapolis, Minnesota.

Opposite below left A cult figure of the Mende people of Sierra Leone. These idealized and carefully decorated sculptures of women symbolize the guardian spirit of the female secret-society, which prepares girls for the life they will lead as adult women. Horniman Museum, London.

Opposite below right The ancestral shrine of the Oba of Benin. The bronze heads, with representations of coral headdress and necklace, represent past obas, and the ivory tusks which surmount them depict scenes in tradition and legend. The Palace of the Oba, Benin City.

Illustration page 63

Illustration page 63

'mountain of brightness'. The importance of the earth appears again in social groups and secret societies, which use symbols of the earth in their rituals.

Illustration page 63

Water-spirits are believed to dwell in springs, wells, streams, rivers and the sea. Olokun, the god of the sea at Benin, is thought to be a great king who lives in a palace under the waters with his soldiers and mermaids, and at times it was said that he tried to conquer the earth by a great flood. Peoples who live along rivers or by the sea have many tales of the spirits there and they make sacrifices to propitiate them. On the Upper Niger people that have been under the influence of Islam for centuries still perform dances every week, in which the spirits of the waters (the Zin, perhaps from the Islamic *jinn*) are believed to enter into their devotees. In is often in conjunction with water-spirits that cults of sacred snakes occur, especially the python, and there are temples for their worship on the Atlantic coast, at Whydah and the Niger delta.

Spirits of the forest are less easily described and worship may only occur in occasional offerings of food placed in front of trees and rocks. Hunters seek to propitiate the spirits of the wild and learn from them the secret lore which makes for success in the chase. They also become weathermen and claim to be able to bring or prevent the rain. In the forest many uncanny spirits are said to dwell: those who have died without proper burial, monsters, fairies, and the ghosts of twins which are like red monkeys. Twins are regarded with awe everywhere: in some places they used to be neglected or killed because they would bring misfortune; elsewhere images were made of them and twin pots outside the doors of their houses had small offerings placed in them.

Ancestral and Royal Cults

The gods play a large part in the traditional religious life of many West African peoples, with their temples, festivals and priests, but there are also powerful cults of the dead. In East and South Africa the latter were the dominant feature of religious life. Everywhere belief in the survival after death is unquestioned and many rituals are performed. There is a first funeral a day or so after death, because corpses do not keep in a hot climate, but a second burial ceremony weeks or months later brings all the relatives and friends together, and rites are enacted to give final rest to the deceased and to make sure that the person does not return as a wandering ghost. The head of the family addresses the dead one by name, some belongings are buried with the body, and food and drink may be laid regularly at the grave. Stools which were used in life often represent the dead and offerings are laid or poured upon them at intervals.

The dead provide a powerful sanction for social life, since generally people fear them more than the gods. The dead are the heads of the family and clan, they know their children, and now that they are out of the body they have additional powers. That the dead are seen in dreams is taken as proof of their survival and presence. They make known their will through dreams and visions, or in messages to mediums and special people. Accidents and disease may be attributed to their stern rule, though cures can be effected by pacifying their anger.

The dead are concerned with family life, and especially with the birth of children through whom they may be reincarnated, or some portion of their spirit or their name passed on. Family property belongs to the ancestors and they must be consulted if there is any question of renting or selling it; this consultation is done by casting lots or throwing nuts on the ground and deducing a reply from the pattern that they form. The crops and harvests are ancestral interests, and so is the weather that makes crops grow; therefore the dead are implored for rain in family prayer or great tribal ceremonies.

The importance of the dead is seen in the countless masks, which are some of the most important contributions of Africa to world art. If there are no scriptures of the ancient religion, yet in the many carvings and sculptures there are expressions of religious faith. Nowhere does this appear more strikingly than in the wooden masks which represent ancestors, animals and other powers. Sometimes the masks are naturalistic, calm or fearful, but often they have abstract designs which show that the dead are beyond human imagination. There are many regular ceremonies at which masked figures appear and represent the living dead, speaking in guttural tones, and giving messages and warnings to their relatives.

Initiation ceremonies are held all over Africa in order to introduce young people to adult life and the teachings of the fathers. Secret *Illustrations page 64* societies, such as the male Poro and female Sande in Sierra Leone and Guinea, have this purpose. Young people undergo trials of endurance, receive traditional information in sexual and tribal customs, and learn the secret of the masked figures, before returning to normal life as full adults.

There were great rulers in parts of old Africa who centralized the power of society, from the Zulu and Swazi, to Buganda, Benin and *Illustration page 64* Ashanti. Some of them, like the Rain-Queen of the Lovedu of the Transvaal, were believed to be immortal and the royal line was passed down through sacred rulers who did not die but 'went elsewhere'. Yet even the most powerful were rarely absolute and they could be dethroned if they violated the tribal customs. Other societies, like the Ibo, Nuer or Shilluk, had no real rulers and were loose federations of families.

Magic and the Present

African religion has been compared to a pyramid, of which the top is the supreme being, the sides are nature gods and ancestors, and at the lowest level are magical beliefs and practices.

Magic is of many kinds and it may be considered as personal or social, good or harmful. Magical objects are made by specialists, medicine-men or magicians, and they are thought to possess both material and spiritual powers. They protect the wearer in amulets, necklaces, bracelets, rings and girdles. Others are used to protect houses, crops and property. Social magic protects the village or calls down rain on the crops. The good magician is respected and works in public, but the evil magician is feared and operates in secret. The latter prepares harmful potions, or even plain poisons, and he is punished if his evil work is discovered.

Divination is a popular form of magic, a kind of fortune-telling. There are many systems, of which the Ifa oracle of the Yoruba is famous, using 256 figures marked on a sanded board and interpreted by expert diviners. Elsewhere, as in Mozambique or Lesotho, strings of shells or bones are cast on the ground and an answer is deduced from the forms that appear.

Witchcraft is widely feared, but it is distinct from sorcery or harmful magic. The witch, generally thought to be a woman, is believed to fly at night from her sleeping body and feed on the soul of her victim, who thereupon sickens and dies. A witch-doctor claims to discover witches, by ordeals and poisons, and to release the captive soul. Some of these witchcraft beliefs resemble those of medieval Europe, and it cannot be too strongly stated that there is no evidence for the existence of either witches or witch-craft, they are the product of tensions and fears clothed in gruesome fantasy.

Much of African traditional religion is declining and disappearing before the advance of modern education and commerce. Two great missionary religions, Christianity and Islam, have made powerful inroads into African life in this century. Christianity now claims over 160 million followers in tropical and southern Africa, and there are over 130 million Muslims. Not only foreign missions but many new African Christian prophets and their societies have taken over much of the traditional religious life.

Old gods and their temples have gone, but magical superstitions are more tenacious and will long remain. The Supreme Being of traditional Africa is assimilated to the God of Islam and Christianity, and rituals for life after death are transferred to the memorial services and ornate tombs of today. There are said to be six thousand Christian sects in Africa, and they represent both the diversity of the old cults and the religious energy and zeal of African life. The parallel rapid spread of Islam into the tropical areas shows also that the new religions have adapted themselves to the African climate of thought, in which all life is seen to have a purpose and to give responsibility to men under the rule of the Supreme Being.

Chapter Five

Aztecs and Mayas

Archaic cultures known only through archaeology form the common background of the main Mexican and Central American civilizations such as those of the Olmecs, Toltecs, Chichimecs, Aztecs and the various Maya peoples. On the other hand they are certain to have influenced each other in historic times. Both their archaic common background and their mutual influences in later times account for the numerous points of resemblance between their cultures and societies, the most striking resemblances being found in matters of religion. There exist of course great differences, or the need would never have been felt to study each of these civilizations separately. The large number of resemblances, however, justifies the fact that nearly a quarter of this short survey of the Aztec and Maya religions will be devoted to them.

Both religions distinguish between 'ancient' gods and 'younger' gods. In Central America the god of fire is invariably an ancient god. The Toltecs called him Huêhuêteotl (Old God). The Aztecs also considered the god of the travelling merchants, Yacatecuhtli (Lord of the Vanguard), an old god, probably because the ancestors of these merchants belonged to an indigenous population group. With the Maya peoples the original nature and agrarian deities were the ancient gods, whereas the gods they had adopted from the Toltects, like the great god Quetzalcoatl (Plumed Serpent), were the younger ones, who were more involved in the cosmic and socio-cultural aspects of their civilization.

Illustration page 73

In the religious as well as the social concept of the universe held by all Central American peoples there existed direct associations between space, time and colour, which have similar structures, but show slight variations from people to people. Taking the earth as the centre, they distinguished six cosmic directions: the four quarters of space, above (heaven) and below (the underworld). So, inclusive of the centre (the earth), there were seven divisions in cosmic space.

In fact each religious and each social system in Central America is found to have an order that is often a complicated elaboration of the system of four horizontal directions (the four quarters) and that of three vertical directions (the three cosmic layers). As the principle underlying this order was connected with a dualistic world view based on the man-woman opposition, the nations of Central America were able to find many interesting solutions for the organizational grouping of their deities, chiefs, priests, military leaders and other dignitaries, by arranging them in sets of four or three, representing either the fourfold or the tripartite system. Within each set of four, however, two members were always considered as closely connected, and in some instances even as a unit. This principle penetrated so deeply into Aztec society that the third child in a family of four children was called 'the middle one'.

Each People Had Its Colour

The horizontal directions were associated with different colours, but each people had its own space-colour associations, as is seen in the following survey:

	East	South	West	North
Maya of Yucatán	red	yellow	black	white
Aztecs	yellow red green	blue	white	black
Toltecs	yellow	white	green	red
Chichimecs	green	red	yellow	white

The combination of space and colour was associated with time, and time was closely connected with the gods, especially among the Maya. All this gave rise to associations between direction, colour, time and the cosmic forces (gods) determining these three elements. The universe and consequently life on earth was successively controlled by a particular combination of direction, time and gods. The Toltecs and the Aztecs (who were in a sense one of the twenty Toltec peoples) called the cosmic ages determined in this way 'suns'. This concept also existed among the Maya, and like the Toltecs they distinguished four such cosmic ages, each determined by one of the quarters and the gods belonging to it.

The Aztecs divided the history of the universe into five 'suns', the first being associated with the east, the second and third with the north, the fourth with the west, and the fifth with the south. The four or five different sets of gods, time and direction always existed simultaneously, side by side. The Maya as well as the Aztecs regarded time as a relative concept in that the four or five 'suns' were represented as occurring in a sequence as well as simultaneously. The idea of sequence only consisted in each 'sun' being dominated by one particular combination, which after a certain length of time (one sun) had to surrender its ascendancy to another combination.

An extra dimension was added to the concept of the universe by including the distinction between the 'world above' (heaven) and the 'world below' (hell). The Maya originally distinguished nine spheres in heaven and nine in the underworld. The celestial spheres are to be

imagined as twice four heavens situated in the four horizontal directions and one heaven on top, viz. that of the supreme divine couple
of creators. The underworld contained the reflected picture of this
cosmic arrangement. The Toltecs, Aztecs, and Maya divided heaven
into thirteen parts, adding one step to the pyramid of heaven by
subdividing the older topmost heaven of the Maya and Olmecs into
five heavens.

All the principles underlying the order of the universe are also
recognizable in the social and administrative organizations of these
peoples.

Each Human Has a Counterpart

An entirely different and probably very old fundamental conception
occurring in Central American religious thinking is that of the existence of so-called 'counterparts in disguise'. Every human being was
thought to have one or more 'counterparts', mostly disguised as
animals, whose fates were linked to that of the human being in a
manner conditioned by cosmic forces.

This conception is closely connected with the ritual time-units of
13 × 20 = 260 days, which the Aztecs called *tonalpoalli* (count of
days), and the Maya *tzolkin* (see the comparative survey of the Aztec
and Maya calendars at the end of this section). The 'days' of the ritual
calendars of these two peoples ran from midnight till noon, each day
being ruled by one of the cardinal points in the order: east, north,
west, south, then again east etc. Each day had for its companion the
daily period from midday till midnight. Each day's companion was
one of the so-called lords of the night, the nine gods ruling the nine
parts into which the night was divided, for during that period the
sun passed through the nine spheres of the underworld. For the same
reason there were thirteen gods that ruled the day.

Every human being possessed from the moment of birth a personal
combination of these periods, which to a great extent determined his
or her fate. This combination was shared with the 'animal counterparts', who consequently shared that person's destiny. This used to
be and still is the principle underlying many acts of magic in this
cultural area. By doing harm to or destroying a counterpart one can
kill or make a person ill; by strengthening a sick person's animal
counterpart one cures him or her.

The Evolution of the Universe

The concept of the order of the universe caused all Central American
peoples to look upon the development of the universe as a steady
evolution during the successive periods of the 'suns'. This evolution,
so they thought, could only be interrupted by catastrophic revolutions
or by natural catastrophes during the transition from one sun to the
next. It was also universally believed that within each sun only those
forms of earthly life could flourish that were organized according to
the principles governing the order of the prevalent constellation. The
relations between people and their gods were governed by the principle of reciprocity. Since it was the gods that created people and

made it possible for them to live, people were obliged to feed and strengthen their gods, the extreme consequence of this being the human sacrifices, which were constantly performed by the Aztecs.

Nearly all literature on Aztec religion is concerned with the immediately pre-Spanish religion of the Aztecâ-Mexîcâ and other Central American peoples under strong Mexican influence. In a wider historical meaning, however, Aztec religion covers a period of over nine centuries (from 1064 to the present day), about which historical data concerning the Aztecâ-Mexîcâ have come to hand, and during which the Aztec religion has undergone considerable changes.

The Aztecâ, the 'genuine' Aztecs, were originally one of the twenty Toltec tribes living in the extreme northwest of the Toltec empire (the present-day state of Guanajuato). We know that before the eleventh century at any rate this tribe had united with the Chichimec tribe of Mexitin (afterwards called Mexîcâ) into one religious, social and administrative organization within the Aztec territory (Aztlan). It was the less civilized Mexitin with their tribal god Tetzauhteotl Huitzilopochtli (Magnificent God Humming Bird on the Left) who eventually gained control of the religious system. The Aztec tribe was divided into four groups, the Mexitin into three. Consequently the Aztecs were associated with the horizontal directions, the Mexitin with the vertical, and the tribal god of the Mexitin was thought to be related to the great Sun-god, the Aztec tribal god to the goddess of the earth.

'Waging War is My Duty'

With the magic nature of their religion and its close relationship with the order of the universe, the Aztecâ-Mexîcâ considered themselves destined to execute the task clearly expressed in the mission that the god Tetzauhteotl is said to have assigned to his high priest Huitzilopochtli – who was later identified with the god – at the time of the fall of the Toltec empire:

> *Therefore I decided to leave*
> *the country (Aztlan),*
> *Therefore I have come as one charged with a special duty,*
> *Because I have been given arrows and shields,*
> *For waging war is my duty,*
> *And on my expeditions I*
> *shall see all the lands,*
> *I shall wait for the people and meet them*
> *In all four quarters and I shall give them*
> *Food to eat and drinks to quench their thirst,*
> *For here I shall unite all the different peoples!*

This text unambiguously points to the task laid upon the Aztec-Mexican regime that was to rule over Mexico and Central America in later times. The political as well as religious ambitions of this people implied the control or at least the regulation of war as an

Above Coatlicue is the Aztec goddess of earth, the mother of the gods. Often she is represented with a skull-head, indicating that she is both old and exhausted by all who live upon her. Museo Nacional de Antropologia, Mexico City.

Above centre Quetzalcoatl in his manifestation as the wind god, Ehecatl. This Aztec basalt statue shows him wearing the characteristic wind 'mask', surmounted by his own distinctive conical cap. Philadelphia Museum of Art, Pennsylvania. Louise and Walter Arensburg Collection.

Above left Tlaloc, the Aztec god of rain and of germination. Museo Nacional d'Antropologia, Mexico City.

Left Huêhuêteotl, a form of the Lord of Fire, Xiuhtecuhtli, from Teotihuâcan (first century AD or earlier). His headdress is a bowl in which a temple fire was kindled. This deity was thought to be the pivot of the universe, linking domestic fire with the Pole Star.

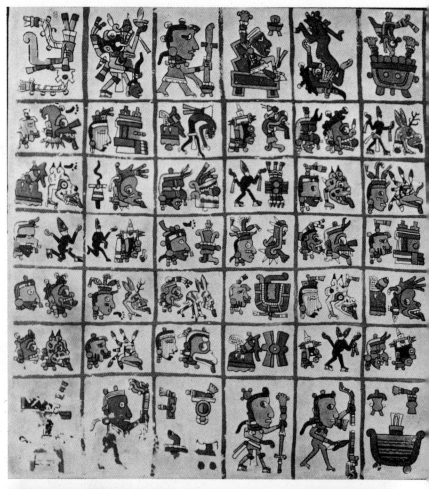

Right The cylindrical tower at Chichen Itza, Mexico, which was probably an observatory.

Left Two folios from a copy of the *Codex Cospiano*. They show the second group of 13-day periods within the 260-day magical calendar known as the *tonalpoalli*. The top and bottom rows of figures represent the fates-above-and-below of the days in the smaller squares between them. Biblioteca Universitaria, Bologna.

Below left An aplite statue of Tlazolteotl, eater of filth and goddess of unbridled sexuality, in the act of childbirth. Despite her own character, she was unusual among Aztec deities in expecting humans to follow a moral code and she received confessions of sexual wrongdoing. Dumbarton Oaks, Washington DC. Robert Woods Bliss Collection.

Below Xipe Totêc, the Flayed One, is a god adopted by the Aztecs from their Huaxtec subjects. The second religious feast of the solar year, Tlacaxipehualiztli, the flaying of men, was dedicated to him. He was a fertility god and originally clearly phallic. Museum of Mankind, London.

Above The pyramid of the Plumed Serpent at Chichen Itza, a sacred city of the Toltecs and Mayas. It probably dates from the sixth century AD. At the top of such pyramids victims were sacrificed to the gods and their bodies thrown down the steps.

Right A stone model of a pyramid (*c.* AD 1500), discovered in the foundations of Tenochtitlán. Being a late Aztec work, all the gods bear speech-scrolls signifying war. The stone codifies the Aztec belief in war as a way of securing captives, some of whom were then sacrificed and their hearts offered to the sun in repayment for the divine sacrifice. Museo Nacional d'Antropologio, Mexico City.

instrument to gain and exercise power, and the unification of all the peoples on earth into one social, religious and administrative organization to guarantee the harmonious preservation of the human race. Again this organization was to be consistent with the order of the universe.

As the Aztecâ-Mexîcâ, urged by their divine mission, migrated further away from their original territory towards the traditional Central Mexican cultural centres, their own culture was increasingly affected.

Alien influences, both religious and social, were more easily adopted; many alien gods were admitted into their pantheon; marriages with members of other tribes and the admission of foreigners into their own tribe widened their concept of the universe. There was a considerable increase in human sacrifices, and the military men gained in power, taking over from the priests more and more administrative functions within the society.

The Needs of a Young Empire

When in 1428 the Aztecâ-Mexîcâ established their domination over the Central Mexican lake area, the development described above culminated in the institution of a state religion which was adapted to the needs of the young empire. It was especially the Cihuacoatl (Female Companion) Tlacayelel, the supreme internal ruler of the empire from 1428 till 1474, who added ideological elements to the Aztec religion. The souls of warriors killed on the battlefield and the souls of victims of human sacrificial offerings rose to the eastern solar heaven. Women who died in childbirth rose to the western solar heaven: the regime looked upon them as heroines because they had died after giving birth to another Aztec. A common metaphor for giving birth to a child was 'taking a prisoner'. The mother on that occasion had as it were acquired a creature dedicated to the gods and as such considered to be equal to a human sacrifice.

Both groups occupied a place of honour within the regime, and on their deaths they were thought to join the train of attendants of the sun-god on his course across the sky; the men from sunrise till noon, the women from noon till sunset. Other people on their death went to the horrible subterranean realm of the dead, exception being made for those who had been fortunate enough to be struck by lightning or to be drowned, for these found a place in the paradise of the rain-god Tlaloc.

The Urge to Conquer

The tribal god Huitzilopochtli was also the god of the south, the god of war, and the protector of the Fifth Sun. Hence the Aztec people considered themselves to be in charge of the regulation of all earthly matters during the fifth cosmic age. This principle may seem easily to lead to an uncontrolled urge to conquer and dominate other nations. But, used as the starting-point for the policy of the Aztec state regime, this dogma was religious in nature and therefore acted as a check on the unlimited exercise of power. For the ideology that had been added to the fundamentals of their religion was aimed only at establishing an overall world-order in agreement with the constellation of the Fifth Sun. This meant that the Aztecs contented themselves with the maintenance on earth of an overall structure incorporating locally many different social, cultural and administrative patterns. It must be admitted that this structure was a very flexible one. The Aztec regime was highly tolerant in religious and cultural matters generally.

Some Central Mexican territories with a high level of culture dating back to Toltec or even earlier times were allowed to join the regulated so-called 'wars of flowers', thereby retaining almost complete internal independence. The wars of flowers were encounters between local armies with a fixed number of warriors, operating within the Aztec world, and fighting ritual battles at fixed times and on predetermined battlefields.

Illustrations page 76 The main religious purpose of these regulated wars, fought according to set rules, was the capturing of prisoners of war who could at some later time be sacrificed to one or more deities of the capturing party or parties. The main social purpose of these wars was to enable the sons of noble families, officers and brave warriors of low descent to win honour and fame, and thus rise on the social ladder. Ideologically wars of flowers might be regarded as an attempt to prevent decadence. The fall of the Toltec empire as a result of the social and cultural decadence of the élite had caused among the Aztecs an almost traumatic fear of it, which induced the leaders of the regime to drive the sons of the élite into one war of flowers after another. Only those who had gained personal success in these wars were eligible for administrative functions.

Concepts of Divinity

The Aztec concept of divinity was rooted in religious principles that had developed in the older Olmec, Toltec and Chichimec cultures. Ancient Central Mexican gods, e.g. Xiuhtecuhtli (Lord of the Year, fire-god), Quetzalcoatl (Venus, saviour, god of wind and science) and Illustration page 73 Tlaloc (Wine of the Earth, rain-god), were adopted by the Aztecs. Yacatecuhtli, the god of the merchants, was probably one of the forms in which Quetzalcoatl was worshipped. The important Aztec god Tezcatlepoca (It Causes the Black Mirror to Shine, the god of the nocturnal sky), often identified with the supreme god, seems to be of Chichimec origin. But as this god was also worshipped by Mixtec and many other tribes, there is no certainty as to his origin. There are indications that he was already worshipped by the Mexitin in Aztlan.

The fertility-god Xipe Totêc (Our Lord, the Flayed One), a phallic god of fertility, was adopted from the peoples living on the Pacific Illustrations page 75 coasts. The Huaxtecs, the most northern Maya tribe on the Gulf, provided the goddess of women in childbed, Tlazolteotl.

The texts referring to the principal Aztec gods and goddesses recorded by Sahagún at Tepepulco reveal a complicated concept of divinity. The Aztecs used the word *teotl* (literally 'stony', but in a figurative sense: permanent, powerful) to denote their gods and goddesses in general. These deities possessed widely differing qualities, and their importance in the pantheon showed great differences. Therefore the concept of *teotl* seems at a first glance to be a rather vague one.

The Pantheon

The following is a translation of part of the Aztec text about the god Tezcatlepoca: 'This one was considered a real *teotl,* he (or it) lived everywhere, in hell, on earth and in heaven. On earth he (or it) brought dust and dung to life, and caused many sufferings among men, he (it) set people against each other, therefore he (it) is said to be hostile on both sides. He (or it) created all things; he (it) brought evil things upon men, thus placing them into his (its) shade, and asserting himself (itself) as their master, he (it) mocked men. Sometimes he (it) gave them riches, dominance and power to rule, nobility and honour.'

This is an almost pantheistic concept of the supreme god, as it is found in several polytheistic religions. No wonder that Tezcatlepoca appears in the Aztec pantheon in more forms than any other god. No other god is referred to under so many different names and with so many metaphors. The best-known are: Om(e)acatl (Two Reed, his principal calender name), Tlamatzincatl (his name as a war-god), Yoalli Ehecatl (Night and Wind, i.e. invisible and evasive), Tloquê Nahuâquê (Ruler of Adjacent and Nearby Things, i.e. the all-embracing vicinity), Ipalnemoani (He or It That Makes Life Possible), Moyocuyatzin (the Self-Creating One) and Moquequeloatzin (the Capricious One). Nature gods, such as Tlaloc (the god of the waters of heaven), Chalchiuhtlicue (Her Skirt Is Made of Jade, the goddess of the waters on earth), Ehecatl (the wind), Tonatiuh (the sun), Chicomecoatl (the maize-goddess) etc., are described by Sahagún's informants as forces with natural effects of their own: rain, irrigation or floods, wind or gale, warmth or heat and drought, etc. These might have occurred in any polytheistic religion.

Illustration page 73

Gods for Each Group

The Aztec concept of divinity is unique, however, in the association of particular gods with particular social groups within a nation, or with entire tribes or nations. Examples are the gods Yacatecuhtli (the god of the merchants) and Huitzilopochtli (the god of the Aztecâ-Mexîcâ), who have been mentioned before. When merchants with their caravan pitched camp on their distant journeys, they made a bundle of all their travelling-canes and laid this on the ground in the middle of their camp. It represented their god Yacatecuhtli. This might lead us to conclude that the Aztecs thought of their group and tribal gods as the suprapersonal unities of collective groups, as the factor that makes the group more important than the sum total of its members. Sahagún's informants at Tepepulco said of Huitzilopochtli that 'he is but subject and prince', a metaphor meaning 'he is no more than the whole people, from the highest to the lowest'. These words also seem to give evidence of a simple way of deifying the supra-personal unity of a group.

It should be remembered, however, that one of the fundamentals of the Aztec concepts of divinity and religion in general was the cosmic interrelationship between all phenomena. This gave to the Aztec concept of both their group and tribal gods a dimension that is not to be inferred directly from the texts quoted above. For the Aztecs considered the supra-individual unity of a group of far greater importance than most Europeans do.

A Predestined Fate

The cosmic relationship embodied in the constellation of the gods, which belonged to the Fifth Sun, gave every individual person as well as every group of persons his or her own predestined fate. Although these forms of predestination might, indeed, have different effects due to the freedom of action allowed to human beings, it was thought that the combined powers and forces in the universe determined the existence of a particular group. This complex of forces, of which the urge to exist and the vitality of the social group concerned forms only one of its component elements, was symbolized by the Aztecs in their group and tribal gods. The complex of forces might in its turn be closely connected with other constellations of power. Consequently the gods with their day-signs could have counterparts, just like a human being.

Considerable differences existed between the gods. There was for instance a wide distance between the supreme god Tezcatlepoca and the group god of the inhabitants of a village-ward, or the god of an extended family. The group god of the feather mosaic workers, Coyotlinahual, differed a great deal from the rain-god Tlaloc. But all Aztec deities had this in common, that they existed longer than man, for they were thought to exist in any case as long as the constellation of the Fifth Sun. Since their existence was comparatively permanent, they were all gods.

Religion and Society

The term 'sacral society' has been used for some present Maya village communities, and is also applicable to the pre-Spanish Aztec society. The religious and social aspects of this society were completely interwoven: its religion, science, philosophy, forms of recreation, arts, wars, agriculture, industry and commerce were integrated in a regime that consisted of structurally uniform sections.

A simple example of the strong resemblance between the state administrative and religious orders was the so-called 'triple throne' of the Aztec empire. There were three capital cities: Mexîco, Tetzcoco and Tlacopan, the capitals of the three central provinces. Each capital city was governed by one royal family, tracing descent through the paternal line. The three royal families formed one large family through regular intermarriage which traced its descent through the female line. The three capital cities were associated with the three vertical cosmic layers: heaven, earth and the underworld. The most important of the three cities, Mexîco, consisted of two parts, Tlal-telolco and Tenochtitlan, each having administrative functions of its own. Tenochtitlan was divided into four parts, each of which supplied the supreme rulers of the four large outlying provinces of the empire. Thus Tenochtitlan, as one of the seats of the central government, was associated with the four horizontal quarters. Besides the three administrative capitals there existed an important religious centre: Cholullan.

The Toltecs had exactly the same system. At first they had three administrative centres: Tollan, Otompan and Colhuacan; their religious capital was Teotihuâcan. The Tecpanec and Tarascan empires showed the same division. The cosmic triple, quadruple and fivefold divisions were also found to underlie their social order.

Aztec Classes

The various social classes in Aztec society had each in its own way a part to play in their religious organization. The Aztec élite consisted of the hereditary nobility, the military nobility, the priests of higher rank, the merchants who traded between the regions both within and without the empire, and some groups of craftsmen, such as the gold and silver smiths, and the feather mosaic workers. The common people were farmers, fishermen and the other craftsmen. Together they were called *macehualtin* (free citizens). The members of the nobility as well as the *macehualtin* possessed the right of landownership. The former often owned private lands; the latter owned land as part of the common property, each family-head being allotted some fields belonging to the common wardlands.

Besides the 'free' classes of society there existed three 'unfree' or tied classes. The *tecpanpouhquê* (servants of the palace) were people who were often ethnically different from the Aztecs and were in the permanent service of government institutions or functionaries. They often enjoyed a pretty high social status, mostly higher than that of the *macehualtin*! The *mayequé* (righthanded ones) were tied farm-workers, who possessed no land. They were former rebels or opponents of the regime and their descendants. Their rebellion against the Aztec government had lost them their right to own land. Finally there were the *tlacotin* (the sold ones), people who had become slaves through unpaid debts.

The Central Importance of Sacrifice

It is understandable that these various Aztec social groupings were differently connected with the Aztec religion. Everybody from time to time sacrificed a little of his own blood to one or more of the gods, usually by piercing tongue or earlobes with a reed, causing considerable suffering. Those who occupied high positions in the social hierarchy brought other, often valuable, offerings as well, such as art objects, rubber balls, all kinds of sacrificial animals, fragrant resin and herbs. Rich merchants also offered slaves in sacrifice, military conquerors offered their war captives. Their hearts were torn out by the priests and offered, still beating, to the god.

For Mayan sacrifice, see illustration page 86.

Every twenty days, that is eighteen times a year, great religious festivals were held. Then each social group, and their leaders in particular, could show the common people their achievements, for an Aztec's social career depended to a great extent on success in organizing these religious festivals. Only those who were prepared to make the most valuable sacrifices were eligible for leading functions. The same principle was applied by Tlacayelel and his followers in dealing with whole nations. The nation that brought the largest number of human offerings enjoyed the greatest prestige.

As everywhere else in the world, the Aztec élite had more varied ideas about their gods than the common people. Farmers worshipped especially the sun-god and the maize- and rain-gods and goddesses and, sometimes more or less under pressure of the government, their tribal god Huitzilopochtli. Fishermen and hunters had their own water- and hunting-gods, the craftsmen had their own group gods, whom they worshipped before all other gods. Slaves worshipped above all Tezcatlepoca, because only his arbitrariness could bring about quick changes in their position. The élite worshipped especially the great gods and goddesses: Quetzalcoatl, Huitzilopochtli, Tezcatlepoca, Tocî-Teteoinnan (Our Grandmother, the mother of the gods, the earth-goddess) etc.

A Philosophy of Life

Religious thinking among the élite developed into a real philosophy with clear formulations of the fundamental questions of life. A concept of the order of the universe was developed that stressed the relative nature of all things. Such a philosophy can only develop in a sophisticated environment. The following strophe of an old Aztec poem may give some evidence of it:

> *Every man on earth*
> *carries with him some conviction;*
> *but it is for a brief period only*
> *that flowers of happiness pass before our eyes*

Within the Aztec élite in particular, but also among the people in general, two important currents could be distinguished: the avowed adherents of the regime established by Tlacayelel with their mystical and military ideology and a large number of prominent people who had got tired of the official ideology of anti-decadence or for some other reason did not believe in it, for instance because they were descended from the leaders in former independent states that had been subjected by the Aztecs.

The first group considered Huitzilopochtli to be their principal god; most members of the second group worshipped especially Quetzalcoatl, the Toltec god who was most concerned with cultural matters and to whom they often also attributed messianic qualities.

The Aztecs were no preachers, nor did they have a well-organized set of religious dogmas. All were free to have their own religious faith, provided it did not conflict too much with the three fundamental principles of the state ideology. These were: the special duty to be fulfilled by Huitzilopochtli (and consequently by his followers) during the age of the Fifth Sun; the readiness to participate in the wars of flowers and/or to bring ritual offerings and do penance for the purpose of preventing decadence; the principle of reciprocity in the relations between people and the gods.

Training the Young

The Aztec youth, boys as well as girls, were indoctrinated with these fundamental principles and the set of connected values, as long as they were at school, from their seventh till their twentieth year, either by priests at scientific-religious boarding-schools, or by army officers at the less strict military and vocational schools. Besides teaching their pupils to believe in the few dogmas of the Aztec religion, the priests and army officers taught them to think. The works left by those who had attended such schools are ample evidence of this. The need for sacrifice made the Aztec religion a harsh one, but it was also a source of order and discipline within the society.

The Maya Religion

The attempt to compare the Aztec and Maya religions is in fact apt to fail, owing to the dissimilarity of the subjects of comparison. The Aztecs, for instance, were a nation belonging to the Nahua group, as were the Toltecs and many other Mexican and Central American tribes. The Maya, on the other hand, were a collection of nations, like the Nahuas. The Maya tribes did not have one common religion, any more than the Nahua peoples had. All Maya peoples indeed shared the same religious background, but this was largely also shared by the Nahuas and other Central American tribes. Yet it is possible to recognize characteristics common to all Maya religions.

A distinction should be made, however, between Maya tribes dom-inated and strongly influenced by Toltecs or other Nahua groups – such as the Maya of Yucatán and the Tzeltal-Tzotzil in Chiapas – and the Maya groups that had undergone little or no Nahua influ-ences, such as the Lacandones. The former groups had generally developed administrative, military and social systems organized according to Nahua principles, whereas the latter groups retained their original character, which laid much emphasis on the worship of nature gods. All Maya groups differed from the Nahuas in that they set a much higher value on time and units of time as subjects of veneration. The concept of time, *kin(h)*, was the centre of Maya religious interest. The Maya religions were and still are more meta-physical in nature than the Aztec religion. In Maya religions 'animal counterparts' (called *chanuletik* in Chiapas) played a far more import-ant part, and each 'animal counterpart' was assumed to be connected with a thirteenfold 'soul' (*ch'ulel*), which was shared by the *chanul* and the person whose counterpart it was.

The following brief survey of the religious system of the Quiché Maya of Guatemala, one of the most important and largest groups of the ancient as well as the modern Maya, may serve as an example of the religious system peculiar to a Maya tribe. The Quiché have left us one of the finest literary accounts in existence of an Indian religion, the *Popol Vuh*. This sacred book of the Quiché contains in succession an account of the cosmogony, some other mythic sagas, and the history of the Quiché tribes.

The Creators

The creator couple, Xpiyacoc and Xmucané, who were also called by thirteen other names, are mentioned at the beginning of the *Book of the Community*. The Toltec dual divinity Tepeu-Gucumatz (= Quetzalcoatl) was also greatly venerated as creator. Another great and ancient god was Huracán, the Triple Heart of the Universe. The creating gods had to fight the Lords of the Underworld (Xibalba) in their efforts to create rational creatures as servants of the gods. After some vain attempts the gods succeeded in making from maize flour the first four men, followed by the first four women. From these four men and three or four women were descended the three Quiché tribes: Cavec with their tribal god Tohil, Nihaib with the tribal god Avilix, and Ahau-Quiché, with the tribal god Hacavitz.

Here too the earthly order had been arranged in perfect agreement with the order of the whole universe. The Cavec tribe was divided into nine *calpolli* (clans) and supplied two of the four supreme chiefs; Nihaib with nine *calpolli* and Ahau-Quiché with four *calpolli,* each supplied one of the four supreme chiefs. This arrangement is another instance of the simultaneous representation of the triple and quadruple partitions of the universe, while the numbers four and nine and their combination thirteen represent the numbers for the earth, the underworld, and heaven.

The most important Toltec-Maya state of Yucatán presents a similar pattern. Three capital cities, Mayapan, Uxmal (later on Izamal) and Chichen Itza, also symbolized the vertical cosmic order. The principal, mostly quadruple, gods of heaven were Itzamná (one of the supreme gods), the Chaacs (rain-gods), and Kukulcán (= Quetzalcoatl). The jaguar god and the ancient god Mam were the best-known gods of the earth. Kisin was the lord of the underworld. The Yucatec religion retained its typically Maya character by its extensive deification of the time signs and the numbers of the ritual calendar.

Illustrations page 85

The present Nahua as well as Maya tribes have lost most of the intricate arrangement of the gods of heaven. But the ancient nature gods, the sun-god and the rain-god, the goddess of the earth and the maize-gods, still play a major part in the daily life of the tribes, sometimes in the disguise of Christian saints. The intricate complex of concepts concerning 'animal counterparts', however, has been preserved nearly everywhere, and acts of magic are still being performed within the framework of these concepts.

The Aztec Calendar

This encyclopedia mentions the Aztecs and Mayas after the preliterate peoples. In a book of reference of this kind this is natural since

Above This Mayan sculpture from Quirigua in Guatemala (*c.* sixth century AD) represents a god. The quetzal-feather headdress suggests that this is the Mayan form of Quetzalcoatl, Kukulcán, in his form as the planet Venus in a phase of invisibility when under the earth.

Above left A large Mayan pottery vase with modelled jaguar head and paws, from the Costa Rica highlands (fourteenth century AD or a little earlier). Museum of Mankind, London.

Left A chac-mool from the Toltec capital of Tula, Mexico. Such reclining figures were placed at temple entrances and depicted attendants of the rain-god Tlaloc (or the Mayan Chaac). The dishes in their laps have been variously interpreted as receptacles for offerings, rain, or the hearts of sacrificial victims.

a kind of writing had evolved. For the Aztecs and the Maya had, independently of the old world, developed such a refined method of registration that it may certainly be called script.

A large part of the pre-Spanish writings that have been preserved is concerned with relations between time-space and the gods. Consequently there exist a large number of documents dealing with the calendar of Central American peoples, which regulated their ritual religious manifestations and were the basis of the entire formal part of their religious life.

The Aztec divinatory calendar was based on the sacred count of days or *tonalpoalli,* by the priests. The twenty day-signs, the corresponding gods and their relations with people were as follows:

Opposite A relief panel used as a lintel in the ancient Maya city of Yaxchilan on the Usumacinta River, Mexico (*c.* eighth century AD). The rain priest (kneeling) is wearing a headdress in the form of a rain-serpent head surmounted by a jaguar mask. He is tearing his tongue with a spiked cord, and beside him is a basket containing cactus spines, which he has also used to draw blood. This is an offering of pain to the god, whose function is shown by the maize-plant staff he carries. Museum of Mankind, London.

	Day-signs	Gods	Relations with people
1	Cipactli (crocodile)	Tonacatecuhtli (maize-god)	good
2	Ehecatl (wind)	Quetzacoatl (wind-god)	bad
3	Calli (house)	Tepeyollotli (earth-god)	good
4	Cuetzpalin (lizard)	Huêhuêcoyotl (fire-god)	good
5	Coatl (snake)	Chalchiuhtlicue (water-goddess)	bad
6	Miquiztli (death)	Tecciztecatl (moon-god)	bad
7	Mazatl (deer)	Tlaloc (rain-god)	good
8	Tochtli (rabbit)	Mayahuel (agave-goddess)	undetermined
9	Atl (water)	Xiuhtecuhtli (fire-god)	bad
10	Itzcuintli (dog)	Mictlantecuhtli (god of death)	good
11	Ozomahtli (monkey)	Xochipilli (god of music)	undetermined
12	Malinalli (dead grass)	Pâtecatl (god of drink and medicine)	bad
13	Acatl (reed)	Tezcatlepoca-Iztlacoliuhqui (supreme god of the north)	undetermined
14	Ocelotl (ocelot)	Tlazolteotl (goddess of fertility)	undetermined
15	Cuauhtli (eagle)	Xipe Totêc (god of fertility)	undetermined
16	Cozcacuauhtli (vulture)	Itzpapalotl (goddess of death)	good
17	Ollin (rotation)	Xolotl (god of twins)	undetermined
18	Tecpatl	Tezcatlepoca	bad
19	Quiahuitl (rain)	Chantico (goddess of the hearth) or Tonatiuh (sun-god)	bad
20	Xochitl (flower)	Xochiquetzal (flower-goddess)	undetermined

The thirteen numbers which in the *tonalamatl* were combined with the twenty day-signs also showed good, undetermined or bad associations in connection with humans: for instance, thirteen was good, but four was bad. Each of the twenty 13-day periods was associated with one of the cardinal points of space and with a particular god. Each period was called after its first day.

Besides the *tonalpoalli* the Aztecs had a system of counting the days of the solar year of 365 days. The system was called *xiuhpoalli*. This solar year was divided into eighteen periods of twenty days (called *metztli* = moon) plus five remaining days, which they called *nemontemi* (useless additions). The eighteen 20-day periods had their corresponding divinities.

In the course of these eighteen 'months' twenty major religious festivals were held annually. There was a festival on one of the last days of every 'month'; in the 'months' of Quecholli and Izcalli festivals were also held halfway through the period. The Aztec solar years were called after the last day of the eighteenth 'month'. In practice this could only be four different day-names, each of which was connected with the thirteen numbers. This gave rise to the *xiuhmolpillis* (bundle of years), each counting fifty-two years. The various Mexican nations had different ways of grouping their years. The Aztecs started each set of years on 2-Acatl, which meant that each *xiuhmolpilli* or 52-year period ended with the year 1-Tochtli.

They regarded the end of a *xiuhmolpilli* as a critical moment, at which the order of the Fifth Sun might be destroyed. During the ceremonies connected with the turn of a 52-year period all fires in the country had to be extinguished. Old furniture and other household implements, pottery, images of gods etc were replaced by new ones. At the moment when the Pleiades rose above the mountain of Colhuacan new fire was made by the high priest on the breast of a sacrificed victim and distributed among all the temples and homes in the country.

In the Aztec empire the beginning and the end of the year differed from place to place. Even the calendars of the twin-cities of Tenochtitlan and Tlaltelolco differed in this respect. At Tlaltelolco the year began with Izcalli, at Tenochtitlan with Atlcahualo. The *nemontemi* or remaining days always followed the 20-day period that was considered the last 'month' of the year. These five days evidently also contained the extra days of leap-years. Besides sets of fifty-two years the Aztecs had even longer time units consisting of two *xiuhmolpillis* (i.e. 2 × 52 = 104 years).

The Maya Calendar

The Maya calendar is based upon the same principles as the Aztec calendars. As has been said, the concept of time and the arrangement of time units formed the central points of consideration in the Maya religion, even more so than with the Aztecs. Hence the Maya had some arrangements unknown to the Aztecs.

Like the Aztecs the Maya reckoned with the ritual time unit of 260 days, divided into 13 × 20 days and called *tzolkin*. They regarded these days as 260 different pairs of combinations of the gods of the thirteen numbers with the twenty gods of the day-signs. The names of the day-signs and their corresponding divinities (as far as we know) were: 1 Imix, 2 Ik (Chac), 3 Akbal, 4 Kan (maize-god), 5 Chicchán, 6 Cimi (Ah Puch, god of death), 7 Manik (god of war), 8 Lamat, 9 Muluc (wind-god), 10 Oc, 11 Chuén (Xamán Ek, Polar Star, god of the merchants), 12 Eb, 13 Ben, 14 (1) Ix, 15 (2) Men, 16 (3) Cib, 17 (4) Cabán, 18 (5) Eznab, 19 (6) Cauac, 20 (7) Ahau (Itzamná).

Fourteen divinites were associated with the numbers 0 and 1 to 13. Only three of these associations are known to us with certainty, viz: 4 sun-god, 10 Ah Puch, god of death, and 13 Chac, rain-god.

In the so-called 'Ancient Empire' in Guatemala, Ik, Manik, Eb and Cabán were the Bearers of the Year, which function corresponded with that of the Aztec days Acatl, Tecpatl, Calli and Tochtli. Besides the ritual sets of 260 days, the Maya, like the Aztecs, had a solar year of 365 days (*haab*), also divided into eighteen periods of twenty days, plus five remaining days.

A peculiar feature of the Maya calendar set of twenty days was that the days of each 'month' were counted in the way we indicate the hours of a day. The first day of Pop was called 0-Pop, the last or twentieth day 19-Pop. The Maya are the first people on earth known to have developed the concept of the number 0, many centuries before the Hindus. The combination of the *haab* and *tzolkin* calendars yielded time units of $73 \times 260 = 52 \times 365 = 18,980$ days, the same sets of fifty-two years that the Aztecs called *xiuhmolpilli*. Besides the sets of fifty-two *haabs* or solar years, the Maya priests applied a count of days by a special adaptation of counting systems based on the numbers eighteen and twenty. This calendar had sets of 360 days, called *tún*. We do not know if the Aztecs had the same system, but, if they did, it was certainly of far less importance to them.

In this system the *katún,* which was a period of 7,200 days, was the most important time unit with regard to religious matters. The Maya priests developed a theory of determinism which was associated with the *katunes*. They were named after their last day, always a day called Ahau, which was, however, combined with different numbers thirteen times in succession. *Katunes* with the same final day were thought to follow similar courses, and to have similar influences on the course of events.

The Maya were continually correcting their calendar, with the result that theirs was the most accurate calendar ever developed.

Chapter Six

Andean Religion

Andean religion – and here we are thinking in the first place of those peoples ruled by the Incas at the time of the Spanish conquest in 1532, from Ecuador in the north, over Peru and Bolivia to northern Argentina and Chile in the south – is still very imperfectly known. In their search for gold the *conquistadores* killed many indigenous priests who could have been good informants. Because of the centralized nature of the Inca state the Spaniards were mostly interested in this tribe of conquerors and in their capital, Cuzco, in southern Peru and paid much less attention to the tribes and peoples dominated by them. But the Incas were really late upstarts on the Andean scene – probably they initiated their expansion some hundred years before the Spaniards came – whereas the other peoples were the descendants of kingdoms and even empires with highly sophisticated religious systems and arts.

In the mountains to the south-east of Cuzco, around Lake Titicaca, originated the culture of Tiahuanaco. It flourished around AD 600 and later its religion influenced most of Bolivia and Peru deeply, probably by way of commerce, conquest and the prestige it held. Somewhat later, around AD 700, another centre – Huari, to the west of Cuzco, near modern Ayacucho – started to influence most of middle Peru. Its original links were to the cultures of the South Peruvian coast, especially that of the valley of Nazca, but soon it became heavily influenced by Tiahuanaco. Notwithstanding Tiahuanaco influence, the original character of Huari religious culture remained distinctive.

Illustration page 95

Tiahuanaco – and, especially, Huari – influences on the peoples they conquered were so great that they caused a radical social upheaval and a complete break in their arts. This is most noticeable in the more important cultures from the Peruvian coast: Moche to the north and Nazca to the south. Moche had used for the expression of its beliefs and symbolic system in its art a very realistic idiom in which figures and motif were modelled or drawn on a flat surface, most in black or brown on white or cream. We can relate the representations easily to reality, although we do not know for what symbols they stood, except where gods and mythical beings are represented. After the interruption by Huari of all these traditions there was a return in art to the old forms, but now the pottery was black, which made it impossible to paint on it scenes of everyday life and of religious ideas.

The best-known culture of this period is that of the kingdom of Chimu, which continued into Inca times and even into early Spanish times.

Nazca excelled mostly in its textiles and in a very stylized non-realistic pottery making use of many different colours. Probably this more restricted area on the coast was never as powerful and independent as the north coast, but its contacts with the mountains seem to have been stronger. Nazca art expressed its religion in a very rigorous system which, on the one hand, makes it more easily discernible than the Moche religious system, but on the other hand, more difficult to relate to Nazca culture, its social organization and everyday life. After the domination of Huari, during which period its art was almost identical to that in Huari, a very different style arose, known by the name of the valley of Ica, which was so geometric and apparently devoid of symbolic meaning that now it gives hardly any help in understanding the religion.

Tiahuanaco art in pottery and stone sculpture had been geometric and, like Nazca, formal. Huari art, mostly known in pottery and textiles, preserved these traits although its pottery had also some forms that were less stylized. This direct expression of an abstract religious model Tiahuanaco had in common with the art of Chavin culture. During the first millennium before Christ, Chavin had influenced the greater part of Peru from the northern highlands. Although superficially its art is rather different from that of Tiahuanaco, it also expressed the religious system mostly in stone (especially in its ceremonial centre known today as Chavin de Huantar). This fact might be the reason why the underlying model is so readily detectable. Chavin art influenced very much the artistic centre of Paracas on the south coast, from which in its turn Nazca art is derived.

No Form of Script
The Incas and the other Peruvian peoples did not leave us any codices – historical, astronomical or religious – or any dated monuments. Nor did they have any script of a hierographical kind, which, like the Rosetta Stone, could have been deciphered. Perhaps this can be explained by the fact that the Peruvians, whose political development was so advanced, were very conscious of the deeper abstract ideas underlying their social and political organization, its religious justification and its functioning through time, but were less worried about an abstraction and the expression in art of concepts on a more superficial level.

Whereas the Mexicans developed a highly articulate iconographic system depicting their many gods of a local, functional and calendrical character, the Peruvians expressed in their art on the one hand only a few basic concepts, to which corresponded the small number of gods they recognized, and, on the other hand, were very advanced in realistic art – as in Moche culture – or in the artistic reproduction – in more stylized conventions like those of Paracas, Nazca and even Chavin – of objects, plants, animals and men from everyday life. In

Inca times the Peruvians had as gods only the Creator, the Sun, the Moon, Venus and the Thunder, the Earth, the Sea and a chthonic dragon – and even these were only considered as being aspects of one and the same religious concept – to which was opposed a multitude of lineal and local ancestors whose direct and concrete relation to their descendants was demonstrated in their mummies or, when these had disappeared, in stone representing them.

Illustration page 97

Although the Peruvian ancestor system, besides pertaining to the social organization, was also a religious system, these ancestors were never completely deified. They were never represented as gods, but they were detached from material being in the form of a mummy or a stone, while preserving certain characteristics due to their origin. All their former kings, the ancestors of the Inca tribe itself, were conserved in the form of their mummies and although their histories incorporated more mythical and religious concepts the older they became, the Incas described them as if all their deeds were only historical. Therefore Inca history is very untrustworthy, historically, and very important religiously. But also, because the Incas preserved their mummies, it seems that they never felt the urge to represent their ancestors as gods in their art or even to develop a technique of codices such as that in Mexico.

Dresses as Memorials

Thus, the mummies or the stones representing them – the *huacas* as they were called – were not dedicated to particular gods. However, they were not disconnected from art and the religious system either. In fact it was not the *huacas* themselves that were considered the most important religious objects to maintain the people's connections with their gods, but their dresses. The Spaniards, destroying the *huacas* in their effort to extirpate the idolatries, only later understood this fact and the Indians were careful not to have the dresses destroyed. They could use them as well on re-collected parts of the old *huacas*. We do not have concrete data of relations between specific *huacas* and specific textiles – although perhaps they might yet be found – but from what we know about these textiles (and we have abundant evidence that throughout Peruvian history textiles were of a very high religious importance), they seem to have represented only the general and basic religious ideas and nothing that could pertain to one and only one *huaca*.

Having first referred to the lack of sufficient evidence on which to base an understanding of the Andean religious system and its history from Chavin times, let us look now at what evidence there is. Although we do not have any chronicle (with perhaps one exception) written by an indigenous priest dedicated to the esoteric knowledge of his people, we know something of the folk religion, especially in relation to social organization. This can help us in our reconstruction of the higher religious forms.

Inca pottery and Inca textiles are highly geometric, but we know that they possessed also a more realistic art in paintings representing their mythological history. Some of these paintings were sent to Spain, but they are lost. Notwithstanding, it seems that the Incas preserved some of their realistic, representational traditions in the lacquered wooden beakers of colonial origin on which scenes of Inca life are depicted in an indigenous style. These paintings, together with the drawings found in two chronicles written by the Indians Joan de Santacruz Pachacuti Yamqui and Felipe Huaman Poma de Ayala, are of the greatest help in connecting the religious system of the Incas to that of their predecessors, from which it must have been derived.

Illustration page 97

The task of reconstructing Peruvian religious history through the iconography in its art will be enormous as there were many different kingdoms and empires with a turbulent history and many different art styles. However, the archaic high civilization of Peru was probably the most isolated one in the world, with a history uninterrupted by any conquest of peoples that could have introduced very different religious concepts. All Peruvian cultures had the same origin and from Chavin times had interacted. The political developments did not alter the fact that all religious systems were based on the same general and abstract concepts.

Illustration page 98

It was perhaps due to this isolation, physical and spiritual, of Peruvian civilization that the influence of the Spanish conquest was more disruptive here than anywhere else. The population on the coast died out almost completely and in the mountains only a couple of hundred thousand Indians were left at the end of the eighteenth century. However, especially in southern Peru and Bolivia, the indigenous population has grown enormously since and has preserved intact its religious ideas, even allowing for an integration into its own system of Spanish influences. The study of modern indigenous religion is therefore of great importance to our subject.

Peruvian Customs

As has been said, because of the ancestral system, Peruvian religion was intimately interwoven with its political and social system and even with its kinship system, and no understanding of the one is possible without that of the other. The primary concept on which the Peruvians based their social organization was that of conquest. It was the custom when a man killed another that he could occupy as much land of this latter's *ayllu* (a kind of clan) as he could reach in all directions with his sling, keeping the dead man's mummy in his house as if it were one of his own ancestors. Even if we have to do here only with a legal concept, it forms the basis of the *ceque* system: a system by which Peruvian villages, provinces and even the whole Inca empire gave religious expression to their social and political organization. On the mountain, sacred to the village or province in question, was placed a central *huaca* representing its first conqueror, surrounded by the *huacas* of the families or *ayllus* conquered by him and his family.

These hierarchical relationships were also maintained by way of marriage, the conqueror marrying the daughters of all the families or of their chiefs conquered by him. In fact the Inca king considered all the women in his empire to be his wives, whom he could subsequently redistribute as wives to his male subjects. It seems that on this idea is based the institution of the *acllas,* the chosen women, who were considered to be the wives of the Inca and of his father the Sun, and who lived like nuns in their special houses in Cuzco and in all the provincial Inca capitals. In the case of the conqueror who married the daughters of his conquered chiefs, his sons by these wives became especially important, as they maintained the ties with their mother's village or province, representing there the power of their father, and in the latter's capital representing their mother's village or province.

The *ceque* system in Cuzco and in the other cities and villages was intimately interwoven with all religious activities, even those that had a calendarical character like those of agriculture, and others that were important in the boys' initiation rites. Major religious activities pertained to conquered *huacas,* who had to be sent to the capital in order to partake in state ceremonies. The most sacred Inca religious ceremony was that of the *Capac cocha* or *Capac hucha* (the translation of this word is not known). A chronicler from Cuzco states that during this rite a sister of the Inca king was sent to one of his conquered cities; a provincial chronicler, however, states that a local ruler, in order to ascend in the Inca political system, had to send a daughter as an *aclla* to the capital. Later she was sent back to her father for the *Capac cocha,* in order to be offered and buried alive.

Notwithstanding these customs, there was also a clear separation and even opposition and animosity between conquerors and conquered, expressed in moieties on the village or province level, and by ceremonial or real battles between them. These moieties and battles exist even today. The conquerors considered themselves to be of heavenly origin, or from fruits of trees dropped on earth, whereas the ancestors of the conquered had come out of the earth.

'Foam on the Sea'

The central and most basic religious concept throughout Peruvian history was that of the creator. His best-known name was that of Viracocha – Foam or Fat on the Sea – describing how his power to create the earth (priestly power was generally symbolized by fat on water boiling in a pot) floated like the earth itself on the unlimited waters surrounding it. He was the first to rise after the recurring floods out of the water and to create the world, the sun, moon and stars, the plants and animals, and humankind, for which reason he was called Pachayachachic. He was the real invisible Sun, male and female, but he also lived on the slopes of the pyramid, symbolizing the Cosmos, and was the dirty, low base (*Ticsi*) of the world and as such was Pachacamac (Lord of the Earth), originating the earthquakes in the interior of the earth. Viracocha was the one indivisible creative power of which all the other deities were only aspects, represented as his sons and descendants. In a more mythological way, he was said

Above A feline deity flanked by snakes on a Moche ceramic stirrup vessel which was designed to contain the liquid needed by the dead in their afterlife. Museum of Mankind, London.

Above left A Chimu vase, double spouted, with two prostrate figures worshipping the head of a crowned deity or a human king. Kemper Collection.

Left A Chimu twelfth to thirteenth-century gold plate, bearing the central figure of the earth goddess and around her symbols of maise, yucca and sweet potato. It may represent an agricultural calendar, and the circle of figures may depict a sequence of time. Señor Mujico Gallo, Lima.

Right A detail of the sun door at Tiahuanaco (*c.* AD 600). This city lies on the Bolivian plateau, near Lake Titicaca. There is evidence that sun worship was of central importance. It is possible that the Incas destroyed the city and dispersed the population.

Below The monument known as the Huaca del Sol (Temple of the Sun), outside the modern town of Trujillo, Peru, the most impressive of the Moche people's enormous ceremonial structures in the form of platforms surmounted by terraced pyramids built of adobe bricks.

Left A female mummy bundle. Burial was normally in this position, the process of mummification generally being the result of natural dessication due to the dryness of the air. This richly dressed female mummy comes from the central coast of Peru. Musée de l'Homme, Paris.

Below left Ornaments for a Chimu mummy pack from the north Peruvian coast (thirteenth-century AD). The headdress represents an axe-blade with puma-head decorations. Nose and ear pendants were normal wear for important Chimu men. Señor Mujico Gallo, Lima.

Below In this drawing by Felipe Huaman Poma de Ayala Indians bring offerings to the *huaca* Cocopona. Customary sacrifices included gold, silver, flamingo feathers, black llama kids and twelve-year-old children.

Right The Inca town of Machu Picchu, high in the Peruvian Andes, may have been a sanctuary for the young women known as the 'virgins of the sun' who served in the Inca temples. The excavation of the remains of a large proportion of young women supports this theory.

to be born in Lake Titicaca, creating there the sun and the moon and the different peoples of the earth whom he sent first underground to their respective localities.

Viracocha had three sons or servants. One was bad, reversing all the creations of Viracocha by making lakes into mountains and mountains into lakes. He was sent away and so became the underworld power of destruction, causing earthquakes and landslides in the rainy season. He was also the god of death and fertility, of the time when the seeds are in the ground. The two other sons represented the two forces in the society, the conquerors and the conquered.

On the basis of this myth were also built all those of particular tribes, in which the local chief represented in society the same position as Viracocha in the whole cosmos. The chief's two sons were those by a woman of his, the conqueror's, family and by a woman of the conquered. Just as the sun was created in Lake Titicaca to travel from there through the skies to the west, so Viracocha went west through the mountains to Ecuador to create men and women, i.e. to bring the different peoples out of their caves. His two sons also travelled west, but one to his right, along the slopes of the Andes, where he created the rivers and plants, especially the useful ones, and the other to his left creating the same on the coast. They all came together on the coast in Ecuador where they disappeared, again like foam, on the waters of the ocean.

Children of Viracocha

The Sun and the Moon, the visible ones, were the children of Viracocha. Generally they were considered to be his son and his daughter, but in a modern version they are called, as in many other parts of South America, older and younger brother to each other. Just as in Cuzco, Manco Capac, the ancestor of the Inca kings, was related there to the conquerors as son of the Sun and his wife to the conquered as daughter of the Moon, so these gods were also related to conquerors and conquered. The Moon originally was the brightest, but the Sun threw ashes in her face and thereafter the Sun was the brighter and more powerful one.

The Peruvians used their cosmological model also as a conceptualization of their own social hierarchy and in this the king and the queen were related to the Sun and the Moon. The secondary children of the king by foreign women or those of conquered peoples were related to the children of the Sun and the Moon. As such were considered Venus – the Morning Star being their son and the Evening Star their daughter – and the Thunder and all the conquered *huacas*.

These were the heavenly deities although in the lowest of these – Venus or the Thunder – we notice already the connection with the earthly deities. The highland peoples identified themselves with the heavenly deities whereas the lowland peoples of the eastern slopes were connected with the lower gods which to the highland people were only minor deities.

On the coast the major temple and pyramid, from Huari times on, was that of Pachacamac, Lord Earth, some 30 kilometres (19 miles) south of Lima. He created the earth and made earthquakes. He was adored in the form of a fox and his female counterpart and wife was the skunk, both the lowest of animals. To the mountain peoples, this lowest of all deities was Pachamama, Mother Earth, who was also represented as the Amaru, a mythical dragon, originating in the eastern lowlands. The Amaru was the archetype of all the low and powerful animals, especially serpents, felines, pigs and, as today, bulls. Pachamama or the Amaru was a priestess and sorceress, who slept with all men. The Amaru lived under earth and in the rivers, and just as thunder and lightning were the destructive powers of Viracocha descending from heaven, so Amaru manifested itself in earthquakes, in a lightning that goes upwards from earth to heaven, in the fire that erupts from volcanoes, and in the landslides occasioned by the overflow of water and mud during the rainy season.

Earth, Sea and Sky

Of this undivided chthonic force, we must consider Pachacamac and Mamacocha, Mother Sea, as the two subdivisions just as the Sun and the Moon were those of Viracocha. The sea was the most important god of the Chimu, whereas they related the Sun to their *huacas*. Venus was to them a child of the sea. To the Incas the wells were subdivisions, children, of the Sea and they had a strong female character.

The connection between Heaven above and Water and Earth below was established by the Milky Way and the Rainbow, whom we can consider as the nightly and daily, the female and male, aspects of the same concept. They both protect the world from the flood, especially in the dry season, by drinking its excess of water. But because of this ability they are also very dangerous. Once they abstain from doing this, the Earth will be immersed again in the water just as in the beginning during the flood. Only a well-integrated and stable society, keeping the established order of the *huacas,* can maintain the functioning of the Milky Way and the Rainbow. But war and not living by the laws of religion can make the flood recur again.

These were the basic elements around which the Andean peoples constructed their religion. But to understand this completely we would have to consider also their architecture, their theory on kinship, and their calendar system, which was far more complicated than has generally been realized.

Chapter Seven

Northern Europe in the Iron Age

The Celts were a group of people whose culture, including the use of horses and iron weapons, appeared in the early seventh century BC in central Europe east of the Rhine. They spread into the Balkans, north Italy and France, and reached the British Isles in successive waves from the third century BC. Eventually their culture was destroyed by Roman power and by the spread of Germanic tribes.

One of the most important Celtic settlements was at La Tène, on Lake Neuchâtel in Switzerland, where substantial remains have been found. It has consequently given its name to an early period of Celtic culture. Our main sources of knowledge about Celtic religion are the material remains of this period (from *c.* 500 BC), the comments of classical writers on this culture, monuments erected after the Roman conquest of Gaul and Britain, and medieval Irish writings which, though no earlier than the eighth century AD, do preserve traditions from earlier times. The evidence is thus widely scattered in space and time, but a fairly coherent picture may be cautiously reconstructed from it.

One recurrent feature is the importance of natural sites as focal points for ritual, notably sacred groves, forest clearings, hilltops and expanses of water. Many objects have been recovered from votive deposits in lakes, marshes, wells and rivers; they include weapons, jewellery, coins, potsherds, ritual objects, bones of animals and men (presumably sacrificed), and pots that may have held food offerings. Some deposits are the accumulated offerings of many years, others of a single occasion; some are the booty of victors, others *ex votos* of the sick: one, at Llyn Cerrig Bach on Anglesey, may in part reflect a particular event – the vain British attempt to rally there against the Romans in AD 61. Ordinary rural rites could take the same form; Gregory of Tours describes how, in the fourth century, peasants gathered every year at a lake at Gévaudan, sacrificing animals in a three-day festival and throwing pieces of cloth, fleeces, cheeses, wax and various foods into the lake.

It was formerly thought that natural sites were the only sanctuaries known to Celts uncontaminated by Mediterranean influences, but archaeology has revealed an ancient native tradition of man-made enclosures, shrines and temples. At Libenice in Czechoslovakia there is a long rectangular enclosure of the third century BC; at one end stood a stone altar and several pairs of wooden posts (one pair very probably carved in human shape), around which many pits held human and animal bones and much broken pottery.

In Germany there are square enclosures defined by earthworks, containing deep shafts into which offerings were thrown. Indeed, shafts, pits and wells are a widespread and long-continued type of ritual site, both in continental Europe and in Belgic Britain. They are carefully constructed, often lined with wood and clay or, in post-Roman times, with masonry; their contents include human and animal skeletons, skulls and other bones, various artefacts, potsherds, images, altars, and other ritually significant objects. Sometimes these are systematically laid out, sometimes dropped in haphazard. Clearly, such openings in the earth were believed to be means of access to an underworld of supernatural powers.

Temple Buildings

Pre-Roman temples also existed. These are small rectangular or circular wooden shrines, often underlying the sites of later Romano-Celtic buildings. Typical is the 'double-square' temple at Heathrow, near London, with its small inner shrine to house the cult images, and a surrounding colonnade for processions and display – a plan frequently used in temples of the Roman period. Far more elaborate temples were built along the south coast of France, under the stimulus of contact with Greeks and Etruscans; despite their sophistication, these have many authentic Celtic features, notably stone heads and *Illustration page 107* actual skulls displayed in niches around the doorways. The Celtic fondness for head-hunting is well attested by classical authors and Irish tales; skulls have been found not only in temples but over the gateways of Gaulish and British forts. Besides being trophies, they may have served magical and necromantic purposes.

Cult Images and Symbols

By far the greater number of images must have been of wood, and a few of them have survived. There are also bronze masks to be mounted on wooden bases, and even some pre-Roman stone statues. Moreover, the ornamental metalwork of the La Tène period is rich in religious symbols. The wheel, swastika and spiral were attributes of a sky-god who controlled sun and lightning; the torc (neck-ring) symbolized authority, and often appears on representations of gods; Janus-headed statues and a four-sided column with four identical faces may symbolize omniscience; many animals, particularly boars, rams and snakes, possessed supernatural significance.

The Gundestrup Cauldron

One outstanding instance of religious art is the Gundestrup Cauldron, a large bowl set with silver plaques, probably made in the Danube area about 100 BC. Round the outside are gods and goddesses, shown as huge heads with small upraised arms, and accompanied by subsidiary figures and animals. Inside are more complex scenes: representations of bull-baiting; a large-breasted goddess surrounded by animals; a god with a wheel, worshipped by a warrior; a god with stag's antlers, accompanied by a stag, a horned snake, and other beasts; a procession culminating in human sacrifice. The bowl itself was obviously a cult object; certain tribes used cauldrons to catch the blood of sacrifices, and Irish myths mention cauldrons of abundance, probably indicating their use in ritual meals.

Illustration page 107

Celtic religion clearly had elaborate ritual, so it is not surprising that Britain, Ireland and Gaul had an organized priesthood, the Druids. Their chief functions were to preserve and transmit myths, legends and poetry, and probably also tribal history and law; to organize sacrifices, interpret omens, and carry out magical rites; and to act as arbitrators in lawsuits and bloodfeuds.

The aspect of their teaching which most impressed classical writers was their doctrine of immortality; indeed, the lavish grave-goods in aristocratic Celtic burials testify to a strong belief in an afterlife, whether inside the grave or in an otherworld like the Scandinavian Valhalla. The regular provision of pork and wine for the dead shows a particular interest in an otherworldly feast. This is of course by no means peculiar to the Celts; rather more unusual is a belief ascribed to them by Posidonius that after the lapse of some years the soul passes into another body. This has been plausibly compared with a Scandinavian belief that people may live again in a child descended from and named after them.

Celtic Divinities in Roman Times

Roman rulers tried to suppress human sacrifice and the organized Druidic priesthood; they encouraged the Celts to identify their gods with those of the Roman pantheon, to build temples, and to dedicate altars in the Roman manner. Consequently, over 370 names of Celtic deities are known from Britain and Gaul in this period, besides numerous statues and reliefs with characteristically Celtic iconography. The vast majority of these names are strictly localized (305 occur only once), and some may be variant titles for the same divinity. No myths are recorded for this period.

Julius Caesar states that the chief Gaulish god protected travellers, craftsmen and traders, and gave wealth. Then came a healer, a goddess of arts and crafts, a sky-god, a war-god, and an underworld ancestral god. Caesar unfortunately gives no native names. Lucan does name three gods – Taranis (Thunderer); Teutatis (God of the Tribe); Esus (possibly Master). These names are not frequent in dedications, however, and they may not have been particularly important figures. Visual representations are a safer guide to the bewildering mass of Romano-Celtic gods than names.

Two figures seen on the Gunderstrup Cauldron frequently recur in Gaul. One is the god with the wheel, now identified with Jupiter (Taranis may be a title of his); the other is the antlered god, usually depicted as a giver of wealth, and on one altar named as Cernunnos (Horned One). Antlers probably symbolize virility, and also the annual renewal of nature; wild beasts still appear with him. Another popular deity was Sucellus, Good Striker, who carried a large mallet

Illustration page 108

and a cup or purse; he seems benevolent, though the mallet might indicate association with thunder, or with the underworld.

Dedications to Mars coupled with various Celtic names indicate the existence of warlike, or partly warlike, gods. Northern England has an armed, bull-horned, and sometimes phallic god; this implies his multiple function as warrior, protector of cattle, and bestower of fertility. As Celts were also keen huntsmen, many local gods and goddesses are shown as hunters, or in company with wild beasts.

Illustration page 108

There was much devotion to gods and goddesses of healing, especially at thermal and medicinal springs. One was Sequana, goddess of the Seine; another was Nodens, worshipped at Lydney Park near the River Severn in the west of England; and there were many others. Such deities were offered coins, statuettes, and representations of the worshipper or of the diseased organ. Another widely venerated group of benevolent goddesses were the Matres or Matronae; they were often shown as a group of three, holding a baby, fruit, or a cornu-

Illustration page 109

copia. Epona too carried fruit, but was mainly a protectress of horses. In contrast to these kindly goddesses were a few goddesses of war – a type better known from Irish myths.

A marked trait of Romano-Celtic iconography is the representation of deities as three-faced or three-headed, or as three identical figures; this indicates complete power. Gods can also be shown as heads only, the head being particularly sacred. Animals still figure prominently, among them the ram-horned serpent, the boar, symbol of ferocity, and favourite meat for feasting; the bull, sometimes shown with three horns, and the raven, bird of divination and warfare.

Irish Divinities

Ireland, which never underwent any Romanization, preserved many archaic myths and hero-legends. This is a world of magic, portents and taboo, where the supernatural and the human constantly interact. The otherworld is not remote; it lies beneath Irish lakes and mounds; it can invade human lives, or be invaded by men and women. Such notions tally well with cult practices of earlier periods.

Among various gods, two are described in considerable detail. One is the Dagda (the Good God), warrior-chieftain, father and magician. He is gigantic and grotesque, with immense appetites; his weapon is a huge club which slays or resuscitates, and he owns an inexhaustible cauldron. He has been compared with the club-wielding phallic giant at Cerne Abbas, and also with the more refined Gaulish Sucellus. The other outstanding god is Lug (also known in Gaul); he too is a warrior, magician, poet, and master of every craft. It is typical of Celtic gods to combine varied functions, reflecting all the qualities of an ideal leader.

Irish Goddesses

Many Irish goddesses are maternal figures, bestowing fertility on crops, herds and men; some are also river-goddesses; others personifications of Ireland itself, who grant their love to kings. Others, more macabre, haunt battlefields, appearing as hags or in bird form, and decide the outcome by sorcery; these include Morrigan (Queen of Phantoms), Badb Catha (Battle Crow), and Nemain (Panic). Yet even these have a favourable aspect; gods and heroes who mate with them learn magical arts of war, though he who rejects them meets a rapid doom.

Irish sources speak of four major festivals, which were probably common to the whole Celtic world. The chief was Samain, 1 November, marking the start of winter and hence of the Celtic year; on this day, and especially on its eve, the natural and supernatural worlds mingled, and the forces from the otherworld threatened humanity. Little is known of Imbolc, 1 February. The spring feast was Beltane, 1 May; cattle were driven to pasture, passing between bonfires to avert disease. The fourth feast was 1 August, Lugnasad, 'Lug's Wedding'; it was linked with goddesses, and may have involved a ritual marriage to assure good harvests.

All these festivals were celebrated by gatherings at the main sacred site in each Irish kingdom, with bonfires, dancing, horse-racing, and no doubt sacrifices too. Irish texts, being written by Christians, say nothing about ritual and worship; but they preserve lightly disguised myths which both illuminate and are illuminated by material remains from earlier periods.

Germanic Religion

Our fullest information on Germanic religion relates to western Scandinavia in the ninth and tenth centuries AD, and comes from oral poetry transmitted through thirteenth-century Icelandic texts, and from the work of Snorri Sturluson (c. 1179-1241). There are also the comments of Tacitus on continental Germans in the first century AD, archaeological and place-name evidence, and scattered remarks by chroniclers, travellers, and missionaries. Moreover, archaeology indicates many links between Germanic religious practices and those of the Celts and of Bronze Age peoples, but within the limits of this section one can only examine evidence from Roman and post-Roman times.

Roman writers alleged that the Germans used only simple rituals in sacred groves and similar natural sites, and though this was not universally true even in Roman times, sanctuaries were probably for many centuries merely fenced areas and small wooden shrines. Possibly even the 'temples' of the tenth and eleventh centuries served merely to house images, not to accommodate worshippers, and sacrifices were still performed in the open. When ceremonies involved feasting, they were held in the homes of local leaders, not in special buildings. It is unlikely that priests ever formed a separate social group; in general it was the king or local chieftain who carried out public rituals at assemblies and festivals, though shamanistic seers also had a place in religious life.

The simplest images were mere wooden posts with human faces; Icelandic sagas also describe elaborate life-size wooden figures, wearing jewellery and carrying their attributes. Nothing comparable has survived, though a 46 cm. (18 inch) figure, probably of the fifth century, may be a miniature copy of an idol; so too may be various small metal or bone statuettes, probably carried as amulets, and dating from the later part of the period.

Several peat bogs in Denmark, Sweden and Germany were the sites of repeated votive offerings, often continued for decades or centuries, of many different types: jewellery, pottery, harness, agricultural tools, smashed bones apparently left after ritual feasts; skeletons or skulls of men, horses and other animals slain in sacrifice; and numerous large deposits of weapons. Several tribes in Roman times used to destroy all captives and booty as a thanks offering for victory, and some finds are clearly sacrifices of this type. Yet besides these, and often on the same sites, offerings of tools and domestic animals bear witness to the cults of peasant communities.

War Gods

The cult of war-gods is clearly attested among Germanic tribes in Roman times; Tacitus mentions two, Mars and Mercury, to whom sacrifice was made for victory. 'Mars' was probably Tiwaz (known in England as Tiw, and in Iceland as Tyr), after whom Tuesday is named. Snorri describes him as wise and valiant, and relates a myth telling how, at the cost of his hand, he fettered a monstrous wolf. A rune named after him was engraved on weapons to ensure success. Tiwaz must once have been more than a war-god; his name (related to Zeus and *deus*) shows that he was originally a sky-god, and there are signs that he assured law and justice. Yet, though once important, by the Viking age he was almost forgotten.

Tacitus's 'Mercury' must be the complex deity called Wotan in Germany, Woden in England, and Odin in Scandinavia; Wednesday is named after him. He bestowed victory and protected princely heroes, but his power was that of a divine sorcerer, master of occult terrors; he was also lord of the dead, and death in battle was the ultimate fate of his worshippers. Human victims sacrificed to him were despatched by simultaneous spear-thrust and hanging, and cremation was associated with his cult. He carried a spear, and was accompanied by eagles, ravens or wolves.

In some tales he had nobler aspects as leader and father of the gods, full of deep wisdom won by self-inflicted torments, and he was also god of poetry. Yet the dominant impression is of a mysterious, sinister and capricious divinity, and it may well be that he was chiefly honoured by aristocratic warriors and their poets; place-names indicate that his cult was practised in Sweden, Denmark and England.

The Valkyries

Myths and poetry speak of Odin's female emissaries, the Valkyries, who grant men victory or summon them to Valhalla. They are often described as beautiful women in armour riding through the air, bestowing their love on living heroes, and serving wine to the dead. Yet there are also gigantic hags who appear before battle, riding wolves, sprinkling blood, or weaving on a loom of human guts and skulls.

Left The portico of the Celto-Ligurian temple at Bouches-du-Rhône (third or fourth century BC), its three pillars furnished with niches for human skulls. Classical writers testify to the Celts veneration of the human head and especially to their practice of taking the heads of slain enemies and preserving them as trophies. Musée Borély, Marseilles.

Left The Gundestrup Cauldron (probably first century BC). One interior plaque shows a procession, with some warriors carrying a tree and others blowing trumpets, while a large figure plunges a smaller one head first into a tub, or possibly a well. A fertility goddess and a hunter god appear on two of the outer plaques. Nationalmuseet, Copenhagen.

Right A funerary stele, Reims (second century AD). Cernunnos, with antlers and torc, sits cross-legged between Apollo and Mercury; coins flow from his bag. Bulls and stags were associated with his cult. Musée Saint-Denis, Rheims.

Below Coventina, a goddess of healing waters, shown as a three-fold figure at Carrawburgh, Northumberland. Museum of Antiquities of the University and the Society of Antiquaries, Newcastle upon Tyne.

Left An eleventh-century ithyphallic figure from Rällinge, Sweden, representing a fertility god, probably Freyr. Statens Historiska Museum, Stockholm.

Far left A statuette of Thor, from Iceland (*c.* AD 1000). The god grasps his beard, which merges into a hammer-like form. Thodminjasafn Islands, Reykjavik.

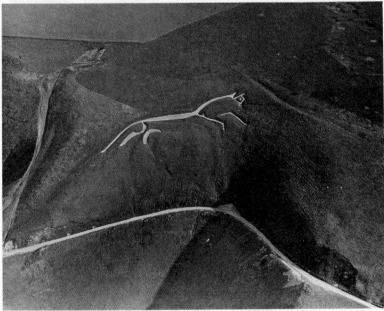

Left The White Horse at Uffington in Berkshire, England. Over 115 metres (370 feet) long, this gigantic figure was probably cut into the chalk hillside close to an Iron Age fort in the first century BC. The horse was held sacred by the Celts and was particularly associated with the horse-goddess Epona.

Above The Oseberg funeral ship (buried in the late ninth century) at the time of excavation in 1904. The burial chamber was in the centre, and contained the remains of one woman, traces of a second woman, and some superb carved wood, all preserved in the soil. Norsk Sjøfartsmuseum, Bygdøy, near Oslo.

Right Viking Age burial place at Lindholm Hills, Nørresundby, Denmark. There are some 628 graves on the site, two hundred of which were marked by the outline of a ship in stones.

This may well be an equally valid conception of Valkyries, for deities of war necessarily present a dual aspect.

Certain sixth- and seventh-century Swedish helmets bear embossed figures, presumably as magical protection. They include a horseman with spear and birds; men fighting with or fettering monsters; men whose helmets have a boar or bird as crest; and men in horned helmets, sometimes naked, dancing with weapons in their hands. Such figures may be simply certain human initiates enacting rituals in a warrior cult – perhaps forerunners of the berserks, who fought naked and frenzied, deriving their strength from Odin. Yet the armed rider may well be Odin himself (quelling monsters is a feat for gods or heroes) and the horned dancers too might be divine, possibly male counterparts to the Valkyries. Perhaps the distinction between human and divine was blurred when initiates copied superhuman prototypes in these warrior cults.

Thor

Thor, whose name means 'Thunder', was widely venerated in Scandinavia in the Viking age, and earlier as Donar in Germany and Thunor in England; Romans identified him with Jupiter, and probably also with Hercules. He was a sky-god, especially a storm-god, whose hammer symbolized the thunderbolt; oaks were often dedicated to him. As he ruled the weather, he was invoked by seafarers and farmers. He also enforced law and justice; oaths were sworn on rings sacred to him, and the Icelandic Assembly always began on a Thursday. His consecrating and protective power was invoked at marriages and burials; his image was carved on hall pillars and ships' prows, as the hammer was on memorial stones.

Illustration page 109

In myths Thor is a mighty fighter, forever crushing giants and monsters who would otherwise destroy the world; sometimes he cuts a comic figure, but he was much loved and invoked. His cult is attested by widespread place-names, by numerous personal names, and by the many miniature hammers used as amulets. By the close of the period, Thor was the god most widely revered, both in Scandinavia and in Viking settlements, as a universal protector.

Fertility Deities

In Roman times Germanic tribes, like the Celts, worshipped the Matres, who gave fertility to men and women and to nature. Tacitus also describes Nerthus, a benevolent 'earth mother', whose symbol was carried round the fields in a covered wagon, and then washed in a lake by slaves who were drowned forthwith. In later centuries we glimpse many goddesses: Nehalennia, worshipped at Walcheren in the third century; the Anglo-Saxon 'Mothers', whose festival was at midwinter; Frija, protectress of the Lombards; the Scandinavian Frigg, Freyja, Gefion and others. They had much in common; they gave fruitfulness to the land, wealth, love and fertility to men and women, and luck to children. The best known is Freyja, goddess of sexual love, magic and divination; but Frija/Frigg, Odin's wife, was originally a more important figure.

Illustration page 109

A chief fertility-god was Freyr, brother and lover of Freyja, and like her a patron of love, marriage, fruitfulness, peace and plenty; in myth, his love for an underworld giantess indicates his marriage with the earth. A late saga says his statue was taken about in a wagon by a priestess, his 'wife'; ritual marriages and processions were a frequent feature in fertility cults.

Other similar gods are described, though in less detail. Njord, father of Freyr and Freyja, ruled the sea, a major source of wealth; he must be in some way related to the early goddess Nerthus, whose name is the same as his. Various legendary Danish and English kings may well be euhemerized fertility-gods; some also had warlike aspects, as indeed Freyr himself must have had, since the boar, a protective emblem used on armour, was associated with him.

Besides major gods, there were several types of lesser male and female deities – elves, 'earth-spirits', guardian-goddesses, and the like – whose protection extended only to particular areas, families or individuals. They gave prosperity, fertility and luck, and in some cases seem to be akin to spirits of the dead.

The Dead

Beliefs concerning the afterlife were very diverse. One was that the dead lived on inside their graves with whatever goods were buried with them. They could bestow prosperity and wisdom on the living, but might also return as fearsome corporeal ghosts. Another conception was of distant otherworlds – the dark realm of the goddess Hel, or Odin's Valhalla, where heroes would feast till the end of the world. The dead were imagined as journeying through eerie regions on horseback, in a wagon, or on foot; or as swept away in the smoke of their pyres. Whatever was burnt or buried with them would be theirs in the afterlife. There are also traces of belief in reincarnation.

Archaeology reveals similar complexity; the basic rites were burial and cremation, but each had wide variations. In Denmark in the first century the rich were buried with sets of food vessels, apparently for feasting inside the grave. In Sweden in the fifth and sixth centuries huge mounds with internal wooden chambers held buried or cremated chieftains. Less wealthy men and women were buried or burnt with a few weapons, clothes, ornaments and tools; their graves might be plain, or covered by a mound or cairn, or surrounded by stones forming a circle, square, or outline of a ship.

Illustrations page 110

The burial of the dead in actual ships was practised in seventh-century Sweden and East Anglia, in ninth-century Norway, and throughout the Viking settlements. Some Swedish families tenaciously maintained the custom till the eleventh century, laying the dead man on a couch near the stern, with his weapons beside him, goods piled in the prow, and slaughtered dogs and horses round the ship. Norwegian ship-burials are equally lavish and include a wooden chamber on deck to shelter the corpse; in England the buried ship at Sutton Hoo held unparalleled treasures, but no sacrificed animals, and apparently no corpse. Ships were cremated too, and probably also set alight on the sea, as floating pyres. Their powerful symbolic importance is confirmed by numerous poorer graves containing small or fragmentary boats; almost certainly they signified the soul's journey to the otherworld.

Cosmic Myths

Few cosmic myths are known from Germanic sources; one, a Saxon belief, was that the universe was upheld by a World Pillar, Irminsul. But Icelandic cosmology is rich and complex; its creation myths include the mingling of ice and fire in the void, the dismemberment of a primeval bisexual giant, a flood, and the creation of humans from tree-trunks. The completed universe consisted of various worlds – of gods, people, giants, and underworld beings – all linked by, or indeed contained in, the World Tree, Yggdrasil. This archetypal sacred tree, life-giving and protective, decaying yet ever renewed, would endure eternally.

At length would come the 'Doom of the Gods', when monstrous forces of evil, breaking from their chains, would attack the world of gods and people, and earth and sky would be destroyed. Loki, in other myths a comparatively harmless trickster, here plays the role of demonic foe. The chief gods would perish, each slaying but also slain by a monstrous adversary. Yet the earth would rise again from the sea and a few surviving gods and people would found a better world; evil then would reappear, and the cycle presumably begin again. This grandiose myth is only found in its entirety in a late tenth-century poem, but its component parts can often be proved to be much older; cosmic myths are certainly an authentic part of the Germanic heritage.

Conclusion

The amount of mythological information recorded in medieval Iceland was very great, and attention has here been chiefly directed to gods whose cult can be shown to have played a part in religious practices; others such as Balder, Loki and Heimdall figure in memorable stories, but their religious significance is obscure. Most Icelandic gods emerge as sharply defined individuals, in contrast with the vaguer 'all-purpose' Celtic divinities; however, the marked shortage of Celtic myths makes it hard to determine whether this is a genuine original difference between the two cultures, or merely due to the polished art and detail of Icelandic texts. The parallels and contrasts between these, the last two great pre-Christian religions of Central and Northern Europe, form a subject that is still far from exhausted.

Chapter Eight

Mesopotamia

The early civilizations of the ancient Near East afford a unique opportunity to study the rise and development of religion in a region of mixed races and cultures which later gave rise to the major monotheistic religions of Judaism, Christianity and Islam. All of these owe some debt to the earlier stages of religious thought in Mesopotamia, the home of the Sumerians, Babylonians and Assyrians.

Archaeologists have uncovered remains of the earliest village settlements (Jarmo in Iraq, Catal Hüyük in Turkey and Jericho in Palestine) which already existed in the seventh—sixth millennia BC. By the fourth millennium larger groups of men in southern Mesopotamia (modern Iraq) had learned to control the waters of the rivers Tigris and Euphrates and irrigate the surrounding plain. This control of their environment enabled cities to be maintained on the banks of rivers and major canals.

From prehistoric times such men were conscious of the spiritual forces on which their existence depended, and the remains of their shrines, places of sacrifice, offerings, symbolic figurines, representations of deities and burial customs attest this. With the advent of writing, first found at Uruk (Erech) about 3000 BC, a new source of evidence, yielding almost half a million documents written on clay and writing-boards using the cuneiform script, make it possible to trace the development of their thought up to the arrival of the Persian and Greek conquerors of the area.

Throughout the third millennium the Sumerians developed views which were to have great influence not only on their contemporaries, the early Semites, but on the succeeding Babylonians and on the Assyrians, Hittites, Elamites and inhabitants of Palestine among the neighbouring peoples who took over their basic beliefs. In essence, their principal concept was that the universe was characterized by order and whatever man could perceive reflected supernatural activity and revealed the divine mind.

For the Sumerians the major components of the universe were the sky (*an*) and the earth (*ki*), the latter being like a flat circular disk surrounded by water and surmounted by the vault of heaven beneath which moved the atmosphere (*lil*) or spirit. They thought that from the primeval sea as first cause sprang the created universe, in which was fashioned the sun, moon, planets and stars, each moving in its divinely ordered and observable path. As in heaven so on earth. Then there came plant, animal and human life.

The superhuman and invisible beings who controlled, and were represented in, the great universe were necessarily described in human terms. Like men and women, they had passions and weaknesses – they ate and drank, married and bore children and possessed servants and dwellings. Unlike people, however, they were immortal for 'when the gods made mankind they reserved death for humans and kept life in their own hands'.

According to their theology, which survives in detailed texts from the early Old Babylonian period, about 1900 BC, the Sumerians thought that each cosmic and cultural entity had its own rules and regulations, to keep it going forever along the plan laid down by the deity who created it. These were called *me* in Sumerian. A list of these includes 'lordship, godship, the crown, the royal throne, kingship, priesthood, truth, descent into and ascent from the nether world, the flood, weapons, sexual intercourse, law, art, music, power, hostility, honesty, destruction of cities, metal-working, scribeship, leather-working, building, wisdom, fear, terror, strife, peace, weariness, victory, the troubled heart, judgment . . . '. Apparent inconsistencies in their polytheism did not trouble the Sumerian theologians. By the Fara period (about 2500 BC) they listed hundreds of divine names, each classified as a god (Sumerian *dingir;* Semitic *il[u]*) and written with a prefix of the sign for a star. Each had his or her characteristic and defined area of responsibility, though many were secondary deities grouped as wives, children, officials or servants in a family around a powerful god.

The Supreme Ruler

An(u), the heaven-god, was originally the supreme ruler of the pantheon and was primarily interested in rulership, symbolized by an enthroned horned headdress as the mark of divinity. His principal shrine was at Uruk. However, when the neighbouring city of Nippur defeated Uruk, its own god Enlil or Ellil, (lord of the atmosphere/winds) and his temple Ekur became the supreme object of veneration. Enlil was the beneficent and fatherly progenitor to whom the creation of sun, moon, vegetation and implements essential to human control of the earth was ascribed. In some theologies Enlil was held to be the son of Anu, though in another tradition he was the offspring of the first divine pair, Enki and Ninki (Lord and Lady of the Earth).

Enlil, though associated with Nippur, was considered the supreme god of all Sumer and held the tablets by which the fates of all people were settled. Nippur remained a holy city and centre of pilgrimage throughout Babylonian history, though by the middle of the second millennium Enlil's position and function was largely taken over by the god Marduk within Babylonia and by Ashur in Assyria. Enlil's consort Ninlil was by that time identified with the great goddess, the Sumerian Innin, popularly taken as Inanna, Lady of Heaven, the Babylonian Ishtar.

The third of the leaders of the pantheon (though the Sumerians had no conception of a triad of gods) was Enki (Lord of the Underworld), also known by the name Ea, the god of the deep. He ruled the primeval waters and to him was attributed all wisdom. In contrast to the more transcendent and overbearing Anu and Enlil, Ea was favourable to both humans and his fellow-deities. Knowing all secrets he was the one who instructed the first people in all the arts necessary to life and progress. He it was too, who made known divine plans to people, and so to him they turned for elucidation of mysteries. He was thus later the patron of exorcists and artisans. His chief cult centre was Eridu on the Persian Gulf.

His son Marduk was destined to become head of the whole Babylonian pantheon when his city Babylon was the seat of a powerful dynasty which dominated most of Mesopotamia. When this happened Marduk's son, the god Nabu, patron of 'science' and especially of astronomy and the scribal arts, gained a new prominence both in Babylon and in his own temple city of Borsippa nearby. Marduk's elevation was in part the work of a theological school which composed hymns and prayers in his honour and added to the classic *Epic of Creation* a twelfth and final chapter to heap on him the descriptive epithets of all the fifty major deities. Thus in lists, such gods as Adad were explained as 'Marduk of rain' and the moon-god Sin as 'Marduk who illumines the night'. By a process of syncretism and ecumenical fervour this group sought to enforce a type of monotheism. They were never fully successful, for local gods still held the affection of their devotees, though Marduk, like Enlil earlier, was greeted as Bel (the Lord). This movement played its part in an increasing simplification of the pantheon.

A fourth creating deity was Ninhursag or Ninmah (The Exalted Lady and original 'Mother Earth'), associated in Sumerian thought with Enlil and Ea in the creation of the human race.

The Stars and Planets

A second group of gods consisted of the Moon (Sumerian Nannar, Su'en or Sin), the Sun (Sumerian Utu, Semitic Shamash), and the principal planets and morning star Ishtar (Venus). The Moon in his crescent-shaped boat regularly crossed the night sky and divided the year into months of thirty days. Nannar was a son of Anu (or of Enlil according to others) and his wife Ningal bore the sun-god and the splendid goddess Inanna. His main shrines were at Ur and Harran.

Illustration page 119

Shamash, the sun, daily crossed the heavens in his chariot dispersing darkness and evil while he shone equally and relentlessly on all. By night his passage through the underworld continued his role as the great judge and 'lord of decisions'. In Babylonia his symbol was a four-rayed sun, whereas in Assyria he was depicted by the winged sun-disc. While he was predominantly worshipped at Sippar and Larsa, every major city had at least one shrine dedicated to him.

The great goddess Ishtar gradually absorbed the functions of many earlier female deities, and her name became a synonym for 'goddess', while she herself was patroness of war and love. In art she can be seen standing as the Lady of Battle, armed with bow and arrows, wearing her lapis lazuli necklace and placing her foot on her symbol, the lion. As the goddess of love in popular worship she was adored throughout the land under various local aspects.

Illustration page 119

From Nineveh, her main temple, her worship spread to the west where this goddess of love and fertility was known as Ishtar of Erbil. She was considered the Queen of Heaven and attracted Judean women (Jeremiah 7:18; 44:19), Syrians as Anat, Arabs as Atar, Greeks as Astarte and Egyptians as Isis. In Babylon alone there were 180 open-air wayside shrines where she could be addressed by prayer or votive offerings. According to one Babylonian tradition, she descended for a while into the underworld in search of her missing lover Dumuzi (Tammuz) with the result that fertility ceased in the land. In astrology she was linked with the evening and morning star (Venus).

These seven major deities may well have been the inner cabinet of the assembly of the gods, in whose hands lay the fate of all. They were supported by fifty great gods and spirits (*annunaki* and *igigi*), who collectively designated the spiritual forces at work above and in the earth.

Riding on the Storm

In Assyria, other gods were revered. The weather-god, Adad, rode the storm, thundering like a bull, his symbolic mount. In his hand was the forked lightning, for though he was the bringer of judgment and destruction by flood he was also the favourable provider of abundance, through the rain. Worshipped in Babylon and Assyria, his most popular seat was in the cities of hilly Syria where he was designated Ramman or Rimmon (the Thunderer) – or known as Hadad (Addu), or under his Hittite title as Teshub.

Assyria always needed to maintain its political and economic position by constant campaigning to keep open its trade routes through the surrounding hills or deserts. It is therefore not surprising that gods with military characteristics were frequently named. Among these were Ninurta, god of war and hunting, perhaps to be identified with the biblical Nimrod and the Sumerian Girsu, and also Nusku (Gibil) the fire-god. The desert Semites to the west added to the Babylonian pantheon such deities as Amurru and Dagan, who are frequently invoked by their personal names.

Each of the major deities had its own attributes, which were invoked in prayer. Most radiated splendour as an awe-inspiring aura which could prostrate both enemies and worshippers before them. Each had its sumptuously attired statue or symbol which could substitute for the deity itself. In art a deity was recognizable from the horned headdress, for otherwise it was shown as an ordinary man or woman. They might carry an identifying symbol, as Shamash carried his saw of decision, or be shown standing upon or near a symbolic animal. So Marduk stands upon a snake-headed lion-eagle (*mushrushu*)

Illustration page 120

and the goddess of healing Gula can be discerned in art from the presence of her dog. The principal deities were also assigned a number which could be used to write their name: Anu 60, Enlil 50, Ea 40, Sin 30, Shamash 20 and Ishtar 15.

Legends and Stories

Philosophical discussion concerning the relative roles and powers of some of these gods found its expression in legends and stories (mythologies in the widest sense of that term) which traditionally set out to account for cosmological realities and current beliefs. Thus the myth of Inanna and Enki, which recounts the transfer of the arts of civilization (the *me*) from Eridu to Uruk, sought to explain the rise of the latter as the prime spiritual centre of Sumer, with Inanna as the most widely worshipped mother-goddess. She visited Enki 'who knows the very heart of the gods'. In Eridu he regaled her with a banquet and in his cups bestowed on her the coveted *me,* which she thereupon loaded into the boat of heaven and carried off. On coming to his senses, Enki despatched his messenger Isimud to tell her of his change of mind. But despite repeated attacks by the evil monsters sent against her, she ultimately reached her city safely, helped by her vizier Ninshubur.

Illustration page 119

The question of the origin of the world is answered in various myths in which the gods are the participants. The birth of the moon is the subject of a poem, while *Enuma Elish,* the title of one Babylonian epic of creation, named after its opening words 'When on high', ascribes the creation of heaven and earth to the hero Marduk, who fought and slew Tiamat, the dragon of the Deep. He split her in two 'like a shell-fish' (or oyster?), making the heavens of one half and the earth of the other. Another epic describes the formation of the earth more realistically. A god bound reeds together and spread earth over them, in the manner of the formation of villages in the marshes of

Illustration page 122

southern Mesopotamia.

Sumerian versions recount the origin of men and women in terms of birth. In one tale, Anu and Enlil act with the co-operation of the mother-goddess Ninhursag. In another Ea and the goddess Aruru create a man from clay by the power of the divine word. The Old Babylonian *Atrahasis Epic* describes the birth of human beings in some detail. When Enlil made the lesser gods dig canals and work for the agricultural prosperity on which the feeding of the gods themselves depended, they went on strike against such hard labour. Their grievances were upheld by Anu, and the gods, by an act of birth using the mother-goddess (called Mama or Nintu), made people of clay and blood. The later *Enuma Elish* takes up this same theme when it tells of the creation of people to serve the gods, after Marduk's victory. This creation was achieved by the mingling of clay with blood of a slain god, Kingu.

The Golden Age

One Sumerian tale ('Enmerkar and the Lord of Aratta') harks back to the Golden Age when:

Left A seal impression showing the slaughter of the monster Tiamat by the god Marduk, who is armed with a thunderbolt and other weapons. British Museum, London.

Above A seal impression showing the winged sun-god Shamash with rays emanating from his shoulders as he rises between the mountains. British Museum, London.

Left An impression from a cylinder seal showing Ishtar, the goddess of war and love, armed with a bow and other weapons, and standing on a lion (seventh to sixth century BC). British Museum, London.

Right A stone socket for holding the divine standard. The Assyrian king, Tukulti-Ninulta I, kneels before the symbol of the god Nusku (thirteenth century BC). Vorderasiatisches Museum, Berlin.

Right A Babylonian devil. British Museum, London.

Left The Assyrian king
Ashurbanipal pouring a libation
over dead lions before an altar, on
which lie bread, meat, and an
incense-burner, depicted on a relief
from Nineveh (669 – 627 BC).
British Museum, London.

Left The stele of Ur-Nammu of Ur
(*c.* 2100 BC), who waters the Tree
of Life before Shamash the sun-
god, distinguished by the
measuring-line and the rod of
justice. The panel below depicts the
king inaugurating the building of a
temple to the moon-god Nannar.
University Museum, Philadelphia,
Pennsylvania.

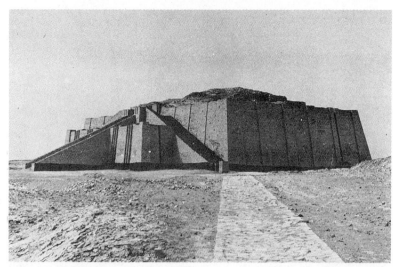

Right The ziggurat or stepped temple-tower of Nannar, the moon-god of Ur, built by Ur-Nammu (*c.* 2100 BC).

Below A marsh village in the region of ancient southern Mesopotamia, constructed on platforms of earth-covered, bound reeds. This is the technique used by a god in one of the creation myths.

Once upon a time there was no snake, no scorpion.
There was no hyena, no lion,
There was no wild dog, no wolf.
There was no fear, no terror.
Man had no rival.

The land Martu dwelt securely.
The whole universe, the people as one
in one tongue gave praise to Enlil.

Another Enki myth involves the 'pure, bright, land of the living', Dilmun, in the Persian Gulf. Here all was peaceful and there was no sickness or old age, though fresh water was lacking. When the sun-god is made to bring this welling up, the place becomes a true paradise for the immortal gods. By the process of birth, Ninhursag brings into being eight plants. When Enki eats these she curses him. Eventually she is persuaded to create eight healing-goddesses, one for each of his sick organs. This she does by painless birth. One of these, Ninti, to heal his rib, has a name which may mean 'the Lady who gives life', and is thus reminiscent of the Genesis account of the birth of Eve.

Human rebellion against the gods is reflected in the story of the gardener Shukalletuda, who committed mortal sin by seducing Inanna. According to the *Atrahasis Epic,* people withdrew their labour, as had the minor gods before them. This deviation from the divinely-given work of supplying the needs of the gods, combined with the noise caused by the multiplication of humankind, deprived Enlil of sleep. He tried to solve the problem by sending plagues, famine and drought, but Enki's intervention enabled men and women to survive these repeated punishments.

Escape from the Flood

The epics of Atrahasis and of Gilgamesh both introduce the Flood as a divine judgement on humankind. In each the hero is a human who gains immortality by surviving, thanks to the warning given by Enki (Ea) to build a boat in which the family and animals may be taken away. Utnapishtim the Faraway tells Gilgamesh, who has just ferried across the waters of Death, how he had escaped the Flood. His ship had eventually landed on Mount Nisir, after he had tested the ebbing of the waters by the despatch of various birds. Enlil was furious that a man had been allowed to escape the destruction, but was prevailed upon by the gods to grant him immortality. 'But who', says Utnapishtim to Gilgamesh, 'will summon the assembly of the gods for you?' In a series of tests he shows how mere man is unable to stay awake even for seven days and nights, or to keep hold of the plant of life when once he has attained it.

Other epics seek to explain abnormalities in the creation, such as imperfect human beings or the distinctive character and customs of the Bedouin Martu. The calamities and sickness brought by the south wind are the subject of a tale of Ninurta and Asag, the sickness-demon. In all these there will be noted certain recurrent concepts concerning journeyings, punishment, divine intervention, the plant of life, and the need for the worship and service of the gods.

Death is the Human Lot

Though there are many myths which emphasize the human search for life, like the story of Etana, the shepherd who tried to reach heaven on an eagle, they all end in failure. Death was the lot of men and women. Even Dumuzi, originally a king of Uruk who was said to have married the goddess Inanna, had to die. When he entered the underworld, his lover sought him in vain and he remained to rule that 'land of no return'. Contrary to popular belief, and the hypothesis of a group of scholars who interpret the myth and ritual to show a resurrection which represents the seasonal dying and revival of vegetation, Dumuzi (Tammuz) did not rise again, according to the later legend of Ishtar's descent to the nether world.

The Mesopotamian view of death and the afterlife is vague. Arallu, 'the great land, the house of shades', lay beneath the earth and was reached by departed spirits by ferry across the River Habur. This belief is reflected in the model boats found in some graves. Here was the realm of Ereshkigal and her husband Nergal, with their entourage of fallen deities and officials, including their vizier Ishum and the goddess scribe Beletersetim who recorded the entrants. All these needed food, clothing and materials, like the gods above the earth and the mortals on it. Status depended on activity during life. The dead were judged by the Sun, whose passage by night provided their only light, and by Nannar, who decreed their lot.

Life was drear and but a pallid reflection of life on earth. Gilgamesh is told by his companion Enkidu how he had been led to the House of Darkness:

> *To the house which none may leave who enter it,*
> *on the road from which there is no way back,*
> *to the house where its inhabitants*
> *are bereft of light,*
> *where dust is their fare and clay their food.*
> *They are clothed like birds,*
> *with wings for garments.*
> *They see no light, residing in darkness.*
> *In this House of Dust which I entered,*
> *I beheld rulers, their crowns now put away,*
> *and royal princes who had ruled the land*
> *in days gone by.*
>
> *(Epic of Gilgamesh VII, 34-42)*

These were fed and given cool water from water-skins, a practical responsibility of the eldest son, who had to provide periodical libations and funerary meals to sustain his ancestors. If a person's ghost or spirit (*etemmu*) lay unburied or deprived of sustenance, it would wander and torment the living. Kings and commoners were buried in cemeteries or beneath their dwellings. The royal graves at Ur (*c.* 2600 BC) included between three and seventy-four followers, musicians, as well as gifts of jewellery, vessels and musical instruments, and the funerary sledge and its draught-animals (as in the grave of Pū-Abi). This may well have been a practice of non-Semitic origin from outside Mesopotamia and similar to that known from Egypt. It does, however, indicate a belief in the need to provide for life in the hereafter.

Personal Religion

The majority of texts relate to the king's official role in the cult. He was the vice-regent of the gods on earth. They invested him with authority to act on their behalf. He was expected to deal justly and without favour, to 'defend the weak against the strong' and to take the part of the fatherless and of the widow. Ethical considerations were guided by what would bring divine approbation and blessing rather than a curse. The proper manner of life and kingship was handed down traditionally and reinforced by texts of counsels and instructions. In the well-being of the king was thought to reside the health of the community, and strict measures were taken to ensure this. To assure continued fertility the king, as successor of Dumuzi, re-enacted the sacred marriage (*hieros gamos*) once or more in his reign. The part of the goddess was given to a selected priestess.

Throughout his life his actions were governed by ceremonies and rituals to guard his purity and person. In certain cases of unfavourable omen, a substitute king would be put on the throne to bear the ill-fortune, or even death, which had been predicted. This was carried out at least once in the reign of Esarhaddon of Assyria (680-669 BC). There is no evidence that the king considered himself divine, though some kings (mainly of the Third Dynasty of Ur) had prayers and hymns addressed to them, perhaps as part of their annual memorial service.

Individuals might rule their lives in some measure like the king. They would address their prayers to a particular deity, whom they would worship with hymns which extolled the divine attributes and achievements and ended with a stereotyped doxology. The Sumerian and Akkadian psalter includes hymns addressed to temples and sacred cities. People might address the intercessory goddess Lama, who took the worshipper into the presence of the god much as one would be introduced to the king on his throne. Protective spirits (*shēdu* and *lamassu*) could also be invoked. Individual responsibility in religion is clearly demanded:

> *Worship your god every day*
> *with sacrifice and prayer which*
> *properly go with incense offerings.*
> *Present your freewill offering to your god*

for this is fitting for the gods.
Offer him daily prayer, supplication
and prostration
and you will get your reward.
Then you will have full
communion with your god.
Reverence begets favour.
Sacrifice prolongs life,
and prayer atones for guilt.

(Counsels of Wisdom, 135-145)

Instead of a prayer or lamentation made in person, a wealthier devotee would deposit in the temple a suitably inscribed object (statue, bowl, *stela,* seal, piece of jewellery or model). These would be placed near the god's statue as a reminder of the request or as thanks for favour received. Prayers might also be written in the form of a letter suitably addressed and usually detailed in its complaint, protest, prayer or petition. Gestures of prayer, apart from kneeling and prostration, were the raising of both hands or holding of one hand before the mouth with the palm towards the face.

The Cult

The temple was the focal point of religious activity. The earliest so far excavated, Enki's temple at Eridu, was a rectangular structure with a niche for the divine statue or emblem, before which stood an offering-table. The building followed the pattern of the earlier reed shrines and was succeeded by ever larger and more substantial buildings. Each had a *cella,* the god being raised on a platform or pedestal in a dark inner shrine before which was placed the altar or table. In a central courtyard beyond the main entrance there might be situated lavers or a well (*apsu*). The building included side-chapels and store-rooms. The main entrance of the temple was sometimes set at right angles to the inner shrine to give greater privacy.

The largest and most celebrated temple was that of Marduk at Babylon, called Esagila (the Temple whose head is raised high). Here stood the massive statue of Marduk and his couch, weighing fifty talents of gold. Within the panelled and pillared hall, but at a lower level, were fifty-five chapels dedicated to the remaining gods of the pantheon. Successive kings paid due attention to the renovation and embellishment of this temple as they did to those in all cities under their control.

At Uruk the temple of Anu (*c.* 3000 BC) was raised on an artificial hill consisting of a series of mud-brick platforms of decreasing sizes and reached by a stairway, This type of construction had evolved from a small shrine raised upon a small platform which at Uqair was 4.5 metres (15 feet) above the surrounding plain. Thus developed the characteristic Sumerian ziggurat or temple tower. At Ur the ziggurat built by Ur-Nammu in 2100 BC was of three stages, the base 60 × 30 metres (200 × 100 feet) and the whole 21 metres (70 feet) high.

Illustration page 122

Each stage was a different colour, with a silver shrine to Nannar on the top. According to Herodotus, the temple tower of Babylon, named Etemenanki (the building which is the foundation of heaven and earth), was of seven stages with the ascent diagonally from level to level.

More than thirty ziggurats have been identified, some, like the twin-towered Anu-Adad construction at Ashur, being of unusual formation. Their purpose has been debated, and some scholars consider them to be representations of the cosmic mountain, a giant altar, or the divine throne. Here god was thought to come down to earth and in the summit temple decorated like a green bower, the sacred marriage ceremonies on which the fertility of earth depended may have been performed.

Priest and King

The cult required numerous and trained personnel to sustain it. Originally the head of the community, the *en*, acted as a priest-king, living in the *giparu* — apartment of the temple. The *en* would be a man or woman according to the sex of the deity to whom the temple was dedicated. Thus the goddess Inanna at Uruk had a male *en*, and the moon-god Nannar at Ur was served by a succession of the daughters of Mesopotamian rulers. When the *en* moved into a secular palace and became the *ensi* (later king), the spiritual role was combined with the function of city-ruler, who was thought to rule the temple estates on the god's behalf. He had to ensure the maintenance of the proper rites and ceremonies on which harmony with the god depended.

Illustrations page 121

The king soon delegated special duties to specialist priests (*shangu*) under a superior. Those who entered the sanctuary (*erib biti*) were accompanied by those whose tasks were to sacrifice, pour libations, lustrations or anointing. Others were concerned with appeasing a wrathful deity with incantations and exorcisms, singing and chanting, and music. Incantation and divination priests worked within and outside the temple, often going to private homes.

Around the temple were housed eunuchs, temple slaves, and sacred prostitutes, in addition to the numerous army of tradesmen, butchers, bakers, metal, silver and woodworkers who prepared the sacrifice and maintained the building and its statues. Herdsmen kept the temple flocks and cultivators the fields, until with increasing secularization after the Old Babylonian period their numbers were much diminished. Certain temples had groups of female priestesses or nuns living in cloisters. All this activity was backed by a large administrative staff of scribes, storekeepers, and guards. Entry to the higher classes of the priesthood was by patronage, which demanded that a candidate be of sound health and body and of good education.

Like humans, the gods required regular supplies of food and drink, which were set out on tables before them morning and evening. The choicest meat was provided from sacrifices (*niqū*), the blood having first been poured out and selected parts, the lungs and the liver, examined for omens. In addition to the staple foods, barley bread, onions and dates, the gods were given fruit, fish, fowls, honey, ghee, and milk. Oil, drink and incense were liberally provided and everything was meticulously recorded by the scribes and their accounts lodged in the temple archives. The statues received fresh ornaments and garments for their particular festival day.

Festivals

Special sacrifices and feasts were made on days sacred to a particular deity. These were in addition to the regular monthly feast-days on the first (new moon), seventh, fifteenth (and later twenty-fifth) days as well as the day of the full moon (*shabatu*) and of its disappearance (*bubbulu*). Since the Sumerian calendar varied in each major city, it provides evidence of the local festivals. At Lagash, the first month (March-April) was the Feast of Eating the Barley of the god Ningirsu and the sixth month the Festival of Dumuzi. At these and other sites the various harvests and sheep-shearing called for festivities and processions.

The major festival was that of the New Year (*akitu*) when, at least at Babylon, Uruk and Ashur, it was celebrated by inviting all the gods of the surrounding region to come in. Detailed rituals survive, like those for most cultic operations such as the making of a statue, and clothing it, or for the foundation of any building. At Babylon the rites began at dawn on the first day and were followed by sacrifices and the making of special statuettes. On the fourth day there followed a recitation of the Epic of Creation and special prayers to Marduk. The next day the king rose and bathed in pure river water before entering the temple dressed in fine linen. After prayers he opened the doors to the priests and administered the morning sacrifice. The king engaged in a long prayer attesting his innocence and good stewardship, but later in the day was approached by the chief priest who, having removed the royal insignia, struck the king on the cheek. If tears flowed, all was well, for Marduk showed that he was well-pleased and all would be well with the land. The king prostrated himself in prayer and his regalia was restored before he offered the evening sacrifice. On the eighth day the king 'took the hand of Bēl' to lead the god out of the temple along the sacred procession route, followed by the visiting gods, priests and the populace. The special New Year festival house, upstream on the river bank outside the city, was reached via the Ishtar Gate and a trip by decorated barge. Here the gods decided the fate of the country for the following year and re-enacted Marduk's victory over the forces of evil. The whole festival ended after the celebration of the sacred marriage between Marduk and his consort Sarpanit, accompanied by much public feasting.

Sin and Suffering

The Babylonians, with their liking for order, listed all categories of observed phenomena, including the errors which seemed to bring on divine retribution in the guise of sickness, trouble and even death. The results of favourable actions were equally recorded. An incantation text describes the sinner as 'one who has eaten what is taboo to his god or goddess, who has said "no" for "yes" or has said "yes" for "no", who has pointed his finger (falsely accusing) a fellow-man, who has said what is not allowed to be said, who has scorned his god, despised his goddess, caused evil to be spoken, has judged incorrectly, oppressed the weak, estranged a son from his father or a friend from friend, who has not freed the captive. . . '. (*Shurpu* II 5ff).

Such sins could be remitted by a penitential psalm, prayer or lament, or discharged by providing an expiatory sacrifice in which 'the lamb is substitute for the man'. This was expensive for the common folk who could, in their direst need, call in an exorcist priest to recite the appropriate incantation taken from his reference manual. Where the cause was unknown, or in such sickness as seizure by the hand of a god, ghost or demon, the accompanying ritual was usually that of transferring the evil to an inanimate object. It was rendered powerless by symbolic action such as binding or piercing a small clay or wood figurine of the sufferer or melting a wax effigy before the fire. The priest was also called in whenever it was necessary to gain power over an enemy or supernatural dangers threatened a building.

Illustration page 120

Collective suffering was the subject of laments and rites but the individual sufferer posed a problem. One composition, called after its opening line *Ludlul* ('I will praise the Lord of Wisdom') has been compared with the biblical Job, since it describes a rich man who loses possessions, health and perhaps sanity from some unknown cause. He vainly attempts to discover the reason through the medium of exorcists, interpreters of dreams, and other priests. He is taunted by his friends and family as he soliloquizes over the mysterious causes of evil. No solution to the problem is given but the praise and healing attributed to Marduk imply that he found the answer in the will, and whim, of that god.

The Babylonian *Theodicy* treats the same subject in the form of an acrostic poem, being a dialogue between the sufferer and a friend. When the former expounds his views of the prevailing injustice, he is answered with the usual and apparently contradictory argument that since the gods order and control the universe their ways are imponderable, but that piety always pays in the long run.

Divination

Despite the fatalism of the sufferer, the prevalent outlook of the ancient Mesopotamian thinker was that people could ascertain the will of god. Since what went on in heaven was reproduced on earth, they had only to observe and examine the evidence to find their answer. This early led to the listing of terrestial phenomena related to the position of the heavenly planets. When the same event recurred, the records, when duly interpreted by a qualified specialist, would give the concomitant happening to be expected, be it foe, flood, revolution, death of a king or the like. Astrology, which did not include horoscopes until the fourth century BC in Babylon, early fathered the science of astronomy, in which the Babylonians excelled.

Other methods of divination in use included the observation of patterns formed in the liver and lung of a slaughtered animal (hepatoscopy). This was the method commonly used when state decisions, such as those on warfare or international agreements, had to be made. Omens from monstrous births (teratology) or physiognomy, such as moles or mannerisms of gait or speech, or from the detailed examination of patients led to diagnosis and prognosis recorded by exorcist and physician alike. The methodology employed brought an empiricism which laid the foundation for the first steps in true scientific progress. Diviners also observed the patterns of oil on water or the flights of birds or the movement of animals.

A whole series of over a hundred tablets records omens from public happenings, from which developed historiography. As with most religious practices, these were primarily related to the king. It is therefore not without interest that the literary form of the omen text (given that *x* happened, then *y* will come to pass) was the basis of recorded case law. All legal decisions and agreements were ratified on oath before the gods and subject to their divine penalty in case of infringement. Since law and order were identified with truth and justice (*kittum u mesharum*) and these were the responsibility of gods, king and ordinary men and women, the whole of life was thought of as a unified religious exercise.

Above A part of *The Book of the Dead* in the Papyrus of Nu. The book consisted of many spells intended to secure the salvation and comfort of the dead in the next world. British Museum, London.

Top The earliest big stone building erected by man, the Step Pyramid at Saqqara, was planned for King Djoser (*c.* 2700 BC) by the architect Imhotep.

Right During the night the sun-god Re was believed to visit the underworld, the realm of demons and of the dead. Dawn signified the triumph of Re over his enemies, and the dead person who joined him in his boat was born again. British Museum, London.

Above The monotheism of
Akhenaten was concerned with the
Aten, the god of the sun's disk,
and this tomb relief shows the king
and his family worshipping the
Aten, whose rays are conceived of
as ending in beneficent hands
conferring the gift of life. Egyptian
Museum, Cairo.

Above left A stele dedicated to the
great triad of Horus, Osiris and
Isis. Osiris carries the royal crook
and flail, while Horus, his son, is
represented as a falcon-headed
man. Musée National du Louvre,
Paris.

Left The largest temple of Horus
was at Edfu. In its present form it
was built in Ptolemaic times. This
court leads to the inner sanctuary.

Above Although the jackal was much dreaded as the disturber of graves, the Egyptians made the jackal-god Anubis a protector of the dead. Here he is represented as a watchful guardian-god on the wooden shrine from Tutankhamûn's tomb. Egyptian Museum, Cairo.

Right The rite of 'Opening the Mouth', performed by King Ay on the dead Tutankhamûn, who bears the insignia of Osiris, from a wall-painting in Tutankhamûn's tomb in the Valley of the Kings.

Below The heart of the deceased is weighed in the scales in order to determine his fate in the afterlife. In the opposite scale is a figure of the goddess Maat (Truth). The gods Thoth, Anubis and Horus conduct the ceremony in front of the enthroned Osiris (from a papyrus of *c.* 300 BC).

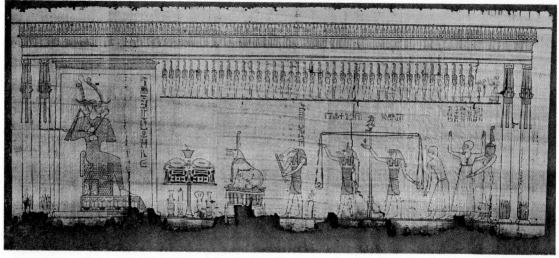

Ancient Egypt

Archaeology has preserved from the remains of ancient Egypt much more that relates to religion than to secular life, and this religious material is very often funerary in character. If graves, pyramids and mummies are what comes to mind first of all in thinking of this civilization, it should be remembered that an undue emphasis has resulted inevitably from the nature of the material available. Most of the cities, palaces, towns and villages are not accessible to the excavator because they have been built upon in later times; further, the material used in their construction was often flimsier than that used in tombs. The latter were built in the desert, away from the cultivated and inhabited land, so that the chances of funerary buildings surviving were always superior, apart, of course, from the danger of tomb robberies. That the Egyptians consciously aimed at permanence in their tombs is shown by the phrase 'house of eternity', used several times of the tomb (e.g. *The Book of the Dead* ed. Naville, 170,8).

The pyramid seemed the best method of achieving this endurance. The first of these was the step pyramid of Djoser in the Third Dynasty, planned for him by his architect Imhotep. It is the first big stone building in history. Before this the Egyptians buried their dead in a structure mostly of brick which is today called a 'mastaba', from the Arabic word for bench. It is an apt word to indicate the shape, and a plausible theory to account for the form of the huge step pyramid at Saqqara is that the basic idea was to pile a number of mastabas of decreasing dimensions on top of each other. Around the pyramid was an elaborate complex of other stone buildings intended for use in religious ceremonies during the burial and afterwards.

Illustration page 132

The main concept behind the step pyramid was probably that of ascent to the heaven and to the sun. In the Fourth Dynasty the design was modified in favour of the true pyramid, the best-known examples being the pyramids of Cheops, Chephren and Mycerinus in Giza.

The Heliopolitan worship of the sun was still the inspiration of the building: in Heliopolis an ancient conical stone called the *benben* had long been venerated as the object on which the sun had first appeared. It was the shape of the *benben* that was being imitated, it seems – though not precisely – by the pyramids.

The Great Pyramid of Cheops, like the others, was associated with a mortuary temple in which the cult of the dead king was provided for. A stone causeway led from this temple to the edge of the desert, and here was located the Valley Temple, which received the king's dead body with due ritual before it was carried on the causeway to the pyramid. In essence, then, the pyramid was a huge tomb aiming at the secure preservation of the dead king, both physically and spiritually. It is ironic, therefore, that not one of the royal mummies of the Old Kingdom has been found. Grouped around the pyramids were the tombs of the king's noblemen in the form of mastabas.

By the end of the Old Kingdom, however, a new type of tomb had appeared in Upper Egypt which was based on the ability to cut into rocky cliffs. A chapel cut into the upper rock face led to a shaft which in turn led to the burial chamber. Several features of this plan were used in the burial of many pharaohs of the New Kingdom, including Tutankhamûn, in the Valley of the Kings near Thebes; one of these rock-cut tombs, that of Sethos I, proceeds into the rock for about 210 metres (700 feet), and the walls of its chambers are inscribed with the text of *Amduat* (The Book of Him Who Is in the Underworld), which describes the nocturnal journey of the sun-god through the underworld until dawn brings his emergence in the world above. The dead king was believed to accompany the sun-god on this journey, and to emerge with him in a new dawn – clearly a guarantee of his survival after death.

Writing

The invention of writing was a significant part of the advance made at the beginning of the historic era (*c.* 3000 BC), and the Narmer Palette exhibits an incipient stage of the hieroglyphic script. The Egyptians regarded the god Thoth, the scribe of the gods, as the inventor of writing, but they also associated the function with the goddess Seshat, the archivist of royal annals. Writing was certainly always important in religious ritual, and its role was believed to transcend the immediate purposes of recording and communication.

A development is discernible already in the Old Kingdom. Spells were doubtless recited in the early temples and tombs, and the priests probably read from versions on papyrus. Inscriptions on stone preserved the names of persons buried in tombs, and they added short spells which ensured the perpetuation of offerings as well as the eternal good fortune of the deceased. These inscriptions, we may assume, did not merely record pious hopes, but were believed to ensure, by their permanent presence, the magical endurance of the physical and spiritual blessings mentioned.

A notable expansion in the use of such inscriptions occurred in the pyramids of the Fifth and Sixth Dynasties at Saqqara, the earliest of which is that of King Wenis (*fl. c.* 2350 BC). The walls of the burial chamber and the passages leading to it are crowded with hieroglyphic texts dealing with the king's future life and adducing in the process considerable evidence from theology, ritual and mythology. These writings, called *The Pyramid Texts,* form the earliest corpus of material relevant to Egyptian religion, and their impact on later writings was also profound, for their content recurs often in later funerary texts, especially in *The Coffin Texts* and *The Book of the Dead*.

The Coffin Texts, as the name implies, were written on sarcophagi, usually of wood, and they derive from the period following the collapse of the Old Kingdom up to the end of the Middle Kingdom. From the beginning of the New Kingdom it became customary to give the benefits of such writings to the deceased in quite a different form: the text was written on a roll of papyrus and inserted in the tomb. As compared with *The Pyramid Texts,* both *The Coffin Texts* and *The Book of the Dead* are much wider in their application, for they proffer their privileges to non-royal persons. The use of papyrus as a medium also led to a further innovation: the text was often illustrated with beautifully coloured vignettes, as in the papyri of Ani and Hunefer. Much of Ancient Egypt's religious literature is thus funerary in character.

Illustration page 132

Other categories include temple inscriptions, which were especially prominent in the Ptolemaic era, hymns to the gods, many of which are found on *stelae*, and mythological tales. Some of the last-named category exhibit a curious frivolity of tone, such as 'The Contendings of Horus and Seth' in Papyrus Chester Beatty I; the more recently published Papyrus Jumilhac includes stories about the gods which do not flinch from ascribing to them some very coarse and vulgar behaviour.

History

Egyptian religion can be traced back, in its prehistoric origins, to as early as 4000 BC, when the careful burial of bulls, jackals and other beasts indicates animal worship. It was in the middle of the sixth century AD that the last temple of the goddess Isis was closed on the island of Philae, so that the time-span covered by Egyptian cults is considerable.

A stable united kingdom was first achieved under Menes about 3000 BC. During the Old Kingdom (*c.* 2686-2181 BC) a strongly centralized monarchy held sway at Memphis, but a period of disruption followed, and when a united Egypt was re-established in the Middle Kingdom (*c.* 2050-1786 BC), the capital was now Thebes in Upper Egypt. Thebes remained the capital in the era of imperial expansion which took place under the New Kingdom. There had been invasion and infiltration from Syria and Palestine by people known as the Hyksos, who introduced Asiatic influences in religion.

In the Late Dynastic period there were several changes in the ruling families. The sixth century BC saw a conscious revival of ancient glories in both religion and art. In spite of this renaissance Egypt was militarily weak and in 525 BC fell to the onslaught of the Persians. Although the Persian yoke was thrown off for a time, the conquest of Egypt by Alexander the Great in 332 BC meant the end of Egyptian independence.

Greek influence was now naturally extensive, but the native cults were allowed to flourish, and a new cult, that of Sarapis, was mainly based on Egyptian foundations. The cults of Sarapis and Isis spread throughout the Greek world. When Egypt became a province of Rome in 30 BC the lands of the temples were put under government control. Under Byzantine rule (AD 395-640) Christianity had become firmly rooted in Egypt, and the old religion was directly under attack. It was in Egypt that Christian monasticism arose, and the old religion may well have influenced this development. Judaism and Gnosticism were also influential forces, especially in the city of Alexandria.

For the origins of Christian asceticism, see page 429.

Local Gods

Historical and political conditions always had a clear impact on religious trends in Egypt. To have separate local gods was a natural tendency in an area which, south of the delta, was nothing but a long river valley extending for some 1000 kilometres (600 miles). With the political unification of the country the god of the capital city became *ipso facto* the leader of all gods and his cult tended to assimilate others. Thus, while there were many falcon-cults, the dominance of the cult of Horus, the falcon-god who was identified with the living Pharaoh, meant that the royal cult subsumed the others. The god Horus is shown on the early Narmer Palette, where an Upper Egyptian victory over Lower Egypt is depicted as happening under the god's tutelage. In other early palettes the god seems to be leading a clan and he is identified with the clan's ruler. This suggests a prehistoric system akin to totemism.

For a definition of totemism, see page 16.

The Egyptians instinctively avoided the deletion of local traditions even when a process of assimilation occurred. As a result their religious ideas show some confusion and even contradiction, as in the different concepts of creation or in funerary beliefs. In a developed stage this evolution seems to suggest that a variety of beliefs was thought to enrich and fortify one's spiritual equipment, and so Henri Frankfort explains the attitude positively as implying pleasure in a 'multiplicity of approaches'. Historically, however, the reason for the complex amalgam is the combination of a large number of local cults and traditions.

Creation Myths

Primacy in any pantheon belongs to the gods responsible for creation, and the Egyptian pantheon is no exception, although there were several different creation myths. That of Heliopolis was undoubtedly the most widely accepted. According to this doctrine the primal creator-god was Atum, who was identified with the sun-god Re.

Atum was said to have emerged from a chaos of waters, called Nun, and to have appeared on a hill; he procreated, without a consort, the deities Shu (air) and Tefenet (moisture), the former of whom separated the sky from the earth, so that Geb (earth) and Nut (sky) now came into being. A natural procreation was here envisaged, and the same is true of the children of Geb and Nut, the gods Osiris, Isis, Seth and Nephthys, although their cosmic import is initially less clear. Together these nine gods formed the Ennead of Heliopolis, a concept which was afterwards applied to other local groupings and sometimes extended to include more than nine deities. That the physical creation began with the emergence of land from water would seem to be an idea which came naturally to the inhabitants of the Nile Valley, who sometimes saw islands of mud appearing in the Nile. Indeed, before the High Dam at Aswan was completed, it was a common experience in Egypt during the annual inundation of the Nile to see the existing villages looking like elevated islands in the surrounding water.

Another aspect of the Heliopolitan doctrine concerns the creative powers of the first god, Atum. All cosmogonies have to face the teasing problem of explaining how creation proceeds if there is only one originator; and also how he himself was created. Atum, whose name means 'The Perfect One', is said to have come into existence by himself (*Pyramid Texts, 1587b*, referring to his form as Khepri). He is, then, self-begotten. But how did he become the father of Shu and Tefenet? It was by masturbation (*ibid. 1248a–d*) or by expectoration and coughing out (*ibid. 1652c* with word-play on the gods' names). In the first connection Atum's hand is personified as a goddess (the word 'hand' is feminine in Egyptian); and in one text the god describes himself as bisexual: 'I am he who engendered Shu; I am he-she' (*Coffin Texts,* II, 161a).

The Doctrine of Memphis

Bisexuality is also ascribed occasionally to Ptah, the creator-god of Memphis, who is called both father and mother in *The Memphite Theology,* a remarkable document deriving ultimately from the Old Kingdom. The creation of the world is here said to have been planned by the god's intelligence and to have been implemented by his spoken word – a striking anticipation of the much later Greek doctrine of the divine *logos.* At Hermopolis, on the other hand, the theology of creation had some affinities with the Heliopolitan teaching. Thus creation began, it was said, with the emergence of a primeval hill from the waters of chaos. Four pairs of deities were associated with cosmic qualities – Nun and Naunet with the waters of chaos, Huh and Hauhet with endlessness, Kuk and Kauket with darkness, Amun and Amaunet with invisibility. This Ogdoad consisted of marital couples in which the males and females were conceptually undiscriminated; perhaps four bisexual deities were the original forms. Amun was the head of the Ogdoad, and his name translates as 'The Hidden One'.

The creation of living beings, as opposed to that of the cosmos, is often ascribed to the artisan-god Khnum, who is said to have fashioned people on his potter's wheel. Again, the earth is sometimes described and depicted as emerging from a lotus-flower, which has itself emerged from the primordial waters, in the form of the young god Nefertem. 'The pool with the lotus' is mentioned in the temple-texts of Edfu as an early abode of a creator-god; these also venerate the 'Perch' in a similar way – the slip of reed on which the falcon-god Horus first alighted.

Gods of Nile and Sun

When the Egyptians considered the exceptional fertility with which their land was endowed, they doubtless saw that the Nile and sun were mainly responsible, and the gods associated with these natural forces are understandably prominent.

It was the annual inundation of the Nile that was especially connected with the god Hapy, and many local Nile-gods, who are traditionally depicted carrying plants, represented the same beneficent power. Since the beginning of the inundation of the Nile in July was signalled by the appearance of the star Sirius with the sunrise, this bright star, called the goddess Sothis by the Egyptians, also symbolized the vegetation produced by the fertilizing flood. The crocodile-god Sebek and the personified Year had similar associations, and the god Osiris assumed, in a funerary context, a close relationship with both the Nile and vegetation.

Illustration page 132

As for the sun, it was Re of Heliopolis that mainly represented his power in the pantheon, and the Egyptian name was also used as a common noun with the meaning 'sun'. Re was identified with Atum in the form Re-Atum, and with the sky-god Horus (the falcon-god whose name means 'The Distant One') as Re-Herakhty, a deity depicted with a man's body but the head of a falcon. Re's chief symbol was the obelisk, and like Horus he was firmly linked to the living kingship since the pharaoh was called, from the Fifth Dynasty onwards (with one example in the Fourth), 'the son of Re'. Ideas of justice and world-order were associated with Re, and the goddess Maat (Truth, Justice, Concord) was regarded as his daughter.

The Helpers of the Dead

The Egyptians always gave prominence to the gods who were believed to help the dead. Among these were Anubis, Sokaris, Khentamenthes, Wepwawet and Osiris, a group attested in the Old Kingdom. Of these the god Anubis, who is figured as a wild dog or jackal, was associated with the process of embalming the dead, and he maintained a consistent measure of importance throughout the

Illustration page 134

long history of Egyptian religion. Osiris, on the other hand, emerged from comparative obscurity to a position of overwhelming importance in the funerary cult. A significant stage in his rise to spiritual power was his identification with the dead pharaoh, which occurred in the Sixth Dynasty. Osiris was primarily a god of the dead and his earliest cult-centre seems to have been at Abydos. The motive behind the identification of the dead king with Osiris was clearly to ensure the perpetuation of the king's sovereignty after death: by becoming Osiris the dead pharaoh would rule over the realm of the dead.

Inanimate objects were often worshipped by the Egyptians, especially in the early dynasties, examples being the crossed arrows of the goddess Neïth, the obelisk of Heliopolis, and the fetish of the god Min, which remains somewhat of a riddle. These fetishes were subordinated to the worship of the gods with whom they were associated, and so their importance diminished. Thus Min, a god of sexual fertility, is usually shown both in human form and as ithyphallic.

Few of the gods are depicted in purely human form. In addition to Min, the gods Ptah of Memphis, Atum of Heliopolis and Amun of Thebes are thus shown, as well as the funerary god Osiris and the Nile-gods. In most cases, however, animal forms appear, and the god is represented either in purely animal form, as with the bull-god Apis, or as a being with human body but animal head. The latter amalgam was a development often pursued as a compromise, and instances are found in the forms of Anubis the dog, Horus the falcon, and Khnum the ram. Sometimes the theriomorphic element is reduced still further, as when the sky-goddess Hathor, the celestial cow, is shown with human body and head, but with a crown of cow's horns embracing a sun disc.

Animal Cults

Animal cults are indeed a basic part of Egyptian religion and they point to an origin in the teeming life of Africa's river-valleys. Several of the cosmic and anthropomorphic gods derive from the region of the eastern delta, and a Semitic influence has here been plausibly suggested. Many other religions, of course, show prominent animal cults. What is remarkable in Egypt is that there was an intense revival and extension of these cults in the Late Period. One of the earliest of the animal cults to be attested is that of the Apis bull of Memphis, who was worshipped as early as the First Dynasty. The worship of Apis illustrates a development which was fairly common. Beginning as an autonomous cult, it was later associated doctrinally with the major gods Re and Osiris as well as with Ptah, the chief deity of Memphis. A further step was exceptional. At the beginning of the Ptolemaic era the cult of Osiris-Apis was consciously deployed in the establishment of a new cult, that of Sarapis, intended mainly, perhaps, for the Greeks in Egypt. Sarapis, however, lost the bull shape of Apis.

Whereas the pharaoh himself was officially a god, only a small group of other men attained this status, and even then it was a veneration accorded to them after their death in recognition of their outstanding qualities. Imhotep, the brilliant architect of King Djoser in the Third Dynasty, was deified in this way, and so was Amenhotep, the son of Hapu, a vizier of the Eighteenth Dynasty. In its final stage the worship of Imhotep reveals him, rather unexpectedly, as a god of medicine, identified with the Greek Asclepius. A very different category of gods comprises a series of personified abstractions, e.g. Sia (Understanding), Hu (Utterance), and Hike (Magic).

Triads

In their local cult-centres the gods were often grouped in nines, on the Heliopolitan pattern. Another favourite grouping was the triad, in which the chief local god was linked with a spouse and a son. In   *Illustration page 133*
Memphis we find Ptah, Sakhmet and Nefertem grouped in this way, while in Thebes we find Amun, Mut and Khons. Another triad, however, is found in Memphis, and in this group Ptah, Sokaris and

Osiris, three male funerary deities, are joined together. A striking feature of the texts concerned with this Memphite triad, as well as of some others, is that the trinity is regarded as a unity. An anticipation of Christian doctrine is here evident, even if a specific influence on the Christian formulation has yet to be proved.

Illustration page 133

Although it has been argued by H. Junker that a primitive monotheism appears in Egyptian religion (the main point adduced being that the epithet *Wr* [The Great One] is used of certain gods), an abundant polytheism is what is usually manifest. In the reign of Amenophis IV or Akhenaten a true monotheism was nevertheless developed, probably under the leadership of the pharaoh himself. Recent research has shown that several elements in his teaching are attested before, but the uncompromising monotheism of his final doctrine was highly distinctive. It was inevitably short-lived, and attempts to find its influence in the early religion of the Hebrews have not succeeded.

Illustration page 133

In spite of the almost endless variety exhibited by the worship of gods in different local settings and traditions, the externals of cult and ritual show a basic cohesion. The Egyptian temple from the Middle Kingdom onwards followed a common plan. A large rectangular space was enclosed by a high wall, and the entrance gate was flanked by two big pylons. First, one entered a large open courtyard with colonnades on three sides; from this there was access to a covered hypostyle hall; a third unit, behind the hall, was the inner sanctuary, in which the statue of the god was kept in a shrine placed on a boat.

It was only the king or the most important priests who were allowed to enter the inner sanctuary; the tradition in this matter was closer to that of Israel than that of Greece, since the Greeks allowed all worshippers to see the god's statue in the *naos* of the temple. A concept often expressed is that the temple is an image of the created world and that its origin reverts to the first emergence of the ordered creation from primeval chaos.

Daily Liturgy

Two versions are extant of the daily liturgy which was performed in all temples. It began with the purification of the priest in the sacred pool near the temple. Entering the temple itself, the priest lit a fire and prepared a censer with charcoal and incense. He proceeded then to the statue of the god in the inner sanctuary, and after due obeisances and offerings he undressed the statue, purified it, and adorned it again with suitable garments and insignia. A sacred banquet followed before the statue was finally replaced in its shrine. Two ideas are linked with the offerings: they are regarded as pleasing gifts, and as such identified with the Eye of Horus; at other times, especially when slain victims are involved, they are identified with the enemies of Horus and Osiris, that is, with Seth and his followers.

Distinctive rites were naturally found in the special festivals of the pharaoh and of the gods. The king's jubilee-festival, called the *Sed,* re-enacted ritually the unification of Egypt under Menes, and its climax was a dance performed by the king in a short kilt with an animal's tail hanging behind it. A procession or 'coming forth' was usually a conspicuous feature of the festivals of the gods, whose statues were carried by priests to other sacred places in order to visit other deities or in order to enact a mythological episode connected with these places.

In the case of Horus of Edfu in the Ptolemaic era the god was paid a festive visit by Hathor of Denderah, and a sacred marriage between Horus and Hathor was celebrated. In the Great Festival of Min the god's procreative power was associated with the harvest and with the kingship, and an act of sexual union between the king and queen was probably a part of the rites. The Festival of Opet for the Theban god Amun entailed a journey by Amun with his consort Mut and their son Khons from their temples in Karnak to Luxor (Opet) and back. It was a journey on the Nile and was followed by large crowds on the river and on its banks. Another festival of Amun, the Festival of the Valley, meant crossing the Nile to visit the mortuary temples of the pharaohs on the west bank; the outward journey finished in the valley of Deir el-Bahari, where the beautiful temple of Queen Hat-shepsut and of Hathor had been built.

Illustration page 131

It was in connection with Osiris that the dramatic enactment of myth was most evident. A text from the Twelfth Dynasty describes a fight on a lake between Osiris and his enemies; the scene is the vicinity of Abydos, and the death and burial of the god are portrayed, followed by his triumphant return to repel his enemies. Much later, in the Ptolemaic era, a text in the temple of Denderah describes a festival of Osiris that was to be celebrated throughout Egypt. The death of the god was mourned, but his rebirth was hailed in the symbolism of barley which was made to sprout from an effigy of the god. A connected rite was the 'raising of the *djed* (pillar)', also symbolic of resurrection.

Funeral Rites

Great importance was always attached to due ceremonial in the burial of the dead, and the future bliss of buried persons was considered to depend on this and on the beliefs bound up with the ritual. The dead were always buried and never cremated, and the rite of opening the mouth was performed for the dead body or for a statue of the deceased; this rite included acts of purification and offering, but the central ceremony was to touch the mouth with an adze, thus conferring, it was thought, renewed life for all the bodily faculties.

Illustration page 134

At the same time the Egyptians believed that it was important to preserve the body itself, and in this aim they were assisted by the dry soil of their desert burial-places. In its most elaborate style mummification entailed removing the brain and the intestines as well as sometimes, in the case of the male, the sexual organs; natron (natural sodium) was then applied to the body externally, and a mixture of natron, spices and oil was inserted into the cavities vacated by the viscera, the space being then filled with wads of linen. Fragrant spices and oils were applied externally too, and the whole body was carefully bandaged with linen before it was placed in a coffin. The removed organs were also preserved, the viscera being kept in four jars, which were said to be protected by the four sons of Horus.

Doctrinally the whole embalming of the body seems to have implied an imitation of what was done, in the legend, to Osiris by Anubis in Abydos, so that the dead person was thereby identified with Osiris: see *Pyramid Texts,* 1122 *c-d.* Amulets were usually placed within the wrappings of the mummy, and special importance was attached to the heart scarab which was placed on the chest. Clearly the heart was regarded as the medium of spiritual understanding; it was not removed like the other inner organs, and a short text on the scarab usually requested the heart not to testify against the dead in the judgment before Osiris.

A Priestly Caste

In funerary rites the chief part was played by the priest who impersonated Anubis. In general the priests were at first appointed by the king. In the New Kingdom and afterwards, however, a priestly caste was evolved and the important offices became hereditary. These professional priests were called 'servants of the god', and below them was a class of lay priests called 'pure ones'. There were naturally numerous subdivisions according to function, and the administration of the considerable property owned by the temples was not the least of the tasks allotted.

The role of women in the priesthood was subsidiary: it was confined in the main to the provision of music and dancing. At Thebes, however, the chief-priestess of Amun bore the title of 'god's wife'; she was the leader of the female music-makers who were regarded as the god's harem and she was identified with the goddess Hathor, who was associated *par excellence* with sexual love and with music. In the Twenty-third Dynasty and afterwards these priestesses were practically rulers of a theocratic city.

Moral Concepts

The concepts of morality embedded in Egyptian religion can be better appreciated by reading the 'Wisdom Literature' than by analysing the texts devoted directly to myth and cult. Upright conduct, according to the *Instruction of Ptahhotep,* has the sanction of a moral order established by Maat at the very beginning of creation. Maat, as we have seen, implies truth, justice and concord, and this text states: 'Maat is good and its worth is enduring, and it has not been disturbed since the day of its creator!' Other virtues praised in similar texts are humility, self-restraint, patience, and wisdom. A funerary inscription of a nobleman in the Old Kingdom makes this claim: 'Never did I say anything evil to a powerful one against any people, for I desire that it might be well with me before the Great God. I gave bread to the hungry, clothes to the naked.' Here the allusion to 'the Great God' implies a belief in judgment after death, and the Egyptians' moral ideas were firmly linked to this belief.

In its developed form it was expressed in the conviction that every-one after death would face a 'weighing of the heart' before Osiris and his forty-two assessors. There are many representations and texts dealing with the idea. In one of the scales a symbol of Maat (Truth) is shown; in the other is the heart of the deceased, and if his virtues enabled him to achieve a balance with Truth, then the verdict was favourable and eternal happiness was secured. If not, a monster called the 'Devourer of the Dead' was waiting to destroy the condemned one. Spell 125 of *The Book of the Dead* is devoted to the theme of judgment, and it contains a number of 'declarations of innocence', such as: 'I have not stolen rations of bread, I have not pried into the affairs of others, I have not disputed save for my own concerns, I have not had intercourse with a married woman'.

Illustration page 134

The Book of the Dead was a means of conveying magical protection and some have argued that all this does not transcend the limits of primitive magic; even the deceased's identification with Osiris, which was the final guarantee of vindication in the judgment, is regarded, from this viewpoint, as devoid of moral depth. A magical element is certainly present, but it can be argued that there is equally evident an underlying anxiety about morals and ethical standards, if not a vague approach to the idea of forgiveness of sins.

Life after Death

The identification with Osiris was likewise the main hope of im-mortality, and from the Middle Kingdom onwards it was a privilege extended to everyone who undertook the proper rites. In the Roman era the act of 'becoming Osiris' is given pictorial expression in that the deceased person is sometimes shown with Osirian attributes. It had long been a custom to prefix the name Osiris to the deceased's name. The renewal of vegetation, as we have noted, became a symbol of revived life. A similar belief was also based on the idea of renewal of life in the sky since the sun after setting is able to rise again. Moreover, the soul's external manifestation, the *ba,* was credited with the possibility of many transformations, enabling it to roam at will from the tomb.

It was probably the vigour of its belief in life after death that empowered Egyptian religion to persist in some form as late as the sixth century AD, even if the contact with conquering cultures had modified and changed some of its shape and content. Thus the religion of Isis and Osiris as presented by the Greek writer Plutarch in the second century AD is freely interpreted with the aid of the Platonic and Stoic philosophies. Fortunately, however, the numerous archae-ological remains and the great mass of native writings allow us to appreciate the earlier tradition in its unalloyed form.

Chapter Ten

Ancient Greece

For an explanation of the cult of the mother goddess and her consort, see page 34.

Over much of the Near East a goddess prevailed; she represented the power of fertility in nature, a projection of the feminine archetype. She went by a variety of names: the Mother, Great Mother, or (later) Mother of the Gods; she might be called Inanna or Ishtar, Anat or Atargatis, Rhea or Dictynna, Baubo, Ma, Allat, or Cybele. Often she had a consort, the young god, who died and was mourned and rose again or was miraculously preserved; he was Dumuzi, Tammuz or Adonis, the vegetation spirit who dies in winter.

The Mother was already in Greece when the Hellenes arrived. At Argos she went by the name of Hera (the Lady) and ousted Dione as Zeus's wife. At Delphi as Ge, the Earth, she had an ancient oracle. At Eleusis she was also Mother Earth (Demeter), and at Sparta she was Orthia. She also came from Asia across the Aegean in various guises. At Ephesus she was Artemis and her temple became one of

Illustration page 151

the wonders of the world. From here she must have reached the island of Delos, and from there Arcadia in the Peloponnese and Brauron in Attica.

The Greeks tamed her, and made of her a goddess of wild nature, a virgin huntress, and tales of her child-bearing were foisted onto an attendant such as Callisto. As Aphrodite (the Foamborn) the Mother reached Paphos in Cyprus. The name 'Foamborn' has a double meaning: it speaks of the sea from which she emerged, as in Botticelli's famous painting, and also of the foam surrounding semen.

Moving on from Cyprus her cult reached the port of Corinth. Here her temple, high on the acropolis, was staffed by over a thousand temple prostitutes, the 'girls of hospitality' who were, says Strabo, the city's chief attraction. The verb 'to Corinthianize' became synonymous in puritan eyes with sexual immorality, and Paul's indictment of pagan society in the first chapter of *Romans* is based on his two years in Corinth. But strip away the commercialism, and the power of the Great Mother is revealed. The Greeks knew also the story of the death of the vegetation-spirit in the myth of Aphrodite's beloved Adonis, who was killed in a boarhunt.

Minoan Religion

Crete was a major centre of early culture and here the Mother was supreme: early figurines are predominantly, though not exclusively, female. By the second millennium BC the goddess had been fully established; she was associated with animals, birds and snakes, the pillar and the tree, the sword and the double-axe, and was dominant in all spheres of life and death. A famous representation shows her standing on a mountain flanked by two lions; another with snakes encircling her arms. Her young consort, whom the Greeks recognized as Zeus, was born on Mount Ida.

The cult was a fertility-cult, and the goddess was associated with the moon (with its connection with menstruation and the power of women) and her consort with the sun; these in turn were represented by cow and bull, and the myths of Pasiphae's love for a bull and Europa's rape by a bull both belong to Crete. The sacred marriage was an important part of the ritual, and in one form of the associated myth Iasion embraced Demeter in a ploughed field; here the link with the land's fertility is inescapable. The general prominence of animals has led some interpreters to suspect totemism.

There were important sanctuaries in caves; excavations of the cave of Kamares have produced fine pottery and a mass of grain, seemingly offered to the Mother. The cave below the summit of Mount Ida survived into Roman times as a sanctuary of Zeus, and animal offerings and impressive bronze work have been found there. The cave of Psychro yielded a bronze votive tablet of about 1500 BC with a cult scene showing the goddess as a bird on a sacred tree with the sun and moon in the background, horns of consecration, and a devotee.

Zeus

The invading Hellenes who came south in the second millennium BC brought with them the great Indo-European sky-god Dyaus, or Zeus. It has been said that this is all we know about them. It was natural for migrant nomads to retain reverence for the overarching sky: land might change but the sky did not. With him came a shadowy consort, Dione, and a valkyrie-figure, Pallas, the Maiden.

In Greece they encountered the Earth Mother. With the first wave of Hellenes she retained her pre-eminence; the sky-god became Posis-Das, husband of Earth. Later Hellenes did not recognize their own god here, and, as Zeus asserted his authority, this proto-Zeus became pushed out to the sea as Poseidon. In general there was compromise. Dione disappeared and Zeus accepted the Earth Mother in her different forms as his bedfellow: hence the numerous amours. The marriage of Sky and Earth secured fertility. The Mother's consort might become a son of Zeus, like Heracles. At Athens the Maiden took over, and the Mother was transmuted into the virgin warrior Pallas Athene. A sky-god is naturally worshipped on mountains and Zeus took the highest mountain, Olympus, as his palace, with a sanctuary later on one of the lower peaks, though he found many thrones: on the acropolis at Argos, on Mount Coressus at Ephesus, on the two mountains at Antioch.

It was natural that the great god himself should experience some blending; in Crete, where there were legends of the birth of Zeus, he was fused with the local fertility-spirit. His numerous titles suggest

ANCIENT GREECE
Illustration page 151

For a definition of totemism, see page 16.

Illustration page 151

Illustration page 151

that he took over the functions of more specialized gods. The Greeks were unusually early in recognizing a universal supreme god. Zeus became a god standing for righteousness, and there was a movement to virtual monotheism. His festival at Olympia demanded a truce even from the belligerent Greeks. In Aeschylus's *Oresteia* he broods in the background. He was Zeus the Saviour, Zeus the Fulfiller, and in passing from Zeus the Protector of Hospitality to Zeus of the Political Assembly, he fulfilled himself. Pheidias portrayed him in a statue which Quintilian thought added something to traditional religion, a statue which called out a noble sermon from Dio of Prusa. To the Stoics Zeus was all, and in all, and it was natural to call the universe 'the city of Zeus'.

The Olympic Pantheon

In the poetry usually ascribed to Homer, society on Olympus appears as human society written large. Zeus is the overlord, the commander-in-chief, the father of gods and men. There is some specialization of function. Hera is the guardian of marriage; Poseidon rules the sea; Aphrodite is the power of love; Artemis is a goddess of wild nature; Athene, besides her martial qualities, is a goddess of wisdom and skills; Demeter, the Earth Mother, became particularly associated with the grain-harvest. Apollo is complex and contro-versial: his double name, Phoebus Apollo, his double headquarters at Delos and Delphi, his double association with north and east, all

Illustration page 152

point to a complex origin. The name Phoebus suggests a sun-god, whose rays spread pestilence like arrows, and who can cure the plague as he can cause it. In classical times he presided over culture in the widest sense, music, literature and higher thought. Hermes is 'the cairn' or heap of stones placed by the roadside for veneration; so the god Hermes becomes the guide of travellers and traders, the messen-ger of the gods, the escort of the dead, and in general a lively trickster like Coyote in America or Anansi in West Africa; a *hermaion* was a lucky find; herms or square pillars bearing a face and the male sex-organ lined the city streets. Hephaestus has been traced to the Near-Eastern oilfields; as a fire-spirit he is naturally linked with smiths and technology. Ares seems to have come down from Thrace. Whatever his origin he was to the Greeks a war-god, and Aphrodite's lover. Finally Hestia, the spirit of hearth and home, makes up the divine twelve.

But she was pushed into the background by Dionysus. His name appears on a Linear B tablet in the Mycenaean period, so that he was known early. However, he must have been suppressed for a period (he scarcely appears in Homer) to make a cataclysmic re-entry. He came from Thrace, a power of wild nature, of religious ecstasy, of

Illustration page 152

the vine and its fruits. The ecstatic cult, spreading among women, who, roving over the mountains in divine frenzy, caught and de-voured their god in the form of an animal, is marvellously recreated in Euripides's play *The Bacchae*.

The Homeric poems have been called 'the Bible of the Greeks'.

That they were not, but more than any single factor they were responsible for fixing and maintaining in the popular mind the picture of these anthropomorphic deities. It is, however, important to remember that in the background is the power of Fate (*moira*). It is implied that Zeus can defy Fate, but that he had better not try.

Some of the gods became state-gods and were caught up in political religion: Athene is an obvious example, and in 405 BC a decree giving Athenian citizenship to Samians is illustrated by Hera of Samos and Athene of Athens shaking hands. Hera also represented Argos, Apollo represented Sparta, Miletus and Cyrene, Artemis Ephesus, Heracles Thasos, and Priapus Lampsacus.

The Power of Nature

For the Greek all of nature was instinct with life. A mountain was the sky-god's throne; worshippers went to the hilltop to pray for rain. Every tree had its dryad, and the oak was sacred to Zeus, the olive to Athene, the bay to Apollo, the myrtle to Aphrodite, the poplar to Heracles. Groves were especially sanctified; they were places of refuge, as in Aeschylus's *The Suppliant Women*. Each spring had its nymph, each river its god; James R. Smith compiled a truly monumental volume on *Springs and Wells in Greek and Roman Literature* with their myths and sacred stories.

Those who strayed in the country might encounter goat-footed Pan or the satyrs and centaurs, half-men, half-beasts. The sea was the home of Poseidon, of Proteus with his magic changes of form, of the sea-grey spirit Glaucus, of the divine nymph Ino Leucothea, of exquisite nereids, monstrous tritons, deadly sirens. Above in the sky Zeus exercized his thunderous power; the divine sun and moon moved serenely, though an atheistic scientist might declare the sun to be a red-hot stone. The constellations had their popular mythology, and a philosopher as profound as Plato declared them to be endowed with soul; as time went on the firmament between sky and earth was peopled with intermediate powers.

Illustration page 152

This affects our understanding of a number of passages in Greek literature. There is little appreciation of natural beauty for its own sake; the Greeks did not climb their mountains to look at the view. Nature gave food and drink, warmth or cool shade; she was useful, or she was awesome and destructive. But basically nature meant living power. So nature was sacred. The famous scene near the beginning of Plato's *Phaedrus* is an account not of natural beauty but of a sacred grove with convenient shade, grass and water added; Diotima in her catalogue of beauty in *The Symposium* does not mention beauty in nature.

In fact the countryside was almost littered with shrines, statuettes and offerings. Strabo described the mouth of the river Alpheus thus: 'The whole tract is full of shrines of Artemis, Aphrodite, and the Nymphs, in flowery groves, due mainly to the abundance of water; there are numerous herms on the road, and shrines of Poseidon on the headlands by the sea.' And Martin Nilsson has commented that one could hardly have taken a step out of doors without meeting a little shrine, a sacred enclosure, an image, a sacred stone, or a sacred tree. This may not have been the highest form of Greek religion, but it was assuredly the most persistent.

Purification and Holiness

Much of Greek religion had to do with purification and holiness. The *temenos* or sanctuary was 'cut off', set apart. The temples we admire were not places for public worship in the modern sense; some might be entered only once a year, or only by priests, or only by a veiled priestess (the temple of Sosipolis at Elis); the inner shrine was called the *adyton* (not to be entered). There were other places not to be trodden, like the grove of Demeter and Kore at Megalopolis, or any place where lightning had struck.

Illustration page 153

Impurity was a grievous offence. A good example from tragedy is Oedipus's parricide and incest; that the offence was unwitting makes no difference. Orestes too had to be purified; on a vase we see him being sprinkled with pig's blood. Sometimes material objects associated with some offence were removed. At Cos after a suicide by hanging, rope and tree were banished. In the curious Bouphonia, a festival of Zeus at Athens, after a formal sacrifice, the priest fled and the axe was tried, condemned and thrown into the sea.

Scapegoats were a form of purification. At Athens and other Ionian cities, at the Thargelia, a festival of Apollo, the sins of the community were loaded on an individual called Pharmakos (the Remedy), who was then driven out. There were many simpler purifications – the sacrifice of pig, dog or cock, or bathing in the sea – and they extended to many recurrent experiences which were redolent of divine *mana:* thus disease had to be wiped away, or the clothes of a woman in childbirth might be dedicated to Artemis of Brauron.

The Mysteries

Among the cults which offered a more personal religion, two stood high. At Eleusis they told the story of the rape of Kore, the Maid, by the god of the underworld, the sorrowing search of her mother Demeter, the blight that Demeter laid on the land, the restoration of the girl to her mother for part of the year only, and the reunion of the goddesses. The myth reflects the burial of the seed-corn underground in storage jars during the dark blight of winter and its reappearance for the spring sowing.

A great festival took place in September. It began with an invitation and a baptism of regeneration in the sea; then on September 19 came the procession from Athens and the initiation. The mystery has been well-kept, but it is a reasonable deduction that there was a dramatic performance of the myth, leading to a sacred marriage, a revelation which was accompanied by a brilliant light and centred on an ear of corn, and a communion meal. There was some kind of identity with the goddess; to commemorate his initiation the emperor Gallienus put the feminine Galliena on his coins. The promise was the same as that expressed by Jesus: 'Unless a grain of wheat falls into the ground

Left A marble statue of Athene (*c*. 480 BC) from the temple of Aphaea on Aegina. Both pediments show Athena presiding over scenes of battle. Aphaea was identified with Britomartis, one of the forms of the Artemis worshipped in Crete. Alte Pinacothek, Munich.

Far left Artemis of Ephesus. The mother goddess is shown with many breasts – some scholars have interpreted them as the ova of the sacred bees which can be seen adorning the figure. Museo Archeologico Nazionale, Naples.

Below left The Mother Goddess in Cretan skirt and hairstyle, supported by goats on either side, in an ivory carving from Mycenae. Musée National du Louvre, Paris.

Below A metope showing Zeus, in the form of a bull, carrying Europa off to Crete over a sea symbolized by dolphins. Museo Nazionale, Palermo.

Above A statuette from Dodona of Zeus brandishing a thunderbolt (*c.* 470 BC). Dodona was the site of an ancient oracular shrine of Zeus, the thunder-god, who gave omens by the rustling of the leaves of the sacred oak tree. Antikenmuseum, Berlin.

Above right The sun-god, Apollo, represented as a young man subduing a centaur on the western pediment of the fifth-century temple of Zeus at Olympia. Archaeological Museum, Olympia.

Right A vivid and energetic portrait of Dionysus, by an unknown vase painter, shows him with vine leaves in his flowing hair and wreathed around his staff. Museo Nazionale di Villa Giulia, Rome.

Left The purification of Orestes depicted on a fourth-century south Italian vase. Orestes clasps the navel stone with his left arm as he wards off an invisible Fury, while Apollo performs the purification with two laurel leaves dipped in the bowl, which is probably full of pig's blood. British Museum, London.

Left Oedipus confronts the Sphinx (early fifth century BC). The elegant hybrid creature with the charming nose portrayed in this vase painting is very different from the vast Egyptian monolith known to most people, but they are both representations of the same idea – the foretelling of the unknowable future. Musei Vaticani.

and dies, it remains alone; but if it dies, it bears much fruit.' It was the promise of Demeter's hymn:

Opposite A view of the sanctuary of Apollo from the highest tier of the theatre at Delphi. Here people came to hear the wisdom of the gods.

> *Blessed among men on earth is*
> *he who has seen these things.*
> *But he who is uninitiate in the holy*
> *rites, who has no lot in them,*
> *does not enjoy a share in like things*
> *when in death he lies*
> *beneath the spreading darkness.*

As Cicero said: 'We have learned to live with joy and to die with a better hope.' Outside the mysteries there was little hope beyond the grave: the Homeric Hades is a place of shadowy wraiths.

The other cult was that of Orpheus. Orpheus was a legendary musician, a kind of double of Dionysus. We meet the Orphics in Sicily and Greece in the fifth century BC; in the gold tablets buried at Petelia giving instructions to the souls of the dead; and in the so-called Orphic hymns from some rather different Dionysiac fraternity of the Roman empire. We know (though only from a late period) of a complex myth which told how Dionysus was killed and eaten by the wicked Titans; how his heart was rescued, and a new Dionysus born from it; how the Titans were annihilated by Zeus's thunderbolt, and mankind born from the ashes. Man was thus compounded of a titanic element, the body, and a Dionysiac element, the spirit. To purify the self of titanic influence required religious observance, including vegetarianism. There was a doctrine of reincarnation, a 'sorrowful weary circle' of death and rebirth, from which initiation offered an accelerated escape; the yearning of the initiate was to hear the words: 'Happy and blessed one, you have become divine instead of mortal.'

'Is Pataecion the thief to have a better fate than Epaminondas merely because he has been initiated?' It is the oldest of questions; it is just to say that initiation was not enough, and the religious demands on the initiate had a strong moral element; a character in one of Menander's comedies contrasts on these grounds the demands of Demeter with those of the Asiatic Cybele.

Philosophical Speculation

Many cosmogonies tell of the forcing apart of sky and earth, who are regarded as united in sexual union. In Hesiod's *Theogony* (eighth century BC) Chaos, the yawning gap, simply 'came into being', so did Earth, Tartarus (the underworld), and Love. These are taken as given: only with the existence of Love can a mythology of sexual union and birth take over. We are at the beginning of rationalism.

Thales of Miletus (early sixth century BC) was the originator of scientific philosophy: he asked questions about cosmogony and looked for an answer in material terms, seeing all things as modifications of water, which is necessary to life, and can solidify or become gaseous. This was the beginning of the process by which Zeus was dethroned and Vortex took his place.

Yet these scientific speculations were not free from myth. Water in the guise of Oceanus was a primal being in Greek myth, and Thales, impressed by magnetic properties in matter, declared 'Everything is full of gods.' Anaximenes, who substituted air for water, declared it to be divine, and there was a general belief in a divine mindstuff which surrounded the cosmos, and seeped through to form the upper air or aether. Some looked for a motive power: the Love and Strife of Empedocles, the Mind of Anaxagoras.

But the move was towards rationalism. Xenophanes attacked anthropomorphism, suggesting that oxen would make similar idols of oxen, lions of lions, and Anaxagoras denied the divinity of the sun, declaring it to be a red-hot stone bigger than the Peloponese. Critias wrote a play in which law was said to be an invention to keep the strong under control, and gods an invention to intimidate the cunning. Later, Euhemerus (*c.* 300 BC) put forward the view that gods were glorified humans: we still call this Euhemerism. One of the doctors denied that epilepsy was a sacred disease due to divine visitation, as was generally held, and said it was called sacred only because it was not understood.

The theological dimension was restored by Plato (427-347 BC). His account of creation involves a divine craftsman, the unchangeable eternal forms which are the blueprint and pattern of the world, and the 'receptacle', which we should call matter. The material world is perishable, and the body which perceives it likewise perishable. The world of the forms, of true piety, perfect justice, beauty-in-itself, is everlasting, and the soul, which perceives it, is immortal. The world of the forms alone is real; even behind that, beyond reality, is the norm of all existence, the form of the good.

Plato's most brilliant pupil, Aristotle (384-322 BC), also propounded a religious philosophy. There is a great chain of being, from pure matter, which is unknowable, at the bottom, to pure form, which is god, at the top; it is a chain from mere potentiality to perfect actuality. God is engaged in unending self-contemplation. He is not involved with the world; he moves it as the beloved moves the lover, without needing to stir; he is the Unmoved Mover. It is one of the paradoxes of history that the profound and subtle medieval scholastics succeeded in identifying this Unmoved Mover with the ever-working Father of Jesus.

Oracles

Illustration page 154 The most famous of Greek oracles was that of Delphi. Here there was originally an oracle of Mother Earth, but Apollo later took over her functions. Normally consultation was through the priestess or Pythia, who, in a trance induced by sheer spiritual and mental intensity (there were no mephitic vapours), uttered unintelligible sounds. The priests, using an efficient information service, reduced these to appropriate advice in intelligible, though sometimes ambiguous, prose or verse. A celebrated ambiguity was the answer to Croesus of Lydia: 'If Croesus crosses the Halys, he will destroy a mighty empire.' He did – his own. There was another method of consultation by drawing a different-coloured bean for yes or no; in one instance a king was chosen for Thessaly by drawing a bean inscribed with the successful candidate's name.

We naturally hear more about the great political consultations, but Euripides in *Ion* shows that private consultations were frequent, and were expected to deal with harvests or children; we may add consultation about illness, and we have even a record of a question from a slave who wants to know how to please his master. Plutarch (*c.* 45-125 AD) says that in his day the *pax Romana* has made the old political consultations unnecessary, and individuals are asking about marriage, travel and finance.

We should remember that the Delphic oracle, like the Yoruba's Ife oracle, was the repository of gathered wisdom. There are some delightful answers: 'How do I cure my son of love-sickness?' 'Treat him gently.' It was Delphi which fostered the two great precepts 'Know yourself' and 'Avoid excess'.

There were other oracles. In Zeus's Dodona the rustling of the oakleaves and other sounds were interpreted for the god's will. Questions were written on lead, and some have survived. Lysanias wanted to know whether he was the father of the child Annyla was carrying; Nicocrateia, to which of the gods to sacrifice for health; a boy, whether to follow his father's profession of fishing; the Corcyreans, how to avoid civil war. At Lebadeia there was an ancient oracle of Trophonius; the enquirer, after purification and sacrifice, was snatched into an underground cave and granted a direct, awe-inspiring revelation. Apollo had some famous oracles in Asia – that at Didyma went back to the sixth century BC, but it was later eclipsed by Claros, which in the Roman period had a large staff, including a choir. The reputation of the oracle spread, even to remote parts such as Dalmatia, Numidia and Britain.

Illustration page 153

Superstition

In his delightful work *The Characters,* Theophrastus sketches a comic picture of the superstitious man: 'Obviously, superstitiousness would be generally defined as a kind of cowardice when confronted with the supernatural. The superstitious man is the sort of person who won't go out for the day without washing his hands and aspersing himself at the Nine Springs, and putting a piece of laurel-leaf from a temple into his mouth. If a cat runs across the road, he won't go any further until either someone else passes or he has thrown three stones across the road. If he sees a snake in his house, he calls on Sabazius, if it is one of the red variety; if it's one of the sacred sort, he builds a shrine on the spot. When he passes one of those smooth stones which stand at cross-roads, he pours a little oil from his flask over it, and won't go on till he has knelt down and bowed his head to the ground. If a rat gnaws a bag of meal, he goes straight to the medicine-man to ask what to do, and if the answer is "Take it to be patched", he pays no attention, but finds some ritual aversion. He is always ceremonially purifying his house, saying that it has been enchanted by Hecate. If he hears an owl hoot while he's out walking, he is much shaken and won't go past without muttering "All power is Athene's." He refuses to set foot on a tombstone or go anywhere near a dead body or a woman in childbirth, saying that he doesn't want to suffer pollution.

'Every month on the fourth and seventh he gives instructions for wine to be mulled for his family; he goes out and buys myrtle-boughs, incense and holy pictures, comes in again and spends the whole day making garlands for the hermaphrodites and offering them sacrifices. Every time he has a dream he rushes to the dream-experts, prophets, or augurs to inquire what god or goddess he ought to appease. When he is about to be initiated into the mysteries of Orpheus, he visits the priests once a month, accompanied by his wife, or, if she is not free, by his children and the nursemaid. Everyone would agree that he often goes down to the sea to asperse himself. If he ever sees one of the figures of Hecate, which stand at the cross-roads, with a wreath of garlic, he goes straight home to wash his head, and sends for the priestesses, and tells them to purify him by carrying round a puppy or squill in ceremonious procession. If he sees a madman or an epileptic, he shudders, and spits into his own lap.'

If this be thought caricature, we do well to remember that the leading Athenian soldier and statesman after Pericles's death, Nicias, lost two armies in 412 BC because two medicine-men advised him that after the lunar eclipse of August 27 he should wait 'thrice nine days' before moving his troops. The humane Plutarch five centuries later condemns his superstition, but makes it clear that there were plenty in his own day whose superstitious 'words and gestures, sorcery and magic, running backwards and forwards, beating drums, impure purifications, filthy puritanism, exotic and illegal asceticism' drove reasonable men to atheism. Yet Plutarch himself was not above seeing an omen in a sneeze.

Hellenistic Religion

Alexander the Great's brief career (356-323 BC) pushed back the frontiers in many ways. The old gods were shaken. The Greeks had honoured as semi-divine 'heroes' the founders of cities. Alexander was certainly a city-founder; he tried to make his divinity the cement of the empire; he failed, but set a precedent. When Demetrius the Besieger visited Athens in 307 BC they sang him a remarkable hymn, declaring that the other gods were absentees, deaf, indifferent or nonexistent, he was manifest, the one true god; they gave him the Parthenon for a palace. Later rulers took such titles as Euergetes (Benefactor, cf Luke 22:25), Soter (Saviour), Epiphanes (God Manifest, cf epiphany), even Keraunos (Thunderbolt).

The old gods might persist, but there was a new stress on the demons, the intermediate spirits, and new gods from the east and south came in alongside the old. Astrology was introduced from Babylon. Gods of healing were in demand; the sanctuary of Asclepius at Epidaurus was immensely popular. The uncertainties led to the exaltation of Tyche (Luck or Chance). Or perhaps there was an anti-god as well as a god; hence such dualistic philosophies as Gnosticism. Yet there was another side to this.

There was a greater unity than ever before. This too called for a new religious expression. There was a tendency towards monotheism, or at least virtual monotheism, in the exaltation of Zeus, and an increasing moralization of religion. Syncretism is an expression of the same mood. One of the most interesting inventions of the age was Sarapis, formed apparently by a fusion of the Egyptian saviour-god Osiris and bull-god Apis, yet with some strange connection with Sinope on the Black Sea. He was identified with Zeus, a healing-god, a saviour-god, a father figure, whose kindly, bearded features are familiar from many representations, and who formed an object of love and devotion to meet the needs of a changed scene.

Tyche

Men are not consistently logical, and the modern who recorded his success 'thank God, touch wood' can be amply paralleled from the ancient world, where Tyche, or Chance, was not merely believed in but worshipped alongside the other gods and goddesses. The two greatest historians of antiquity, Thucydides and Polybius, took chance (with a small 'c') as a cardinal element for historical analysis; the two greatest philosophers, Plato and Aristotle, taking an ultimately teleological view of the universe, equated chance with all that did not belong to the directly purposive act of god and man, that is, in effect, with physical law.

If chance had such hold on the imagination of the intellectual, it is not surprising that Chance received the worship of the man in the street. Being capricious and unpredictable, she was regarded as feminine. She is represented with symbols of the prosperity which she gives or withholds, such as the cornucopia, or the wings appropriate to Victory, of lubricity, such as the wheel on which she unstably stands, or of her direction of life, notably the rudder. The orb on which she sometimes stands is an ambiguous symbol. It may be the globe of the universe which she dominates, but it is a slippery platform, and her position is insecure.

Her greatest period is the Hellenistic age, but she is singled out long before that. In the Homeric hymn to Demeter she is a nereid, in Hesiod's *Theogony* a daughter of Ocean; Archilochus says that chance and fate control our destiny, and Pindar identifies Chance with one of the Fates. She is prominent in Euripides. In the Hellenistic and Roman periods she plays an important part in the novel. She is blind, personal, and malevolent. Chariton's *Chaereas and Callirhoe* is the story of a tug-of-war between Chance, who causes all the disasters, and Aphrodite, who rescues the lovers. In Apuleius's

Golden Ass the pattern is similar, except that Isis, not Aphrodite, is the saviour. That such novelists were expressing popular opinion is seen in the epitaphs. There, the references to Tyche are, with one solitary exception, expressed in terms of bitter and despondent hatred. Typical is this:

Here I, Phileremus, lie a dead body, the object coveted by Tyche's tyranny, dragged from life by the very spirits.

Three modifications of this picture are of some importance. In the first place, there was an ancient fertility spirit known as the Good Spirit, Agathos Daemon; he needed a consort, and acquired Agathe Tyche, Good Chance. The Good Spirit was sometimes identified with Zeus; hence the astonishing relief from Athens, now in Copenhagen, dating from the fourth century BC and depicting Zeus with the cornucopia, and Good Chance as his consort. Secondly, in Asia where the mother-goddess has long reigned, it was natural that Tyche should be regarded as another of her many guises. Thirdly, in the public life of Hellenistic and Roman times, Chance became a city-goddess. A famous bronze statue by Eutychides depicted the Tyche of Antioch, seated on a rock representing the Mother's mountain throne, with a sheaf of wheat, symbolizing prosperity, in her hand, and a battlemented crown for the protection of the city on her head. Similarly Antiochus I of Commagene put up a colossal inscription, with statues in which Commagene is personified as Tyche.

The Roman encyclopedist, the elder Pliny, who knew the Greek world well, has an excellent summary of the general position of Tyche. All over the world Chance alone is invoked, he says, the one defendant, the one culprit, the one thought in men's minds, the one object of praise, the one cause. 'We are so much at the mercy of Chance that Chance is our god.'

Hellenistic Philosophy

All the philosophies of the Hellenistic Age in different ways pursued *autarkeia* (self-sufficiency, non-attachment). The Stoics were pantheists; the end of the first book of Pope's *Essay on Man* is a magnificent exposition of Stoic doctrine:

All are but parts of one stupendous whole,
Whose body Nature is, and God the soul.

'Would you call him Fate?' asks Seneca. 'You will not be wrong . . . Would you call him Providence? You will be right . . . Would you call him Nature? You will not be speaking falsely . . . Would you call him Universe? You will not be deceived.' The favourite name was Zeus: under this name the most religious of the early Stoics, Cleanthes (331-232 BC), hymned him; his counterpart in the Roman empire, Epictetus (*c.* AD 55-135), said that his proper work was to hymn god. The Stoics were determinists: all is in the hands of God, and our task is to accept. We are players in the divine drama, and whether our role is that of king or slave it is essential to the whole. And Stoic leaders include slaves like Epictetus and emperors like Marcus Aurelius (AD 120-180).

To the Jews, Epicurean and atheist were synonymous, but this was unjust. Epicurus (341-270 BC) attacked superstition and the evils it counselled, but he was a religious man. His fourfold prescription for health ran: god is not to be feared; death is not to be felt; good can be easily attained, evil can be easily endured. The Epicureans held to the mortality of the soul, which is an atomic structure, dissolved with the body. They denied that the gods reward the righteous or punish the wicked. But gods exist; consensus says so, and we perceive them in dreams. They live in untroubled bliss and philosophic conversation in the interstices of the worlds, caring nothing for men; but the soul which is 'in tune with the infinite' can pick up from them emanations like radio waves, to its own benefit and bliss.

After a period of scepticism and preoccupation with epistemological problems the Platonists returned to theology. Numenius blended Plato with Pythagoras, Albinus with Aristotle, Justin, Clement and Origen with Christianity. The greatest religious genius of the ancient world, Plotinus (AD 205-270), stood foursquare in the succession to Plato. His thought centres on the One, beyond personality, beyond reality, beyond thought, beyond definition, beyond comprehension. All things aspire to It; from It the whole universe is derived by a process of efflux or emanation. The highest life is the ascent of the soul to God by the aspiration called Love (Eros); Plotinus actually says that God is Eros, but this is hardly more than a counter-slogan to the Christian 'God is *Agape*' (Christian Love). The true end of the soul is mystical and ecstatic union with the One, the flight of the Alone to the Alone, and Plotinus, himself a mystic, experienced this more than once.

Chapter Eleven

Ancient Rome

For divination and astrology in Mesopotamia, see pages 129–30.

The Etruscans are the most important and controversial of the peoples of early Italy. Where they came from, nobody knows: Herodotus said from Lydia, and religious parallels with the astrology and divination practised in Mesopotamia offer some support for this. But the essential facets of Etruscan culture developed in Italy north of the Tiber in the seventh and sixth centuries BC. Economically, it depended on agriculture and metallurgy; politically, it was based upon city-states linked in a league with its religious centre near Volsinii, where there was a shrine of a god whom the Romans called Vertumnus.

The Etruscan deities fall into three groups. First there are those who bear pure Etruscan names. We know little about them; some were identified with Greek and Roman deities, which suggests parallel functions. Thus Tinia was treated as one with Jupiter, Setlans with Vulcan, Turms with Mercury, Turan with Venus (often on mirrors), Nortia with Fortuna. A second group appears to have been taken over from their Italic neighbours: we recognize familiar Roman gods among them. Such are Ani (Janus), Uni (Juno), Mnrva (Minerva), Nethuns (Neptune). A third group is derived from the Greek colonists

Illustration page 171

to the south: Aite (Hades), Aplu (Apollo, whose statue from Veii is one of the masterpieces of Etruscan art), Aritimi (Artemis), Charun (Charon), Hercle (Hercules), and Persipnai (Persephone).

The predominance of underworld deities in the last group is notable. Preoccupation with the afterlife is a major feature of Etruscan religion. Funeral games were held in honour of the dead, and it has been argued that herein lies the origin of gladiatorial displays. Tombs

Illustrations page 171

were elaborately furnished and regarded as the houses of the dead. Some of the magnificent frescoes which survive show the dead journeying to the underworld under sometimes horrific divine escort. When Lucretius, the Epicurean poet of the first century BC, was seeking to disperse fear of punishment after death, he may have been writing not for the sophisticated society of Rome so much as for the villages to the north.

There is some evidence that sexual symbols were associated with tombs; if so, it suggests that to the Etruscans it was the lifeforce in each individual which constituted the essential being and the part which survived death; this is close to the Roman concept of the *genius*

Illustration page 173

and the *iuno,* the male and female sex elements.

The other aspect of Etruscan religion which proved immensely influential was divination. There were many ways of divining the will of the gods, such as thunder and lightning, or through the flight of birds, but the Etruscans were especially famed for hepatoscopy, the study of the liver.

The sacrificial victim was slaughtered and opened up, and the liver examined for markings or other peculiarities. The right side of the liver was the area denoting good luck, the left bad luck. But the discipline was one of great complexity: a remarkable bronze liver from Piacenza is divided into no less than forty regions, each marked with the name of a different god. Some of the finely engraved mirrors show the diviner or *haruspex* at work; one depicts a scene from Homer in terms familiar and contemporary to the artist. Furthermore the reputation of the diviners lasted centuries after the Etruscans had disappeared as a political force. When the Capitoline temple was destroyed in the civil war of AD 69 Vespasian called in Etruscan diviners for the reconstruction. Three hundred years later Julian was still consulting them.

Early Roman Religion: the Numina

When the priest in classical Rome sacrificed to Tellus Mater, the earth-goddess, and Ceres, the corn-spirit, he invoked Vervactor, Redarator, Imporcitor, Insitor, Obarator, Occator, Sarritor, Subrincator, Messor, Convector, Conditor and Promitor. These curious godlings derive their names from the several operations of agriculture, the breaking of the fallow ground, the second ploughing, the furrowing and sowing and on through top-dressing, harrowing and hoeing to harvesting, gathering, storing and withdrawing from store. They are powers, *numina,* each presiding over a limited but necessary operation, and having no existence apart from that operation. Hence their German name *Sondergötter,* gods of a special function, or, more picturesquely, *Augenblickgötter,* gods of the twinkling of an eye. We are back beyond the anthropomorphic deities at a more primitive and basic level of belief.

These powers are particularly associated with agricultural operations and with family life. We may take birth as an example of the latter. Alemona had care of the foetus, Nona and Decima (Ninth and Tenth) watched the critical months of gestation, Partula had parturition for her field. Lucina, Candelifera and the Carmentes offered the charm and the light needed for safe birth. Then in a magical ceremony evil spirits were dispersed with axe, stake, and broom by Intercidona (Cleaver), Pilumnus (Staker), and Deverra (Sweeper). There was Cunina rocking the cradle, Vagitanus calling out the first howls, Rumina for breast-feeding, and, as the child grew, Edusa and Potina superintended eating and drinking. Fabulinus guided the function of speech, Statulinus the first attempts to stand, and it was Abeona and Adeona who preserved the child's going-out and its coming-in.

Some of these *numina* preside not so much over functions as over the operation of power in some other sense. Thus the *genius* of the man and the *iuno* of the woman are present all through the period of fertility, not just during the act of procreation. Others enjoyed a local habitation and a name: Vesta in the hearth, the Penates in the storecupboard, Janus in the door, Terminus in the boundary-stone; the Genius resided in the head of the father of the family, since the seed was believed to emanate from the head.

The Lares are an important relic of this stage of belief. Theorists have attempted too tidy an explanation of them; parallels from other parts of the world suggest that they are ancestral spirits who preside over the fertility of the farmland; the *Lar familaris* came into the farmhouse with the farm-workers, the *Lar compitalis* guarded the cross-roads where several farms met.

Again, these are not gods; they are 'powers'. But some of them took on personalities and became gods. The name Venus is neuter in form; Venus was a sexless garden-spirit before becoming the great goddess of love. Juno was always closely associated with nubile women, but became the queen of the gods also. The name of Saturnus looks like a power of sowing, Neptunus a power of water. In the countryside the old religion of field and farm remained strong. It was a relevant religion with a beauty of its own; it dealt with the things that matter in life and revealed a desire to be right with the power behind the universe in life's central concerns. It had lasting power; it persisted well into Christian times, and the name 'pagan' really means 'countryman'.

The Emergence of the Gods

The word *numen* is a neuter word meaning 'nodding'. Its use is connected with the idea that fertility resides in the head: the concept is becoming anthropomorphic but has not gone all the way. Gradually the *numen* was transformed into the fully anthropomorphic god, male or female, and sometimes with uncertain sex: the shepherds' god Pales is found in the masculine and in the feminine. The function, which was once the whole god in embryo, now becomes an attribute, and the new god might gradually attract a variety of attributes represented by cult-titles.

It seems that the first great god of the Romans was Mars. In later times he is familiar as the war-god. But earlier he was equally involved with agriculture. As Marmar he was invoked to shield the fields from pestilence; as Mamurius he was a year-spirit driven out with peeled wands, and returning as the New Year. He had his own leaping priests, the *salii*, and parallels suggest that they were leaping for taller crops. The festival of the shields may be preparation for war, but the clanging of spear and shield may equally represent thunder-magic. The champion war-horse was sacrificed to him, and its blood was used in fertility-magic. He received the sacrifice of pig, *Illustration page 172* sheep and bull, the *su-ove-taurilia,* for the prosperity of the land. March, the old beginning of the year, the start alike of military campaigns and farming operations, was his month. Perhaps, though this is but one speculation of many, he was originally a storm-god.

Quirinus is a mysterious power, later identified with Romulus, the legendary founder of Rome. He is associated with Mars; Servius calls him 'Mars in charge of peace', and the Romans assembled in their civil capacity were called Quirites.

The third member of the trinity originally worshipped on the Capitoline Hill became supreme. This was Jupiter, like Zeus, the Indo-European sky-god, who came down to Rome from his hill-shrine at Alba Longa. From the time of the Etruscan kings he dominated the pantheon under his title 'Best and Greatest', and became uniquely associated with the destiny of Rome. The old power of femininity, Juno, became his consort and queen.

Illustration page 172

Two of the other former *numina* are prominent in the Pantheon as 'indigenous gods' – Janus, the spirit of the door, later represented as looking both ways, and Vesta, the spirit of the hearth, whose national shrine was tended by Vestal Virgins who began service between the ages of six and ten and continued (in classical times) for thirty years.

Other gods were called *Di novensiles;* these were the expatriates or immigrants. Most prominent was the Italo-Etruscan goddess of technological skill, Minerva, associated with Jupiter and Juno in a new Capitoline trinity. Others were Hercules, a god of success in practical affairs; Mercury, whose name shows his association with merchants; Apollo, a healing god; Fortuna, a power of fertility and an oracle-goddess from Praeneste and Antium; and Diana, a tree-spirit, who was invoked by Catullus in a wonderful hymn, and whose worship at Nemi was the starting point for Frazer's *The Golden Bough*.

Some of the deities were identical with Greek gods as originating from the same Indo-European deity. As Zeus is Dyaus, so Jupiter is Diupiter, Father Dyaus. Others, like Hercules (Heracles) or Apollo, were taken over directly from the Greek settlements. As contact with the Greeks developed, further identifications were made. Juno naturally was one with Hera. Minerva became Pallas Athene, Diana Artemis, Venus Aphrodite, Mercury Hermes, Neptune Poseidon, Vulcan Hephaestus, Ceres Demeter, Liber Dionysus, and so on. Sometimes the transition was easy, but Venus and Mercury experienced a considerable metamorphosis. With the change the legends adhering to the Greek deity became attached to the Roman; strings of them are told in Ovid's *Metamorphoses*. But it is in general true to say that such legends are always an indication of Greek influence; a *numen* has no legends.

Pax Deorum

Religion was a matter of securing the *pax deorum,* the favour of the gods, by observing the appropriate festivals, sacrifices, and rituals. Sacrifices were in the hands of the college of *pontifices*. The *pontifex maximus* had considerable political prestige, and the sceptical Caesar undertook the office for this reason. With the *pontifex maximus* served the four high priests, *rex sacrorum, flamen Dialis, flamen Martialis* and *flamen Quirinalis*. Jupiter's priest, *flamen Dialis,* was subject to especially disabling taboos. He might not ride a horse, see an army, take an oath, wear a ring or knotted fastening, go out without a cap, use iron to cut his hair or nails, pass under a vine, touch a dog: these are a few examples of many restrictions which can be traced back to magical beliefs. There was an elaborate calendar, officially published in 304 BC but going back much earlier in effect, of days on which public business might or might not be transacted: this was the *Fasti*. For each sacrifice the appropriate victim had to be selected, the exact ritual observed, the precise formula recited. Under the empire new *flamens* were appointed to administer the imperial cult.

The other great priestly colleges were the augurs, whose task was to ascertain Jupiter's will by means of auspices, and the Board of Fifteen (*quindecimviri*), who had special care of the Sibylline books. But there were others: the twelve Arval Brethren, who had charge of the fertility of the fields and whose ancient hymn survives; the Fraternity of Titus, who guarded the ancient Sabine rites, and had some responsibility for augury; the Fetials, whose province was treaties; the *luperci,* who celebrated a New Year ritual each February; the *salii* or leaping priests, who served Mars and Quirinus.

Political Religion

The Greek historian Polybius praised, and the Christian theologian Augustine condemned, the Roman aristocrats, for using religion as an opiate for the people. In Republican times innovations under political pressure in times of crisis were brought about through the Sibylline books. A legend told how King Tarquin had acquired the last three for a price which might have commanded nine, being outwitted in haggling. The Sibyl was a mysterious mantic figure, to whom miscellaneous oracles were ascribed. These may have been systematized in 367 BC, or earlier. They introduced the *lectisternium,* in which pairs of deities represented by sculptured busts were set on couches, and banquets set before them, and the *supplicatio* or religious procession to the temples. Here we see the consolations of food, spectacle, and novelty. Similar consolations were provided in the form of dramatic and athletic contests.

The books were also responsible for new cults: as early as 496-3 BC there was a temple to Ceres, Liber and Libera (Demeter, Dionysus, and Persephone) decreed by a Sibylline oracle; in 293 the healing god Aesculapius (Asclepius) came in the form of a snake to the island in the Tiber where the hospital of S. Bartolomeo still stands; in 205 BC the Great Mother was brought by the soldier mystic Scipio in the form of a black betyl from Pessinus. It was in fact during the war with Hannibal and its grim disasters that the books were busiest; people turn to religion in time of war.

The common people took this seriously, but the upper classes were increasingly sceptical. Claudius Pulcher, told that the sacred chickens would not eat (a grievous omen), said, 'Then let them drink' and threw them into the sea. Flaminius wilfully neglected his religious duties. Marcellus, the noble augur of the Second Punic War, rode in his litter with the blinds down so as not to see the evil omens, as if that annihilated them. By the first century the augurs were a laughing stock and an atheist held the pontificate for political purposes.

Augustus

The general scepticism was arrested by Augustus. He was too calculating to be sincere; superstitious he was, but hardly religious; but his political sense advised a religious basis for his rule. In 29 BC the temple of Janus was closed, signifying the end of war; in 28 BC the senate entrusted the monarch with the restoration of the temples, and he could later boast of the eighty-two he had renovated. In addition there were his new foundations. Incomparably the greatest was the temple of Palatine Apollo. The god of light and culture, who had presided over the final victory at Actium, was an excellent emblem for the new reign. Other temples were to his adoptive father the divine Julius, to Jupiter the Thunderer, to Mars and Venus, to Mars the Avenger, and to Vesta.

There was a parallel restoration of ceremonial. Augustus honoured office by holding it himself, *pontifex,* augur, and member of the Board of Fifteen, becoming *pontifex maximus* on Lepidus's death in 12 BC. The office of *flamen Dialis,* vacant for more than half a century, was filled again. The priests were set sacrificing, the colleges revived, the rites restored. The Secular Games of 17 BC, heralding a new age, are a good example; we happen to possess Augustus's autobiographical note, the text of the Sibylline oracle prescribing the ritual and an account of the ritual, an inscription including a letter of Augustus, two senatorial decrees and the records of the Board of Fifteen, and Horace's skilfully contrived hymn. We can trace the dominant notes of death and new life, purification and renewal, religion, fertility, and morality. Another important witness is the Altar of Peace with the solemn sculptured procession and the panels representing Mother Earth, Aeneas sacrificing to the Penates, the nurture of Romulus and Remus, and the divine figure of Rome on a pile of armour. The poets, Epicurean though they might be in upbringing, shared in this. Horace contributed his demand for temple restoration and his hymn; Virgil set his vision of Eternal Rome in the context of a religious experience; even Ovid interested himself in the religious calendar.

Illustration page 173

Emperor-Worship

Rome learned the attribution of divine honours to individuals from their contact with the Greeks. In 212 BC Marcellus had a festival in his honour at Syracuse. In 195 BC at Chalcis, Flamininus was accorded a priesthood, which survived for three centuries, and a hymn was sung to Titus, Zeus and Rome, ending 'Hail Paean Apollo, hail Titus our Saviour'. At Ephesus there was a shrine to Rome and P. Servilius Isauricus, proconsul from 46 to 44 BC. The notorious Verres was honoured in Sicily; Cicero and his brother Quintus were offered honours which they refused. A year or two BC Paullus Fabius Maximus received a festival jointly with Apollo Smintheus; the Smintheia Pauleia was still celebrated in the Troad two centuries later.

Further east and south the oriental divine monarch was familiar:

the Romans regarded the thought with fascination and fear. Pompey aped Alexander, who had accepted divinity for political purposes; Caesar was at least toying with the deification he received after death; Mark Antony became unabashedly Dionysus-Osiris, consort of Cleopatra-Isis, queen of Egypt, and they named their children Sun and Moon.

With his consummate political flair Augustus established the pattern for the future. In Egypt he had to be the divine monarch, but elsewhere he was more cautious; he did not want the Romans to sin a second time against statesmanship. The Greeks had societies for various purposes, called *koina;* these were adapted to the ruler-cult. But Augustus did not allow himself to be honoured alone; his name must be coupled with Rome or the Lares. At Rome he took the title *divi filius,* son of the divine (Julius). This suggested a parallel with Hercules, the son of a god, who was admitted to the company of the gods for his services to humanity: this is the point of Tiberius's rebuke to the flattering courtier who spoke of the emperor's 'sacred duties'; the emperor snapped 'Laborious', and the rebuke to flattery pointed to future not present divinity.

Only megalomaniacs like Caligula, Nero or Domitian demanded worship in their lifetime, as *dominus et deus,* slave-owner to slaves and god to mortals; it was in answer to Domitian's pretensions that John the evangelist made his Thomas assert that Jesus was the true *dominus et deus,* Lord and God. As so often, the structure in heaven reflected the structure on earth, and the assembly of the gods was depicted in a kind of celestial super-senate, with additional members co-opted on merit. Hence the practice arose of the deification of good emperors after their death, and the blunt soldier Vespasian, feeling his death-agony approaching, had the humour to exclaim 'Oh dear, I'm afraid I'm becoming a God.'

Illustration page 172

Of course this was a political religion. The Olympian gods could not unite a world-empire, the divine emperor might. The emperor was god because he was emperor; he was the centre of worship as Aeneas was the centre of *The Aeneid* – only as symbolical of Rome. This meant that the cult received particular emphasis on the fringes of empire, in Britain, where a cult of Claudius was introduced from the first, or in Asia, where the cities squabbled over the right to the title of *neokoros* or temple-warden of the official provincial cult. The imperial cult lasted well into the third century, till Aurelian changed to the principle of rule by the grace of God, which paved the way for the Christian empire, though Constantine's person still received veneration.

A Province of Empire

As Rome's empire spread, she assimilated what she met: this was her secret. Religiously the process is called the *interpretatio Romana,* the Roman understanding of foreign gods as their own; we must remember that there was a corresponding process by which the assimilated provincials represented Roman gods as their own.

Britain provides a convenient example. There were numerous Celtic gods, some purely indigenous, some known from Europe. We find them alike in their own right and identified with the Roman pantheon. At Bath the goddess of the hot springs, Sulis, was identified with Minerva: the architecture of her temple is classical, the sculpture is not. At Lydney on the Severn, Nodens, who survives in mythology as King Lear, acquired a fine temple in the fourth century AD; this may represent an Irish settlement. Brigantia in the north was accepted as a nymph; Maponus or Mabon, a god of youth, was identified with Apollo. Mars, a natural god for the soldiers to introduce, finds many identities. Sometimes the Romans honoured a local god as the Genius of the Place. The Celtic mother-goddesses became assimilated to the Fates. Jupiter the Best and Greatest was important in official cults, and there was naturally emperor-worship: the foundations of Claudius's temple at Colchester may still be seen.

For further details of Celtic divinities in Roman times, see pages 103–4.

In addition the soldiers and traders brought with them a variety of eastern cults – Mithras and Jupiter of Doliche, and Isis, and Cybele, and the Syrian goddess. How Christianity came we do not know, but three British bishops attended the Council of Arles in 314 AD, and there are remarkable memorials in the house-chapel at Lullingstone, the word-square at Cirencester, and the mosaic at Hinton St. Mary.

Magic and Superstition

Astrology came west from Babylon; the Stoic polymath Posidonius encouraged it. Stoics and Platonists were behind it; Epicureans and Christians opposed it. The theory of astrology posited a mystical kinship between men and stars: 'we share powers and passions with the planets.' Saturn's course was slow; hence it was believed to make men sluggish. The planet Venus presided over love; Jupiter offered power; Mercury blessed trade. The snake was associated with the healing gods; the constellation of that name helped the healing process. Astrology was a pseudo-science; the calculation of horoscopes was an intricate business, and the astrologers were called *mathematici,* (mathematicians).

The movement exploded in the reign of Tiberius, who retired to Capri 'with his Babylonian horde'. It was now that the Stoic Manilius wrote his astrological poem. Astrology with its fatalism might buttress the *status quo;* it might also encourage dangerous ambition, and from time to time the astrologers were suppressed, though never for long. Under Marcus Aurelius, Vettius Valens wrote ecstatically of the communion of the astrologer with the gods; in the fifth century AD Stephanus of Byzantium was using much the same language.

Astrology was a widespread superstition, but it was only one of many. Four examples must suffice.

Magic was used for medical purposes; magical amulets were a protection against disease, and we have such incantations as 'flee, demon hydrophobia from the wearer of this amulet'. Pliny is full of curious superstitions: thus, to cure a headache, pick a herb growing

on the head of a statue, wrap it in a piece of cloth and tie it round
your neck with a piece of red string.

The second example is curses, often inscribed on tablets of lead and
buried. They cover a variety of occasions: sometimes they are written
by those who are crossed in love, sometimes by punters seeking to
nobble the race-horses they have not backed. A typical example,
found by a spring near Arezzo, put a curse upon a certain Q. Leturius
Lupus, also called Caucadio, and called on the nymphs or boiling
waters to destroy him within a year.

The third example relates to an interesting discovery at Pergamum
of a sorcerer's equipment, a three-legged bronze table, elaborately
engraved with the dark divinity of Hecate, a round dish with magic
markings, and two rings: evidently the rings would be hung from a
thread over the bowl and indicate the appropriate symbols as they
swung. We know of a *cause célèbre* in the fourth century involving
similar equipment, which was used to determine Valens's successor.

Finally we may mention Apuleius. His *Golden Ass* is full of magic
and witchcraft; this may be merely part of the tradition of story-
telling, though it is significant that it found a ready audience. But he
himself married a wealthy widow, whose family accused him of
bewitching her. The charge was ludicrous, and Apuleius was a skilled
enough pleader to laugh it out of court. That it reached court at all
reveals the superstition of the age.

The elder Pliny is here of special interest. Something of a rationalist,
who attacks magical uses, he none the less believes in the evil eye,
invisibility, sex-changes, lunar influences, the awesome power of
menstrual blood, odd numbers, magic circles, the power of iron, the
protective effect of spitting and the use of mystic formulae.

Life after Death

The general beliefs about life beyond death in Roman society were
as complex as those in most societies. The ancestors were as important
to the traditional Roman as to the traditional African. The aristocrat
kept the ancestral busts or masks to be produced on the appropriate
occasions; the Lares were the general ancestral spirits; the moral norm
of Rome was the *mos maiorum,* the way of the ancestors; the *Di Manes*
were the spirits of the dead and were feared and honoured; the
Parentalia in February was a festival of the dead, All Souls, and was
mainly celebrated in families rather than publicly. Popular belief extended to ghosts (there are excellent ghost stories in Cicero and Pliny),
and to witches who could call up the dead.

Etruscan demonology and Greek myth combined to foster a fear
of punishment beyond the grave, which Cicero and Seneca might
scoff at, but which the Epicureans felt imposed on others. But on the
whole the epitaphs show neither hope nor fear. Some express regret
at having left the pleasures of life, others satisfaction at having escaped
life's troubles. A common formula for the latter is NF F NS NC *non fui
fui non sum non curo* I did not exist. I existed. I do not exist. I do not
care. Another speaks of 'eternal sleep'. The main evidence for regret

Above Vespasian, the emperor who joked of his approaching godhead on his deathbed. Museo Archeologico Nazionale, Naples.

Above right A scene from an altar, showing the *suovetaurilia*, the sacrifice at which a pig, sheep and bull were offered. The word itself is made up of a combination of these three words in Latin. Musée National du Louvre, Paris.

Right Jupiter, the supreme god of the Roman pantheon was protector of the city and the state and guardian of public morality, being concerned with oaths and treaties. Originally a sky-god, he was later identified with the Greek Zeus, his cult being introduced to Rome by the Etruscans shortly before their fall. Musei Vaticani.

Left A wall painting at the House of the Vetii in Pompeii, showing the head of the family with his *genius*, represented by a snake. The *genius* and *iuno* were the male and female forms of a family's power to continue itself, and cult was paid to them.

Below The west side of the Emperor Augustus's magnificent Altar of Peace, erected in 13 BC on the Campus Martius as part of his campaign to revive the ancient Roman virtues. Two legendary scenes are depicted on this side: Aeneas's sacrifice on his return to Italy and the suckling of Romulus and Remus.

Above A tetradrachm minted at Antioch shows the child king of Syria, Antiochus VI (145-42 BC), wearing the crown of the sun-god. British Museum, London.

Right A frieze from the series illustrating the Dionysiac mysteries, in the Villa of Mysteries at Pompeii (*c.* 50 BC). The neophyte is preparing for her initiation, which will culminate in a mystical marriage.

Below Dionysus wakes the sleeping Ariadne to take her as his bride, one of a series of Roman sarcophagi which depict allegorically mortal beings putting on immortality.

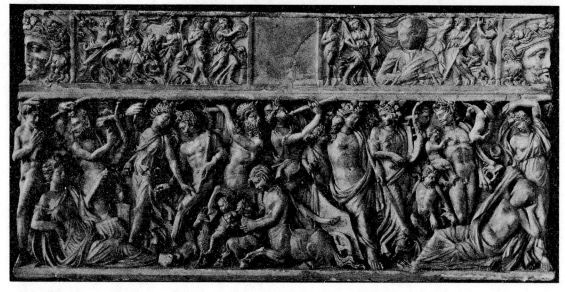

is associated with tombs such as flank the Via Appia, which are plainly designed to be the House of the Dead. Sometimes they have dining-rooms and kitchens attached, so that the living might share in a banquet with the dead man on his birthday.

Furthermore, from the Hadrianic period to the third century a magnificent series of sarcophagi depicts scenes which symbolize the mortal putting on immortality. Dionysus takes Ariadne as his bride, *Illustration page 174* or appears in triumph; Castor and Pollux ride with Leucippus's daughters through the door to new life; the Muses symbolize the touch of divine inspiration; Prometheus forms man and gives him life; Hercules is shown fulfilling the labours for which divinity was the reward. The battle scenes and hunting scenes speak of triumph; Endymion awakens to Selene's kiss; the round of the seasons tells of the rebirth of the year; Nereids and Tritons depict the journey to the Isles of the Blest, which becomes stylized in a wave ornament; flowers and garlands assert life.

The Sun

In many parts of the east the sun was a prominent object of worship. In Illyria there was an ancient tradition of sun-worship; in Egypt the Sun had long been chief of the gods; in Syria the town we call Baalbek was known by the Greeks as Heliopolis, Sun-city; in Persia the Sun *Illustration page 174* was one of the chief lieutenants of Ahura-Mazda in his struggle against darkness. Sol, the sun-god, had an ancient cult at Rome, but under Augustus Sol was displaced by Apollo. It was natural that as the centre of gravity of the Roman empire moved eastwards, sun-worship should grow in power. It was already strong in imperial propaganda; Nero's Golden House was an appropriate home for the incarnate sun, and Antoninus accorded the sun peculiar honour.

Under the Severan dynasty sun-worship became dominant; the sun-god was portrayed with Severus's characteristic beard, and the emperor took the title INVICTVS (unconquered), which was the peculiar epithet of the sun. It was a natural development. The sun was a superb unifying symbol and rallying-point for the whole empire; the old religion was devalued, and the usurpations had made it difficult to treat the emperor as a central point for worship. Even the excesses of Heliogabalus could not destroy the power of the symbol, and in AD 274 Aurelian established the sun-god as the supreme god of the Roman empire.

Ernest Renan once said that if Christianity had collapsed the world would have been Mithraist; this is not true; sun-worship would have been dominant, but not in its Mithraic form. In fact the emperor Constantine's Christianity was ambiguous. His family owed traditional allegiance to the sun-god; the famous vision of the cross as he marched on Rome came to him from the sun; the sun continues to appear on his coins through the decade, and on his arch at Rome; his own statue at Constantinople bore the rayed crown of the sun-god, formed, as he believed, from the nails of the true cross; his god was a god of power, never of love. The sun was not wholly defeated.

Personal Religion

For personal religion men turned to the mystery religions, those whose secret rites were known only to the initiated. Eleusis was the best-known; it was still potent for Cicero and for Plutarch. The power of Dionysus is mightily revealed in the Villa of the Mysteries at Pompeii, where a magnificent series of wall-paintings shows the whole process of initiation, presided over by the god – the reading of the liturgy, the offerings, the symbolic suckling of a kid, divination, the unveiling of the mystic phallus, the flagellation or ritual death, the dance of resurrection, and the preparation for the holy marriage – a marvellous record of devotion.

Illustration page 174

The mysteries of Isis and Osiris came from Egypt. Isis was a saviour-goddess, Osiris the god who was rent in pieces and reborn. In Egypt the dead man was identified with Osiris, and addressed as Osiris. Isis and Osiris offered protection in this world and life in the world to come, and the *Golden Ass* of Apuleius, which has a serious purpose underlying its picaresque adventures, is the testimony of a Romanized African to the fascination of the cult of Isis.

For reincarnation of Osiris and identification with the dead, see pages 143–4.

Cybele, the great mother-goddess of Asia Minor, also had her mysteries. Admission was by the *taurobolium* or baptism in bull's blood, which some believed to bring eternal life, though others repeated the ceremony after twenty years. The baptism is recorded at Puteoli in the early second century AD; our most vivid description comes from Prudentius in the fourth. Originally those who gave themselves to the Mother were expected to castrate themselves, offering their fertility for the fertility of the world, but from the time of Claudius this can no longer have been true, and under the Empire the cult was popular.

Mithras was a Persian saviour-god, a spirit of the firmament and ally of Ahura-Mazda. Initiation was in seven steps: the lower grades, or Servitors, were Raven, Bridegroom, Soldier; the upper grades, or Participants, were Lion, Persian, Courier of the Sun, Father. Initiation involved real or symbolic tests of endurance. Mithraism never commanded large numbers. The chapels (with the relief of Mithras killing the bull whose blood meant life) were always small, and the members largely soldiers and traders with some civil servants. Astrology was mixed up in the cult, which made moral demands and promised bliss beyond the grave.

For Mithraism in Ancient Iran, see pages 182 and 187.

Christianity was an eastern mystery. Its appeal was various: the strong, magnetic personality of its founder; the quality of life and fellowship, and all that was meant by the new word *agape* (Christian love); the position accorded to women (Prisca, Phoebe, and Nympha were followed by the second-century martyrs Blandina, Perpetua and Felicitas); the sturdy organization of the churches; the conviction which cut away the multiple choices of the ancient world and faced martyrdom with courage (the blood of Christians is seed); the message of hope for all men. The scholar A. D. Nock put it well when he wrote 'It was left to Christianity to democratise mystery.'

Chapter Twelve

Ancient Iran

Iran, or Persia as it was once called, is enclosed within a triangle of mountains and has at its heart two salt deserts which are so barren that the Gobi Desert appears fertile in comparison. With the mountains towering up to a height of 5500 metres (18,000 feet) Iran is a land of great contrasts: tropical jungle near the Caspian Sea and a Mediterranean climate in the river valleys of the southwest. These differences have given rise to various cultures, and the mountains have made contact between them difficult. While western Iran is subject to influence from Mesopotamia, Greece and Rome, the east is under the influence of India and even China. Iran thus stands as a bridge between east and west, a fact which has not only influenced her religion, but has also made Iran a watershed of history.

About 1000 BC waves of Aryans, a nomadic warlike people, moved into Iran from the north and northwest and by 800 BC occupied the land. The religions of India and Iran, both under Aryan influence, display a number of similar characteristics; a number of gods appear in both (Mithras for instance), their concept of cosmic order is similar, and their rituals have many common features.

The Aryans' religion reveals their manner of life. It is the religion of a people living close to nature, at once revelling in it, and yet afraid of it: struck by its life-giving goodness and yet afraid of its life-destroying cruelty. The abstract character of the religion is suggested by the names of its gods: Contract (Mithras), True Speech (Varuna), Hospitality (Aryaman), and so on.

Zoroastrianism

Zarathustra or Zoroaster (the more commonly used Greek form of his name) is thought to have worked in northeast Iran. Traditionally dated 628-551 BC, he may in fact have lived earlier than that. Of the details of his life we know very little, although piety has, inevitably, lovingly embellished the narrative. His early teaching aroused great hostility and he was forced to flee. In his new home he found a disciple in a local ruler, Vishtaspa, and from this time on Zoroaster became a figure of some importance in local affairs. He was married with one daughter and two sons. Tradition records that he was murdered in his seventies.

Zoroaster's teaching has come down to us in seventeen of his hymns, *The Gathas*. Although they are difficult to translate, his zeal, love for God, and wisdom are striking. To Zoroaster God is the Wise Lord, Ahura Mazda, the one who creates heaven and earth, the first and the last, yet also a friend, the one who has called him from the beginning. God can have nothing to do with evil. His Holy Spirit establishes life, and creates men and women. He is opposed by the Evil Spirit, the destructive force, who is characterized by the Evil Mind, the Lie, and Pride. Between these opposing forces, these twin spirits, people must choose. If they follow the path of evil, their lives are full of evil thoughts, words and deeds. But if they follow the path of truth, then they share in the Good Mind and attain integrity, immortality, devotion and the kingdom, all of which are aspects of God.

The conflict between truth and falsehood, however, is not eternal. There will come 'the last turning point of the world', when the 'two great hostile armies come together'. Men and women will have to submit to 'the great test' by fire, and 'justice shall be realised'. The whole will be 'renovated' by the 'benefactors' or saviours of the good religion, who will suppress passion by just deeds and the spread of the wise teaching. All who work for the suppression of falsehood are saviours, a term which applies particularly to Zoroaster himself.

Although Zoroaster condemned much of the old tradition he did not break with it completely. As a priest he composed a number of his hymns in the traditional form. In the old fire-ritual he saw a symbol of light and the cosmic law of God and used it in his devotions. At least some of the aspects of God are adaptations of Aryan ideas, the idea of Truth for example. He was also prepared to use the customary imagery of the individual judgment at death. But all that he took over he refashioned and remodelled in a unique way. His love for God demanded of him that he work for social justice and harmony. He opposed the destructive work of the nomadic invaders, seeing in the settled pastoral life a pattern of peace and truth.

The teaching of any founder of a religion is inevitably developed and adapted by his followers. Zoroastrianism is no exception. Zoroaster's thoughts were codified, modified and brought into harmony with the thought and needs of the times. His followers did not deliberately pervert his teaching, but there seems to have been a 'coming-together' of his teaching and the traditional faith. The result was a profound faith expressed in mythical terms.

The Sources

The holy book of the Zoroastrians is the Avesta. It was probably not written down until the fifth century AD, but some of the material goes back to a much earlier date, even to the pre-Zoroastrian period. Unfortunately the whole Avesta has not weathered the ravages of time. All that remains are the hymns of Zoroaster (*The Gathas*), the main liturgical texts (*The Yasna* and *Vendidad*), other hymns (*The Yashts*), and prayers.

In the ninth century AD a number of Zoroastrian books were written to defend the 'Good Religion' against Christian and Islamic propaganda and to expound the faith to laymen. Written in Middle Persian, or Pahlavi, they were extracts, précis and comments on the Avesta and often turn out to be exciting stores of ancient beliefs.

But this is not all. Folklore, inscriptions, coins, reports of foreign observers, and the faith of modern Zoroastrians, all add to our knowledge of the religion of Iran.

The Concept of God

A Zoroastrian catechism teaches that the 'System, Order, Principle, and Rule' which is to be seen in the heavens and on earth 'makes us recognize and believe in the infinite being of the Almighty Lord'. Zoroastrians love the world, and believe life teaches us that God is the 'Greatest, the Best, and the most excellent in Virtue, Righteousness and Goodness.' (J. J. Modi, *A Catechism of the Zoroastrian Religion*, Bombay, 1962, pp. 6ff).

'The original word of false religion is that evil comes from the creator' (Denkart, edited by D. M. Madan, 1911, translated by R. C. Zaehner, *The Teachings of the Magi*, London, 1956, p. 94). God cannot be responsible for evil. Evil is a substance, as is good, and both are taken back to a first cause, God and the devil, Ahriman. The devil, who has always existed, is responsible for all evil in the world, disease and death, anger and greed. As the two are fundamentally opposed substances they inevitably come into conflict.

In the conflict both have their respective forces. The 'aspects' of God such as Integrity, Immortality etc., which Zoroaster propounded, became, if they were not so already, distinct individuals, the six Bounteous Immortals, or Amahraspands. They sit before the throne of God, have a special place in Zoroastrian ritual, and guard the elements of the world (fire, earth, water etc.). They are not the only heavenly beings, however. There are also the Yazatas, or Adorable Ones. The position of these two classes of beings has often been compared to the position of archangels and angels in Christianity. In theory the number of Yazatas is legion, but naturally certain ones dominate, usually the old Aryan figures. Despite the mythology the abstract character of the heavenly forces remains; they still represent the Good Mind, Truth, Peace, etc.

Opposed to the heavenly forces are hordes of demons and evil spirits. They are rarely depicted in such individual terms as their heavenly counterparts, but their vile nature is forcibly expressed. The greatest detail occurs in the picture of the chief demons who are opposed to the Amahraspands: they are the archdemons of Apostasy, Anarchy, Vile Thoughts, Disobedience, Hunger and Thirst, and, above all, the Lie.

The Understanding of the World

The history of the world is the history of God's conflict with the devil. It is divided into four periods, each of three thousand years. In the first two periods God and the devil prepare their forces, in the third they come into conflict, and in the last the devil is finally defeated. At creation the devil broke through the rampart of the sky and attacked the first man and beast with disease and death, capable as he is only of destructive action. But at the moment of his apparent victory both man and beast emitted seed, which gave rise to human and vegetable life. As life came through their death so the perpetuation of the good creation and the defeat of the devil are assured. The world belongs to God himself, so that Zoroastrians, unlike members of some religions, do not believe matter to be evil. Indeed it is the devil, not human beings, who is in an alien material world. He can have no material form, but remains in the world parasitically, vainly trying to destroy God's work.

Men and Women in the World

People, the human forms of his heavenly self or *fravashi,* are free agents. They may choose to follow God or the devil. If they choose right, they assist God in his ultimate victory. Choosing right means accepting the world for what it is, God's world. The Zoroastrians do not contrast the spirit and the flesh as St Paul did. The soul and the body are a unity, and to withdraw from the world as a monk is to reject God's world. Asceticism is as great a sin as over-indulgence. Men have a religious duty to take a wife, have children and so increase the Good Religion. Equally it is a holy act to till the soil and breed cattle. Since health is the gift of God, bodily health is to be sought by all. 'A healthy body enables man to have a healthy good mind, which in turn enables him to do good works' (Modi, pp. 29ff).

Essentially the Zoroastrian religion is a joyful religion. On the day of the month dedicated to the god of judgment, for example, one is not advised to be morbid, but 'on the day of Rashn, life is gay: do, in holiness, anything you will.' (*Counsels of Adhurbadh,* Zaehner, *Teachings,* p. 108.) Out of respect for others, bad manners and being a bore are reckoned as sins! To enjoy life one's self and to help others to do so is fundamental to the religion. The Zoroastrian must act justly in all he or she does, for so is God's order established.

Zoroastrianism, then, has a strong social ethic, and, in contrast to Hinduism, an essentially activist one. Work is 'the salt of Life'. But a person's character is expressed not only by what he or she does and says, but also by his or her thoughts. People must 'overcome doubts and unrighteous desires with reason, overcome greed with contentment, anger with serenity, envy with benevolence, want with vigilance, strife with peace, falsehood with truth.' (*Counsels of the Ancient Sages,* Zaehner, *Teachings,* p. 25).

The Formal Expression of the Zoroastrian Faith

Like Hindus and Sikhs the Zoroastrians have, as part of their daily dress, symbols to remind them of their religion. The first is the sacred thread, the *kushti* with seventy-two threads symbolizing the chapters of *The Yasna.* This is untied and reknotted several times a day expressing both a moral and a religious resolution. Secondly they wear the shirt, *sadre,* symbolizing the religion. The priests wear white robes with turbans and masks over their mouths during certain ceremonies *Illustrations pages 183, 184* to avoid defiling the sacred fire with their breath.

There are prayers for the five divisions of the day, for example at sunset, and ceremonies for all the great moments of life: birth, puberty, marriage, childbearing and death.

Death is the work of the devil, so a corpse is the abode of demons. The more righteous the deceased the more powerful the demonic work has been. To cremate or bury the corpse would defile the elements, so bodies are exposed in 'Towers of Silence', *dakhmas,* where they are devoured by the vultures. Since childbirth can so easily bring death, that, too, is hedged around with prescriptions and prohibitions. Before all major acts of worship one must undergo a purificatory ritual. Confession of sins committed in thought, word or deed is often made.

Illustration page 184

There are two central rites: the fire-ritual and the *haoma* sacrifice. Fire is the symbol and son of Ahura Mazda, and must be kept free from all defilement. Neither the sun or unbelieving eyes must see it, and it is preserved in a fire temple. There are a number of sacred fires constantly and lovingly attended by the priests. The chief fire is the Bahram, or king of fires, which is crowned and enthroned, not simply installed. When the Parsis visit the fire their foreheads are marked with the ash as a symbol of humility, equality and as a source of strength.

Illustration page 184

Haoma is a plant, but more than that, it is the god Haoma on earth. In the *haoma* ritual, the god is pounded and from the juice comes the drink of immortality. In this bloodless sacrifice the offering is at once god, priest and victim, and the faithful consume the divine sacrifice in anticipation of the sacrifice at the end of the world which will make all humans immortal.

The Goal of History

At death one's actions are weighed in the balance. If the good outweigh the bad, one passes on to heaven, but if not, to hell, where the punishment is made to fit the crime. But this is still not the end. Eternal hell is an immoral teaching in Zoroastrian eyes. A good God would never allow his creatures to suffer eternally. The purpose of punishment is to reform so that on the day of resurrection all may be raised by the saviour to face the final judgment. Then, when all are finally pure, the devil and all his works are finally destroyed and the distinction between heaven and earth is overcome so that all may worship and live with God in the full glory of his creation.

Other Religious Movements in Iran

Zurvanism

To many Iranians Zoroaster's God was unsatisfactory. Although he was all good, he was limited by the power of the devil. For the Zurvanites Zoroaster's twin spirits become Ohrmazd and Ahriman, emanating from an undifferentiated One beyond all duality called Zurvan, Infinite Space and Time. Zurvan is the 'four-faced god', his faces or aspects, represent procreation, birth, ageing and the return to the Infinite, or the World Ages. Thus within the One are seen all aspects of life, light, dark, heat and cold.

The basic Zurvanite myth tells of Zurvan wanting a son, but after sacrificing for a thousand years, doubting the fulfilments of his desire. At the moment of his doubt twins are conceived. Ohrmazd (i.e. Ahura Mazda) is the manifestation of all that is good, Ahriman (the devil) the manifestation of Zurvan's doubt. Because Ahriman is the first to enter the world he is made the ruler for 9,000 years, but to Ohrmazd is given the priesthood and ultimate victory. This theoretically equal status of the two figures resulted in the offering of sacrifices to Ahriman as a power to be propitiated, and may explain the offerings to Deius Areimanius in Mithraism.

With Zurvanism a variety of influences can be detected: Babylonian, Indian, and Greek. The result was more than one school of thought. The Fatalist School, believing the world to be the limitation of Time (Zurvan), viewed human beings as puppets in the hands of Fate, and denied Zoroaster's basic concept of free will. Others denied that the world could have been created out of nothing by an act of will and accepted the idea of an evolutionary development of matter, a denial of the Zoroastrian creator God. This Materialist Zurvanism also denied a belief in future reward or punishment in heaven and hell. These 'modernizations' of Zurvanism may have been only fringe movements.

Of Zurvanite ethics we know little. Perhaps under Buddhist influence Zurvanites believed the fundamental evil of humankind to be 'wrong-mindedness', or greed, manifesting itself physically as lust and mentally as ignorance. Women were thought of as the immediate sources of much evil in the world, seducing men onto the path of wrong-mindedness, a movement away from the Zoroastrian ethic and in common with a variety of religions.

The reconstruction of Zurvanite belief, however, is tenuous. No Iranian text mentions the sect, much less expounds its belief. The evidence is derived from foreign authors whose sources date back to the fourth century BC and odd texts which may be taken as accommodations of orthodox belief to Zurvanism. When this school began we cannot say. Some scholars suggest Zoroaster's twin spirits were adaptations of Zurvanism, and others have identified a fourteenth-century BC bronze as a portrayal of Zurvan, but this is speculation. The movement certainly grew during the Achaemenid (c. 550-333 BC) and Parthian (250 BC-AD 247) periods. The Sassanian period (AD 247-635) may have been a time of conflict between two churches, Zurvanite and Zoroastrian, or, perhaps more likely, there were within the Zoroastrian Church different movements all practising the same ritual. Zurvanism may have been such a movement rather than a distinct sect, but if so it was a powerful and influential one.

Mithraism

Originally an Aryan god, Mithras was worshipped in Iran as the god of contracts (*mithra* actually means contract). He preserves truth and order, destroying the disruptive forces of evil, anger, greed, pride and procrastination, all evil gods and men. He is described as a

Left This fifth-century BC portrayal of magi offering sacrifice comes from Dascylium, or Eregli, in Asia Minor. The accurate representation of the scene – the barsom twigs and the covered mouth – is evidence of how widely Zoroastrian practices were known. Istanbul Arkeoloji Müzeleri.

Left A ritual meal among Irani Zoroastrians.

Above The *dakhma* of Cain near Yazel, where dead bodies are exposed. To cremate or bury the body would be to defile the elements.

Above right Ervad Fireze M. Kotwal holding strips of metal that symbolize the sacred barsom twigs. The mask worn over his nose and mouth is to prevent contamination of the twigs by his breath.

Right A Persian miniature (*c.* AD 1600) showing worshippers at a fire altar and before a shrine. British Museum, London.

Left A silver plaque from Luristan (1200-900 BC) which some scholars believe represents the god Zurvan giving birth to the twin spirits (the opposing principles of good and evil). On either side are figures symbolic of the three ages of human life. Cincinnati Art Museum, Ohio.

Below One of Mithras's trials of strength with the sun-god was the capture and sacrifice of a wild bull. This sacrifice is made in his honour. Musée National du Louvre, Paris.

Right A scene showing Mithras hunting, from Dura-Europos. The style of the clothes, the position of the figure and horse, and the arrangement of the animals are completely Iranian. The scene has been interpreted by some as symbolic of the god hunting the forces of evil.

Right It has been argued that the faithful reproduction of Iranian dress on this sixth-century Ravenna mosaic of the three magi suggests that the artist knew of a Mithraic birth myth.

Below Mithraic worshippers wearing masks attend the priest in a communion meal celebrated on a table covered with a bull skin.

'mighty, strong warrior', and it is he that 'the warriors worship at the manes of their horses' before going into battle (stanzas 140 and 10f, I. Gershevitch, *The Avestan Hymn to Mithra,* pp. 145, 79). As guardian of truth he is the judge of the soul at death, and as preserver of contracts determines when the period of the devil's rule is at an end. His coming 'amid the homage of the meek and lowly' in days of victory is awaited (sts. 117f).

The later *Oracle of Hystaspes* mentioned by Christian writers has been identified as a Mithraic oracle foretelling the god's coming at the end of the world to destroy the wicked with fire and to save the righteous. A number of Roman monuments depict his birth and some fifth-century Christian texts imply that there was a Mithraic myth foretelling the appearance of a star which would lead magi to the birthplace of the saviour.

Illustration page 186

Mithras is an important and popular deity in Iranian history. He was invoked by the Achaemenid kings in their inscriptions, and both kings and commoners had names compounded with Mithras (Mithradates for example). He still occupies an important place in Zoroastrian ritual.

Whether there was ever a separate Mithras cult in Iran it is difficult to say, but from Iran his worship spread as a distinct cult east into India and west into Mesopotamia and Asia Minor. Armenian legends, theophoric names, reliefs, and Egyptian and Anatolian inscriptions all testify to the god's widespread popularity in the ancient Near East in pre-Christian times.

Mithraism first entered Rome in 60 BC, and in the second century AD it spread through the empire as far as Britain. Carried mainly by soldiers, it was an exclusively male cult. At baptism, when the initiate had to submit to both physical and spiritual tests, he renounced all crowns but Mithras, and was expected to adhere to a strict moral code. In return he was promised a share in the resurrection.

The central belief of the cult was the sacrifice of a bull by Mithras. This act was both creative and redemptive. The worshipper looked back to a sacrifice at the beginning, when life had come out of death, and forward to the final sacrifice by Mithras when the last animal to die would give men the elixir of immortality. A foretaste of this divine gift could be shared in the regular communion meal of bread and wine in which the priest represented Mithras.

Illustration page 185

Illustration page 186

The Mandeans

The Mandeans, or Nazoreans, are a small sect still in existence in south Iraq and neighbouring Iran. They claim descent from John the Baptist, and believe that their ancestors fled to Parthia at the Fall of Jerusalem. Their vocabulary and symbolism is a mixture of Semitic and Iranian elements, with much Gnostic content. The first redaction of their texts, written in Mandean, dates from the eighth century AD, but their content is much older. They are a very esoteric group, and only the priests are granted permission to read the more important religious texts.

Afraid of anthropomorphic language, the Mandeans describe the Absolute as a supreme formless entity, and call it 'the King of Light', 'the Lord of Greatness', 'the Great Mana'. The King of Light is set over against the realm of darkness. The world is created by emanations from the King of Light, one of the most important of these being the saviour, Manda d'Hayye (the Knowledge of Life), whence the name of the sect.

Everything in the material world has its heavenly counterpart. The cosmos itself is similar in shape to its creator, the archetypal Man. As in many religions the Mandeans believe that the physical limitations of the body are not expressive of a human being's real nature. The soul, they believe, is in exile in the world, a particle of light which became imprisoned in matter at the creation. Whereas the body is created by the planets, life and breath come from the world of light. But the soul is not released from the body through the subjection of the body in asceticism; people may enjoy the good gifts of life in moderation. The soul's release is hampered by the planets, stars and what are considered to be such false religions as Judaism and Christianity. At the end of the world, when the earth and planets are done away with, the souls of the pious will be liberated. Liberation can also be achieved here and now as a result of the work of Hibil-Ziwa, a saviour who entered the underworld and defeated the evil spirits.

Baptism wards off evil spirits and is essential to salvation. It is both a washing of the body and soul and a resurrection to the new life. A sacramental meal forms part of the baptism, as of other important rituals. Another essential rite is the *massiqta,* the rising up, or ascent, in which the passage of the soul to the world of light is made possible by rites of purification celebrated at a person's death. As shown in a number of Iranian reliefs the handshake is in general an act of religious significance; it plays an important part in the Mandean cult where it is known as the *kushta.* Very detailed prescriptions are given for all ritual, and an incorrect performance can have extremely dire consequences for both initiate and priest.

An outbreak of plague in the nineteenth century killed virtually all the priests. Although a new hierarchy has been formed the priests now are almost all old men, and replacements do not seem to be forthcoming.

The Manicheans

Mani (AD 216-274) was born of a princely Parthian family and spent his youth in Mesopotamia, then a melting pot of many major religions. He had his first vision at the age of twelve and at twenty set out to establish his new religion. Having access to the royal court he converted a number of influential leaders and received the favour of the Sassanian monarch, Shapur I, whom he accompanied on his western wars. The royal favour was renewed until the last days of Bahram I when the Zoroastrian priests, the Magi, led by Kartir, opposed his teaching and, afraid of his success, plotted his downfall. Mani died in chains.

Mani proclaimed himself the fulfilment of the work of Zoroaster, Buddha and Jesus. All had incomplete fragments of the truth, but even this had been corrupted by their followers. As the 'apostle of light' for all men Mani identified his gods with those of his hearers, so when addressing Christians the saviour is called Jesus, when addressing Zoroastrians the First Man is called Ohrmazd (Ahura Mazda). The God of the Old Testament, however, was repugnant to Mani. In times of persecution Manicheans were thus able to present themselves as Christians or Zoroastrians. It may have been this characteristic which appealed to Shapur.

Dualism lies at the heart of Mani's teaching. God, the Father of Greatness, is opposed by the Prince of Darkness. The two are primary elements. The world is created from the bodies of the rulers of darkness, the Archontes, and imprisoned within matter are sparks of light, fragments of the First Man dragged down by the demons. In this present world of mixture the soul seeks escape from the fear of death, the vulture-like enemy which separates it from its true home.

Release is achieved by asceticism, knowledge of the true nature of the self, and the defeat of the demons by the saviour, who has himself been saved by God from their clutches. On release the soul ascends to the New Paradise ruled by the First Man, and at the end of the world, when all the sparks of light are released, the whole body returns to the Eternal Paradise. Meanwhile, those who do not achieve release in this life are subject to rebirth.

The initiates were divided into two classes: the 'hearers' (the lower grade), who collected food and necessities for the 'elect' (the upper grade), who were expected to follow a higher religious code. Mani consciously created a new religion, and provided it with canonical literature and ritual. Idols were banned, but Mani, believing in the educational value of art, decreed that the books be beautifully bound and illustrated and that the ritual should have beautiful music and hymns. It is not clear whether the Manicheans had a sacramental system.

Manicheism spread thoughout the Roman Empire, Arabia, India and China. Although physical and intellectual persecution destroyed the religion centuries ago, it has been a source of influence on a number of movements, for example on the Albigenses of medieval France.

A Short History of Iranian Religion

The two basic elements of Iranian religion are the traditional Aryan faith and the teaching of Zoroaster. Iranian religious history is the story of the interaction of these two beliefs under the influence of outside forces. The Achaemenid period (c. 550-333 BC), one of the peaks of Iranian political history, was a time of Zoroastrian infiltration into the traditional and state religion. A number of royal inscriptions suggest Zoroastrianism was a source of influence at the court, particularly during the reigns of Darius and Xerxes.

The official priests of Iran were the Magi, a hereditary priestly caste whose duty it was to look after 'religion'. Whatever rites were offered were performed by them. As Zoroastrianism became more popular it seems to have been the Magi who carried the teaching, perhaps without considering it a distinct religion or cult. As Zoroastrianism was spread through Iran by the Magi, so the teaching of the prophet was synthesized with the traditional faith, a synthesis which characterized both Achaemenid and later times. The Achaemenid Empire was a vast one, and the intermingling of cultures had its effect on religion. Greek statues were introduced into the cult and Babylonian astrology became a major factor. This may well have been the milieu which gave birth to Zurvanism.

For Babylonian astrology, see pages 129–30 and 169.

Alexander the Great's invasion in 333 BC and the advent of Hellenism provided a tremendous shock to the Iranians, despite Alexander's attempts to unite East and West, and his adoption of many Iranian customs. When Iran again became independent, it was under the Parthians, (*c.* 250 BC to AD 247). The Parthians, having a less advanced civilization, naturally retained much of the Hellenistic 'technology', architecture, monetary system, etc. But gradually in the second and first centuries BC their Iranian culture came to the fore. This can be seen in their art and coins, but perhaps mainly in the influence they exerted on others. If Roman Mithraism grew out of the Iranian form of the god's worship, and not from an Iranian satellite such as Pontus, then it spread to Rome as a result of the Parthian expansion westwards. It was during the Parthian period that the Mandeans are thought to have come to Iran.

Although Zoroastrianism was the state religion in Sassanian Iran (AD 247–635), there were a variety of minority religions: Buddhism, Judaism, Christianity, Mandeans, and Manicheans. On the conversion of Constantine the Great to Christianity there was an urgent political need for a faith to unify the vast empire against Christian Rome and other threats. But it would be wrong to present the struggle between the various Iranian religions simply in political terms. From early times Iran has struggled with the problem of evil in the world, and this is the basic question for many of the movements. The Manicheans rejected matter as of evil origin, the Mandeans and Zoroastrians affirmed that life was the gift of God. The Zurvanites and Mithraists were similarly divided. Zoroastrianism may have been the official Sassanian religion, but beneath the surface of the orthodoxy and ritual of a state church theological differences continued.

The unity which prevailed may have been the result of the common threat of Islam. The Islamic Empire incorporated Iran in AD 635. After the fighting there seems to have been little organized persecution. Nevertheless to advance materially, one had to become a Muslim, and there were many defections. Zoroastrianism survived, however, locally, especially in Fars, and in the intellectually free atmosphere of the tenth century many books were written in defence of the Good Religion.

The situation in Iran became so difficult in time that groups of the faithful emigrated to India and there formed Zoroastrian communities, the Parsis or Persians, later centred mainly on Bombay. Although they are basically conservative, being subject to different influences the Parsis have been led to modify certain practices and beliefs. Their position at the present time is very difficult. Through hard work many are wealthy, but in a country with strong socialist tendencies this is not always an advantage. Their identity has been preserved largely through having their own schools, but these now have to admit non-Parsis. Quite what the future holds no one knows.

Not all the faithful Zoroastrians emigrated to India, however. Many remained behind, and although times have been hard small communities still exist, mainly in Yazd, Kerman and Tehran. They have been granted freedom of worship, and at the fire temples and shrines the ancient faith is still practised. Even some of the ostensibly Islamic shrines appear to be adaptations of Zoroastrianism, and the last shah used ancient Iranian titles. The position of Zoroastrians is still very difficult, however, scattered as they are, with few priests.

Influence of Iranian Religion

Despite the small number of practising Zoroastrians in the world today, just over 125,000 in India and according to a 1976 census 25,000 in Iran, Iranian religion, especially Zoroastrianism, has in fact played one of the major roles on the stage of world religious history.

Zoroaster was known and respected in Greece at the time of Plato, and the worship of Mithras spread throughout the Roman Empire as far as the north of England. Turning to the East, Iranian art and religion has long been a source of influence for India. Mithras worship spread from Iran to the Magas of India in the sixth century AD and after, but before that Zoroastrianism may well have stimulated the growth of a saviour concept in Buddhism, in the form of Maitreya Buddha. Iran has played a particularly important role in the religion of Islam, helping it to develop from an Arabian into an international religion; the growth of the mystical movement, the Sufis, and the saviour concept may owe something to Iranian influence. Perhaps Iran's greatest influence has been on the development of Judaeo-Christian belief. It is widely accepted by biblical scholars that the later Jewish concepts of the devil, hell, an afterlife, the resurrection, the end of the world and the saviour imagery were all coloured by Zoroastrianism, beliefs which, of course, have affected the very foundations of Christianity. Theologically as well as geographically, Iran, the bridge between East and West, has contributed immensely in the field of religion.

Chapter Thirteen

Hinduism

Hinduism is a vast subject and an elusive concept. To describe a religion which has a history of some 3,000 years (and perhaps many more), which is embraced by hundreds of millions today, a religion, moreover, without a defining creed, a group of exclusive adherents, or a centralized hierarchy, is to be put in the position of a blind man trying to describe an elephant. Even to define it is difficult. For the purposes of Hindu family law, the Republic of India defines a Hindu as an Indian (we must add, Pakistani, Nepali, Singhalese, etc.) who is not a Muslim, Christian, Parsi or Jew! For our purposes we should have also to exclude the Buddhist, the Jain and the Sikh. But this tells us only what Hinduism is not.

Positively, we might say that Hinduism is adherence to or worship of the gods Vishnu, or Shiva, or the goddess Shakti, or their incarnations, aspects, spouses, or progeny. We thus include the many adherents of the cults of Rama and Krishna (incarnations of Vishnu), Durga, Skanda, and Ganesha (the wife and sons of Shiva). We would, however, exclude Brahma and Surya, the Sun, who once had cults and temples of their own. We would exclude those few for whom the vedic heritage is the chief expression of religion, a heritage, however, which is strictly pre- or proto-Hindu. But most importantly we would exclude by this definition the great mass of persons who are unable to tell the census-takers whether they are Vaishnava or Shaivite, whose principal deities are the *gramadevatas,* goddesses of the locality, not to mention the followers of the purely tribal religions of the hill and jungle peoples in several parts of the Indo-Pakistan sub-continent.

Perhaps the best we can do is to follow the medieval philosopher who states that those teachings are righteous (*dharmika*) which do not obstruct the Veda, i.e. which do not deny the efficacy or the pre-eminence and eternity of those oldest of the Indian religious texts. Such a definition is sufficiently broad; for while the Veda is today little read and less followed, every Hindu pays it homage, and only those who explicitly deny it (Jains, Buddhists, Sikhs) are recognized as heterodox.

In any case, Hinduism comprises a multiplicity of cults and sects more or less closely affiliated with a high tradition. While the concepts and practices fostered by the high tradition influence and give to these cults and sects a recognizably Hindu shape, the high tradition itself is the end result of continental enrichment through the absorption of local and tribal gods, rites and philosophies. If we concentrate our attention on this high tradition, and especially on its custodians, the Brahmin priests and scholars, and their extensive literature, it becomes possible to write a connected account of Hinduism.

The Domestic Religion of the Aryan Invaders

In scattered pockets of eastern India live people speaking languages of the Munda or Austro-Asiatic family, comprising also some of the languages of South-East Asia and of Australia; in South India and parts of Central India and Pakistan, languages of the Dravidian family are spoken; and in the remainder, that is, all of India north of the Vindhya Mountains, and down the western side of the peninsula to Goa, the Indo-Aryan languages predominate, languages akin to Persian and those of Europe, including English.

The Munda contribution to Indian civilization and to Hinduism is entirely unknown, and, though it is not likely to have been great, it is probably substantial enough to repay the patient labours of linguists and anthropologists which will be required to elucidate it. By contrast the Dravidian contribution is certainly substantial, and the prospects of determining it are much brighter, thanks to the fact that four of the Dravidian languages have literatures, one of them, Tamil, going back almost 2,000 years. Nevertheless, Dravidian studies are still in their adolescence, and little can yet be said with certainty on the question of Dravidian elements in Hinduism. With the Aryans the case is different. Their contribution to the formation of Hinduism is enormous and in most cases obvious.

The Aryans invaded India during the movements of Indo-European-speaking peoples all over western Asia and parts of the Mediterranean region in the second millennium before Christ. They possessed several decisive military advantages over the indigenous inhabitants of the sub-continent: a superior bronze weaponry and, shortly, iron, and horse-drawn chariots with spoked wheels, thus lighter and swifter than the solid-wheeled, ox-drawn carts of the natives. They were altogether highly mobile and military in character, equipped to conquer and rule a cultivating population, and were themselves engaged in agriculture and the herding of cattle. In many respects the Indus Valley civilization which had preceded the Aryan was superior to it, and it was perhaps 1,500 years after its demise that India regained an urban civilization of comparable standard and scope; but more of the Indus Valley civilization later.

The *Rig Veda*

Somewhere between the years 1500 and 1200 BC, Aryan tribes invaded India, settled in the Punjab, and composed hymns which make up the *Rig Veda*. This is a document of inestimable historical importance. Not only is it the oldest work of literature in an Indo-European language, it is the oldest living religious literature of the world. Among Indo-European-speaking peoples the Indians are unique in adhering to a religion in direct descent from that of the parent culture, and their ancient religious literature, beginning with the *Rig Veda,* is astonishingly rich in contrast to the almost complete absence of surviving religious literature of ancient Greece and Rome.

The collection consists of 1,028 hymns to the vedic deities. Other collections (*samhitas*) were made to serve the needs of chanting (*Sama Veda*) or the manual operations of the sacrifice (*Yajur Veda*), in which the hymns played a vital role. While these secondary collections reproduce much of the Rig Vedic material, reorganized for their particular purposes, a fourth collection, the *Atharva Veda,* stands apart from the others in that it contains numerous spells and incantations for medicinal purposes, magical aids to victory in battle, and the like. The vedic collections are complemented by a series of works called Brahmanas (*c.* 800–600 BC), devoted to the explanation of the hymns, their ritual application, their mythology, and speculations on the mystic homologies between the macrocosm and the sacrifice itself. Vedic literature is completed by a third series of works, the Aranyakas (*c.* 600 BC) and Upanishads (*c.* 600–300 BC), which carry these speculations further, to the brink of monistic philosophy. Finally, a series of ancillary works, much of them now lost, provides the scientific stratum of vedic scholarship, all of them deriving from the sacrifice and its requirements: grammar, phonetics, metrics, astronomy, ritual, etc., the last comprising both the greater public sacrifices and the domestic ritual, out of which later grew a legal literature.

Although the Aryan domestic religion is served by only a fraction of the vedic literary corpus, it is more important to the Hinduism that emerges at the close of the vedic age than the great hieratic sacrificialism, or even the Upanishadic gnosis, that the bulk of this priestly literature presupposes. This domestic religion, in its essential outlines and even in some of its details, is recognizably akin to that of other Indo-European-speaking peoples, especially the early Greeks and Romans. And it is this Indo-European heritage, developed on Indian soil under Indian conditions, which is the part of vedic religion which survives today, in the marriage ceremony and the offerings to the dead.

Kindling the Sacred Fire

In the Aryan household there is a sacred fire, kindled at the time of the establishment of the household, that is, during the marriage ceremony. This is no ordinary fire: it must not be used for cooking and other mundane purposes; it must be fuelled with certain kinds of wood; it must be kindled in a special manner, by the rubbing of sticks; it must not be allowed to burn out. In this fire the householder must make daily offerings to the gods. He is, in fact, obliged to perform three times daily what is called the 'Five Great Sacrifices': the worship of Brahman, the world-spirit, which consists in the teaching or recitation of the Vedas; the worship of the fathers with offerings of food and water for their nourishment; the worship of the gods with burnt offerings; the worship of *bhutas* (living beings or

Left The burning ghats at Varanasi (Benares) on the River Ganges. Cremation is the prescribed method of disposing of the dead. Afterwards the ashes may be scattered in the river.

Below Ritual bathing in the Ganges at Varanasi. Thousands of Hindu pilgrims perform this act of purification in the sacred river each year.

Right Brahmin priests chant hymns at a vedic fire-ritual to ensure a good harvest.

Right A ritual performed before a pantheon of gods at a simple shrine of popular prints.

spirits), by scattering grain in the four directions and the centre, in the air and on the household utensils, and by placing food on the threshold for outcasts, animals, birds and insects; and the worship of men by extending hospitality to an Aryan, by preference a Brahmin learned in the Vedas.

By far the weightiest obligations the householder owes are those to the fathers, or ancestors. Not only must he make daily offerings of food and water to them, and to the house spirit which dwells in the northeast corner of the house, but he must offer them the *pinda*, rice-ball, on the new-moon day of every month.

The essential elements of this ceremony, called *shraddha*, are as follows. Learned Brahmins of unimpeachable character take their places on seats strewn with sacred grass in an open place. The householder opens (and closes) the ceremony with burnt offerings to the gods in the sacred fire; but the principal episode is the offering to the fathers. He forms three rice-balls and places them on a strewn carpet of sacred grass after having sprinkled the place with water; these go to his three deceased ascendants, father, grandfather and great-grandfather. He wipes the rice clinging to his hand on the grass; this is the offering to the three previous ascendants, great-great-grandfather, etc. He then pours a water libation on the ground near the *pindas;* this gratifies the more distant agnatic ancestors. He then divides the *pindas* among the Brahmin guests, who eat them, and the remainder of the *shraddha* mainly consists in a feast for the guests.

A Link with the Ancestors
The theory of the *shraddha* is that the living nourish the ancestors who dwell in the World of the Fathers with the offerings of rice-balls and water, while the ancestors confer blessings and benefits on their living descendants by conferring prosperity, progeny, and the like. Thus the *shraddha* is the point of meeting between the living and the dead, the expression of their interdependence. But this relationship may be inverted if the proper funeral rites are not performed for the deceased; for until installed in the World of the Fathers, the ghosts of the dead are liable to visit misery on the heads of descendants who do not nourish them with offerings or secure their passage to their proper sphere.

Thus shortly after death, the corpse is borne to the burning-ground in a procession of the relatives headed by the eldest son, the chief mourner and successor to the deceased householder. The corpse is cremated and the mourners circumambulate the pyre, not in the auspicious clockwise direction, but anti-clockwise. They then bathe and proceed homeward, led this time by the youngest son. On the third day after the cremation the bones are thrown into a river, preferably the Ganges on whose banks the burning ghats still have a brisk traffic, as they have had for thousands of years. For ten days libations of water and offerings of rice-balls and vessels of milk are made to the deceased. At this time, or on the completion of a year, the *sapindikarana* is performed, which makes the deceased a sharer of

Illustration page 195

the *pinda* with his or her ascendants in the monthly *shraddha*. It is believed that by this the ghost acquires a subtle body by which to make the journey to the World of the Fathers or, according to later thought, to another birth.

One did not accede to this domestic religion by the mere fact of the birth, nor were all the Aryan dead candidates for worship and entry into the World of the Fathers. When the deceased was a young child, an unmarried girl or an ascetic, the body was buried or cast into a river, not cremated, and no offerings were made. Initiation into full Aryanhood was required. For the boy, this was the conferring of the sacred thread and the *mantra;* for the girl, it was marriage; and the ascetic was regarded as having become dead to the world of the householder and his religion. The initiation was regarded as birth into the religious life, so that the upper castes who wore the sacred thread were called 'twice-born'.

Initiation

Initiation was one of a series of rites called *samskaras,* or what an anthropologist might term 'life-crisis rites'. Three of these took place before birth, to promote conception, procure a male child, and ensure the welfare of the foetus. Between the birth ceremony and the name-giving ceremony mother and child observed ten days of ritual impurity. Other stages in the child's development marked by such *samskaras* were the piercing of its ears, the first journey out of the house to see the sun, the first meal of solid food, and, in the case of a boy, the first tonsure, in which the head was shaved except for a tuft on the top which was to remain throughout his life.

Initiation was the next *samskara,* normally occurring when the boy was between eight and twelve years old. The nub of the ceremony was the investiture of the candidate, wearing the garments of an ascetic and holding a staff, with the sacred thread, placed over his left shoulder and slung under his right arm. The officiating priest communicated the Gayatri Mantra, a verse from the *Rig Veda,* which is used by upper-caste Hindus in all their rituals:

Tát Savitúr váreṇiaṃ	Let us think on the glorious
Bhárgo devásya dhīmahi,	splendour of the god Savitri,
Dhiyo yó naḥ pracodáyāt.	that he inspire our minds.

The initiate was then required to beg for alms and place himself under the tutelage of a learned Brahmin (his *guru*) for instruction in the sacred lore, chiefly the Vedas. The pupil had to show extreme deference to the *guru,* even greater than to his own parents, for while mother and father confer life, the *guru,* through his religious knowledge, confers immortality.

The student had to remain strictly celibate, constantly to guard against falling into ritual impurity, and to subordinate himself to his *guru's* every dictate while following a course of study which, for a Brahmin, might last twelve years or longer. Its end was marked by a ritual bath. The Aryan was then expected to marry immediately.

Life-long celibacy played no part in early Aryan religious conceptions, and indeed was repugnant to them. To permit celibacy would be to destroy the cult of the ancestors; denied nourishment, the fathers would wreak their vengeance on the living. Thus in a later time, when asceticism had become widespread and had gained admission into Aryan religious ideas, the life cycle was expressed as a series of four stages: student, householder, forest hermit and wandering ascetic, of which only the first two were incumbent on all the twice-born, a compromise between two conflicting modes of life. It was further laid down that people were born with three debts: to the gods, to the fathers, and to the sages, which they must acquit before abandoning the world for asceticism. These were satisfied by recitation of the Veda, procreation of a son, and performance of sacrifice; thus in theory at least one could only become an ascetic after having been a married householder.

The Marriage Laws

Not only did the cult of the ancestors require a man to marry and beget a son to continue the cult and offer up the *pinda* for his soul's repose, but it required marriage in its own right. There is no reason to think that only the married man could perform the *shraddha* for the ancestors, and on becoming a widower he relinquished his headship of the family and priesthood of its sacred fire to his son, and went into retirement.

He could not marry at random; for only a wife of equal birth, that is, coming from an Aryan family in which the initiation and other rites were performed, could participate in the domestic rituals without defilement, and give birth to an untainted son, competent to perpetuate the worship of the ancestors. Moreover, the prospective bridegroom had to seek a bride who was unrelated to him on his father's or mother's side, someone, that is, whose family did not offer the *pinda* and water oblations to any of his ancestors. The bride, then, must be a stranger; but, equally, she must be initiated into the bridegroom's family to take part in its religion and give birth to its son, and cease to be a member of her family of birth.

The wedding ceremony symbolizes this conception of marriage as gift, sacrament and initiation. The bridegroom and his party travel in procession to the bride's house, where they are received hospitably by the bride's father. The couple is seated in a temporary pavilion, either side of a small curtain, which is then removed, to the accompaniment of sacred verses murmured by the officiating priest. The bride's father then formally gives his daughter to the groom; the couple clasp hands and offer grain in the sacred fire; they circumambulate the fire with the ends of their garments knotted together; and they take seven steps together, and are sprinkled with holy water. Further rites take place after the couple's recession to the groom's home, and the marriage is consummated. The funeral rites, already described, complete the series of *samskaras*.

Hindu Family Law

Certain fundamental characteristics of Hindu family law are traceable to this domestic religion. The head of the household was the priest of its religion, that is, its ancestor-cult; and inheritance of his property devolved upon those competent to make offerings to him and his ancestors after his death, his married sons in the first instance. Failing descendants in the male line, inheritance would fall to those who offered the *pinda* to one or more of the ancestors the deceased had also offered to, that is, a *sapinda* or sharer of the *pinda,* because inheritance carried with it the obligation to make offering to the deceased.

A daughter, for that reason, could not inherit, since only males could perform the *shraddha,* but a man without sons could adopt one who thereby severed his links with his natural father, or appoint a daughter, if he had one, to beget a grandson who would become his heir. One could not serve two domestic fires, worship two sets of ancestors, inherit from two different families. Thus the bride, the adopted son, and the son of the appointed daughter lost membership and rights in their natal family, and became members and acquired rights in their adoptive one.

The Aryan domestic religion, heavily Brahminized and in an attenuated form, is still widely followed in India by the upper castes. Many of the minor *samskaras* have fallen into disuse, and regular *shraddha* offerings are rare; the theory of the ancestor-cult and passage to the World of the Fathers has been qualified, in fact superseded, by the doctrine of the reincarnation of the souls of the dead. But the main features of this religion remain; the caste system has, if anything, intensified the Aryan concern for ritual purity and the measures one must take to secure and retain it; and its legal implications have until recently governed Hindu inheritance and adoption.

The Vedic Religion of Sacrifice

An early Aryan analysis of society divides it into the four estates (or *varna*) of *brahmin* (priest), *kshatriya* (warrior, king), *vaishya* (merchant class), and *shudra* (serf), of which the first three take the initiation and are thus called twice-born. The word *varna* or 'colour' has been held to signify that this functional division has a racial basis, at least in so far as the lighter, twice-born Aryans were distinguished from the darker native population, some of whom the Aryans made their serfs. A similar functional division of society by their Iranian cousins suggests that from the start the Indo-Aryans had a priesthood and forms of sacrifice which were in its special care and custody, beyond the domestic rituals.

The religion of the bulk of vedic literature is priestly and public, not domestic, and the objects of its worship are not the deified Fathers but the *devas,* radiant celestial gods, the word for whom is cognate with Latin *deus.* Some of them derive from Indo-European antiquity. One such is the Sky Father, Dyaus Pitar (Greek Zeus Pater, Latin Jupiter). These deities are mainly connected with the heavens and meteorological phenomena, and almost all are male. Exceptions are the Earth Mother and her daughter Dawn (Ushas, Greek Eos), both Indo-European, and a handful of others; but the relative absence of goddesses in the vedic pantheon is one of the more striking differences between its religion and the Hinduism of later times.

By the time of the *Rig Veda* the figure of the Sky Father was fading and his place had been taken by the vedic god *par excellence,* Indra. Indra is pre-eminently a war-god, a king of the gods and their leader in battle. He destroys the fortified cities of the aborigines, recalling the experience of the Aryan warriors during the conquest of the Punjab. Like his human counterparts, Indra is given to feasting and drunken rowdiness. He rides the sky at the head of his host, the *maruts,* lesser storm-gods, and in this is especially connected with lightning, his weapon, with which he ripped open the belly of the dragon Vritra, releasing the life-giving rains.

Illustration page 205

Solar deities abound. Surya, whose name is the common word for 'sun', drives a fiery, one-wheeled chariot drawn by seven horses across the sky. Vishnu is a minor deity with solar characteristics, destined to become one of the two major deities of later Hinduism; the vedic Vishnu is a dwarf who traverses the universe in three giant strides, to the delight of the gods and the vexation of the demons.

Illustration page 205

Agni, the fire, was the axis between the world of men and the world of the gods; he conveyed the burnt offering to the gods. He dwelt hidden in many places, affording an object for proto-philosophical speculation: in the waters of the sky, appearing as lightning; in the fire-sticks, his parents, with which the sacred fire was kindled, and elsewhere.

Illustration page 205

As custodians of the sacrifice, the Brahmins were especially fond of Agni, but more particularly theirs was Soma (Iranian *haoma*), the apotheosis of an inebriating drink prepared from the juice of an unidentified plant, but probably like cannabis or some other narcotic. The preparation of *soma* was elaborately ritualized, and the special character of this god in relation to the Brahmins, who called Soma their king, was marked by the devotion of an entire book of the *Rig Veda* to hymns to this deity. Later, Soma was identified with the moon and acquired the lunar jurisdiction over the growth and health of crops and foetuses.

Varuna and Mitra

Two other gods of Indo-Iranian, if not Indo-European provenance were Varuna and Mitra. Both, like so many of the Vedic deities, had solar associations. One of Mitra's chief offices was to guarantee oaths and compacts; his Iranian counterpart survived Zoroaster's reform of Iranian religion and was worshipped in the Roman Empire in Christian times as Mithras. Varuna was known as an *asura,* (originally a class of deities, but later demons opposed to the *devas*), a term which in its Iranian form is the first part of the name of Zoroastrianism's god of light, Ahura Mazda. Varuna is perhaps older than Indra, and like Dyaus is upstaged by the boisterous war-god in the *Rig Veda,* but the highly ethical character of Varuna is much in advance of the amoral Indra. Varuna is the guardian of *Rita,* the physical and moral order of the universe, without which the seasons would not follow in due succession and the fabric of society would fall apart. Varuna is omniscient; his ubiquitous spies report to him the conduct of men and women; wherever two are gathered together, Varuna is present as the third. The hardy, optimistic vedic warrior adopts a different stance before Varuna than before any other of his gods, the stance of the penitent sinner begging deliverance from Varuna's just wrath.

The vedic pantheon abounds in lesser divinities too numerous even to list. Two others are of some general interest, Yama, the first mortal, who guards the World of the Fathers with his brindled dogs, and Rudra, a god to be feared since his arrows bring disease, and to be supplicated since in his inverse aspect he is a god of healing herbs. As Shiva, the propitious, he was the vedic contribution to the personality of the great deity of Hinduism, though his role in the Veda, like that of Vishnu, was minor.

The Royal Sacrifices

The sacrifices were many and varied. The grandest were the royal sacrifices: the *Rajasuya,* the *Vajapeya* and the *Ashvamedha.* The first was a royal consecration, the high-point of which consisted of sprinkling the king's head with water and other spiritually potent fluids. The 'Drink of Strength' (*Vajapeya*) was a kind of rejuvenating ceremony which included a sham chariot race and an 'ascent to heaven' up a ladder by the king and queen. The 'Horse Sacrifice' (*Ashvamedha*) is of special interest for its long survival in Indian history and its political implications. A consecrated stallion in the company of 100 other stallions and a bodyguard of mounted warriors, was set free to wander at will for a year. The princes in whose territory it wandered attempted to capture or kill it, thus subjecting the sacrificer to unpleasant divine retribution, or were obliged to submit to his overlordship. At the end of the year the horse was sacrificed and passed on its accumulated potency to the queen, thus securing the health and prosperity of the kingdom and the ruling family.

There were besides less costly and ambitious sacrifices open to the patronage of the Aryan householder. These rites had several common features. The householder who paid for the sacrifice and received its benefits was the sacrificer, and he and his wife had an essential role to play, however minimal, as compared to the role of the Brahmin technicians of the sacrifice. The required priestly corps increased as the rites themselves became more complex. The *Rig Veda* contemplates eight priests, including the sacrificer; sixteen or seventeen are required in later times. The sacrifice begins with a consecration of the sacrificer, lifting him from the profane to the sacred sphere, a sphere charged with danger for those not ritually insulated, and ending with a deconsecration for the descent from the sacred.

The sacrifice itself takes place round a sacred fire kindled on a specially constructed brick altar out in the open; the only associated buildings are at most temporary affairs, not temples. The materials offered may be milk, ghee, various vegetable substances, wine, and the flesh of animals, including, at this early date, cattle. The benefits derived may be many. Typically the sacrificer is promised gold, cattle, long life, the birth of sons, immortality, but it is essential that the priests be properly fed and paid.

The Gods Join the Feast

The original theory of the sacrifice was no doubt the one of simple reciprocity which underlay the offerings to the ancestors as well. When it was properly performed, the gods descended to the sacrificial field where, invisibly seated on the sacred straw, they joined the sacrificial feast as honoured guests, nourished by the oblations which Agni consumed; or, in a later formulation, men 'pour upwards' by pouring on the fire the offering which Agni conveys to the gods while the gods 'pour downwards' the rain on which agriculture and thus human life depends. Guilt-offerings, thanks-offerings and propitiation were rare or absent, and the vedic literature has little place for direct, spontaneous prayer.

As the sacrifice evolved and Brahmin dominance over it increased, sacrificial theory was elaborated and extended in novel ways. The hymns and other formulae were regarded as possessing a magic power, *brahman,* which was also viewed as a pervasive, neuter spiritual force sustaining the universe, a derivative of which is Brahmin (*brahmana*), the priest-magician who has mastery of sacred utterance. The efficacy of the sacrifice was purchased by the exact recitation of the formulae. The emphasis on the role of speech led to minute phonological analysis and, ultimately, to the earliest grammatical science of the ancient world, with an analytical penetration unsurpassed until modern times.

Illustration page 196

The elements of the sacrifice were speculatively identified with the parts of the cosmos, and the sacrifice itself was regarded as a re-enactment of creation, playing an indispensable role in the sustaining of the cosmos and preservation of its order. The simple reciprocity of early sacrificial theory yields to the notion that precision of performance compels results; the simple objects of the earlier sacrifice yield to the claim that the whole universe and its moral order depend upon the sacrifice.

'The Trembling Ones'

The vedic poets composed under inspiration; they are sometimes called 'the trembling ones', and their visions were gained by inward mental concentration. Their compositions are intricate in style, and in language and form archaic: an esoteric literature, tortuous and, after more than a century of modern vedic scholarship, still imperfectly understood. Most of the hymns are in praise of the gods, but several speculative hymns, precursors of Indian philosophy, centre upon the problem of cosmogony.

The oldest cosmogonical myth in the Veda is the Indo-European one of the union of the Sky Father with the Earth Mother to produce the *devas;* but the prevailing myth in the *Rig Veda* is that of Indra and Vritra. According to this myth, previous to the creation there was no *Sat* (Real) or *Asat* (Unreal), no *Rita,* no separation of Sky and Earth. There were only beings called *asuras,* in two classes: those led by Varuna, the *adityas* (whose name signified release and burgeoning), locked in warfare with the other class, *danavas* (signifying bondage, inertia), under the leadership of Vritra (whose name, a 'covering' or 'lid', evokes a similar sense). The *adityas* arranged the birth of a champion, Indra, apparently from Mother Earth and Father Sky, and made him their king. Fortified by draughts of the intoxicating *soma* and armed with the thunderbolt forged by Tvashtri the Artificer, Indra slew Vritra. Out of the burst belly of Vritra flowed seven streams pregnant with the embryonic Sun; thus the life-sustaining elements of moisture, heat and light were won. The earth, the abode of men, was spread out; sky, the sphere of the gods, was secured and supported above it. Indra separated the hemisphere of the *Sat* (earth and sky) from that of the *Asat* (the nether world). Order was established in the one and the demons were confined to the lower world of chaos. The sun's course was set; the heavenly waters sent rain to earth; the *adityas* were assigned their functions; and Varuna oversaw the cosmic order.

Indra is Supplanted

The Indra-Vritra myth was certainly old in Rig Vedic times, probably traceable to the period of Indo-Iranian unity, since the Persians knew a 'Slayer of Verethra', and perhaps earlier: Indra himself is invoked by a Mitanni ruler in a treaty dating from the fourteenth century BC, from the Middle East. In the later *Rig Veda* scoffers appear, who say, 'Indra is not! Who ever saw him? Who is he that we should praise him?'

Against this background of decaying faith in Indra the search for the cosmogonic agent is pressed further. Indra is supplanted variously by Prajapati, Lord of Creatures; Vishvakarman, the All-Maker; Brahmanaspati, Master of the Magic Potency Which Sustains the Universe; and Vach, the Word. In a very important hymn the creation is attributed to the sacrifice by the Primeval Man (Purusha) of himself, by the dismemberment of his own body. From his head sprang the Brahmins, from his shoulders, the warriors, from his thighs the merchant class, and from his feet the servile *shudras,* thus fixing the functions and rank of the four estates; in this way the animals, earth, air and sky, moon and sun, the hymns, chants, metres, and prose formulae, and Indra, Agni and Vayu (Wind) were also created.

The most penetrating speculations of the *Rig Veda,* however, are those which posit some neuter principle, such as the One Real (Ekam Sat) which, we are told, is variously called Indra, Mitra, Varuna, Agni, etc., as much as to say the gods are phenomenal aspects of the Absolute. Elsewhere creation is attributed to That One (Tad Ekam), who presides over the universe and who is known only through the insight of saints, not from tradition or the gods; indeed the poet is

Left The sun-god, Surya, driving his chariot, from a Bundi painting of the eighteenth century. Victoria and Albert Museum, London.

Below left Agni, the god of fire (left), and Indra (right) from a South Indian wood carving. These two were rivals for popularity in the early pantheon. Agni is accompanied by a ram. His two heads symbolize domestic and sacrificial fires. Musée Guimet, Paris.

Below Shiva Lingobhava, a tenth-century granite carving from Chola, South India. The *lingam*, an ancient fertility symbol, has long been associated with Shiva and is the most popular representation of him. This shows the anthropomorphic image inside the symbol and depicts the myth in which Shiva reveals to Brahma (top) and Vishnu (bottom) that he is the origin of both. British Museum, London.

Above Angkor Wat in Kampuchea, the sanctuary of the god Vishnu and the mortuary chamber of its royal founder. This twelfth-century temple is the masterpiece in a series of large-scale Hindu structures built by the kings of ancient Cambodia.

Right The temple complex at Bhuvaneshvara in Orissa, eastern India, seen across the sacred pool. Once a year, an image of the god Shiva is immersed in the water.

Above A mother goddess from Bengal (*c.* second century BC). Such fertility figures are still the primary objects of worship for many peasants. Victoria and Albert Museum, London.

Above left The 'prototype Shiva' figure on a seal from the Indus Valley settlement at Mohenjo-Daro, Pakistan, seated in a yoga position and surrounded by animals (*c.* 2500–1800 BC).

Left Eighth-century shore temples at Mahabalipuram: examples of pyramidal South Indian temple-towers capped by octagonal roof forms.

Above A holy man rests in a yoga pose within the great Shiva temple at Kanchipuram in Tamil Nadu. Built in AD 1509, it claims a hall of a thousand pillars (really 540).

Right Mortification of the flesh at the festival of Thiapusam. As a form of penance, this man has embedded a pattern of small barbed hooks in his torso.

unsure whether this deity himself knows the facts about the creation. Thus a true monism is achieved by the close of the period of Rig Vedic composition. Later texts carry on the search for the single principle underlying the universe.

Religions of Gnosis and Release

The problem of death is the beginning of philosophy. The highest felicity which the vedic Aryan had sought through his sacrificial religion was a place for his soul among the blessed dead in the World of the Fathers at the top of the sky. In the Brahmana literature, that stratum which immediately follows the four collections (*Rig Veda, Sama Veda, Yajur Veda, Atharva Veda*) and precedes the Aranyakas and Upanishads the idea of redeath appears. The nagging conviction that the soul's repose in heaven was not guaranteed seems to have been the source of much fruitful speculation in the early Upanishads.

It is in the Upanishads that we first find three related doctrines of capital importance for all later Indian religious history: the doctrine that the soul repeatedly dies and is reborn embodied in a new organism (*samsara*), that one bears the effects of one's deeds in this or a future life (*karma*), and that there is an escape from the weary round of redeath and rebirth (*moksha, nirvana*).

The classic doctrines are not unequivocally formulated or systematically expounded in the Upanishads. The enduring charm of that literature derives from its very lack of system, in contrast to subsequent philosophical literature. In the early Upanishads, we find a bold, speculative urge to try out new and unheard-of ideas without much concern for rigorous verification or fixing their interrelations. Some of these ideas are put in the mouths of vividly-drawn characters, and it is significant that not all of those who teach the new ideas are Brahmins. Parables and metaphors are freely employed. Although the philosophy of these works is still in a formative, experimental stage, they later came to be regarded as the canon upon which it was the business of philosphers to comment, interpreting them in such a way as to lend authority to one philosophical system or another.

The Gods Must Die

The three doctrines mentioned illustrate well the new direction which Indian religion was taking in this period. The vedic Aryan had hoped for material blessings in this life, and heaven after death, but now it appeared that the very gods must die and be reborn again and again, and that one's birth as a god, Brahmin, ordinary man, animal or vegetable is contingent upon the virtue or sin acquired by one's deeds in a previous incarnation. The universe so conceived is strictly just and impartial, and the individual is solely responsible for his or her destiny through the ethical choices which determine it.

There is here the possibility of an activist and individualistic response, but on the whole this has not been the result. The weal or woe of life are the end product of deeds done in a previous life, as unchangeable as they are inescapable. So vast is the time scale through which the individual soul travels from birth to birth, so heavy are the odds against escape, that one must take radical steps to gain release – casting off all worldly entanglements for a life of ascetic meditation. Only to the ascetic is a kind of activism and individualism open, and that activism is paradoxically quietism.

The possibility of release arises from the doctrines of the identity of the inmost self or soul (*atman*) with the Absolute (*Brahman,* neuter). This relationship is variously expressed in the 'Great Utterances' of the Upanishads: 'I am Brahman'; 'That (*Brahman*) art Thou'; the Absolute is characterized as 'Not this, nor that', i.e. it is incommensurate with any element of the phenomenal world. The means by which release from transmigration and reunion of the soul with Brahman may be achieved are also various in the Upanishads, but the constant requisite is knowledge of the relation itself. In some passages this knowledge is sufficient and it is a closely-guarded secret; in others, meditation, ascetic abstention, and good conduct are added qualifications.

Wandering Ascetics

The *Rig Veda* speaks of 'the silent ones' and 'the long-haired ones', and the inward concentration by which the vedic poet attains his vision no doubt is a paradigm of the ascetic search for gnosis, but the ascetic is a very minor religious type in the early vedic period. In subsequent times we hear increasingly of *shramanas,* wandering ascetic teachers, a term which comprehends the founders of Jainism, Buddhism and other heterodox sects; and when the grammarian Patanjali describes Brahmins and *shramanas* as natural enemies like the snake and the mongoose, it seems likely that asceticism developed outside the Brahmin vedic tradition, and may even be originally non-Aryan.

From the time of the Upanishads asceticism emerges as the highest form of the religious life. Where the vedic Brahmins had held that the performance of the sacrifice sustained the cosmic order, Indians of a later day ascribed the stablility of the universe to Shiva's eternal penances in his Himalayan fastness. The powers generated by penances were thought to be so great that the gods in jealousy and fear sent celestial damsels to seduce the ascetic from his meditation and cause him to expend his accumulated potency. The virtue of a great ascetic could protect a city from an enemy, so that it was fruitless to give battle until the ascetic had been corrupted by some stratagem or other. Ascetic penances were sometimes severe in the extreme – lying between fires, staring at the sun, standing one-legged or in other awkward postures for great lengths of time.

These profound changes in Indian religious life, from the time of the Upanishads through the lifetime of the founders of Buddhism and Jainism (around 500 BC), cannot have been unrelated to the equally profound changes which North Indian society was undergoing. With the waning of the power and the prestige of the old vedic Kuru and Panchala tribes of the Delhi region, there grew up powerful kingdoms along the Ganges in the modern states of Uttar Pradesh and Bihar, kingdoms ruled by non-vedic Aryans or perhaps even non-Aryans, only lightly Brahmanized, if at all. The tribal kingdom was giving way to the territorial state, incorporating indigenous non-Aryan populations.

The ancient vedic aristocracy decayed, as upstarts without pedigree established successful kingdoms with aggressive territorial ambitions; cities made their reappearance on the sub-continent; the introduction of coinage led to the creation of fortunes by merchants and bankers out of all proportion to the rank to which their birth assigned them, according to the notion of the four estates. The profound feeling of insecurity which these changes wrought on large sections of the population are eloquently expressed by a king quoted in the Upanishads:

'[The great kings and heroes of the past] have abandoned their glory and passed to the next world. . . . The oceans dry up, the mountain-tops fall, the Pole Star trembles, the stars are loosened, the earth founders, the gods leave their stations. . . . In this flux, I am like a frog in a dry well.'

Many Time Schemes

Of the countless ascetic movements of this age, two have survived, Jainism and Buddhism, discussed elsewhere in this volume. In the times of their founders the classic doctrines of transmigration, retribution and release, which were in their formative period in the Upanishads, had become axioms upon which to build a philosophy, no longer subject to doubt. A further axiom common to all subsequent systems was that time is cyclic, that the universe undergoes growth, decline, destruction and re-creation endlessly. One variety of the many time-schemes may be found in the *Laws of Manu*. The four succeeding ages through which the quality of life, morality and religion decline are respectively 4000, 3000, 2000 and 1000 years long, each preceded and followed by a 'dawn' and a 'twilight' of as many hundreds, 12,000 years in all, at the end of which the world is destroyed and reconstituted. But the entire period is only one age of the gods, a thousand of which make a day of Brahma, the creator, whose night is of equal duration. The exact computation is of little significance; the point is that time dwarfs the human scale, and that by the time the doctrine is formulated, humanity is well into the Iron Age.

Another fundamental principle common to the ascetic movements, one antithetically opposed to vedic notions and only faintly represented in the Upanishads, is that of *ahimsa* or non-violence. The idea that the taking of animal or human life under any circumstances is sinful and results in rebirth as a lower organism can play no role in a religion based on sacrifice. On the contrary, it is especially strongly associated with the explicitly anti-sacrificial, anti-vedic ascetic movements, Jainism above all. Since in an extreme view all action, good or bad, leads to entanglement in the web of *samsara,* these movements tend to quietism and non-violence. The legacy of this doctrine has been the very widespread vegetarianism of India; the cow's special

For the role of ahimsa in Jainism, see page 248.

inviolability is first evident in this period, the vedic Aryans having used the cow to feast their guests and sacrifice to their gods.

The Origins of Hinduism

If we compare the Hinduism of the past two thousand years with the religion of the early Indo-Aryans as it can be known from the Vedas, the contrasts are dramatic. Where the Hindu worships an iconic representative of the deity whom he or she chooses to regard as supreme, the vedic Aryan had no icons and no personal relationship to a single supreme deity. Where the Hindus worship in a temple, vedic religion centred about the sacred fire, in the domestic hearth or on the brick out-of-doors altar. The Hindu makes offerings of goods and praise, in a spirit of loving devotion, hoping for acts of grace which mitigate or even transcend the harsh justice of the doctrine of retribution (*karma*), whereas the vedic Aryan looked upon his offerings as (at first) the fulfilment of his end of a cosmic partnership between himself and his gods and ancestors, or (later) as a means of compelling the gods to grant his wishes.

Illustrations pages 206, 207

For an explanation of the law of karma, see pages 245–6.

The Aryan pantheon was, with few exceptions, entirely male and preponderantly celestial; the Hindu pantheon adds mother-goddesses, earth-goddesses, theromorphic divinities such as cobras, and tree-spirits. The Vedas revile worshippers of the phallus, whereas the worship of Shiva in the form of a stone *lingam* has long been widespread. One may even descend to smaller matters: the vedic gods ride horse-drawn chariots, the Hindu gods ride mounted on the beasts peculiar to them.

Illustration page 196

Illustration page 205

These differences serve to distinguish Hinduism from what precedes it, which it is customary to call Brahmanism (not forgetting Jainism, Buddhism and other non-Brahmin movements); they also call for explanation.

Failing to find sufficient explanation of the origins of these novelties in the vedic literature, or in foreign influence due, for example, to the presence of Asiatic Greeks who ruled northwest India in the second century BC, we look to the countryside, where 80 per cent of Indians live today, a percentage which cannot have been smaller in earlier times. Here millions of peasants follow what might be called 'country Hinduism', a collection of cults which bear little or no relation to the Veda. The popular worship of snakes and tree-spirits is attested in early Buddhist art as in country Hinduism. For the great majority of peasants the most important deity is not Vishnu or Shiva, but the village goddess (*gramadevata*), often called Earth-Goddess or Mother, significantly always feminine, who presides over fertility of vegetable and animal life, and over pestilence and disease as well. To the peasant, petitionary prayer and propitiation come naturally. The shrines and cults of these purely local deities, whose parochialism dissolves into vastly-dispersed general types, are often attended by non-Brahmin, even low-caste priests.

Country Hinduism

The silence of early Indian religious literature on country Hinduism is no proof that it was not in existence from earliest times. It is important to remember that this literature is Brahmanical, which is to say, priestly, or ascetic. It is significant that the Aryan cult of the ancestors and its accompanying life-crisis rites, the direct source of what we can call domestic Aryan Hinduism, only achieves literary expression at a later stage, when it has fallen under Brahmin domination, though its origins go back to the period of Indo-European unity. It is significant too that though some Brahmins eventually became temple priests, they are often regarded as inferior to other sorts of Brahmins, and *The Laws of Manu* forbids their presence at the funeral feast.

We are warranted then in believing that idols, temples and the like are un-Aryan or at least un-Brahmin contributions to Hinduism, and in the silence of the texts we are further free to hypothesize that country Hinduism has always been practised, long before it became Brahmanized and thus achieved a literature; free, be it noted, in the sense that we have no facts to dispute this view – or support it. We may even consider that India was Hindu long before the arrival of the Aryans.

Before the Aryan invasions India had possessed the most widely dispersed urban civilization the world had yet known, the Indus Valley civilization, lasting a good five hundred years from about 2300 to 1800 BC. As at present known the cities of this civilization were strung along the River Indus in Pakistan, reaching into Indian Rajasthan, the Punjab, and as far east as the Upper Ganges-Jumna Doab, and spreading either side of the mouths of the Indus along the Makran coast to the west and Gujarat to the south; a thousand miles separate the most distant sites. These cities, with their baked-brick houses and citadels, grid-iron pattern of streets and elaborate drainage systems were marvels of the antique world, and their material civilization, except in respect of military technology and metallurgy, was much superior to that of the Aryans who arrived after their demise (if they did not cause it).

Male and Female Gods of the Indus Valley

Sir John Marshall, one of the excavators of Mohenjo-Daro in Sindh (which with Harappa in the Punjab is one of the largest Indus cities), has excellently formulated the argument for an Indus contribution to later Hinduism, or even an Indus Hinduism, and we cannot do better than to summarize his theory.

The evidence consists of steatite seals and figurines of various materials – though some of the buildings revealed by excavation are thought to have been shrines or temples, none contained images. First comes 'The Great Mother Goddess', some representations being pregnant female figurines, the majority being nude female figures with high collars and headdresses. They are of the same class as female figures found in the peasant cultures of the Baluchistan foothills which preceded and co-existed with the Indus civilization, and also with similar figures distributed all over Neolithic western Asia to the

Illustration page 207

Aegean. Next comes 'The Male God', 'recognisable at once as a prototype of the historic Siva', seated with the soles of his feet touching (a yoga posture), ithyphallic (recalling the *lingam* cult), surrounded by animals (depicting Shiva's epithet, 'Lord of Beasts'). Stone representations of phallus and vulva abound, either in conventionalized or realistic form, which point to the cult of the *lingam* and *yoni* of Shiva and his spouse, and non-phallic stones may be connected with the historic *shalagrama* stone, a device of Vishnu. The worship of trees, snakes, and bulls (i.e. the bull of Shiva), though not the cow, suggests continuity with the Hinduism of historic times, and ideas of ritual pollution and purification by water may be implied in the existence of a great bath, and may explain Hindu concepts of pollution.

This attractive hypothesis would account for the existence in Hinduism of the non-vedic cults centring on the figures of Shiva and the great goddess, both in her rustic version as Earth Goddess and her Tantric version as Shakti, Shiva's spouse. But it must be remembered that there remains a 1500-year silence in the archaeological and literary record between the end of the Indus civilization and the evidence of the emergence (or re-emergence) of these cults in Hinduism. Since its systematic excavation in the 1920s, the Indus civilization has added a whole new chapter to Indian history, but it is still too early to be certain how that chapter fits in with what follows. It is up to archaeology, which raised the problem in the first place, to solve it.

Philosophy, Mythology and Ethics

Three important features of Hinduism give it a distinctive shape and consistency: the six *Darshanas* or systems at the intellectual level; the Epics and *Puranas,* in respect of legend and mythology; and the caste system, in the area of day-to-day behaviour.

The *Darshanas* are doctrinal systems which, each in their own way, lead to release from the fetters of earthly existence. There are six of them, in complementary pairs: Nyaya and Vaisheshika, Sankhya and Yoga, Mimamsa and Vedanta. Nyaya is a school of logic and epistemology. Vaisheshika teaches that nature consists of eternal atoms distinct from the soul, by knowledge of which the soul can achieve release. Sankhya opposes matter (*prakriti*) to soul (*purusha*). As in Jainism the individual souls are infinite and discrete, and salvation consists in recovery of the soul's original purity in isolation from matter. Sankhya's doctrine of the three *gunas* or constituent characteristics, causing goodness (*sattva*), passion (*rajas*) and lethargy (*tamas*) in things and beings, is very influential in many departments of Indian thought.

Yoga has a similar metaphysics with the addition of Ishvara, an exalted and remote deity forever beyond the bonds of matter. The discipline of a *yogi* leads from the practice of an austere moral code through postures conducive to meditation and the control of breath to absorbed meditation. The Yoga known to western enthusiasts is a late elaboration of these early practices, with heavy emphasis on more difficult physical postures (Hatha Yoga) and a physiological theory according to which the *yogi* in meditation seeks to raise the *kundalini*. This is a spiritual force conceived as a dormant snake lying coiled at the base of the spine, up the central vein (*sushumna*) which lies in the vertebral column, through six 'circles' of psychic power along the column to the 'lotus' at the top of the head, by accomplishing which he wins salvation (Laya Yoga).

Mimamsa stands apart from the others in that it is a school of vedic exegesis, a perpetuation of Brahmanical sacrificialism. Vedanta is the most important of the six, constituting the central Hindu philosophical tradition to this day. Its greatest expositor was the South Indian philosopher Shankara (*c.* 788-820), who crystalized the monistic tendency of the Upanishads into a system which treats the soul as an aspect of the impersonal Absolute (Brahman) and the world as illusion or trickery (*maya*), from knowledge of which the soul may realize its identity with the Absolute. Several of these systems, especially Sankhya and Yoga, originated outside the vedic tradition, and at a very early time; they may well have been allied to the *shramana* movement.

Hindu Poetry and Myth

The great mythological works of Hinduism are the Epics, namely the *Mahabharata* (a heroic poem in 100,000 couplets describing the fratricidal conflict of the Pandavas and Kauravas, rulers of the Delhi region in vedic times) and the *Ramayana* (a lengthy poem on the deeds of King Rama of Ayodhya) and the compendia of creation myths, king lists, legends and religious doctrines called *Puranas* (Antiquities). These are non-sectarian, composite works in which rival deities and dogmas mingle easily; they are common property of all Hindus, in which each may find a chosen deity and preferred mode of achieving salvation. Though written in Sanskrit, and therefore in the special custody of the Brahmins, their language is of a more popular variety, and their contents bespeak the Brahminization of popular religions.

A chaste, even ascetic, ethical code is a prerequisite of all the systems of salvation, and of most of the Hindu sects, though in that the religions seeking release from the world strive for a state in which conventional distinctions between good and evil are resolved, ethics play the role of a prelude or first movement in the religious life. In the day-to-day life of the Hindu, on the other hand, ethics are of the first importance, and to a large extent may be reduced to the avoidance of pollution.

By the beginning of the Christian era, and probably considerably earlier, Indian society had come to consist of thousands of castes which placed restrictions on dining, drinking, marrying, fraternizing, and later, smoking with the members of other castes. Breach of such rules brings pollution, for which a penance is required by way of purification; in extreme cases, the offender may be excommunicated. Even pollution unwittingly incurred must be remedied, and one becomes polluted willy-nilly in some unavoidable circumstances, such as a family death. The caste system, which ranks castes according

Illustrations pages 195, 208

to inherent purity and susceptibility to pollution, from the various sorts of Brahmins to the untouchables at the bottom of the scale, and regulates the duties of each, has given to Hinduism and to Indian society its durability, its conservatism and its acceptance of the peculiarities of other groups.

Hindu Sects

The Hindu sects rise like small islands, giving structural relief to the vast ocean of Hinduism. Proportionally few Hindus are members of a sect; it is not necessary to belong to one to make offering to the village deities, to bathe at places of pilgrimage or to worship in temples. But because they are more amenable to historical study than the Epics and *Puranas,* for instance, and because, from their appearance in the last centuries before Christ, they are an important part of the development of Hinduism, we must trace their rise.

Sectarian Hindus may be identified by the marks they bear. If they are Vaishnava (devotees of Vishnu), they have two parallel marks of a special white earth drawn from the hair-line to the bridge of the nose, with a perpendicular connecting line at the bottom, and some additional mark distinctive of the particular sect added; also they will typically have a necklace and rosary, the beads of which are made of the *tulasi* shrub, sacred to Vishnu. If they are Shaiva (devotees of Shiva), they bear three parallel horizontal lines of ash on their foreheads. A Hindu joins a sect by undergoing initiation, the crucial element of which is the communication of the sacred formula (*mantra*) of the sect to the initiate by the *guru* or religious preceptor. This initiation is a copy of the Brahmanical initiation with sectarian adaptations. The *mantra* is generally of the form 'Om, homage to *x*', where *x* is the name of the god to which the sect is devoted. Since knowledge of it is the true sign of membership, and since it is endowed with redeeming efficacy, the *mantra* is not to be revealed to outsiders. However, if an outsider should overhear or read the *mantra* in a book, it is of no value since the special potency of the *mantra* is only present when it has been communicated orally by a qualified *guru.* Thus the sects involve distinguishing marks, initiation, *mantras* and *gurus,* and this implies a succession of *gurus* and a well-defined body of adherents who have been initiated – in effect a church. Finally, of course, the sect has its peculiar precepts, modes and times of worship, and a particular god or aspect of a god to which it directs it devotion and from which it hopes to derive its salvation. Hindu sects may be classed according to the object of their devotions: Shiva, Shakti or Vishnu.

Illustration page 217

Shiva

Whatever the truth of the theory of his Indus civilization origin, Shiva, or rather Rudra, as he is there called, is found in the *Rig Veda.* His functions in the early Veda are two: he is the Howler accompanied by the divinities of the storm, the *maruts,* sending down lightning; and he has sovereignty over disease and, therefore, over healing herbs. He is a turbulent and terrible divinity, to be propitiated. When,

Above Kali, the black earth-mother whose rites involve the sacrifice of animals and at one time of humans (*c.* eighth century AD).

Above left An eighteenth-century painting of Shiva and Parvati, a benign aspect of Shiva's wife, enthroned in their heaven on Mount Kailasa. Pilgrims climb the mountain with their offerings while gods and sages honour the divine couple. Museum of Fine Arts, Boston, Massachusetts.

Far left A devotee of Shiva in Sri Lanka.

Left Nataraja (the Lord of the Dance), a form of Shiva, in an eleventh-century bronze from Tiruvelangadu, Madras. As he dances, he crushes the dwarf, a symbol of ignorance, underfoot. State Museum, Lucknow.

Right A shrine to Kali at Mathura,
Uttar Pradesh. Kali was one of the
destructive aspects of Shiva's wife.

Below An eighteenth-century
Kangra painting of Durga slaying
the demon Mahisha, who
threatened to dethrone the gods.
Durga was another of the
aggressive forms adopted by
Shiva's wife. Unlike Kali, she was
young and beautiful and was born
as a fully-grown warrior goddess
to destroy demons, each of her ten
arms being provided with weapons
borrowed from the gods. Victoria
and Albert Museum, London.

through prayer to him, cattle are not struck by lightning, he is called Pashupa, Protector of Cattle; and when illness is averted he is credited with healing powers. In later vedic texts Rudra's qualities are expanded upon – he has a blue neck and red complexion; his jurisdiction extends over forests, robbers, outcasts, medicinal herbs, cattle; he is the Wearer of Matted Hair; but when appeased he is Shambhu, Shankara, Shiva (the Benignant, the Beneficent, the Auspicious). One worships him to keep him at a distance; to avert cattle epidemics a bull is sacrificed to Rudra outside the boundaries of the village, and with every mark of an inauspicious rite. The horrendous and ambivalent character of Shiva has never entirely disappeared.

Illustration page 217

Rudra is a minor figure in the *Rig Veda,* and the rise of Shiva to a position of eminence and as the centre of a cult was gradual. By the second century BC we hear of devotees of Shiva, who appear to have constituted a sect. Clear evidence of the *lingam* or stone phallus, in which form Shiva is widely worshipped, comes later; but in addition to the supposed *linga* of the Indus civilization, there is in the *Rig Veda* a prayer to Indra, not to permit those whose god is the phallus to destroy the Aryan supplicants' rites.

The earliest historical Shaiva sect was the Pashupata, founded by Lakula, who lived in about the first or second century AD, and who was regarded as an incarnation of Shiva himself. The Pashupata novice, according to the literature of this sect, moves through several stages to salvation. In the first stage he bathes and lives in the ashes of funeral pyres, and performs acts of worship in the temple: laughing, dancing, singing, uttering the sound 'huduk' like a lowing ox, and incantation. At a higher stage of spiritual proficiency he abandons the sectarian marks and wanders alone, provoking the censure of ordinary people by snoring, shaking as if afflicted by the 'wind disease', making amorous gestures to women, by moronic behaviour and nonsensical speech. There follow higher, more decorous stages in which meditation comes to the fore. The eccentric behaviour of the second stage is explained on the theory that the Pashupata's bad *karma* is exchanged for the good *karma* of his censurer, but it is in addition an extreme expression of the ascetic's rejection of the world and his self-isolation from it.

We learn of several Shaiva sects appearing in the subsequent centuries. The Kapalikas (Skull-bearers) again illustrate the ascetic 'transvaluation of all values' in that they purposely adopted the marks of the slayer of a Brahmin, namely the staff and skull begging-bowl, to court dishonour; in further indulging in the drinking of wine, the eating of meat and illicit sexual intercourse in ritual contexts, they are identifiable as Tantrics of the Left Hand variety (see below). Such extreme ascetic movements survived the vilification of the many and flourished for centuries; in fact, solitary Shaiva ascetics, or *siddhas,* were distributed all over northern India in the centuries previous to the Muslim invasions, and contributed greatly to the religious and philosophical movements of Tibet as well as India.

Methods of Achieving Salvation

The approval and acceptance of Shaivism by respectable society (of which we have certain evidence by the seventh century), as well as by large numbers of ordinary people, however, assumes the development of sects in which eccentricity of the sort practised by the early sects was eliminated and a less ambiguous or shocking mode of behaviour was enjoined. One such is the Shaiva or Shaivasiddhanta system widely followed in South India, whose methods of achieving salvation – periodic devotions, meditation, yogic meditation, penance, worship of the *lingam* and the like – are considerably Brahmanized and wholly unobjectionable. The same may be said of Kashmir Shaivism, and both have theological literatures of considerable interest and importance. The Kalamukhas formed a sect which flourished in South India for a time but has since disappeared. Though unfairly maligned by their Vaishnava opponents, they carried on the study of the Veda as well as the sectarian texts at their large temples and monasteries, eschewing the startling behaviour of other Shaiva sects and taking the vow of non-injury, truth, non-theft, chastity and poverty. The Virashaiva or Lingayat sect, founded in the twelfth century, may be a reformed version of the Kalamukhas, who disappeared about that time and some of whose temples are now in Virashaiva hands. Sanskrit learning and *lingam* worship play an important role in both; indeed, both Kalamukha and Virashaiva priests are described as Jangamas ('moving *linga*' or the *lingam* incarnate), and Virashaiva initiation confers the small *lingam* in a silver box which all members of the sect wear on the neck. Basava, the 'founder' of Virashaivism, was minister under the Kalachuri king Bijjala (AD 1145-67), and is said to have incurred the king's wrath by depleting his treasury through benefactions to the Jangamas, and to have arranged his assassination with popular support after a period of royal persecution. The Virashaivas today form a caste or rather a group of castes with their own priesthood, the Lingi-Brahmins, with a ritual strikingly and significantly similar to the Brahmanical.

In Tamil Nadu, in the far south of India, the devotional songs in Tamil of the Shaiva saints called Nayanars testify to the penetration of popular devotional Shaivism to the limit of the sub-continent from perhaps the seventh or eighth century, where Buddhism and Jainism had preceded it, and where it still flourishes.

Shakti and Tantricism

We have seen that there is good reason to believe that goddesses of fertility have been worshipped in India since the beginning of the Neolithic Age, and that their cult forms an important part of the non-Aryan background of Hinduism. Bana, a seventh-century author, informs us that tribesmen of the Vindhya Mountains of Central India make offerings of flesh and wound themselves to offer their own blood to the goddess Chandika; in another passage a queen of Ujjain in western India, to procure the birth of a son, offers worship to this same goddess, though in a less gruesome fashion. We see here a mother-goddess shared by aboriginals and the upper classes. Whatever the origins of the cult of a great goddess or *shakti,* we can say that between the fifth century, when a temple was established 'filled with demonesses, sacred to the Mothers, who shout most loudly in the darkness' to the present, her worship has flourished.

Mythologically, the Great Goddess is conceived of as the spouse of Shiva, and like Shiva she has both a pacific and a terrifying aspect: as Parvati, the Lady of the Mountains, she is Shiva's beautiful bride; as the ugly and bloodthirsty Kali she demands animal (and at times human) sacrifice; as the Dweller of the Vindhyas she waylays travellers and is patron saint of robbers; as Durga she slays the Mahisha, the demon in the form of a buffalo, and so is at once an awesome combatant and a saviour to humanity. The cult of Durga is today very characteristic of Bengal, where her return to her paternal home as a young bride is celebrated annually with much affection. Durga is indeed something of a symbol of Bengali nationalism and regional identity.

Philosophically, the Great Goddess is the *shakti* or power of Shiva, who represents the opposite pole of maleness, consciousness and rest; in fact the special efficacy of any god is his *shakti* and is personified as his wife. The somewhat surprising association of femininity with both matter and energy and maleness with passivity in this dichotomy may have its roots in the ancient Sankhya metaphysics, in which the world results from the union of *prakriti* (matter, feminine gender) and *purusha* (the individual souls, masculine), which is the passive spectator. In Sankhya, however, salvation consists of extricating the soul from the entanglements of matter, whereas Tantricism attempts to overcome the essential polarity in union. Without *shakti,* Shiva is a corpse.

Tantricism is the religion of the *tantras.* Any Shaiva or Vaishnava canonical treatise is liable to be called a *tantra,* in distinction from the *shastras* of Brahmanical religion, science and law, but it is to that religion whose texts consist of a dialogue between Shiva and the Goddess that the term 'Tantricism' refers. Followers of the *tantras* are often called Shaktas along with other worshippers of the Great Goddess. Tantricism in a broader sense characterizes the Vajrayana Buddhism of Tibet, and tantric elements have penetrated Jainism and Vaishnavism to some extent; but among Hindu tantrics Shiva and his *Shakti* are the principal deities.

The philosophical equipment of Tantricism is not exceptional among Indian religions and most of the elements of its religious life can be found in other Hindu sects as well. There is the usual initiation by a *guru* and the communication of the *mantra,* rituals, prayers and meditation. What is remarkable is the degree to which *mantras* and rituals have been multiplied, and the complexity of the result; also remarkable is the systematic and deliberate reversal of dietary and sexual taboos in the ritual of a few tantric sects, as we have already noted of the Kapalikas.

For an explanation of the cult of the mother goddess and her consort, see page 34.

Illustrations pages 217, 218

Illustration page 218

Stages to Supreme Bliss

Persons are classified according to their spiritual capacity as *pashu* (beast), *vira* (hero), or *divya* (divine), and for each capacity there is an appropriate mode; or again these three are the stages on the way to supreme bliss through which the novice successively passes. Among the Kaulas, for example, at the first stage vedic sacrificialism, Vaishnava *bhakti* and Shaiva gnosis are successively elevating modes, followed by consecration and *nyasa,* pointing to the various parts of the body and uttering the *mantras* peculiar to the divinities which by so doing are made to enter the worshipper, provided it is done with an inner attitude of adoration. The stage of hero includes the most distinctive of tantric modes: the ritual of the 'Five Ms' (*panchamakara*), in which he successively partakes of wine (*madya*), fish (*matsya*), meat (*mamsa*), parched grain (*mudra*) and sexual intercourse (*maithuna*). At the highest stage the aspirant becomes dead to the world and its antinomies, liberated while yet in the flesh. Laya Yoga is very prominent in all forms of Tantricism.

Practices such as the Five M's ritual were only intended for the adept, who had the passions firmly under control, and they were followed by only a few sects, called Left-Handed, to distinguish their methods from those of the more conventional and numerous tantric sects of the Right Hand, which substituted harmless symbols for the forbidden things, or simply ignored them altogether. Left-Handed rituals derived their force from the deliberate reversal of the established morality. The explicit aim of the Five M's ritual is to raise the worshipper above praise, censure, shame, pride of family and caste as a step toward liberation from the bonds which keep one from the supreme bliss; at the same time the ritual testifies that the prevailing morality rigorously forbade such things as wine, meat-eating, and sexual intercourse outside of wedlock.

Vishnu

Unlike Shiva and Shakti, in whom the terrifying aspect of deity is always present, Vishnu is on the whole a consistently benevolent deity, an Apollo to Shiva's Dionysus, as befits a god with solar origins.

There are a few references to Vishnu's measuring of the universe in the *Rig Veda,* but a full version of a variant of the legend is found in the *Shatapatha Brahmana.* The *asuras* agreed to give their enemies the *devas* for the performance of sacrifice only so much ground as could be covered by a dwarf. The gods chose Vishnu, who lay down, and swelled so large as to cover the entire earth, thus transferring it to the possession of the *devas*.

From fairly modest beginnings Vishnu contrived to grow in stature until he comprehended and synthesized in his own person the cults of many diverse deities and came to be recognized as the supreme deity by many millions of Indians. According to the classic and Puranic iconography, Vishnu lies sleeping in the primeval waters on the coils of the thousand-headed cobra. From his navel grows a lotus

Illustration page 227

bearing Brahma, who creates the world. Here Vishnu incorporates
the creator Narayana into his person; other divinities have been subsumed to him as avatars or earthly incarnations.

According to the *avatara* doctrine Vishnu takes on an earthly form
to save the world when its destruction by the forces of evil is threatened. Ten avatars are generally recognized:

1 The Fish (Matsya), which saved Manu (the first man), the Sages
and the Veda from the great Flood.

2 The Tortoise (Kurma) on whose back the gods placed Mount
Mandara, with which they churned the milk ocean to recover the
ambrosia they had lost in the great Flood.

3 The Boar (Varaha), who killed Hiranyaksha, and rescued Earth
from the cosmic ocean into which the demon had thrown her.

4 The Man-Lion (Narasimha). The demon Hiranyakashipu had obtained a divine boon that he could not be killed indoors or out, during
the daytime or at night, by god, man, or beast. Vishnu burst from
a pillar in the demon's palace in the form of a Man-Lion, at twilight
when it was neither day nor night, and killed the demon on the
threshold.

5 The Dwarf (Vamana) is a variant of the vedic episode. The Dwarf
appears before the demon Bali and is granted the boon of as much
space as he can cross in three strides; in two he covers earth, air and
sky, generously refraining from taking the third, nether region, which
he leaves to Bali.

Illustration page 227

6 Rama of the Axe (Parashu Rama), who cleared the earth of *kshatriyas*
twenty-one times in succession, in defence of Brahmins against royal
depredations.

7 Rama, king of Ayodhya, hero of the *Ramayana,* who killed the
demon Ravana of Sri Lanka.

8 Krishna (see below).

9 The Buddha, perhaps included to draw heterodox elements into
Vaishnavism.

10 Kalkin, the incarnation of the future, variously described as a
horse, a horse-headed man, or a man seated on a white horse with
flaming sword in hand. He will bring judgment to earth and restore
the golden age.

Of these figures only Rama, Krishna and Buddha have followings
today. The cult of Rama appeared only about the time of the Muslim
invasions; in the *Ramayana* he is the epitome of *kshatriya* chivalry and
heroism, and his queen Sita of chastity and fidelity, raised to a high
pitch but not yet divinized. Krishna, on the other hand, is the object
of an early cult.

Krishna

As a child Krishna delights in naughty pranks, and astonishes his
elders by performing many miracles; as an adolescent he is the
amorous cowherd, playing a flute and summoning the wives and
daughters of the place to sport with him, especially Radha, his favourite; as man he is the hero who slays his maternal uncle (or

Illustration page 228

cousin), King Kamsa of Mathura, as foretold by a prophecy which had made Kamsa order a slaughter of the innocents at Krishna's birth. Krishna rules Mathura for a time but political vicissitudes force him to lead his Yadava followers to Dvaraka, on the west coast, where he marries Rukmini and establishes his kingdom. After a time the kingdom breaks up in a drunken feud, his son is killed and Krishna himself dies when a hunter, mistaking him for a deer as he wanders dejectedly in the forest, shoots him in the heel, his one vulnerable spot.

Illustration page 228

The story of Krishna is a composite of elements added to the main stock at different times and from different sources. His name itself means 'the Dark' or 'Black', suggesting a hero-god of the darker aborigines of India, and various distinct tribal groups are associated with him in legend. Krishna first appears as hero and slayer of Kamsa; his erotic adventures with the *gopis* (cow-girls) play an important part in legend and religious literature only in medieval times, and as an object of worship the infant Krishna was born only after his maturity and adolescence had been defined.

In the *Mahabharata,* Krishna appears as the charioteer of Arjuna in the fratricidal struggle. On the first day of battle Arjuna, seeing many near relatives in the opposing ranks, refuses to fight and incur the sin of fratricide, however just the cause. His dialogue with Krishna in the course of which he is convinced that he must fight, is called the *Bhagavad Gita* (approximately, *The Song of the Blessed One*), the most widely-read and cherished of Hindu classics.

Arjuna's Dilemma

Put very briefly, Arjuna's perplexity arises over the question of *dharma* (righteousness, religion, law, duty), which, as a warrior, bids him fight and, as a kinsman, forbids him to kill the enemy Kauravas. The resolution of the dilemma is in two parts. On the one hand, Krishna reminds him that it is a *kshatriya's* sacred duty to fight in the defence of goodness; that, indeed, it is better to perform one's own duty, which is to say, the duties of one's caste and station in life, even if it is lowly, than to perform the duty of another, however well. As to killing his relatives, on the other hand, Krishna points out that the self (*atman*) is never slain but sheds the body at death and takes on a new one, in birth after birth. The two teachings together give the caste system a religious sanction, and make of the performance of caste functions and usages a religious duty; but there are further implications. Would not Arjuna do better to lay down his arms, leave society and its duties, and seek his salvation in a life of ascetic quietism? Since action leads to rebirth (*karma*), the avoidance of action appears the proper course. Krishna teaches that this is so: those who seek salvation through the actions of performing vedic sacrifice continue to be reborn, whereas to seek liberation through the path of ascetic meditation and renunciation of action is much superior.

So far the argument is Upanishadic; but on closer inspection, the ascetic deludes himself if he thinks he has ceased from all action (for he must still breathe, eat, etc.) and so total non-action is unattainable. However, the effects of action, causing successive rebirth, may be avoided by giving up the fruits of action, by the disinterested performance of duty; for desire, not action *per se,* is the agent which binds the soul to the ephemeral world. Thus the householder need not become an ascetic to achieve liberation from *samsara.* He need only renounce the fruits of action, and perform his duty, caring nothing if it turns out well or ill.

This is the main teaching of the *Gita,* and the answer to Arjuna's dilemma; but there is a further teaching, somewhat gratuitously joined thereto, which is of the greatest importance: the teaching of *bhakti* or devotion to God. He who adores the Lord Krishna with his whole soul is the greatest ascetic. Those who meditate on the Lord at death achieve union with him; there is no rebirth when a man devotes his whole heart to the Lord. The wicked man who adores the Lord becomes holy; even women, *vaishyas* and *shudras* attain salvation if they resort to him.

The Vaishnava Movement

This warm, devotional religion, drawing women and members of the low castes to itself, is first announced in the *Gita* and is destined for a long and fruitful career through Indian history. The Vaishnava saints of Tamil Nadu of the seventh to twelfth centuries (the Twelve Alvars) significantly included members of the lower castes in their ranks, and wrote ecstatic poetry in praise of the Lord in the vernacular, a phenomenon which was to reproduce itself in North India under the Dehli sultanate and early Mughals.

The Vaishnava *bhakti* movement of South India was given a theological basis by Ramanuja (eleventh century). The monist (Advaita) system of the great Shankara, crystallizing the Upanishadic tradition, had held that the soul was identical with the impersonal Brahman and that the world was the trickery or illusion of Brahman, real only in a qualified, practical sense. This prestigious philosophy left no place for *bhakti,* since its Supreme Soul was impersonal and not an object of love or devotion; and the individual soul was a part of it, so that knowledge of this identity, not love of God, was the means of salvation. Ramanuja returns to the Upanishadic tradition and finds justification for a qualified monism (Vishishtadvaita) according to which the Supreme Soul is a loving, personal god, from which matter and the individual proceed, but which remains distinct from them; through *bhakti* one returns to the bosom of God, yet the soul retains its separate identify.

Ramanuja Brahminizes *bhakti* by restricting its practice to the three twice-born estates as a culmination of knowledge of vedic rites and vedantic philosophy. He adds a new mode, however, which is open to all: *prapatti* or throwing oneself completely on God's will. The followers of Ramanuja divided over the question of the nature of self-surrender, and formed themselves into two groups. The northern school says that salvation is attained on the analogy of the monkey, which carries its young clinging to its belly, i.e the individual must make some effort to acquire grace. The southern school uses the analogy of the cat which carries its kitten by the neck, i.e. God's grace needs no human effort.

Madhva, a thirteenth-century Brahmin, carried Vaishnava theology into frank dualism (Dvaita): Vishnu, the individual souls, and the material world are eternally distinct; the latter depends entirely on Vishnu's will, and the Lord saves whom he pleases, though he pleases to save only the pure. The ordinary man is destined to transmigrate without cease; the naturally wicked are destined for the outer darkness. The possibility of Christian influence on Madhva's doctrines is not excluded.

The earliest Vaishnava sectarians of which we hear are called Bhagavatas, and their earliest known inscription is on a pillar surmounted by Garuda, the mystical bird on which Vishnu rides, inscribed by a Greek Bhagavata named Heliodorus, ambassador from the Indo-Greek kingdom of Taxila to the Shunga king of North India in the late second century BC. The Bhagavatas seem to have worshipped Vasudeva (Krishna), his brother Sankarshana, his son Pradyumna, and his grandson Anuruddha as emanations of Vishnu; in any case this doctrine of emanations, as hypostasizations of the elements mind, soul, etc., was characteristic of the Pancharatra system, which Ramanuja took as point of departure.

Other Deities

Other deities have or have had cults of their own. The Creator Brahma (as distinguished from the impersonal Absolute Brahman) for a time had temples erected in his honour. Sarasvati, his wife, presides over music and speech, and is worshipped by musicians, writers, and students taking examinations. Surya, the sun, was for a time widely worshipped in western India through the offices of the Maga-Brahmins, who must be connected to the Magians of Persia. *Illustration page 229* Shiva's elephant-headed son, Ganesha, the Lord of Obstacles, is prayed to at the outset of any enterprise or ritual, though he no longer *Illustration page 228* has a cult of his own. Another son of Shiva, Skanda (Karttikeya, Subrahmanya) is extremely popular in the Tamilnad, where he was identified with the pre-Aryan god Muruhan. Vishnu's wife Lakshmi (Fortune) is a popular figure, though without a cult of her own. Hanuman, the monkey-god and helper of Rama, is a guardian spirit widely worshipped by villagers; as representatives of him, monkeys are widely protected in India.

Medieval Hinduism

In the eighth century AD, Islam's second century, Arab power expanded into the Indus Valley but succeeded only in establishing a small and soon independent province. In the eleventh century, Islam's fourth, the religion of the Prophet reappeared under the auspices of the Central Asiatic Turks, who, in the person of the military slave Qutb-ud-din Aibak, established by 1206 the Sultanate of Delhi. By the beginning of the fifteenth century the sultanate had brought most

Left Vishnu's three strides, which encompass the universe and confine the demons to the nether world, from the second cave temple at Badami, Mysore state (AD 550–580).

Left A nineteenth-century painted clay depiction of Vishnu and his wife Lakshmi, on the serpent Ananta, afloat on the primeval waters. From Vishnu's navel grows a lotus, from which Brahma is born. Victoria and Albert Museum, London.

Opposite above left The boy Krishna steals butter from the womenfolk, one of his numerous childhood pranks depicted in an eighteenth-century Rajput painting. Pergamon-Museum, Berlin.

Opposite above right Krishna lifts Mt Go-vardhana on one finger to protect it from the floods sent by Indra in a seventeenth-century tempera painting. Victoria and Albert Museum, London.

Opposite below A village festival in honour of Skanda, the god of war and one of Shiva's sons. Shiva created six children to deliver the gods from a demon, but Parvati hugged them so hard that they became one. However, the six heads remained, and most statues represent Skanda thus.

Left Ganesha, one of the most popular Hindu gods. The human head of this son of Shiva was reduced to ashes soon after his birth, and Shiva made up the deficiency with the head of Indra's elephant.

Right Sri Aurobindo, who abandoned politics for the life of a holy man and founded a religious centre near Madras.

Far right Rabindranath Tagore, the Hindu whose poetry won him the Nobel Prize for Literature.

Right Mahatma Gandhi, the greatest Hindu of modern times, and the architect of Indian independence.

of the sub-continent under its sword, and its provincial governors had as quickly established themselves as separate, independent powers; in the sixteenth century, the Dehli sultanate succumbed to another Central Asiatic military elite, the Mughals.

India was for the first time confronted with an invader it could not assimilate, whose rulers and whose Persian administrative cadres had access to a mature religious and cultural tradition of their own. Shut up in walled towns, their only contacts with Hindus were, with a few notable exceptions, through the revenue-collection machinery, the lower levels of which remained in native hands, and the armed suppression of rebellion, which is to say refusal or inability to remit the very heavy taxes they imposed. The auguries for a fruitful interchange of ideas were bleak indeed, and the very foreign religious concepts of orthodox Islam perhaps added to the self-imposed isolation of the rulers from the ruled. That in the course of time over one-fifth of the inhabitants of the sub-continent have embraced Islam is scarcely due to the awesome institution of the Dehli sultanate. The Muslim rulers never entertained a policy of conversion and did little to encourage it, though they were given to justifying the spoliation of temples and the suppression of revolts under the plea of iconoclasm and the extension of the faith.

Conversion must have come from a very different source, from the Persian Sufi *pirs* or *shaykhs* who wandered the countryside preaching a religion of ecstatic love for God and human beings and establishing retreats open to all orders of society for communal worship and mystic meditation. Sufism struck many responsive chords in Hinduism, especially the *bhakti* movement in Vaishnavism: in the necessity for and worship of the guide (*pir, guru*), the approach to God through love and dependence on his grace, the importance of absorbed meditation, and the stages on the path to union with God. Where they did not result in conversion, the currency of Islamic ideas through Sufi agency powerfully influenced Hindu thought.

A Tendency to Monotheism

Among the earliest strata of the literatures of the North Indian vernaculars are to be found the poetic effusions of Vaishnava *bhakti* saints of this period. Bringing to fruition the tendencies of their Hindu heritage in the religious climate provided by the presence of Islam, many of them spoke out against idolatry, against the religious sanctions surrounding the caste system, and against the efficacy of rituals of any kind. Several of these saints were of humble station and little education; their means of expression was poetry, not systematic philosophy; their religion was *bhakti,* not gnosis; they tended toward monotheism and a personal god, not an impersonal absolute; and they hoped for union with God, not absorption into the Godhead.

Ramananda, in the fourteenth century, is a seminal figure in these developments. Though a Brahmin, he went about northern India preaching in the vernacular to all sorts and conditions of men. Communal meals and worship among his followers of all castes was a bold innovation; and among the traditional lists of his disciples we find the names of a Rajput, a barber, a leatherworker, a woman, and a Muslim weaver. This last was a man named Kabir, who flourished in the fifteenth century during the last days of the Dehli sultanate; it is unlikely that the two were in fact contemporary. Kabir's teachings, couched in vigorous Hindi verses, have had a wide influence, and they are preserved among others, in the sacred books of the Sikhs, whose founder, Nanak, was a younger contemporary, and the Dadupanthis, a Hindu sect whose saint Dadu was a Muslim cotton-cleaner from Gujarat in the sixteenth century.

Kabir's strong assaults on idolatry, the rituals of the Brahmins and the distinctions of birth reflect the Muslim side of his teaching; Hinduism provides the background and foil of his thoughts; and the religion of the heart combines the two. Legend has it that on his death his Muslim and Hindu adherents contended over his corpse, the one to bury, the other to cremate it, when a voice told them to draw back the shroud. Doing so, they found a heap of flowers which they divided, the Muslims burying their portion, the Hindus cremating theirs. There remain distinct Muslim and Hindu institutions perpetuating Kabir's memory to this day, but his verses are a common heritage of North Indians, far beyond the confines of the sects which sprang up after him. Tulsidas of the sixteenth century is another leading figure among the worshippers of Rama, and his version of the *Ramayana* occupies a central position in Hindi devotional letters.

The Adolescence of Krishna

Side by side with the cult of Rama, which first appears at this time, the older cult of Krishna developed in new directions, and the two cults together encompassed the Vaishnavas of North India. Common to both, however, was the inclination to regard the favoured object of devotion as the supreme god, rather than as an avatar of Vishnu, of whom little mention was made. During this age the adolescence of Krishna and his amorous sport with the milk-maids and with Radha in particular comes to the fore. In Vrindavana (Brindaban) near Mathura, the scene of Krishna's boyhood and erotic adventures, a Brahmin of the late fifteenth and early sixteenth century received a revelation from Krishna directing him to erect a shrine and gather together the latter-day reincarnations of Krishna's companions that he might again sport with them. Vallabha's school teaches that the highest forms of *bhakti* are involuntary and come directly from God; and the most advanced of the initiates gather together to re-enact the sports of Krishna. The descendants of Vallabha, now in western India, are the *gurus* of the sect and have a great hold over their laity.

The Radha-Krishna cult quickly established itself in eastern India, especially in Bengal; one of Krishnaism's finest literary works is the Sanskrit *Gitagovinda,* of the twelfth-century poet, Jayadeva, and the hymnody of subsequent Bengali and Maithili poets is still the basis of Vaishnava devotional singing. Chaitanya, a contemporary of Vallabha, is the patron saint of Bengali Vaishnavism, and like Vallabha

is regarded by his followers as an incarnation of Krishna. A prominent
feature of his life were his song meetings, through which he attracted
a following to himself and to devotion to Krishna.

Union with God

The Radha-Krishna literature employs an erotic metaphor to explain
the relation of humans to God and to encourage *bhakti,* in the manner
of the Sufi mystics and the biblical *Song of Songs*. Here the soul is
feminine in relation to God, for whom it yearns. It describes the pains
of separation from the beloved and the bliss of union with him. For
Chaitanya and his followers the emphasis falls on separation and the
hope of union, and so the metaphor remains only a metaphor. For
another, smaller sect, the Sahajiyas, the bliss of union with God is
experienced through erotic practices, perhaps under tantric influence,
and is parallel with Vallabha's movement. In Maharashtra the cult of
Vithoba (Vishnu-Krishna) and his wife Rukmini prevails, and the
lover Radha is little heard of. Jnaneshvara, the founder of the cult,
and his successors, Namdev in the thirteenth and fourteenth centuries,
and Tukaram, in the seventeenth, are the greatest saints of Maratha
bhakti.

Like others of the age the Maratha saints taught that the experience
of the Highest was open to everyone regardless of caste, that the
sinners who repented and loved God purified their whole family, and
that *bhakti* alone was the way to salvation. Also like others of the age,
they composed devotional songs of great force and beauty which
remain the basis of religious devotion in their region to this day.

As the Mughal age progressed the creative period of North Indian
bhakti passed, and by the eighteenth century innovation and reform
were entirely at an end. In the early Mughal period new, bolder,
pantheistic forms of Sufism had entered India, and, under the great
emperor Akbar (r. 1556-1605) and especially in the teachings of his
grandson Prince Dara Shikoh, the tendency to merge Islamic mysticism with Hindu *bhakti,* or even with Upanishadic gnosticism went
its furthest and gave the orthodox Muslims their greatest alarm.
Under succeeding emperors, especially Aurangzeb (1658-1707), reaction set in as the party of the *ulama* (the scholars, which is to say,
the doctors of the Law) gained the upper hand to a degree they had
never achieved in the past. On the Hindu side, the *bhakti* poet-saints
had gathered followers who spontaneously turned into sects and with
the passage of time became castes. It is not surprising that this should
have happened; for, once the followers of a particular saint had sub-
joined communal dining to communal worship and hymn-singing,
they were liable to be excommunicated by their caste fellows; seeking
husbands for their daughters they would be obliged to look to other
members of their sect; and once inter-dining and inter-marriage is
established, the difference between a sect and a caste becomes fine
indeed. Thus Hindu society in general frustrated the potential for
social reform inherent in the sects; and the sects themselves frustrated
the anti-ritualistic and anti-idolatrous teachings of their founder-saints

by developing a distinctive ritual and by making of their saint, his descendants, or his writings an object of veneration.

Hindu Nationalism

In the times of Aurangzeb a Maratha prince named Shivaji raised the banner of the defence of religion and homeland against the Muslim rulers of India, and created a Maratha state in the Deccan which rapidly eroded the Mughal power. Hindu and Maratha nationalism thus arose in opposition to the Islamic presence. Although, under its later rulers, the Maratha state came to stand for Maratha imperialism over non-Marathas, Hindu and Muslim alike, until it succumbed to the British, it set many precedents for later Hindu nationalism.

Hinduism in Modern Times

As medieval Hinduism had developed in relation to the presence of the Islamic religion and to alien rule, so from the beginning of the nineteenth century modern Hinduism emerged in response to the presence of missionary Christianity and British rule. The novel modes of worship, the missionary programmes and some of the theological and ethical conceptions of the new Hindu movements of the nineteenth century drew inspiration from Christian example; and the organized social concern of the movements parallel European sentiment and missionary example. European oriental scholars have provided an external source of influence for the recovery of India's past on scholarly principles.

The Hindu response to these influences and to the threat of conversion to Christianity has been, variously, to try to ignore them, to revive and revitalize Hinduism, or to reform it in ways congenial to the needs of the times and a humanitarian outlook. The salient fact of nineteenth-century Hinduism is that radical reform of religion appeared first, while movements at once more widely popular and more outspoken in the defence of traditional religion arose in the second half of the century as the pressures of modernity mounted and touched more and more Indians. The most momentous event of that century was the Mutiny of 1857, whose watchword was, 'religion is in danger'. In the twentieth century, until the independence of India and Pakistan, religion was inextricably enmeshed in nationalism and the burning questions it posed from day to day. After Independence religious nationalism lived on, as did the earlier fruits of contact with, and reaction to, British administration and Christian missionaries.

Rammohun Roy

Raja Rammohun Roy (1772-1833), rightly called 'The Father of Modern India' by later generations, was a man of remarkable scope in an age of remarkable men. Schooled in Persian and Arabic for service under the Mughal governors, and in Sanskrit for religious study, he acquired a perfect mastery of English in the service of the East India Company; and when his interest in Christianity was aroused, he learned Hebrew and Greek from the Serampore missionaries, near Calcutta.

Rammohun Roy's relations with the missionaries were not uniformly cordial. He collaborated with them for a time on the translation of the Bible into Bengali and Sanskrit; but his book *The Principles of Jesus: The Guide to Peace and Happiness,* published in 1820, which praised the moral teachings of Jesus, offended them with its denial of the doctrine of the Trinity, and he defended Hinduism against the unfair and uninformed polemics of Christian publicists.

Rammohun Roy lent powerful support to several measures of social reform which were intimately bound up with religious conceptions. The prohibition of *sati* (widow-burning) and the introduction of English education, accomplished in his lifetime, owe much to his efforts; many other reforms he urged have since been effected.

In 1828 Rammohun formed the Brahmo Samaj, a group of educated Bengalis which met weekly for readings from the Upanishads, sermons and hymn-singing, not unlike Protestant services in form. The group might not have long outlived the death of its founder in Bristol in 1833 had it not been reconstituted in 1843 by Debendranath Tagore, a son of one of the wealthy charter members, under whom it acquired a more distinctly sectarian and theistic character, and who established a school for Brahmo missionaries who now began to attract new members in greater numbers. Under the magnetic leadership of its third director, Keshab Chandra Sen, it reached its apogee and began its decline; for Keshab in 1879 preached a 'New Dispensation' which he had received from God to crown the old dispensations of Judaism, Christianity and Islam, and thereby caused a schism.

Soon after the founding of the Brahmo Samaj, similar movements appeared in the other coastal metropolises of British India, Madras and Bombay, many of which affiliated with the older body and whose unity survived the secession of the New Dispensation.

The Arya Samaj

Much less urbane in its origins and its appeal is the Arya Samaj, which was founded in 1875 by a religious mendicant, Dayananda Sarasvati, who was born a Shaivite in Gujarat, on the western side of India. Dayananda's slogan was 'back to the Veda'. In that this implied the rejection of idolatry and the full-blown caste system, it was a reformist slogan, and indeed he admitted all classes of society to the study of the Veda, which had hitherto been the monopoly of the twice-born. He was also in favour of scientific technology for India, and by a peculiar exegesis succeeded in finding the railway and telegraph in the ancient texts. On the other hand the modern cow-protection movement derives from Dayananda, and remains a potentially explosive issue in politics. The overall tendency of Dayananda's teaching was to reform Hinduism and defend it pugnaciously from attack, to strengthen India with modern technology, and to reject Western dominance in thought, religion, mores and, by implication at least, politics.

If Dayananda combined modernity with tradition, Ramakrishna Paramahamsa (1834-1886) was entirely of the type of the great medieval saints. An uneducated Bengali who lived in a Kali temple in

Calcutta, he would go into trances through constant devotion to and meditation on the deity; on one occasion he was in a trance more or less uninterruptedly for six months, and was only saved from starvation by his followers who forced food on him during his more lucid periods. He found mystical experience whether the object of his meditations was the Great Mother, Sita, Rama, Krishna, Mohammed or Jesus, and taught, therefore, the validity of all religions.

This homespun figure lived a life of extreme renunciation and used apt and homely parables in his discourse. He soon attracted the interest of a number of the educated, reformist members of Calcutta's upper classes, especially the Brahmos, through Keshab Chandra Sen, who held him in great admiration. One young man, Narendra Nath Datta, met him as a sceptic and parted a convert. He became an ascetic under the name Swami Vivekananda and founded the Ramakrishna Mission, whose monks carry on good works, scholarship, and the spread of their master's teachings throughout India, with centres in Europe and America as well.

Indian and the West Must Help Each Other

Vivekananda did more than any one man to propagate Hinduism in the West, and simultaneously to refurbish its image among the Indian intelligentsia, when in 1893 he attended the Parliament of Religions in Chicago. He spent the following four years in America, teaching a band of admirers, and when he returned in 1897, with a handful of Western disciples, he immediately became a national hero. Vivekananda's belief that India must learn science from the West, while the West must learn spiritually from India, to overcome its materialism, has been very influential.

On the involvement of Hinduism in Indian nationalism, we must note the role of Theosophy, a movement which reached India in 1879, some four years after its foundation in New York. Theosophy espoused reincarnation and *karma* as teachings of its own 'ancient masters', and defended Hinduism and Sri Lankan Buddhism from its European critics. After the death of the founder of the Theosophical Society, Madame Blavatsky, at the end of the nineteenth century, Theosophy became more directly involved in nationalist politics under the leadership of Annie Besant, who in 1917 became president of the Indian National Congress.

The first generation of Indian nationalists did not overtly appeal to religion in their politics. They were men of position and substance, humanitarian and often religious in private life, who sought social reform, responsible government and, one day, a self-governing India within the British Empire. One such was Gopal Krishna Gokhale, who besides serving on the Legislative Council of Bombay and later in the Indian Legislative Council, founded the Servants of India Society in 1905, to train and sustain workers who dedicated themselves to a life of simplicity and practical social uplift. The most notable of these Servants of India was the young Mohandas Karamchand Gandhi (1869-1948).

Anarchy and Assassination

An extremist faction surfaced in the first decade of the twentieth century, particularly in opposition to the partition of Bengal into Muslim and Hindu provinces in 1905 under Lord Curzon. Anarchy and assassination in the cause of expelling the British were sacred duties in this faction: nationalism and Hinduism were merged. This heady mixture, besides causing enough unrest to force the reunion of divided Bengal in 1911, contributed to its second partition in 1948, when Pakistan was separated from India; the identification of Hinduism with nationalism rendered Hindu-Muslim relations extremely hostile.

Hindu nationalism also had distinctly provincial or regional overtones, especially in Bengal where its patron was the Mother Goddess, and in the Bombay state, where Bal Gangadhar Tilak (1856-1920) established annual celebrations in honour of Ganesha, coinciding with the Muslim festival of Muharram, and Shivaji, the Maratha hero whose memory Tilak revived as a symbol of Marathi Hindu nationalism. Tilak's commentary on the *Bhagavad Gita* carried the message that political action was a teaching of Krishna, and the implication that violence in furthering that action had divine sanction.

The three great leaders of Hinduism in the first half of the twentieth century include a former extremist (Aurobindo Ghose, 1872-1950), a moderate (Rabindranath Tagore, 1861-1941) and a mediator between those two poles (Mahatma Gandhi, 1869-1948). Ghose's career *Illustrations page 230* as an extremist during the agitation over the first partition of Bengal was short-lived, and after release from prison he renounced political action and founded a religious hermitage in the (then) French enclave of Pondichéry, and became *guru* to a large following who call him Sri Aurobindo. Rabindranath Tagore was not a politician at all, rather the greatest of Bengali poets, who won the Nobel Prize for Literature in 1913. Born in the illustrious Brahmo family, deeply religious, highly cultured and broad of vision, through his writings and lectures he warned of the dangers of the worldwide rise of nationalism, and could not accept Gandhi's version of it, which seemed to him xenophobic and backward-looking.

Mahatma Gandhi

Very different was Mahatma Gandhi, whose simplicity of life and religious appeal stirred the masses, and whose abhorrence of violence and desire to make reform and moral uplift an integral part of the freedom movement ennobled that struggle. Like Tilak, he believed that the *Bhagavad Gita* taught that religion consists of a life of purposeful action; unlike Tilak, he rejected violence and brought the notion of *ahimsa* to bear on political life. His technique of non-violent non-co-operation proved uniquely embarrassing to British rulers, and his virtual control of the Indian National Congress from the death of Tilak made him the architect of Indian independence. Gandhi's thought draws variously on Thoreau, Ruskin and Tolstoy, but mostly on the Vaishnavism and Jainism of his native Gujarat. He was very active in the cause of the Untouchables whom he called *harijan* (children of god) and their relief from social disabilities; he promoted cow-protection, prohibition, and the use of Hindi as a national language. Gandhi's vision was an India of self-sufficient villages unsullied by the evils of modern industry, spinning its own cotton to clothe itself, raising its own food, living in harmony and contentment; his success was to bring into being an independent Republic of India.

His successor, Acarya Vinoba Bhave (d. 1982), furthered the Gandhian vision by seeking to persuade villagers and rich landlords to pool their lands, working them and enjoying their produce communally (the *Bhudan* or 'land-gift' policy), and nearly four million acres have been so dedicated. His was a kind of village communism, with love and moral suasion replacing the class struggle.

Gandhi was deeply grieved by the Hindu-Muslim emnity and its result, partition, which Hindu nationalism had helped to foster, and he undertook fasts and conciliatory actions to bring the antagonists to their senses. On January 30, 1948, he was assassinated by a Maratha Hindu nationalist. The deep currents stirred by Tilak continue to move some sections of Hindus, and they are not likely to fade quickly.

The Spectrum of Hinduism

In the India of today the whole spectrum of Hinduism may still be seen, though few sects have been untouched by modern influences. Most have now opened schools, recovered and printed neglected texts, initiated reforms of clergy, temple management and practices, and undertaken apologetic or missionary work. The Ramakrishna Mission stands out as the representative of liberal, modern Hinduism; but side by side more ancient orders and sects survive and preserve their traditional characteristics. What the future holds only a prophet can say. The dissolution of the caste system will change Hinduism profoundly and in unknown ways; agnostic humanism could, in the long run, severely reduce its numbers; but, on the record of its long past, its chances of survival are good.

Left Stone sculpture from the twelfth or thirteenth century of two Tirthankaras: Rishabha the first and Mahavira the last of the present era. British Museum, London.

Above The consecration of
Mahavira by Indra, the king of the
gods, after attaining enlightenment
beneath the sala tree. Indra gave
Mahavira a beautiful robe at his
initiation, which was later taken by
a greedy Brahmin priest. A
fifteenth-century miniature from
the *Kalpa-sutra*, Gujerat. British
Museum, London.

Above right A Sthanakavasi
Shvetambara nun making a
pilgrimage on foot in Rajasthan.
Note the cloth across the mouth to
prevent her from breathing in, and
so destroying, insects.

Right A ceiling and columns of the
Rishabhanatha temple on Mount
Abu (eleventh century AD) in
Rajasthan.

Chapter Fourteen

Jainism

Jainism is perhaps the only heterodox religion surviving in India today that derives from the Shramanas, the ancient religious teachers distinguished from the Brahmins (see Hinduism) by their doctrine of salvation through atheism and asceticism. Essentially an Indian religion on account of its adherence to the twin beliefs of transmigration and liberation of the soul, it is nevertheless alienated from Hinduism by its rejection of the Brahmanical institutions of caste and sacrifice. It thus has many affinities with Buddhism, particularly the Theravada school, with which it also shared the Ganges Valley in its early days, and a Magadhan language (Ardha-magadhi) – as opposed to Sanskrit – for its original scriptures. But whereas Buddhism, despite its spectacular spread outside India, was effaced from its motherland, Jainism, albeit with a small scattered minority of only three or four millions of followers, managed to survive and still continues to exert its influence on the cultural and social life of modern India.

The Jains, known in ancient times as Niganthas, the Unattached, derive their name from a Sanskrit word *jina*, the victorious, applied to their great teachers, also called the Tirthankaras – 'ford-makers' to cross the river of transmigration. The Jains believe that the universe, which has neither a beginning nor an end, passes through an infinite number of cosmic cycles, each divided into two alternate phases of ascent and descent, during which time there is respectively a gradual rise and fall of human civilization. In each such phase, twenty-four Tirthankaras appear, who not only attain liberation for themselves but also teach the path of salvation to others. Rishabha was the first *Illustration page 239* of the twenty-four Tirthankaras of our present age of decline. Being the first law-giver he is also called Adi-natha or the First Lord. Only a legendary account of Rishabha and his successors is preserved by the tradition. But the last three are well within the known history of ancient India: the twenty-second Jina, called Nemi, was a cousin of Krishna of the Mahabharata War.

Nemi's successor was Jina Parshva of Benares, who flourished around 850 BC. The last of the Tirthankaras of our age and the supreme teacher of the present-day Jains is Vardhamana Mahavira (599-527 BC or 540-468 BC), a contemporary of Gautama the Buddha (624-544 BC or 564-484 BC).

The Life of Mahavira

According to the *Kalpa-sutra*, a semi-legendary biography compiled in the third century BC, Mahavira was born at Kundagrama, near modern Patna, Bihar, to Siddhartha, a chieftain of the Licchavis, and his wife Trishala. He was, according to one tradition, a life-long bachelor. According to another, however, he married a princess called Yashoda, who bore him a daughter called Anoja. At the age of twenty-eight, on the death of his parents, Mahavira renounced his family life and became a mendicant (*muni*) in the tradition of the Jina Parshva.

His renunciation was complete. He discarded even his loincloth and went about naked, for a full twelve years, in silence and meditation, practising the most severe austerities to attain the state of a *jina*. In the thirteenth year, after a prolonged fast, Mahavira, outside the town of Jrimbhikagrama, on the bank of the Rijupalika, in the field of the householder Samaga, under a sala tree, in deep meditation, reached completely and fully the unobstructed, unimpeded, infinite

Illustration page 240   and supreme best knowledge and intuition, called *kevala*.

The scriptures claim that he knew and saw all conditions of the world of gods, men and demons; whence they came, whither they are born, as men or animals or become gods or hellish beings, the ideas, the thoughts of their mind, the food, doings, desires, the open and secret deeds of all living beings in the whole world; the Arhat (Holy), for whom there is no secret, knew and saw all living beings in the world, what they thought, spoke, or did at any time.

With the attainment of omniscience, the *summum bonum* of Jainism, Mahavira had liberated himself from the forces (or *karma*) that lead one into the cycle of transmigration. He was now acclaimed a Tirthankara, a leader of an order, a fact testified to us by the rival scriptures of his contemporary Buddhists. Mahavira spent the remaining thirty years of his life propagating his faith and organizing the vast community of his followers, consisting of laymen, laywomen, nuns and monks, a large number of whom might have belonged to the ancient order of Parshva. He entered *nirvana* or final rest at the age of seventy-two at Pava, a small town not far from his birthplace.

The Path of Non-Violence

Mahavira is said to have preached his first sermon at a congregation of Brahmins engaged in performing a sacrifice and to have converted them to his path of non-violence. Eleven of these Brahmins became his chief disciples, called the *ganadharas*. Chief among these were Gautama, Sudharma and Jambu, who received his teachings and transmitted them to posterity in the form of an oral tradition. This was first codified at a council of monks called by the pontiff Sthulabhadra at Pataliputra, the capital of the Mauryan Emperor Chandragupta (*c.* 317-293 BC), who is believed to have abdicated the throne to become a Jain monk. The canon compiled at this council consisted of certain portions of the *Purvas* (the ancient texts, possibly going

back to the times of Parshva), the eleven *Angas* (limbs or sections),
and several texts of a miscellaneous character. These were further
revised and finally written down at a second council held at Valabhi
in Saurashtra in the fifth century AD.

A Major Schism

The Pataliputra council also witnessed a major schism that divided
the community of the Jains into two sects. Tradition maintains that
Bhadrabahu, the eleventh pontiff, foreseeing a long period of famine
in the north, migrated to the south, to the present site of the Jain
colossus at Shravana-Belgola in the state of Mysore, leaving Sthulabhadra in the charge of those monks who had opted to stay behind.
When, after a lapse of twelve years, Bhadrabahu returned to Bihar,
he found that the northern monks had abandoned the austere ways
laid down by their master and had even taken to the practice of
wearing white robes, a concession inadmissible, in the opinion of the
orthodox section, to Jain monks, who had to renounce all bonds,
including the emotion of shame, to attain the condition of passion-
lessness (*vita-raga*).

The community of monks and their lay followers thus split into
two sects, the Digambaras (the sky-clad) and the Shvetambaras (the
white-clad). The Digambaras maintained that the vow of nudity, a
mark of total renunciation as exemplified by Mahavira, was a binding
condition on a Jain monk. The Shvetambaras considered this vow to
be purely optional and claimed, on the evidence of a scriptural passage
(*Uttaradhyayana* XXIII), that the practice of wearing clothes obtained
under the order of the previous Tirthankara Parshva. The Digambaras, led by Bhadrabahu, declared the Shvetambaras to be apostates
and declined to accept the canons compiled by Sthulabhadra as
authentic.

The Sects Diverge

Ever since then the two sects have drifted away from each other,
extending their activities in different parts of India. The Digambaras
still depict the images of the Tirthankaras shorn of all clothes, and
due to the rigours of their rules have all but lost the order of monks,
their laity being guided mostly by householders advanced in spiritual
discipline. On the other hand, the Shvetambaras still have a sizable
community of monks, but their practice of worshipping at the Jain
shrines with the images of *jinas* highly decorated with silk and jewels
gave rise in AD 1653 to a reform movement called the Sthanakavasis
(dwellers in halls), who condemned all forms of iconolatry and temple
worship as inconsistent with the teachings of Mahavira.

The schism, harmful as it was for the unity of the community, did
not result in any significant departure from the fundamental teachings
of Mahavira. All Jains, irrespective of their sectarian practices, adhere
to the three basic doctrines that characterize their religion: the *ane-
kantavada*, the belief that there are no absolutes; *karma-vada*, efficiency
of action; and *ahimsa*, non-violence. These describe respectively the
nature of reality, the causes of bondage and the path of salvation.

The Nature of Reality

The doctrine of non-absolutism distinguishes the Jain from the other traditional systems of Indian philosophy. The latter tend to define reality either as eternal or as momentary. Both fail to account for the phenomena of change and eventually resort to a doctrine of illusion with which they deny the reality of bondage itself. The Jain abandons both these extremes and maintains that the nature of reality is complex, defining the existent as that which is characterized by a simultaneous operation of origination, destruction and permanence.

Accordingly, an object of knowledge must consist of three inseparable aspects: a substance, innumerable qualities that inhere in it, and an infinite number of forms or modifications through which the substance passes in the infinity of time and space. In the process of this constant flux, a substance like soul (*jiva*, corresponding to the *atman* of the vedic schools) acquires a new form, while at the same time abandoning its old form, and yet remains eternal by not relinquishing its essential quality of consciousness. The soul is thus eternal when looked at from the point of view of substance, and is at the same time momentary if one considers only its modifications. In like manner, the Jain maintains that the soul is both finite and infinite, bound and free, corporeal and incorporeal etc., if looked at from different viewpoints. The same is true of the remaining categories recognized by the Jains: matter, and the principles of motion, rest, space and time.

The Doctrine of Maybe

Since no speech is capable of simultaneously describing the manifold aspects of the reality without incurring contradiction, the Jains advance a theory of qualified speech as a corollary to the doctrine of non-absolutism. This is called *syad-vada* or 'the doctrine of maybe'. A statement like '*x* is eternal' is not only dogmatic but also wrong, since it denies its impermanence. The correct thing would then be to say 'Maybe the *x* is eternal', which would indicate the existence of other properties not expressly stated by the speaker. Seven such predications are possible: maybe yes, maybe no, maybe yes and no, maybe indescribable, and three more combinations of these.

Whereas the doctrine of *anekanta* affirms the reality of the manifold states of the soul, the doctrine of *karma* explains the state of bondage. Jains believe that in its natural state, which is potentially present even in a blade of grass, the soul knows all things, and is in a state of perfect bliss, unhindered by any material contact. In its unnatural state, it suffers varying degrees of limitation, conditioned by its body. The soul has no form of its own. But in its state of bondage it is capable of contraction and expansion, and is coextensive with the bodies which it inhabits in the course of transmigration, which has no beginning in time, nor any agent like a creator or a god.

The number of souls is infinite and they are classified into five divisions according to the number of sense-faculties they possess. The largest number consists of those invisible beings who are at the lowest level of consciousness, and have the very elements – earth, water, air and fire – as their bodies, and the vast vegetable bodies, which possess only the faculty of touch. The next group consists of various animalculae which possess two senses, that of touch and taste. Insects like ants and fleas have one more faculty, that of smell. The larger insects like the wasps and butterflies have in addition the faculty of taste. All other beings, including the higher animals, men, and the infernal and heavenly beings, possess five faculties which they are liable to lose at the termination of their life, in the same way as the lower species may gain the higher states, all according to the inexorable law of *karma*.

The Law of Karma

The law of *karma* assumes that every deliberate action has its own consequence and pursues the doer, often beyond the grave. The gross bodies that a soul inhabits in the course of transmigration are thus caused by its own acts of will, the morally good ones resulting in heavenly and human bodies and the evil actions yielding the infernal and animal ones.

All Indian religions believe in this efficacy of *karma* (deed), and also in a psychic body as a mechanism for the transference of deeds from one birth to the other. But the Jain is distinguished by his doctrine of a karmic body, consisting of a special kind of extremely subtle atom of matter by which the soul is enmeshed during the state of transmigration and from which it is not separated even at the time of death. This subtle matter, when bound with the soul, obstructs its innate qualities of omniscience and perfect bliss. The process of its operation is explained in the following manner. Molecules composing the organs of mind, speech and body, when activated, produce vibrations (*yoga*) in the soul and attract the karmic matter that pervades space. This influx alone is not sufficient to bind the soul. If the soul is actuated by passions (*kashaya*) such as attachment or aversion, and indulges in evil actions, then this karmic matter is absorbed by the soul, as a wet cloth absorbs dust.

The Jain canonical texts, called the *Karma-granthas*, dwell at length on the varieties of will and action that bring about the influx of particular categories of *karma*, their duration and consequences to the soul. Broadly speaking the *karmas* are divided into eight kinds. Concealment of knowledge out of envy, for instance, attracts the knowledge-obscuring *karma*, which will produce lack of intelligence in that person on the maturity of that *karma*. Compassion and self-pity will give rise to the feeling-producing *karmas*, which will cause pleasant and unpleasant feelings respectively. The faith-deluding *karmas* cause disbelief in the true nature of reality. Intense feelings induced by the rise of passions cause conduct-deluding *karmas*, which produce want of restraint from evil acts. The life-determining *karma* determines the span of life, and the status-determining *karma* determines a high or low status within those states. Censuring others and praising oneself, for instance, is said to result in that *karma* which brings about a low status. The obstructive *karmas* stand in the way of success in any undertakings, particularly those concerned with giving, gaining and enjoyment.

The *karmas* thus incurred remain in the soul, embedded as it were, sometimes for a few moments only and sometimes for an aeon, awaiting the time of their maturity. They then disassociate of their own accord from the soul, after yielding their fruits according to the intensity of will and the nature of the actions that had caused their influx. They will be subsequently reabsorbed by a new series of passions and actions and thus the wheel of transmigration will be kept in constant movement. Each soul indeed has taken in (enjoyed) successively all the molecules of matter in the entire universe and has cast them off. And each soul has been revolving innumerable times in the cycle of matter. There is no point in the entire space of the universe which has not been the seat of a birth of a soul. In this way each soul has been many times roaming, occupying all points in the cycle of space.

The Way of Salvation

This process of transmigration may be without a beginning, but it is not endless for those beings – and the number of such souls is also infinite – who are endowed with an innate capacity for salvation. But the way to freedom is not automatic, nor is it to be had by the saving grace of a deity, for the Jains do not admit of a creator or a god who might intervene and lift the souls from the mire of transmigration. There exists, however, an interminable line of Tirthankaras who, by the dint of their exertion, have realized the path and have shown it to other beings out of compassion. Although few would aspire to be a Tirthankara, which is merely a worldly status accomplished by the special discipline required of a teacher, all those who follow the path are also assured of complete liberation with the full glory of omniscience.

Arresting the Passions

Salvation is possible only by stopping the influx of *karmas*, by arresting the passions and by guarding the channels of their activity. This calls for right faith, right knowledge and right conduct, which together constitute the path to liberation. Right faith is defined as an enlightened belief in the true nature of the soul as distinct from the body and the forces of *karma*. It is attained by intuition or by instruction from those who have fully realized it. This cannot be had from the false gods of the theists who are, as the Jains are wont to prove, clearly subject to passions; nor from the fallacious scriptures like the so-called 'revealed books' that propound absolutist views; nor from those teachers who worship false gods, perform sacrifices, or indulge in mortifications that are not conducive to the eradication of passions. A true Jain therefore takes refuge only in a *jina* who is omniscient and passionless (*vita-raga*), in a scripture that is consistent with the doctrine of non-absolutism, and in a preceptor who has renounced all possessions and attachments.

Temples without a Deity

The Jain temples do not enshrine the images of gods but only of the Tirthankaras, depicted either as seated or standing, rapt in meditation. The bathing of their images, the waving of lamps in front of them to the music of devotional hymns, and the celebration of the five auspicious occasions of their lives (conception, birth, renunciation, enlightenment and *nirvana*) are parts of popular ceremonies for the laity; but in the absence of a deity there is no real worship in these acts.

The Litany

The impersonal relationship between the devotee and the Tirthankaras can also be seen from the famous Jain litany called the *Namaskara-mantra*, which makes no mention of a historical person, not even of Mahavira. It refers to five kinds of beings worthy of worship: the *arhats* (the holy ones), the *siddhas* (the perfect ones), the *acaryas* (the leaders), the *upadhyayas* (the preceptors) and the *sadhus* (the aspirants). The first group includes all beings who have attained enlightenment, particularly the Tirthankaras, and who preach the Law while they are still in a state of embodiment. The *siddhas* are those beings, infinite in number, who have attained final liberation and whose pure spirits permanently reside at the summit of the universe. The last three groups refer to the members of different ranks within the order of the Jain monks.

Right Conduct

Right conduct consists of renunciation of all activities, whether mental, vocal or physical, which proceed from passions such as anger, pride, deceit and greed, and thus set in motion the cycle of *karma*, thereby causing great injury to oneself and others. For the laity this renunciation is by necessity of a partial nature, and consists of a series of progressively severe vows which prepare the individual for the life of a monk or nun, whose renunciation is then complete. First in the series are the five 'limited' vows: non-violence, truthfulness, non-stealing, chastity (*brahma* — faithfulness to the vows of marriage), and non-attachment (the limitation of worldly goods). By three additional vows called the *guna-vratas* the laity confine themselves to a well-defined region, such as a town or country, and to a direction within it such as east or west, and avoid all futile activities that might hinder the observance of the five basic vows. The last in the series consist of vows of fasting on the eighth and the fourteenth days of a lunar fortnight, the dispensing of charity, for which the Jains are renowned, and certain other vows pertaining to the spiritual exercises suitable to a householder.

The foremost among these is the *samayika*, an act of meditation, aimed at the realization of the true nature of the self. During this act, which may last an hour twice or even thrice a day, the aspirant retires to a secluded place, and temporarily renouncing all bonds, including those of family and of possessions, makes a confession of the infringements of the vows, forgives and asks forgiveness of all beings, and thus experiences great peace and tranquillity. Laypeople in this act are indeed ascetics, albeit for a short period; the peace they enjoy sustains them throughout their austere lives.

All Life is Sacred

The moral basis of the entire Jain discipline is *ahimsa*, or non–violence. All life is sacred and inviolable, even that of the unfortunate beings who are born as animals, and are but suffering the consequences of their own *karma*. The Jain scriptures, deploring the almost universal habit of eating meat, attach great importance to dietary rules. The widespread vegetarianism of present–day India is very much the result of the Jain emphasis on the evils of destroying animal life for sport, food or sacrifice. For, whereas the Brahmanical schools condone animal sacrifices and even approve of certain meat dishes on particular occasions, and the Buddhists freely partake of meat provided by others, the Jains absolutely forbid meat, and alcohol and honey as well, for the members of their community.

Even in their vegetarian diet, Jains, as they advance to the higher stages of their spiritual career, called *pratimas*, are expected to avoid certain varieties of food, notably fruits with many seeds and fermented products of milk, and to refrain from eating after sunset, lest they cause injury to the innumerable insects that come to life at dusk. For the same reason the means of livelihood open to a devout Jain exclude professions that involve destruction of plants or the use of fire and poisonous stuffs, and trades connected with slavery and animal husbandry. This accounts for the fact that the Jains, today as in the ancient days, are mostly to be found in the middle classes of *vaishya* rank, the merchant castes of India.

Total Renunciation

A householder well trained in the earlier stages of devotion is considered fit to receive the advanced vows of a monk (or nun). These are called the *maha-vratas* (the great vows). A monk renounces everything, including his family, property and his civil rights, and, in the case of the Digambaras, even the loincloth. The Jains celebrate the occasion of such 'going forth' (*pravrajya*) with fitting pomp and solemnity, by taking the aspirant in procession to a Jain temple, where he is initiated into the order of the monks either by the head of a local order or by a senior monk. The aspirant pulls out his hair in five handfuls as a symbolic act of his indifference to physical pain, and receives a new name from his teacher signifying his spiritual rebirth. He also receives a whisk, made of peacock feathers (in the case of a Digambara) or of yarn (for a Shvetambara) with which he removes insects from his path, and which also serves as a mark of his ascetic status; the Sthanakavasi Shvetambaras further wear a cloth over the mouth for the same purposes.

Illustration page 240

He must henceforth beg for his food and, except during the rainy season, must not take a permanent residence in any one place. He is not allowed the use of any means of conveyance, nor an umbrella, nor even a pair of sandals. He must spend his wandering life actively engaged in the study of the scriptures, in penances like silence and fasting, and in meditations, arresting the influx of new *karmas* and bursting the bonds of the old. When he perceives that his end is near, he should court death by fasting so that he may die the death of a saint with peace and mindfulness. Such an aspirant is nearer the goal; he is destined to break the cycle of rebirth and attain the state of perfect bliss.

The Achievement of the Jains

Despite their preoccupation with renunciation, the Jains claimed several eminent kings of ancient India as members of their faith, and were prominent in the courts of many medieval dynasties of the Deccan and Gujarat. Several fine pieces of temple architecture speak of their ancient glory, notably the magnificent colossus of Bahubali in the south, and the Delawara temples at Mount Abu in Rajasthan, famous for delicate workmanship in marble. Their monks were renowned for scholarship and maintained fine libraries that still survive, and which contain rare works of great antiquity on almost every branch of learning. They contributed immensely to the fields of logic and philosophy, and were pioneers in developing vernacular literature in Tamil and Kannada. They were also zealous in the propagation of the doctrine of non-violence and obtained even from the Mughals decrees prohibiting the slaughter of animals on days sacred to the Jains.

Illustration page 240

In modern times as well the Jains have continued their activities in these directions with added emphasis on the application of non-violence on a wider scale. It was greatly due to the influence of the Jains, particularly of a Jain saint called Rayachand, that Mahatma Gandhi, in the early days of his career, formulated his political and socio-economic philosophy on the foundations of truth and non-violence.

Chapter Fifteen

Sikhism

Sikhism as we know it today is the evolved product of three primary elements. The first of these is the devotional system taught by Guru Nanak in the Punjab during the early decades of the sixteenth century; the second is the structure of Punjab society, particularly of the rural society of the Punjab; and the third is the period of Punjab history which extends from the time of Guru Nanak to the present day. No understanding of Sikhism is possible without reference to all three of these elements. To the fundamental base provided by the teachings of Guru Nanak sociological patterns and the pressure of historical circumstances have added doctrines, customs, and social observances which together constitute a distinctive way of life. This society finds a coherent religious expression in the system which to the Sikhs themselves is known as *Gurmat* and which the West calls Sikhism.

Before an attempt is made to describe this system a note of caution must be entered. It is important that lines should not be drawn too sharply, for clear-cut divisions will misrepresent the true nature of Sikh religion and society. There is certainly an area of doctrine and practice which is distinctively Sikh, but the further boundaries of Sikhism shade imperceptibly into the broad expanse of North Indian religious tradition. This is at once evident in social terms where we find common caste lines running horizontally through Hindu and Sikh society. It is also true in doctrinal terms.

Areas of common doctrine and practice should not, however, prompt an excessive blurring of distinctions. Sikhism is neither totally identified with Hindu tradition nor totally distinct from it. A considerable measure of identification is to be found in the antecedents of the thought of Guru Nanak in the common acceptance of such concepts as the doctrine of transmigration and in the observance of closely related customs. The distinctions are to be found in a rejection of some important Hindu conventions: notably the religious significance of caste divisions; in the existence of the Sikh brotherhood, the Khalsa; and in the Sikh's own insistence upon a distinction.

The Life of Guru Nanak

Illustration page 257 Abundant material is available relating to the life of Guru Nanak and until the twentieth century the most popular of all Punjabi prose forms was the *janam-sakhi*, or 'birth-evidences' of the *guru*. The *janam-sakhis* are, however, hagiographical writings, pious tales which idealize Nanak but which communicate little concerning his actual life. From them and from occasional references in other works it is possible to reconstruct no more than a bare outline.

Guru Nanak was born in AD 1469. His actual place of birth is disputed, but there can be no doubt that his parents belonged to the village of Talvandi, forty miles west-south-west of Lahore and now known as Nankana Sahib. In this village Nanak spent his childhood and early manhood. Before leaving it he was married and had two sons.

While still a young man Nanak moved to the town of Sultanpur and there entered the service of the local nawab. At some point close to the year 1500 he left Sultanpur and adopted the life of a wandering ascetic. The *janam-sakhis* describe his travels in considerable detail, but offer very little that can be satisfactorily established. It is, however, clear that the *guru* must have spent many years moving around India in this manner, and it is possible that his travels may also have taken him outside India to more distant places.

From references which he makes in his own works it is apparent that he witnessed something of the incursions of the Mughal emperor Babur, and it seems likely that his travels must have terminated during the period of Babur's invasions. An area of land situated on the right bank of the River Ravi had been donated to him and there he built the village of Kartarpur. He evidently spent most of his remaining years in this village and died there towards the end of the fourth decade of the sixteenth century, probably in September 1539.

Antecedents of the Thought of Guru Nanak

The teachings of Guru Nanak have commonly been represented as a syncretic blend of Hindu tradition and Muslim belief. This is a gross over-simplification and when expressed in terms of 'a mixture of Hinduism and Islam' it must be totally rejected. The teachings of Guru Nanak do indeed represent a synthesis, but the elements which constitute the synthesis can never be defined, however loosely, as Hinduism and Islam.

The synthesis to which Guru Nanak gave such clear expression was a system which, in its essentials, had already evolved. There was in existence a variety of religious belief which is now referred to as the Nirguna Sampradaya, or the Sant Tradition of Northern India. Of its exponents, by far the most important prior to Guru Nanak was Kabir. This tradition is commonly but erroneously confused with Vaisnava *bhakti* (devotion to the incarnations of Vishnu). This certainly provided some of the fundamental components of the Sant tradition, but the two are by no means identical.

For Kabir's teachings, see page 232.

To the Vaisnava inheritance was added an important though transformed element of tantric yoga and also a slight Sufi (mystical Muslim) influence. The result was a pattern of belief which affirmed the characteristic Vaisnava emphasis upon devotion, but which diverged from Vaisnava *bhakti* at significant points. The doctrine of the divine avatar was rejected, idol-worship was spurned, and a strictly inward

For the incarnations of Vishnu, see pages 222–3; for tantricism, see pages 221–2; for Sufism, see pages 493–6.

devotion was affirmed. This pattern of inward meditation was declared to be not the easy road of traditional *bhakti* but a narrow path which few could ever hope to follow.

It was this synthesis which Guru Nanak inherited and which he transmitted to his followers. This acknowledgment must not, however, suggest that the teachings of Nanak lack originality or that they do not represent a point of new departure. The originality of Guru Nanak lies in his recasting of the Sant synthesis in the light of his own experience and insight, and his genius in the clarity and the beauty with which he expressed it.

The Teachings of Guru Nanak

At the very beginning of the first composition recorded in the Sikh scriptures there stands the figure 1. The figure represents the unity of God, a concept which Guru Nanak interprets in monotheistic terms. God is for Guru Nanak single and personal, the transcendent creator with whom those who seek salvation must develop the most intimate of relationships. It is this quest for salvation which concerns Guru Nanak and repeated declarations of the way of salvation constitute the burden of his teachings.

Guru Nanak expresses his understanding of God by means of a number of oft-repeated terms. A primary one is *nirankar*, 'without form', and God is most characteristically referred to as 'the Formless One'. Another is *akal*, 'eternal', and a third *alakh*, or 'ineffable'. Considerable emphasis is laid upon this latter doctrine and numerous words are used by the *guru* to express it. How can one know God? Guru Nanak's first answer is that one cannot know God, for God in his fullness is far beyond the understanding of mortal beings.

There is, however, a second answer. God, who in his fullness is unknowable, is not wholly unknowable. Because he is also a god of grace he has imparted a revelation which is perceptible to the limited mind of man. This is the revelation in creation. God is *sarab viapak*, 'everywhere present', immanent in all creation and visible everywhere to the eye of a spiritually awakened person. This general revelation has a particular focus, namely the human heart. A person must be able to see with the outward eyes and likewise he or she must be able to see with inward eyes. It is inwardly that meditation must take place and for the person who meditates in this manner there will come a progressive enlightenment which ultimately issues in salvation. The revelation in creation is, for Guru Nanak, of crucial importance, for it is at this point that there can exist communication between God and human beings. Only if this insight is apprehended and rigorously applied can the divinely-given way of salvation be found.

The Way of Salvation

The chief obstacle which impedes the quest for salvation is the human condition. People in their unregenerate condition are in bondage to the world. Their loyalty is to the world and its values, and this attachment imprisons them within the endless transmigratory round of birth and death. The great enemy is *maya* (unreality). For Guru Nanak, *maya* does not imply a doctrine of the ultimate unreality of the world itself, but rather an unreality of the values which it represents. The world offers qualities which are accepted as both good and desirable, but which constitute a deception. Those who accept the world in this way and who accordingly seek fulfilment in attachment to worldly values are victims of *maya*, of the illusion that these attachments, if not actually Truth itself, are at least not inimical to Truth. The result of this attachment is transmigration, the suffering of death upon death instead of the eternal joy of the beatific vision. The fate of the unregenerate is protracted separation from God.

The condition of the unregenerate is desperate, but it is not hopeless. God in his grace has revealed himself in his creation and by appropriating this revelation salvation can be won. The key terms employed by Guru Nanak to express this divine revelation are *nam*, *shabad*, *guru*, and *hukam*. The first two of these, *nam*, the divine Name, and *shabad*, the divine Word, are synonymous, each serving to summarize the revelation in its totality. Anything which can be affirmed concerning God is an aspect of the divine Name or of the divine Word. In an unregenerate condition, however, people will fail to perceive the manifestations of the divine presence. These are made clear to them by the *guru*, or divine Preceptor, which in Guru Nanak's usage designates the voice of God mysteriously uttered within the inward understanding of the awakened and receptive seeker. The term *hukam*, or divine Order, expresses the nature of the revelation. People must comprehend the divine order of the universe, both physical and psychical, and strive to bring themselves into harmony with it. The attainment of this harmony means salvation.

A Devotional Discipline

For the fulfilment of this objective the seeker after salvation must enter a devotional discipline and persist in its regular application until the ultimate harmony has been attained. This discipline, as Guru Nanak makes very clear, has nothing to do with external observances such as temple rites, mosque worship, pilgrimages, or asceticism. The only approved destination for the pilgrim, the only acceptable house of worship, is the human heart wherein the *guru* utters the divine *shabad*.

The term most commonly used to express the discipline taught by Guru Nanak is *nam simran*, (remembrance of the divine Name). The mechanical repetition of a particular word or sacred syllable was an established devotional practice, but the meaning imparted to the term by Guru Nanak goes far beyond this. There is first an insistence upon the absolute interiority of the discipline, and secondly an extension from the single word to a developed doctrine of meditation. Even this is inadequate as a description of the practice. The ideal is a total exposure of one's whole being to the divine Name, and a total conforming of all that one is and does to the divine Order which finds its expression in the divine Name.

Growing into God

The result of a disciplined application of *nam simran* is a growing towards God and a growing into God. It is a gradual process which Guru Nanak represented as a series of ascending stages. The fifth and last of these, *sach khand* or 'the Realm of Truth', is the final consummation wherein the soul finds mystical union with God. In this condition of ineffable bliss the chains of transmigration are sundered and by merging the soul in God ultimate release is obtained.

The First Successors of Guru Nanak

Before his death Guru Nanak appointed a disciple to follow him and for more than one and a half centuries the leadership of the new community was exercised by a series of successor *gurus*. This line eventually terminated at the death of the tenth *guru*, Gobind Singh, in 1708. The followers of the *gurus* were at first called Nanakpanthis but soon assumed the name of Sikh, a word which in its literal sense means 'learner' or 'disciple'.

The period of the second *guru*, Angad, was relatively unimportant, but some significant developments marked the term of his immediate successor, Guru Amar Das. It is during this period that we find unmistakable signs of a loose religious following crystallizing into a distinctive community. Guru Nanak's emphasis appears to have been laid almost exclusively upon the quest for salvation and the technique of obtaining it. This emphasis was evidently maintained by Guru Angad, but by the time of Guru Amar Das the need of greater cohesion was being increasingly felt. Guru Amar Das met this need by providing distinctive ceremonies for birth, marriage and death, and by instituting a rudimentary system of pastoral supervision (the *manji* system). Three Hindu festival-days were designated Sikh festivals also and the *guru*'s establishment in the town of Goindval became a centre of Sikh pilgrimage.

One other factor of primary importance which seems to have been emerging by the time of Guru Amar Das was the rural base of the developing Sikh community. The *gurus* themselves all belonged to the urban-based Khatri (or mercantile also administrative and priesthood) caste and during the period of the *gurus* many of their disciples were also Khatris. During the same period, however, their following began to come increasingly from the Jats (or agriculturalists) and eventually the Jats developed a strong predominance within the community. It is at this point that the relevance of rural sociological patterns, and particularly the distinctive Jat cultural patterns, becomes so clear. Later political and military developments within the community are in part a response to this constituency and during the eighteenth century these developments found theoretical expression in the evolving doctrines of Sikhism.

Guru Amar Das was succeeded by his son-in-law Ram Das, the founder of the city of Amritsar, and he in turn was followed by his youngest son, Arjan. This established the succession within the male line of a particular family (the Sodhi Khatris) and all the succeeding

gurus were direct descendants of these three. The period of Guru
Arjan is important for two other reasons. It was Guru Arjan who
was responsible for the compiling of a definitive scripture (the *Adi
Granth*, or *Granth Sahib*); and it was during his term that the growing
strength of the movement first attracted the unfavourable attention
of the Mughal authorities. At the Emperor Jahangir's order Guru
Arjan was arrested and in 1606 he died in captivity.

Military and Political Involvement

The early seventeenth century was the period of the Naqshbandi
reaction in Mughal India. Set against the developing strength of the
Sikh community, this led quite naturally to a growing official interest
and a corresponding deterioration in relations between the Sikh *gurus*
and the state. The death of Guru Arjan and a series of three minor
skirmishes with Mughal troops prompted the sixth *guru*, Hargobind,
to assume a measure of political and military authority. The community thereby underwent a highly significant change of direction,
though not at the cost of abandoning the religious system of the first
guru. The changes which followed the increasing political and military
involvement of the community resulted in significant extensions of
Sikh doctrine, but not in any renunciation of the original base.

Conflict with the Mughal authorities was revived during the period
of the ninth *guru*, Tegh Bahadur, and continued to intensify during
the lifetime of the tenth and last *guru*, Gobind Singh. During this
latter period the conflict also extended to the rajahs of the Shivalik
Hills, an area renowned for the prominence which it accorded to
shakti (power) concepts. It was in this area that Guru Gobind Singh
spent most of his life and within this context that he made a momentous decision.

The Khalsa

Guru Gobind Singh's decision was the evident result of a conviction
that his followers required a much firmer organization, and its product was the founding of the Khalsa in 1699. The Khalsa is best
described as an order, as a brotherhood in which religious, military,
and social duties are merged in a single discipline. Precisely what
happened at the actual founding of the order in 1699 is not known,
although later works purport to describe the ceremony in some detail.
This is, however, of secondary importance. Primary importance
attaches to the fact that for the Sikh community of the eighteenth
century the Khalsa brotherhood became the focus of needs, ideals and
ambitions which developed rapidly during the course of that century.

The tumultous eighteenth century was for the Sikhs a period of
widening hopes and expectations. Mughal power in the Punjab was
assailed by the Sikh leader Banda Bahadur (d. 1716), by Nadir Shah
of Persia, and by Ahmad Shah Abdali of Afghanistan. Under the
impact of these blows it eventually crumbled and upon the ruins there
arose the military power of the Sikhs. During the middle years of the
century the Sikhs emerged as a loose confederation of irregular warrior bands called *misls*. Towards the end of the century the leader of

Opposite above left Worshippers in the Golden Temple at Amritsar. Upon entering the temple worshippers offer coins and each receives a small portion of *karah prasad* (sanctified food). They then sit and listen to the singing of passages from the scriptures. The singing is continuous except for a brief period during the middle of the night. Entry and exit are permitted at any time.

Opposite above right A particular sanctity attaches to the waters surrounding the Golden Temple, and pilgrims to the shrine often bathe there. The breeches worn by the Sikh constitute one of the 'five Ks'.

Illustration page 257

one of the *misls*, Ranjit Singh, established a total ascendancy over all the others and formed a Sikh kingdom covering most of the Punjab.

It was during this disturbed century, extending from 1699 to the rise of Ranjit Singh, that the principal transformation took place, and it is primarily to the events of this period that the term 'Sikhism' must be related. The Sikh community enters this period with a loose organization and a rudimentary discipline. It emerges from it with the tight organization and the distinctive discipline of the Khalsa.

Prominent among the features of this discipline are a number of prohibitions, notably a ban on the use of tobacco and a rigorous insistence upon the wearing of the 'five Ks'. These are the *kesh* (uncut hair), the *kangha* (a comb to hold the hair in place), the *kirpan* (dagger), the *kara* (steel bangle), and the *kachh* (a pair of breeches which must not come below the knee). The wearing of a turban is not explicitly enjoined, but is rendered necessary by the insistence upon uncut hair. All Sikhs baptized into the Khalsa must also assume the name Singh in the case of men and Kaur in the case of women. Sikhs who have been baptized and who subsequently abandon their observance of the Khalsa discipline are referred to as *patit* (fallen) by their orthodox brethren. Others who have never taken baptism but who claim to be followers of the *gurus* are called *sahaj-dhari* Sikhs (slow-adopters).

The extent to which these developments lay within the intention of Guru Gobind Singh remains a largely unexplored issue. Certain features must undoubtedly have been promulgated by him, but it is likewise beyond doubt that others evolved in response to the events which followed his death. By the end of the eighteenth century the pattern is clear and it has ever since dominated Sikh history and Sikh religion. There have been many *sahaj-dharis*, claiming to be Sikhs without accepting the baptism or the discipline of the Khalsa, but it is the Khalsa ideal which has ever since sustained an overwhelming claim to be the true image of the Sikh faith.

The Sikh scriptures

Two collections of sacred writings rank as scripture in the Sikh community. Although only one of these, the *Adi Granth*, enjoys an undisputed canonical status, its later companion the *Dasam Granth*, possesses its own distinctive importance.

The *Adi Granth*, literally the First Volume, is the collection which was assembled during the years 1603 and 1604 by Guru Arjan. For this collection the *guru* used another compilation which had earlier been prepared at the behest of Guru Amar Das, adding to it his own compositions and those of his father, Guru Ram Das. Subsequently a few works by Guru Tegh Bahadur were appended and the canon was definitively closed during or soon after the period of Guru Gobind Singh. In addition to the hymns of the *gurus* a number of compositions by earlier figures of the Sant tradition have been included. Prominent among these are Kabir, Namdev, and Ravidas. A collection of couplets ascribed to Sheikh Farid of Pak Pattan has also been included.

Left A Sikh family gathered before the *Guru Granth Sahib*.

Below A modern Sikh picture of Guru Nanak. Prints of this kind are very popular and few Sikh homes are without one.

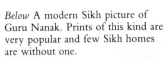

The bulk of the volume is classified according to *rag*, or metre, and within each *rag* further subdivisions according to length and author have been introduced. Most of the material consists of the hymns which were employed by the *gurus* as vehicles for their religious instruction. Almost all are composed in Sant Bhasha, a language closely related to both Hindi and Punjabi, which during the later medieval period was extensively used throughout North India as a lingua franca by the exponents of popular devotional religion. The script is Gurmukhi, which today is used only for Punjabi.

The status which is now accorded the *Adi Granth* represents the final stage in the development of the Sikh doctrine of the *guru*. In earlier Indian tradition the *guru* was invariably a human teacher. For the Sant tradition and for Nanak, however, the *guru* was the voice, or the Word, of God. Within the Sikh community the role was soon transferred to the line of men who gave authoritative expression to that Word and so reacquired its personal connotation. According to Sikh tradition Guru Gobind Singh, immediately prior to his death, declared that the line of personal *gurus* had come to an end and that thereafter the functions of the *guru* were to be jointly vested in the corporate community and the scripture.

It seems likely that this interpretation developed over a period of time, for we find hints of it before Guru Gobind Singh, and the leadership vacuum which followed his death will have strongly encouraged the definitive formulation of such a doctrine. There can be no doubt, however, that during the eighteenth century it acquired a fundamental importance. With the rise of Ranjit Singh the corporate aspect fell into disuse while the scriptural aspect ascended to a position of ultimate authority. This status it has retained ever since. In the daily life of devout Sikhs and in all Sikh ceremonies the *Adi Granth*, which is generally known as the *Guru Granth Sahib*, has an absolutely central significance.

Its later companion is, by contrast, little read nowadays. The *Dasam Granth* is an eighteenth-century collection of miscellaneous works attributed to Guru Gobind Singh. The attribution appears to be accurate in the case of a few compositions, but the bulk of the collection, consisting of Hindu legends and tales of the wiles of women, cannot possibly have been his work. The particular importance of the *Dasam Granth* lies in the testimony which it offers to seventeenth- and eighteenth-century Sikh ideals, and as a source for this period of Sikh history it possesses a considerable value.

Sikh Worship
The regular worship of a devout Sikh finds expression in three observances. The first is the daily recitation of certain appointed passages from the *Guru Granth Sahib*, notably the Japji of Guru Nanak which should be recited from memory immediately after rising and bathing. Secondly, there is the daily family observance. Although this is by no means universal, many families will gather each morning in the presence of the *Guru Granth Sahib* and read a passage selected at

Opposite above A gathering of Sikhs at Gurdwara Sis Ganj, Delhi's largest Sikh temple.

Opposite below A rear view of the Golden Temple of Amritsar (1765), seen across the Pool of Nectar. Beyond it is the gatehouse and the dome of the Akal Takht (Throne of the Timeless God), the centre of the administrative organization of the Sikh religion.

Illustration page 257

259

random. Thirdly, there is attendance with the wider family of the Khalsa at the *gurdwara*, or temple.

From the days of Guru Nanak the *gurdwara*, or a building corresponding to it, has occupied a position of considerable importance in the life of the Sikh community. The pattern of worship which is followed within a *gurdwara* consists chiefly of the singing of passages

Illustrations pages 257, 258 from the *Guru Granth Sahib*. When first entering a *gurdwara* a Sikh will go before the *Guru Granth Sahib*, touch the ground with the forehead, and make an offering. At certain appointed times all who are present will join in reciting the *Ardas*, or Sikh Prayer, a set form which invokes the divine grace and recalls the past sufferings and glories of the community. This prayer first evolved during the eighteenth century and has since undergone occasional minor amendments. It concludes with a reference to the *Guru Granth Sahib* as 'the manifest body of the Guru' and with the famous proclamation: '*raj karega khalsa*', (the Khalsa shall rule!).

The Sikhs Today

According to the most recent figures the total number of Sikhs living in India is approaching 12 million, or 3 per cent of the country's population. Of this total number approximately 90 per cent live in the portion of the Punjab which was left in India following the partition of 1947 (i.e. the area now covered by the states of Punjab and Haryana). Almost 4 per cent live in the adjacent areas of northern Rajasthan and Delhi, leaving only 6 per cent spread over the remainder of India. A large number have migrated to other countries, but emigration figures are not available.

In no part of India do the Sikhs possess a numerical preponderance. Even in the state of Punjab they constitute a bare 50 per cent of the population. They do, however, possess an influence much in excess of their statistical strength, not only within the state of Punjab but also within certain wider areas of Indian life. These include the armed forces, transport, political activity, and sport. The Sikh community also enjoys a relatively high economic status and is well above all-India averages in educational attainment.

Several reasons may be held to account for this favoured condition. One of the more important of these is the fact that a majority of Sikhs live in an unusually fertile area. This environment, allied with progressive farming techniques, has brought economic sufficiency and in many cases a considerable prosperity to the Jat Sikhs. No aspect of the Sikh faith inhibits this advancement. On the contrary, the Sikhs' general freedom from cramping custom has placed them at a considerable advantage, an advantage which they have not been slow to exploit.

Khatri and Arora (inferior urban caste) Sikhs have also enjoyed a wide measure of economic success through industry and the professions. This may be explained partly in terms of an inherited mercantile skill and partly by the emphasis which Sikhs have laid upon education. Nowadays it is only the Sikhs belonging to outcast groups who suffer from extensive economic insecurity, and their condition is generally better than that of Hindu or Christian depressed classes.

Relationships between Sikhs and Hindus have, on the whole, continued to be friendly and intercommunal marriages along caste lines are by no means unknown. Sikh leaders have occasionally claimed the existence of malicious Hindu intentions, but such claims normally have a political purpose and have affected relationships only slightly. A more serious cleavage in Punjab society is the rift dividing the Jats from certain urban classes. This rift is basically economic. Associated religious distinctions are secondary.

A prominent feature of the Sikhs' freedom from restrictive custom has been their willingness to migrate to other countries. Today Sikhs are to be found in almost every part of the world, particularly in the United Kingdom, East Africa, Malaysia, and the west coast of Canada and the United States. A large number of the immigrants who have entered the United Kingdom from India are Sikhs and there are now fifty *gurdwaras* in the country. The fact that a large number of these immigrants are no longer recognizable as Sikhs points to one of the community's great anxieties. Recent years have shown a marked willingness on the part of young Sikhs to abandon the outward symbols of their faith when living outside India. Even within the Punjab there are distinct signs of a trend in this direction.

Chapter Sixteen

Buddhism

What in the West has come to be known as Buddhism, by analogy with other 'isms' is, in its home in Asia, known as the *Buddha-sasana*, that is, the way of life, or discipline, of the Awakened One, the Buddha. It is known also as the *Buddha-Dhamma*, that is – as near as it is possible to get to an English meaning for the word *Dhamma* (in Sanskrit *Dharma*) in this context – 'the eternal truth' of the Awakened One. This translation is, of course, ambiguous, and represents the ambiguity, or rather the plurality of meanings, in the original term. 'The eternal truth of the Awakened One' means both the truth *concerning* the fact of the Awakened, and that such awakenment is possible, and also the truth *proclaimed* by the one who is regarded as pre-eminently the Awakened, the Buddha, or *Gotama* (Sanskrit *Gautama*), who lived in northern India in the sixth century BC.

Some explanation at this point may help to avoid confusion about the variety of names and titles by which this man is known to history. As the English Elizabethan dramatist is referred to as 'Shakespeare', so this man is known as Gotama; it was his family name. His personal name was Siddhattha (in Sanskrit Siddhartha). His family were of a republican clan which claimed a noble and ancient lineage, the Sakyas. A title by which Siddhattha came to be known, therefore, was 'the Sage of the Sakyas', Sakyamuni. Other epithets and titles are applied to him in the Buddhist scriptures, such as 'the Tathagata', the meaning of which is obscure; but best known is the title by which he is generally known in the West, the Buddha. This, the reader will by now have realized, is not a personal name, and should not be used as such. Indeed, according to the Buddhist tradition, a Buddha has appeared from time to time throughout human history, and will continue to do so, whenever people's knowledge of the *Dhamma* is lost and practice of the *sasana* ceases altogether. In conventional terms, this happens approximately every 5,000 years.

Buddhist tradition records the names of at least twenty-four Buddhas who preceded Buddha Gotama. There is no evidence for their existence as historical personages; their existence is affirmed as 'revealed truth', proclaimed by the Buddha Gotama. Buddhist tradition thus envisages a period of at least 120,000 years of history prior to the time when Gotama lived in the sixth century BC. But this is only a token-figure.

The time-scale of Buddhist, and of Indian thought generally, is vast by Western historical standards, and reaches back infinitely into the past and infinitely forward into the future. The process of clock-time is not of primary significance though it is not altogether without significance. If clock-time can be thought of as a horizontal dimension, stretching backwards and forwards from the present, the dimension of ultimate significance for the Buddhist is the vertical one. They are concerned with what happens in this dimension, within the ongoing process of time, and in particular that there should be aroused in people some awareness, however dim, of this other dimension, which will lead to the state of awakenedness, to another realm of being. But this is to anticipate what must be said concerning the teaching of Gotama the Buddha. First some account of his life and experiences must be given.

The Life of Gotama

What is known of the Buddha's life is based mainly on the evidence of the canonical texts, the most extensive and comprehensive of which are those written in Pali, a language of ancient India. These form the canon of scripture for the Theravada Buddhists of Sri Lanka, Burma, Thailand, Kampuchea and Laos, although they are regarded with respect by the Mahayana Buddhists of China, Korea and Japan also. (The differences between these two types of Buddhism will be dealt with later.) The Pali texts provide evidence also for the general conditions of social, religious and political life in North India in the early period of Buddhist history, evidence which has been corroborated at some points by archaeological discoveries in the area.

According to the tradition, Gotama the Buddha was the son of one of the leaders of the Sakya clan, whose home was the Himalayan hill-town of Kapilavastu in what is now Nepalese territory. Here in the foothills of the Himalayas the young Siddhattha grew up and spent his early manhood. He married, and had one son, Rahula. While his son was still a baby, Siddhattha began to be disturbed by the perennial problems of why men are born, only to suffer sickness, the decrepitude of old age, and eventually death.

Illustration page 267

The texts describe how he encountered successively a man tortured by disease, a man in the last stages of senility, and a corpse being carried out to the cremation ground, followed by sorrowing relatives and friends. Reflecting upon the fact that this is the fate of every man, he then saw a fourth figure, that of a shaven-headed holy man, a religious wanderer, one who had dedicated himself to the pursuit of the ascetic life in order to find some way of release from the apparent futility of life. Such men, known as *shramanas*, were not uncommon in ancient India, and it was to this life of the wandering ascetic that Siddhattha now turned, in hope of finding a solution to the problems of human existence.

The Religious Leaders of Sixth-Century BC India

These *shramanas* or religious wanderers are often contrasted with the other major religious figures of the time in India, the Brahmins, or priests. Very often the *shramana* would be a teacher of some particular religious or philosophical doctrine. The doctrines varied and the *shramanas* engaged in religious controversy among themselves, but what united them generally was that they represented an alternative to Brahminism and ritual sacrifice. Since the sacrificial system over which the Brahmin presided was complicated and costly it did not offer very much that was relevant to ordinary householders, cultivators, small tradesmen, and so on. It was to these that the teaching of the *shramanas* appealed more strongly. A dominant motif in their various doctrines was the idea of liberation from the weariness of life, most frequently through personal discipline or asceticism.

Siddhattha joined himself to a group of ascetics and for a time engaged very seriously and strenuously in the pursuit of spiritual truth by the method of asceticism. Finally, finding himself no farther forward in his quest, even although his ascetic discipline had been so rigorous that he was reduced to skin and bones and brought very near to death, he decided that what he was seeking was not to be found in this way, or indeed in any of the ways represented by contemporary religious leaders.

The Awakening

Siddhattha left the ascetics, and went on his way until he came to a place on a river bank near Gaya, on a tributary of the middle Ganges, where, beneath a bo-tree, he began to meditate earnestly after the method of Indian contemplative and holy men, and resolved that he would remain thus in meditation until he reached the enlightenment he was seeking. The tradition tells how he was assailed by Mara, the Evil One, who, with his three daughters, sought by means of various *Illustration page 267* stratagems to deflect the Buddha-to-be from his purpose. Mara's efforts were, however, all in vain, and after a night of spiritual struggle, all the evil factors which, in the Buddhist view, tie men to this imperfect, mortal existence were overcome, and he became the Awakened, the Buddha, and entered a transcendental, eternal realm of being.

The tradition makes it clear that it would have been possible for him at this point to remain thus, and to have had no further concern with the transient, mortal world. But out of compassion for the mass of humankind this possibility was set aside by the Buddha in order that he might devote himself, during the remainder of the life-span of his mortal body, to proclaiming the *Dhamma*, the eternal truth into which he had 'awakened'.

He remained in meditation, therefore, for a further week only, and then spent a time walking to and fro in the neighbourhood of the bo-tree. During this time he was again approached by Mara, who urged him, now that he was Buddha, to abandon this world of mortals and enjoy the bliss of *nibbana* (the Sanskrit *nirvana* is more commonly used). The Buddha replied that he must first proclaim the *Dhamma* to others, must see the order of monks established, and only then, in due time, depart finally from the mortal scene.

The first preaching of the *Dhamma* is said to have been in an open place, a deer-park, near Benares. The discourse is known in Buddhist tradition as 'The Discourse of the Setting in Motion of the Wheel of Dhamma' (*Dhamma-cakkappa-vattana Sutta*). The form in which the text of this now survives in Pali is probably the product of a somewhat later period, although it contains some of the essential principles of early Buddhist thought and practice. (The main feature of this early doctrine will be described later. See page 271.)

The Beginning of the Buddhist Community

From this time, the Buddha began to attract disciples who were eager to hear more of his teaching and to be instructed in 'the way' or 'path' (*magga*) of which he spoke. Unlike the teaching of the Brahmins and other philosophers of ancient India, such as those whose philosophy is preserved in treatises known as Upanishads (a title which indicates that it was given confidentially to a circle of initiates), the Buddha's teaching was addressed to all and sundry, high and low, and was expressed in terms which would have some meaning even for the simplest.

It was set forth in a great variety of parables, similes, anecdotes and similar devices of popular instruction, yet always in such a way as to arouse an interest and encourage people to commit themselves personally to 'the path', by means of which alone they could hope to enter at length into full apprehension of the truth. This emphasis on the need for personal verification of what is at first accepted in faith has remained a dominant feature of Buddhist practice to the present day.

Among those who became the Buddha's disciples during the forty years of his public activity were people of all classes and occupations. The growing Indian caste-system was disregarded by Buddhists; when a man entered the Sangha, the order of those who were engaged in a full-time pursuit of the Buddhist holy life, it made no difference from what class or caste he came; deference was afforded to members of the order only on account of their saintliness, or length of experience in the Sangha. Besides those who entered the order there were many others who remained 'lay-followers' (*upasikas*), and who practised the Buddhist rule of life for householders, until such time as they might decide to engage in the life of the Buddhist monk, the man without home and possessions, devoting himself primarily to the life of meditation.

The Development of the Order

At first the Buddha and his disciples were a group of wandering *shramanas*. Only later did the order adopt a settled way of life. The whole of the area of the middle Ganges Valley with its various towns, large and small, was covered by their wanderings back and forth, and throughout this area and beyond the name of the Sage of the Sakyas became well known and respected.

The circumstances of the time were favourable to the growth of the Buddhist community. The tribal federations were disappearing before the advance of new, more vigorous and aggressive monarchies, such as that of Magadha, with its capital at Pataliputta (Patna). With the disappearance of the republics went also the old familiar ways of life. The organization of the monarchies was larger and more impersonal, and men were glad, therefore, to find in the Buddhist community, organized as it was on the lines of the old federations, something of the common life they had lost. Moreover, the disturbed nature of the times had the effect of raising with greater acuteness such questions as: Why do men suffer? What is the ultimate purpose of human life? and so on. To such questions many found satisfying answers in the Buddha's teaching.

The Buddha and his disciples did not travel about for the whole of the year, however. For three months or so, during the period of heavy monsoon rains in North India, travel was impossible, and during this period groups of Buddhist monks resorted to places of shelter where they lived a community life. At the end of the rains they went their several ways again, but in the course of time this practice of the common life during the rains-retreat was extended to the time after the rains had finished, and settled communities of Buddhist *shramanas* began to be established.

The Establishment of Buddhism in India

No clear chronology of the Buddha's ministry can be discerned from the evidence that is available. It appears from the tradition that by the time of his death at the age of eighty he had become a famous and much respected figure, and had allies and supporters among rich and poor. A king of Magadha named Bimbisara was one of his most devoted friends. The Buddha's attitude to the institution of monarchy appears to have been somewhat ambiguous. Some of the sayings attributed to him indicate that he regarded the exercise of kingship as a hindrance to the pursuit of the religious life and a destiny to be avoided if possible. On the other hand he seems to have taken the view that a monarch who was well disposed towards the *Buddha-Dhamma* could do much to facilitate the effective practice of the Buddhist life by his subjects, by ensuring that there was social justice within his realm, that none were in dire want or poverty, and none had the opportunity of becoming excessively rich.

In this is seen the application of the characteristically Buddhist principle of 'the middle way' – that is, between a life of extreme sensuality and luxury and one of extreme asceticism. The Buddha himself had, in the course of his own approach to Buddhahood, rejected both of these in turn. The creation of ideal conditions for the pursuit of the Buddhist life by the maximum number of citizens was something which the Buddha appears to have regarded as the proper task of a pious monarch. The just social order is presupposed in the Buddha's teaching rather than prescribed, although there is no lack of hints in the Buddha's teaching that this is the pattern of social life to be aimed at. It is for this reason that modern Indian historians such as D. D. Kosambi and Romila Thapar see early Buddhism as 'a social

Left A stone panel (second to third century AD) showing Gotama sitting awake beside his sleeping wife, surrounded by courtiers exhausted by their revels. According to legend, it was then that Gotama decided to set out and seek the real meaning of existence. British Museum, London.

Left A carving from the fifth-century Ajanta Caves showing the temptation of the Buddha by Mara and his three daughters. The Buddha resisted all their devices and as a result of his endurance he attained perfect awareness and became the Awakened.

Right The *stupa* built over the place at Sarnath, Uttar Pradesh, where the Buddha preached for the first time. The ruins in the foreground are those of the first Buddhist monastery.

Below One of the *stupas* at Sanchi, Madhya Pradesh (mid first century AD). Its significance lies in what it contains: in this case the relics of two famous disciples of the Buddha. The notion of a processional way around the *stupa* probably derives from a frequent ritual in solar cults.

Left A late Hellenized representation of the Buddha, from Paitava, Afghanistan (third or fourth century AD). Iconographically, this sculpture is interesting because it marks the shift away from the humanistic Western tradition towards a more hieratic Indian style. Musée Guimet, Paris.

Far left An eighteenth-century Tibetan *tanka* (or cloth painting) representing the Buddha in the act of passing into *nirvana* at his death, surrounded by disciples. The event, which promises salvation for all creatures, is portrayed as a celestial festival. Gulbenkian Museum of Oriental Art, Durham.

Left A medallion depicting the transportation to heaven of the bowl of the Buddha. Although Buddhism itself was a highly intellectual concept, the common people soon created a series of myths and legends about the Buddha.

philosophy' with which any good ruler would have found it necessary to come to terms.

The Death of the Buddha

The last few weeks of the Buddha's life, unlike the preceding years, are recorded in some detail in the *Mahaparinibbana Sutta* (Discourse Concerning the Entry into Final *Nirvana*). Once again Mara the Evil One confronted the Buddha as, according to the tradition, he had done on many occasions during the years since he became Buddha, always however retiring defeated and disconsolate. On this occasion he again urged the Buddha to retire from the earthly scene and enter into final *nirvana*, and this time he received what might appear to have been a favourable response; he was assured by the Buddha that his decease would occur in three months from that day.

The narrative makes it clear however that there was no comfort to be derived from this fact by Mara, since the Order of Buddhist Brethren and the Order of the Sisters, as well as lay disciples of both sexes, were now thoroughly established. They had become 'true hearers, wise and well-trained, ready and learned, . . . able to tell others of the doctrine, preach it, make it known, establish it . . . and make it clear.' In other words there was in existence a Buddhist missionary community able to witness to the *Dhamma* and instruct converts in the Buddhist way. The Evil One could find little comfort in the Buddha's decease now.

Seven days after the Buddha's death at Kushinagara (Sanskrit *Kusinagara*), a small town (modern Kasia) to the northwest of Patna and just to the south of the border of Nepal, the body was cremated. The occasion was marked by ceremonies of the kind which in those days were observed at the death of a king. After the cremation the relics were divided equally among eight clan-groups; each of these built a sacred cairn over their portion of the relics, a form of memorial known in India as a *stupa*. For lay Buddhists the *stupa* became the focus for their devotions, and eventually, as will be mentioned later, developed into the form known in Sri Lanka and South-East Asia as a pagoda.

The Buddha's Doctrine

It would be foolish to suppose that any genuinely religious doctrine could be encapsulated in a few printed pages and handed out to interested enquirers for sampling. This is nowhere more true than in the case of the Buddha's doctrine. For it is not simply an ideological system intended for intellectual evaluation. Buddhists frequently and rightly insist 'If you wish to *understand* the Buddha's doctrine, you must *practise* it!' The teaching of the doctrine was from the first meant to be carried out by those engaged in the Buddhist life, and was to be related to the life-situation of the disciple, step by step; this is how it is still done in Asia today. What can be conveyed in print, however, is a general description of the Buddhists' view of the human situation and of human spiritual needs, which is acknowledged by them as having in its essentials been delivered to them by the Buddha.

Opposite above left Avalokiteshwara, the *bodhisattva* of compassion, in a fifth-century Gupta-style sculpture from Sarnath.

Opposite above right Buddhist monks execute a mystical diagram or *mandala* in Ladakh, Kashmir. This form of aid to meditation probably derives from traditional folk religion.

Opposite below The monastic centre of Mahayana Buddhism at Nalanda in Bihar, which reached its greatest splendour in the seventh century AD. It resembled a cluster of colleges in a university complex, each monastery (or *vihara*) consisting of small cells around an open courtyard.

Illustration page 269

Illustration page 268

The Four Holy Truths

An exposition of this body of doctrine could start from any one of a number of points. It is convenient here to use one of the best-known introductory expositions, namely that which begins from what are known to Buddhists as 'the four holy truths'.

The first of these is the affirmation that all mortal existence is characterized by *dukkha*. This term covers the whole range of meanings conveyed by the words 'ill', 'evil', 'unsatisfactoriness', 'imperfection' and 'disease'. There are times in life, even long periods, when one is unaware of this characteristic, but ultimately it will assert itself and one will experience the bitter sense that things are not what ideally they should be, nor as one could wish them to be. The more refined the sensibilities, the greater is the awareness of this basic characteristic in all mortal existence.

The second truth is that of *samodaya*, or the 'arising' of this sense of unease; it arises out of craving or desire. By this is meant the perpetual thirst of the human spirit to be consuming – whether things, or experiences, or ideas; it is, in fact, the tendency of the human individual to lay hold upon the environment and make it minister to his or her pleasure.

The third truth is *nirodha*, or 'cessation', that is, the cessation of desire. The cessation of individualistic desire is also the cessation of the experience of *dukkha*. This cessation is also equated with *nirvana*, the ideal state of being. To be in this ideal state is to be *nibbuta*, a word which in everyday use in India in the Buddha's day meant 'cool', in the sense of being cool after a fever, that is, healthy and well. In its special Buddhist usage *nibbuta* was an epithet of the ideal humanity – 'cooled' from the heat of the principal passions, hatred, greed and illusion (or better, spiritual darkness or blindness).

The fourth holy truth is that there is a way to such cessation of desire, to such health, to such a pure state of being, and that this is the path (*magga*) pioneered by the Buddha, which others may also learn to tread.

The Buddhist Path

Morality

The earliest and most basic description of the path is that it is threefold, consisting of morality, meditation, and wisdom. These are not successive stages, to be gone through one after the other, but are pursued simultaneously. Morality however has a certain priority: without serious effort to observe the moral precepts there would be no effective practice of meditation.

For monks and lay-people alike the five basic moral observances are expressed in the formula which is used regularly in daily devotions, and which may be translated approximately as follows: 'I undertake to refrain from causing injury to living things, from taking that which is not given (i.e. stealing), from sexual immorality, from falsehood, and from the use of alcohol and drugs as tending to cloud the mind.' A more advanced degree of moral discipline is followed by some lay-people and consists of the observance of an additional three precepts: to abstain from taking food after midday, to abstain from dancing and singing and amusements, and to abstain from the use of garlands, cosmetics and personal adornments. These additions to the rule of life for lay-people are often made on sabbaths and holy days, as an expression of deeper devotion.

It is this set of eight observances which is referred to when the more serious Buddhist speaks of 'taking the eight precepts' at the monastery or temple on holy days. These eight precepts should not be confused with the Eightfold Path. This is a later elaboration and expansion of the original three-fold structure of morality, meditation and wisdom, and will be described in the following section. The eight precepts are to be observed also by members of the order, the Sangha, at all times, with the addition of a further two: to refrain from accepting gold and silver, and from the use of a luxurious bed. There are other social and moral obligations and duties for lay-people and monks, to which reference will be made in connection with social responsibilities.

So far, however, it may seem that the Buddhist way is largely negative, that is, it appears to consist in refraining from various kinds of activity which are considered inimical to spiritual progress. It may also seem that not much has yet been said about the Buddhist doctrine. In fact, the first important point of the doctrine is that a good moral life is the basis from which understanding of the true nature of things must begin. And the teaching of the Buddha was that *this* is the kind of pattern of moral life which must be followed.

Meditation

The second major aspect of the way outlined by the Buddha is meditation. With right conduct must go right thought or right attitudes; together, action and thought are correlated in right being. The cultivation of right thought or right (i.e. morally wholesome) attitudes is one of the primary purposes of meditation. The interrelation of thought and action is implied in the fuller description of the Buddhist life as an Eightfold Path. The eight items, and their relation to the threefold scheme of morality, meditation and wisdom, may be set out as follows:

1 Right understanding	Faith	Wisdom: III
2 Right thought	(initially)	(ultimately)
3 Right speech		
4 Right bodily action	Morality: I	
5 Right livelihood		
6 Right moral effort		
7 Right mindfulness	Meditation: II	
8 Right concentration		

It will be seen that the sequence, morality-meditation-wisdom, is preceded initially by faith. At the beginning of the Buddhist life, that is to say, right understanding (i.e. of the nature of the world and the human situation) and right thought (i.e. a right inner mental attitude) depend on acceptance of the account of things given by the Buddha. Ultimately, however, after living the Buddhist life of morality and meditation, what was at first accepted in faith becomes a matter of direct knowledge or wisdom. Personal apprehension of the truth is now possible, where first it had to be accepted in trust with a view to this ultimate verification through the course of Buddhist living.

With regard to meditation, it must suffice here to say that while there is in the Buddha's teaching much reference to meditational practices, the necessity of meditation, and its various stages and benefits, the subject itself is one which in Buddhist tradition is regarded as best taught by personal instruction by a meditation-master. The pupil's own personal situation, temperament, and type of personality have all to be taken into account and the appropriate course of meditation prescribed. In so far as this aspect of Buddhism can be investigated with the aid of books, the reader is recommended to E. Conze's *Buddhist Meditation* (London, 1956).

Wisdom

The wisdom into which the person who, taking the Buddha's prescription as guide, lives the Buddhist life eventually enters, can be described in its main features, as it is set forth in the Buddha's teaching. It must be emphasized, however, that in the Buddhist view the truth about the nature of things which the Buddha perceived and proclaimed will not command the immediate assent of the worldling. The personal apprehension of this truth is wisdom, the goal of the Buddhist way, but its attainment requires the travelling of the path.

The essential features of the truth proclaimed by the Buddha are as follows. We have already noted that all life is *dukkha*. To this must be added another universal characteristic of mortal life: all is *anicca* (Sanskrit, *anitya*) or impermanence. There is *nothing* which remains the same. The whole of the cosmos which presents itself to sense perception is in a state of continual flux. Only mistakenly do people take certain things to be permanent, remaining essentially the same through all contingent events. The realization of this truth leads to another, the third 'mark' or characteristic of earthly existence, namely *anatta* (Sanskrit *anatman*), the supremely important truth that there is no permanent, unchanging, real 'soul' (*atman*) residing within the human individual.

In their folly, according to the Buddha, people believe that there is such a real unchanging entity within each individual. They think and act accordingly, striving and fighting one another to defend or to save these supposedly eternal individual souls. In opposition to some contemporary Indian philosophers who taught that ultimate cosmic reality (*brahman*) was identical with the soul (*atman*), the Buddha proclaimed that human individuals consist of a temporary conjunction of five groups of factors (*khandhas*), one group being physical and the other four non-physical.

Constant Flux

The association of these five groups lasts only momentarily. They are in constant flux, and finally, at the death of the individual, the association of the factors ceases, without remainder. These five groups of factors are: 1 physical form, 2 sensation, 3 perception, 4 volition, and 5 consciousness. It should be noted that the Buddha's doctrine does not affirm that there is nothing that is eternal, only that it is not to be found in the isolated human individual.

It was the Buddha's denial of the reality of the individual soul which more than anything else distinguished his doctrine from that of other religious philosophers in India. All these, therefore, regarded his views as heretical. If the soul is denied, they argued, moral striving is pointless, and moral justice has no basis. If there is no enduring soul, there is no bearer of merit or demerit, punishment or reward. If a man does not reap the consequences of his own good or evil deeds, why should it matter to him how he lives?

This appeal to self-interest as the motivation for a moral life seemed to many then, as it still does now, a perfectly commonsense view of things which could only be abandoned at the risk of social and moral chaos. So powerful was this commonsense argument that there arose even among the Buddhists an unorthodox sect known as the Personalists, who argued that, although the Buddha denied the reality of the soul, he must have affirmed the reality of the person as the enduring basis of being.

But the Buddha, in rejecting what he held to be the illusion of selfhood, which must be dissolved by means of the moral and meditational disciplines of the Buddhist life, was affirming the reality of a wider realm of being, not confined within the bounds of 'I', 'me', and 'mine'. He was urging upon people the importance of destroying this egocentric view, in which spiritual reality must consist of a multitude of ego-centred beings, so that people might live a wider, freer life – the life which transcends the narrow confines of the individual's cravings and desires, the transcendental, desire-free life which is *nirvana*. It was the seeking of this transcendent state which provided all the motivation necessary for moral striving, according to the Buddhist view. This was the path that people were invited to tread. The Buddha spoke from the position of one who experienced that of which he spoke. From a vantage point of this kind it was possible only to say what in fact the Buddha said: '*Ehi passiko*' (Come, and see!).

The Community of the Buddha

The invitation was, in the first instance, an invitation to lose one's individual existence in the common life of the Sangha, the Buddhist order of *bhikkhus*. This latter word is commonly translated 'monks' or 'nuns' and this is certainly nearer the meaning of *bhikkhu* than is the word 'priest', which is sometimes erroneously applied by Europeans to the members of the Buddhist community in Asia today. Literally the word means 'a sharer', and referred initially to the fact that the *bhikkhu* depended for daily sustenance on the share of food put aside by lay well-wishers and supporters of the community. It has also the sense of one who shares in the common fund of 'alms', whether of food or goods, which were given to the community in any one locality.

The life of the *bhikkhu* was one which entailed (as it still does) the renunciation of all personal possessions and preferences, and a willingness to live a common life of poverty and chastity. Within this common life, with its recognized disciplines and meditational practices, the individual ego was dissolved, and the truer Buddhist perspective was gradually made apparent.

From a very early stage a rule of life was developed and codified in what came to be known as the *Vinaya* – the Discipline. In the first instance the separate items of the code were rulings given by the Buddha upon specific questions of conduct as they arose in particular situations. Later these rulings came to be accepted as standard and were given institutional form in a vast collection which now occupies the first of the three main sections of the Buddhist canon of scripture. These three are: 1 the Discipline; 2 the Discourses; and 3 the Essence of the Doctrine (*Vinaya-Pitaka*; *Sutta-Pitaka*; and *Abhidhamma-Pitaka*). One of the important functions of the Sangha was to preserve and transmit these collections, at first orally, and then in written form. This is still the function of the Sangha today, and one which is regarded very seriously, especially in the Theravada Buddhist countries of Sri Lanka and South-East Asia.

Offences to be Avoided

Within the whole collection known as The Discipline the most important section for the *bhikkhus* is a list of some 250 items of conduct known as the *Patimokkha*. This consists in fact of a list of offences to be avoided, beginning with the most serious, for which the penalty is expulsion from the order, and followed by those for which the penalty is suspension for a time, and then offences of diminishing seriousness, down to matters of etiquette and decorum. This list is recited in the full assembly of the *bhikkhus* at 14-day intervals, and confession is required of any infringement. This recital is an ancient practice of the Buddhist order and is still faithfully observed in the monasteries and convents with due solemnity. It constitutes a continual reminder to the monks and nuns of the standard of behaviour which is proper to members of the Sangha.

An important difference between the Buddhist Sangha and religious orders in the West is that in the Buddhist case membership may or may not be for the rest of a man's (or a woman's) life. If at any time a *bhikkhu* feels that he or she can no longer remain in the order, and should return to lay life, that person is at liberty to do so, after signifying this intention to the abbot. In some countries in South-East Asia it is not unusual for a person to become a member of the Sangha for a certain limited period; this is regarded as worthy of merit and beneficial. If he or she is able to remain in the Sangha for life, so much the better. Many of course do, and become respected and valued members of the social-religious complex of Buddhist society in Asia.

A mistake which Westerners easily make is to think of the Buddhist Sangha as withdrawn from the world. This is partly due to the use of the somewhat misleading word 'monk'. Buddhist monks are not usually men cut off from society, nor is a Buddhist monastery a place separated from the wider community. There is a reciprocal relationship between monks and lay people. The people provide the monks with their food and robes, and maintain the monastery in various ways. The monks provide various services for the local people.

One of the most obvious of these is, traditionally, education. The monastery is the school where the village boys and girls come to learn to read and write, with the result that the Buddhist countries of Asia have generally had a higher than average rate of literacy. Other services which the monks provide are of a ceremonial nature, especially at festival times, or occasions such as funerals. They give regular public instruction in the Buddhist way of life; they act as spiritual advisers and moral counsellors; and in addition to this may also take a leading part in local community affairs and undertakings, especially in Thailand, for example, where their co-operation is often sought by government agencies (agricultural, medical, etc.) in implementing official policies.

The Social Duties of Lay People

In addition to the moral precepts for lay people which have already been mentioned, there are certain recognized moral and social obligations. These are described in one of the discourses of the Buddha, known as the *Sigalovada Sutta*. This sets out the duties of children to parents, and parents to children; of pupils to teachers, and of teachers to pupils; of husbands to wives, and wives to husbands; of servants to employers, and employers to servants; and finally of lay people to their religious preceptors, i.e. monks, and of monks to lay people. These sets of duties, which appear to go back to a very early period of Buddhist history, have in many cases a curiously modern appropriateness; this particular *sutta* is well-known in Sri Lanka and South-East Asia, and on the whole is more faithfully observed than many such ancient codes of morality.

The Expansion of Buddhism in India

To return now to the story of the development of the Buddhist community after the Buddha's decease (*c.* 484 BC), it is sufficient to note that for the first two centuries there was a steady growth in numbers and influence of the Sangha, and that there was also a certain decline in religious zeal. This kind of reaction is not unknown in other traditions after the early years of enthusiasm. Some of the monks became excessively preoccupied with the literal details of the disciplinary code and out of a spirit of legalism began to criticize other monks, whom they accused of laxity in the observance of the discipline. This brought about a major division in the order about a century after the Buddha's decease, when those who stood for a strictly literal observance parted company from those who favoured a more liberal outlook. The second main development of the first two centuries was a development of the analytical method of Buddhist philosophy which had been initiated by the Buddha.

The Abhidhamma

The Buddha's teaching, aimed as it was at popular audiences, had been largely in the form of dialogues, parables, anecdotes, similes and so on. But in some of the discourses attributed to him, particularly those in which he was teaching the *bhikkhus*, summaries of the essential matters were given in lists or groups of headings intended as mnemonic aids. This was particularly so in the analysis of the five groups of factors (*khandha*) which constituted the so-called 'person'. These groups of factors were subject to further analysis and it was the resultant list of mental and psychic phenomena, their interrelationships and interactions which made up what was known as the *Abhidhamma* (Essence of the Doctrine).

The study of these abstractions became one of the major interests of Buddhist monks in the period following the Buddha's decease. Disagreement on points of interpretation arose, and after about two centuries there developed a major division of schools of thought. The intricacies of the *Abhidhamma* are beyond the range of the present work. Some idea of the nature of the issues may be gained from E. Conze's *Buddhist Thought in India*, Part II, and T. R. V. Murti's *The Central Philosophy of Buddhism*, chapter III. It is appropriate here to indicate only that the controversy was largely over the question of whether past and future events could be regarded as real, after or before they had happened. The Sthaviras, or Elders (the traditionalists), maintained that only present events were real. Their opponents, the Sarvastivadins, affirmed that past, present and future events are all equally real: hence their name, from *sarva* (all), *asti* (exists), *vadins* (affirmers).

Buddhist Developments in the Reign of Ashoka

It was of no little consequence for the future development of the Buddhist community that one of India's most powerful rulers, the Emperor Asoka (r. 273-232 BC), became a Buddhist in the early part of his reign. This happened after he had engaged in a campaign against Kalinga, the conquest of which gave his empire an extensive eastern seaboard. The bloodshed involved in the campaign, however, produced in Ashoka such revulsion that he underwent a personal crisis, and vowing that henceforth there would be heard in his domains no longer the sound of the drum, but only that of the *Dhamma*.

The many rock- and pillar-edicts which he had erected throughout the empire, and which have been discovered in modern times, are a rich source of information for Ashoka's subsequent policies and actions. Although he was personally a supporter of the Buddhist Sangha, as emperor he extended his patronage to various other religious communities. The edicts indicate his desire to see piety, justice

Left The Sleeping Buddha at the Gal *vihara*, Polonnaruwa, Sri Lanka. This colossal rock-cut image of *parinirvana* is an enlargement of the standing images of Anuradhapura.

Centre A 50-metre Buddha at Wewurukannala *vihara*, just outside Dikwella, Sri Lanka. Completed in 1968, it conceals an 8-storey building. Inside the head are all the Buddhist scriptures, a small *dagoba* (or *stupa*) and a circle of figures.

Below left The temple and sacred lake of the Isurumuniya *vihara* near the ancient Sri Lankan capital of Anuradhapura.

Below Praying at a domestic shrine in Colombo, Sri Lanka.

Right A north Indian Hindu-style tower with smaller pinnacles crowns the eleventh-century Ananda temple at Pagan, Burma.

Right An eleventh-century Burmese Buddha from the Sulamani temple, Pagan, one of five thousand temples and pagodas at this great Buddhist site.

and social welfare in the society of which he was the ruler. Ashoka's special connection with the Buddhist community had the consequence of further stimulating its growth in numbers and extent, with the result also that with its considerable increase in popularity the Sangha came to include in its ranks men who had entered it for less than the highest motives.

About the year 250 BC, that is midway through Ashoka's reign, a council of Buddhist monks was held at Patna, one of the primary purposes of which was to debate the philosophical issue which, as has been mentioned, divided the Sthaviras and the Sarvastivadins. In the end, the matter was decided in favour of the former, and from about this time the Sarvastivadins appear to have moved away from the capital, northwestwards up the Ganges Valley, eventually making Mathura (modern Muttra, south of Delhi) on the River Jumna their centre. Ashoka's empire extended to the northwestern borders of the Punjab, and as Buddhist monks were free to move throughout the whole area the community had, by the end of Ashoka's reign, probably reached the borders of his territory, where it met the Hellenized kingdom of Gandhara.

This contact with Hellenized culture was not without its effect on Buddhism. One result may have been the development of the devotional artform, the Buddha statue, sometimes referred to by Westerners as a Buddha-image, but by Buddhists called a *buddha-rupa* – that is the 'form' of the Buddha. Until this period there had been no plastic representation of the Buddha, and it was from about the time of the contact with Mediterranean culture in northwestern India that the use of the *buddha-rupa* seems to have begun. Some of the earliest examples, in which the Buddha is represented by a standing figure, strongly resemble representations of the Greek figure of Apollo. Another view, however, is that the development of this form of *Illustration page 269* Buddhist art was not due to foreign cultural contacts but was an indigenous development which centred around Mathura.

Until this time the way in which devotion to the Buddha was given symbolical expression was by means of the *stupa* – the solid stone or brick memorial-mound enshrining a relic of some sort, which has already been mentioned in connection with the events following the Buddha's decease. Many such *stupas* were built in northern India during Ashoka's time, as expressions of Buddhist piety. Some examples of this ancient form of architecture are still to be seen in India.

Missionary Activity

One of the ways by which Buddhism grew in extent during Ashoka's reign was by planned missionary activity. A number of missions were sent out from Patna during this period. They went to all the frontier regions of the Ashokan empire. Some of the places to which they were sent, mentioned in the records, are difficult to identify with certainty now. There is one, however, which is in no doubt, and that was the expedition of monks sent to Sri Lanka, about which more will be said later.

Throughout Ashoka's territory the settled communities of Buddhist monks grew in number, and probably also in size and in dignity. While the Sangha had always been open to men and women of all social classes and while there had been some notable additions to the Sangha from the ranks of the Brahmins, these had not formerly been so numerous as they seem to have become from the time of Ashoka onwards. This was a contributory cause of the emergence of a new trend in Buddhist thought and practice which came eventually to be called the Mahayana. What this was, and how it developed, we must now consider.

The Growth of Mahayana Buddhism in India

The term Mahayana means 'the Great Method', that is, of achieving the Buddhist goal; the name was adopted by the adherents of this school in conscious distinction from what they called 'the Little Method', or Hinayana. The difference between the two was that the Mahayana was more consciously universal in the sense that it provided for a wider sector of society. The older, more traditional form of Buddhist life involved a sharper differentiation between monks and lay people, and in its emphasis on the monastic life and the strict observance of the *Vinaya* code implied that it was virtually only in the living of the monastic life that the Buddhist goal of *nirvana* could be achieved. This, the Mahayanists held, was an unnecessarily narrow view of the matter; although they did not deny its validity, they simply thought it was unnecessarily restrictive. There was, however, some criticism by the Mahayanists that the Hinayana, with its religious élitist emphasis, tended to encourage spiritual pride, pride which, in their view, was sometimes ill-founded.

In some degree the populist emphasis of the Mahayana was a continuation of one of the two main divisions which had emerged about a century after the Buddha's decease, that is, the party who had followed a less strict and literal interpretation of the monastic discipline. Between this early liberalism of the fourth century BC and the Mahayana there is an affinity, but the historical connection between them is difficult to trace. The Mahayana is difficult to date with any precision, but its rise can probably be placed within the first century BC or early AD, that is, about five hundred years after the decease of the Buddha.

The Bodhisattva Concept

One of its major characteristics, then, was its wider popular basis. This, together with the more liberal attitude to prescribed rules and practices, meant that popular forms of religious belief and devotion found readier acceptance. Buddhism has always adopted a fairly tolerant attitude towards the indigenous beliefs and practices of the peoples to whom it has come, and does so still in the rural societies of Asia. This tendency was, however, more marked among the adherents of the Mahayana, and as a consequence there came to be allied with traditional Buddhist practice of the stricter sort a good deal of local cult-material and the absorption of local deities. How this came about has to be explained with reference to another development in the Mahayana, the *bodhisattva* concept.

The *bodhisattva* is thought of as a being who, upon the threshold of *nirvana*, deliberately sets aside entry into this final blissful state out of compassion for the mass of ordinary beings. Instead of becoming fully *buddha*, he or she remains in the temporal realm, devoted to the salvation of others. This emphasis upon compassion which the *bodhisattva* concept represents was not something radically new. Compassion for others had been regarded as a virtue in earlier Buddhism, but it had there a somewhat subordinate place to wisdom. In the Mahayana development it came to receive an equal emphasis with wisdom, as a principal virtue in the spiritual ideal which the *bodhisattva* represented. Even this, however, was a recovery of what the earlier spiritual ideal, the *arahat*, had represented – that is, a person who had transcended the limiting notion of 'self' and who because of this was a source of beneficent moral and spiritual influence. The *arahat* ideal had become corrupted in the centuries immediately before the rise of the Mahayana, and needed to be given this new formulation.

The *bodhisattva* was thought of also as a being no longer subject to the physical limitations of human life. He or she inhabited a 'celestial' realm, a spiritual 'field' brought into being by his own saintliness. It was into this blessed realm of being that he was believed to be able to bring others by his spiritual power. There was in theory no necessary limit to the possible number of *bodhisattvas*, and there thus developed belief in a number of such beings, each known by his or her own name. Some of the more prominent of these were Avalokiteshwara ('He Who Looks Down in Mercy'), Amitabha ('Boundless Light'), and Manjushri ('Beautiful Lord'). For lay people in India at this period each of these became the central figure in a cult which, phenomenologically, was very similar to the cult of a deity. In this way Mahayana Buddhism provided a transition from the indigenous cults of local Indian deities to Buddhist doctrines and practice.

Illustration page 270

The Development of Mahayana Philosophy

At the same time that Mahayana was developing a wider Buddhist appeal to the lay people of India, its monks were developing a highly abstract religious philosophy. The increasing number of men of Brahmin family who had been entering the Buddhist Sangha was reflected in the increasing degree to which the earlier system of *Abhidhamma* was subjected to Brahmin intellectual criticism.

The Brahmins were the masters of ancient Indian logic, and it was on logical grounds that the *Abhidhamma* theories of the Hinayana schools were criticized. The *Abhidhamma* method of analysing what seemed to be real objective entities into their constituent, transient factors had crystallized into a final pattern of *dhammas*. These were thought of as the ultimate, real 'atoms' of all mental and psychic and physical events, and were held to be a certain limited number (the exact number varied from one school to another).

This theory of existence was criticized by Mahayana philosophers as being rather inconsistent with the analytical method. This, they said, had been intended to show that there are no ultimate, real entities so far as the empirical world is concerned. It is, they argued, as illogical to regard any of these *dhammas* as real as it is to regard the human 'soul' as real. All is flux, and the method of the Buddha was intended to show this, providing no final resting place at all within the empirical world – not even in so-called *dhammas*. They therefore pursued the analytical method relentlessly. The *dhammas* named by Hinayana monks were purely arbitrary stopping places.

Logically there could be no termination of the process of analysis and further analysis. Nothing existed to which any permanent properties could be attributed. Only when every positive property had been denied was reality attained, for every attribution of property involved a degree of relativity and hence could not be regarded as absolute. What they were seeking, in fact, was an absolute, and they described the goal of the Buddhist analysis as that which is reached when every positive attribute has been made void. It is by the word 'Void' that the term which they used for the absolute (*shunyata*) is sometimes translated.

This school of Mahayana thought is called the Madhyamika, a name which may be translated roughly as 'neutralism'. It is known also as Shunya-vada. The great exponents of this school were a Buddhist monk of Brahmin family from South India, Nagarjuna and his disciple, Aryadeva, both active in the early third century.

Reaction

While this kind of issue may seem far removed from the practice of religion, it has to be remembered that it was in the context of the devotional and meditational life of the monastery that such intellectual exercises would have been carried on. Even so, however, there was a certain degree of reaction in Buddhist circles against so excessively intellectual an emphasis. This showed itself in one form in the emergence of a school known as Yogacara, which arose in India at about the end of the fourth century AD. Its principal literary exponents were Asanga (AD 310-390) and his brother, Vasubandhu (AD 320-400).

The Yogacara represented a shift of emphasis within the Mahayana, and a return to the moral and meditational aspects of religion. In contrast to the Madhyamika insistence on the Void as the only absolute, the Yogacara affirmed the reality of pure consciousness (*vijnana*). It is for this reason that the school is known also as the Vijnana-vada. The aim of the Buddhist life was seen to be the purification of consciousness, by means of moral striving and meditation, and the attaining of the pure state of consciousness, which was the real, and the absolute.

The Spread of Buddhism to China and Japan

By the time the Vijnana-vada had developed in India, Buddhism had already been carried to China and had begun to establish itself there. By about the middle of the second century AD Buddhist monks were travelling along the busy trade-route that led from northwestern India through Central Asia to western China. In that part of India there were then large and populous Buddhist centres, for it was one of the areas of great strength of the developing Mahayana. The missionary task, laid on the first monks by the Buddha himself, of spreading the *Dhamma* to all peoples, was in certain respects easier for Mahayana than for Hinayana monks. They did not regard themselves as strictly tied to the letter of the monastic disciplinary code, and could, for example, when they ventured into colder climates, use warmer clothing than the monk's robe which was prescribed for use in India. The unsettled condition of China at the end of the Han dynasty (latter half of the second century) was such that people were in a receptive mood for the coming of a new religion. Even although upper-class Confucian scholars might view it with contempt, many of the Chinese masses were prepared to welcome the new teaching, especially its message of celestial *bodhisattvas* to whom appeal might be made for help and salvation from the ills and sorrows of this life.

Becoming well established in China, Mahayana Buddhism spread from there into Korea, and thence into Japan by the end of the sixth century AD. Particularly popular was the cult of the Bodhisattva Amitabha, known in Japan as Amida. Belief in his power to save men by his grace and to bring them at death to his paradise or 'Pure Land' became one of the dominant strands of Japanese Buddhism and remained so up to modern times.

For Buddhism in China, see pages 343–9; in Japan, see pages 363–70.

The Decline of Buddhism in India

Meanwhile, in India, the Yogacara emphasis had aided the development of a variety of meditational cults and yogic practices in which extensive use was made of mystical diagrams or *mandalas*, sacred formulae or *mantras*, and various other aids to the cultivation of states of trance. Many of these practices were derived from traditional Indian folk-religion, and were incorporated, with or without much adaptation, into a nominally Buddhist context. Thus developed the form of Buddhism known as Tantra, or Mantra-yana, which was characteristic of the early medieval period in India, and which preceded the virtual disappearance of Buddhist religion from most of the sub-continent. The trend in monastic life played a part in the decline of Buddhist observance and belief among the lay people, for, with the increase in the number of great monastic centres where philosophical and secular learning were pursued for their own sake, there went a corresponding decrease in the number of small, local or 'parish' monasteries which had until then served as focal points of Buddhism for the people of the countryside and small towns.

Chinese Buddhist pilgrims were now coming to India, the Holy Land of the Buddha, and the accounts which some of them have left of their travels provide valuable evidence of the state of Buddhism in India from the fifth to the seventh centuries AD. Some of the more famous Chinese pilgrims, who came in search of holy relics, sacred texts, and knowledge of Buddhist practice and monastic organization, were Fa-hsien (in India from 399 to 414), Hsüang-tsang, whose journey from China until his return there covered the years 629 to 645, and I-tsing (in India from 671 to 695). Between Fa-hsien's visit and that of Hsüang-tsang Buddhism was clearly declining. Monasteries which the former had found inhabited were by the latter's time ruined and forsaken. Lumbini, near Kapilavastu, the Buddha's birth-place, was found by Hsüang-tsang to have suffered thus. This fact is noteworthy in view of the veneration which had been accorded in earlier Buddhist practice to the four 'holy places': namely Lumbini, the birth-place; Buddha-Gaya, the scene of the Awakening; Sarnath, the place of the first preaching of the *Dhamma*; and Kushinagara, the place of the Buddha's decease. The neglect of Lumbini by the seventh century AD would seem to suggest not only the decline of local monastic life but also in this particular case a loss of interest in the localities associated with the historical Buddha, Gotama, perhaps as a result of the shift of emphasis to the notion of present *bodhisattvas*.

A Few Centres Flourish

Meanwhile a few great monastic centres where Mahayana philosophy and, later, Tantric speculation flourished were increasing in size and status. The outstanding centres were Nalanda in Bihar, Vikramasila in West Bengal, and Amaravati and Nagarjunakonda in South India (Andhra Pradesh). Sukumar Dutt, in his book *Buddhist Monks and Monasteries of India* (London, 1962), has characterized this shift in the centre of gravity from small local monasteries to large institutions akin to universities as a movement away from 'study for faith' to 'study for knowledge'.

Illustration page 270

It was during this period that the spread of Buddhism to Tibet occurred. Its effective founder in that country was Padma-Sambhava, and the form of Buddhist religion which he introduced was predominantly tantric, that is, the form of belief and practice which gave great prominence to mystic symbols, sacred chants and various other esoteric devotional activities. This had an appeal for the Tibetans, a people whose religion until this time had been of a kind in which magical practices had played a large part. After a period of opposition and some persecution, Buddhist religion was re-established at the beginning of the eleventh century. One of the outstanding figures in this reintroduction of Buddhism was Atisha, a Bengali monk from the monastic centre at Vikramasila, and again it was the tantric form which was conveyed to Tibet from northern India, and gave to Tibetan Buddhism the characteristic features by which it came to be known to Europeans in modern times.

For mystical symbols in Kashmir, see illustration page 270.

Buddhism in India Since 1200

There is something to be said for the view that Buddhism had disappeared altogether from India by about 1200. We have seen that the decline of local Buddhist centres of influence had been going on for some centuries, and the institutional forms of Buddhism gradually came to be concentrated in the great centres such as Nalanda. When, by reasons of their great wealth and magnificence, these eventually attracted the plundering activities of the Muslim invaders from the northwest, their fall meant the virtual end of Buddhism as a recognizable institution in India. But the responsibility for this certainly does not rest upon Islam, or even upon the savagery of the particular representatives of Islam who seem to have dealt Buddhist institutions in India the *coup de grâce* at that time. As a religious system separate from the Hindu cults and sects Buddhism had already largely been lost to sight.

Some take the view that the religion of the Buddha lives on in the devotionalism of the Hindu *bhakti* cults. Certainly the complex of ideas and practices known as Hinduism owes much to Buddhist influences and ideas. Having bequeathed its treasures to Indian religion in this way, it is said, Buddhism as a separate religion gracefully disappeared from the scene. Some aspects of the worship of the god Vishnu, in particular, would seem to support this view, especially its relative laxity with regard to caste-distinctions, its devotionalism, its doctrine of avatars, of whom the Buddha is one, its vegetarian observances, and so on. Again, even in the prestige enjoyed by the Hindu philosopher Shankara some have seen an indirect influence of Buddhist thought, since he seems to have been influenced by some Mahayana ideas in the working out of his monistic philosophy of Advaita Vedanta, and was even regarded as a 'crypto-Buddhist'.

For the god Vishnu and his worship, see pages 222–3 and 225–6.

It is from considerations of this sort that E. Conze, for instance, takes the view that the separate existence of Buddhism no longer served any useful purpose and that its disappearance was no loss to anyone. It, too, was subject to the universal law of change and impermanence which the Buddha had proclaimed. In this view of the matter 'what Buddhism in India died from was just old age, or sheer exhaustion' (E. Conze, *A Short History of Buddhism*, 1960, p. 86).

Nevertheless, in Sri Lanka Buddhism did not die of exhaustion or old age, however close it may have been to doing so at some points in its history, and today it is far from feeble after twenty-two centuries of continuous existence in that island. From the point of view of the historian it seems more likely that the fate of the Buddhist community in India was due to a complex set of circumstances, a number of which can be identified: the trend towards centralization, the loss of distinctiveness as Mahayana grew closer to Hinduism, the loss of royal patronage, and finally attacks by the Muslim invaders.

It did not disappear entirely, however, but persisted in out of the way places on the borders of India, especially in the north. In the twentieth century there has been a growth in the number of Buddhists in India, owing to the mass conversion of many of the class formerly known as 'Untouchables' These conversions were considerably stimulated by the public adherence to Buddhism of Dr B. R. Ambedkar, a former cabinet minister in independent India, in 1956. Ambedkar was leader of the Untouchable class and many of them followed his example.

Monks from Sri Lanka and elsewhere have gone to India to assist this growing community of new Buddhists, a large proportion of whom are found in the state of Maharashtra, and now number some five million. In addition to this, and at a quite different level, is the renewed interest in Buddhism among some of the more sophisticated and Westernized citizens of India, although this is largely intellectual and hardly amounts to anything that could be called a popular revival of Buddhism.

Buddhism in Sri Lanka

Illustrations page 279

So far as is known, Sri Lanka was the first country outside Ashoka's India to receive Buddhism and it is certainly the country with the longest continuous and unbroken history of Buddhist practice. For most of the story of Buddhism's introduction into the island by the monk Mahinda and his companions we are dependent on the Pali historical chronicles. While there may have been some embellishment of the details of the story, in general there is little doubt that Buddhist beginnings in Sri Lanka go back to at least the third century BC. Some would date them even earlier.

The king of Sri Lanka at the time was named Devanampiya Tissa, that is, Tissa Beloved of the Gods. His name is an indication of the religion of Sri Lanka prior to the introduction of Buddhism; it consisted of the worship of a number of gods, many of whom bore the same names as the vedic deities worshipped in ancient India. Brahma, Indra, Yama, Varuna, and Kuvera were the major ones; others included Baladeva, Rama, Vasudeva and Shiva. According to the tradition, the king himself became a lay Buddhist, as did many of the people of Sri Lanka. Worship of the gods did not cease, but was gradually adapted to a system which was basically Buddhist and in which the vedic deities were supposed to have been converted to Buddhism, and were now subordinate to the Buddha, to whom the highest respect was given.

Devotion to the Buddha was expressed symbolically by worship of the *stupa* or relic-mound and the bo-tree. The first *stupa* in Sri Lanka was built by Tissa in the capital city (at that time Anuradhapura) and is still venerated by Buddhist pilgrims. A shoot of the original bo-tree was brought from Buddha-Gaya with great pageantry and planted with due ceremonial in a specially prepared place to the south of the city. Most important, however, in the establishing of Buddhism in the island was the entry into the ranks of the Sangha of Singhalese men and women. A monastery was founded at Anuradhapura. It was known simply as the Maha Vihara (the great monastery) and from that time became the most important centre of Buddhist religion in the island.

The school of Buddhism which came to Sri Lanka was that which prevailed at the Emperor Ashoka's capital, namely that of the Sthaviras or Elders. This became known later as the Theravadin school, and has remained the dominant type of Buddhism in Sri Lanka. Its monks are conservative in their attitude to the central teachings of Gotama the Buddha and in their interpretation of the monastic code. It is they who have preserved the scriptures in the Pali language.

Left Thai Buddhist monks carry prayer-sticks to the funeral pyre of a friend. Funerals are traditionally happy, often including a band which plays as the body burns.

Left Wat Po in Bangkok. This towered-temple illustrates the typical spired *stupa*, or *praprang*, adopted in Thailand after the eighteenth century.

Right A plan of ninth-century Borobudur in Java. One of Buddhism's greatest stupas, it is constructed in the form of a mandala. Five closed square galleries and three open circular inner terraces combine in an ascending and concentric scheme which conveys the universe geometrically.

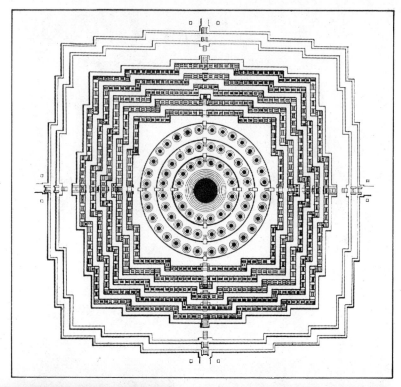

Below right A Buddhist monk in Vietnam burns himself to death in 1963 as a protest against the war being waged there. This is an ancient custom intended to indicate faithfulness to the peaceful Buddhist tradition.

Below Barefoot women and children at evening prayer in Penang, Malaya. The wearing of shoes would be an act of desecration.

Left The Dalai Lama with advisers and attendants at a religious ceremony in the Potala Palace, Lhasa, before the Chinese invasion of Tibet in 1959 forced him to flee into northern India.

Left The Wheel of Life, depicted on an eighteenth or nineteenth-century *tanka*. Said, by one early text, to have been described by Buddha himself, it represents the principles of Tibetan Buddhism and, possibly as a teaching aid to the illiterate, is often found painted on the wall beside a temple's main entrance. Symbols of the three cardinal sins, the cock (passion), the snake (hatred) and the pig (stupidity), appear at the centre. Then come the victims of bad *karma* (right) and good *karma* (left) and the six spheres of existence. The rim of the wheel represents the twelve *nidanas* or links in the chain of causation, the culmination of the Buddha's search for truth. Clasping the wheel is the animal symbolizing impermanence or death. Victoria and Albert Museum, London.

Above Prayer flags bearing printed Buddhist texts fly from a stone cairn high in the Tibetan Himalayas. Left by pilgrims, they are a continuation of ancient folk practices.

Right A Tibetan woman clutches a prayer wheel. During the Chinese Cultural Revolution, possession of such an object would have been punished: many were destroyed, others hidden.

Somewhat later in the history of Buddhism in Sri Lanka there was an attempt, successful for a while, to introduce the Mahayana form from South India. Serious rivalry developed between the Theravadin monks of the Maha Vihara and the monks of the newly established Mahayana monastery, the Abhayagiri. For some centuries this rivalry continued, first one party and then the other gaining the support of the ruler. The people seem on the whole to have been more in favour of the Theravadin monks. Eventually, in the fourth century AD, the rivalry was brought to an end by the king in favour of the Theravadins, who remained thereafter the dominant, and eventually became virtually the only, school of Buddhism which continued to exist in Sri Lanka.

This ascendancy was greatly assisted in the fifth century by the work of the great Buddhaghosa, whose achievements in the realm of commentarial exposition of scripture and the composition of a great symposium of doctrine may be likened to that of Aquinas in the Christian tradition. Pali Buddhist scholarship had been in decline for some centuries and had been almost eclipsed by the prestige of Sanskrit, the language of the Indian Brahmins and of the Mahayana school of Buddhism. It was Buddhaghosa who restored Pali learning and literature to a place of honour, and in so doing became a figure to whom the greatest respect was paid by Buddhists not only in Sri Lanka but subsequently throughout South-East Asia. Possibly his greatest work is the *Visuddhimagga* (The Way of Purification), which is both a compendium of Buddhist scripture and a systematic exposition of Buddhist spirituality.

For a thousand years after Buddhaghosa, Buddhist practice in Sri Lanka continued to follow the pattern which he had received from the older monks from whom he learnt the tradition, but which he then so masterfully formulated and embodied in literary form. During these ensuing centuries the fortunes of the Sangha in Sri Lanka waxed and waned. Sometimes it was required to revive the Sangha in the neighbouring Buddhist countries of South-East Asia, namely Burma, Thailand and Kampuchea. At other times, when it had sunk low, it was itself revived by Theravadin monks from those countries.

The Portuguese Come to Sri Lanka

The most difficult period in the history of Buddhism in Sri Lanka probably began with the coming of the Portuguese Catholics in the sixteenth century. During the century or so during which they dominated Sri Lanka, and then under the rule of the Dutch for a further two centuries, and finally that of the British from the beginning of the nineteenth century, Buddhism passed through a period when its monasteries were deprived of their lands, its relationship with the state was broken, its lay adherents were either forced or cajoled into renouncing their religion in order to embrace another, and the delicate fabric of Buddhist society, lay and monastic, suffered serious damage. Nevertheless, by the end of the nineteenth century Buddhism in Sri

Lanka, then undoubtedly at its very lowest ebb, began to revive.

New movements, monastic and lay, began to appear. New interest in the treasures of Pali literature began to be aroused, partly by the enthusiasm of Western orientalists and students of religion; new centres of Buddhist higher education were established. The practice of Buddhist meditation began to be revived in newly established forest-retreats and monasteries. By the time Sri Lanka became an independent nation again in 1948 Buddhism had been largely, though not entirely, restored to its place as the principal guiding and directing *Illustrations page 279* force in Sri Lankan culture. From Sri Lanka Buddhist influence is now extending once again, mainly through publications and the missionary activities of monks, not only to other Asian countries but to the West also.

Buddhism in Burma

Both the Hinayana and the Mahayana were introduced into South-East Asia by missionary monks during the early centuries of the Christian era. The whole area of southern Burma and southern Thailand was inhabited by a people called the Mons. These followed the Theravada form of Buddhism, which came to them probably from eastern India. In central and northern Burma an important school of the Hinayana, the Sarvastivada, had considerable influence, and so, by the fifth century AD, had the Mahayana. There is archaeological evidence that both forms of Buddhism flourished in upper Burma at that period. They may have reached Burma overland from Bengal. The phases of development through which Mahayana Buddhism in India passed seem to have been reflected in Burma. Certainly by the eleventh century the Buddhism of upper Burma appears to have been largely of the Tantric kind.

At that time the northern part of Burma was ruled by kings of Tibeto-Burmese race, ancestors of the valley Burmese of today. One of these, Anawrahta, whose rule began in AD 1044, was converted to the Theravada form of Buddhism by a monk from southern Burma. Anawrahta then embarked on a programme of reform of the tantric Buddhism practised in his realm by a priesthood called the Aris (literally, the 'holy ones', a title which in this case seems to have been rather inappropriate). He obtained from a neighbouring kingdom, by the rather un-Buddhistic use of armed force, a complete copy of the Pali canon of scripture, and made this the norm for the practice of Buddhism in his realm.

In this way the Theravada became the dominant form of Buddhism throughout Burma, and the Mahayana disappeared, surviving only in occasional practices which have been incorporated into the blend of indigenous and Buddhist belief and practice which go to make up the distinctive pattern of what at the lay level should be called Burmese Buddhism. The religion practised in the monasteries of Burma is, however, identical with the Theravada of other South Asian countries (Sri Lanka, Thailand, Kampuchea and Laos) and is based on the Pali canon.

Burma has many monasteries; they are found adjacent to almost every town and village, especially in the lowland areas, which is where most of the Burmese live. The monasteries have exerted a strong influence on the moral life of the country and have provided through the centuries the local centres of education. Monastic scholarship in Burma has specialized in the study of the *Abhidhamma* literature, that is, the third section of the canon, which deals with the analysis of mental and moral phenomena. The background to this kind of scholarship is, as M. H. Bode pointed out, a considerable measure of support from wealthy pious lay people, since 'literary work required a more spacious, convenient vihara (monastic building) than was needed for the simple round of the mendicant's ordinary life, besides a whole library of sacred texts. To supply all these and other necessities of scholarship was a highly meritorious act, and rich laymen were as eager to acquire merit in such ways as monks were content to accept their gifts' (M. H. Bode, *The Pali Literature of Burma*, 1909, reprinted 1966, p. 35).

In the fifteenth century there was a further revival of Buddhism in the southern part of Burma, for which the king, Dhammaceti (1460-91), appears to have been largely responsible. He had earlier in his life been a monk, and was as a king renowned for his piety. He continued to act as protector of the Sangha throughout his reign, and was concerned to reform some of its less orthodox aspects. He sent a mission of monks to Sri Lanka to study and equip themselves in order to return and revive the monastic life of his kingdom. Towards the end of the fifteenth century the exclusive use of Pali as the language of religion began to yield to the use of Burmese, a process which was to gain momentum in the sixteenth century as more and more scriptures, commentaries, and devotional literature began to be produced in the vernacular (a curious parallel to a similar process which was taking place at about the same time in India and Europe in connection with the use of Sanskrit and Latin respectively).

The British Rule Burma

Burma was, unlike Sri Lanka, only lightly affected by the coming of the Portuguese. It was not until the early nineteenth century that European colonialism began to affect Burma, in this case in the gradual extension of British rule by three stages (1826, 1853 and 1885). The last Burmese king was deposed and removed from Mandalay and the British became the rulers of the whole country. The exploitation of the natural resources of the country, with very little in the way of compensating economic benefits, had a disruptive effect on Burmese life from which it has not yet recovered. The old pattern of royal patronage and protection of the Sangha was broken. Nothing was done by the British to make good the damage they had caused in this respect, and the life of the Sangha suffered severely as a result.

Although the social and institutional fabric of Buddhism in Burma suffered damage from colonial rule, the physical fabric survived virtually intact both the British rule and, more briefly, that of the Japanese. Some of the most magnificent Buddhist pagodas in Asia are to be found in Burma, the most notable being the Shwe Dagon, the Golden Pagoda, on the northern outskirts of the city of Rangoon. This great focus of Buddhist devotion consists of a central circular mass of masonry, covered entirely with pure gold leaf, about the same height as the dome of St Paul's Cathedral in London. It is surrounded by a circular open marble pavement, on the outer edge of which are various monastic buildings and shrines. It is a place of pilgrimage for Buddhists from all over South-East Asia, and especially from the towns and villages of Burma. Other famous pagodas are in Moulmein, and the former capital Mandalay.

Throughout the vicissitudes of the colonial period some of the monks maintained the tradition of *Abhidhamma* study, for which Burma was famous, and also certain methods of meditation, based on discourses of the Buddha in the Pali canon, in which Burmese monks have specialized. A notable feature of the period since independence has been the growth of meditation centres for lay people, especially around the city of Rangoon. To these come civil servants, teachers, merchants, and so on, to spend a period of two, three or perhaps four weeks in the practice of meditation under the close supervision and guidance of a meditation master.

Thailand

The earliest evidence of Buddhism in Thailand is in connection with the Mon peoples (already mentioned in connection with Burma). Archaeological evidence from sites in the plain of South Thailand, such as Nakorn Pathom, where there is a large and ancient *stupa*, suggests that Buddhism was practised here from the second century AD. *Buddha-rupas*, inscribed pieces of terracotta and *Dhammacakra* (wheel of the doctrine) symbols which have been found appear to belong to this period. During these early centuries, up to about the end of the seventh century AD, the type of Buddhism in this region was mainly of the Hinayana kind.

From the eighth century onwards, however, the neighbouring kingdom of Shri-Vijaya (in Sumatra) became increasingly powerful and exerted an influence on what is now southern Thailand. This included the influence of the religion which was at that time predominant in Sumatra, namely an amalgam of Mahayana Buddhist and Hindu elements. *Buddha-rupas* found in Thailand which date from this period of dominance by Shri-Vijaya reflect the Mahayana characteristics. Similarly, eastern Thailand came under the dominance of the Khmers (a Hinduized kingdom in the area which is now Kampuchea) between the eleventh and fourteenth centuries and as a result there was an influx of elements of Hindu culture. Already, however, in the thirteenth century the Thai people were moving into the north of the country from southern China, and by the fourteenth century were expanding southwards. As they did so they absorbed the largely Hinayana form of Buddhism of the Mons of the central plain.

From that time onwards a similar pattern of relationships to that which existed in Burma between king and monks seems to have developed in Thailand, with the ruler in most cases acting as supporter and protector of the Sangha in his realm. Theravada Buddhism was undergoing a reform in Sri Lanka during the fourteenth century, under the rule of the renowned King Parakkama Bahu, and this drew a number of monks from Thailand to Sri Lanka who, returning to their own land, introduced there the reformed Theravada practices and learning; since then the Theravada form has predominated in Thailand.

A New Capital

At the end of the eighteenth century a new capital was established in the south of the country, on the Chao Phya (or Menam) River, first at Dhonburi on the west bank, and then on the east bank opposite Dhonburi at Krung-thep or Bangkok. The line of Thai kings who established this new capital are known by the name 'Rama', followed by a numeral. One of the most famous of these was Rama IV, known also as Mongkut. Before becoming king on the death of his brother in 1851 Mongkut had for some thirty years been a Buddhist monk, and for the latter part of this period, the abbot of a *wat*, or temple, *Illustration page 289* in Bangkok. As such he had introduced a number of reforms and had sought to develop a reinterpretation of Buddhist ideas in terms of contemporary thought. He was himself a scholar, and conversant with Western learning of the time. One of his most important achievements was the founding of a reformed school of the Sangha called the Dhammayutika. It was, in fact, not until the reign following Mongkut's, that of his son Chulalongkorn (Rama V), that the Dhamamayutika was recognized as a separate school of the Sangha.

It grew out of the following of monks which Mongkut began to gather when he was appointed abbot of the Wat Bovoranives in Bangkok in 1837. During the fourteen years that he remained there Mongkut gained a well-deserved reputation as a preacher and teacher, expounding Buddhist ideas in terms which all his listeners could understand. From a neighbouring Catholic bishop, Pallegoix, he learnt Latin, and from an American Presbyterian missionary, English. He was particularly interested in contemporary scientific knowledge and its practical applications. As a monk on his daily round he came constantly into contact with the ordinary people of the city of Bangkok. By the time he left the monastery to take over the responsibilities of king at the death of his brother in 1851, Wat Bovoranives had become one of the most influential centres of the Buddhist Sangha in Thailand.

Mongkut not only sought to interpret the *Dhamma* in contemporary terms; he also succeeded in restoring to the life of the Sangha some of the essential emphases which had been lost sight of. His purification of its life and his reform of its discipline had a reinvigorating effect which spread from his monastery to many others, a process which has continued up to the present time.

The Lasting Effects of Buddhism

Illustration page 289

Thailand provides a good example of the kind of life (religious, moral and social) Theravada Buddhism has been capable of promoting and maintaining in South-East Asia when left free from the disruptive effects of colonialism and communism. The people are well satisfied with the opportunities which the Theravada provides for expressing and practising the religious life. Christian missionaries have worked among the Thais for many years; they have been well received and are generally respected, but less than two per cent of the people have thought it necessary to change to another religion.

In 1982 there were in Thailand 24,000 *wats* (monasteries), 175,000 monks and nuns, and some 100,000 novices; the numbers fluctuate as many people take up monastic life only in the rainy season, July to October. Since 1902 the Sangha has administered its affairs independently of the secular government through the Sangha Supreme Council, although the king remains a Buddhist and the patron and protector of the order. The monks are active in preaching and explaining Buddhist doctrine and the Buddhist way of life throughout the country by means not only of local assemblies in temples, but also through radio and television. Monks have been sent as Buddhist missionaries to Malaysia, India, Laos and England. Some of the monasteries are centres of social welfare, and include within their compounds schools, libraries and hospitals.

Kampuchea, Laos, Vietnam

The former colony of French Indo-China had, prior to its colonization by the French in the latter part of the nineteenth century, for many centuries existed as a number of independent kingdoms, in each of which the predominant religious tradition was Buddhist: Theravada in the case of Kampuchea and Laos, and Mahayana in the case of Vietnam. Prior to the thirteenth century, however, Kampuchea and Laos also had a tradition of Mahayana, with which were mingled elements of Brahminism. By the end of the thirteenth century the three main religious groups represented in Kampuchea were Hindu Brahmins and worshippers of the god Shiva, and Theravadin Buddhists. As a result of Thai influence from the fourteenth century onwards Kampuchea came to be more and more a Theravadin country. The state of Laos was founded in 1353 by a Thai prince who had been educated by a Buddhist monk in Kampuchea. Since that time Laos has developed into a predominantly Theravadin country. Its monks have close ties with those in the neighbouring country of Thailand.

Mahayana Buddhism had reached Vietnam prior to the eleventh century AD and Buddhist monks were respected for the quality of their lives as well as for their learning. In AD 1010 a Buddhist named Ly Thai-to became ruler of Vietnam, and from that time onward Ch'an (Zen) Buddhism enjoyed a special prestige. His successors in the Ly dynasty in the eleventh and twelfth centuries, up to 1225, were also zealous adherents of Zen Buddhism. Early in the fifteenth century the country fell under Chinese domination, with a consequent

For the teaching of the Ch'an school, see page 347.

growth of Confucian and Tao influence, and a restriction of the activities of Buddhist monks. As far as the common people were concerned, this resulted in the development of a religious syncretism. In the latter part of the nineteenth century, under French colonial rule, Buddhism was again subjected to severe restriction, as a result of the growth of Catholic influence. A faithful minority of monks continued the practice of their religion in seclusion, while the more publicly involved 'bonzes' supported a syncretism of elements of tantric Buddhism with primitive religion and polytheism.

During the twentieth century, up to the outbreak of the hostilities which devastated the country in the nineteen-sixties, there had been a steady recovery of Buddhism in Vietnam. The most prominent revival was that of the Amida (Pure Land) form of the Mahayana, which increased at the expense of Zen, but Theravadin influence was also growing. In 1951 an All-Vietnam Buddhist Association was formed; for some years Buddhist monks in Vietnam had been meeting together not only with their own compatriots, but also with Buddhists from other countries, and had been increasingly aware of Buddhism as an international religious community. After 1962 Buddhist leaders in Vietnam had a much more public and political role thrust upon them, and some revived the ancient Chinese Mahayana practice of self-immolation for the sake of the Buddha. In this modern form the practice was intended as a witness to their faithfulness to the Buddhist tradition and a protest against the destruction of the country and people of Vietnam.

For the cult of Amida, see pages 366–7.

Illustration page 290

Indonesia

Not a great deal is known of the early history of Buddhism in the territory now designated Indonesia, but it is safe to say that it had been introduced into Java by the fifth century AD, and that it played an important role in succeeding centuries in most of the other regions of present-day Indonesia. Its entry into this area appears to have been as a result of the same missionary motive which characterized Buddhism in India. It had become well established in Sumatra by the seventh century, under the Srivijaya kings who at that time ruled the island. The importance of the Srivijaya kingdom as a centre of Buddhist learning is testified by a Chinese Buddhist pilgrim who visited the island of Sumatra in 671 in the course of his travels.

Contact with eastern India resulted in the developments in Mahayana Buddhism in India being reflected in Sumatra; by the eighth century the Tantric form had spread there. From the early ninth century Buddhism was well established in the Malay peninsula, which was then under the rule of the Sailendra dynasty. In Java the massive structure known as Borobudur, a great sculptured pyramid, dates probably from the eighth century and indicates the great prestige which Buddhism had gained in Java.

Illustration page 290

Throughout the period of its public prestige in Indonesia Buddhism coexisted on friendly terms with the Shaivite form of Hinduism. The Tantric form of Buddhism made possible also a certain degree of syncretism with native Indonesian and Malay religious beliefs and practices. Its eventual displacement by Islam from the thirteenth and fourteenth centuries onwards was very gradual and peaceful, the more so since the form of Islam which entered Indonesia from India was strongly penetrated by Sufi mysticism. Buddhist monasteries became Muslim religious centres. The pattern of religious life which these Indonesian Muslim centres sustained was so similar to that of the Buddhist social order that there was no great or dramatic change.

Although the majority of the inhabitants of Indonesia are today classified as Muslims, some Buddhists are still to be found, and while their number may be small the influence of Buddhism has not by any means been entirely effaced. The festival of Vesak, celebrating the Buddha's birth, awakening, and *parinirvana* (final *nirvana*), is still observed annually, and there is a centre, with a monastery, at Bandung. But apart from this Buddhism has left its imprint on many facets of Indonesian culture, and has played a central part in giving Muslim Indonesia its own characteristics.

Tibet

As we have already seen, Buddhism was established in Tibet in the eleventh century. In AD 1076 a council was held at Tho-ling in western Tibet to which monks are said to have come from all parts of the country, so it seems clear that by that date Buddhism was widely spread in Tibet. The period of growth from the eleventh to the fifteenth centuries was marked by the emergence of a number of different movements. These, as in other religious traditions, arose very largely as a result of social and psychological differences between different adherents of the religion. Their growth may have been also a sign of the great vitality of Buddhist religion in Tibet during that period.

Certainly there was in neighbouring Bengal something of a revival during the eleventh century; during this and the three succeeding centuries many monks made their way from Bengal to Tibet. To some extent this movement of Bengali monks was due to the increasing difficulty of maintaining the monastic centres in Bengal during the period of the growth of Muslim power in North India. During the latter part of the period it was mainly the Tantric form of Buddhism which was transmitted to Tibet. The monks carried with them something also of the spirit of the great centres of learning such as Nalanda and Vikramasila, with the result that similar centres of monastic learning became a characteristic feature of Tibetan Buddhism, and remained so until the twentieth century.

One of the great figures of eleventh-century Tibet was a monk named Mila, to whose name is added the epithet '*repa*' (i.e. 'the cotton-clad'). This was an allusion to his extremely austere way of life; in disregard of the cold climate of Tibet he wore a cotton robe, so great is said to have been the quality of his asceticism. He was a poet too, the author of 'one hundred thousand songs', many of which became and remained familiar to the people of Tibet. He was himself a disciple of a teacher named Marpa, the founder of one of the most popularly based sects, the Ka-gyu-pa. The characteristic concern of his sect was with yogic and other spiritual practices, rather than with philosophical wisdom.

Another sect, by way of contrast, was concerned with strict adherence to the traditional monastic code of discipline; another with the pursuit of profound philosophical ideas; yet another was characterized by its social organization, which incidentally had the effect of providing a stable basis for the social organization of the country after the destruction of the monarchy. These various sects within Buddhism did not exist in competition or rivalry, but in harmony. It was accepted that their diversity together comprised a unity, each sect esteeming the others as parts of the totality which was Tibetan Buddhism.

An important reform movement which began in the fourteenth century under the leadership of a teacher named Tsong-Kapa (1357-1417) resulted in the formation of the Gelug-pa, a sect popularly known as 'the Yellow Hats'. This sect revived the tradition of strict monastic discipline. Its members drank no wine, did not marry (unlike some other Tibetan monks) and maintained a high level of personal morality. It was believed that one of its leading abbots, who died in 1475, was reincarnated in a young monk, and that he in turn was at his death reincarnated in another. It was to this reincarnated and highly revered *lama* that the name Talai (Ocean) was given, and hence began the line of the Talai, or Dalai Lamas.

In 1642 the Yellow Hats became the ruling power in Tibet and continued so until the Chinese takeover of Tibet in 1950. As spiritual head of the Yellow Hats the Dalai Lama was thus head also of the Tibetan State. The position of Dalai Lama has been compared with that of the Pope in Catholic Europe; there are some similarities, but the essential difference is that the Dalai Lama is held to be an incarnation of the heavenly being or *bodhisattva* named Avalokiteshwara (the most celebrated of all the Indian Mahayana *bodhisattvas*). It is believed that when a Dalai Lama dies the next incarnation is a child born forty-nine days later, and there is a well-defined routine for seeking out and identifying the child who is to become the new Dalai Lama, and for training him for his spiritual duties.

Illustration page 291

Following the tradition of the monastic universities of India, many of the monasteries of Tibet were for some eight centuries, until 1950, great centres of learning. Among lay-people one of the major preoccupations was the study of history. It was a Tibetan, Bu-ston, who composed a very valuable and famous history of Indian Buddhism.

The Buddhism of Tibetan lay people absorbed many features of earlier, pre-Buddhistic religion. This was known as Bon, or Pön, and was a kind of shamanism, with worship of spirits and tutelary deities of various kinds. One of the most important of these was the Lord of the Soil, who was venerated by means of an upright stick or pole, often decorated with pieces of rag or with coloured cloth. The

Illustration page 292
For shamanism in Central Asia, see pages 47–8.

Tibetans have been described by travellers as continually engaged with prayer wheels, offering prayers to these deities whenever they are free from other pursuits; this too is a feature of pre-Buddhistic religion. The most characteristic Buddhist symbol, however, namely the *stupa* or pagoda, has its Tibetan form in the *chö-ten*, a familiar sight in Tibet.

A modern historian of Tibet, H. E. Richardson, has pointed out that it is the more spectacular features of Tibetan Buddhism which have too often captured the attention of the West, whereas less is heard about the considerable piety and moral influence of the quiet life of the monasteries. He adds that in lay life, too, there is much unspectacular but real religious devotion, practised in the context of the family, and providing a stabilizing and cohesive element in Tibetan life.

One of the effects of Buddhism upon the people of Tibet was to convert formerly warlike and aggressive tribes into a people so pacific that they have been unwilling as well as unable to resist invasions by non-Tibetans from the north. The latest instance of this is the Chinese domination of the country on the grounds that Tibet is politically an integral part of China, a claim based on earlier instances of such rule. From this event followed the radical reshaping of the structure of traditional Tibetan life, which appeared almost to have disappeared, at least within Tibet itself. It maintains a precarious existence among Tibetan émigrés in the Himalayan foothills of northern India, where a friendly Indian government has made provision for the refugees to salvage something of their traditional culture. It is conceivable, however, that the Tibetan community of northern India could in the future play some part in the re-establishing of Buddhism there, from whence it originally came. In 1980 the Potala Palace in Lhasa was reopened to Tibetan Buddhists and some pilgrimages were permitted.

Conclusion

Certain general observations may be appropriate in concluding this brief survey, to assist the reader to put into perspective what has been said of Buddhism in the successive periods of its history and the various lands into which it has spread.

While a distinction can be made between the two main divisions, the Mahayana and the Hinayana (the latter represented now solely by one of its original eighteen schools, the Theravada), it would be a mistake to regard these two divisions as constituting anything like the schism which has existed in Christian history between the Roman Church and the Greek Orthodox, or between Roman Catholicism and Protestantism. Although at certain periods local conditions (as in Sri Lanka) led to some fairly vigorous rivalry between Mahayana and Hinayana monasteries, at other times, in India, monks of the two schools could be found living together in the same monastery. Today, just as often in the past, there is considerable sharing of learning and experience between representatives of both wings. The differences between them are strictly differences of emphasis, and in countries where one is dominant (in Burma or Thailand, for example, where the Theravada is the prevailing form) there is no lack of evidence of Mahayana ideas and practices.

It is in fact alien to the character and spirit of Buddhism to be harshly intolerant of those with whom one disagrees. This can be illustrated at another level in the hospitality which both the Mahayana and the Hinayana have afforded to indigenous beliefs and customs. These have not been violently rejected and condemned out of hand, but have been allowed to continue, combining gradually with the Buddhist beliefs and practices of the monasteries until they have become vehicles for the expression of what is essentially Buddhist.

This may be held by Western observers to have serious dangers for the preservation of the 'pure' form of religion, but the evidence provided by 2,200 years of Buddhist history in Sri Lanka for example is that tolerance, when combined with serious missionary concern and compassion, does not lead to the disappearance of the original insight, or to a diminution of the quality of religious experience and practice. The attitude which is summarized by saying, 'What you believe and practise is different from what I believe and practise, and since my form is right, yours must be wrong, and should be abandoned', is not appropriate in the Buddhist context, wherever else it may find a home. In a choice between tolerance and benevolence on the one hand, and exclusiveness and hostility on the other, Buddhists generally prefer the former.

The fortunes of Buddhism have therefore waxed and waned and will no doubt continue to do so. Sri Lanka's history provides a representative example of this. There are always *two* possibilities: in times of decadence, difficulty, opposition, or unpopularity there is the prospect that the Buddhist tradition may suffer yet greater adversity; but there is also the possibility that it may revive and recover, and it has shown this capacity on a number of occasions throughout its history. In general it is true that Buddhism has never spread by the use of armed force, and that it has sometimes suffered loss of influence by its spirit of gentleness. This may be a disadvantage; on the other hand it may prove to be an aspect of Buddhism which will tell in its favour.

The Buddhist monk is not merely a man of peace in a passive sense; by his inner attitude he is an active force making for peace, as the internal history of Buddhist countries demonstrates. Buddhism flourishes in times of peace, and it has always used the arts of peace most successfully in its service. Buddhist sculpture, painting and architecture provide eloquent testimony to its ennobling and refining influence on human society. But in the last analysis the Buddhist horizon, like the Christian, is not limited to the transient world of time and physical sense; the peace which is proclaimed by the Buddha, the *Dhamma*, and the Sangha is that of a realm which is eternal.

Chapter Seventeen

China

China stands alone among the world's great civilizations, having developed in almost total isolation from the rest. Her achievements have thus a uniqueness which makes them at once a marvel to behold, but a puzzle to understand. Isolated by geography, at the extreme eastern end of the ancient Euro-Asian world, hemmed in by mountains and deserts, lying across no trade routes, China developed by itself.

The Chinese speak a language which has no affinities with any other language group and which is written in a script – a Chinese invention – unlike any other. The script, however, has a great virtue: its ideographs represent ideas rather than sounds: thus it can be read all over China irrespective of the 'dialect' of the speaker. Further, books written in this script two thousand years ago are easily readable today. The language and its script have played a powerful role in giving the people a sense not only of unity and identity but of continuity.

The Chinese people have traditionally thought themselves to be the centre of the universe (*Chung-kuo*, the Chinese name for China, means the 'kingdom in the middle'). Like the Greeks, they have regarded themselves as an island of culture in a sea of barbarity. Unlike the Greeks, and more like the Romans, the Chinese have long understood the arts of large-scale administration. Beginning with a civil service selected on the basis of merit, Chinese bureaucrats kept the empire intact for two thousand years. Despite the replacement of the empire, firstly by the republic from 1912 to 1949 and then by the Communist regime, the uniqueness and continuity of the Chinese ethos have remained astonishingly alive.

Like the West, China too has had its formative age of philosophers, its imperial periods, its intellectual renaissances, but Chinese civilization contrasts at almost every point with Western experience. In religious and philosophical ideas, as in so much else, the Chinese experience embraces the feelings and aspirations of all humankind, but expresses them always in a peculiarly Chinese way.

Three Major Religions

Three religions have played a major role in China's three thousand years of history. They are Confucianism, Taoism and Buddhism. Confucianism and Taoism are indigenous to China. They had both been in existence for some five hundred years before Buddhism was introduced from India. But even before the rise of Confucianism and Taoism, an earlier religion (from which both Confucianism and Taoism each in its own way grew) had held sway in China for nearly a thousand years. Religion in China had thus a history extending over a millennium and a half before its notions were challenged by a foreign tradition.

So powerful was this indigenous tradition that, after the introduction of Buddhism to China, Buddhism became increasingly Chinese in character. Purely Chinese schools of Buddhism were born. But again, so influential was the impact of Indian thought and religious experience upon Chinese minds that Confucianism and Taoism also underwent change. They re-emerged in such forms as Neo-Taoism and Neo-Confucianism – reformulations of the indigenous tradition, made to meet the challenge of a new and alien one.

In a civilization as long-lasting, as coherent and relatively speaking, as uninfluenced from outside as that of the Chinese, many other cults and sects have flourished. Other alien religions have also been introduced, particularly, though belatedly in comparison with other countries, the Western forms of Christianity. But in the long run Confucianism, Taoism and Buddhism have played the major roles in Chinese religious experience.

In speaking of Confucianism and Taoism as religions it is important to remind the Western reader that, in the Chinese mind, they are *chiao* (teachings), and teachings which are not exclusively or specifically religious though they are concerned with much that we should think of as religion.

The writings of the founders of Confucianism and Taoism have been regarded as part of the collective cultural heritage of the Chinese. In the case of Confucianism its sacred canon, consisting not only of the writings of the Confucian founders but also of secular documents pre-dating Confucius, forms a classical corpus. For nearly two thousand years the Confucian canon was the mainstay of the curriculum in Chinese education. Familiarity with the canon, for example, was one of the principal requirements of the civil service examinations. For much of Chinese history, Confucianism and Taoism have been thought of by the Chinese themselves as manifestations *par excellence* of the national ethos, and not specifically as religious faiths inviting conversion, membership and personal commitment.

On the other hand, with the introduction of Buddhism at the beginning of the Christian era, the notion arose of religion as a formally organized institution. As a riposte to Buddhism, Taoism evolved similar institutions, acquiring, as Buddhism already possessed, a priestly order and a hierarchy, temples and monasteries and a sacred canon. Each attracted its own adherents as converts to a faith. There have been times in Chinese history when the sectarian loyalties thus engendered have been critical. This is particularly so in those rare periods when members of the imperial house have espoused either Buddhism or Taoism. But the imperial house and the Chinese ruling establishment have been pre-eminently Confucian, and Confucianism as the dominant philosophy of the administrative classes became institutionalized in official rites and ceremonies and in the imperial sacrifices. In this way, it became part of the apparatus of government. It became the state cult. But both Confucianism and Taoism were, in origin, simply philosophical systems which were devoid of any cult element, followed by 'schools' and individuals, and were neither institutionalized nor particularly religious.

To confine inquiry to the religious aspects of Confucianism and Taoism, however, is to ignore many expressions of Chinese religious thought and feeling, whether of a 'higher' or of a 'lower' kind, which do not specifically relate to either of these two philosophical systems. There are, or have been, religious elements present in many facets of family and social organization, in the cults and practices of economic and other groups, and in political theory and action at almost all levels from local to national government. The multiplicity and variety of temples and shrines in every city and village across the land and the presence in countless households of the domestic gods and their altars provide tangible evidence of this.

The World of Divination

Chinese recorded history begins with the Shang dynasty, which covered the period from the sixteenth to the eleventh centuries BC. Its records are the oracle bones discovered towards the close of the nineteenth century and since then the main source for the history of the Shang. These bones, of which some hundred thousand fragments have been recovered, are divination enquiries. The enquiries were engraved on animal bone and shell. They were addressed to the spirits for guidance. The request having been inscribed, the diviner then applied heat to holes bored in the bone and the resultant heat-cracks were interpreted as being either an 'auspicious' or 'inauspicious' re-

Illustration page 309 sponse from the spirits.

From the nature of the enquiries made, we gain a picture of a society regulated in almost every aspect of daily life by divination and governed by considerations of good and bad luck. The 'powers' consulted in divination were the spirits of the deceased kings, the *ti*, and the spirits of the ancestors. From traces still discernible in the shape of the written ideographs, we know of a phallic element in such worship. But from requests made about the propriety of making sacrifices and performing rites, we know that, in addition to the spirits of the dead, the deities of the hills and streams and other nature gods and tutelary spirits were worshipped. Not only were the dead asked for guidance in matters of conduct, but their *mana* (their inherent power) was invoked in ensuring the fertility of men and women, crops and beasts.

The Ancient Religion

Animism (the worship of the nature deities), fertility rites and cults, and in particular ancestor worship are not only features of the earliest

recorded Chinese religious practices, but recur in a variety of different forms in the 'popular religion' of subsequent times.

The Shang dynasty was superseded by the Chou dynasty in 1027 BC. Until 771 BC, the Chou royal house ruled as 'priest-kings', in undisputed sway over the Chinese world. Some documents have survived from this period and a considerable body of inscriptions made on bronze sacral vessels. Together these tell us something of the religion of the Chou royal house.

Illustration page 310

The royal religion of Chou assumes an importance out of all proportion to its intrinsic interest because the period was regarded as a golden age by Confucius. Certain of its documents were cited by him as ancient precedents, and were included in the Confucian canon. Many elements of the Chou royal religion thus passed into Confucian orthodoxy.

Early Chinese monarchs were both priests and kings, and sovereignty consisted in being invested by heaven with its 'charge'. When Wen (posthumously made king by his son) revolted against the Shang dynasts, his son, King Wu (1027-25 BC), ascended the throne and founded the Chou dynasty. The Chou ruled, as the documents of their era insist, in the belief that their mission was foreordained by heaven – that heaven had relieved the Shang kings of their 'mandate' to rule, and that they, the Chou royal house, were invested by heaven with its 'charge'. This charge is the 'mandate of heaven'.

In Chou belief, the highest deity was the Supreme Ancestor (Shang-ti), a term synonymous with *T'ien* (heaven). Heaven, so belief ran, holds the entire universe (the natural world and its inhabitants – the 'known world' of the Chinese) in its hand, foreordains the occurrence of the seasons in their courses, orders the cycle of death and renewal, and ensures the fertility of men and women, crops and beasts. But heaven invests the responsibility for ordering the universe in its regent upon earth, the Son of Heaven (T'ien Tzu). This role, the Chous claimed, had fallen to them. The 'ordering of the universe' was a matter of 'being ritually acceptable' (*p'ei*) to heaven, and, through the performance of rituals, sympathetically inducing the realities of the natural order and its sequences in the universe and among mankind.

The Role of the King

Heaven showed its displeasure by untimely weather or other supernatural signs such as thunderbolts (a disturbance in the orderly cycle), and by a failure in fertility (a withdrawal by the powerful dead of their *mana*). The priestly functions of the kings therefore consisted in sacrificing to the dead kings and to Shang-ti – the most remote and therefore most powerful of them; in reporting to God on the course of secular events; and in engaging in such mimic rites as a ritual ploughing and sowing (in the case of their queens, a ritual spinning of the silk cocoons from the mulberry) to ensure fertility and to begin again the round of life and renewal of the year.

Being 'ritually acceptable' to heaven, *p'ei* was the king's patent of sovereignty and provided the powerful political sanction that bound his vassals in allegiance to him. Assisting the king in the proper performances of his duties were the priests and intoners. They were the experts in the forms of ritual, and important among their duties were the astronomical observations that made possible the fixing of the calendar.

The semi-deified nature of kingship, attested by the choice by heaven of the king as its son, gave the king political hold over his vassals, who were in their turn invested with 'charges' by him. Just as the king ruled by virtue of heaven's 'charge', so too did his feudal underlords hold local sovereignty under the king's charge (*wang ming*). The feudal lords in their turn enfeoffed sub-feudatories with a lord's charge (*kung ming*), so that the entire feudal pyramid of western Chou, from top to bottom, was held on tenure to the will of heaven.

The king ruled directly in his own domain and by delegation to feudatories in 'the states of the four quarters'. Within his own jurisdiction, each feudatory had the sole right to worship and invoke the tutelary deities. 'The great affairs of state are sacrifice and war,' says an ancient rubric and, in the Chou royal religion, the patricians were the priests and warriors of the state.

Royal Worship

The royal worship took place in the ancestral temple, the central building in the palace complex. Oriented by the sun to face south, the palace precincts were approached through the south gate, and opened up into the great court, on the north face of which was the shrine to the Chou ancestors. To the rear, through two further gates, was the centre court, on the north side of which was the residential palace.

A victorious general, in an inscription on a sacral vessel, describes a typical ceremony, partly worship, partly royal *levée*, in which he took part. On the first day before dawn the chief ministers prepared the king in his palace. The king then proceeded to the ancestral temple. The feudal lords, returning from a military campaign, appeared at the south gate and were summoned to the great court, where they presented their captives. The captives were then sacrificed in the ancestral temple. The party proceeded to the centre court and an account was given of the campaign. The king went from the centre court to the temple to sacrifice to the royal ancestors. On the following day the meat and wine offered in sacrifice were eaten in a feast given to the assembled vassals, who were rewarded by the king.

The rituals employed in such services are preserved in the earliest section of the *Book of Songs*, an anthology of early Chinese poetry. These are hymns of the Chou kings and, apart from being the earliest poems in the Chinese language, they have an importance as the first literary expression of Chinese religious feeling.

The hymns consist of invocations and confessions addressed to the royal ancestors, and recitals to the gods of deeds of valour. Other pieces celebrate before the gods the presence of vassals and feudatories

Above Oracle bones of the Shang dynasty (*c.* sixteenth to eleventh century BC). Thousands of these bones have been found, engraved with requests for help and guidance addressed to the spirits. The bone is scorched where it was heated to produce cracks and auguries were read from the results. Royal Ontario Museum, Toronto.

Left A Shang dynasty ceremonial jade sceptre combining the *pi* disc, symbolizing heaven, and the axe as the symbol of royal power. Narodni Galeri, Prague.

Right Ceremonial and sacrificial vessels in bronze show a style of great strength and authority. This tripod vessel dates from the Western Chou dynasty, Honan province (*c.* 1028-771 BC). Royal Ontario Museum, Toronto.

Far right A shaman-inspired wooden tomb guardian from Ch'ang-sha (*c.* third century BC). There was a great gulf between the primitive superstitions of the people and the Confucian philosophy of the nobility. British Museum, London.

Centre Yü the Great, successor of Shun and hero of the primeval flood in a painting by Ma Lin (Sung dynasty). Yü was held to be the ancestor of the Szu and was said to have dammed 233,559 streams and built mountains at the corners of the earth to prevent flooding. National Palace Museum, Taipei.

Right A statuette in bronze of Hou-chi, Prince of the Millet, supposed to be a descendant of Huang Ti and ancestor of the house of Chou. Beginning as a cult hero, he was later written into Chinese history as an historical figure. Musée Guimet, Paris.

Above Li, the rites of early religion which Confucius transformed into a code of righteous behaviour, are illustrated here in a stone rubbing from the Wu family shrine in Shantung province.

Far left A pottery figure of an exorcist which bears witness to the fact that the primitive faith in the shamans and their spirits lingered on (Western Chin dynasty, AD 267-317). Royal Ontario Museum, Toronto.

Left A statuette of Confucius dressed as a mandarin (late Ming or early Chhing dynasty). Musée Guimet, Paris.

Above Tung Yung, one of the examples of filial piety in Chinese legend, is shown here tilling the earth and then meeting the spinning maid in a rubbing of a detail from a sarcophagus (sixth century AD). William Rockhill Nelson Gallery of Art, Kansas City, Missouri.

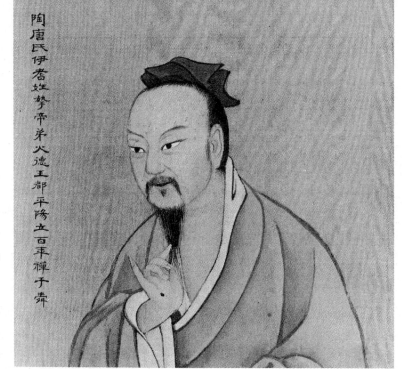

帝堯真像

陶唐氏伊耆姓勢帝弟火德王都平陽立百年禪于舜

Right Yao, the mythical king famous for his benign rule. He was supposed to have lived the simple life of a common farmer. This was painted on silk during the Chi'en Lung period as part of an album containing twenty-four portraits of the Chinese emperors. Metropolitan Museum of Art, New York. Gift of Mrs Edward S. Harkness, 1947.

at the ceremonies. There are songs of welcome addressed to the vassals and songs of fealty addressed by them to the king. The whole comprised the liturgy of the royal worship. Poetry begins in China with the chanting of this liturgy and the first attempts at prosody derive from the fitting of prose paragraphs to the percussion beat and dance mime of the temple rituals.

Something of the religious feeling of the temple liturgy can be gained from the excerpts which follow:

With stately calm and reverent accord,
The ministers and attending knights
Record the virtues of their founding Lord
Our heavenly ministrant, the great King Wen.

O Lord, may you in your great majesty
Find in measured act and formal word
Praise not displeasing from mere mortal men.

Majestic, never ending
Is the Charge of Heaven.
Your virtue descending,
Oh, illustrious King Wen,
Overwhelms with blessing
Your servants on earth.
We have only to receive your favour.
May it be preserved by those who come after.

Our offerings
Of oxen, sheep
We humbly bring.
May from these spring
Heaven's keep
And the favour of the king.
May we always
Fear the wrath of Heaven
So to keep his favour
And our ways even.

To bring peace to the land we must
Follow the precepts of King Wen, and trust
To his statutes; from afar he will watch and approve.

His robes of brightest silk,
His cap encrusted
With precious stones,
The wine so mellow and soft;
He moves without sound
In reverent modesty among

The sacred tripods and the drinking horns;
He moves from Hall to Threshold with measured pace,
And for the aged brings at last the gift of grace.

The charges of the Chou kings and the ritual hymns of their priestly worship provided for Confucius the 'documents of antiquity', ancient authority for his own religious and political ideas. Certain of the notions of the royal Chou religion became basic religious beliefs for Confucius and the Confucian state which came later. Principal among these are the notions of a supreme being (Shang-ti, 'God-on-high'), the notion of kingship being held at heaven's pleasure (the 'mandate of heaven'), and the notion that heaven withdraws its mandate from the wicked and sanctions the overthrow of a dynasty when its 'virtue' runs out, and justifies its replacement by a new dynasty 'acceptable to heaven'. The centrality of the royal ancestors in the royal pantheon and the worship and sacrifice made to them in the royal religion led to the centrality of ancestors in subsequent religious practice. Reverence for the powerful dead and the invoking of their *mana* for the sustenance of the clan became part of Chinese social mores, and filial piety a central Confucian teaching.

Confucius invested much of the early religious practice with moral sanctions, but (as the large-scale human sacrifice mentioned above reminds us) this was a pre-moral age. Its ideas were motivated not by moral good and evil, but by the ritual manipulation of powers to ensure good luck and to avert bad luck and to invoke the collective power of the departed dead.

While kings and aristocrats engaged in 'sacrifice and war' and performed their priestly functions in the royal religion, belief in the countryside – as hints in the later poems in the *Book of Songs* show – took the form of fertility rites, at which in spring and autumn the common folk invoked the *mana* of the dead for the fertility of their land, their livestock and themselves.

Aristocratic Religion

In 771 BC the kings of western Chou moved their capital to the east and, with the shift of capital, came a decline in their power and influence. Real political power, as opposed to titular power, passed to the princes of the city-states. Originally the feudatories of the Chou royal house, the city-state rulers gradually asserted their independence and, with growing independence, increasingly took upon themselves kingly privileges. Among them were the priestly functions of the ancient kings. Presiding over the 'altars of the soil and crops' (that is, the worship of the fecundity deities of the locality over which the princes enjoyed dominion) and maintaining the ancestral cults in family shrines became the symbols of authority in city-states.

Feudal princes attached their genealogy to local cult-heroes of the past. Thus, Hou-chi, the Prince of Millet, became the putative ances-
Illustrations page 310 tor of the Chi clan; Yü the Great, the hero of the primeval Flood, was the putative ancestor of the Szu. In this way a number of culture

heroes, hitherto of local significance and unknown to the royal religion of western Chou, were introduced to the Chinese pantheon. Later, historians created a historical basis for these cult-heroes and they were arranged in a historical succession. This happened in the great period of historical writing, the second to the first centuries BC, and thus the 'legendary emperors', with their fictional dates, entered Chinese 'history' and pushed back its time span several millennia. These 'emperors' became of great cultic importance, particularly in the Han dynasty, and figure prominently in the local cults and popular religion of the time. In actual fact there is little evidence prior to the Shang for any historical ruling figures.

Thus, through their possession of the local altars and their right to attend to the divinities of fertility, together with their access to the *mana* of their divine ancestors, the princes of the city-states asserted political domination over their subjects.

The city-states maintained archives of which one in its entirety and others in fragments have survived. The *Spring and Autumn Annals* (*Ch'un-ch'iu*) of Lu and the commentaries which have accrued around them provide our principal source for the religious ideas current in the period. The archives themselves contain brief sentence-length entries which record matters of dynastic concern – the marriages and deaths of the princely house, treaties entered into with other states and ominous happenings (untimely weather, the appearance of freaks and the like) and observations of eclipses and meteors. These archives had the ritual purpose of placing on record for the ancestors matters of dynastic concern. Ritualistic conventions governed the phrasing of their entries. Confucius is credited, implausibly, with having a hand in the compilation of the *Spring and Autumn Annals*, with the consequence that the *Annals* have been included in the Confucian sacred canon. An esoteric interpretation of them, written in Han times, became part of Confucian teaching.

Shamanism in the South

Almost all of our eastern Chou sources are concerned with the religion of the city-state princes and with that of the aristocratic classes. We know little of the popular religion of the period. But, from the city-state of Ch'u, which by the fourth century BC dominated the upper Yangtze Valley, and included parts of what are now Anhwei, Honan, Hunan, Hupeh and Szechuan, a collection of shaman songs has survived as part of the *Elegies of Ch'u*. These, the *Nine Songs*, are shamans' hymns.

The religious practices described therein are of a very different kind from the religious rituals of the princes in the city-states. The gods invoked are from the local cults of areas in Ch'u – mountain and river goddesses and local heroes. The shamans, either men or women, ritually washed, perfumed and decked out in gorgeous dresses, sing and dance accompanied by music in a courtship ritual, inviting the gods to descend in erotic intercourse, and then, when the gods depart, lament the sadness of their departure. The rites described in the *Nine*

Songs, barbarous from a Confucian standpoint with their sensuality, magnificence and sadness, produced exquisite poetry. The following is an example:

With a faint flush I start to come out of the east,
Shining down on my threshold, Fu-sang.
As I urge my horses slowly forward,
The night sky brightens, and day has come.
I ride a dragon car and chariot on the thunder,
With cloud-banners fluttering upon the wind.
I heave a long sigh as I start the ascent,
Reluctant to leave, and looking back longingly;
For the beauty and the music are so enchanting
The beholder, delighted, forgets that he must go.
Tighten the zither's strings and smite them in unison!
Strike the bells until the bell-stand rocks!
Let the flutes sound! Blow the pan-pipes!
See, the priestesses, how skilled and lovely!
Whirling and dipping like birds in flight!
Unfolding the words in time to the dancing,
Pitch and beat all in perfect accord!
The spirits, descending, darken the sun.
In my cloud-coat and my skirt of the rainbow,
Grasping my bow I soar high up in the sky;
I aim my long arrow and shoot the Wolf of Heaven;
I seize the Dipper to ladle cinnamon wine.
Then holding my reins I plunge down to my setting,
On my gloomy night journey back to the east.

In Ch'u the court appears to have enjoyed these religious performances, and it is possible that the *Nine Songs* owe their survival to the fascination of the court with such religious spectacles. But underlying them is a shamanistic cult, which was not confined to the south, but was widespread as the popular religion of the peoples throughout the city-states. Shamans played the role of exorcists, prophets, fortune-tellers and interpreters of dreams. They were also the medicine-men, the healers of diseases.

Sporadic references to them in the literature of the period suggest that they were everywhere. In proposals for new colonization measures, for example, in the first century BC, the new colonists are to be provided with 'doctors and shamans, to tend them in sickness and to continue their sacrifices', suggesting that the shaman was a customary member of village society. The phrase 'shaman family' hints that the calling of the shaman was hereditary. But with the rise of Confucianism there was prejudice against shamans, and beginning with the saying of Confucius that the 'spirits should be revered, but kept at a distance', literature, being largely in the hands of Confucians, becomes increasingly reticent about the shamanism of the people.

The Age of the Philosophers

The roots of both religious Confucianism and Taoism were laid during the Age of Philosophy. From the sixth to the third centuries BC, in the city-states of the north-central plain, China enjoyed an extraordinary period of the flowering of the human mind. Philosophers proliferated, travelling from one court to another, gathering adherents, propounding their theories and arguing them in open debate, each seeking a prince who would 'put their way into practice'. The father of Chinese history, Szu-ma Ch'ien (fl. 145-90 BC), described them as the 'Hundred Schools'. From among the Hundred Schools, there gradually emerged the schools of Confucius and of the Taoists, upon whose teachings the philosophy and religion of Confucianism and Taoism would in subsequent centuries be based.

But thought depends on environment. The devolution of power from the Son of Heaven, ruler of a unified China, to the princes of a China divided into independent principalities did not cease there. Within the city-states themselves, power passed from princes to oligarchs, groups of powerful nobles, and from the oligarchs, in at least one case, to a plebeian dictator. From a religious point of view, this raised the problems of the sanction of heaven for political power, and the rights to the custody of the altars.

Then too, to the disconcerting political position of the city-state rulers was added the problem of social and economic change. For Chinese society was changing. The economic historian would observe that many of his key dates occurred in the seventh century BC. Iron was introduced; coins minted, with a legend indicating the mint town. Groups of merchants, sufficiently organized to negotiate terms of status and operation with their princes, appeared in the city-states. Mention is made too at this period of state monopolies in the manufacture and distribution of salt and of state-controlled marketing of fish.

In short, into the comparatively simple agrarian economics of locally self-sufficient communities, whose only external obligation was the sending of tribute to the supreme ruler, there were suddenly thrust those disconcerting complications of specialized production, inter-regional trade, and of a basis for the economy other than that of the storing of commodities for the accumulation of wealth. These shifts in the economic sphere produced deeply rooted disturbances in the social equilibrium, and social change led to political unrest. It was above all to the rise of the city-state and to the problems of its polity that Chinese philosophy addressed itself.

Social mobility among the aristocracy also increased. Certain aristocrats turned mercenary and attached themselves as clients to patrons. Others became merchants engaged in interstate trade (the word for commerce is *shang*, perhaps from the descendants of the rulers of the Shang settled in the state of Sung). Others hired themselves out as tutors to the sons of the nobility, or opened schools. They called themselves the *Ju*, 'the gentle' or 'the yielding'. They taught the arts of city-state life, ceremonial and ritual, reading and writing, using the ancient anthologies of court and popular songs and of state documents as their textbooks. Their pupils formed a coterie, later becoming their followers or patrons. Soon distinctive schools and leading figures appeared among them. They began to circulate among the city-states, offering to the princes their theories of government and the services of their pupils. By the fourth century BC the peripatetic philosopher was a familiar figure at the courts. Some rulers staged public debates for them, and rival theories were thus argued and aired. One ruler, the Lord of Ch'i, opened an academy, at which the leading philosophers of his day lectured. This foreshadowed the academies of the imperial period – the direct ancestors of the modern Chinese university.

The Philosophical Age was thus ushered in during a bewilderingly complex period of change and innovation. Economic and social forces were abroad, the natures of which were but faintly understood at the time. But they posed problems for which nothing but a prolonged period of thought and speculation would provide an answer. The problem, however, was always thought to be political: how to restore order and equilibrium to the city-state, an equilibrium which was still alive in the memory but which had been shattered by recent events.

Of all the schools of the Philosophical Age those which most concern the student of religion are that of Confucius and his successors in the Confucian school, Mencius and Hsün Tzu, and that of the mystics, Chuang Tzu and Lao Tzu. For Confucianism and Taoism arose above the struggles of the Hundred Schools and bequeathed to the Chinese empire its two principal philosophies and its two indigenous religions.

Confucius

Confucianism was the earliest of the many philosophies that comprise the Hundred Schools. Confucius, its founder, was China's first philosopher. He was born in 551 BC in the city-state of Lu, and died in

Illustration page 311

579 BC. His name is a Latin form of the Chinese K'ung Fu-tzu, (Master K'ung). He was of aristocratic descent. As tutor to the sons of the city-state aristocracy, he taught the arts of city-state life, the study of the *Book of Documents*, a collection of archives concerned mainly, though not exclusively, with western Chou, and the *Book of Songs*, which contained, among other things, the ritual hymns of the early Chou kings. He thus instilled into his princely pupils the system of the Chou royal religion.

But Confucius conceived of these documents not so much as a bible of kingly religion – though of course they are much concerned with religion and provide the ancient precedents for the practice of religion for rulers – as the relics of a golden age. It was the restoration of the values and practices of this age that Confucius saw as the political answer to the problems of the city-states. To Confucius, the heroes of this golden age were its founder-kings Wen and Wu and the Duke of Chou, regent of King Wu's son Ch'eng. The restoration

of the policies of the early Chou kings was Confucius's political
platform. As a philosopher, Confucius appealed to the texts of the
Book of Songs and the *Book of Documents* as his authority. His method
was scriptural. As a political theorist his approach was conservative
– his programme was one of the restoration and preservation of an
earlier tradition. He protested that he merely 'transmitted what was
taught to me without making up anything of my own' (*Analects*, 7.1).

An Ethical and Moral System

In reality, by using these documents as scriptures and by interpreting
their archaic language in a contemporary sense, he evolved an ethical
and moral system from writings that are auguristic, dominated by
magic, and amoral. Thus *tê*, the magical force, the *mana* of antiquity,
became 'virtue' in an ethical and moral sense. The power that *mana*
exerts became the force of example which in Confucian thinking
converts the 'good' into an irresistible force. The prince of the ancient
texts, *chun-tzu*, becomes for Confucius 'a prince indeed' – a gentleman, as ideally a gentleman should be. *Jen*, the attributes of members
of the tribe in good standing, becomes for Confucius an almost
transcendental quality of goodness – attained only by the sages of
antiquity.

It was the genius of Confucius to have converted much of the
language of primitive religion into a vocabulary for ethics and to have
transformed that religion into a moral system, as society passed from
a concern with good and bad luck to a concern with right and wrong.
As the originator of a moral and ethical system, Confucius has influenced and been revered by the Chinese for two thousand years. But
the piety of his followers has credited him with worldly success as a
statesman and diplomatist and even hailed him as 'the king they never
crowned'. The historical Confucius, in contrast to the Confucius of
piety and legend, was in fact a disappointed itinerant teacher, who,
despairing that the ruler of his own city-state would ever put his
teachings into practice, travelled to neighbouring states, only to meet
the same indifferent and hostile reception. Unrecognized in his own
day except by a small band of devoted adherents, it was to be centuries
before his teachings prevailed. He died a disappointed man.

The Analects

The teachings of Confucius are contained in the *Analects* (*Lun-yü*).
They contain twenty books, each consisting of a collection of
sentence- or paragraph-length sayings of the master recorded by his
pupils. Certain parts of the *Analects* probably predate Confucius, but,
as with religious scriptures generally, these problems concern specialists. To the ordinary Confucian, the *Analects* are the words of Confucius and, as such, the *Analects* form part of the Confucian sacred
canon. The *Analects*, as they have been studied century by century,
have gathered commentaries elucidating and expanding on their interpretation. Latter-day Confucians have found authority in the *Analects* for ideas foreign to their original meaning. As originally taught,
the ideas of Confucius might be summarized as follows.

There is a way for a prince to follow. It is the 'Way of the Former Kings'. Since the former kings, in the Confucian view, ruled and behaved as heaven decreed, they provided exemplars for later generations to follow. They did so by being *jen*. Originally a word connoting a member of the clan in good standing (cf. Latin *gens*), *jen*, for Confucius, meant being good in an extremely wide and general sense. Such qualities as unselfishness, deference towards others, courtesy and loyalty to family and prince are attributes of *jen*. The good (*jen*) do not repine in adversity and are bold in the cause of right. But these are merely aspects of *jen*. For Confucius, *jen* itself was an almost transcendental ideal attained only by the sages of antiquity. It was a mystical entity – the essential quality of sainthood.

Virtue

If *jen* is the attribute of sainthood, *tê* (virtue) is the power by which sainthood is achieved: virtue, not as opposed to vice, but rather as the inherent virtue, the power or efficacy of something, was closer to Confucius's meaning. Thus princes should rule by virtue, a prestige the force of which far transcends physical force and coercion. The good person exercises virtue and others turn to the good. The man who seeks to be *jen* by cultivating his *tê* attains the princely ideal. This princely ideal, *chün-tzu* (lit. a prince), becomes in Confucian teaching the embodiment of the ideals of human conduct: it is man at his very best, as a man should be. The *chün-tzu* is governed in all his conduct by *li* (ritual). *Li* – the rites of the early religion – becomes for Confucius an entire code for gentlemanly conduct, governing dress and social punctiliousness, good manners generally, and also demeanour and gesture, so that to moral conduct is added an appropriate outward manifestation. Beneath the surface of the Confucian emphasis upon the minutiae of day-to-day living is the older belief that the rite itself has its own magical potency.

Illustration page 311

In speaking of goodness and the cultivation of the power which engenders it and the performance of the appropriate gestures which are its outward signs, Confucius is concerned with personal ethics and morality. This is the 'way of the true gentleman' – the Confucian ideal. It is Confucius's own distinctive contribution to the ancient religion. He invests religion with an ethical and moral content.

In his concern with personal conduct and personal duty, Confucius seems to suggest that he has little concern with the spirit-world and the supernatural. 'The Master did not talk about the will of Heaven, or about prodigies or disorders [of nature]' (*Analects*, vii:20) and 'did not talk about spirits' (*Analects*, xi:2). But this is a matter of emphasis. 'How can there be any proper service of spirits until living men have been properly served?' was Confucius's reply to a question about the costliness of religious rites. In short, service to god becomes meaningless if service to other people is neglected. And it is the ethical and moral problems of a man's relationship to his fellow-man with which Confucius was primarily concerned. This is the quintessence of his teaching.

Filial Piety

One further teaching of Confucius, and one that came to have an important emphasis in certain schools of Confucianism, is filial piety. *Hsiao* (filial piety) originally meant piety to dead parents and ancestors, and the duties owed to them of sacrifice and sustenance. For Confucius, whose emphasis was upon duty to the living, *hsiao* became serving parents 'while they are still living' and thus there grew up the five relationships of Confucian teaching: that of prince and subject, of father and son, of older and younger brother, of husband and wife, and of friend with friend. For most Chinese in practical terms filial piety embraces those attitudes of respect for the senior and a reciprocal attitude of love and affection on the senior's part to his junior – both as a part of daily conduct among the living and, after death, as a religious obligation in ceremonial worship.

Mencius

After the death of Confucius in 479 BC, his disciples scattered (tradition has it that he had seventy disciples), and from among them several schools of Confucianism arose. The most important figures among them are Mencius and Hsün Tzu. A modern Chinese philosopher has likened the place in Chinese history of Confucius to that of Socrates in the West, of Mencius (an idealist in temperament and philosophy) to that of Plato, and of Hsün Tzu (a realist) to that of Aristotle. Confucius, Mencius and Hsün Tzu form a sort of trinity as the founding fathers of Confucianism.

Mencius was born a century after the death of Confucius. His Chinese name was Meng K'o, but he was referred to in deference as Meng Tzu (Master Meng). He was born in 390 BC in the tiny principality of Tsou, not far from the city-state of Lu, the birthplace of Confucius. He died *c.* 305 BC. Like Confucius he was a member of the aristocratic classes, though very little is known about his personal antecedents. Tradition improbably makes him a pupil of Tzu-szu, the grandson of Confucius. Mencius, like Confucius, was a teacher. He aspired ultimately to hold office in the courts of the city-states. He sought a prince who would 'put his Way into practice'. Like Confucius, he had the disappointing experience of failing to find such a prince. After having served a brief term as minister in the state of Ch'i he retired into private life, there to continue to teach his way to his dedicated pupils.

After Mencius's death, his teachings and sayings were gathered together by his followers. A text has survived, the *Works of Mencius*, which contains much that was gathered in this way. The *Works of Mencius* follows the pattern of the *Analects* – short sentence- or paragraph-length sayings of the master, illustrative anecdotes, maxims and the like. But the paragraphs are extended and the treatment is much fuller than that of Confucius. There is no perceptible attempt at arrangement by topic or sequence. The reader, who is not directly addressed in *Mencius*, is, as it were, invited to eavesdrop on the conversations of a master and his pupils, ranging at random across the entire spectrum of Mencius's thought. Instead of being given any direct instruction, the reader must piece together, from allusion, parable, anecdote and maxim, an ordered statement of Mencius's philosophy. The *Works of Mencius*, like the *Analects*, form part of the Confucian sacred canon.

Mencius's avowed aim, like that of Confucius, his mentor, was to pass on the wisdom of the ancients without 'making anything up of myself'. But the process of 'transmitting without creating' became, as so often in the history of Confucianism, 'creating by transmitting'. Mencius was speaking for his own day and age, for which the 'wisdom of the ancients' had to be newly interpreted. In the process he made his own distinctive contribution to Confucianism.

Notions of History

For Confucius, the 'way of the former kings' was the way of the early Chou emperors (eleventh and tenth centuries BC). For Confucius, the Shang and Hsia dynasties that preceded Chou were shadowy eras. The heroes Yao and Shun he barely mentions. By Mencius's day Chinese notions of their prior history had grown. They reached very much farther back into antiquity. In this view the world began with a deluge and was made habitable by the work of three heroes,

Illustrations pages 310, 312

Yao, Shun and Yü the Great. Of them Yao and Shun appointed their own successors, but with Yü the Great the principle of hereditary tenure was created and Yü became the putative founder of the Hsia dynasty. Later, historians organized these heroes into dynasties, and regarded them as secular rulers. But in Mencius's day the golden age, the era of primordial perfection, was the 'days of Yao and Shun'. In this more ample utopia, Mencius's ideas of sainthood became more secular. 'Any man can become a Yao or a Shun.' And too, in this more secular spirit, *jen*, the almost unattainable ideal of Confucius, became for Mencius 'humane conduct' – an ideal readily attainable by any one. Mencius's principal teachings concerned the ideals of *jen*, and *yi*, originally a word meaning 'immemorial rights', becomes for Mencius justice – social and economic justice. Humanity and justice thus became the mainstays of Mencian teaching.

Humanity and Justice

In stressing justice Mencius introduces a concern for the common people, that is, the *min* in contrast to *jen* (the aristocracy). Confucius had very little to say about the *min*. Ensuring that the common people got what was due to them became, for Mencius, a prime duty of the prince. Further, heaven is the guardian of the common people and heaven shows its displeasure when they suffer. This emphasis upon the well-being of the common people in Confucianism and the notion that it is the yardstick of the ruler's virtue was one of the contributions of Mencius to the 'way'. Mencius has much to say about economics, and for him the link between ethics and economics was a close one. 'A constant mind without a constant livelihood is impossible' (*Mencius*, 3a: 5), and so it becomes the purpose of government 'to produce the necessities of life in sufficient quantity' (*Mencius*, 7b: 12).

To Mencius, the gentleman 'who is a gentleman indeed' not only may, but does, assiduously cultivate *jen*. For the prince who has these qualities the goals of true kingship are realized – the prosperity of the state, the perpetuating of his line, and ultimately the allegiance of the whole world. *Jen* engenders 'power' (*tê*), a prestige and moral persuasiveness which is the very opposite of *pa* (physical force and coercion). *Wang* (true kingship) and *pa* (rule by force) are thus opposed. To rule by superior virtue rather than by force becomes a very influential element in later Confucian political thinking.

The obligations of filial piety also receive a special emphasis in Mencius. A rival philosophy taught that 'all peoples should love each other equally'. Mencius however, saw an antithesis between his own 'familial duty', the hierarchy of affections with their priorities of seniority and the social cohesiveness that this ensured, and 'love for all humanity', which he thought destructive of the social organization of the family and of the state.

Illustration page 312

Human Beings and Their Fate

Mencius engaged in a debate current in his day on the subject of human nature and human fate. Confucius is silent on this subject. Human nature, *hsing* (about which several theories were held in Mencius's day), was to Mencius innately good and this was attested by the universality of a sense of kinship and of right and wrong. It is in this that humans differ from other living creatures. But the *hsing* can be mutilated and atrophy and disappear if not nurtured aright. Nurturing the *hsing* consists in guarding the mind (*ts'un hsin*), for the mind is the repository of humanity and justice. It is the *hsing* (nature) and *hsin* (mind) that determine what we are. It is our *ming* (fate) that governs our fortunes and determines our lease on life. *Ming* was originally a patent to a fief-holder, given by the Son of Heaven as heaven's deputy to a feudatory. In extended usage it became our lot in life – the fate ordained by heaven. While people can guard their minds and determine their conduct, they cannot determine their fate, which is in heaven's hands. Thus Mencius believed that though all humans are innately good, the realization of that good comes with self-cultivation and self-knowledge.

Hsün Tzu

Hsün Tzu (*fl. c.* 312-238 BC), the third member of the trinity of the founding fathers of Confucianism, lived towards the close of the Age of the Philosophers. Confucius, as a pioneer of the age, offered his teaching unchallenged by rival philosophers. Mencius developed Confucius's teaching under attack from the Utilitarians and the Hedonists (see page 325). Hsün Tzu defended Confucianism in the full knowledge of the claims of competing philosophies and, armed with the superior techniques of philosophical debate that had developed as the age drew to its close, presented Confucianism in a way that made his presentation the most complete and well-ordered philosophical treatise of the Philosophical Age.

While Mencius admired Confucius's virtue, Hsün Tzu admired his learning. Hsün Tzu attacks Mencius for his idealistic tendencies, preferring himself a tougher-minded, realistic approach to problems. In this approach, Hsün Tzu reinterprets Confucianism in ways which differ from Mencius in important respects.

Hsün Tzu, like his predecessors, appealed to antiquity. But, unlike Mencius, and closer to Confucius, he preferred the age of the early Chou kings. He called them the 'latter kings' in contrast to Mencius's 'former kings'. For Mencius, antiquity *par excellence* was the days of the lengendary Yao and Shun. For Hsün Tzu it was the historical and documented period of the early kings of Chou. This placed authority on the firm ground of historical documentation rather than in the utopian world of myth and legend.

In this tougher intellectual atmosphere, Confucianism, for Hsün Tzu, became more rationalistic and materialistic. Heaven became impersonal – it is nature and the natural process. Human nature, far from being innately good, as Mencius averred, was in the view of Hsün Tzu basically evil.

Hsün Tzu's Confucianism is perhaps the least transcendental and most human-centred of all. Beginning with the harsh premise that human beings are born evil, Hsün Tzu laid great stress upon the belief that by education and moral training they can become good. Education and training derive from the study of classical texts, with the sages of the past as exemplars. These sages differ in no way from human beings in their basic nature and endowments but are examples of what can be attained in moral understanding and insight when the mind is employed aright. This done, Hsün Tzu offers almost unlimitedly bright hopes for improvement through study. This elevation of the virtues of study and scholarship gave Confucianism, as it developed later, one of its most characteristic features. So too did Hsün Tzu's insistence that the end process of education and the proper function of the educated man was to govern. In later Confucianism it became an axiom that the best educated were the best able to serve the state – a notion which found expression in China's famous civil service, recruited by examination.

This optimistic, if severe, view of human prospects in this life led Hsün Tzu to see in heaven not the transcendental god of Confucius or the personal and ethical god of Mencius – but impersonal Nature and the natural process.

The Human Mind – the Centre of the Universe

Since moral order and human perfection begin in the mind, the human mind becomes central in Hsün Tzu's universe, and this led him to a humanistic, rationalistic view of religion. Certain religious practices he condemned outright as superstition – such things as praying for rain, exorcizing sickness and reading a person's fortune in the face. Other forms of divination he allowed, provided that the interpretations were made in the light of human reason. He denied the existence of harmful spirits and ghosts. The spirits of the ancestors and the powers of nature became, for Hsün Tzu, manifestations of moral excellence. By a perfect understanding of nature, people can control their environment and universe. Hsün Tzu was thus the most rational of the Confucian philosophers.

We have seen that, for Confucius, *li* (the rites of the early religion) became a code for human conduct. The observance of *li* came to play an important part in later Confucianism. Hsün Tzu provided a new and rational justification for the part that *li* plays in life. Observing the appropriate gesture, wearing the proper dress, maintaining the correct mien and demeanour – all that is involved in *li* – were for Hsün Tzu a regimen for restraining the desires and for rectifying the evil conduct that the untutored human being is prone to. *Li* was a useful training device in refining and beautifying human emotions.

This thorough-going rationalism, and the pessimistic views on the original nature of human beings, in contrast to the teachings of Mencius, led, in later Confucianism, when the views of Mencius became orthodox, to a certain diminishing in esteem for Hsün Tzu. But in his emphasis upon the virtues of education, and the duty of the scholar to govern, Hsün Tzu expressed an idea that became central in Confucianism.

In the writings of Confucius, Mencius and Hsün Tzu we have the kernel, as it were, of the philosophy and religion later to be known as Confucianism. During the Age of the Philosophers, early Confucianism had to compete with rival systems. It had not yet been accepted as an official philosophy and religion – that was not to be for another two or three centuries, and Confucianism itself had still to undergo further refinement at the hands of later philosophers before its orthodoxy was fully established.

Utilitarians and Hedonists

Mencius complained that, in his day, the whole world had succumbed to the teachings of Yang Chu and Mo Tzu. These rival philosophies, the utilitarianism of Mo Tzu and the hedonism of Yang Chu, were serious challenges to early Confucianism.

Mo Tzu (*fl.* 479-381 BC) and the philosophical schools that developed among his pupils exercised a powerful influence in the Age of the Philosophers. This influence declined under the empire and Mohism suffered a virtual eclipse. In modern times, interest in Mohism has revived largely because certain ideas in Mohism seem to have parallels in both Christian and Marxist teaching.

Mo Tzu, unlike Confucius, had little use for authority or antiquity. He was not above citing ancient precedents but he affected to prefer the Hsia dynasty to that of the Chou. Neither had he any use for mystical intuition, and the long passages devoted to refuting Mohist logic in the writings of the mystics show how formidable was the opposition that the Mohist schools were able to set against mysticism. To Mo Tzu the problems of society could only be attacked by rejecting authority and precedent and by starting anew in the pure light of reason. He arrived at his axioms deductively and then proceeded to argue inductively from given premises.

He argued that the sum total of human experience attests to the existence of a deity. The deity has a purpose, a will. That will and purpose are conceived in love and compassion. Order is the ultimate manifestation of the divine compassion. The secret of the successful prince lies in enquiring into the causes of disorder, for then only can he cure its evils. Since all people have the ear of heaven, it follows that all are equal in the eyes of heaven. Heaven rains upon the just and the unjust. Heaven manifests its love upon all regardless of person. It therefore follows that people should love one another without discrimination and with equal intensity.

The idea that people should love each other equally, with no regard for the priorities of affection due to family and prince, seemed to Mencius to be subversive of life itself. 'It outrages all human feeling,' he protested. In recent centuries, with the propagation of the Christian gospel in China, some Chinese scholars have discovered in Mo Tzu another preacher of a gospel of love.

But, despite Confucian objections to the doctrine of 'loving all people equally', Mo Tzu proceeded to demonstrate that people understand what conduces to their benefit and what conduces to their harm, and if given the choice they would opt for universal love. The criterion should be the consensus of the common good and the consensus would be for universal love.

The consensus of the common good – this idea led Mo Tzu to his two political axioms, that of the common weal (the greatest benefit to the greatest number) and that of the common accord (the theory that the policy producing the greatest benefit must be acceded to by all). It followed that only the most able, irrespective of class or family, were fit servants of the commonwealth and to them should go its highest honours and greatest rewards.

In Mo Tzu's system the highest moral act of the individual was to be found in making sacrifices for all. To this end he and his pupils formed a sworn band of brothers, engaged in extreme asceticism, wore a distinctive dress and regalia, and rendered total submission to the leader of the order. We are reminded of the religious orders of the Christian West. To the Mohist order, war was the very antithesis of universal love. The order therefore declaimed forcefully against aggression of any kind. Its opponents argued that war was a scourge in the hands of the righteous and fighting in a righteous cause was itself righteousness. The Mohists argued that war itself was evil. But this did not prevent them from also arguing that the greatest good might conceivably lie in warding off aggression.

To this end, a branch of the school devoted itself to the arts of the defence of the city. One of their oddest byproducts was the invention of a number of fortification devices. The Mohist *Canons of Logic* contains references to mechanics and optical principles – doubtless arising from a concern with military engineering – which are among the earliest scientific observations in the language. In their day, any city which invited the Mohist order to undertake its affairs was assured that the defence of the city would be conducted by men devoted to the idea that its greatest good might lie in the sacrifice of the defenders' own lives. There is an interesting trace of this notion in the Chinese language to this day, for *mo-shou* (Mohist defence) is a term for stubborn, unreasoning defence. But it was pre-eminently in the defence of doctrine that Mo Tzu's disciples excelled. The study of the means and techniques of demonstration which they undertook was the main purpose of the manual *Canons of Logic*.

Yang Chu the Epicurean, the second of Mencius's two main rivals, argued that the city-state, far from being redeemable, was past recovery. People's main concern, therefore, should be for themselves. They should seek in a perilous age for the preservation of their own person and the cultivation of their own integrity. They should refuse to become involved in material things and should offer no hostage to fortune by indulging unfruitful desire. Above all they should avoid involving themselves with their fellows. Against the virtues of social order, Yang Chu raised the banner of individualism. Rather than save the city, he thought it more important to save a single life.

Yang Chu left no writings. His philosophy is recovered only from the references made to it by his opponents. A work sheltering under his name called the *Garden of Pleasure* is a much later and perhaps spurious compilation. His reputation has suffered like that of Epicurus and largely for the same reasons. Nevertheless, the contemporaries of Yang Chu attest to his influence in his own day, and it is very possible that he was the precursor of the contemplatives and mystics who followed shortly after him, who are known best through the names of Chuang-tzu and Lao-tzu.

Philosophical Taoism

Confucianism and Mohism were 'activist' philosophies. They were concerned with the arts of the government of the city-states and with social morality. They were 'this-worldly'. They were to lead eventually to the state religion of Confucianism, the aspect of Chinese religious life we might think of as ethical.

But while the 'activist' philosophers were advocating their theories in the courts and capitals of the city-states, philosophical activities of a quite different kind were taking place in the countryside, as it were, outside society. These were the philosophies of the Quietists.

Their concerns were 'other-worldly'. They sought self-awareness and self-cultivation in the transcendental through yogic practices. In the transcendental, they saw the unchanging Oneness underlying a world of change, which at the same time gave both impetus and motion to life. This they called *tao*. All philosophers in ancient China spoke of their *tao* – their way – but the Quietists spoke, as it were, of *Tao*-ness itself. They came to be called, as a result, Taoists, and it was the speculations of these Taoists that were to inspire eventually the religion of Taoism – the aspect of Chinese religious life we might think of as mystical.

Confucianism inspired a religion of ethics and of social behaviour.

It had its historical roots in the aristocratic religion of antiquity. Taoism inspired a religion of mysticism. Its origins lie closer to the popular religion of antiquity – for it sought access to knowledge in the trance-state of the shaman rather than in the documents of antiquity. In their later religious forms, Confucianism and Taoism reflect something of these origins. Confucianism was predominantly a religion of the court and of the gentry, while Taoism never lost sight of its more popular roots.

The Core of the Taoist Scriptures

Two collections of Taoist works have survived from the Age of the Philosophers. They are the *Chuang Tzu* and the *Lieh Tzu*. Further, towards the very end of this period a brief Taoist work appeared anonymously, highly polemical in tone, known as the *Tao Tê Ching*. These three works form, as it were, the core of, and certainly are the earliest works in, a vast collection of Taoist treatises that form the Taoist Canon, the scriptures of religious Taoism.

The *Chuang Tzu* and the *Lieh Tzu* differ in style and treatment from the *Tao Tê Ching*, in ways not dissimilar to those of the *Analects* of Confucius and Mencius on the one hand and of Hsun Tzu on the other. The former are anecdotal and aphoristic, with little attempt at orderly sequence, while the latter are formal philosophical treatises.

Illustration page 329

In the Taoist tradition, the authorship of the *Tao Tê Ching* is attributed to Lao Tzu – a figure the very historicity of whom is in doubt, and so is the case with Lieh Tzu's work. Chuang Tzu (?369-?286 BC) on the other hand was a historical figure and a contemporary of Mencius. The work that bears Chuang Tzu's name, however, comprises writings from different hands and from differing periods. Regarded as philosophy, these works must be seen in this severe historical view. But, as the scriptures of a later religion, they are regarded as the canonical works of Lao Tzu and Chuang Tzu, the putative founders and patriarchs of religious Taoism, for whom later piety provides a great deal of hagiological detail.

In their various parts the *Chuang Tzu*, the *Lieh Tzu* and *Tao Tê Ching* represent branches of Taoist thought, but there are certain fundamental notions and certain grounds common to them all. This is philosophical Taoism.

The *Chuang Tzu* describes, in the form of parables, imaginary dialogues between Chuang Tzu and his critics, parodies of the discourses of the logicians and stories of Taoist saints, a form of knowledge known only to the adept. To speak of it, let alone to argue about it with any but an adept is pointless, for just as the river-gods know nothing of the sea, or an insect cannot conceive of the flight of the great migratory birds, so too the man of 'lesser knowledge' (of mundane thought) cannot conceptualize 'greater knowledge' (the vision of the mystic). This knowledge the adept gains in trance, a state in which 'I lose me'.

In trance, the adept takes off on a journey, 'riding upon the wind', borne by 'cloud chariots' to the infinite. He sees that 'Heaven and

Left Lao Tzu, with a scroll in his hand, riding an ox. An ink drawing by Chang Lu (Ming dynasty, 1368-1644). National Palace Museum, Taipei.

Above 'Legendary Emperors', a detail of a Taoist temple fresco from Southern Shansi province (Yuan dynasty, 1280-1368). Royal Ontario Museum, Toronto.

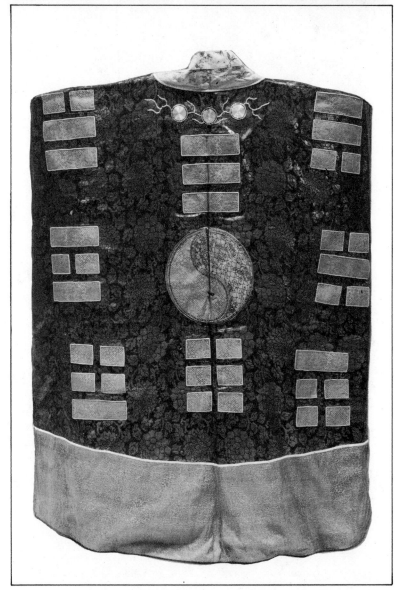

Right A Taoist priest's robe, in blue brocade with applied symbols of the eight mystic trigrams and the *yin-yang* in gold-patterned red satin (late eighteenth or early nineteenth century). Metropolitan Museum of Art, New York. Gift of Joseph J. Asch, 1936.

Above The Temple of Heaven or Hall of Annual Prayers in Peking. Here prayers were offered for good crops in the spring, and here the emperor, the Son of Heaven, received his mandate to rule China from God, the Supreme Emperor.

Above left A Ming dynasty painting of a Taoist priest in his ritual garments. Religionskundliche Sammlung der Universität, Marburg.

Left A fragment of a wall painting showing the Buddha, from Qoco (seventh to eighth century AD). The style of the painting is distinctively Indian but each country came to see the Buddha in terms of its own art and characteristic physical features. Museum für Indische Kunst, Berlin.

Earth came into being with me together, and with me all things are one'. In this vision all things are relative, all opposites blend, all contrasts are harmonized. The One is *tao*. It is the total spontaneity of all things. All is so-of-itself. *Tao* therefore can 'do everything by doing nothing'. *Tê* (the virtue or morality of the Confucians) is, for the Taoist, the *tao* inherent in anything. It is its 'power'. *Tao* (the way) and *tê* (its power) are fundamental conceptions of philosophical Taoism. Since everything is 'so-of-itself' – has, as it were, its own spontaneity – any human interference is damaging. The adept therefore opposes institutions, moral laws and government as human artifices, obstructing the free-play of *tao* and the working of *tê*. The best way to govern the world is not to govern it. Similarly, in the art of living, happiness is achieved by letting alone – by allowing *tao* free-play – by engaging in the activities which are actionless. Qualities and values are relative. What is, is good.

Finally, death is but an aspect of existence, as life is. It is the exchange of one form of existence for another. As the *Chuang Tzu* says, 'Life and death are one, right and wrong are the same.' It is this that 'frees a man from his handicaps and fetters'.

The *Tao Tê Ching* (*The Way and Its Power*) is the classic book of Taoism. Most of it is in verse and its method of exposition is essentially that of poetry. Composed towards the close of the Age of the Philosophers, its author abandons the method of fable and story used in the *Chuang Tzu* and compresses the quintessence of Quietist teaching into a single whole. Taken in its historical place in early Chinese philosophy, the *Tao Tê Ching* can be read as a statement of the philosophical position of the Quietists and the Quietists' refutation of rival philosophers of their time. But as a scripture the *Tao Tê Ching*, attributed to Lao Tzu, the patriarch of Taoism, has pre-eminence in religious Taoism. There are more than thirty versions of the *Tao Tê Ching* in English translation and it has been generally recognized as a classic of mysticism far beyond China.

Other Schools

Among the Hundred Schools of the Age of the Philosophers, mention so far has been made of the schools from which the two major indigenous religions of China sprang, namely the schools of the Confucians and of the Taoists. Mention too has been made of Mo Tzu and his school. Mo Tzu's conception of heaven was the closest to the notion of a personal god to be met with in ancient Chinese thought, but this has not been important historically in the development of Chinese religious notions. Interest in Mo Tzu, however, has revived in modern times, partly on account of it.

Two further philosophical movements must be mentioned which have an important bearing on Chinese religious history. The first of these is that of the Cosmologists.

At some time in the early part of the third century BC, speculation began about a theory of the universe as an ordered whole and about the laws which govern it. Prominent in this movement were Tsou

Opposite above The Buddha Vairocana, of whom the cosmos is the expression, at Lungmen in Honan province (AD 672-75).

Opposite below Barbarian royalty worshipping the Buddha, depicted in inks and colour on a silk hand-scroll and attributed to Chao Kuang-fu (*c.* tenth century AD). Cleveland Museum of Art, Ohio.

Yen and his school, which profoundly affected the course of philosophy in the Han period and in subsequent times.

Tsou Yen posited a cycle of five elements: earth, wood, metal, fire and water. Each element in turn conquers its predecessor in recurring cycles. Each in turn governs a period in history and from this Tsou Yen posited a cyclical theory of history – very influential in later Chinese thought. But each element in its period of rise and decay governs the natural world, so that both natural and human events are explicable (and predictable) in these terms. Tsou Yen's followers are known as the Yin-yang school. *Yin* means literally the 'dark side' and *yang* the 'sunny side'. At about the same time as the theory of the five elements appeared, the terms *yang* and *yin* occur as categories in a dualist cosmological theory, in which *yang* and *yin*, the light and the dark, the male and the female, the strong and weak, occur as two cosmic principles, through the interaction of which all phenomena of *Illustration page 330* the universe are produced.

The *yin-yang* dualism entered into Confucian orthodoxy by its incorporation into the *I Ching* – a late compilation from, and rational arrangement of, earlier works on divination. The *I Ching* or *Book of Changes* is arranged around eight trigrams, each composed of combinations of three divided or undivided lines. By combining two trigrams sixty-four hexagrams were obtained, and to these sixty-four signs descriptions were added of their supposed symbolic meanings. The hexagrams and their interpretations were thought to have come down from remote antiquity. Certain appendices to the *I Ching* traditionally, though erroneously, attributed to Confucius, were included and thus the *I Ching* with its *yin-yang* cosmology entered the Confucian canon.

Yin-yang and the five elements inspired much of later Chinese natural philosophy, but they also entered into the popular religion through Taoism and their symbols became a common part of the iconography of popular Chinese art.

The School of Law
Finally, there was a school of thought called by the Chinese the School of Law because it advocated that law should replace morality. It arose from the teachings of the Lord of Shang in the state of Ch'in, the state which at the close of the Age of the Philosophers conquered the rest of China and set up, under the first emperor, the unified nation-state of dynastic China. The School of Law rejected all appeals to tradition, reliance on supernatural sanctions and trust in supernatural guidance. It was concerned only with 'the reality of the world as at present it exists'.

It advocated the abolition of feudal privilege and the precise encoding of the peoples' duties, an encoding which was to be enforced by rigorous punishments and encouraged by heavy rewards. Armed with this severe advice, the rulers of Ch'in imposed upon the whole of China a unity and a peace, thus saving the country from the crippling depletions suffered during the wars of the contending city-states. However, such was the ferocity of the totalitarian regime of the first emperor that Legalism, as a philosophy, was in the end discredited.

Pre-Imperial Religion

The religious heritage of the Chinese in the pre-imperial age (prior to the second century BC) had two quite distinct elements. The first, prominent as an influence in the religious aspects of Confucianism, was the cult of heaven and the divine ancestors, in which princes and the aristocratic classes propitiated and sought the aid of the powerful dead who ruled, as it were, as a political hierarchy in the heavens and conferred their mandate to govern on their regents below. This worship, designed to keep heaven and human beings in accord, at first by magical rituals and later by moral precepts, became, under Confucian guidance, the state cult of Imperial China.

Illustration page 309

The second was the world of augury and magic, in which the spirit-medium, the shaman, acted as intermediary between humans and the spirits. This was a religion kept alive among the people, preserving the elements of a more primitive religion, in which exorcism, fortune-telling and the like performed for the peasant classes the function of religious practice. Closely parallel to the trance-state of the shamans was the transcendental state cultivated by the Taoists, a state which became the epistemological basis of Mystical Taoism. Many of the functions of the early shamans were later taken over by the Taoist priesthood.

Illustrations pages 310, 311

Religion under the Ch'in and Han Dynasties

The Age of the Philosophers closed with the collapse of the city-states and the establishment of the empire under the Ch'in. China was united for the first time for half a millennium. The Ch'in rulers, under a totalitarianism largely inspired by Legalism, united the city-states into a single nation-state. The First Ch'in emperor succeeded in subjugating the princes and peoples of the erstwhile city-states as subjects to himself alone, but also sought to demonstrate to them that his overlordship extended to their altars and to the gods they worshipped as well.

In a series of peregrinations he toured the empire, ascending its sacred mountains, visiting its shrines, making the appropriate sacrifices to the local deities and thus asserting his sovereignty not only over men but over all the gods of the land. This assumption of religious no less than temporal power he symbolized in the title by which he designated himself: Ch'in Shih Huang-ti. Ch'in is the name of his ruling house; shih signifies 'the first', the first of a line he imagined would continue for ten thousand generations; *ti* was the term by which the god-kings of antiquity were called; and *huang*, 'illustrious', suggested that he was the most illustrious among the *Ti*.

Under the advice of Legalist ministers, Ch'in Shih Huang-ti ordered the burning of all books save those concerned with the useful arts, hoping to destroy the teachings of the Hundred Schools.

As the first emperor grew older, he cultivated both shamans and magicians from various parts of the empire, seeking of them the herb of immortality, hoping to prolong his own life indefinitely. In this process, elements of the popular religion in all their original varieties came to the court. The emperor died a megalomaniac, regretted by no one.

The Han dynasty (202 BC to AD 220), which followed the Ch'in, inherited the structure, the institutions and the unity of the Ch'in. But it rejected both the harshness of Ch'in's laws and Legalism with its intolerance. The Han ushered in a period rich in intellectual and cultural achievement. Chinese today like to call themselves 'men of Han'. During this period Confucianism was established as the state orthodoxy, Taoism became a popular religion, and, toward the close of the Han, Buddhism made its debut in China.

The Triumph of Confucianism

The Ch'in came to power as a result of military conquest, and the Han succeeded the Ch'in through an armed uprising. But from the first emperor down to the time of Emperor Wu of the Han dynasty, the kings were plagued by the problems of the religious sanctions that legitimized kingship. We have seen how this affected the behaviour of the first emperor. The early Han emperors were beset with similar problems. The history of this concern was chronicled by the father of Chinese history, Ssu-ma Ch'ien, in a treatise called 'The *Feng* and *Shan* Sacrifices'. Writing in the time of Emperor Wu, he reflects the belief then current that the mandate of heaven requires that the ruler be fit to perform the *feng* and *shan* sacrifices. In attempting to trace the history of these sacrifices he gives what is, in effect, a history of royal religious belief which, while fanciful in its earlier parts, gives a great deal of information on religious belief in his day.

In fact, there is no evidence that the *feng* and *shan* sacrifices were part of the observances of kingship in antiquity, but the search for the formula led the early Han kings to explore the extent of religious belief over the entire empire, and in the records of this search much was set down which is recorded nowhere else.

It was in the conflicting advice given to the early Han emperors on the rites, the ceremonies and the sacrificial duties of kingship that Confucian scholars began to assume that ascendancy in the Han court which resulted in the ultimate triumph of Confucianism as the state orthodoxy and as the guardian and arbiter of the religious rites of its sovereigns. Confucians tutored the princes of the royal house and became prominent in state service. By the time of Emperor Wu (r. 140-87 BC), himself educated by Confucians, the suggestion had been made that Confucianism should be the sole philosophy of government. Court officials were appointed to specialize in the study and explanation of the Confucian classics. An imperial university was established to teach Confucianism, from among the graduates of which the officers of state were to be chosen. Gradually, under this pressure, the followers of non-Confucian philosophies were dismissed. Finally, under Emperor Hsüan (r. 73-49 BC), a council of the empire's Confucian authorities was summoned and for three years they discussed the problems of the interpretations of the classics. Their deliberations were contained in a memorial to the throne. In 51 BC the emperor ratified its contents. Henceforth there was an official orthodoxy – an official interpretation of the Confucian classics which became authoritative in government.

Thus Confucianism, proscribed under the Ch'in and a small and local movement at the beginning of Han, came, as the dynasty ran its course, to triumph over all the Hundred Schools. It became the state and court orthodoxy. Its classics became the stuff of the curriculum for the educated classes. Proficiency in the classics was the criterion for selection for state service and preferment. Confucian religious notions and prescriptions for the rituals of worship became the official religion of the royal house. Confucianism had become the state cult.

Need for Personal Gods

During the Age of the Philosophers notions of a personal god and of individual intercession and worship had gradually been replaced, among the 'activist' philosophies, by quasi-scientific and materialistic notions of the universe and by a ritual of human behaviour devoid entirely of the transcendental. The elements of the Chou royal religion which had been turned to ethical advantage by the earlier philosophers were eliminated altogether by the later philosophers. Among the Quietists the techniques of ecstasy and trance and the goals of the Quietist initiate were far removed (whatever their earlier connection) from those of the shamans of the popular religion, who, as the medium between humans and gods and spirits, provided for popular religious needs.

But belief in personal gods persisted, and personalized spirits and shamans, sorcerers and magicians abounded. Whatever the official religion taught, people still sought for relationships with gods and spirits of a personal and individual kind. And belief in such deities and spirits, as also in the possibility, through the mediation of shamans and others, of personal intercession with the gods, provided for those religious needs which philosophers and the official religions had bypassed.

For those unhappy about their fate after death or the fate of their loved ones, the official religion offered no consolation. At death, so belief ran, a person's several souls separate and the body disintegrates. Shamans, sorcerers and magicians on the other hand, affected to be able to recall the wandering souls of the dead, and by various techniques and drugs claimed to be able to ensure the immortality of the body, so that scattered souls could be reintegrated into an immortal body and the obliteration of death be averted.

It was in the search for such immortality that the first emperor engaged in a nationwide search for the 'men of recipes' – for those who, among the popular priesthood, sought to provide such solace. And in this search it was revealed how widespread beyond the circles of a small intellectual elite the beliefs and practices of the popular religion were. A century and a half later, a Han emperor, Emperor Wu, in later life engaged in a similar quest. The magicians and sorcerers who appeared at his court, to the strong disapproval of the growing Confucian court elite, were eloquent testimony to the persistence and popularity among the people of the old religion.

The Yellow Heaven

Towards the close of the Han dynasty a group of men practising alchemy and healing arrived at the conclusion that the 'blue heaven' would shortly be replaced by the 'yellow heaven' as the presiding power in the universe. They prophesied that in the year AD 184 a new and revolutionary era would be ushered in – a millennium of universal peace. This apocalyptic vision occurred at a time of almost universal political unrest. It became, for an aroused peasantry, a rallying point for revolt. The rebels wore a yellow-coloured kerchief on their heads as a token of their association with the yellow heaven. Because of this their rebellion came to be known as the Revolt of the Yellow Turbans.

Whatever the causes for the revolt, the movement was Taoist-led, its ideology was Taoist-inspired and the reforms it sought were to be found in the formation of a Taoist state. The revolt was suppressed, but it revealed the existence of a religion calling itself Taoist, which was well organized with a large popular following. It had evidently been established long before the revolt of AD 184.

In Taoist history, Chang Liang, who had served the first Han emperor and was a student of Taoism, is mentioned as seeking in vain to 'attain immortality'. Seven generations later a reputed descendant of his, Chang Ling, emigrated to West China and wrote a treatise on Taoism. He gathered a coterie of disciples, said to have been numbered in tens of thousands. He was reputed to have attained immortality. In the second century AD a Taoist Church was already in existence, in which the Chang surname and the reputed descendants of Chang Ling were prominent leaders.

The Taoist Church was divided into two regional groupings, that of the east under the direction of Chang Chüeh and his two brothers (the 'Three Chang') and that of the west under the direction of Changs descended from Chang Ling. At the time of the Yellow Turban Revolt, the eastern Church was said to have the allegiance of eight provinces, two-thirds of the Han Empire, and to have mustered 360,000 followers. In those eight provinces the Taoist Church had thirty-six districts. At the head of the hierarchy were the three Chang brothers: General and Lord of Heaven, General and Lord of Earth, and General and Lord of Man. Under them the larger districts (with over ten thousand converts) were in charge of a Great Adept, the smaller districts of a Lesser Adept. A similar regional organization existed in the western Church under Chang Heng and Chang Lu. A religious hierarchy extended down to the individual community, forming ranks of priests and laity.

Rites and Services

The Taoist Church developed rites and services for atonement for sin, and for the expiation of sickness (thought to be caused by sin). The priests recited incantations over water and gave it to the penitent to drink. If this failed to secure relief from sickness, it was attributed to lack of faith. In the western Church, the faithful paid five pecks of rice as redemption money (for centuries after, the western Church was known popularly as 'The Five Pecks of Rice Doctrine'). Sins were written down and the confession recorded. Three copies addressed to heaven, to earth and to water, were placed on a mountain, buried in earth and submerged in water respectively. Sins such as drunkenness, debauchery and stealing were atoned for in this way.

The Taoist religion and the Church that propagated it at the end of the Han dynasty were far removed from the school of mysticism that bore the name Taoist in the fourth and third centuries BC. From being a philosophical theory based on mystical intuition, Taoism had become a religion of salvation. From being a matter for private and personal speculation, Taoism had become an organized Church with its hierarchy and adherents. At the close of the Han, Taoism was a religion as was Buddhism and as Confucianism had become. Its appeal was broadly based and popular. It was to grow in importance and popular appeal through the six dynasties and until T'ang, and it even at times enjoyed brief periods of imperial patronage.

Illustration page 330

As a religion Taoism offered a way of salvation. It provided for the faithful a variety of routes to paradise. At its most popular and simple, the devotee, too poor to engage in costly techniques of diet and breathing, in drug-taking and abstinence, and too uneducated to follow the treatises on mystical union and ecstasy, could, by piety, by confession and atonement acquire the necessary merit by which, at death, after a stay in the underworld, he or she could be saved and escorted to paradise.

Similarly, by pious observances and by attending special services for their redemption, the faithful could pray for the souls of the dead, who, through the merit of the living, might finally gain release from the underworld and entrance to paradise.

At a higher stage of devotion, by charity, by abstinence and by service in the religious community, the faithful could attain a stage whereby they joined the ranks of officialdom in the underworld, and through service in its hierarchy secured entrance to paradise.

The Avoidance of Death

The true initiate, however, sought to avoid death altogether and to pass to the land of the immortals directly by translation. There were multitudinous techniques and regimens by which the ranks of the immortals could be attained, but this was reserved only, of course, for the most advanced.

In the broadest terms these regimens of dietary practices, breathing exercises, sexual disciplines and the like were designed to replace, in the mortal body, those elements which were gross and mortal by the

Opposite above left Ancestor worship has been one of the most deep-rooted elements in Chinese religion. This woman is lighting candles in an ancestral shrine in Kwangdung province in 1981.

Opposite above right Consulting a spirit medium. Ah Wei, the medium, writes down the messages he receives from the dead while in a trance.

Opposite below left The 'Paradise of Amitabha', a hanging scroll in ink and colours on silk. Amitabha ruled in the paradise of the Buddhist, part of the mythology which grew up around an originally austere and intellectual religion. British Museum, London.

Opposite below right A Chin dynasty twelfth-century wooden carving of Kuan-yin. As a symbol of fecundity and the healer of sickness, she is still immensely popular. Her image is found in almost every home, and many make the pilgrimage to her temple of Miao Feng Shan outside Peking. Royal Ontario Museum, Toronto.

ethereal and incorruptible. It was said that at the creation the nine vapours were mixed in chaos. They separated, the purest forming the heavens and the coarsest forming the earth. The human body is made up of the coarser elements. What endows it with life is the primordial vapour which enters the body at birth. It joins with the essence and this forms the spirit – the principle of life. At death vapour and essence separate. The body is governed by spirits as is the universe. If the body is not to disintegrate, these spirits too must be retained, preventing the parting of spirit and essence. Thus immortality is reached.

Three principal groups of techniques were employed to do this. These were 'nourishing the life principle', 'nourishing the spirits', and 'preserving the One intact'. One of the causes of death was held to be the consumption of cereals because their 'vapours' nourished evil spirits in the body. These spirits resided in the brain, the heart and the stomach. By diet, the use of drugs and breathing exercises these could be repressed. The coarser vapours and spirits were replaced little by little by the primordial vapour, which is eternal. When pure cinnabar was absorbed, the bones turned to gold and the flesh to jade – another promised escape from corruption. By breathing one could force the essence to rise through the marrow to the brain and strengthen the union of vapour and essence, thus nourishing the spirits which prevent dissolution. Then, too, by meditation, by deep concentration and by Quietist ecstasy, one could enter into communication with the good spirits within, which gradually, as the vision progressed, led to the vision of the Great Triad, at which immortality was assured.

The Taoist Community

Finally, of course, there were the greatest of all adepts, those who, taking the road of Chuang Tzu and Lao Tzu, renounced personal immortality for the higher state of being identified with *Tao* itself, a state in which no corporeal containment is possible.

Under the papacy of the Changs, life in the Church centred on the local communities of the faithful. In charge of the community was the teacher (*shih*). Below him were the community officials, ranked, with suitable titles, in three grades: those who were both pious and rich, those who were rich, and those who were pious but poor. They conducted initiation rites for those of eighteen years of age and assisted the needy especially in case of sickness. They raised the money for feasts and ceremonies and in general were the patrons of the community. The ordinary members of the community were known as the *Tao-min* (Taoist people). The teacher was an office held hereditarily and passed from father to son. Within living memory, the descendants of these teachers still had charge of Taoist communities and properties and were still addressed by the title *shih kung* (respected teacher).

Life in the community was a full one. Each year had its calendar of feast-days and festivals, some obligatory and fixed, some held at

Right The dragon is the ancient symbolic animal of China, and recurs again and again in Chinese legend and myth. This one is part of a funeral procession and decorates the gaily-coloured hearse. Behind can be seen mourners wearing white, the traditional colour of mourning in China.

Right Prayer before a household altar. Many Chinese conduct religious rites in their homes at a personal family shrine.

the particular request of a member of the community. Three times a year the congregation met to celebrate the three agents, heaven, earth and water – assessors of rewards and punishments. There were five services a year for the departed faithful. Certain services were religious banquets offered to the teacher by pious families on occasions of birth and death. Some were, in a sense, masses to seek for particular favours – a son, a cure for sickness, rain, promotion in rank – or celebrations for favours received.

The rites of the Church gradually increased in both number and complexity. Among those to appear later was the Festival of the Gold Amulet, celebrated for the emperor and designed to avert such natural disasters as floods, the ill effects of eclipses and the like and to ensure the nation's well-being. There was also the Festival of the Jade Amulet for the health and well-being of all, believers and non-believers. The Festival of Dust and Ashes was celebrated to expiate sickness. The Festival of the Yellow Talisman sought to ensure the release from Hades of ancestors going back to the seventh generation.

Illustration page 331

Thus, for the members of the community who lived in piety, repented of their sins and were zealous in attendance, the Church offered salvation and an escape to the Mystical Garden (Paradise) after a sojourn in the Shades.

The Coming of Buddhism

It was during the Han dynasty that, as we have seen, Confucianism triumphed as the official cult of the ruling house and that of its officials, whereas in the countryside among the masses, Taoism in a religious form was rapidly becoming the popular, national religion of China. While this was happening, however, quietly and almost unremarked, a foreign religion was brought to China from India, which was to pose a serious challenge both to Taoism and to Confucianism. This was Buddhism.

It is not known precisely when Buddhism reached China. But China was in touch with India and the West by the middle of the first century BC. The Han Empire, by this time, was firmly established in Central Asia and dominated the silk road to the West. A century later, in AD 65, a Buddhist community is recorded at the court of a Han prince. But before this Chinese envoys and soldiers had served in the Buddhism countries of Central Asia. Moreover, colonies of non-Chinese from these Buddhist countries resided in the trading cities of China proper. Further, towards the end of the first century AD a Buddhist community existed in Loyang, the capital, itself.

To this community, in AD 148 a Parthian missionary, An Shih-kao, came. He was the first unequivocally historical personage in the history of Chinese Buddhism. An Shih-kao, with his co-missionaries in the Buddhist Church at Loyang (Sogdians, Parthians, Yueh-chih and Indians), began the long work of the translation of the Buddhist scriptures into the Chinese language. In AD 166 Emperor Huan of the Han dynasty had Taoist and Buddhist ceremonies performed in the palace: a formal announcement that Buddhism had come to China.

Buddhism, like Taoism, was a religion of salvation. But it must not be supposed that the Buddhism which took root in Han China was an organic whole of doctrine and practice as it was in India, where, divided into its several schools, it was already well developed. Buddhism was received by the Chinese as a foreign form of Taoism.

Contradictory Doctrine

As doctrine, Buddhism and Taoism are contradictory in a number of fundamental ways. Taoism pursued the perpetuation of human personality. Buddhism denied its very existence – for Buddhists there is no 'me'. Taoism looked for the immortality of the physical body. Buddhism regarded the human body as it regarded all created things, as impermanent.

But in Chinese eyes these doctrinal differences were at first obscured. In its practices Buddhism had certain seeming similarities with Taoism. It engaged in public worship without sacrifices. It gave importance to meditation and to yogic practices, to fasting and to abstinence. For several centuries it was popularly believed in China that Buddha had been taught by Lao Tzu, the patriarch of Taoism, and that Buddhism was simply a foreign form of Taoism.

The problems of propagating the faith were formidable. It was a faith evolved in a social milieu very different from that of China. It made many assumptions, universally held in India, but utterly alien to China. It was expressed in a language as different from Chinese as is Sanskrit, by monks few of whom could express themselves well in Chinese (before the late fourth century AD no Chinese knew Sanskrit).

Beset by these problems, both doctrine and practice tended to be reduced to those elements which, by supposed or real similarity, had their counterparts in Chinese religious life and thought and were amenable to adaptation and incorporation with Chinese practices.

The Age of Faith

For the next four centuries the unity of the Han was to be replaced by a period of disunion, that of the three kingdoms and the six dynasties. Disunion was to persist until, under the Sui and the T'ang dynasties, China was unified again.

The period of political disunity was to be the beginning of China's Age of Faith. The uncertain fortunes of the courts loosened the hold that Confucianism held over the intelligentsia, and in this looser, freer soil the Taoist Church was to flourish, and the Buddhist Church gradually to take firm root.

Confucianism in the Age of Faith

Under Han political supremacy Confucianism had served the state and Confucians had succeeded largely in excluding rivals from the influential positions. With the collapse of Han power and the descent of China into political disunity, Confucianism lost prestige and the scholar-administrators revived interest in some of the rival schools – in Legalism, in Mohism, and in Mystical Taoism. In the middle of the third century AD, from within Confucian circles, a new learning, the 'dark learning' (*hsüan hsüeh*), appeared. Among the cultured gentry the 'dark learning', an intellectualized Confucianism drawing heavily from re-interpretations of the *Chuang Tzu*, the *Tao Tê Ching* and the *Book of Changes*, became a leading way of thought. With its intellectual curiosity and its metaphysical bent, it became the philosophy and pastime of the leisured, aristocratic classes. The intellectual climate thus created was to have important repercussions on the development of Buddhism. For the rather legalistic and dogmatic form of Confucianism that informed the ruling families under the Han was to give place to a more speculative, frankly intellectual Confucianism, creating in its adherents a mind more sympathetic to the subtleties of Buddhist thought.

Buddhism in the Age of Faith

During the troubled third century the Buddhist Church in China, still largely in the hands of aliens, confined most of its energies to translation of the Buddhist scriptures, often in conditions of great difficulty. In doing so, the foreign missionaries, by this time often born and educated in China, greatly improved the sophistication and style of the translations.

This activity was of first importance. Buddhism had brought to China a new form of social organization – the monastic community, the Sangha – which was to become a social phenomenon of immense significance in medieval Chinese society. It provided for intellectual activity in a way not previously known in China. But the Church needed the permission and patronage of the ruling classes essential for so revolutionary and costly an institution. Buddhism had to make inroads among those classes who were the guardians of wealth and patronage. Despite the immense activity in the procuring and translation of scriptures in the third century, Buddhism had made little progress in this direction. But during the fourth and fifth centuries the Buddhist Church succeeded in forming an intellectual clerical elite of Chinese and domesticated foreign monks, propagandists of a Buddhism adapted to the country, which thoroughly penetrated the Chinese upper classes. From this time Buddhism became vigorous and a serious challenge to Taoism.

One of the most important cultural gifts Buddhism made to China was the enrichment of its literature, not only by Buddhist writings but by much else of scientific and philosophical value from India's literary riches. And one of the most moving testimonies to the piety of the Buddhist faithful in China is the amount of energy and talent which they brought to the work of translation. We have spoken of the difficulties of the earlier translators.

The work of translation took a new turn at the beginning of the fifth century, when Kumarajiva, a Buddhist from Central Asia, with the help of the emperor, organized a translation bureau better than anything that had existed until then in China. Here, with a large corps of assistants, he produced new scriptures, retranslated bad translations and propagated them abroad. Both he and his collaborators translated some ninety-eight works, of which fifty-two survive and are included in the Buddhist canon. The elegance of Kumarajiva's translations gave the Buddhists scriptures a new appeal to China's literature-conscious intelligentsia.

Many Translations

From this time forward, translations in ever-increasing number and with greater accuracy were made. Various bureaus of translators continued the work of Kumarajiva. Special mention should be made of Paramartha, an Indian of a Brahman family, who in the middle of the sixth century translated some seventy works; of Hsüan-tsang, a Chinese of an official family who, on returning from a famous pilgrimage to the holy places of India in AD 645, devoted the rest of his life, under imperial patronage, to the translation of the sacred texts that he had collected on his travels (they are said to have been about twenty-five times as voluminous as the Christian Bible); and of I Ching, who shortly after Hsüan-tsang's death made a similar pilgrimage, going to India by sea from southern China.

The work of bringing scriptures to China and translating them, a work that had proceeded steadily from the debut of Buddhism in China until the eighth century when access to Central Asia and India by land was cut off, added much to Chinese philosophy and thought. But the propagation of the faith among the populace was largely of the kind that had come to China at the end of Han and the period of the Three Kingdoms, a Buddhism much modified by Taoist practices and adjusted to indigenous ideas, which was acceptable among the Chinese people. But monastic Buddhism itself was evolving in China its own distinctive forms, and these slowly penetrated to the laity.

For definitions of Mahayana and Hinayana Buddhism, see pages 282–4 and 275–7.

Illustrations pages 331, 332

The doctrine and practices of Buddhism were firmly established in India and Central Asia long before Buddhism reached China. But, as we have seen, Buddhism, whether in its Hinayana (the lesser vehicle) or Mahayana (the greater vehicle) form, as a religion for monks or laymen, came to China through a process of propagation, often piecemeal, by scripture and by preaching, in both simple and sophisticated forms, over a period of some five centuries. It was received in a land with a native system of religious beliefs at least a millennium old. It was interpreted in a language, the very vocabulary of which was replete with Chinese notions often at serious cross-purposes with the vocabulary of Buddhist Sanskrit. Despite these difficulties, it brought to China a religion based on belief in the Buddha and the essence of Buddha's doctrine, the Four Holy Truths.

The first holy truth is that life is ill and being is suffering. The second is that life is perpetuated by rebirth. It is craving and desire that bring about rebirth. The third is that liberation from rebirth is to be had by the elimination of desire and craving, and the fourth is that eight steps lead to the stopping of the ill of life. The eight-fold path consists of right understanding, right thought, right speech, right bodily action, right livelihood, right moral effort, right mindfulness and right concentration.

There is only one way of escape from this suffering, the way discovered by the Buddha. It is the way that leads to *nirvana*, that is, to unconditioned being, which is permanent and does not lead to death and rebirth. Deliverance comes with faith in Buddha, and with the practice of the law (*Dharma*) as preached by the community of monks (the Sangha). Hence its confession of faith: 'I take refuge in the Buddha, I take refuge in the Law, I take refuge in the community of monks.'

For a fuller description of Buddhist doctrine, see pages 271 and 274–5.

Monks and Laity

Like Taoism Buddhism has two modes of religious life, monastic and lay. While the monks, the intelligentsia as it were of both religions, disputed doctrinal differences and in their disputes influenced Chinese intellectual life generally, both religions competed for the souls of the people of China. Both reduced doctrines which were highly subtle and metaphysical to simple proportions whereby the layperson, too untutored to engage in scholastic disputation and too poor to renounce the world for the Buddhist monastery of the Taoist phalanstery, might enjoy the solaces of religion – help in this life and a hope of paradise in the next.

In China Buddhism, in its interplay with Taoism and as it came to find expression within the Chinese genius, produced a number of purely Chinese Buddhist sects. Principal among these are Ch'an Buddhism, that of the T'ien-t'ai School, the Pure Land School, and the Tantric sect, Chen-yen.

The Ch'an School

The first of these Chinese schools is that of Ch'an (Chinese for the Sanskrit *dhyana* 'meditation' and *Zen* in Japanese). Ch'an in essence teaches that salvation comes from inner enlightenment and that enlightenment comes in an instant, as it had to the Buddha. It is a sudden conversion, obtainable here and now. It teaches that the only reality is the Buddha nature. By turning the gaze inward this can be seen and in one final vision it is suddenly revealed. Ch'an is thus hostile to much that had become traditional in Buddhism. Images and scriptures were viewed with hostility. Metaphysical speculation and theory were discarded for concrete thought. Gradual processes and levels of religious experience were set aside for one instant and total experience. In these things Ch'an had much in common with the teachings of mystical Taoism.

Ch'an became a separate school at the beginning of the eighth century, and by AD 750 had its own monastic rule and organization. It claimed very much earlier origins, tracing its beginnings to Chu Tao-sheng (*fl.* AD 397-434) and his pupils, students of the *Lankavatara Sutra*, who attacked the idea of 'merit'; to Bodhidharma in the early sixth century, whom legend credited with gazing at a blank wall for nine years; and to such famous monks as those who surrounded Hui Neng (637-713 AD). It was, however, Shen Hui, a pupil of Hui Neng, who founded the school in South China from which Ch'an thereafter flourished. In the eighth and ninth centuries Ch'an enjoyed its heroic age and it was at this time that the great Ch'an masters worked. By AD 1000 Ch'an was rivalled only by Pure Land Buddhism. In the Sung dynasty the influence of Ch'an was powerfully envinced in landscape painting. It had thoroughly permeated China's aesthetic life.

The Pure Land School

The second of the Chinese schools is that of the Ch'ing T'u (Pure Land), or Lotus, or Amidist School. Pure Land is the Buddhism of simple faith. One of the differences between Mahayana and Hinayana was that the former taught that those unable to achieve enlightenment of themselves could achieve it through faith in the efficacy of *buddhas* and *bodhisattvas*. Certain *buddhas* had created Buddhalands, that of Amitabha being the Pure Land in the west. By simple invocation of the name of Amitabha, coupled with faith in his efficacy, the devotee

Illustration page 341

of his cult was assured of rebirth in the Pure Land.

The cult of Amitabha (the Buddha of Infinite Long-life) had originated in India. In China, in the fourth century AD, Fa-t'u-teng (d. AD 349), a missionary from Central Asia, arrived in Loyang and with imperial patronage built many temples and engaged in widespread evangelism to form a Church that would appeal alike to the masses and to his court patrons. A pupil of his, Tao-an (AD 314-385), carried his work of evangelism further. A former Taoist, Hui-yuan (AD 334-416) became a pupil of Tao-an. It was Hui-yuan who, using Taoist figures of speech, founded the Pure Land School.

For the concept of the bodhisattva, see pages 282–3.

The cult of devotion to *buddhas* and *bodhisattvas* was widespread. (*Bodhisattvas* are the *buddhas*-to-be, who refrain from entering *nirvana* to remain as saviours of others.) In China the *buddhas* and *bodhisattvas* acquired names that were purely Chinese and were represented in paintings and images by a formal iconography. Gotama the historical Buddha, became Shih-chia-fu (Sakyamuni), represented as seated on a lotus in meditation, or in a recumbent position (the 'Sleeping Buddha'), or as an ascetic. The Bodhisattva Avalokitesvara became Kuan-yin (a name found in mythical Taoism), originally male, but

Illustration page 341

usually represented in female form as the goddess of mercy who intercedes for those in peril. Kshitigarbha became Ti-tsang, the *bodhisattva* who travels through purgatory delivering the souls of the damned. Maitreya became Mi-lo-fu, the messianic *buddha*, who, when the Law is forgotten, will bring back to earth the teachings of Buddha.

But, though the cults of these and others spread from the fourth century onwards, that of Amitabha (in Chinese O-mi-t'o) and Kuan-hin became firmly associated with the Pure Land School. Amitabha's paradise stirred the Chinese imagination in much the same way as did the fairyland in the Kun-lun Mountains, the home of the queen mother of the west, the paradise of the Taoists.

Pure Land provided a simple faith and a simple invocation for the humble believer, tied by daily work and too poor to study and engage in elaborate ritual. It was the most popular form of Buddhism among the laity until within living memory. By AD 1000, Ch'an and Pure

Land had attracted the allegiance of the vast majority of Chinese monks.

The T'ien-t'ai and Chen-yen Schools

The T'ien-t'ai School was founded by Chih Yi (AD 538-597), a pupil of Hui Ssu (d. AD 577), a monk who worked hard to ensure the survival of Chinese Buddhist literature. Chih Yi, who early in life had been a Ch'an exegete, taught that salvation lay, not in any one process alone, but in a careful balance of meditation, concentration, the study of scriptures, moral discipline and ceremonies. This refusal to go to extremes and the part given to the study of the sacred canon had a particular appeal to Confucians. The school produced many scholars. Chih Yi wrote a number of commentaries and treatises on Buddhism which by their moderation and systematic and simple exegesis had a particular appeal to the classes trained in the Confucian disciplines.

Of a quite different sort is the second school. This is Chen-yen (True Word), a sect deriving from that aspect of the faith known as tantric or magical Buddhism. It was sometimes called *mi-chiao* (the secret teaching) because of its esoteric nature. In this school salvation begins with an initiation of the would-be believer into the circle of a teacher to whom must be given total obedience and from whom the truth – the secrets – are to be had. Salvation lies in the possession of the 'secrets'. These are sought by the use of spells, the performance of gestures and mime, and identification by meditation with the numerous deities of the tantric pantheon.

The Chen-yen school was introduced in China in the eighth century, and is based on the system of Amoghavajra (AD 705-774). From China it found its way soon after to Japan, where it still has a large following as the Shingon sect. Tantric Buddhism appeals to a feeling for the occult that goes back to the dawn of history and in China provided for Buddhism charms and magical rituals which were already a part of religious Taoism.

For the Shingon sect in Japan, see page 366.

Taoism in the Age of Faith

It was during the Age of Faith, and particularly during the Six Dynasties, that the Taoist Church reached its apogee. Despite its successes in the Sui and early T'ang, thereafter began the long and slow decline to the moribund state it has reached in modern times.

At the close of Han the Church was in political opposition to the throne. By the fourth century AD it enjoyed patronage at court and among the great families. Famous poets, such as T'ao Yuan-ming (AD 375-427), and artists, such as the caligrapher Wang Hsi-chih (AD 321-379) and the painter Ku K'ai-chih (AD 344-406), were influenced by Taoism. During the Sui and early T'ang dynasty it enjoyed imperial favour, partly through the elixirs that Taoist alchemists experimented with. The second T'ang emperor sent a copy of the *Tao Tê-ching* in Sanskrit to the Prince of Assam. The T'ang emperors, whose surname coincided with that of Lao Tzu (i.e. Li), showed Taoism particular sympathy. In AD 748 the Taoist papacy was accorded official recognition. But, despite this rise to official favour, after the Age of Faith Taoism lost the popular hold it had exercised over the people and was gradually reduced to a religion of monks and sorcerers.

Taoists and Buddhists quarrelled fiercely during the Age of Faith for the conquest of the souls of China. The Taoists found it difficult to forgive the Buddhists for drawing so largely from among their own converts. The Buddhists, on the other hand, resented the imputation that their religion was but a foreign form of Taoism. A question fiercely argued was whether Buddha had been the teacher or the disciple of Lao Tzu.

As Buddhism became more Chinese, it became in some ways more Taoist. But the Taoist Church as it developed had also drawn much from Buddhism.

The New Confucianism

Confucianism never lost its hold over the *literati*, for all their preoccupation with the 'dark learning' during the Age of Faith. Its canon continued to enshrine, for the educated, the quintessence of Chinese culture. The study of the Confucian classics after their official recognition by the imperial house in Han times continued. In the second century AD, Ma Jung and Cheng Hsuan wrote commentaries on the classics, thus starting the tradition of meticulous scholarship and study the better to expound the ideas of Confucius. In the seventh century AD, K'ung Ying-ta wrote further commentaries from which there gradually emerged a unity in Confucianism, each book of the classical canon being thought of as a facet of a whole, unified teaching. The *literati*, thus trained, wrote the histories of China, a tradition that began in Han times, and which, dynasty by dynasty, has been maintained until the present century. With the restoration of unity in the Sui and T'ang dynasties, despite the fascination of certain rulers with Taoism and Buddhism, Confucianism maintained its influence as the classicism of the educated classes. The work of large-scale administration called for bureaucrats with Confucian training, rather than of Buddhist or Taoist faith.

The Confucian elite at the courts, even during the Age of Faith and increasingly thereafter, maintained a steady opposition to Buddhism and Taoism. Buddhism they thought of as foreign and from T'ang times onward as unpatriotic. Taoism had been a rival to Confucianism from classical times. But, apart from its social ethic, Confucianism failed to meet religious needs, or to compete satisfactorily with the challenge with which Buddhist and Indian thought was able to confront it.

All this changed under the Sung dynasty. During the eleventh century AD there was a particular efflorescence of Confucian scholarship and a determination upon reform in policy of a peculiarly nationalistic kind. Broadly speaking, its philosophers, Shao Yung and Chou Tun-i, and the Ch'eng brothers, set out under challenge from Buddhism and Taoism to evolve from Confucianism an orderly

whole which would express for the educated ideas about humankind
and the universe. This speculation was put in final form by the
greatest figure of the age, Chu Hsi (AD 1130-1200). After his death
the new Confucianism became official orthodoxy and remained so
until within living memory. Chu Hsi has been called the Thomas
Aquinas of Confucianism.

Neo-Confucianism is difficult to summarize. In Chu Hsi's words,
it proclaimed that 'in every human mind there is the knowing faculty
and in everything there is its reason. The incompleteness of our
knowledge is due to our insufficiency in investigating the reason for
things. The student must go to all things under Heaven beginning
with known principles and seeking to reach the uppermost. After
sufficient labour has been devoted to it the day will come when all
things will suddenly become clear and intelligible.' Such is the Confucianism of Chu Hsi which, from the thirteenth century AD to the
twentieth, officially took the place of belief for most educated
Chinese.

With the triumph of Neo-Confucianism which, under the state
system of education became the common ground for belief of the
educated classes, Taoism and Buddhism slowly declined. Much of
their thought had become part of the Chinese ethos and they lost
their distinctive characters.

Minor Religions
Taoism, the indigenous religion, and Buddhism, the religion from
India, both became thoroughly assimilated into the culture of the
people. Other religions have entered China with less success. Nestorian Christianity came in the seventh century AD and Manichaean-
ism a little later, and so did Mazdaism and Islam and the Jewish
religion as the religion of foreign traders during the T'ang period.
Under the Yuan Islam flourished, especially among the Muslim com-
manders in the Mongol army. Muslims are found today in scattered
communities throughout China but in large numbers only in the
extreme west and northwest.

None of these religions have made any serious impact on Chinese
life. Even the vast missionary enterprise of the Christian Church in
China in the last three centuries has, from a religious point of view,
had disappointing results. But missionary activity closely allied with
educational enterprise has done much to bring Western learning to
China. It came, however, at a time when the West itself was becoming
increasingly secular and missionary influence upon the educated
classes in China, themselves the heirs to the secular tradition of
Neo-Confucianism, had a greater influence in secular education than
in religious ideas.

Under Communist Domination
Since 1949 the mainland of China has been under Communist domination. The regime campaigns vigorously against certain religious
groups as 'counter-revolutionary'. But, since time immemorial, the
popular religion has been present among the Chinese, interwoven in

Illustration page 341

all the social practices of kinship groups, social and economic groups and local communities. This is attested by the presence in every village and hamlet throughout China of local ancestral shrines, local deity fanes, shrines for local heroes, temples in the hands of Buddhist and Taoist monks, a temple of Confucius or, more frequently, temples of a common pantheon in which elements of all religions are found, sometimes betraying an eclecticism that defies analysis. Revolutionary movements since the turn of the present century have attacked the popular religion in *p'o mi-hsin* (breaking down superstition) movements, but the temples and shrines remain, sometimes in a sad state of repair, all bearing lively testimony to the omnipresence within living memory of the popular religion.

In their heyday the Buddhist and Taoist Churches had an articulate elite and a tangible organization. The popular religion had neither. After the decline of Buddhism and Taoism, a slow process from the thirteenth century onwards, communities of monks in isolated centres have maintained their faith with some of its original purity, traces of which still remain. But the large popular hold of these religions upon the masses declined rapidly. Elements of Buddhism and Taoism were absorbed into the popular religion.

Surprisingly little is known of that religion, though elements of it are present in every Chinese community. The attention of scholars has been directed to the religions of the articulate classes, in whose writings, century by century, it has been recorded. From the secularism of Confucianism and from the fate of the Taoist and Buddhist Churches some scholars have concluded that the Chinese are not particularly religious. But religious beliefs and practices among the people, though poorly articulated, have been present since time immemorial.

Illustrations pages 341, 342

Toleration (Ed.)

For Buddhism in Tibet, see pages 300–2.

After the death of Mao Tse-tung in 1976 more tolerant attitudes appeared towards religion, which had suffered repression during his Cultural Revolution. In 1980 the largest Taoist temple in Peking was repaired at government expense, along with a number of historic Buddhist temples and monasteries. The Dalai Lama remained in exile from Tibet in India, but his Potala Palace in Lhasa was reopened to Tibetan Buddhists and some pilgrimages were permitted. Certain important mosques and churches were allowed to reopen. In 1981 the official paper *Red Flag* suggested both support and some opposition to religious freedom by stating that 'at present quite a large number of people in China believe in religion. We must respect this objective fact.'

Chapter Eighteen

Japan

Japan presents us with a mingling of religious traditions similar to that which we find in China, although the pot-pourri is different. The principal religion in the historical period – and written history for Japan begins only with the fifth century of the Christian era – is undoubtedly Buddhism, but even then, as will be evident, a Buddhism which already reflected its composite Chinese form and which was to be largely accommodated to the ethos of Shintō, Japan's older religious tradition.

During the Stone Age, what inhabitants there were in Japan's four main islands were largely of Ainu stock, whose religion, involving blood-sacrifice and bear ritual, seems to have had no influence on the invading Japanese who entered the country both from the direction of Korea and Siberia to the north and the Pacific islands to the south. The Yamato clan, who were dominant later and from whom the imperial family emerged, belonged to the southern group of invaders.

The earliest records we possess are the *Kojiki* (The Record of Ancient Things), written in AD 712 in Chinese characters which phonetically portray the native Japanese, and the *Nihongi* (Japanese Chronicles), a document written in Chinese in AD 720, which purports to give the history of Japan from its beginnings to AD 697. The latter is much influenced by the Chinese emphasis on its imperial line, and seeks to emphasize both the antiquity of Japan and its imperial family in particular. Both works would suggest that Japan has a divine mission upon earth, and so pass smoothly from myth to history, presenting the merely mythological as though it were verifiable history. The age of the *kami* (which had begun with the emergence of the cosmos out of chaos) gives place to the age of human history, when Ninigi, the grandchild of the sun *kami* (Amaterasu-O-mikami), descends to the lower realms and his great-grandson, Jimmu, becomes the first emperor of a unified Japan.

The date given for this event is 660 BC, but historians would hardly accept such precision for a period one thousand years before the use of writing and, by comparing the Chinese records, date the emergence of the Yamato clan to importance in the first century BC (or even later). They would regard the unification of the country as not complete until six or seven hundred years later. It would appear from Chinese documents that authority lay with women rulers who acted

353

as shamans or mediums, thus preserving in their person the unity of the regal (or political) and the priestly (or religious) function, which subsequently became the emperor's role.

The *Kojiki* and *Nihongi* both give valuable variants of the ancient mythology, whilst the *Engishiki* (Regulations of the Engi period), dating from AD 927, incorporate the ancient *Norito* (Ritual Prayers), as used by the priestly families.

Buddhist and Shinto Ideas Interact

Once we come to the introduction of Buddhism into Japan in the sixth century, we have written documents to draw upon, and we can observe not only the wide sectarian variety that had already marked Mahayana Buddhism, but also a merging of the newer Indo-Chinese religions with the older Japanese religious traditions and the emergence of new syncretic forms. Even the older Buddhist sects took on a new dimension on Japanese soil, and against the background of feudal conflict there was a widespread blossoming of Buddhist culture and a proliferation of sects, which was most marked in the thirteenth century.

The interaction of Buddhist and Shintō ideas continued, and the national religious consciousness was deepened by the appearance of Europeans in AD 1549, when Francis Xavier first sought to introduce Christianity into Japan. Feudal rivalries permitted the Christian mission to advance, and the number of converts reached more than 300,000 by the turn of the century, but first the anti-Christian legislation of Hideyoshi in 1587 and then the more forthright and exclusivist policy of the Tokugawas (from 1612) led to Japan's isolation and reversion to older patterns – an isolation which persisted until 1853. The return of Westerners to Japan in that year was followed by the resumption of Christian missions in 1859 and the repeal of the anti-Christian legislation in 1873.

State Shintō

The new Western-style constitution of 1889 granted religious freedom, but this only meant formal permission for Christianity to organize itself in addition to Buddhism and Shintō. Other Japanese religious movements, of which a number had arisen since early in the nineteenth century, still had to thrive under the umbrella of Shintō or Buddhism, and register themselves as Buddhist or Shintō sects. Meanwhile, however, the Imperial Rescript on Education (1890), making use of Shintō mythology and Confucianist ethics, had introduced that aspect of state Shintō which sometimes goes by the name Tennoism (*Tennō* meaning 'Heavenly King' and being the title given to the emperor). According to the new creed, state Shintō, despite its incorporation of regular Shintō mythology and religious ceremonial, was declared to be non-religious and incumbent upon all Japanese citizens.

It remained for the Allied occupation in 1945 to remove Shintō from government patronage and for the new constitution of 1947 to guarantee freedom of religion with the right both to registration as independent religious bodies and to the propagation of the beliefs of any religious bodies. Because of this new freedom hundreds of movements that are often called the 'new religions' have been registered, although it will be seen that they largely reflect the syncretic character of popular religion in Japan and bring to the surface many of the ideas and practices that had long been present within the older Shintō and Buddhist traditions. The presence of Christianity has brought a new set of ideas, but, as with Confucianism at an earlier date, it has tended to provide the ethical basis which was not always explicit in the other two religious movements.

First, however, we must turn back to Japan's past – to Shintō, and see how that past is built into the present.

Shintō is not itself a Japanese word, but was coined in the sixth century, when Buddhism entered Japan, to express the older religious tradition, 'the way of the *kami*'. It is often described as Japan's 'indigenous faith' not because its strongly naturalistic worship has no parallels elsewhere, but rather because it enshrines the distinctive ethos of Japanese religiosity, which has influenced the Japanese version of other faiths as well. A conspicuous feature is its intuitiveness – with far greater emphasis on religious experience than on the reasoning out of theological principles. Shintō worshippers rarely ask ontological questions; they feel rather the reality of the *kami*, for a direct experience of divinity and a sensitive recognition of mystery are for them far more important than an intellectual approach to doctrinal niceties.

The Meaning of *Kami*

The word *kami*, although often translated 'god' or 'gods', should probably be left untranslated. It is applied to beasts, birds and plants; to seas and mountains; to natural phenomena; to the storm, the wind and the awe-inspiring echo which resounds through the gorge or the grove; and to the clan ancestors or warriors. The eighteenth-century Shintō savant, Motoori Norinaga, after stating his inability to understand the meaning of the term, goes on to define it largely in terms of the numinous: 'All . . . things whatsoever which deserve to be dreaded and revered for the extraordinary and pre-eminent powers which they possess are called Kami.' 'They need not,' he says, 'be eminent for surpassing nobleness, goodness or serviceableness.' (quoted in W. G. Aston's *Shintŏ: The Ancient Religion of Japan*, pp. 6-7). A modern Shintō scholar must still say: 'The Japanese people themselves do not have a clear idea regarding the Kami. They are aware of the Kami intuitively at the depth of their consciousness and communicate with the Kami direct without having formed the Kami-idea conceptually or theologically. Therefore, it is impossible to make explicit and clear that which fundamentally by its very nature is vague.' (Ono Sokyō: *The Kami Way*, p. 8).

Even though there is a Japanese word *kami* which means 'above' or 'superior', it would seem wiser to link it etymologically with the particle *ka*, which is the expression of wonder or puzzlement, evoked by the fearful or the incomprehensible. The passage of years may have brought some refinement to the notion, but the refined and the unrefined still co-exist.

Conceptions of the Divine

Bellah, in his general analysis of Japanese religion, refers to two basic conceptions of the divine. The first is of a 'superordinate entity' who dispenses 'nurturance, care and love'. This view of the divine, however, does not make a keen distinction from the human, as it 'shades off imperceptibly into political superiors and parents, both of whom are treated as in part, at least, sacred'. The second is the ground of being or the inner essence of reality. To this category belong the concept of the *buddha* nature (said to be present in all) and the more philosophical interpretations of *kami*, which arose as a result of Buddhist influence.

Confucianist ideas about *T'ien* (Heaven) influenced a seventeenth-century writer in his ethical view of *kami*: 'To say that the Kami dislike what is unclean is equivalent to saying that a person who is impure in heart displeases the Kami. . . . This is because the Kami embody Essential Uprightness and Honesty, and therefore it is a Heavenly Ordinance that we should lead an honest and happy life in harmony with the Will of the Kami.' One writer wished to see a link with the word *kagami* (mirror): 'That which in Heaven is Kami, in nature is Spirit, and in man is Sincerity' (the basic virtue in Shintō thought).

Shintō Rites

Originally Shintō rites were extemely simple, and no special buildings were required. Prayers were offered and rites performed at natural shrines, such as the sacred *sakaki* tree which even now is present within every shrine precinct. The divine word would be uttered through the shaman in a state of *kami*-possession (*kami-gakari* or *kangakari*), which often manifested itself in an ecstatic dance. (In present-day shrines the successor of the female shaman is seen in the *miko*, the female shrine-attendants, who are responsible for the *kagura*, the mystic dance which usually symbolizes the identification of the worshippers with the *kami* of the shrine.) Gradually there evolved not only a specific priesthood but also a set pattern of shrine construction. There is no image representation of the *kami*, but simply a *shintai*, a symbolic representation of the *kami* who may be any one of the *yao-yorozu no kami* (literally 'eight million *kami*') of whom the *Kojiki* and *Nihongi* speak.

Worship was originally a family affair, and, the clan being but the extension of the family, there are a large number of shrines set apart for *ujigami* (clan *kami*). The *ujigami* is concerned for the communal interests of the clan. The fact that the community derived its oneness from its relationship with the *ujigami* as *ujiko* (children of the clan) would immediately suggest both that the *ujigami* was *in loco parentis* to the community (i.e. its *Oya* or 'parent') and that the petition for material needs had significance because a parent is ready to bestow bounty upon children. The shrine of the *ujigami* was called *uji no jinja* (shrine of the clan) or in some instances *ujigami no yashiro* (shrine of the clan *kami*).

Although movements of population have broken up old family and clan associations, there is still a sense in which the community shrine becomes the focal point of identity, and its festival achieves the solidarity of the local grouping. When a child is taken to the shrine, it is not that it may participate in common worship or receive instruction. It simply recognizes that there is a fundamental link between itself, its community and the *kami*.

Special Shrines

The influence of ancestor worship meant, of course, that the *ujigami* could be regarded as the ancestor of the local chief or leader, or the reverse could occur – an actual ancestor could be invested with the status of the *ujigami*. The former seems to have been the case with the imperial family, which had leadership in the Yamato clan. The emperor would be his own priest in his 'family' cult, which was transferred at an early date to the Grand Shrine of Ise. The guardian *Illustration page 359* *kami* of the family came to be regarded as the ancestress of the emperor. (The older shamanistic pattern was long preserved, in that the emperor was represented at the shrine by a princess from the imperial family.)

Similarly the Taisha Shrine of Izumo was the shrine of the Izumo clan, and the storm *kami*, Susanoo-no-Mikoto, is described as being in conflict with Amaterasu-Ō-Mikami, the *kami* of the Yamato clan. The Izumo province is often called the 'land of the *kami*' as it was the *Illustration page 359* centre of religion in ancient Japan. The shrine there is the oldest in Japan. It is said that, every October, the *kami* from all over the country assemble there for a great meeting and arrange marriages. Accordingly October is called in Izumo *Kami-ari-zuki* (the month with the *kami*), whereas other parts speak of *Kannazuki* (the month without the *kami*).

Shrines usually face towards the south, but occasionally the east; the west and the north, however, are regarded as the unlucky regions. As the worshipper approaches, he or she will pass through the *torii* (the gateway to the shrine), and may pass through a whole cluster of *torii*. The gateway is such as any house might have possessed, and may be made of wood, stone, bronze and even of concrete. Ancient shrines uniformly use cypress wood. Often the natural character of the tree is preserved, although the later Chinese-Buddhist influence is seen in the painted (usually red) *torii* and shrines. Apart from the *torii* the pathway may be lined with stone lanterns, donated by worshippers, and guarding the shrine will often be found two Korean dogs or two Chinese lions – except in the case of the Inari shrines (dedicated to the *kami* of the rice-fields), which are guarded by fox images, because the fox is regarded as the messenger of the *kami*, and is also the symbol of fertility, to which end the Inari shrines are largely directed.

Correct Behaviour

If the visit to the shrine is a private one, the worshipper will proceed on foot once past the first *torii*, and must wash hands and mouth either at a natural spring in the shrine compound or in a rock-hewn pool, using utensils provided by the shrine. Then he or she will clap hands and bow the head in reverence while making the petition. A petition may, however, be written on paper, and attached to one of the sacred *sakaki* (*Eurya ochnacea*) trees.

More formal worship will involve four elements: the act of purification (*harai*), when, in addition to the washing, the priest will wave a branch of *sakaki* (or a paper equivalent) over the worshipper's head; the offering (*shinsen*), which may be a cereal or drink offering, but is now usually in money, or may be symbolic, in the form of a *sakaki* twig; the ritual prayer (*norito*); and the symbolic feast (*naorai*), indicative of eating with the *kami*. The last would often involve sipping a few drops of rice wine (the sacred *miki* which had first been offered up at a kind of harvest festival), given by the priest or one of the *miko*. Groups of worshippers may also ask for a performance of the shrine *kagura* (sacred dance), of which there are thirty-five, typifying the ancient mythology.

The *norito* are almost exclusively concerned with human needs. One, for example, supplicates the *kami* for a successful harvest:

First of all, in your sacred field, O Sovereign Deity,
. . . May the latter grain harvested by them,
May the latter grain to be harvested,
With foam dripping from the elbows,
Pulled hither with mud adhering to both thighs –
May this grain be prospered by you . . .
In ears many hands long –
Then the first fruits in both liquor and stalks. . . .

(D. L. Philippi, *Norito*, p. 26).

Until the Meiji era, when the state began to use Shintō for national ends, the priests of each shrine would compose prayers thought appropriate for the occasion, but from 1875 the state provided official prayers for use in stated rites and festivals. Since 1946 the Association of Shintō Shrines, with which more than 80,000 shrines are linked, has drafted prayers, but the priests are free to compose their own if they so desire.

Worship in the Home

Shintō worship comes to the home through the *kami-dana* (*kami-shelf*), which is the home-shrine. It is customary for amulets from the Ise Shrine (which became the national shrine, as the nation came to be considered one family with the emperor as the father-figure), the shrine of the *ujigami*, or the shrine of the locality to be placed there. Each morning and evening offerings would be made both to the shrine tablets and ancestral tablets. After ceremonial ablutions,

Left Shinto shrine at Izumo. There has been a shrine on the site for centuries, the first mention being in an early eighth-century history when it was built on the emperor's order as a symbol of his power.

Below left Shrine of the Shinto supreme sun-goddess at Ise, the most sacred site in Japan. The vestige of a tree (called the heartpost) lies beneath the shrine, which has been rebuilt on the same plan every twenty years since the fourth century.

Below A procession through the streets of the Gion quarter of Kyoto celebrates an annual Shinto festival on 17 July to commemorate deliverance from plague. The child on the horse, called a *chigo*, is a pageboy to the god. Now the son of an actor, the role was once played by a samurai's son.

Above The seventh-century Horyuji temple complex at Nara. The pagoda and golden hall are enclosed on three sides by covered corridors and on the fourth by the tenth-century lecture hall (extreme right).

Opposite A gilt-bronze triad of the Buddha Sakyamuni, with two attendants, surrounded by *bosatu* (or *bodhisattvas*), from Horyuji, Nara (AD 623).

Far left Shaka, the Buddha Sakyamuni, emaciated by austere exercises performed in the attempt to attain enlightenment. Drawing in ink on paper of the Kamakura period (*c.* 1200). Seattle Art Musem, Washington. Eugene Fuller Memorial Collection.

Left Fugen-bosatu, the protector of all who worship the sacred text of the Lotus Sutra and the prolonger of human life. His image is most often found in the monasteries of the Tendai and Shingon sects. Silk hanging scroll (thirteenth or fourteenth century). Private Collection, Tokyo.

Right A votive hanging of painted and lacquered wood from the Kamakura period depicting Monju, god of wisdom, one of the eight *buddhas* surrounding the supreme Buddha in the lotus diagram adopted by the Shingon sect. In his hand is the sword of wisdom, round his neck the wheel of the law. Seattle Art Museum, Washington. Eugene Fuller Memorial Collection.

Right A vision of paradise in the Amida Hall at Chusonji, North Japan. Lacquer, gilding and mother-of-pearl decorate the shrine. Amidist sects called on Amida at the approach of death to enter his paradise, and such shrines derived from the habit of embodying the paradise to come.

the devout worshipper would bow before the shrine, clap the hands twice and bow again for a moment in silence.

Shintō Symbols

The religion is basically imageless, but symbols are abundant. The commonest is the mirror, which mythology links with Amaterasu-Ō-Mikami. It is one of the three symbols – the others being the sword and the jewel – which she bestowed on her grandchild when he descended to earth. Ninigi-no-mikoto was instructed to honour and worship it as 'her spirit'. As a result it has become the sacred symbol (*shintai*) of many shrines – and notably of the Great Shrine of Ise.

Shrine Festivals

Many types of shrine festival are held, and, apart from the seasonal festivals which reflect an agricultural society and the New Year festival, they will be linked with local traditions or circumstances. During the dedication festival the portable *mikoshi* (the 'sacred palanquin' of the *kami*) will be carried by the youth of the locality on long poles to the accompaniment of a large amount of spontaneous merriment. The procession may recall some historic event, or may be simply an *Illustration page 359* indication that the *kami* is there with his people to bless them.

Until its disestablishment in 1945 shrine Shintō tended to be synonymous with state Shintō. The latter was 'founded on the idea that the prosperity of the nation, the safety of the imperial house, and the happiness of the people are blessings given when human politics coincide with the will of the gods.' (Association of Shintō Shrines: *Basic Terms of Shintō*, p. 33). The principle of *saisei itchi* (the unity of religious rites and politics) is derived from an implicit conviction in Shintō that life should not be departmentalized, and that there should be no sharp lines of distinction between the sacred and the secular.

The Beginnings of Buddhism in Japan

It appears that Buddhism was first introduced to Japan in AD 539, when the ruler of a small Korean kingdom sought an alliance with the ruler of Yamato and to please him sent a statue of the Buddha and some of the Buddhist *sutra* (texts), describing them as 'the greatest treasures' he could send.

Japan had already been influenced by Chinese thought and culture – to a large extent through the introduction of the Chinese system of writing in AD 405. Chinese ancestor-worship had also influenced Japanese attitudes to the past, and had been incorporated, together with some elements of Taoist magic and divination, into native Shintō beliefs.

It would be true to say that the early Buddhist sects, of which three still survive, with a total membership of about 130,000, made their main impact upon those in the community who were most ready to accept the foreign culture. The Nara sects (so called because Nara was then the capital) were strongly foreign and made little attempt to accommodate themselves to Japanese culture or to the needs of the common people.

For definitions of Mahayana and Hinayana Buddhism, see pages 282–4 and 275–7.

Although the introduction of Buddhism had been from Korea, the continuing links were with China, where Buddhism had already accommodated itself to Confucianist and Taoist thought-forms. It was only natural, therefore, that the Buddhism introduced into Japan should be the Chinese version of Mahayana Buddhism, even though some of the schools had a commixture of Hinayana teaching.

At first the Shintō priesthood was much opposed to the new faith, and when a pestilence broke out it was attributed to the fact that worship was being rendered to foreign *kami*. The accusation led to the burning of Buddhist temples and the destruction of images of the Buddha.

The new religion had support, however, in court circles, and one of the prominent leaders in the cultural and religious revolution was Prince Shōtoku (574–621), the prince regent, who introduced a new constitution based on Buddhism, whereby Buddhism was practically recognized as the state religion. (Both then and subsequently there was a tendency to identify Buddhism and the nation's law, which at once made the state sponsor for religion and granted religious sanction to the state.) As a pious Buddhist, Prince Shōtoku built temples and established monasteries, and showed his erudition in publishing commentaries on some of the *sutras*. Alongside the temples were the visible signs of Buddhist compassion – dispensaries for people and animals, hostels for the sick, the orphaned or the aged. The beautiful

Illustration page 361

temple, Hōryūji, still survives as a witness to his zeal.

A modern writer has contrasted the beginnings of Buddhism with modern times, asserting that 'today Buddhism is always associated with melancholy temples, anachronistic priests and the chanting of sutras for the dead', whereas the Buddhism of the early days represented a progressive cultural movement. The *sutras* were then considered to be 'advanced' in their thinking, and the revolution in art, literature, architecture, music and politics, too, was linked with Buddhism.

Popular Buddhism

In so far as Buddhism was accepted by the common people, it was largely through its tantric aspects that it made its impact. For many the scriptures, the images and the temples were (and still are) means of securing material benefits – whether recovery from illness, rain for the rice-fields, or peace in the community or the nation as a whole. There was (and still is) a demand for relevance and for 'signs following' the promulgation of the faith. It was to take as long as seven centuries for Buddhism to be assimilated to the point where it no longer appeared foreign. For the majority it was far easier to grasp the cultural aspects of Buddhism than its more difficult ideological or metaphysical aspects.

Holy Men

As we have seen, the shamanistic tradition in Shintō was very strong, for through the intermediary the people felt that they could have rapport with the unseen powers. Although at the official level the entrance of Buddhism into Japan had meant a widespread development of organized religion, the more unorthodox tradition of the charismatic leader persisted, and 'holy men' outside official religious structures sought to provide a religious life for the common people.

Such people, called *hijiri* (holy men), laid great emphasis on individual piety. Many followed Buddhist ascetic practices and were called *ubasoku* (from the Sanskrit *upasaka* 'ascetic' or 'magician'), and their strict discipline became the basis of Shūgendō (the ascetic way). It was thought that the *shūgensha* (the ascetic) could attain superhuman or magical power as a result of the merit acquired through religious austerities. Some of the *ubasoku* passed from village to village, acting as the local shamans. Shūgendō linked up with primitive Shintō mountain worship, and the *yamabushi* (mountain-climbers) are still essentially the magicians of the mountains, who seek 'inspiration' (in the sense of 'ecstasy') on their mountain climbs. A Buddhist explanation was added to the effect that the ascent of the mountain was parallel with the ascent through the eightfold path, leading to the goal of enlightenment.

One of the early unorthodox *ubasoku* was Gyōgi (670-749), who became the Buddhist equivalent of an archbishop and was responsible for the construction of Todaiji in Nara, in which temple is enshrined the enormous statue of Vairocana Buddha. On that occasion the shrine at Ise is said to have given its approval for the erection of the temple in 742 and soon afterwards there was erected within the temple compound a shrine to Hachiman, the Shintō war *kami*. Under a reciprocal arrangement an image of the Buddha was deposited in a shrine-temple within the precincts of the great shrine at Ise. Even during his lifetime, Gyōgi was held to be a *bodhisattva*, and through his successors Buddhist magic and ritual, together with popular Taoist superstitions, were combined with older Shintō forms.

For the concept of the bodhisattva, see pages 282–3.

In the tradition of 'holy men', ideas of '*kami* possession' or '*buddha* possession', were commonly held. In some cases the charisma might pass from generation to generation within families, as was the case amongst the Yamabushi, or, as in the case of the *miko* of the Shintō shrine, they might practise as mediums because of a special gift.

The Establishing of the Tendai and Shingon Sects

Tendai is named after the Chinese T'ien t'ai sect of Buddhism, and was introduced into Japan by Saichō (767-822), who was known posthumously as Dengyō Daishi. He established a temple on the slopes of Mount Hiei near the city of Kyoto, which became the capital in 798. This temple (called Enryakuji) was to be the centre of Japanese Buddhist activity for almost 800 years, and during the days of its chief influence the mountainside was full of temples and monks who could also exercise an influence on politics by invading the capital in armed bands.

Tendai was fundamentally an eclectic form of Buddhism, which sought to embrace the apparently contradictory interpretations of the road to salvation. Basically it held that reality is one and yet the one reality can be known through three thousand manifestations. Its teaching accordingly incorporated esoteric mysteries, the element of meditation which was to be later emphasized in the Zen tradition, and the notion of faith in Amitabha Buddha, which was to come alive in the Pure Land sects of the thirteenth century.

Illustration page 361

The Lotus Sutra lay at the heart of Tendai teaching with its emphasis on the *ekayana* (the single vehicle) which was to supersede, and yet embrace, the other 'vehicles', whether Hinayana or Mahayana. The stress on one ultimate reality (*ichijitsu*) encouraged the Tendai sect to seek a relationship with Shintō on the understanding that the Japanese *kami* had their place within the ultimate unity.

The Mystery at the Heart of the Universe

Shingon (Pure Word) Buddhism was introduced by Kūkai (774-835), who received the posthumous name of Kōbō Daishi. The original Sanskrit word from which Shingon is derived means 'a magic formula', and so the title indicates the esoteric character of this sect. Like Saichō, Kūkai studied in China and, on his return, he established his monastery on Mount Kōya.

According to its teaching, mystery lies at the heart of the universe, and this mystery is expressed through symbols and ritual. Kūkai produced two *mandala* which gave a symbolic representation of the cosmos – the one portraying the realm of indestructibles and the other pointing to the womb world, where there is the conflict of becoming and the ideal Oneness is not yet attained.

Illustration page 362

Kūkai was regarded as a *bodhisattva* and the representative on earth of Maitreya (*Miroku* in Japanese), the Buddha of the Future. Shingon is the most syncretic form of Buddhism, and Kūkai is regarded as the author of Ryōbu-Shintō, the fusion of Buddhism and Shinto which became the feature of Japanese religious life. Subsequently there emerged the '*Honji* (homeland) *Suijaku* (footprints) Theory',

Illustration page 360

whereby Shintō *kami* (as well as the historical Sakyamuni himself) were seen as derivatives of the ultimate metaphysical reality represented by the *Honji*. Shintō and Buddhist apologists were able to argue concerning the position of the *kami* and the earthly *buddhas vis à vis* the ultimate, and *vis à vis* one another.

Pure Land Buddhism

As we have seen, Tendai teaching had already incorporated elements of the Amida (Amitabha) faith, which epitomized the aspect of compassion in Mahayana Buddhism. Hōnen (1133-1212) was, however, responsible for its becoming a powerful movement within Japanese Buddhism. He was concerned to make salvation available for all, and so asserted that, to attain buddhahood, help from outside (*tariki*) was an inevitable requirement. *Tariki* avails, where *jiriki* (self-help) has failed. This help comes from Amitabha Buddha (*Amida* in Japanese), the Buddha of boundless light and infinite life, the very embodiment of compassion, the lover of humankind, the protector and refuge.

Amida was said to be none other than a monk, Hōzō, who, many ages ago, had vowed that he would not enter *nirvana* until his merit had become universally applicable. His boundless compassion had created, it was held, a Pure Land which all could attain through his grace. Salvation was through the transference of the merit he had gained, and his eighteenth vow referred to the possibility of being born in the Pure Land through the repetition of his name. The Jōdo (Pure Land) Sect which was established by Hōnen's followers held that Amida's name was to be repeated constantly and that the *nembutsu* (the petitioning of Amida through the cry '*Namu Amida Butsu*') was the way to the Pure Land. Despite this stress on the grace of Amida, Jōdo teaching encourages good works as helpful in bringing the devotee into the Pure Land.

JAPAN

Illustration page 362

Shinran (1173-1262), however, who was a disciple of Hōnen, saw in this a residue of *jiriki*, and, in establishing Jōdo Shinshū (The *true* Pure Land sect), taught faith as a complete passivity. For him Amida's compassion makes no distinction between the 'good' person and the 'evil'. 'No evil,' he says, 'is strong enough to avoid being embraced with Amida's infinite love.' Whereas Hōnen had said: 'Even a bad man will be received in Buddha's Land, but how much more a good man!', Shinran reversed the notion to 'Even a good man will be received in Buddha's Land, but how much more a bad man!' Faith becomes the sole requisite for salvation: all moral effort is swept aside.

He teaches that faith and the vow are one. The power of faith proceeds from the vow, and the continuous repetition of Amida's name is itself a revelation of the presence of faith. The *Nembutsu* is the vehicle of salvation, being Amida's gift to humanity, for it reminds people of their *karma* – the unworthiness which makes human achievement of salvation through personal merit an impossibility. It is the cry of joy, we are told, which recognizes the grace of Amida.

Faith in Jōdo Shinshū has been compared with Luther's teaching, but there are basic differences, for Shinran is still wedded to Buddhist philosophy, and Amida is fundamentally no more than an expedient (*hōben*) – a personification of the principle of compassion. The former president of one of Shinshū's universities in Kyoto writes: 'Through the *Nembutsu* . . . Shinran tried to grasp the whole essence of the Indian Mahayana Buddhism in which the wisdom and the mercy was one.' (S. Yamaguchi, *Dynamic Buddha and Static Buddha*, p. 10). For the ordinary devotee, however, Amida is a real object of worship:

Day in, day out, I am with Amida:
Let the sun set whenever it pleases,
How grateful indeed I am! Namu-amida-butsu!'
(D. T. Suzuki, *A Miscellany of the Shin Teaching of Buddhism*, p. 74).

Because the gift of Amida is held to have no conditions attached to it, Shinshū is very much the religion of the laity for the laity. It has no special discipline for its followers, and has encouraged the overthrow of older Buddhist asceticisms. Shinran himself married, and this led to the establishing of a hereditary priesthood which has gradually influenced other sects as well. The popular appeal of its teaching was great, and the universalist character of its message was seen in the fact that the Ēta (the outcasts of Japanese society) became adherents.

Zen Buddhism

For the teaching of the Chinese Ch'an school, see page 347.

Zen is the Japanese rendering of the Chinese *Ch'an*, itself derived from the Sanskrit *dhyāna* which means 'meditation' or 'contemplation'. Meditation had always been an important aspect of Buddhism, and, on its introduction into China (by Bodhidharma, as legend has it – an Indian monk who died in AD 528), had come to terms with the quietist aspects of the Taoist tradition.

Zen had been incorporated into Tendai teaching, but it did not flourish as a separate school till the monk Eisai (1141-1215) founded the Rinzai school of Zen in 1191. Eisai was himself somewhat eclectic and was more interested in the cultural aspects of Zen, when one compares him with Dōgen (1200-1253), one of Japan's greatest philosophers, who, although he himself had no intention of founding a specific school, was later reckoned as the founder in Japan of the Sōtō School of Zen.

Illustration page 361

Zen looks to the apostolic succession of enlightenment from the time when Sakyamuni was first enlightened to the time when a young disciple in the hall of meditation – a feature of every Zen temple – enters into the meaning of the *kōan*, given him by his master. The *kōan* is a teaching device introduced in China about the eleventh century, and is used by the Rinzai school, whereas the Sōtō school emphasizes the meditation as such leading to the sudden entrance into the truth. When students have spent twelve to fifteen years in a monastery in the practice of meditation and satisfied their masters that they have attained the inner meaning of Buddhism, they can be given the stamp of approval which permits them to be teachers in turn.

Young monks (not yet ordained as priests) study and meditate under a resident master, and are also instructed in temple management and ceremonies. They live frugal and disciplined lives. In a Rinzai temple the trainee will have interviews with his master and indicate his present understanding of the *kōan*. Lectures are given – not for instruction, but for inspiration.

Laypeople, too, are accepted for temporary sessions, but there is not the kind of pastoral concern that one finds in the Honganji temples of Shin Buddhism, where counselling often takes place.

For many, however, Zen is linked with the arts – with flower arrangement, the tea ceremony, or the calm and mystic serenity of the seemingly formless garden. But some might say that through these there can be 'a direct insight of a profound awakening' – an

Illustrations pages 373, 374 intuitive and existential leap into the ultimate.

Nichiren Buddhism

The Nichiren sect was formed by Nichiren (1222-1282) when (in 1253) he gathered together a few followers in Kamakura. He criticized all the Buddhist sects of his day, and was consequently persecuted by the monks and laymen as well as by those government officials who were votaries of those sects. His devotion to the Buddhist *Dhamma* (which he considered to be uniquely and finally portrayed in the Lotus Sutra) and to the prosperity of his own country appeared in the title of his thesis in 1260 – 'Risshō Ankoku-ron' (a thesis which holds that 'national security' depends upon the 'establishing of the Buddhist Law'). He held that only in the establishment of the ortho-dox religious tradition could Japan achieve internal peace and be secure from the threatened Mongol invasion. At the same time he was anxious to see in the teachings of the Lotus Sutra the fulfilment of national religious movements, and the *mandala* he produced were brush-drawn Chinese characters, in which Shintō *kami* and Indian *devas* (gods) joined with the Buddhist *bodhisattvas* in the paean in honour of the Wondrous *Dhamma*, as taught in the Lotus Sutra – *Namu myōhō rengekyō* (Reverence to the Wondrous Law of the Lotus Sutra).

The sect, throughout its history, has been marked both by its nationalistic emphasis and syncretic tendencies and by its exclusive claims and absolutist demands. Nichiren's call to *shakubuku* (a kind of forceful proselytism) has been of late taken up by Sōka Gakkai.

The majority of Nichiren groups believe Nichiren to have been a manifestation of the Bodhisattva Jōgyō, who is depicted in the Lotus Sutra as appearing in the age of the decline of Buddhist teaching. Sōka Gakkai, however, claims that Nichiren is an incarnation of the Eternal Buddha.

The Lotus Sutra would seem to give the layperson equal status with the monk, and it is important to note that within the Nichiren tradition there has emerged the so-called Zaike Bukkyō (Lay Buddh-ism) – a revolt against over-clericalism. Lay Buddhism is the corollary of the assertion that it is the ordinary people who are in reality the *bodhisattvas*, who have compassion in their hearts and who can aspire to the enlightenment of the Buddha. At the same time, an emphasis on the laity means a simplification of ceremonial and teaching and an attempt to get at the kernel of the teaching. Both the popular maga-zine and the temple sermon accordingly seek to reinterpret the ancient faith in a contemporary idiom directed to actual situation.

The Worship of the Temple

A temple is always constructed inside an enclosure, and the compound may include not one but a whole series of temples. The entrance is usually guarded by forbidding statues with scowling faces, which are *Illustration page 374* thought to ward off evil. They are customarily covered with paper, because worshippers write their petitions on bits of paper, and, after chewing them, throw them at the figures. If they stick, it is thought that the prayer will be answered. The temple will often have a pagoda, *Illustration page 371* three to five stories high, usually with elaborate ornamentation. The main sanctuary contains an altar with lighted candles – with images of the *buddhas*, *bodhisattvas* and *devas*, and around the altar are boxes containing the *sutras*. No sect will have the entire Chinese canon, but each will make its own selection of those regarded as normative. The central image upon the altar differs according to the sect.

The *sutras* are chanted and prayers offered by the priests to the accompaniment of drums and bells and the burning of incense. The ordinary worshippers rarely attend. Their devotions will be largely private and more often than not confined to the home *butsudan* – a replica in miniature of what there is in the temple.

Many of the temples will, however, cater chiefly to popular demand. They will provide souvenirs, inscribing the names of contributors to temple funds on some sacred article or ornament which will find its place on the *butsudan*. The mystical atmosphere of the temple will be emphasized, amulets and charms distributed – with one temple specializing in the Buddhist equivalent of a St Christopher's medallion for Tokyo's busy taxi-drivers. In most temples the priests will be available for the performance of specific rites, where the petitioner may have little more than a superstitious respect for the validity of the *sutra*.

Despite the fact that the Anatta (non-soul) doctrine lies at the heart of Buddhism, the strength of ancestor worship is such that funerals and memorial services for the departed occupy the priest far more than regular instruction on what Buddhism actually teaches. As a result, the most popular festival is the Ō-Bon (held on the fifteenth day of the seventh month), when the departed spirits are believed to return to their native place, and are welcomed there with lanterns and fireworks.

Since the thirteenth century, ancestral tablets in which the ancestral spirits are supposed to reside have had their place on the family *butsudan* to be adored together with the statuette of the Buddha and copies of the *sutras*. Just as the Shintō worshipper looks to become a *kami* when he dies, so the Buddhist expects to become a buddha; and it is doubtful whether there is any conceptual difference.

In the matter of votive offerings there is little difference at the popular level from Shintō practice. There are the offerings for healing, for an easy pregnancy or the safe development of a child. The model of a breast will be offered in prayer for abundant mother's milk. A ladle is offered in prayer for a child, but, if the bottom of the ladle is knocked out, an abortion is the object of the petition. Figures of Dharma (i.e. Bodhidharma, the supposed founder of Zen Buddhism) are offered – eyeless until the plea is answered.

New Religions: Their Background

Until recent times, new movements were not able to receive public recognition. For two hundred and fifty years, during the Tokugawa shogunate, Buddhism had been the official faith, although at the popular level Shintō and Buddhist ideas were intermingled and the

Illustration page 383

Left In Japan, the Buddhist *stupa* took the form of the pagoda. This one, at the Kofukuji temple at Nara, has five storeys and dates from the Kamakura period (AD 1186–1335).

Below left An eaves-bracket detail from the gateway of the seventeenth-century tomb of Tokugawa Ieyasu at Nikko, a most elaborately decorated and coloured building.

Below This ancient fountain feeds the basin for the ritual ablutions performed by visitors in the garden of the Buddhist Horyuji temple at Nara.

Opposite above left The tea
ceremony reflects the influence of
Zen Buddhism upon everyday life
in Japan. The calm and orderly
ritual seems to free the mind and
induce a sense of peace.

Opposite above right Zen monks
practising kyudo. The aim is that
archer, bow and target become one
with the universe through the
concentration of mental and
physical forces so that the archer
shoots at him or herself whilst
aiming at the target.

Opposite below A garden of
contemplation at the Ryoanji
temple in Kyoto. This relatively
small Zen garden of the
Muromachi period encompasses
fifteen rocks set in white gravel
arranged to imitate water.

Right A gilded copper *shari-tō* or
miniature pagoda containing the
shari or sacred ashes of holy people.
Veneration of the *shari* was popular
in the late Heian and early
Kamakura periods. Many such
reliquaries were made, though this,
from Saidaiji, Nara, is probably the
finest.

Right One of the Nio, the two
kings who watch over the
entrances of monasteries to protect
them from evil influences.

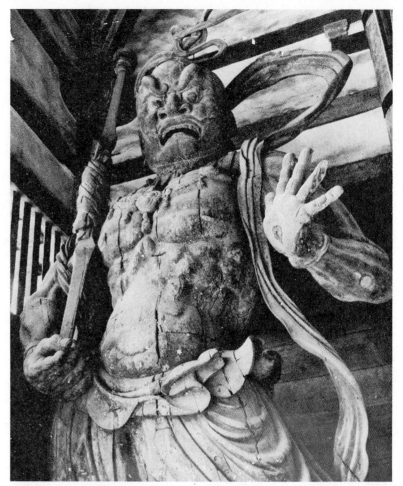

Right The Ginkakuji temple at
Kyoto set amidst beautiful gardens.
In the upper storey are the Zen
study-rooms.

fusion was also given official sanction. As far as public and social ethics were concerned, the inspiration came from Confucianism rather than the Shintō-Buddhist religious tradition.

The age was one of severe restrictions, and a visit to the local shrine or temple festival or pilgrimages to different shrines, particularly the Shrine of Ise, were the only occasions when the ordinary person could break away from conventional patterns of behaviour or travel beyond a limited locality. The pilgrimages were especially popular and were called '*okage mairi*' – 'going to give thanks'.

After the restoration of imperial power in 1868, the common people developed folk chants, patterned after Buddhist *sutras*, and even used them as a means of propounding a new social gospel. At the same time there developed dances with magic formulae, called *ee ja naika* (it's good, isn't it?) dances. When it became obvious that political or social reform would not occur, it was natural for the populace to cast in their lot with religious movements which began to emerge in the middle of the nineteenth century. These movements were not completely new, and could not really be called new religions, because they reflected the undifferentiated character of popular religion, where the ecstatic and charismatic had a great influence. A movement like Tenrikyō incorporated dances as a source of inspiration, whilst the social concern comes out in the utopian vision of the future and the critique of contemporary patterns.

Illustration page 383

Sectarian Shintō

When, in 1882, the Meiji government divided religious organizations into three categories – Buddhist, Christian and Shintō – those that could not be classified as Buddhist or Christian were classified as Shintō sects, and this meant a distinction between *jinja* (shrine) and *kyōha* (sect) Shintō. The sects were quite heterogeneous, and eventually thirteen were permitted to register. They belong to five groups. Some like Taishakyō which claims more than 3,000,000 members and centres in the ancient Izumo Taisha shrine, are pure Shintō sects; some are Confucianist in inspiration; some look to ancient mountain-worship as their basis; others concentrate on special rites for purification.

Most interesting, however, are the three sects of peasant origin, for they set the pattern for many other movements that have arisen in the twentieth century. The three are Kurozumikyō, Tenrikyō and Konkōkyō. Certain common features seem to mark them and the so-called 'new religions':

1 The movements arise in time of social crisis.
2 There is a charismatic leader.
3 There are 'apocalyptic' signs and wonders.
4 There is ecstatic behaviour, and a free rein is given to the members for a full participation in the worship and activity of the cult.
5 There is a tendency towards syncretism, and the diffused character of popular religion is evident.

Kurozumikyō looks, for its starting point, to the personal religious experience of Kurozumi Munetado (1780-1850), who had an intense devotion to Amaterasu-Ō-mi-Kami. He regarded her as the source of universal life, and, believing that he had attained Oneness with the *kami*, he came to be regarded as an *ikigami* (a living *kami*). The *kami* is called *Oya* (Parent), and Kurozumi believed that, through prayer, the believer could penetrate to the source of life.

The Religion of Heavenly Wisdom

Tenrikyō (The Religion of Heavenly Wisdom) was founded by Na-kayama Miki (1798-1887) who was very much a person of her age and environment. The *Kyōsōden* (Life of the Foundress) speaks of her contact with Buddhist temples (chiefly Jōdo Shinshū) and Shintō shrines, of her interest in the Ise pilgrimages and of her appeal to the Yamabushi for the healing of her son.

Her sudden *kami*-possession on 26 October, 1838, marked the beginning of a new religion. The canonical scriptures of Tenrikyō emphasize the 'revelatory' character of her experience. They relate that, when she was used as a medium, a *kami*, later identified as Kuni-toko-tachi-no-Mikoto (one of the primary *kami* of the *Kojiki* and *Nihongi*, who is linked with the act of creation), spoke through her. This *kami* was later equated by Miki with the Moon (*Tsuki*), and a subsequent *kami* who 'spoke' through her was identified as the Sun (*Hi*). The story says that eight pairs of *kami* followed, of whom the last were Izanagi and Izanami, the creator-progenitors of the popular Shintō myth and also the progenitors of the human race in Miki's own creation myth, commonly called the 'Ancient Record of the Sea

Illustration page 384 of Mud'.

Whilst Tenrikyō was compelled, during the strongly nationalistic period before 1945, to approximate its teaching to official Shintō, there is now much more effort to identify the deity as unitary. Tsukihi is regarded as one divinity, also called Tenri-Ō-no-Mikoto, and the other eight *kami* are said to be the instruments of Tsukihi and to have no separate existence.

The basic scriptures are the *Ōfudesaki*, written over the period 1869-1882, the *Mikagura-uta* (Song for the Dance) written between 1866 and 1882, the *Ancient Record of the Sea of Mud*, composed from notes taken from memory of Miki's oral account, and the *Ōsashizu* (Guidance), which professed to be the transmission of divine oracles even after Miki's death which is described as her 'ascension'.

Tenri is the name now given to the town where the chief sanctuary stands, and it is also called Ōyasato, the town of the Parent. It is understood as the locus both of creation and the consummation of all things, when the heavenly dew will descend upon the central pillar. Apart from the main shrine, there is a memorial chapel dedicated to the foundress and one where the ancestors of members are enshrined.

Emphasis is laid upon *yokigurashi* (joyous living), which results from regarding life as lent from God, and from sweeping away the 'dust' that collects, and upon voluntary labour, which demonstrates gratitude to God and which has been largely responsible for the extensive building programme in Tenri. Here there are educational, medical, cultural and sporting facilities in addition to the chief shrine and the dormitories for tens of thousands of visitors.

The Religion of Metal Lustre

Konkōkyō (The Religion of Metal Lustre) was started by an uneducated farmer called Kawade (1814-1883), better known as Konkō Daijin, who claimed in 1859 to be an *ikigami*, saying that he was the intermediary of Tenchi-Kane-no-Kami. He proclaimed this *kami* as supreme and 'the origin of the universe'. Humans owe duty to the parent *kami*, and must cultivate his god-given nature. At the same time the very existence of *kami* seemed to be dependent upon humans. Kawade emphasized divine favour: 'By virtue of the divine favour man is blessed and saved, and the world moves on in peace and prosperity!' We are told that the consequences of the new attitude to life are twofold: there is peace of mind in life and death, and there is harmony in the home and society because 'there is no such thing as a non-relation under the sun'.

Here we have a motif that has become common to almost all the new religions – that religion must impinge upon ordinary life and also that it must produce the 'good life'.

The Ōmoto Group of Religious Movements

Whilst it is impossible to examine all the newer religious movements, the Ōmoto group of religions are indicative of the highly syncretistic character of much of Japan's modern religious thinking. Ōmoto's story begins with Deguchi Nao, who in 1892 was possessed by a *kami* and was thought to be mad. Under possession she wrote the *Ōfudesaki* (With the Tip of the Brush), later to be interpreted by her younger associate, who became her son-in-law and took the name Deguchi Onisaburō. The *Ōfudesaki* and Onisaburō's *Stories of the Spirit World* form the basic scriptures. In the latter, Onisaburo spoke of himself as a John the Baptist.

At times Ōmoto's teaching sounds monotheistic, but then asserts that its doctrine is based upon a view of God comprehending simultaneously the contradictions of monotheism, pantheism and polytheism. It lays claim to finality: 'All religions of the world are the forerunners of Ōmoto.' Whilst basically Shintō in its inspiration – and it is now included in the Sect Shintō Association – Onisaburō is said to have become host to the spirit of Miroku. This reference to Miroku adds a note of Messianism, and we are introduced to the idea of God as both judge and saviour, the one who both overthrows the old order and establishes the coming kingdom. The prewar persecution of Ōmoto, leading to its suppression by the government in 1935, encouraged the notion that 'Messianic woes' must precede the coming of the kingdom.

Illustration page 383

Ananaikyō was founded by Nakano Yonosuke in 1934, when he broke away from Ōmoto, but the present organization dates only from 1949. He, too, is an enthusiastic follower of spiritism and professes to receive messages from the spirit world and so to be the successor of Deguchi Onisaburō. Nakano accepts the popular Messianism of the Maitreya cult within Buddhism, and speaks of the unification of all religions at that point. The very name *ananai* is an indication of his universalism. One explanation of the word, which is used of the hempen rope which hangs from the gong in front of the Shintō shrine, is that the rope binds the believer to the realities of the world beyond. The word is written with the numerals '3' and '5', and one explanation is that the '3' represents the three religions of Ōmoto, Hung-wan-tsu-hui, and Bahai, whilst the '5' represents the five world religions, interpreted as Christianity, Islam, Confucianism, Buddhism and Taoism. The religion emphasizes meditation, and the establishment of observatories throughout the country is regarded as a means of communication with the cosmos.

Power in a Pearl

Sekaikyūseikyō (Religion of World Messianity) was founded by Okada Mōkichi (1882-1955), when he broke away from Ōmoto. He believed himself to be endowed with the wonder-working power of Kannon (the Bodhisattva of Mercy). One story had it that this power was contained in a small pearl within his body, and that a light was radiated from this pearl which would kill bacteria! Through his charisma, he was believed to have the power to heal the sick and enrich harvests. As a result he was called Hikari-San, 'Man of Light', and it was supposed that he could transfer the healing power to pieces of paper on which he had written the character for 'light'. At the centres of the religion there is an attempt to establish the 'kingdom', for it is its concern 'to eliminate sickness, poverty and war from this world and transform it into an earthly paradise'.

The deity is called Miroku, and health, riches and peace are said to be the marks of his kingdom. One of the hymns says:

Miroku the Great God, comes forth, endowed with the great strength of the three in one — Fire, Water, Earth. Miroku, the Great God, from of old has planted the heaven upon earth.
Miroku, the Great God, even as comes a thief, has secretly been born below.
Leaving behind the highly exalted throne, to bring salvation Miroku has been born below.

He is also called Kōmyō Nyōrai (Buddha of Light – Amida).

The House of Growth

Seichō no Ie (The House of Growth) claims to be a 'non-denominational movement of truth, teaching that all religions emanate from one universal God'. It was founded by Taniguchi Masaharu in 1928, when he became convinced that there was only one True Being, to which he gave the title 'Jissō', and that all other things were simply the product of man's own thought. For the Shintō worshipper this True Being could be thought of as Kami; for the Buddhist as the Buddha or Amida, etc., and for the Christian it would be Christ.

At the Tokyo headquarters meditation is commonly carried on in 'The Tower of Light' and is called *shinsō kan*, 'seeing the mind of God'. From the headquarters *nempa*, 'waves' of spiritual desire, are thought to issue forth. Central to the teaching is the Holy Sutra, entitled 'The Nectarean Shower of Holy Doctrines', which is supposed to have an active force in effecting man's realization of his true status.

Nichiren Movements

We shall refer to only three of the many movements that have received their inspiration from Nichiren and the Lotus teaching. Reiyūkai (Soul-Friend Association) was founded in 1925 and has achieved a wide popularity. Although it claims to follow in the Nichiren tradition and uses the Lotus Sutra in its daily offices, its chief attraction is its emphasis on ancestor worship. The attraction is largely for married women who are permitted to maintain links with their own ancestral past. Both the founder and his successor, Kotani Miki, showed shamanistic traits, and through them contact with the spirit world is promised the adherents. Membership of Reiyūkai is non-exclusive, and the majority of the two to three millions claimed as adherents are simultaneously members of other Buddhist (or Shintō) groupings.

Risshōkōseikai, an 'association' for the establishment of 'right law' in the world, for 'fellowship' in the faith, and for 'completeness', came into being in 1938, when Niwano Nikkyō and Naganuma Myōkō seceded from Reiyūkai. Mrs Naganuma had a reputation for her psychic powers and her healing gifts. These gained great publicity for her and she was regarded as a living Buddha. Since her death in 1957 the shamanistic elements have not been so prominent, and emphasis has been rather placed upon the *hōza* (counselling groups) and upon the attempt to present Buddhism in modern dress, as a creed that brings about peace and goodwill. Hence, in his popular commentary on the Lotus Sutra, Niwano speaks of people looking to the attainment of buddhahood, when 'the black cloud' of error will be done away. Men and women's daily life is to manifest an acceptance of Buddha's command, for only so can a person show the true repentance that will enable the *karma* to be broken. The life of faith will mean union with the Buddha, which is union with the 'great life of the universe' and an entrance into the Buddha-world.

This movement shows nothing of the exclusiveness of ordinary Nichiren Buddhism, but displays desire for relationship in all directions, typified by Niwano's visits to the Vatican, Geneva and Lambeth!

The vast Sacred Hall in Tokyo, which was opened in 1964, is the result of the contributions of more than one and a half million members, and is the scene of huge rallies.

Remarkable Growth

Sōka Gakkai has had the most extraordinary development of any of the new religious movements. Whereas it numbered only 50,000 in

1951, at the inauguration of the Shakubuku programme, it now claims to have nearly 16,000,000 adherents, and the Clean Government Party which is associated with it has the third largest representation in the two chambers of the Diet (fifty-nine members in 1980).

The name means 'Scholarly Association for the Creation of Value' and reflects the utilitarian aim of Makiguchi Tsunesaburo (1871-1944), the founder. Originally it was to have been a system of pedagogy for the creation of goodness, beauty and utility, but he and his younger associate, Tōda Josei (1899-1958), came under the influence of Nichiren Shōshū, a small, but fanatical group within the Nichiren tradition, who claimed to be the sole exponents of Nichiren's orthodox teaching. This group identified Nichiren with the Eternal Buddha to the neglect of Sakyamuni, and the *mandala* in Daisekiji (its chief temple near Mount Fuji) was claimed to be the only genuine one produced by Nichiren, and so efficacious for the salvation of mankind. The sect has as its aim the recognition of its tenets as the national religion.

Only a small proportion of the members of Sōka Gakkai are also members of Nichiren Shōshū, but the exclusiveness and messianic fervour of the larger movement are undoubtedly derived from the teaching of the smaller group. The success of Sōka Gakkai is largely derived from the desire to express Japan's national consciousness. The structure is well designed to alleviate individual anomie and yet permit the organization to grow massively without the disadvantages of a large organization. The primary groupings are so strong that the organization can stand, whilst the inter-relationship of the primary groups ensures that the movement does not split up, as has been the case with Shingon Buddhism and many of the new religious movements, into innumerable schismatic groups. Because of the smallness of the primary groups the individual never feels lost.

The conversion link brings the members into a complex of vertical relationships leading up to the headquarters in Tokyo, but, in addition, there are the horizontal links through the 'block' system of growing houshold units together. At the same time there are a series of interest or peer groups.

Absolute Truth

The theological premise is that the movement is based upon absolute truth, and happiness is said to be ensured by the truth. It is strongly lay in its organization, and yet skilfully combines the traditional with the new. It is practical and 'this-worldly'– with no ethic of renunciation, but rather one easily within reach of the ordinary well-adjusted person. Daily prayers are expected, but they are simple and repetitive, and the pilgrimages to Daisekiji are anything but ascetic. A further strength is the rejection of the regular hierarchies in society, and a ranking in the movement which is dependent upon individual effort.

Other New Movements

Of the miscellaneous new religious movements that have flourished in the past twenty years P.L. (Perfect Liberty) Kyōdan is a good example. It was founded by Miki Tokuharu (1871-1938) as Hito ṇo Michi (The Way of Man), but this movement was suppressed in 1937, and Miki Tokuchika refounded it in 1946 as the Perfect Liberty Association. The very use of English shows the claim to modernity, and its creed follows the fundamental premise that 'life is art'. The practical side is seen in the golf courses, the pottery kiln and the sporting stadia at the headquarters of the movement. Sport, education, social concern and prayer are all symbols of the human expression of and striving towards harmony. Human activity has meaning because it expresses divine creation, and through this activity peace and harmony are secured.

Man Reflects God

The idea of the human being as a microcosm is, of course, common to most religions, but Japanese religions, in the main influenced by Shintō's strong world-affirmation, are concerned very much with human activity – more so than with human thought. So P.L. links activity with personality. People reflect God in their creative work, and this work itself reveals them and preserves, too, the notion of individuality which a postwar 'democratic' age would wish to incorporate. 'Man', we are told, 'can express his individuality in every act he makes. . . . There is nothing in human affairs that cannot become art. Man's life begins and ends in self-expression.' (*Perfect Liberty*: *How to lead a happy life*, p. 17).

In the case of the new religions, it can be argued that they are restoring the solidarity of the group for those who, in an era of rapid social change, are experiencing the breakdown of the old systems which had made for individual or social security. In the fellowship of the new movement the individual finds a new warmth and a new sense of community. The Shintō shrine may also be the symbol of community solidarity, but its tradition lacks appeal for those who demand some measure of modernity. However, dependence is not the last word. There is also the call to an active self-realization, which means the growth of self-confidence. Personal problems are resolved and the group pilgrimages and voluntary social-service leave less time for the morbid introspection which leads to the state of *fuan* (unease), while the large building-programmes which have led many to call the new movements *tatemono shūkyō* (building religions) give the feel of success.

Religious Statistics

Religious statistics are not always reliable, and cannot, in any case, show whether adherence to a religion is genuine or simply nominal. Many of the Buddhist sects number the families whose tablets are lodged with their temples, and then allot five to a family. It is obvious that family allegiance may differ from personal allegiance, and it is not surprising that total statistics amount to almost 180,000,000, although the total population of Japan is only a little over 110,000,000.

The Shintō shrines tend to list all within the community who contribute towards the shrine festival, which explains a figure of almost 85,000,000 adherents. There are, however, not more than 22,000 priests to minister at the 80,000 shrines. Figures for the sects are more accurate, with Tenrikyō claiming almost 2,500,000 members. They have 15,000 churches and more than 100,000 who have received the minimum training for conducting services. Konkōkyō has upwards of 600,000 members, worshipping in 1,350 churches and served by 3,600 priests, whilst Kurozumikyō claims more than 700,000, although there are only 300 churches served by 3,400 priests.

Of the Buddhist sects (which altogether claim upwards of 37,000,000 members) Jōdo Shinshū and Nichiren are the most popular, with more than 9,000,000 members each. The various groups associated with Shingon number more than 7,000,000, the Zen sects about 4,500,000, Jōdo upwards of 4,000,000 and Tendai about 2,000,000. The figures for Nichiren Buddhism would probably include new religions such as Risshōkōseikai, although they would be much higher if statistics for Sōka Gakkai were included.

Of the new religions P.L. Kyōdan has a membership of about 1,000,000, Sekaikyūseikyō just under 500,000. Seichō no Ie claims more than 2,500,000 members, but that total simply marks the number of subscribers to their literature! Ōmoto has about 100,000 members and Ananaikyō about 200,000.

Christians in Japan form a tiny minority, just over three million, some 3 per cent of the population.

Above An early seventh-century representation of Miroku in contemplative attitude. Miroku-bosatsu (Maitreya or the Buddha of the Future) was very popular in the sixth to eighth centuries. His chief devotees today are the Shingon and Zen sects. Koryuji, Kyoto.

Above centre Jizo-bosatsu, a wooden sculpture of the Muromachi period. Jizo is the counsellor and consoler of the dead and the protector of children. He is worshipped by all but the Pure Land and Nichiren sects. Seattle Art Museum, Washington. Eugene Fuller Memorial Collection.

Above left Bishamon (possibly of Taoist origin) is one of the seven deities of luck, and is also thought of as a *kami* of war. As such, he is represented as guardian of the temple. The small pagoda he holds indicates that he is the protector of Buddhism. Seattle Art Museum, Washington. Eugene Fuller Memorial Collection.

Right A late nineteenth-century silk scroll depicting Izanagi and his sister Izanami, the eighth of the early Shinto couples. Izanagi is plunging his celestial spear into the ocean of chaos to create the island of Onogoro. Museum of Fine Arts, Boston, Massachusetts.

Chapter Nineteen

Judaism

Judaism is the religion of the Jewish people. The formation of the Jewish people, which may be traced back to the Exodus of the Hebrews from Egypt, is closely bound up with a divine revelation, and with the commitment of the people to obedience to God's will. This close connection between religion and peoplehood gives Judaism a unique character which is not shared by its daughter religion, Christianity. But at the same time, it complicates the analysis of Judaism, because it is difficult, if not impossible, to separate the history of Judaism from the history of the Jews. However, an attempt is made here to portray Judaism in its historical development by considering its own organic growth, and by showing how the vicissitudes of historical experience have affected the very fabric of the religion. This naturally involves a selection, for only those aspects of Jewish history and culture which have directly influenced religious development or been associated with it can be considered here.

Over its long history of 3,000 years, Judaism has changed both in theology and in practice. The Jewish people have been called 'the people of the Book', which means not that their religion is determined literally and exclusively by the contents of the Bible, but that that book has been the authority, guide and inspiration of all the many forms which the religion of the Jews has taken in different periods and in different lands.

Judaism therefore has its roots in the Hebrew Bible. This collection of books (the Greek word *biblia* means books) was written over a period of nearly 1,000 years and established in its full canonical form by the end of the first century AD.

The Hebrew Bible is divided according to the Jewish tradition into three sections: the Torah, that is the Pentateuch, the 'Five Books' of *Genesis, Exodus, Leviticus, Numbers* and *Deuteronomy*, which were believed to have been written by Moses from divine instruction on Sinai; the Prophets, sub-divided into Earlier Prophets, *Joshua, Judges, Samuel, Kings,* and Later Prophets, *Isaiah, Jeremiah, Ezekiel,* and twelve 'minor' prophets; and the Writings. The Writings were normally arranged in the following order: *Psalms, Proverbs, Job, Song of Songs, Ruth, Lamentations, Ecclesiastes, Esther* (these last five being called the five *megillot,* or small scrolls), *Daniel, Ezra, Nehemiah* and *Chronicles.*

Illustration page 393

The Bible is basically a record of the Hebrews' aspiration to understand God and his ways both in relation to the natural world and to humanity. The name Hebrew (*Ivri*) is derived perhaps from the root meaning 'to cross', and refers to the people who came to Canaan from the eastern side of the Euphrates. It is also associated with the name Ever, grandson of Shem (*Genesis* x:24). 'Shem' is the root of the word 'Semite'. In recent years archaeological discovery and scholastic research have shown how biblical texts may fruitfully be compared with traditions emanating from the civilizations of ancient Egypt and Mesopotamia, Phoenicia and Canaan, Assyria and Persia. These comparisons show how, on the one hand, the authors of the Bible were men of their time, sharing similar cosmological and legal ideas, and how, on the other, they rose above their contemporaries through the power of prophetic insight, to propound new dimensions in ethical and universal monotheism.

Common Assumptions

Because the Bible reflects a religious outlook stretching over a long period of time and in contact with many cultures and religions, it displays a variety of ideas and practices. These, however, are built on common assumptions. God's existence and power are taken for granted. The dilemma of the Hebrew is not the question whether God exists, or why he exists, but rather how he acts in the world, and what he requires of people. The natural world is a manifestation of God's glory. This is the core of the first chapter of *Genesis*, and also of Psalm 19: 'The heavens declare the glory of God. . . .' The fate of nations and the experience of individuals reflect the power of God in the affairs of human beings.

The Bible moves from a restricted view of God as a national deity to a more universal conception of him as the God of all nations which are but instruments in his hand. This may be seen in the several names of God which are found in the Scriptures, ranging from Shaddai, which seems to signify storm-god, or god of power, Elo'ah, Yah, and Adonai, to the more common Elohim, and YHVH, the tetragrammation, the last becoming the most sacred divine name (usually translated 'Lord') which was not pronounced by the Jews. (The name 'Jehovah' is a medieval misreading and does not occur in the Hebrew Bible.)

The God of the Bible is both a remote, transcendent being, imposing his awe upon the universe, demanding absolute obedience under the sanction of severe penalties, and also a loving and compassionate father, who has a close personal relationship with those who revere him. 'I dwell in the high and holy place, and with him also that is of a humble and contrite spirit' (*Isaiah* lvii:15). This paradox is a reflection on the ambivalent attitude that the Hebrews had towards a world which could appear to be at the same time both stern and bountiful. And this paradox has remained an essential and realistic part of Jewish theology down to our times.

From the ritualistic point of view, the religion of the Hebrews was centred round a sanctuary or shrine, at first movable and finally established in Jerusalem. This sanctuary, first the Tabernacle, later the Temple, was considered to be the special place where the God of the Hebrews was to be worshipped. It was here that animal sacrifices, and offerings of other kinds, were offered by the priests – a special hereditary class descended from Aaron, the first high priest, elder brother of Moses. Offerings were made upon the altar daily, and special offerings were made on holy days. In addition individuals were obliged to bring offerings as an atonement for sin, or as thanksgiving on special occasions, after childbirth for instance. The priest, as well as being an officiant in the sanctuary, was also consulted by the sick, since certain diseases conveyed ritual uncleanness. And he also apparently taught the law: 'For the priest's lips should keep knowledge, and they should seek the law at his mouth' – (*Malachi* ii:7).

The Prophets

However, since all institutionalized religious observances are prone to become automatic practices, without full understanding or spiritual awareness on the part of the practitioner, so among the Hebrews spokesmen arose who denounced the insincere practice of Hebrew ritual. These spokesmen were the prophets. The prophet was a man who believed himself to be specifically summoned by God to preach his message. The actual origin or nature of the prophetic experience is not clear to us, but it is evident that it was an experience that was both irresistible, overcoming the protests of a Moses (*Exodus* iv:10), an Isaiah (*Isiah* vi:5), and a Jeremiah (*Jeremiah* i:6), and transforming, turning as it did Saul 'into another man' (I *Samuel* x:6). The Hebrew word for prophet – *navi* – comes from a root signifying 'to well up, to gush forth', as if the prophet were a passive instrument for the expression of God's will. It is possible that the prophetic experience was of many types, ranging from the obscure mystical vision of Ezekiel to the clear ethical conviction of Amos.

Illustration page 393

But the main burden of their pronouncements concerns the righteous life, whether it be the life of the individual, or the life of the nation; and this passion for righteousness compelled them, when necessary, to confront both priest and monarch. Indeed, one is tempted to set the prophet entirely against the priest, on the one hand, and the ruling class, on the other, but this would be an over-simplification, for the early 'seer' Samuel had priestly functions also, and Ezekiel the prophet was deeply concerned with the ritual and fabric of the Temple, while it is within the priestly legislation of Leviticus that we find one of the highest expressions of social morality in the Bible – 'you shall love your neighbour as yourself' (*Leviticus* xix:18). Furthermore, at least one prophet, Isaiah, belonged to the nobility, and not all the kings of Israel and Judah defied the canons of the Hebrew faith.

In all aspects of the religion portrayed in the Bible there is an overriding consciousness of the religious purpose of the Hebrew people. The early narratives of the patriarchs, the 'fathers' of the Jews, were written down primarily in order to inculcate the doctrine of the close relationship that existed between God and the Hebrews. This relationship was emphasized even more thoroughly in the experience of the Exodus, which, from one point of view, was but a necessary preliminary to the divine revelation at Sinai.

Illustration page 394

Thenceforth this specific characteristic of the people was the main burden of prophetic exhortation, imposing as it did upon the Hebrews a special responsibility to fulfil the divine mission. 'Ye shall be unto me a kingdom of priests, and a holy nation' (*Exodus* xix:6); 'You only have I known of all the families of the earth; therefore I will visit upon you all your iniquities' (*Amos* iii:2). This relationship was described in the terms of a covenant or agreement (*brit*) between God and the Hebrews, which was to be renewed publicly on several occasions between the Mosaic era and the time of Ezra.

From Hebraism to Judaism

The period from the completion of biblical writing (*c.* 150 BC) to the compilation of the *Mishnah* (AD 200 – see page 391) was one of transition in the history of Judaism. A long and slow transformation took place, at the end of which biblical Hebraism emerged as rabbinic Judaism. There are many unanswered questions concerning this period, but it is clear that the religion of the Jews was not at this time the stable, codified system that it was later to become.

According to the rabbinic tradition itself there were a number of Jewish sects, some of which were considered to be beyond the pale of 'normative' Judaism. There were disputes between the Sadducees – reputed to be descendants of Zadok, the priest, and belonging mainly to the priestly, aristocratic class – and the Pharisees – literally perhaps meaning 'separated ones', those who considered themselves to be specially devoted to the study and practice of the Torah. These disputes concerned such questions as the resurrection of the body and the date of the festival of Pentecost. The sect of the Samaritans, who rejected rabbinic interpretation of Scripture and confined themselves to the literal application of the Pentateuch, became more and more removed from the centre of Jewish tradition, while both the testimony of Josephus and recent archaeological discovery provide evidence that during this period there existed organized Jewish communities which shunned urban life and constituted a more ascetic, almost 'monastic', society. Such were the Essenes and the community of Qumran, if these two are not, in fact, to be identified with each other.

Illustrations page 394

The literature discovered among the Dead Sea Scrolls, especially that dealing with the 'Wars of the Sons of Light against the Sons of Darkness' and the 'Teacher of Righteousness', must be considered together with those books of the Apocrypha and other literature called Pseudepigraphic (which did not become part of the Jewish canon of Scripture) which deal with 'the end of days'. Eschatological ideas and visions are already found in the later strata of the Bible (e.g. in *Daniel* and *Zechariah*), but in this period they proliferated (especially in the Hebrew *Enoch*) and signify the emotional and imaginative power released at a time of political and spiritual disorientation and even breakdown. The influence of Persian and Hellenistic ideas and practices was marked, and, although the attempt (in 168 BC) by Antiochus Epiphanes to destroy the Jewish religion had been thwarted by the Maccabees, nevertheless the Hashmonean dynasty itself soon fell prey to oriental megalomania, with disastrous results for the faith of the people. And when this was followed by the oppression of Roman rule the result was a proliferation of new religious concepts and movements, some of which were later to form the foundation of Jewish mysticism (*kabbalah*), while others found a home within the rival faith of Christianity.

The Rise of Christianity

Messianic speculation in religious movements is usually at its height when anti-religious pressures are at their most acute. Such was the case in the period with which we are dealing. The Jews looked forward to the coming of a Messiah (literally 'anointed one'), who would be descended from the house of David, who would break the yoke of political oppression, re-establish Jewish national sovereignty, and usher in a period of peace, the establishment of the Kingdom of God. From the Gospel writings it would appear that Jesus of Nazareth considered himself, and was considered by many Jews, to be the Jewish Messiah. From this point of view he was acting within the Jewish tradition, and, indeed, there is little in his teachings that contradicts the established Jewish religious ideology of his time. He certainly would not have thought of himself as belonging to any other religion but Judaism.

His death was encompassed both by those Jews (mainly Sadducees) who saw in his powerful preaching a danger to the established Temple practice, and hence to their own position, and also by the Romans in power, who considered him to be a potential national rebel, precisely because of his messianic pretensions. His execution at the hands of the Romans marked the end of his influence for the majority of Jews, who would have interpreted his death as evidence for their own misapprehension of him as the Messiah.

Relations between the followers of Jesus and their opponents became more than an internal affair when the Pauline interpretation of the life of Jesus established itself as the basis for a new religion – Christianity – and when Gentiles in large numbers became converted to the new faith. The new elements introduced by Paul, including the divine incarnation, vicarious atonement, the abrogation of the law, and the doctrine of the basically sinful nature of man, could not be accepted by Jews who wished to remain within the fold of Judaism. Indeed, the growth of these new ideas served to emphasize the corresponding opposite concepts in the later history of Judaism.

In other ways, too, the expansion of Christianity had lasting effects on Jews and Judaism. It assumed the role that Judaism had previously played in the conversion of Gentiles. Soon, in Christian (and later in

Muslim) lands Jewish proselytism was to become a capital offence. But the most important result of all was that, in the centuries that ensued, the Jews were considered in the eyes of the Christian Church to be guilty of deicide, and an accursed people, their very existence and the practice of their faith being merely a living testimony to their blindness in not recognizing the advent of the true Messiah. This was the official attitude of Christianity for many centuries and it caused great physical and spiritual suffering to the Jews. Only in recent times has there been an attempt on the part of the Christian Church to mollify the harshness and severity of this attitude.

The Pharisaic Achievement

It was the great achievement of the rabbis called *tannaim* (100 BC–AD 200) that they were able, with a remarkable spiritual creativity and a fine sensitiveness to changing circumstances, to transform Hebraism into Judaism. It was they who, by reshaping the biblical core, laid the foundations of modern Judaism.

There was one single overriding factor which led to this transformation – the destruction of the Temple in Jerusalem by the Romans in the year AD 70. Hitherto the religion of the Jews had been based in matters of worship and ritual on a sacrificial system, and the official representatives of the people before God were the priestly class – the *cohanim*. But once the Temple had gone the sacrificial system disappeared, since it was forbidden according to priestly legislation to offer sacrifice in any place other than the central sanctuary, and, together with the system, the priestly caste lost its overall domination. The priestly hierarchy was to all intents and purposes terminated and Jewish religious leadership became far more 'open' and democratic, depending for its worth on learning rather than birth. The main place of worship for the Jews was now no longer the Temple in Jerusalem but the synagogue of the locality. (The priestly class continues, however, in traditional Judaism, to occupy a special place in synagogue ritual, marriage law, and some other fields.)

It is true, of course, that this transformation did not take place overnight. The synagogue, as an institution, had been founded long before the Roman era. There is also no doubt that scholars in Jewish law, variously described in the tannaitic period as scribes, or rabbis (*rabbi* = my teacher), flourished side by side with the Temple cult for many years before the Temple's destruction. But the dividing line for practical purposes still came at the year 70, when the long preparations for a new form of Hebraism finally came to the fore. The transformation may be epitomized by the story concerning Rabban Yochanan ben Zakkai. When a disciple of his asked despairingly how the Jews could achieve atonement now that sacrifices could no longer be offered, Rabban Yochanan replied that the place of sacrifice would henceforth be taken by deeds of charity.

The rabbis were able to reconcile these changes with the eternal unchanging authority of divine writ through their belief that God, at Mt Sinai, gave Moses not only a written law (*torah she-bi-khtav*) – the

Illustrations pages 395, 418

Illustration page 395

Pentateuch – but also an equally authoritative oral law (*torah she-be-al peh*), which was an interpretation of the former, and which was transmitted intact by Moses's successors right down to rabbinic times. This oral tradition was committed to writing by Rabbi Judah ha-Nasi in the *Mishnah* (literally 'repetition') about AD 200. Therefore, the teachings of the rabbis were authentic and true to the original Torah because of the fidelity of the oral tradition. Indeed, the tradition as a whole was also given the name Torah (literally 'teaching'). This combination of scriptural and oral tradition allowed the rabbis considerable flexibility in their interpretation of the Bible, and made Judaism into an extremely resilient and sensitive instrument for the expression of religious experience.

The Great Influence of the Bible

The influence of the Bible on later Jewish writing cannot be exaggerated. It is as if all subsequent religious literary activity among Jews were but an extension of the scriptural word. The Jewish attitude to the Bible may be summarized by the statement in the *Ethics of the Fathers* (v:25): 'Turn it, and turn it, for everything is in it; contemplate it, and grow old and grey over it, and do not stir from it. You can follow no better course than this.' New ideas and attitudes were continually being discovered in the biblical text, new inspiration derived from it, further elaboration embroidered round it. And the whole was, and is, a labour of love, as well as a religious duty.

Illustration page 396

Midrash, or biblical interpretation, was originally of two types: halakhic (i.e. legal) and aggadic (homiletic and anecdotal). And these two types, which were mostly written anonymously, existed side by side for many centuries, so that Judaism possesses a rich anthology of Bible interpretation, which provided a foundation for later rabbinic commentators. These commentators were able to use the Bible as a medium for expressing their own personal religious ideas.

The Mishnah

The *Mishnah* was a systematization of previous attempts to summarize the heterogeneous mass of custom, concept and legislation which had grown up among the Jews in the centuries before its compilation. But at the same time it bears the stamp of a mastermind whose intention it was to formulate Jewish law for posterity, and shield it from the destruction threatened by political upheaval and persecution. The *Mishnah* comprises six orders (*sedarim*) and each order is subdivided into a number of tractates (*massekhtot*) on individual subjects. The six orders are: *Zeraim* (Seeds) – mainly agricultural legislation, but including an important tractate on the liturgy; *Moed* (Festivals); *Nashim* (Women); *Nezikin* (Damages), i.e. civil law, but containing also a collection of moral and theological statements; *Kodashim* (Sacred Things) – legislation connected mainly with the Temple; and *Tohorot* (Cleannesses). Besides the *Mishnah* there existed in this period other legal traditions, called *baraitot*, which were taken into account by later rabbis when they, in turn, attempted to standardize Jewish tradition.

The *Mishnah* reflects many different opinions and often does not make a firm decision in matters where rabbinic authorities conflict. This, together with the fact that new traditions were constantly springing up, made it necessary for the book to be subjected to intensive study and commentary. This was done in the schoolrooms of Palestine and Babylonia, and their discussions and decisions formed the basis of the two versions of the *Talmud*: the Palestinian (or the Jerusalem) *Talmud*, and the Babylonian *Talmud*.

Each *Talmud* (literally 'teaching' consists of the *Mishnah* together with the comments upon and elucidation of it (called *Gemara*, literally 'completion'). The Babylonian (completed *c.* 500) is more comprehensive than the Palestinian and has served as the foundation for Jewish law and practice since that time. The *Talmuds* and other contemporary rabbinic literary works contain not only law but also a great deal of theological and ethical discussion, as well as historical and anecdotal material; for the rabbis were concerned with the broader and more fundamental moral issues of their times, as well as with the minutiae of the law. Problems such as the conflict between individual freedom and divine foreknowledge, the question of evil, immortality and the life after death, the nature and destiny of man, the will of God, and the role of the people of Israel, all these were thoroughly investigated, and the resulting statements and discussions provide some of the finest Jewish religious literature ever composed. This period also witnessed an efflorescence of liturgical writing.

Development of the Law

After the completion of the Babylonian *Talmud*, Jewish law continued to develop in two major areas. Firstly, new legal decisions had to be made in those circumstances which were not covered by earlier legislation. Secondly, the unwieldy mass of rabbinic law needed to be arranged in a way which would enable a student to consult it with comparative ease. The first requirement was met by the growth of *responsa* (Latin 'replies') literature. Questions on Jewish practice were addressed to the Geonim, as the leaders of Babylonian Jewry were called, and later to other acknowledged rabbinic authorities, and the questions together with the replies have often been preserved. The result was a body of legal decisions which were to act as guide and precedent for future discussion. This activity has continued to the present day. The *responsa* of rabbis the world over have been collected into several hundreds of volumes, and they shed light on, among other things, the daily lives, social circumstances, and religious practices of the Jews. They are therefore indispensable to the historian of the Jewish people.

Codes

The second problem – that of the unmanageable proportions of the legal material – was solved by the codification of the law. The first major systematic code of the whole material was produced by the Spaniard Moses Maimonides (1135-1204), the greatest Jewish thinker of medieval times, who spent most of his life in Egypt. This code was called the *Mishneh Torah* (Repetition of the Law). The author

Left A scroll containing the Torah, the 'Five Books' supposedly written by Moses. The Jews are traditionally known as the people of the Book, and their sacred literature has had a great effect on religions which came after them, notably Christianity and Islam. The Jewish Museum, New York.

Below Ezekiel's vision of the Valley of Bones in *Ezekiel* xxxvii, as represented in the synagogue at Dura-Europos, copied by Herbert J. Gute. Yale University Art Gallery, New Haven, Connecticut.

Left Synagogue architecture was influenced by the cultures with which the Jews came in contact. The ancient synagogue at Capernaum in Galilee shows strong Roman influence.

Opposite above left Moses receiving the tablets of the law on Mount Sinai, from the Rothschild *Siddur*. The Library of the Jewish Theological Seminary of America, New York.

Opposite above right Scholars work on fragments of the Dead Sea Scrolls. Since the Six-Day War in 1967, they have been lodged in the Shrine of the Book, Israel Museum, Jerusalem.

Opposite below An ideal hiding-place for the treasures of the ascetic Qumran community before they were wiped out by the Romans in AD 68. The Dead Sea Scrolls were rediscovered in 1947 by a goat-herd.

Below A relief on the Arch of Titus in the Roman Forum, showing the aftermath of the Jewish Revolt: spoils from the ravaged temple of Jerusalem are carried in procession at Titus's triumph.

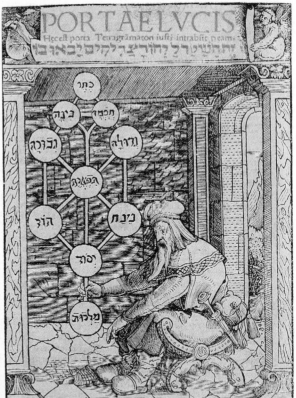

Above A synagogue school in the Mea Shearim quarter of Jerusalem. Constant discussion and analysis of the scriptures as the source of knowledge and as a guide to conduct has long been an essential Jewish practice.

Above right A Jewish kabbalist holding the Tree of Life, from the frontispiece of *Portae Lucis* by Paulus Ricius (1516). The ten spheres of the tree represent the emanations from God.

Right A thirteen-year-old boy in a reform synagogue in Jerusalem becomes *bar-mitsvah*, and is held to be an adult, responsible for fulfilling the commandments of the Torah.

states that it was originally intended to spare the student the trouble of picking a way through talmudic argument. But it met with vehement opposition from critics who accused Maimonides of giving his own opinions unsupported by argument, of failure to quote sources, and also of introducing philosophical matters which were not part of the original legal system. Nevertheless, the *Mishneh Torah* soon established itself as a work of erudition and lucidity.

As an authority, however, it was superseded by a later code, the *Shulchan Arukh* (Prepared Table) of Rabbi Jospeh Karo (1488-1575). Karo was born in Toledo, but grew up in Asia Minor, and later settled in Safed in Palestine. After an exhaustive study of two earlier codes, that of Maimonides, and the *Arba'ah Turim* of Jacob ben Asher (1270-1343), he published his own code for the use of students. It was at first criticized by the Ashkenazim (i.e. Jews of northern and eastern Europe), who alleged that the code was based only on the practice of the Sefardim (Mediterranean Jews), and therefore could not be accepted by the totality of world Jewry. But, after the Polish rabbi Moses Isserles (1525-1572) had added to the code his own comments, which included references to Ashkenazi ritual and practice, the code was universally accepted as authoritative, and it has remained so for traditional Jews down to this day.

Karaites

While these internal developments were taking place in the field of *halakhah* (Jewish law), disputes with Jewish sects, as well as relationships with other peoples and other faiths, compelled the rabbis to continue to rethink their theology, and to study their traditions from new points of view.

While the Samaritans remained an ever-diminishing group whose links with Judaism became more and more tenuous, a new sect emerged in the eighth century in Persia, called the Karaites (more exactly *benei mikra* – adherents to [literally 'children of'] Scripture). This sect denied the validity of the rabbinic oral tradition, and based its ideas and its practice solely on the written word of Scripture, as communicated by God to Moses. This involved the Karaites in departures from rabbinic practice. They refused to allow any lighting on the Sabbath; they did not observe the post-biblical festival of Chanukkah; and they were more restrictive in their dietary laws and in their marriage regulations.

The growth of this sect, therefore, threatened to undermine that very unity of Jewish thought and practice which the Geonim were endeavouring to preserve, as well as imperilling the basic structure of rabbinic Judaism. The Rabbanites (as the opponents of the Karaites were called) did all that they could in polemical writing and in legal ordinance to counter this threat. This meant, however, that they had often to fight the Karaites on their own ground, the ground of Scripture, and this entailed a new objective study of the Torah, using all the tools of grammar which were available to them. Sa'adia (882-942), the most distinguished of the Geonim, was among the first to adopt this new approach to the Bible. He compiled a lexicon, translated the Bible into Arabic, and also wrote commentaries in Arabic to a number of biblical books.

Sa'adia's lead in composing a personal, thoroughgoing commentary on the Bible was followed by others. The foremost among them were: Rashi (Rabbi Solomon ben Isaac of Troyes, 1040-1105), whose work is printed in every edition of the rabbinic Bible, and characterized by a laconic style and a humble piety; Abraham ibn Ezra of Spain (1089-1164), who concentrated on literal and grammatical elucidation, but who also added lengthy disquisitions of a philosophical and astrological character; and Moses ben Nachman (Nachmanides) of Gerona (1194-1270), who was of a more mystical frame of mind. Scores of other commentaries have been written to the Bible, and the works of the major commentators have themselves been the objects of elucidation and interpretation – all with the aim of clarifying the word of God for successive generations of Jews.

The Karaites increased in numbers gradually throughout the Middle Ages, reaching as far west as Spain and as far north as Lithuania. Their numbers were drastically reduced as a result of Nazi persecution in the Second World War and only a few thousand now remain. Their direct influence on modern Judaism has been only minimal.

Further Confrontations

Just as confrontation with the Karaites caused 'normative' Jews to re-examine the Bible, so disputation with other faiths, particularly Christianity and the younger religion of Islam, caused the Jews to re-examine their theology, and to review it in the light of contemporary philosophy. This concerned more than the problem of public disputation with protagonists from the two rival faiths, which consisted usually of charge and counter-charge concerning differing interpretations of crucial scriptural verses. What was at stake was the validity of a revealed religion when challenged by the revelations claimed by other faiths and by knowledge of the world arrived at by the use of human reason. Judaism saw itself threatened from three sources: Christianity, Islam, and a man-centred philosophy.

The Rise of Jewish Philosophy

Although the early work of the Alexandrian Jew Philo (c. 20 BC-AD 40) sought to bridge the gulf between revelation and reason by the extensive use of philosophy in an allegorical interpretation of Scripture, no systematic attempt to present a reasoned Jewish theology was made until the Middle Ages. The Karaites, indeed, were among the first to attempt to accommodate the results of Greek philosophical enquiry, and their work, at least partially, motivated Sa'adia to write (in Arabic) his *Sefer Emunot ve-Deot* (Book of Beliefs and Opinions), the first major Jewish philosophical treatise.

Sa'adia, very much influenced by Islamic philosophers, states that the truths of religion may be arrived at by reason alone and, indeed, that it is a religious duty to use one's reason in order to verify those truths, but that it is a mark of God's love for humankind that he granted them, both learned and unlearned alike, immediate awareness of those truths through revelation. Sa'adia proceeds to discuss creation, the nature of God, divine justice and foreknowledge, repentance and immortality. He thereby set the pattern for future works of this genre including the foremost of them – the *Moreh Nevukhim* (Guide for the Perplexed) of Moses Maimonides.

This book had immense influence on subsequent Jewish thinkers (and on some Christian scholars too, including Thomas Aquinas). It is marked by a rationalism which was considered extreme by many of his contemporaries. Maimonides attempted to show that traditional Jewish theology could be reconciled with the prevailing Aristotelian philosophy of his time (i.e. an Islamic interpretation of Aristotle). In order to do this he reinterpreted both biblical and rabbinic texts in a severely rationalistic way, maintaining that miracles were not an interruption in the natural process, that prophecy could be accorded to any who were both intellectually and morally prepared for it, that the scriptural human encounter with the divine took place in a vision or dream and not as literally described. He even went so far as to say that if it could be proved rationally that God created the world from pre-existent matter then the Bible would have to be reinterpreted. He also gave rational explanations for the observance of the commandments. His ideas were not accepted without a great deal of discussion and debate throughout Mediterranean Jewry, but his work gradually established itself as the authoritative medieval philosophical presentation of Judaism.

Philosophy in the Middle Ages

The flourishing of Jewish philosophy in the Middle Ages, which involved many rabbis in addition to those mentioned, shows that Judaism, even in this period, was not concerned only with the minutiae of the law, as has been commonly supposed. That it has tended to give this impression is due to a number of factors. Firstly, the Jews' *raison d'être* was to perform the *mitsvot* (commandments), i.e. to fulfil the word of God as revealed in the Torah, and this could be accomplished more tangibly in the practical matters regulated by law than by philosophical or dogmatic assertion. Secondly, it should be remembered that the 'law' regulated the moral and ethical life, as well as specifically ritual practice, although the latter being more distinctive has naturally appeared to be the more dominant feature. Thirdly, for purposes of Jewish identity and association with the community, the practice of Judaism was a more objective criterion than a theological state of mind. Although various attempts have been made to formulate a Jewish creed, Jews have generally resisted the imposition of a system of belief as distinct from a system of practice. This has resulted in a remarkable freedom of thought among Jews coexisting with, until recent times, a uniformity of practice.

Jewish Mysticism

Yet, concomitant with both the legal and philosophical preconceptions of medieval Jewry, was the mystical aspiration of the Jews, which assumed many forms in different communities of the European and Mediterranean world. *Kabbalah* (literally 'tradition') is the word customarily used for this aspect of Judaism, although it is sometimes limited to describe the Jewish mysticism which developed particularly in thirteenth-century Spain and which had such a great influence on subsequent generations – specifically in sixteenth-century Palestine. Jewish mysticism, like many other kinds of religious mysticism, seeks as its end personal union with God, achieved through spiritual exercise, meditation and contemplation. But there is, in addition, what one might call a social messianic purpose behind this aspiration for union – a belief that the mystic can influence God in his way with the world, and so hasten the time of redemption.

The origins of Jewish mysticism may be seen in those areas of biblical literature which lend themselves in particular to imaginative elaboration, and which, from early rabbinic times, were accorded a special place in the study of Torah, namely the first chapter of *Genesis* and the first chapter of *Ezekiel* – the creation and the chariot. The mystery of creation, which is founded basically on the problem of how a transcendent incorporeal God can create a temporal physical world, gradually resolved itself into the construction of a system of divine emanation, much influenced by Neo-Platonic ideas, by which the world emerges through successive stages, each one further removed from the godhead. These stages or spheres (*sefirot*) were also accorded the status of divine attributes. The mystery of the chariot was concerned with the nature of God himself, and the human contemplation of God. The 'ascent to the chariot' consisted of the journey of the soul of the mystic through the various celestial palaces to the throne of God. Preparation for such a journey involved prayer and meditation, particularly on the letters of the Torah, as well as bodily exercises.

Illustration page 396 The literature of Jewish mysticism is very extensive. We may single out for special mention: the *Sefer Yetsirah* (Book of Creation), a seminal work written before the sixth century, which describes how the world was created by means of the twenty-two letters and ten numbers of the Hebrew language; the *Sefer Hasidim* (Book of the Pious), written by Judah the Pious (d. 1217), which is a compilation of mystical thought, legend, and homiletical material, reflecting the inner life of the Jews of the Rhineland, and which is distinguished by a marked penitential character; and the *Sefer ha-Zohar* (Book of Splendour), a collection of writings, the core of which is a mystical commentary on different parts of the Bible, composed mainly by Moses de Leon at the end of the thirteenth century in Spain, but attributed to the second-century rabbi, Simeon ben Yohai. The *Zohar* became the fundamental work of *kabbalah*, and future mystical literary creativity was an extension and interpretation of it, extremely wide-ranging in character. A distinct mystical school grew up in Safed in Palestine round Joseph Caro, Moses Cordovero, and particularly Isaac Luria (1534-1572) and his pupil Hayyim Vital.

The Hasidim

One of the results of the growth of this mystical tradition was the emergence of the *hasidim* of central Europe at the end of the eighteenth century. The founder of the hasidic movement was Israel ben Eliezer (d. 1760), known as Baal Shem Tov (or Besht). Based on Lurianic *kabbalah*, hasidism preaches the striving for communion with God through the cultivation and experience of joyful fervour in prayer, study, and the natural world. It emphasized the traditional Jewish concept of simple delight in the service of God, and appealed particularly to those Jews in eastern Europe who were unable to participate in the legal dialectic of traditional study of the Torah.

The leader of each hasidic community, known as the *tsaddik* (the righteous one), was credited with the possession of a special relationship to the divine spirit, and often with the power of working miracles. The movement was opposed by the more learned traditional rabbis, who perceived in it the danger of pantheism and the discouragement of learning in favour of an ignorant piety. But the movement flourished quickly, and, despite the destruction of countless hasidic communities by the Nazis, it still boasts of thousands of adherents, particularly in the United States and Israel.

Illustrations page 416

Jewish Belief

We may at this stage give a brief outline of the major beliefs and practices of Judaism, which have for the most part remained unchanged in traditional orthodox Judaism since the codification of the *Shulchan Arukh* in the sixteenth century.

Judaism holds that there is one eternal God, who created the universe, and who remains master of it. God is both omnipotent and all-loving. He created human beings as free agents, giving them the ability to choose between good and evil. ('Everything is in the hand of Heaven, except the fear of Heaven' – Talmud Berakhot 33b.) God communicates with humans through revelation, and humans can communicate with God through prayer and meditation. Through these media of communication God has given human beings a divine law, the Torah, the fulfilment of which will hasten the establishment of God's kingdom on earth. This will be heralded by the arrival of a personal Messiah, who will be human, and descended from the house of David. The Jewish people have a special role in this divine scheme, since it was to them that God revealed his Torah through Moses on Mt Sinai.

Obedience to the Torah is central to Judaism, and it is enacted through fulfilment of the commandemnts, both moral and ritual, of which the Torah is composed (traditionally there are 248 positive and 365 negative commandments). Although in different ages attempts have been made to explain the reasons for, and purposes of, the *mitsvot* (commandments), no rationalization can equal in effect the original concept of the *mitsvah* as being simply the expression of God's will, and as such binding on the believing Jew. The Jews therefore have a duty in the sight of both people and God to lead a life in accord with the divine will, and through that life to bear witness to God and his purpose in the world. This is the kernel of the idea of the Election of Israel.

All People are Equal

In the Jewish view of society all people are created equal. As the rabbinic tradition has it: 'the first man was created alone, so that none of his descendants would be able to say to another, "my father was greater than your father".' Therefore each human being is precious and has dignity simply because he or she was created by God in his image. This underlies the Jewish conception of each person's relationship to his or her fellows – a relationship ideally based on love, respect and understanding. The Torah commands that particular concern should be shown to the under-privileged, the sick, the widow, the orphan, the stranger, the distressed, the captive and the poor. This is emphasized through constant reference to the history of the Jews themselves: 'you know the heart of a stranger, seeing you were strangers in the land of Egypt' (*Exodus* xxiii:9).

People, being free, have the ability to master their evil inclinations. They are born with propensities for both good and ill, and do not 'inherit' a burden of sin. The world in which they are born is a good world, created by God, and Judaism requires of the Jews that they enjoy the bounty of this world, and use its gifts as far as lies in they power for the betterment of humankind, and the service of God. Judaism is, therefore, a world-affirming, not a world-denying faith. Salvation is to be achieved in this world and through this world.

Belief in the physical resurrection of the dead and the immortality of the soul have for long been cardinal tenets of traditional Judaism, but there is far more emphasis on the care of body and soul in this world than on preparation for eternity (one of the most frequent images of heaven is that of the righteous sitting with crowns on their heads, studying the Torah, with the Holy One as their master).

The moral duties of the Jew are aptly summarized in this extract from the *Mishnah Peah*, ch. 1, which is included for reading in the traditional morning service:

'These are the things, the fruits of which a man enjoys in this world, while the stock remains for him for the world to come: viz., honouring father and mother, the practice of charity, timely attendance at the house of study morning and evening, hospitality to wayfarers, visiting the sick, dowering the bride, attending the dead to the grave, devotion in prayer, and making peace between man and his fellow; but the study of the Torah leads to them all.'

The Life of the Jew

The welfare of society depends to a great extent on the welfare of the individual unit of that society – the family. Judaism lays great stress on the desirability of preserving a loving and peaceful relationship within the family, an aim whose realization is aided by the fact that the home, even more than the synagogue, is the chief centre of Jewish religious life. The festivals are celebrated mainly in the home, and the many distinctive features of Jewish family life help to ensure its cohesiveness. Parents, as well as setting high moral standards for their children, are enjoined particularly to educate them in the study of the Torah, a knowledge of which is indispensable for the correct observance of the *mitsvot*.

Childhood

Male children are circumcised at the age of eight days, a rite which derives from the command given to Abraham (*Genesis* xvii) to circumcise himself and his son Ishmael. The ritual is therefore called the 'covenant of circumcision' (*brit milah*), since the child is brought into the covenant which God made with 'Abraham, our father'. The operation is performed by a *mohel* (or circumsiser), and the prayer is offered that the child 'may commit himself to the Torah, to marriage, and to good deeds'. The first-born male child, who, according to biblical law (see *Numbers* iii:11-13, and elsewhere), was to be devoted to God, is symbolically redeemed from the *cohen* (priest) in a ceremony called *pidyon ha-ben* (redemption of the first-born son).

Formal Jewish education, in addition to that which children receive within the family, commences usually at the age of five or six, when they are brought to the religion school (*cheder*, literally 'room') attached to the local synagogue. Whereas in medieval times this would be the focus of their entire education, for most Jewish children today the *cheder* is regarded as an adjunct to their daily secular instruction. However, both in the United States and Europe, there is a growing movement to establish Jewish day-schools, many of which have already been founded.

The age of majority for girls, according to talmudic tradition, is twelve years and one day, and for boys thirteen years and one day. At the age of thirteen the boy becomes *bar-mitsvah* (son of the commandment), that is, he is regarded as entirely responsible for his religious acts and liable to fulfil all the commandments of the Torah. Indeed, in talmudic times the technical term used for him was *bar-onshin* (son of punishment), meaning that he was liable to punishment for transgression of the Torah. The ceremony associated with the attainment of the age of *bar-mitsvah* originated later than the talmudic period. In it the boy is 'called up' to the reading of the Torah in the synagogue, and reads himself from the Hebrew text, and sometimes the prophetical portion also. This symbolizes his graduation to adult status in the eyes of the Law and of the assembled congregation. Since study of the Torah is an essential, ongoing process for the Jew, *bar-mitsvah* represents only one stage in Jewish education and not its culmination.

Illustration page 396

Marriage

Marriage (*kiddushin*) is one of the most important of the practical *mitsvot*. The rabbis emphasized that the first commandment in the Torah was 'bear fruit and multiply' (*Genesis* i:28), and that it was God's will that the first man should be provided with a helpmate. Marriage is essential both for procreation and for the mutual comfort and companionship of man and woman. Marriage is for the Jew the 'natural' state, and a tradition of celibacy existed from time to time only in sects which were on the periphery of Judaism, such as the Essenes. Generally speaking, a marriage may be contracted between two Jews (a Jew being defined as a child of a Jewish mother) provided that neither of them is already married, and provided that there are no obstacles deriving from a consanguineous relationship between them. (Marriage between cousins, and between uncle and niece is permitted.) Among the more important ritual prohibitions is that of a marriage between a *cohen* (priest) and a divorcee or a proselyte.

Jewish marriage is essentially a legal contract entered into willingly by two parties in the presence of valid witnesses. The main element of the marriage ceremony is the giving of an object of value, usually a ring, to the bride by the bridegroom, followed by his declaring: 'Behold, you are betrothed to me by this ring according to the law of Moses and Israel.' The bride and groom share a cup of wine, and the bridegroom breaks a glass, to symbolize the destruction of the Temple. The marriage takes place beneath a canopy (*chuppah* – a word which has come to signify the ceremony as a whole), which is a symbol of the couple's first home and also of the spirit of God which hovers over them. The bridegroom gives the bride a marriage document (*ketubah*), duly witnessed, in which she is granted certain property rights should he predecease or divorce her.

Jewish marriage may be dissolved by divorce. The grounds for divorce are variously enumerated by the rabbis, but the general consensus is that it is a procedure which is much to be regretted, and which should be adopted only as a last resort. 'If a man divorces his first wife, even the very altar sheds tears. . . .' (Talmud Gittin 90b). In the divorce procedure the husband gives his wife, in the presence of witnesses, a 'bill of divorcement' (*get*), in which he states that she is free to be married to another. It should be stressed that although, as one would expect from legislation stemming from the ancient world, the wife does not enjoy the same rights as the husband in matters of divorce, nevertheless strenuous efforts were made through the institution of the *ketubah* to afford the wife some protection.

Mourning

The rites of mourning are detailed and specific. The dead body is washed and clothed in a white shroud. Burial (cremation is prohibited) is effected as soon as possible after death. The prescribed 7-day period (*shivah*) of mourning commences after the funeral. The mourners remain at home, sit on low stools (a custom derived from the biblical rite of sitting on the ground as a sign of mourning), and are 'comforted' by visitors. Evening prayers are said in the home on each evening except the Sabbath, when the mourners leave their home to attend the synagogue. During the prayers the mourners' *kaddish* (Aramaic for 'sanctified') is said. Less rigorous periods of mourning follow up to eleven months after the funeral. It is then customary to consecrate a head-stone in the cemetery in memory of the dead

Above A Jewish family gathered together for the *seder* or Passover feast. On the table can be seen the unleavened bread which commemorates the hasty way in which the Israelites left Egypt.

Right A seventeenth-century print showing the various ways in which a *sukkah* could be built. These structures were designed to remind the Jews of how they had lived in the desert.

person. The anniversary of the death is marked each year, and relatives visit the graves of the dead in the period preceding the High Holy Days.

Festivals and Holy Days

The Jewish festivals and holy days present a consistent phenomenon of what one might call 'creative assimilation'. Their origins are often pre-Hebraic, being based on Canaanite or Babylonian prototypes. But when they were adopted by the Hebrews they were transformed in the course of time into apparently indigenous Jewish celebrations, purified of idolatrous and orgiastic elements, and imbued with Jewish historical experience.

The Jewish calendar is lunar, consisting of twelve months, each commencing at the new moon, of twenty-nine or thirty days each, viz. *Nisan* (March-April), *Iyyar, Sivan, Tammuz, Av, Ellul, Tishri, Marcheshvan, Kislev, Tevet, Shevat, Adar*. In order to ensure that the agricultural festivals are celebrated during the correct season of the year an additional month, *Adar Sheni* (Second Adar) is intercalated after the first Adar, approximately every three years. This ensures the correspondence of the lunar year of 354 days with the solar year of 365¼ days.

Traditional Jews outside the land of Israel observe the festivals (except the Day of Atonement) for one day longer than the period prescribed in the Torah. This is because communities a long distance from Jerusalem could not always be sure that the messenger, who came from Jerusalem to announce the advent of the new month, would arrive in time for them to observe the festival on the correct date. This extra day has been discontinued by Reform Jews.

Every festival (Hebrew *Yom Tov*, literally 'good day') and sabbath begins and ends at dusk, following the biblical pattern ('there was evening and there was morning – the first day').

The Sabbath

Illustration page 405

The Sabbath (Hebrew *shabbat*, i.e. day of rest), the most important day in the Jewish calendar, begins on Friday evening, the eve of the seventh day. It commemorates God's completion of the creation of the universe, and his rest after his labours (*Exodus* xxxi:12-17). It is instituted in the home by the lighting of the sabbath candles and the recital of *kiddush* (sanctification), the benedictions over wine and bread and over the Sabbath day itself. Parents customarily bless their children. It is a day both of abstention from work, a subject of much elaboration in rabbinic sources, and of study of the Torah. The Sabbath is terminated by the ceremony of *havdalah* (division), which involves the dousing of a candle in wine and the smelling of sweet spices, which symbolize the beauty of the Sabbath as it departs.

The Days of Awe

The Days of Awe (*Yamin Noraim*) are the first ten days of *Tishri*. The first two days of *Tishri* comprise the New Year (*Rosh ha-Shanah*) and the tenth day is the Day of Atonement commonly known as *Yom Kippur*. The period as a whole is known as the Ten Days of Penitence

(*Aseret Yemei Teshuvah*). The new year festival was originally called 'a memorial proclaimed with the blast of horns' (*Leviticus* xxiii:24), and was apparently not connected with the new year itself, a designation which does not occur in the Pentateuch. And even after the festival came to be known as *Rosh ha-Shanah* the emphasis remained not on the celebration of the new year but on the reaffirmation of the kingship of God, and on the inauguration of a period of penitence.

The day is distinguished by the blowing of a ram's horn in the synagogue, which reflects perhaps the original idea of a trumpet fanfare accompanying the 'coronation' of God, but which was later interpreted as a call to repentance, and as a recollection of the fidelity of Abraham who, during the episode of the binding of Isaac, sacrificed a ram which he had seen 'caught by its horns in a thicket' (*Genesis* xxii:13). This passage is in fact read during the *Rosh ha-Shanah* service.

The Day of Atonement is the most solemn day in the Jewish calendar. It is a day of fasting, this being the traditional interpretation of 'affliction of soul' (*Leviticus* xvi:29; xxiii:27). The rabbis stress the importance of true contrition as an essential accompaniment to fasting, which by itself is not sufficient to obtain atonement. The service in the synagogue continues throughout the day, and is characterized by a recapitulation of the duties of the high priest on the Day of Atonement in the Temple, and by the blowing of the horn at the end of the service with the communal affirmation that 'the Lord, He is God'. The Book of Jonah is read. Just as in biblical times the priest asked for forgiveness both for himself and for the community of Israel, so the Day of Atonement affords opportunity for both personal and communal repentance. The eve of the day is commonly called *Kol Nidrei* (literally 'all vows'), these being the opening words of a prayer which asks for the nullification of all vows made under duress. Although not written originally with this in view, it came to reflect the situation of those Jews who were converted to other faiths by compulsion.

'Pilgrimage Festivals'

On the three pilgrimage festivals, *Pesach*, *Shavuot*, and *Sukkot*, the Jews were commanded to go to Jerusalem to participate in the worship at the Temple (*Deuteronomy* xvi:16). They have additionally in common both an agricultural and a historical significance.

Passover (*Pesach*) is an eight-day festival beginning on the fifteenth of *Nisan*, the first two and the last two days being full festival days (*Yamim Tovim*). It originally marked the advent of the barley harvest, and was a spring festival, and a memory of this is still retained in its observance. But its chief purpose is to celebrate and, to some extent, to recreate the Exodus from Egypt, when the Israelites emerged from bondage to freedom. Another name for the festival, occurring in the special *kiddush* for the day, is 'the season of our freedom'. It has two main features: the abstention from eating leaven during the whole period of the festival, this being a reminder of the fact that the

Israelites left Egypt in such haste that the dough they were preparing did not have time to rise, and, secondly, the celebration of the *seder* (literally 'order') in the home on the first two nights.

The *seder* is fundamentally a festive meal at which the story of the Exodus is narrated by the head of the family to the children. The special prayer-book used is the *haggadah* (literally 'narration'). The story is introduced by the questions of the children and illustrated by the use of symbolic foods. It is customary to invite 'strangers' as well as members of the family to the table, and the whole atmosphere is one of gaiety and thanksgiving, as if the participants 'had just come out of Egypt'. The *seder* accentuates the role of God in history, and is typical of all the major commemorations of historical events in Judaism in that it attributes achievement to the power of God and not of man (cf. the festival of *Chanukkah*). The *seder* concludes with the singing of songs of a popular character. It is customary to read the *Song of Songs* at this festival.

Illustrations pages 405, 406

The second pilgrimage festival is *Shavuot* (literally 'weeks'). It is a two-day festival beginning on the sixth of *Sivan*, seven weeks after the second day of Passover. Hence its other name of Pentecost (fiftieth day). *Shavuot* was originally a celebration of the wheat harvest. An indication of this is the reading of the *Book of Ruth* at this time. But it is now observed as the anniversary of the revelation of the Torah to Moses at Mt Sinai, another name for the festival being the 'Season of the giving of our Torah'.

Sukkot (Tabernacles) is the third and last of the pilgrimage festivals. It is a nine-day festival beginning on the fifteenth of *Tishri*. As with Passover, the first two and the last two days are full festival days. It commemorates the autumn harvest, particularly of fruit, and in addition it is a memorial of the way in which the Hebrews in the wilderness depended on the bounty of God, living as they did in insecure habitations. The festival is observed in the home mainly by the building of a *sukkah*, a temporary structure, with a roof through which one should be able to see the stars. During the festival the family should regard this dwelling as their permanent abode in order to attempt to recreate the conditions which the Hebrews experienced in the desert.

Illustration page 406

In the synagogue the worshippers carry the *arba'ah minim* (four kinds), i.e. specimens of palm, myrtle, willow and citron, in accordance with the rabbinic interpretation of *Leviticus* xxiii:40. The meaning of this practice has been explained in many ways both beautiful and profound. The ninth day of the festival is designated *Simchat Torah* (Rejoicing in the Torah). At this time the annual cycle of the readings from the Torah begins anew, the last section of *Deuteronomy* and the first of *Genesis* being read successively. It is a time of great merriment and joy and is usually characterized by singing and dancing in procession with the scrolls of the Torah. Another name for the festival is 'the season of our rejoicing' but, as if to temper the mood of the festival, the *Book of Ecclesiastes* is read.

Illustration page 405

Other Festivals

The festival of *Purim* occurs on the fourteenth of Adar. It is based on the *Book of Esther*, which is read in the synagogue at this time. Basically, the festival is an occasion for thanksgiving for the salvation of the Jews from the persecution of Haman, a figure who, even more than Pharoah, is seen as a representation of all persecutors of the Jews through the ages. It is customary to send gifts to the poor, in accordance with a command in the *Book of Esther*.

Chanukkah (Dedication) is post-biblical in origin. It is an eight-day festival beginning on the twenty-fifth of Kislev. Since, like *Purim*, it is not an observance which is enjoined by the Torah itself, it does not partake of the nature of a *Yom Tov* and regulations concerning abstention from work do not apply. It commemorates the great victory of the Maccabees over the forces of Antiochus Epiphanes, who in 168 BC strove to destroy the Jewish faith. The observance of the festival, however, is built not upon the military victory as such, but upon a legend which tells of how a one-day supply of consecrated oil which the Maccabees used for the re-dedication of the desecrated Temple lasted for eight days until more could be obtained. Consequently in Jewish homes a candelabrum (*menorah*) is lit, consisting of eight candles (together with an additional 'servant' candle), one candle being lit on the first night of the festival, two on the second, and so on.

Illustration page 415

There are other fast days in the Jewish calendar apart from the Day of Atonement. The most important of these is *Tishah b'Av* (Ninth of Av) which commemorates the destruction of both the first and second Temples in 586 BC and AD 70 respectively. The *Book of Lamentations* is read, and prayers recited for the end of the Exile and the restoration of the Temple. In latter years there has been a tendency to commemorate also on this day the death at the hands of the Nazis of six million Jews during the Second World War.

A day which has seen something of a revival in recent years is *Tu b'Shvat* (fifteenth of Shvat – the New Year for Trees), the celebration of which has become associated with the planting of trees in modern Israel.

Dietary Laws

An area of ritual observance which is of great importance to the traditional orthodox Jew is that of *kashrut* (literally 'that which is fitting' is the noun, *kasher* or *kosher*, fit, being the adjective), a term used for the dietary laws. These are very extensive, but may be summarized as follows. The following may be eaten: animals that both chew the cud and have cloven hooves; fish that have both fins and scales; birds that do not fall into the category of those prohibited in *Leviticus* xii. Animals and birds must be slaughtered in a prescribed manner (*shechitah*). Meat derived from other sources is *terefah* (literally 'torn') and may not be eaten. Milk and meat products should be separated, and the utensils, etc. connected with them. This is derived from *Exodus* xxiii:19 – 'you shall not boil a kid in its mother's milk'. The hind-quarters of animals may not be eaten unless the sciatic nerve

is first removed (derived from *Genesis* xxxii:33). The blood must be
thoroughly drained away (cf. *Genesis* ix:4).

The Synagogue

The synagogue is the centre of public worship and social life for the Jewish community. The word 'synagogue' is Greek in origin, and means 'place of assembly'. This is paralleled by the Hebrew *bet ha-knesset*. It is also designated as *bet ha-tefillah* (house of prayer) and *bet ha-midrash* (house of study). These three names aptly summarize the main purposes of the synagogue.

The chief feature of the synagogue building is the ark (*aron ha-kodesh*), which is basically a cupboard in which are housed the scrolls of the Torah (*sifrei torah*). Each scroll contains the Hebrew Pentateuch, hand-written on parchment. The ark, since medieval times, has been located on that wall of the synagogue which faces Jerusalem. In front of the ark is the perpetual light (*ner tamid*) which symbolizes the eternal presence of God, and also continues the idea of the perpetual altar-fire in the Temple precincts. The conduct of the service proceeds from the *bimah* or *almemar*, a raised platform, which apparently in early times was at one end of the synagogue (and still remains so in most progressive synagogues), but which is now usually placed in the centre of the building. A separation is made between the sexes either by a partition or by the construction of a ladies' gallery. Partly because of medieval legislation which forbade the building of synagogues above a certain height, they are not usually distinguished by their elevation, nor are they normally decorated with pictures or statuary, for fear of transgressing the second commandment. Artistic endeavour was confined to the plan of the edifice itself and to the decoration of the ark and the *almemar*.

Prayer

The original basis for Jewish prayer is to be found in the Bible, and, indeed, a large part of the Jewish liturgy is composed of quotations from the Scriptures, particularly the *Psalms*. Despite the Jew's acknowledgement of God's utter transcendence, there has always existed a very strong, almost personal link between the praying Jew and his God. This sense of close relationship informs the liturgy with an honesty and trust which allows questioning, doubt and dialogue.

There are three set times for prayer: morning (*shacharit*), afternoon (*minchah*) and evening (*ma'ariv*). The basic Jewish prayer is the *shema* ('hear' – from its first word – *Deuteronomy* vi:4-9). This confession of God's unity is recited twice daily, is the first prayer taught to children, and the last to be said by the Jew in his or her lifetime. It is the nearest formulation to a popular creed that Judaism possesses. The *amidah* (literally 'standing'), also called the *tefillah* (prayer), consisted originally of eighteen benedictions (*shemoneh esreh*), now nineteen, recited thrice daily. It is a combination of praise and petition, and affords an opportunity for prayer of a private and personal nature. The *alenu* ('it is our duty'), a third-century prayer, recited at the end of the service, is a strong affirmation of monotheism, and embodies the Jewish hope for the establishment on earth of God's kingdom.

Private prayer may be recited at any time, and in practically any place. Communal prayer should be recited traditionally in the presence of ten adult males (*minyan*, literally 'number'). Male worshippers wear the *tallit* – a prayer shawl – during morning service. The *tallit* has fringes on its four corners (*Numbers* xv:37-41). A smaller version (*tsitsit* or *arba kanfot*) is worn always under the outer clothes. *Tefillin*, small boxes containing the paragraphs of the *shema*, are worn on the forehead and arm during morning weekday prayer to fulfil literally a command in *Deuteronomy* vi:8. For the same reason the *shema* is fastened to the doorposts of a Jewish home in a small receptacle called *mezuzah*. The head is covered during prayer, and orthodox Jews rarely go without some head-covering.

Illustration page 415

Personal prayer and prayer at home are marked not only by the statutory prayers already mentioned but by the recital of grace before and after meals, by the whole range of special Sabbath and festival liturgy and observance, and also by a large number of benedictions to be recited on special occasions (see Singer's Prayer Book pp. 385ff). The prayer book for Sabbath and week-days is called *siddur*, and that for the festivals is called *machzor*.

Modern Trends

Although Judaism of a traditional nature has continued to exert influence upon many Jews and continues the ancient practice of Judaism, to all intents and purposes, as prescribed in the *Shulchan Arukh*, it has had to face new problems in the last two centuries, and to adapt itself to conditions which have been quite different from those of previous Jewish experience. These new circumstances have been brought into being by three main factors: the emancipation of European Jewry and the rise of Reform Judaism; the resurgence of anti-semitism culminating in the Nazi holocaust; and the establishment of the state of Israel.

The Emancipation and the Rise of Reform

Illustration page 415

For many centuries, throughout the medieval period, Jews experienced severe political, social and academic disabilities. Although circumstances varied from one country to another and from one age to another, nevertheless it was generally the case that relationships in Christian countries between Jew and Christian were limited, that Jews were barred from certain trades and professions, and prevented from participating in the normal educational system, both at school and university, and that, furthermore, they were compelled to live in specified areas. (The actual description 'ghetto' however was not used until 1517 in Venice.) They were also often subject to discriminatory taxation. One of the results of this kind of existence was that Jews became inward-looking, more concerned with their own religious traditions, and a deepening of their own Jewish spiritual awareness, than with the outside world.

However, at the end of the eighteenth century and the beginning of the nineteenth, liberal movements swept across Europe, bringing social and political relief to many of the oppressed. The Jews benefited from the implementation of these new liberal ideas, particularly in Germany, France, Britain and the United States. Jews found that they were free to mix socially and intellectually with their non-Jewish neighbours, and were given some voice in political affairs. They were also able, for the first time, to bring contemporary academic objective scholarship to bear upon the sources of Jewish tradition.

This meant that hitherto unchallenged assumptions were now questioned, among them the Mosaic authorship of the Torah, the authenticity of the oral tradition and, hence, the validity of the *Talmud* and the Codes. Great scholars of the calibre of Leopold Zunz, Abraham Geiger, Heinrich Graetz, and Moritz Steinschneider set themselves the task of subjecting the totality of the Jewish achievement to a searching critical enquiry. Together with this new scholarship went an awareness of the need for a new expression of Judaism.

This was demonstrated in the first place in the early nineteenth century in Germany by a demand for the revision of the Jewish form of worship. Hitherto the prayers had been recited entirely in Hebrew, with a sermon in Yiddish, and without instrumental accompaniment. But, gradually, in some congregations, a sermon in the vernacular was introduced, the service was shortened, some prayers were recited in German translation, and the organ was used. This was the beginning of Reform Judaism (also called later Liberal Judaism).

These simple early changes led to more fundamental departures from tradition: an emphasis on the more universal aspects of Judaism which entailed the curtailment of references in the liturgy to the Election of Israel, and to the restoration of the Temple and sacrificial worship; the rejection of the idea of physical resurrection and the coming of a personal messiah; and an expression of the belief in the progressive revelation of God. Greater emphasis came to be placed on the prophetic elements in Judaism in contrast to the rabbinic elements, with a consequent elevation of the ethical above the ritual requirements of the faith. Equality of the sexes was also established in all aspects of Jewish life, including equal educational opportunities for girls and boys.

These developments caused considerable dissension within those communities where they occurred, but reforming tendencies spread rapidly, particularly in Germany and in the United States, where German immigrant Jews belonged mainly to the Reform 'wing'. There are now Reform or Liberal communities in nearly all the countries with a Jewish population, except those of the Communist bloc. The strong Conservative movement in the United States represents a more moderate reform of orthodox Judaism than Reform, while the newer Reconstructionist movement, theologically radical, emphasizes the wider aspects of Jewish culture and civilization.

The New Anti-Semitism

The early reformers were motivated partly by the new ideas concerning the hope for humankind, and the expectation of a speedy

Illustration page 416

realization of the dream of universal peace and human brotherhood, which were characteristic of the age in which they lived. The Age of Enlightenment had seemed to usher in a new era of harmony between Jew and non-Jew. Indeed, a movement had been inaugurated, the Haskalah (Enlightenment) movement, which had affected many Jews in Europe, and been particularly important in Russia in the first half of the nineteenth century. It proposed cultural assimilation with the environment in which its followers lived, and encouraged the writing (in Hebrew) of works in imitation of the contemporary literature of other peoples, giving an impetus to the revival of Hebrew as a living language.

These hopes of reformers and *maskilim* (intellectuals or rationalists) alike were soon to be qualified by the resurgence of anti-semitism, particularly in Germany, Russia and France. This new type of Jewish persecution was based more on concepts of racial superiority (and inferiority), supported by political and economic propaganda, than on specifically religious ideas. European Jewry had been subjected to physical humiliation, torture and death many times in its long history, particularly during the periods of the Crusades, the Spanish Inquisition, and the Chmielnicki massacres in Poland (1648-9). And now in the nineteenth century persecution began anew. Successive attacks against the Jews resulted in large-scale migrations, especially from continental Europe to Britain and the United States.

This new rise of anti-semitism culminated in the Nazi philosophy of Aryan superiority, and of the concept of the 'Final Solution' for the Jewish people living in German-occupied lands during the Second World War. Some six million Jews were exterminated, whole communities were annihilated, academic and religious institutions were destroyed. This was numerically the greatest tragedy that had ever befallen the Jewish people, and the problems that now beset religious thinkers after the holocaust are as profound and demanding as those that faced the rabbis after the destruction of the Temple by the Romans in AD 70.

The Growth of Zionism

One of the ideas of traditional Judaism which had been discarded by the early Reformers was that of the Return to Zion. The new liberal atmosphere prevailing in Europe during the early part of the nineteenth century persuaded them that this was an outdated concept and that their 'home' was the country in which they had been born and reared, and that they had no other national loyalty. But the longing for Zion and Jerusalem, the yearning for the return from Exile, for the gathering of the dispersed Jews, was very deep-seated in the Jewish consciousness, beginning with the promises made to the patriarchs, emphasized during the Babylonian exile, and renewed with vigour after the Roman destruction of the Temple. Judah ha-Levi (1075-1141) in particular made of this concept one of the central themes of his philosophy and his poetry.

The renewal of the persecution of European Jewry at the end of

Left Illegal Jewish immigrants to Palestine wading ashore, having dodged the British Royal Navy's blockade in the late 1930s.

Opposite above left Hasidic Jews in Jerusalem.

Opposite above right Nazi stormtroopers in Berlin enforce the one-day boycott of Jewish citizens on 1 April 1933.

Opposite below A panel of rabbis study the marriage contract at a unique Hasidic wedding in New York. The bride came from a line of miracle-working rabbis.

Below The *kibbutzim*, or communal farms, were the early means of developing arid and uncultivated land in the new state of Israel. Young people still go from all over the world to work on them.

the nineteenth century gave this aspiration a sharper edge. Whereas in previous centuries it had been inextricably linked with a specifically religious orientation, expressed in the hope that God would redeem his people by bringing them back to the Holy Land, it now underwent a more nationalist, political transformation. The Zionist movement was born at the First Zionist Congress of 1897, with Theodor Herzl (1860-1904) as its main inspiration. This movement, whose work culminated in the founding of the state of Israel in 1948, had its spiritual overtones, as evidenced by the work of Rabbi Abraham Isaac Kook (1865-1935), and cultural aspirations, embodied pre-eminently in the work of Asher Ginzberg (known as Achad Ha-Am, 1856-1927). But its fundamental nationalist direction aroused opposition among those Jews who saw their distinctiveness primarily in religious terms.

In latter years, however, there have been few Jews who, whatever their individual philosophies, have not supported their brethren in the state of Israel. In religious terms it would appear that a constructive tension is establishing itself between the Judaism of the Diaspora (or Dispersion), especially that of the United States, and the spiritual consciousness of the Israelis.

Opposite above The Wailing Wall, the remains of the temple in Jerusalem, which was destroyed by the Romans in AD 70. Once the temple had gone, Judaism became a much less centralized religion.

Opposite below A Russian rabbi takes cakes and wine with members of his congregation and the synagogue board. *Illustration page 417*

Illustration page 417

Chapter Twenty

Christianity

Christianity is a way of life, embodied in a corporate society or fellowship and centred on the worship of the One God revealed to the world through Jesus of Nazareth, who lived as a human being for about thirty years in Palestine and was crucified by the Romans at Jerusalem between AD 29 and 33. Christians believe, on the testimony of many contemporary witnesses, that he rose from the dead after three days and was seen by his disciples on numerous occasions during the succeeding forty days, after which he departed whence he came. Thus, Christians do not worship a dead hero, but the living Christ.

During the three years of his earthly ministry of teaching, when he was near to Caesarea Philippi, the ancient Paneion on the slopes of Mt Hermon, the disciple Peter answered his question 'Who do men say that I am?' with the declaration 'Thou art the Christ', i.e. the Messiah, the anointed deliverer, promised to the Jews in the Old Testament (*Matthew* xvi:13, *Mark* viii:29). After his resurrection the apostle Thomas, having first doubted that Jesus was risen, when confronted by Jesus uttered the basic belief of millions of Christians from that day to the present: 'My Lord and my God' (*John* xx:28). Christianity is thus both a historical and a supernatural religion.

It built upon the revelation of the One God given to the Jews and recorded in the Old Testament, but within the first generation of the followers of Jesus it made a tremendous appeal to the non-Jewish or Gentile world of the Hellenized Empire. The Greek language and Greek thought forms were pressed into service by preachers of the new Christian gospel (*euangelion* – good news) from the time of St Paul onwards.

Plato and Aristotle had taught that the time process is unending, each human civilization being succeeded by another, and Stoicism, the most popular philosophy in the first century AD, taught that the universe formed out of the divine fire would be dissolved, after running its course, into the divine fire once again, to be succeeded over and over again by other similar universes for all eternity. Judaism, on the other hand, had taught that this universe is the creation of the one true God, who has throughout its history shown his power (and intervention) through a series of 'mighty acts' which will lead to a final consummation in the future – 'the day of the Lord' (*Isaiah* ii:12, *Joel* i:15, *Zephaniah* i:7, *Malachi* iii:17) – when evil will be conquered and a new world will dawn, in which God will reign as king of peace and righteousness.

This idea of a final goal of history, of a purpose in creation, of redemption from evil, and of salvation for the individual commended itself to those familiar with the many mystery religions and cults of the Hellenistic world as well as to those brought up in the fatalist beliefs of the Greek philosophers. The new faith in a way of life which made moral demands upon individuals, filled them with a new divine power (called by Christians 'Holy Spirit'), and conferred upon them a new quality of being – 'eternal life', which began in the here-and-now but went on in the hereafter – was summed up by St John in terms with which the Gentile Greek would be familiar: 'In the beginning was the Word (*logos*) and the Word was with God, and the Word was God . . . all things were made by him. . . In him was life; and the life was the light of men' (*John* i:1-4 ff).

This new life was to be shared in a community where love of one's neighbour was axiomatic. 'He that loveth not knoweth not God; for God is love' (*John* iv:8); 'we know that we have passed out of death into life, because we love the brethen. He that loveth not abideth in death' (*John* iii:14). It is small wonder that when Paul and Silas preached the new faith of Christianity in the Greek city of Thesalonica, 'and some of them were persuaded . . . and of the devout Greeks a great multitude', the Jews 'moved with jealousy' brought some of the brethren before the rulers of the city, crying, 'These that have turned the world upside down are come hither also' (*Acts* xvii:4-6). To the Jews it was a 'stumbling-block' that the Messiah should be crucified, for the Law of Moses had pronounced a curse on anyone who was hanged: to the Greek philosophers it was foolishness (*I Corinthians* i:23).

Despite this, Christianity is today a world-wide faith. In what follows we shall trace the origins and expansion of the Christian Church, its divisions, its social influence, the main doctrines of Christianity as they have developed in the different periods of Christian history, the forms of worship practised by Christians and the place of Christianity today among world religions.

Origins

Both Jesus himself and the small band of disciples who followed him during his earthly ministry in Galilee and Judaea were all Jews by race and religion. They regularly attended the synagogue, they visited the Temple in Jerusalem, they kept the Jewish feast of the Passover and the other great festivals. The fact that Jesus claimed to be the Messiah foretold in the Old Testament scriptures of the Jews, and was acknowledged by Peter in his confession 'Thou art the Christ' (i.e. *Christos*, the anointed, the equivalent in Greek of the Hebrew *Messiah*), would not have occasioned surprise among his contemporaries, since they were all, like the old man Simeon who received Jesus at his circumcision in Jerusalem, 'looking for the consolation of Israel'

(*Luke* ii:25). There was, indeed, a general expectation of the coming of a Messiah who would free the Jews from the hated rule of the Romans and usher in the rule (or kingdom) of God, the 'Day of the Lord' (*Isaiah* ii:12 and frequently in the Old Testament).

That Jesus identified himself as Messiah with the 'Suffering Servant' of *Isaiah* xlii, liii and *Zechariah* ix:9 mystified his disciples and caused his rejection by the Jewish people when he carried this identification to the lengths of being crucified on Calvary. The reaction of his followers seems to be faithfully reflected in the words of one of the two disciples on the road to Emmaus (*Luke* xxiv:19-21): 'Jesus of Nazareth, who was a prophet mighty in deed and word before God and all the people . . . the chief priests and our rulers delivered him up to be condemned to death, and crucified him. But we hoped that it was he which should redeem Israel. Yea, and beside all this, it is now the third day since these things came to pass.'

The Resurrection

The origin of the Christian Church is not to be sought in the teaching of Jesus, or even in his call of the twelve disciples to follow him. Christianity was born with the resurrection and glorification of Jesus of Easter Day. The historian can neither prove nor disprove the miraculous events of the first Easter Day recorded in all the Four Gospels. What is certain is that something happened and that, as a result, a new faith was born. Even those who question the 'empty tomb' or the accounts of the resurrection of Jesus cannot deny the reality of the 'resurrection faith' on the part of the early Christians. It seems that the risen Christ first appeared to the disciples in Galilee (*Mark* xvi:7, *John* xxi), whither the disciples had forlornly returned, as Peter said, to 'go a-fishing' (*John* xxi:3). After this they returned to Jerusalem to await the imminent second coming of the Lord.

Paul sums up for the Corinthian converts the Easter faith which created the Church: 'that Christ died for our sins according to the Scriptures; and that he was buried; and that he hath been raised on the third day according to the Scriptures; and that he appeared to Cephas (Peter); then to the twelve; then he appeared to above five hundred brethren at once, of whom the greater part remain until now, but some are fallen asleep; then he appeared to James; then to all the apostles; and last of all, as unto one born out of due time, he appeared to me also' (*I Corinthians* xv:3-8). According to *Acts* ii:22-3 and 36, Peter preached the gospel that this Jesus whom 'ye by the hand of lawless men did crucify and slay . . . God raised up . . . let all the house of Israel therefore know assuredly, that God hath made him both Lord and Christ, this Jesus whom ye crucified.' So Peter called upon his fellow Jews to repent (*Acts* iii:19, 21). Many responded and formed the infant Jerusalem Church, under the leadership of

Illustration page 428

Peter, John and James.

The Spread of the Gospel

During the centuries before Christ the Jews had spread far and wide outside Palestine. They constituted the Jewish Diaspora (dispersion), and by the first century AD Jewish colonies existed, especially in the larger towns, such as Antioch, Ephesus, Corinth, Rome, Carthage and Alexandria. It was through the synagogues in the Diaspora that Christianity first spread and came into contact with the Gentile (non-Jewish) world. From Antioch, where the followers of Christ were first called Christians (*Acts* xi:26) by their enemies, in derision, Paul took the gospel to the Jewish centres of Asia Minor and Greece, and ultimately visited Rome, where tradition asserts that he was martyred, with Peter, *c.* AD 64. In the process many Gentile as well as Jewish converts were made, with the result that by the end of the first century AD there were organized Christian communities ('churches') all round the Mediterranean. By the end of the second century they had spread to Egypt, North Africa and Gaul.

CHRISTIANITY

Illustration page 427

The word 'church' (*ecclesia*) means 'an assembly of people'. It was used in the Greek Septuagint version of the Old Testament to translate the Hebrew word for the assembly, congregation, or people of God. In the New Testament it usually means the whole body of Christians (*Acts* v:11, *Colossians* i:18, *Galatians* i:13), but the same word is used of a local Christian congregation – e.g. 'the church in Jerusalem' (*Acts* viii:1), 'the church in Antioch' (*Acts* xiii:1), 'at Corinth' (*I Corinthians* i:2), and even in the plural, e.g. 'the churches of the Gentiles' (*Romans* xvi:4), 'the churches of Asia' (*1 Corinthians* xvi:19). In the thought of Paul there is only one Church, which has many members (*I Corinthians* xii:13: 'in one Spirit were we all baptized into one body, whether Jews or Greeks, whether bond or free'). Thus it is possible to speak of the Church 'at Corinth' or 'in Jerusalem', meaning those members of the one Church, 'the Body of Christ', who are situated in that particular place. The notion of different churches existing side by side, having separate forms of worship, organization, sets of beliefs, and no fellowship with one another dates from a considerably later period in Church history.

Organization and Worship of the Early Church

It was remarked earlier that Christianity arose out of Judaism. Jesus, we are told, was accustomed to enter the synagogue 'on the Sabbath day' and, on one occasion, at least, he read the lesson (*Luke* iv:16). The first followers of Jesus continued to join in the worship of the synagogue, and Paul and Barnabas attended the synagogues in the cities of the Diaspora (*Acts* xiii:5, 14; xiv:1; xvii:2).

It would, therefore, be natural that the primitive Church should model its organization on that of the synagogue, which was everywhere directed by a local body of elders. Thus the *presbuteroi* (presbyters, or elders) of the church in Jerusalem are mentioned along with the apostles as its leaders. On his last visit to Jerusalem Paul was received by 'James and all the elders' (*Acts* xxi:18). In the Gentile world Paul and Barnabas appointed elders in every church on their first missionary journey (*Acts* xiv:23) so the office was not confined to the Jewish-Christian church in Jerusalem. In his letters to these churches Paul subsequently referred to the elders as bishops or *episcopoi* (*Philemon* i:1, *Acts* xx:28, *Titus* i:7), so that in the Gentile churches the terms were interchangeable.

The Role of the Bishop

The term *episkopos* (bishop) connotes a personal function of super-intendence or oversight (*episkope*), which was evidently exercised by one of the college of presbyters in a church, for by the middle of the second century such an arrangement, known as 'mon-episcopacy', was universal. Ignatius (d. *c.* 117) described himself as 'bishop of Syria' in his *Epistle to the Romans* (ii cf. ix). In his *Epistle to the Trallians* he wrote, 'when you are in subjection to the bishop as to Jesus Christ . . . it is necessary that you should do nothing without the bishop, but be ye also in subjection to the presbytery'; 'likewise let all respect the deacons as Jesus Christ, even as the bishop is also a type of the Father, and the presbyters as the council of God, and the college of Apostles.' A three-fold ministry of bishop, priests and deacons is here clearly envisaged.

The deacons may, indeed, have been the first to be established. A unanimous tradition goes back to Irenaeus, Bishop of Lyons (*c.* 178-200), that the seven men appointed to 'serve tables' (*Acts* vi:2) were deacons and so represent the origin of the later diaconate. This was an entirely new office, not derived from the synagogue. The early Christian manual known as the *Didache*, compiled before AD 100, speaks of apostles and prophets (sometimes using the terms interchangeably) and gives detailed directions for distinguishing be-tween 'true' and 'false' prophets. It also gives an instruction to 'appoint for yourselves bishops and deacons worthy of the Lord' (*Didache* xv).

Scholars in the episcopal tradition have tended to see the origin of the episcopate in the appointment of local bishops as direct successors of the apostles by 'devolution' of the apostles' commission from the Lord, or by a process of 'evolution' upwards from the ranks of the presbyters. Scholars in the Presbyterian and allied traditions have tended to regard every presbyter as a bishop on the ground, among others, that Paul uses the terms interchangeably in his letters to the Gentile churches. Irenaeus (*c.* 190) gives a list of Roman bishops from his own time back to Linus in AD 68. According to the Norwegian scholar Einar Molland, this list does not imply any continuity of ordinations: the 'succession from the Apostles' did not derive from an apostolic authority to ordain, sacramentally transmitted through an uninterrupted series of impositions of hands, but it meant a guar-antee of the genuine tradition of the doctrine and teaching of the apostles, handed on through a verifiable series of men, in contrast to the un-apostolic, heretical teaching of the Gnostics.

Consecration

Bishops could not be consecrated until their predecessors were dead. Irenaeus himself was probably chosen and consecrated by his fellow-presbyters at Lyons, in the same way as the bishops of Alex-andria down to the fourth century, just as the Roman cardinals elect the pope to this day. In Milan and Carthage, and probably elsewhere, on the other hand, the bishop was elected by the people (not the presbyters) and consecrated by three bishops from the neighbourhood. Whether the bishop was the successor of the apostles or the prophets, or both, or was elevated from the ranks of the presbyters, by the middle of the second century these functions were universally exercized by the bishop, assisted by presbyters and deacons, but it is probable that different churches may have arrived at the common practice by different routes and at different dates.

Baptism and Circumcision

Membership of the Jewish faith was by virtue of birth and all males had to be circumcized at eight days of age (*Genesis* xvii:2, *Exodus* xii:48). When Gentiles adopted Judaism they were first baptized (since Gentiles were regarded as being in a state of ritual impurity), and then circumcized. Jesus commanded his disciples to 'make disciples of all the nations, baptising them into the name of the Father and of the Son and of the Holy Ghost', according to *Matthew* xxviii:19. This verse may well be a later interpolation into the original gospel of Matthew, but it certainly reflects what the early Church did, in fact, do. Baptism was regarded by Paul as the Christian circumcision (*Romans* ii:29, *Philemon* iii:2-3, *Colossians* ii:11), and the comparison of baptism with circumcision (i.e. initiation into the covenant with God) is frequent in the writings of the early fathers of the Church. Instruction in the faith was naturally required before a candidate for baptism could be accepted.

The *Didache*, before AD 100, already orders baptism in water in the name of the Trinity. By the time that we come to the *Apostolic Tradition* of Hippolytus (*c.* 215), the Church has evolved a full baptismal liturgy, which includes the washing away of sin (symbolically) in the water, anointing with oil blessed by the bishop, the 'sealing' (or confirmation) by the bishop, and first communion of the neophyte. The normal time for baptism was on Easter Eve, followed by the first communion early on Easter Day.

The Sabbath

The Christian Church inherited from Judaism the seven-day week culminating in the observance of Saturday as 'the Sabbath', which was for the Jews a day of rest from all work. A Swiss scholar, Willy Rordorf, has recently published an important study entitled *Sunday* (Eng. trans. SCM Press, 1968) in which he maintains that the early Christians regarded the duty of Sabbath observance as including the whole span of our life, that Sunday (the first day of the week) replaced the Sabbath (the seventh day) as a day of worship from the very beginning, and that 'right down to the fourth century the idea of rest played absolutely no part in the Christian Sunday'.

It is perfectly true that Sunday was observed as a day of worship from the beginning, as a weekly commemoration of Easter, the day of the resurrection, and that Christians could not observe it as a day of rest until the Emperor Constantine decreed in 321 that Sunday should be kept as a rest-day throughout the Empire, but it does not follow that the early Christians abandoned the Sabbath (Saturday). Both days were still being kept as festivals, marked by celebrations of the Eucharist, in the fourth century, as is shown by Gregory of Nyssa's reprimand, 'If you have despised the Sabbath, with what face will you behold the Lord's Day . . . They are sisters' (*De Castigatione* ii) and by Chrysostom (*Homilies on Matthew* v:1). Moreover the first definite mention of regular assemblies for worship on 'the day of the Sun' (Sunday) is in Justin Martyr (*Apology* I, lxvii) about 150.

The Eucharist

The origin of the Christian Eucharist lies in the Last Supper, at which Christ inaugurated the New Covenant in his blood on the night before his crucifixion (*Matthew* xxvi:26-8, *Mark* xiv:22-4, *Luke* xxii:17-20, *I Corinthians* xi:23-5). Whether or not this supper was the Jewish Passover has been hotly debated among scholars. It certainly took place in the Passover season: hence the subsequent fixing of the date of Easter on the Sunday following the Passover full moon. At an early date, however, the Eucharist came to be celebrated every Sunday as a weekly commemoration of the resurrection, and not only once a year at Easter. Indeed, by the early third century a daily celebration is attested by Cyprian in North Africa. Before that time the Eucharist seems to have been celebrated only on Saturdays and Sundays and on the 'station days', Wednesday and Friday, which were fasting days reminiscent of the older Jewish fasts on Monday and Thursday (cf. *Didaché* viii:1).

But there would be gatherings for prayer every day at the times of the ancient Jerusalem temple sacrifices, namely at dawn and at dusk. Services in the synagogues were held at these times and they were continued in the early Church. Thus, Tertullian (*c.* 200), when commending the introduction of prayer at the third, sixth and ninth hours among the ascetics, says that these hours of prayer should be 'of course in addition to the regular prayers which without any reminder are due at the beginning of day and of night' (*De Oratione* xxv).

Daily Worship in the Early Church

The content of the daily and weekly worship of Christians was likewise modelled on that of the synagogue. In both there were four main elements: prayer, psalmody, scripture readings, and a sermon or homily (on the Sabbath) on the portions of scripture which had been read. Greek was the liturgical language of Christians, even at Rome, until the third century. The earliest surviving text of the Eucharist (*c.* 215), in the *Apostolic Tradition* of Hippolytus, shows that the first part of the service still consisted of the four elements derived from the synagogue. After this there followed immediately the consecration of bread and wine, which were offered to God as a sacrificial memorial (*anamnesis*) of the sacrifice of Christ on Calvary and partaken by the baptized members of the Church as the body and blood of Christ – the means appointed by Christ himself at the Last Supper for communion with him (cf. *John* vi). Out of this primitive rite there

Left A view of the supposed Mount of Temptation through an excavation trench at Ain es Sultan, Jericho. Here the Devil offered Jesus the kingdoms of the world and was rejected.

Below left The fourth-century Lazarus Cubiculum in the Catacomb of the Jordani, Rome. Only in times of persecution did the Early Christians assemble in the catacombs; mostly they made occasional visits to celebrate the anniversary of a martyr or for burial ceremonies. The wall paintings portray the Raising of Lazarus (left) and the Good Shepherd (right).

Below Early Christian crosses at Ephesus, Turkey, bear witness to the presence of Christianity in the city.

developed in the course of centuries the Latin Mass in the West and the various Greek and oriental liturgies in the East.

Asceticism had a place in Christianity from the beginning. Fasting and fast days have already been mentioned. Celibacy and renunciation of earthly possessions were practised by some Christians in their own homes before St Anthony, *c.* 285, adopted the life of a hermit in the desert of Egypt. Other solitaries followed his example and for mutual protection lived in loosely organized groups of hermits (anchorites). Then, in *c.* 320, Pachomius founded the first monastery for monks living under a regular rule (coenobites) at Tabennisi on the right bank of the Nile. Soon both anchorites and coenobites were to be found all over Egypt and the rest of the Middle East.

Through Athanasius, Rufinus and John Cassian both forms of asceticism spread to the West. St Basil (in 358-64) composed a monastic rule, drawing on that of Pachomius, which became the basis of the rule still followed by the monks of the East, and in the sixth century St Benedict established the first Benedictine community at Monte Cassino in Italy under a rule drawn up by him, which was the basis of all subsequent monasticism in the West. In all these rules provision was made for a regular cycle of prayer during the day and the night hours. Thus the original times of prayer at dawn and at dusk were elaborated into the seven canonical hours contained in the *Breviary* of the medieval Western Church. Together with the *Missal*, which contained the service of the Mass, this provided the clergy with a regular cycle of prayer.

Relations between Church and State

Julius Caesar granted to the Jews the right freely to practise their own religion and to pay the temple tax for the upkeep of the Temple in Jerusalem. They were, thus, recognized as a *religio licita* (a licensed religion association) and were excused from any duties to the state which might conflict with their religion, e.g. military service, which might involve infringement of the Sabbath rest and their laws about food. The first Christians were regarded by the Roman authorities as a sect within Judaism and Paul was actually taken into protective custody by the military tribune at Jerusalem when he was in danger of his life (*Acts* xxi:30-36). But the influx of large numbers of Gentiles into the Church and the continual hostility of the Jews towards them soon convinced the authorities that the followers of 'Chrestus' (Christ) were not a sect of Judaism, but constituted a new religion.

There were constant outbreaks of mob violence against Christians in Asia Minor and in Rome, because they refused to attend the games (owing to their religious associations) or to worship the Roman gods. They met secretly for worship at night – men and women, behind closed doors – hence charges of immorality and incest. It was rumoured that they partook of the blood of a newborn babe – hence charges of cannibalism – and they were militant proselytizers. The Roman historian Tacitus accused them of 'hatred of the human race' and, when the mad Emperor Nero set fire to Rome in AD 64, he diverted attention by making the Christians into the scapegoats.

There was severe persecution in Rome and the vicinity, in the course of which Peter and Paul are said to have perished. Domitian (*d.* AD 96) also persecuted the Christians. So did Marcus Aurelius (161–80) and other emperors, but these were sporadic persecutions and in the intervals of peace the Church grew in strength and numbers, penetrating all strata of society, including the imperial household, until it became 'an empire within the empire'.

In 249 Decius became emperor. The one-thousandth anniversary of the founding of Rome stirred him to re-establish the ancient worship of the Roman gods, to reunify the empire and so to instigate the first empire-wide systematic persecution of the Christians. Bishop Fabian of Rome was executed in January 250 and the see of Rome was vacant for fifteen months. Bishop Cyprian of Carthage and Bishop Dionysius of Alexandria went into voluntary exile, directing their dioceses from secret headquarters. Many Christians stood fast (the confessors); many conformed to the state religion by taking part in sacrifices or burning incense before the statue of the emperor (the lapsed). There were many martyrs. When the persecution ended in June 251 with the death of Decius, the Church had to deal with the problem of the readmission of the lapsed, and a serious split occurred between Pope Stephen of Rome and Cyprian and the North African Church.

Renewed Persecution

During the renewed persecution under the Emperor Valerian in 258, Cyprian was beheaded. Thereafter the Church endured peace for nearly sixty years, during which many half-converts joined the Church, until the final and most severe persecution under the Emperor Diocletian (284–305), who issued a series of edicts designed to stamp out the Christian scriptures, the clergy, and finally the laity as well. Terrible suffering was endured by the Christians, especially in the eastern part of the empire, until Constantine the Great defeated the Roman usurper Maxentius at the Battle of the Milvian Bridge in 312. The following year Constantine issued, together with the Eastern emperor, Licinius, an edict of toleration of all religions. Christianity did not become the official religion of the Roman Empire until the Edict of Theodosius I in 380.

Nevertheless, after the Peace of Constantine the state, in the person of successive emperors, took an ever-increasing interest in the affairs of the Church. In the fourth century the emperors' objective was to preserve the unity of the empire; hence their efforts to secure unity

Illustration page 427

in the Church, which was torn by schism and heresy. Donatism in North Africa was an anti-Roman, nationalist movement among the Berbers of Numidia, which claimed to be the true Church of the apostles and martyrs and refused (like the later Puritans) to have any dealings with the state. Constantine tried by diplomacy and then by persecution to unite them with the Catholics, but without success. They were finally declared outlaws by the Emperor Honorius in 412, but survived this and the Vandal invasion of North Africa until, in the seventh century, Islam overwhelmed both Donatists and Catholics.

Arguments about the Nature of Christ

From the beginning Christians had asserted belief in one god – the God revealed in the Old Testament – but also in the divinity of Jesus Christ. It could only be a matter of time before the question of the relation of God the Father to his Son, Jesus Christ, would arise. The great Arian controversy of the fourth century, which split the Church in two, stemmed from the preaching of the Alexandrian presbyter, Arius, that the Son was a created being who did not eternally exist and, therefore, was a sort of demi-god, subordinate to the Father. The Emperor Constantine summoned the first General Council of the Church at Nicaea, in 325, to settle this dispute and so reunify the Church. It condemned the teaching of Arius and produced a creed which declared that the Son is of one substance with and co-eternal with the Father. Theodosius I convened the second General Council at Constantinople, in 381, which endorsed his definition (380) of Catholicism, finally condemned Arianism and also Apollinarianism (which had overstressed the divinity of Christ, in opposition to Arianism), and reaffirmed the Nicene Creed.

Illustration page 437

A further dispute arose between the monk Nestorius, who became patriarch of Constantinople in 428, and Cyril, patriarch of Alexandria (412-44), about the two natures (divinity and humanity) in Christ. Nestorius over-emphasized the humanity of Christ and so took exception to the traditional description of Mary as *Theotokos* (mother of god), declaring her proper title to be 'mother of Christ', since she was the mother of the human nature alone. There was a ferocious argument between Cyril and Nestorius, in which Rome joined on the side of Alexandria against the pretentious claims of the upstart see of Constantinople. Thus politics entered into the dispute. Once again the state intervened. The third general council of the Church at Ephesus, in 431, was called by the two emperors, Theodosius II of the East and Valentinian III of the West. It condemned Nestorianism, and Nestorius was exiled to the Egyptian desert in 435.

His teaching was, however, perpetuated in the Christian School at Edessa, which was transferred to Nisibis in 489 and received the support of the Persian king. From there Nestorian schools and missionaries spread rapidly to India, Central Asia and China (where a bilingual inscription in Syriac and Chinese, discovered by the later Jesuit missionaries at Sinangfu in 1625, relates that a Nestorian missionary preached the gospel there as early as AD 636). The Nestorian Church survived the persecutions of Tamerlane in the fourteenth century in Kurdistan down to the First World War, after which many of its survivors moved to San Francisco.

Further Disputes

A further fifth-century dispute between the patriarch of Alexandria (supported by Rome) and the patriarch of Constantinople centred

431

round the archimandrite Eutyches of Constantinople, who held that after the incarnation there was only one nature in Christ. This doctrine is known as Monophysitism (one natureism), and after its condemnation by the fourth General Council of the Church at Chalcedon, in 451, convoked once again by an emperor, Marcian, who attended the final session personally and even resorted to arms to enforce its decrees, the Catholic Church in East and West accepted what is known as the Chalcedonian Definition of the doctrine of the Trinity. This endorsed the famous Tome (or Letter) of Pope Leo I, which asserted that Jesus Christ is one person, the Divine Word, in whom are two natures, the divine and the human, permanently united before and after the incarnation, though unconfused and unmixed.

This statement of belief, together with the other doctrinal definitions of the first four general councils of the Church, have ever since been accepted by Eastern and Western Orthodox, Catholic and Protestant Christians. But, just as the followers of Nestorius seceded and formed a schismatic church (unrecognized by Catholics and Orthodox alike) after the Council of Ephesus in 431, so the upholders of the one nature in Christ after the incarnation seceded from the main body of Christians after 451 and became the Monophysite or 'Jacobite' Church (named after the Syrian monk Jacob Baradai, *d.* 578), which today has a Patriarch of Antioch and churches in Syria, Iraq, Cyprus, Israel, Jordan, Egypt, Armenia and Ethiopia.

The Church in the West

The growth in power and prestige of the see of Rome between the second and the fifth centuries was due to the fact that Rome was the royal city, the capital of the empire, until the seat of government was transferred to Constantinople (New Rome) in AD 337, and thereafter the bishop of Rome became the most powerful personage in the West. It was also due to the consistent support of the orthodox Nicene faith by the bishops of Rome and their increasing claims to authority and jurisdiction over the other churches in virtue of their being the successors of the Apostle Peter. These claims were not always admitted by the other ancient patriarchates of Jerusalem, Antioch, Alexandria and Constantinople, but in the West the jurisdiction of the see of Rome (for a time rivalled by Milan) had been generally recognized by the time of Pope Leo I (440-61). He was the first pope to be buried in St Peter's, Rome.

The Church's organization was modelled on that of the Roman Empire, for, as in every metropolis or chief city of each Roman province, there was a superior magistrate over the local magristrates of the cities included in the province, so in the same metropolis there was a bishop whose power extended over the bishops of the other cities in the province. He was, therefore, called the metropolitan, or the primate. The boundaries of an ecclesiastical province did not always coincide exactly with those of its civil prototype: ambitious prelates sometimes based their claims to extra jurisdiction on imperial grants, and later on papal grants.

Church Revenues

The revenues of the Church were originally entirely derived from the voluntary offerings of the faithful. Tithes and first fruits are occasionally mentioned, but the clear biblical precedent (*Deuteronomy* xiv:22-26) does not seem to have been exploited by the clergy until the second half of the sixth century in Merovingian Gaul. From Constantine's time the property of the churches – at first confined to places of worship and burial grounds – grew rapidly. He himself gave land and houses to the churches and his example was followed by many of his subjects.

In 410 Rome was sacked by the barbarian Visigothic chief, Alaric, who was an Arian Christian. The fall of the 'eternal city' caused consternation throughout the empire and called forth Augustine's famous book *City of God*. Other barbarian tribes, most of them non-Christian, also poured across the Rhine into Gaul, Spain and North Africa. These Germanic invasions produced chaos (and some persecution) in the West. The Franks alone, under King Clovis, were initially converted to Catholic Christianity.

But before 410 Christianity had reached Britain from Gaul, and the ancient British (or Celtic) Church, driven westward into Wales, Cornwall and Ireland, was the agent for the reconversion of much of England after the Anglo-Saxon invasions, and then of northern Holland, southern Denmark and northwest Germany. St Columban (*c.* 550-615), an Irish abbot, went to Gaul, *c.* 590, with some disciples (among whom was St Gall, who gave his name to the canton in Switzerland, where he ministered) and established monasteries at Anegray and Luxeuil, in the Vosges. Driven from Burgundy, they settled at Bobbio in northern Italy, where their house became a great centre of learning. St Boniface (680-754), born at Crediton in Devon, is known as the 'Apostle of Germany', where he laid the foundations of a settled ecclesiastical organization. He had the full support of the pope, founded the famous abbey of Fulda (*c.* 743), was made archbishop of Mainz (*c.* 747), and died a martyr's death in Frisia.

The Holy Roman Empire

The coronation of the Frankish king Charlemagne by the pope at Rome in 800 marked the beginning of the Holy Roman Empire, the successor of the old, now vanished Roman Empire. It also led to a tremendous conflict between the temporal and spiritual powers (the emperors and the popes), under the German and Bavarian emperors. A compromise was reached in the famous Concordat of Worms of 1122 between Pope Calixtus II and Emperor Henry V. The emperor surrendered to the Church all investiture of bishops with the ring and staff, i.e. the symbols of spiritual authority, while the pope granted Henry the right to invest a bishop with the temporal possessions of his office by the touch of the royal sceptre. Lay investiture – the cause of Henry IV's excommunication by Hildebrand (Gregory VII) and his famous submission as a penitent, barefooted in the snow before the castle gate at Canossa (1077) – was at an end, but the conflict as to who should appoint bishops continued throughout the Middle Ages. So too did the struggle to assert the supreme authority of the bishop of Rome in matters spiritual and temporal.

Under Pope Innocent III (1198-1216) the papacy reached the zenith of its worldly power. When King John of England resisted the pope's nomination of Stephen Langton as archbishop of Canterbury, he laid England under an interdict, which meant the cessation of all administration of the sacraments. He threatened Philip II of France with an interdict, excommunicated King John of England and compelled the Holy Roman Emperor to do homage to him. The Fourth Lateran Council of 1215 declared the doctrine of transubstantiation to be an article of faith, so that anyone who denied it would be eternally damned, and required annual confession and communion from all the faithful under the same penalty. Thus, the interdict and excommunication were fearful weapons in an age when people believed that the only defence against the fiends which would assail their souls when they passed out of the body at death was the sacrament of the body and blood of Christ, and that infants dying unbaptized went straight to hell.

Illustration page 428

Rebels against Rome

Gradually the balance of power was to shift, until, by the time of the Reformation in the sixteenth century, the papacy had become virtually the tool of the Holy Roman Empire. Meanwhile a new sense of nationality was arising in England and in France. Both Edward I of England and Philip IV of France defied Pope Boniface VIII, who asserted in *Unam Sanctam* (1302) that temporal powers are subject to the spiritual power and that 'it is altogether necessary to salvation for every human creature to be subject to the Roman pontiff'. Boniface was taken prisoner by Philip's mercenaries and died soon after: the temporal power of the papacy was broken. There followed the Great Schism, a period of French popes settled at Avignon and rival popes in Rome (1378-1417), and a series of general councils of the Church at Pisa, Constance and Basle designed to heal the schism (achieved at Constance) and also to reform the Church. The latter it failed to do and so paved the way for the Reformation and Counter-Reformation of the sixteenth century.

Revival of Learning and Culture

After the barbarian invasions, the conversion of the Franks, and the coronation of Charlemagne there was a renaissance of classical and biblical learning, in which Alcuin of York (?735-804) played a leading part after 796, when Charlemagne made him head of the monastery of St Martin in Tours. Theological discussion developed eventually into the scholasticism of the great medieval thinkers – Peter Lombard, St Thomas Aquinas, Duns Scotus and William of Occam. Tradition has ascribed to Pope Gregory the Great (540-604) the reformation of church music known as 'Gregorian chant' and the reformation of the liturgy. This work was carried on by Alcuin and his successors. Gregory was a monk and monasticism played a great part in the revival and dissemination of Christian art, architecture, music and letters.

Each successive monastic order aimed at reforming the worldliness which had crept into the Church and returning to the simplicity and purity of the rule of St Benedict. The Cluniac Order was founded in *Illustration page 437* 910 at Cluny, near Mâcon in Burgundy; the Cistercian Order in 1098 at Cîteaux, also in Burgundy, its most famous son being St Bernard of Clairvaux (1090-1153); the Carthusian Order in 1084 at the Grande Chartreuse, some 24 kilometres (15 miles) north of Grenoble. 'Canons regular' or Augustinian canons – clerks living a common life – came into being in northern Italy and southern France in the mid-eleventh century. Later came the friars, who insisted on complete poverty for the community as well as the individual member, who earned a living by working, or, if need be, by begging, and who, unlike the monks (who lived in community), engaged in popular preaching and missionary work. They were the Franciscans, founded in 1209, and the Dominicans, founded in 1216.

All these orders of monks and friars spread rapidly throughout Europe. The monks were the purveyors of learning and culture. They said their prayers, sang the daily offices, developing church music to a considerable degree, copied manuscripts, wrote great letters and theological treatises themselves (e.g. St Bernard of Clairvaux, St Anselm), and built marvellous abbeys, many of which are now in ruins. During the thirteenth and fourteenth centuries the great Gothic *Illustration page 439* cathedrals of northern Europe were built. Stained glass and carving in wood and stone embellished both cathedrals and parish churches. They were the chief means of religious instruction among the illiterate masses, supplemented in the fourteenth and fifteenth centuries by mystery plays. Sermons were rare except in the late thirteenth and the fourteenth centuries, the great age of the preaching friars.

Religion in a Feudal Society

The medieval Western Church existed in a feudal society. It took for granted the existence of rich and poor and of different callings which were divinely appointed, yet it strove to achieve a unity of Christendom centred on obedience to spiritual and temporal authority and the Christian ethic as then understood. This unity was very imperfectly realized, but the crusades were one expression of the ideal. A war in which the Christian peoples united to rescue the holy places of Palestine from the Muslims was proclaimed by successive popes to be a work of high merit.

The acquiring of merit in the sight of God by the performance of 'good works' was believed to be a means of obtaining grace. Such 'good works' included attendance at mass, paying for the saying of masses, going on pilgrimages, veneration of the saints, and doing penance. A good deal of superstition was mixed up with the popular Christianity of the later Middle Ages and the sixteenth-century reformers rejected the whole sacramental theology built on the theory of human merit.

Even the powerful monolithic Church of the Middle Ages had been challenged by dissident groups, often persecuted but never entirely suppressed, e.g. the Albigenses or Cathari, who taught a form of Manichean dualism, the Waldenses, the followers of John Wyclif in England (known as the Lollards), and of John Hus in Bohemia, both of whom attacked the papacy and demanded a return to a more scriptural and simple Christianity. These groups prepared the ground for the reception of the seminal ideas of Luther and Calvin.

The Reformation

The struggle for power between the spiritual and temporal authorities, referred to above, aided by the growing spirit of nationalism in England, France, Germany and Bohemia had created an increasing anti-papalism and, ultimately, anti-clericalism in the late Middle Ages. The failure of the General Councils of the fifteenth century to reform the Church, the ever-increasing financial exactions of the papal Curia, the decadence of monasticism, the worldliness of the clergy, paralleled by the revival of learning which we call the Renaissance, the new study of the scriptures, the new demand for intellectual freedom and the right of private judgment – all furthered by the invention of printing – led inevitably to the splitting up of the one great Church of the Middle Ages centred on Rome into those states and churches which remained within the Roman obedience and those which repudiated the spiritual authority and the doctrinal decisions

Illustration page 438 of the Roman pontiffs.

Old Traditions Retained

Despite this colossal upheaval in the sixteenth century a great deal of the traditional teaching and practice of the pre-Reformation Church was kept. All the main Protestant Churches kept the three creeds derived from the General Councils of the fourth and fifth centuries. Thus they continued to profess belief in the Trinity, the two natures in Christ, the fall and original sin, the atonement wrought by the death of Christ, his resurrection and ascension. They retained the belief in the literal, infallible inspiration of the books of the Old and New Testaments, which they thought of as dictated by the Holy Spirit.

The chief difference between Protestants and Catholics was the rejection by the former of the *magisterium* of the Roman Church, with its claim to be the sole interpreter of scripture, and their refusal to allow to Church tradition the same authority as to scripture. God's Word was for them the sole authority and, although individual interpretation of the infallible scriptures led to some diversity of opinion among the reformers, there could be no differences concerning the basic articles of the Christian faith common to all Christians since the days of the apostles. The primitive Church was, indeed, the pattern for subsequent ages.

Salvation through Faith

It was through studying the Bible, and especially Paul's *Epistle to the Romans*, that Martin Luther (1483-1546) came to realize that man

Dégrataf buf uel maur monnechorum.

Above A marriage ceremony in an Eastern Orthodox Church. The priest holds the wedding crowns over the heads of the bride and groom.

Above left A twelfth-century Italian drawing showing St Benedict handing to a group of monks his Rule, composed for the regulation of their lives at Monte Cassino, where he died *c.* 550. This Rule was the basis of all later western monastic discipline. Biblioteca Nazionale "Vittorio Emanuele III", Naples.

Left The Emperor Theodosius I (AD 379-95), the last sole ruler of the Roman empire, who established orthodox Catholic (i.e. Nicene) Christianity as the religion of the empire, proscribing heresy and paganism alike. He is seated between his sons Honorius (left) and Arcadius (right), who became rulers respectively of the western and eastern halves of the empire after his death. Detail from a silver *missorium* or ornamental shield sent as a gift (AD 388). Real Academia de la Historia, Madrid.

Right Pisa Cathedral (1063-92), the finest Romanesque church of northern Italy, faced with marble and richly arcaded.

Opposite The inspiration of Gothic vaulting is amply illustrated by the early fourteenth-century nave of Exeter Cathedral, south-west England, by Thomas Witney.

Above Vamitelli's view of St Peter's Square, Rome (1706). Bernini's square (begun 1656) is a vivid image of the embracing arms of the Catholic Church.

Right Cranach's engraving of 1545 graphically contrasts the spiritual simplicity of the Evangelical Church and the corrupt worldliness of the Catholic tradition.

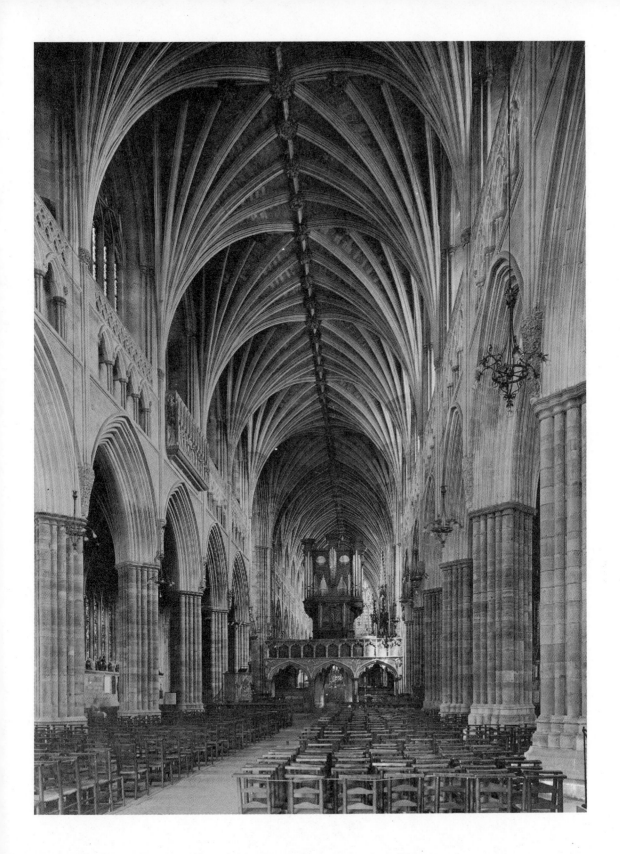

cannot attain justification (a right relationship with God) by his own works – penances, pardons, pilgrimages, masses or any of the observances enjoined by the medieval Church – but only by faith in the sacrifice of Christ offered once upon the Cross. 'The just shall live by faith' (*Romans* i:17; *Galatians* iii:11). By 'faith' Luther did not mean mere intellectual assent (*fides*), but rather child-like personal trust (*fiducia*) in the Redeemer. Grace is freely given by God, not earned by human merit or bought through a papal indulgence.

In 1517 Luther challenged the current teaching on indulgences in his famous *Ninety-five Theses*, and later began the attack on the papacy itself, powerfully reinforced by his *Appeal to the Christian Nobility of the German Nation* (1520), in which he denounced the financial exactions of the papacy. He was excommunicated, then outlawed by the Imperial Diet at Worms in 1521, and hidden in Wartburg Castle by his patron and protector, the Elector Frederick of Saxony. Here he translated the Bible into German and issued tracts which were printed and circulated throughout Germany. After his return to Wittenberg to undo the work of more radical reformers, and still more after the failure of the Peasants' Revolt, many of the German princes and cities accepted the evangelical teaching of Luther and allied themselves with electoral Saxony.

The Latin mass was abolished and replaced by Luther's German mass at Wittenberg (1525). Priests and monks began to marry (Luther himself marrying an ex-Cistercian nun, Katherine von Bora, in 1525). He composed many hymns in German. After the Diet of Speier (1529), the right of princes to organize national churches was recognized, and the formal 'protest' to the Archduke Ferdinand of six princes and fourteen cities, defending the rights of minorities and freedom of conscience, gave to the Reformers the name 'Protestants'.

Already Lutheranism had spread into Scandinavia, France and England. It never took serious hold in France. In England its influence was dead by 1550, after which, first Zwinglianism and then Calvinism left more permanent marks. In Sweden, where bishops were retained (in contrast to the 'superintendents' set over the Land or State churches in Germany) a truly national Lutheran Church was established. After the Confession of Augsburg (1530), drafted by Philip Melanchthon, which marked the final break between the Lutheran states and Rome, and the death of Luther (1546), Lutheran theology developed on confessional lines into a new form of rigid scholasticism.

Zwingli

Meanwhile, a parallel movement of reform had been in progress at Zürich and other German Swiss cities. Zwingli (1484-1531) was educated in the humanist tradition (unlike Luther, who had been an Austin friar brought up on the Nominalist philosophy of the later schoolmen). Zwingli lectured on the New Testament (like Luther), and attacked fasting, clerical celibacy, and the mass. Organs, relics and images were cast out of the churches in July 1524 and the religious houses were dissolved in December. Mass was abolished by the town

Illustration page 440

Opposite above left An interrogation by the Inquisition. Faced with the spread of independent thought and sectarian divisions, the Inquisition fell back on a belief in authority and tradition to test an individual's adherence to Catholicism.

Opposite above right Martin Luther, the ex-monk who caused a major schism in the western Church, painted by Cranach. Kunstmuseum, Basel.

Opposite below left The Virgin in prayer, an Ethiopian miniature from a manuscript of the fifteenth century. She was believed to offer protection against demons. Bibliothèque Nationale, Paris.

Opposite below right SS. Ignatius Loyola (1491-1556) and Francis Xavier (1506-52), both pillars of the Society of Jesus. Loyola was its founder, Xavier a missionary known as the 'Apostle of the Indies and of Japan'.

council at Zürich and was replaced by Zwingli's German service of the Lord's Supper at Easter 1525. This was paralleled by similar action at Berne, Basel and other Swiss towns, which formed themselves into a Christian Civic Alliance against those cantons which remained Roman Catholic. War ensued and Zwingli was killed in the Battle of Cappel (1531), where he carried the banner as chaplain.

The Protestant Reformation in German Switzerland was accomplished by the magistrates in the various city councils, who took their cue from local reforming leaders like Zwingli, Oecolampadius, Myconius and Haller. At the Colloquy of Marburg (1529), where Luther and Zwingli met, agreement was reached between them on fourteen articles of religion, but on the fifteenth (concerning the Eucharist) they could not reach agreement. Luther stoutly maintained belief in the real presence of Christ in the bread and wine (though not by transubstantiation), while Zwingli regarded Christ's words at the Last Supper, 'This is my Body', as purely symbolic.

Calvin at Geneva

In French Switzerland, the Reformation had already started in Geneva under Guillaume Farel when John Calvin (1509-64), the French reformer and humanist scholar, arrived there in 1536. On his death-bed he described the citizens of Geneva as a 'perverse and ill-natured people'. They were ruled by a council responsible to the general council of all the citizens and there were factions and quarrels continuously during Calvin's life. His first attempt to control the situation in Church and State ended with his departure to Strasbourg in 1538, when he and Farel refused to accept the Liturgy of Berne imposed on the ministers by the council without consultation.

During the three years that Calvin spent at Strasbourg, as pastor of the French congregation, he learned much from Martin Bucer (1491-1551), who anticipated Calvin in his stress on the doctrine of predestination, in his restoration of a New Testament fourfold ministry of pastors, teachers, elders and deacons (cf. *Ephesians* iv:11, *I Timothy* iii:8, v:17), and in providing a vernacular congregational liturgy in French in place of, but derived from, the Latin mass. Theologically, Bucer stood midway between Luther and Zwingli. Calvin had already published in 1535 the first edition of his famous *Institutes of the Christian Religion* in Latin. An enlarged second edition appeared in 1539 (the final edition is dated 1559) and a series of French editions from 1541.

In that year he returned to Geneva, secured the adoption by the council of his *Ordonnances Ecclésiastiques*, by which the consistory of pastors presided over by a lay magistrate was set up, and a liturgy adapted from the form in use at Strasbourg. This Genevan liturgy is the basis of all Presbyterian liturgies, in Scotland and elsewhere, as well as of the Reformed Churches of continental Europe until recent times. The institution of Elders is, likewise, characteristic of all Reformed Churches stemming from Geneva. It was not, however, until 1555 that Calvin gained complete control of the Genevan Consistory and established the right of excommunication of heretics and evil livers.

Calvin's Theology

Calvin's theology followed the main lines of that of Luther in regard to original sin, justification and predestination, and the authority of scripture. But he went further in his insistence on the impenetrable mystery of the absolute sovereignty of God and in his doctrine of the Church. Calvin rejected the medieval doctrine of transubstantiation, the Lutheran doctrine of consubstantiation, and Zwinglian symbolism in regard to the Eucharist. In the *Institutes* he accepts it as a mystery which he experiences rather than understands and, in his *Little Treatise on the Lord's Supper* (1542), whilst he insists that there is a real spiritual presence of the Lord (and a real spiritual partaking) in the Lord's Supper, he bids people 'raise their hearts on high to heaven, not thinking that the Lord Jesus may be so brought down as to be enclosed under any corruptible elements'.

Calvinism was the greatest religious force in the development of the Protestant Reformation in Europe and, ultimately, in America, since from it stem the Presbyterian, Congregationalist and Baptist denominations. In the sixteenth century Calvinism (as expressed in the 'Reformed' tradition stemming from the Zürich Agreement of 1549 between Calvin and Farel and Bullinger, the son-in-law and successor of Zwingli, i.e. between Calvinists and Zwinglians) spread rapidly through France, the Low Countries, central and eastern Europe, and also greatly influenced the course of the Reformation in the England of Edward VI and Elizabeth I.

Illustration page 458

England Reforms in Moderation

In England the Reformation did not follow the doctrines of Luther, Zwingli, or Calvin in their entirety. More than in any other European Protestant country, the Catholic tradition of the Middle Ages was retained. Thus, the threefold ministry of bishops, priests and deacons, together with the territorial division of the country into two provinces (Canterbury and York) comprised of dioceses and parishes, was retained, along with the canon law of the Western Church and the ecclesiastical courts inherited from the Middle Ages.

Under Henry VIII Parliament passed various acts abolishing the jurisdiction of the 'bishop of Rome' and recognizing the sovereign as 'the only supreme head in earth of the Church of England', but there were no significant changes in doctrine or worship. The monasteries and other religious houses were dissolved in 1536 and 1539, their lands and revenues being taken over by the Crown. The Bible was translated into English and placed in the churches, while the superstitious use of images was prohibited.

In the reign of Edward VI the Latin mass was abolished by Parliament, which substituted for all previous service books the first *Book of Common Prayer* (1549) in English. Images in the churches were now destroyed, along with the chantries, and, as a result of the increasing influence of the radical Protestants who favoured the theology of

Bullinger and the Zürich Church, a much more Protestant second *Book of Common Prayer* (1552) was enjoined by Parliament.

The accession of the Catholic Queen Mary in 1553 brought about the restoration of the Latin mass and the jurisdiction of the pope over the English Church. The foreign Protestants in England as well as very many English Protestants took refuge at Frankfurt, Strasbourg, Geneva and other continental cities. Cranmer, Ridley, Latimer and a few others were tried for heresy and burnt at the stake.

The Final Break with Rome

The reign of Elizabeth I saw the final break with Rome, the re-establishment of the royal supremacy and the English prayer book, and the introduction of the Thirty-Nine Articles in an attempt to define the dogmatic position of the Church of England in relation to the controversies of the sixteenth century. The Calvinist John Knox was chiefly instrumental in establishing the reformed Church of Scotland on Genevan lines with a 'Confession of Faith', a 'Book of Discipline' (1560) and a liturgy based on *The Forme of Prayers* (1556) used by the English congregation at Geneva and approved by Calvin. Presbyteries were not, however, set up systematically for another twenty years, and for more than a century Presbyterianism and Episcopacy alternated in Scotland until Presbyterianism finally triumphed in 1690.

Elizabethan England also contained many Puritans who were not satisfied that the so-called 'settlement of religion' had carried reform far enough in a scriptural direction, and who wished to replace the episcopal system by a presbyterian one. Having failed to get their way, first through Convocation, then through Parliament, some of them refused to conform to the religion established by law ('Non-conformists'), left the Church of England (hence, 'Separatists'), and fled to Holland. They are the ancestors of the Independents, or Congregationalists, and the Baptists.

The Counter-Reformation

Illustration page 440

Illustration page 440

Meanwhile a Counter-Reformation, or Catholic Reformation, had been taking place in the Roman Church. In Italy and in Spain a great revival of religion took place between *c.* 1520 and 1580, associated with the founding of the Oratory of Divine Love and of various new religious orders (Capuchins, Theatines, Barnabites, Oratorians, and the Society of Jesus). Their objects were to restore the dignity and due observance of divine service; by special exercises and devotions to reawaken the spiritual life; to educate the clergy; and to preach the Catholic faith. The Roman Inquisition was established in 1542 by Pope Paul III to exterminate heresy, and shortly afterwards the 'Index' of prohibited books was set up.

The Council of Trent was in session at intervals between 1545 and 1563. The Canons and Dogmatic Decrees of the Council defined Roman Catholic doctrine, specifically rejecting the Lutheran doctrine of justification by faith alone, asserting the equal authority of scripture and tradition and the sole right of the Church to interpret scripture, but probably the most important legislation was that concerning the appointment and residence of bishops and ordering the setting up of seminaries in every diocese for the training of the clergy. The Jesuits everywhere played a leading part in the Catholic revival which followed in all those countries which had not adopted Protestantism, and even (temporarily) in some which had – e.g. Sweden, Switzerland and parts of Germany.

The Netherlands were divided: the seven northern provinces, under William of Orange, were Calvinist, while the ten southern states remained Catholic. Calvin's teaching had also taken hold in France and the Huguenots (as the Calvinist French Protestants were called from *c.* 1560) were engaged in civil war with the Catholic majority from 1562 to 1598, when they were granted full freedom of worship by the Edict of Nantes. France, however, remained officially a Catholic country down to 1905.

The Struggle for Power

The seventeenth century was filled with wars, sometimes religious wars, and in the course of it the various national churches consolidated their positions. In Germany there were bitter theological disputes within Lutheranism, as well as between Lutherans and Catholics, and Calvinism made big inroads. The enforcement, after the Peace of Augsburg (1555), of unity of belief in Protestant and Catholic territories alike stultified thought. The religion of the monarch became the religion of the state.

In England the Puritans continued to press for the abolition of episcopacy and the prayer book. Some of them, in despair, sailed for America in the *Mayflower* in 1620 and planted Congregationalism in New England (the Church of England had already been established in Virginia in 1607). The Puritan Revolution in England, however, achieved success in 1643 when Parliament abolished episcopacy and, next year, substituted the *Directory of Worship for the Book of Common Prayer*. The monarchy was re-established in 1660 under Charles II, together with the whole episcopal system and a revised prayer book (1662). But the Nonconformists achieved some relief by the Toleration Act 1689, after which parliamentary control over the Established Church superseded royal control.

During the struggle Quakerism was born. These 'seekers', as they called themselves, abandoned all traditional Christian outward forms – ministry, creeds, sacraments, liturgy, systems of theology – and waited in silence, meditating on the Bible until they felt the 'inner light' of God dawning within them and the Holy Spirit enabling them to speak. In their small communities they stressed the comradely life and works of charity, inspired by the mystical experience of Christ through the Spirit. Their great champion in England was George Fox (1624-91) and in America, William Penn (1644-1718). Today they are known as the 'Society of Friends'.

Illustrations page 457

Nationalism in Europe

In the Netherlands the controversy over predestination raised by

Arminius was dealt with at the Synod of Dort (1618–19). In France there was a prolonged dispute between the Jansenists and the Jesuits over the doctrine of grace, which soon assumed political overtones. But the real struggle for power lay between the papacy and the advocates of national absolutism. Gallicanism in France had its counterparts in Sicily, Spain and Portugal and developed through Febronianism to that particular church-state system in absolutist Austria known as Josephinism. The Church was regarded as a department of state.

Scepticism and Revolution

By the end of the seventeenth century the cult of reason had made considerable progress. In England the Deists of the early eighteenth century, who found God's laws sufficiently manifested in nature and denied the need for any supernatural revelation, were worsted by William Law, Berkeley and Butler. In France Deism was championed by Voltaire, Rousseau and the Encyclopedists. When the French Revolution came, many of its leaders were animated by their spirit. The Civil Constitution of the Clergy (July 1790) forced on the clergy an oath of loyalty to the nation, fixed their stipends (the state having taken over all ecclesiastical property), and abolished the old diocesan and parochial boundaries. The religious orders had already been dissolved.

The 'Terror' and the guillotine followed; then total dechristianization – the closure of the churches in Paris, the cult of the goddess Reason, of Robespierre's Supreme Being, and finally the religion of theophilanthropy. Napoleon regarded religion as necessary to France and a guarantee of patriotism. He therefore made a Concordat with Pius VII in 1801 which governed relations between the State and the Catholic Church in France until its disestablishment in 1905.

The revival of Catholicism in France, Germany, Austria etc., which followed the defeat of Napoleon, went hand in hand with the development of Ultramontanism (the centralization of authority in the papacy), which culminated in the declaration of the Vatican Council of 1870 that the pope is infallible when he makes, by virtue of his office, a solemn pronouncement on faith or morals – not, as popularly misunderstood, that everything the pope says is infalliby true.

The Evangelical Revival

In England and in Germany the scepticism about orthodox Christian belief, engendered by the rationalists, was powerfully reinforced by the discoveries of the scientists and the historical and biblical critics of the nineteenth century. The industrial revolution produced social problems which neither Catholics nor Protestants were at first able to deal with. In England, however, the eighteenth century had already witnessed the spiritual awakening of the Evangelical Revival, both within the Established Church and outside it, when the followers of

Illustration page 458 John Wesley (1703-91) left the Church of England and founded the Methodist movement. In America the movement began in the 1760s, but increased rapidly after Wesley ordained two of his laypreachers for work in America and later, in Baltimore, Francis Asbury was made superintendent, or bishop. The Methodist Episcopal Church was destined to become the largest Protestant communion in the world.

The Evangelical Revival was followed by the Catholic Revival known as the Oxford Movement – associated with the names of Keble, Pusey and Newman. Through these two movements a spiritual revolution was effected in English Christianity (for the Nonconformists were influenced by both), and the scepticism resulting from the attacks of scientists and biblical critics was countered by a new generation of scholarly churchmen, such as Westcott, Lightfoot, Hort and Gore, and Lord Acton (Roman Catholic).

Meanwhile, other Christians were deeply concerned by the social conditions revealed in the novels of Dickens, Charles Kingsley and George Eliot. Christian Socialism (a movement started within the Church of England by Ludlow, Kingsley and F. D. Maurice) was continued by Gore, Stewart Headlam and William Temple and gradually roused the conscience of Church and nation to the need for better housing, education and social conditions for the working classes. Throughout the nineteenth century the Nonconformist Churches also strove for improved conditions and the betterment of the poor, for religious equality with the Established Church, and for a share in national education.

The unification of the German states into the German Empire in 1871 had been preceded by the unification of Italy as a kingdom under Victor Emmanuel in 1860, but it was not until 1870 that the temporal power of the pope over Rome and the States of the Church came to an end. The pope withdrew into the Vatican. Only after Mussolini had concluded a concordat with Pius XI in 1929 did the pope come out of voluntary seclusion and assume temporal power once more as head of the Vatican State. Christianity, however, in any of its forms, whether Roman Catholic, Anglican, or Protestant, had not for some centuries been confined to Europe, as must already have been noted.

The Spread of Christianity

We have seen how Christianity spread from Palestine to Syria, Asia Minor, Greece and Rome in the first century AD. By the fourth century churches were established in every province of the Roman Empire and had spread outside the empire into Mesopotamia, Persia and the kingdom of Armenia. The founder of the Armenian Church (which accepts the doctrines of the first three General Councils of the Church, but rejects that of the fourth General Council of Chalcedon) was Gregory the Illuminator (c. 240-332).

Christianity was introduced into Ethiopia about the middle of the fourth century and also among the barbarian Goths who lived north of the Danube. The apostle to the Goths was Ulfilas, who was consecrated bishop by the Arian bishop, Eusebius of Nicomedia. He reduced the Gothic language to writing, translated the Bible and spent forty years evangelizing the Goths, converting them to the Arian form of Christianity. Ireland was outside the Roman Empire. Its

Illustration page 440

conversion began with the work of St Patrick (d. 461) in the early fifth century. Patrick introduced the diocesan episcopal system into Ireland, but Celtic Christianity was famous for its monastic schools in the fifth and sixth centuries and the chief person in a monastery was the abbot, not the bishop.

The fifth century was a period of disaster for the empire, especially in the West. In 404 the Rhine frontier collapsed and the barbarians (wave after wave of peoples pressing westward from the steppes of Central Asia into more fertile lands) poured into Gaul and Spain. The Huns were non-Christian: hence they destroyed the churches and everything Roman. Others, like the Goths under Alaric, who sacked Rome in 410, were Arian Christians. The Vandals were also Arians: they took over the Roman administration and persecuted the Catholics, especially in North Africa. In the sixth century the Eastern emperor Justinian I drove the Goths from Italy and the Vandals from North Africa and recovered the rest of the empire with the exception of Britain, Gaul and northern Spain. Britain had been invaded from c. 449 onwards by non-Christian Angles and Saxons, who eventually occupied most of the country and drove the old Romano-British Christians westward into Cornwall, Wales and Cumberland. In 597 St Augustine, with a party of monks sent by Pope Gregory the Great to evangelize the English, landed at Thanet in Kent and the reconversion of England began. Scotland and Northumbria were evangelized by Irish missionaries.

Europe becomes Christian

Celtic (or Irish) missionaries also were the principal agents in converting large parts of Europe to Christianity after the barbarian invasions (see page 433). Clovis, king of the Franks, had already accepted 'Catholic' Christianity and been baptized with 3,000 of his followers at Reims on Christmas Day, 496. When Charlemagne, king of the Franks, was crowned as emperor in Rome by Leo III on Christmas Day, 800, the fiction of a Holy Roman Empire, to last over 1,000 years, began. Charlemagne was a Catholic Christian, but he 'converted' the Saxons by the choice of Christianity or the sword. Scandinavia was the last outpost to accept Christianity, but by 1200 all Europe (except for a few pockets) was Christian and acknowledged the leadership of the pope.

The first mission to the Slavs had occurred in the ninth century, led by Cyril and Methodius. For some years there was a tussle between Rome and Constantinople as to their allegiance – and whether their liturgical language should be Latin or Slavonic – but from c. 1000 AD the spread of Christianity throughout Russia took its inspiration from Byzantine Constantinople rather than from Rome. Poland was on the borderline and had been divided between Roman and Orthodox Christianity since the tenth century. The Magyars of Hungary (Mongolian émigrés to the West), who at first desecrated churches, were converted to Catholicism in the tenth century and in 1001 their king, Stephen, was crowned by the pope.

The Fight Against Islam

Meanwhile Islam had made serious inroads into Christendom. The Arabs advancing under the inspiration of Mohammed had captured Jerusalem in 638, Alexandria in 642 (followed by the whole of Egypt), the coast of North Africa, including Carthage, in 697, and the greater part of Spain by 715. The Muslim army was checked in central France by Charles Martel at Tours in 732, but Rome itself was plundered in 846 and Sicily, along with parts of southern Italy, fell to Muslim domination in the early tenth century. The final blow was the fall of Constantinople to the (Muslim) Turks in 1453. Thus large parts of early Christian Europe and Africa became Muslim, and the advance of Islam produced the Christian crusades, designed originally to recover the Holy Places from Muslim domination.

But a new power appeared on the horizon of Europe, which produced a new missionary enterprise. The Mongols under Genghis Khan and his successors established a vast empire from China to the Caspian Sea and invaded Russia, Poland and Hungary. Many Christian prisoners were taken into Central Asia, and various missions were despatched by the pope to the Great Khan, the most notable being that of the Franciscan John of Monte Corvino, who laboured in Peking and was consecrated as the first archbishop of the Latin Church of the Far East in 1308. In 1369 the Latins were expelled from Peking after the Chinese recovered the city from the Mongols. By 1400 the ruthless Tamerlane had destroyed all Western and Christian civilization in Asia.

Jesuit Missionaries

A fresh start had, therefore, to be made by the Jesuit Francis Xavier (1506-52), who reached Goa in 1542 and founded a missionary college, from which he preached Christianity through Travancore, Malacca, the Molucca Islands and Sri Lanka. In 1549 he landed in Japan, learned the language, and founded a Church which persisted for a time despite persecution. Goa became an archbishopric in 1557 with authority over the Latin Church in East Asia. The same year the Portuguese settlement at Macao began and thither came the Italian Jesuit Matteo Ricci (1552-1610), who was destined to sow fresh seeds of Christianity in China. Jesuit, Dominican, Franciscan and Augustinian missionaries also carried the gospel to South and Central America and to parts of North America.

For Christianity in Japan, see page 354.

Illustrations pages 458, 459

It was the Augustinians who opened the Philippines to Christian missions in 1565. The Jesuits followed with schools for both Spanish and Filipino children. In 1611 the Dominicans founded the University of Manila. In 1622 Pope Gregory XV established the 'Congregation for the Propagation of the Faith' (known as 'Propaganda') to superintend the work from Rome, but although the Portuguese made repeated attempts to establish Christianity in Africa, there were too few missionaries to make any permanent impact.

Protestant Missions

The Protestant Churches of the Reformation were not unaware of the existence of the lands outside Europe which some of their nationals helped to colonize – notably the English and the Dutch – but beyond caring for their own kith and kin they were in no position to embark upon missions directed towards the native populations, on any large scale, until the late eighteenth century. Pietism in Germany had produced the first two non-Roman Catholic missionaries from Europe to India (they reached Tranquebar in 1706). The British East India Company was generally hostile to missionaries. In England the Society for Promoting Christian Knowledge (SPCK) was founded in 1698, mainly for the dissemination of Bibles and tracts at home and abroad. The Society for the Propagation of the Gospel in Foreign Parts (SPG), which followed in 1701, was at first mainly concerned with the American colonies and sent John and Charles Wesley to Georgia as chaplains.

It is, therefore, all the more remarkable that the German Lutherans sent out to India originally by the king of Denmark were, as Bishop Stephen Neill says, 'taken over by the High Church Anglican Society for Promoting Christian Knowledge, and financially supported with a view to their preaching the Gospel to the non-Christians; and at the same time they were chaplains to British regiments and communities. They used the Book of Common Prayer, and indeed translated it into Tamil, they baptised and celebrated the Lord's Supper according to the Anglican rite . . . but, strange as it may seem, the episcopal Church of England from 1728 to 1861 employed in South India missionaries who had never received episcopal ordination according to the Anglican rite' (*A History of Christian Missions*, 1964, p. 233).

The Nonconformist Effort

The Nonconformist Churches in England took their share of responsibility for spreading Christianity outside Europe. Thus, the Baptist Missionary Society, founded in 1792, sent its first (and perhaps most famous) missionary, William Carey (1761-1834), to India in 1793. It also sent William Knibb (1803-45) and others to Jamaica, where they played their part in the campaign for emancipation of the slaves; Timothy Richard (1845-1919) and others, including the biblical scholar H. H. Rowley (1890-1969) to China; and George Grenfell (1849-1906) to the Congo. The London Missionary Society, founded in 1795 by Congregationalists, Presbyterians, Anglicans and Wesleyans, sent its first twenty-nine missionaries to Tahiti in 1796. Maintained chiefly by the Congregationalists, in recent times it has helped to spread Christianity in China, India, South-East Asia, South and East Africa and the South Sea Islands. The Anglican Church Missionary Society (CMS), originally founded in 1799 as the Society for Missions in Africa and the East and renamed in 1812, was followed in 1813 by the Methodist Missionary Society. Churchmen and Nonconformists had already co-operated in 1804 to found the British and Foreign Bible Society (BFBS), which has now translated the whole, or parts of the Bible, into over 1200 languages.

Many other missionary societies from Great Britain, Scandinavia and all the Protestant countries of Europe have contributed to the dissemination of Christianity throughout the world. The Basel Evangelical Missionary Society dates from 1815, the Danish Missionary Society from 1821, the Berlin Society from 1824. The USA also joined in with the founding, in 1810, of the American Board of Commissioners for Foreign Missions – originally inter-denominational, but later mainly Congregational – which sent missionaries to India as early as 1812. In 1814 the American Baptist Missionary Union was formed; the American Methodist Missionary Society in 1819; and in 1835 and 1837 the Dutch Reformed and Presbyterian Churches broke away from the American Board of Commissioners to form separate missionary societies. Roman Catholic missions also revived and prospered in the nineteenth century.

The first World Missionary Conference was held at Edinburgh in 1910 and its members learned that there were 1,925,205 communicant members of the Protestant and Anglican Churches in Asia, Africa and other non-white areas. Many of the delegates attended not as interested individuals, but as official representatives of the so-called 'younger churches'. The second World Missionary Conference at Jerusalem in 1928 actually produced a whole volume of its report entitled *The Relations between the Younger and Older Churches* – from which the unhappy phrase 'younger churches' derives – unhappy, since the Church is, as St Paul declared, the 'Body of Christ', which exists in various localities, through time and eternity, and cannot, therefore, be 'young' or 'old', but is one in Him. The realization of this truth leads naturally on to an examination of the movements towards unity within the Christian Churches.

The Growth of the Ecumenical Movement

The Methodists were the pioneers in denominational reunion, i.e. the healing of divisions within a denomination. Thus, union was achieved between the Wesleyan and the Methodist Episcopal Churches in Canada in 1833 (the Methodist New Connexion joined them in 1841) and the Methodist Church of Canada was formed in 1884. In 1857 three bodies of English Methodists joined together to form the United Methodist Free Churches, but the English Methodist Church did not come into existence until 1932. In the USA the great schism in American Methodism occurred in 1845 over the question of slavery, resulting in a split between the Methodist Episcopal Church and the Methodist Episcopal Church South. These two Churches joined with the Methodist Protestant Church in 1939 to form the Methodist Church. Since 1891 an International Council of Congregational Churches has existed as an advisory body without administrative or judicial powers. Since 1905 most of the Baptist Churches have been associated in the World Baptist Alliance, which also exercises no judicial control over its member Churches. World Conferences of Pentecostalists have been held since 1939.

The Salvation Army is organized throughout the world on military lines. It demands strict discipline, obedience and sacrifice, but is essentially a revivalist and evangelistic movement which regards the Church's sacraments of baptism and the eucharist as non-essential. It is, therefore, unlikely to unite with any of the historic Churches.

The attempt to achieve wider reunion between different denominations really began with the publication of the so-called Chicago-Lambeth Quadrilateral, adopted by the Protestant Episcopal Church of America in 1886 and reaffirmed by the Lambeth Conference of the bishops of the Anglican Communion in 1888. This asserted that Christian unity can only be restored by 'the return of all Christian communions to the principles of unity exemplified by the undivided Church during the first ages of its existence. Which principles we believe to be the substantial deposit of Christian Faith and Order committed by Christ and His apostles to the Church unto the end of the World.' This deposit was further defined as '(1) The Holy Scriptures of the Old and New Testaments as the revealed Word of God; (2) The Nicene Creed as the sufficient statement of the Christian Faith; (3) The two Sacraments – Baptism and the Lord's Supper; (4) The Historic Episcopate locally adapted in the methods of its administration to the varying needs of the nations and peoples called of God into the unity of His Church.'

It is the last of these which has proved the chief stumbling block to the organic union of episcopal and non-episcopal Churches. Thus, the 'Appeal to all Christian People' issued by the Lambeth Conference of 1920 (which put forward the Quadrilateral as the basis of unity) met with a very mixed reception among the Free Churches in Britain, despite the confession by the Anglican bishops 'in penitence and prayer' of 'our share in the guilt of thus crippling the Body of Christ and hindering the activity of his Spirit'.

In 1925 the formal union of the Presbyterian, Congregational and Methodist Churches of Canada produced the United Church of Canada. In 1947, after long negotiations, the Church of South India came into being through the union of episcopal and non-episcopal bodies, viz. four dioceses of the (Anglican) Church of India, Burma and Sri Lanka, with the South India Province of the Methodist Church and the South India United Church (formed in 1908 of Presbyterian, Congregational and Dutch Reformed bodies, reinforced in 1919 by Lutheran and Reformed members of the Malabar Basel Mission). Other unions have taken place and in 1969 talks between the Presbyterian and Congregational Churches in England and between the Church of England and the Methodists had reached an advanced stage, but, although the Methodist Conference voted in favour of the scheme of union by a majority of 77 per cent, the vote in the Convocations of Canterbury and York reached only 69 per cent; thus the scheme was rejected.

A New Spirit of Co-operation

The ecumenical movement, however, has not been solely concerned with the reunion of the divided Churches. Full intercommunion was agreed between the Church of England and the Church of Sweden in 1920 and with the Old Catholics in 1931. Very friendly relations have been established between the Church of England and the Eastern Orthodox Churches and, although Pope Leo XIII declared Anglican Orders invalid in 1896 and the talks between Anglican and Roman Catholic theologians, led by Lord Halifax and Cardinal Mercier, at Malines (1921-25) came to nothing, a new spirit of co-operation and mutual respect has arisen between the Anglican and Roman communions, largely through the work of Pope John XXIII and the Second Vatican Council.

As we have seen earlier, all the historic Churches of Western Europe sent missionaries to Africa, Asia, the Americas and other parts of the world. It was in the 'mission field' that the problem of intercommunion and common endeavour arose acutely. The World Missonary Conference at Edinburgh in 1910 resulted in the formation of the International Missionary Council (formed in 1921 under the chairmanship of J. R. Mott), whose purpose was to co-ordinate the work of all non-Roman Catholic missions. Behind the organization of the WMC and the resulting IMC lay the experience and ideals of the World Student Christian Federation (founded 1895, which subsequently arranged several World Youth Conferences and produced the first General Secretary of the World Council of Churches (Dr W. A. Visser't Hooft).

Also arising from the Edinburgh Conference was the World Conference on Faith and Order, largely due to Bishop Charles Henry Brent and the Rev. W. T. Manning (later bishop of New York) of the Protestant Episcopal Church in the USA, who recognized the necessity for excluding from a World Missionary Conference all discussion of the doctrinal disagreements underlying the disunion of Christendom, but conceived the idea of a conference called specifically for this purpose. The General Convention of the American Episcopal Church supported them and World Conferences on Faith and Order were held at Lausanne (1927) and Edinburgh (1937), after World War I. But already in 1914, under the shadow of war, the concern of many Christians that the Churches internationally ought to do something to prevent war had produced the World Alliance for International Friendship through the Churches.

Social Problems

International Christian co-operation on social questions, already under way in France, Germany, Switzerland and America before 1914, led to the idea of a World Conference on Life and Work, aimed at bringing the Christian conscience to bear on the practical problems of the contemporary world. The idea was taken up by Archbishop Söderblom of Uppsala, Sweden, and the first world conference was held at Stockholm in 1925. A second World Conference on Life and Work was held at Oxford in 1937 – the same year as the second World Conference on Faith and Order at Edinburgh. Negotiations started in 1937 resulted eventually in the fusion of 'Life and Work' and 'Faith and Order', aided in no small measure by the efforts of

Archbishop William Temple, Visser 't Hooft, the Swedish bishop Yngve Brilioth, and the German pastor Niemöller.

The result was the setting up of the World Council of Churches at Amsterdam in 1948. The aims of the WCC are set out in a report of its first assembly: 'The World Council of Churches has come into existence because we have already recognised a responsibility to one another's churches in Our Lord Jesus Christ. There is but one Lord and one Body. Therefore we cannot rest content with our present divisions . . . we embark upon our work in the World Council of Churches in penitence for what we are, in hope for what we shall be.' The WCC has a permanent organization, with offices in Geneva. Its membership is restricted to those Churches which 'accept our Lord Jesus Christ as God and Saviour', but it is a consultative body which has neither legislative, nor judicial, nor executive power over the member Churches. It is essentially an organ of inter-Church co-operation.

Rapprochement with Rome
The World Council of Churches at its inauguration included representatives of about 150 Christian communions, but no official representatives of the Roman Catholic Church or of the Orthodox Churches. Rome did, however, send to Amsterdam an observer, Charles Boyer, a French Jesuit professor at the Gregorian University, who was convinced that the Curia was wrong in boycotting the ecumenical movement. At Amsterdam Boyer met George Bell, Bishop of Chichester, and so began a series of contacts between the Church of England and the Church of Rome, dating from the visit of Bishop Stephen Neill to Rome in June 1949, through the meeting between Boyer and Leonard Prestige in Strasbourg in September 1950, followed by meetings of Drs A. R. Vidler and J. N. D. Kelly with Boyer at Rome (1957), Cambridge (1958), Assisi (1961) and Oxford (1962), to the meeting at the Vatican of Archbishop Fisher with Pope John XXIII in 1960 and of Archbishop Ramsey with Pope Paul VI in March 1966.

During his visit to Rome Archbishop Ramsey opened an Anglican Institute at Rome, as a place of common prayer for Anglicans and Roman Catholics. Bishop Moorman of Ripon and Canon Pawley were appointed as representatives of the English archbishops in Rome, in consultation with Cardinal Bea, head of the Secretariat for Christian Unity, and they attended, as observers, the Roman Council known as Vatican II. A new spirit has animated the Church of Rome since this council (opened by Pope John XXIII on 11 October, 1962, and

Illustration page 460 concluded by Pope Paul VI on 8 December, 1965). The collegiality of the episcopate was strongly affirmed as well as the apostolate of the laity (for which a universal congress was held at Rome, 11-18 October, 1967).

The revision of the liturgy, begun by Guéranger in 1840, had resulted in the restoration of pure Gregorian chant and the scholarly study of the history of liturgy. Stimulated by liturgical scholars'

researches at Louvain and Maaria Laach, this had produced before
World War II a revival of liturgical worship, through liturgical congresses and the development of the dialogue mass. Its counterpart was seen in the Church of England in the development of the Family Communion, largely stimulated by A. G. Hebert's book *Liturgy and Society* (London, 1936) and E. L. Mascall's *Corpus Christi* (London, 1953, 2nd ed. revised and enlarged 1965). The Church of Wales and the Church of Scotland, as well as the Reformed Church of France and Switzerland (see J. D. Benoit, *Liturgical Renewal: studies in Catholic and Protestant Developments on the Continent*, Eng. trans., London, 1958), had also revised their traditional liturgies in a more catholic direction. All this liturgical revival (including the introduction for an experimental period of Series II Communion Office in the Church of England) helped forward the movement for reunion of the Churches.

The Return to the Bible and the Recovery of Theology

World War I shattered many traditional theological notions. Karl Barth, a German Swiss Protestant pastor (1886-1968), published in 1919 his famous *Commentary on Romans*, in which he challenged the pre-1914 optimistic Christianity that boasted of human capabilities and achievements, its faith in science and progress, its stress on mysticism and feeling. By contrast, he spoke of human folly, ignorance and pride, and sought to lead theology back to the 'Word of God' and the principles of the Reformation, emphasizing 'revelation' to the detriment of 'reason'. His literary output and his influence (especially on the German Confessional Church during the World War II) were immense. Emil Brunner (1889-1966), another Swiss dialectical theologian, author of *The Mediator* (Eng. trans. 1934), *The Divine Imperative* (Eng, trans. 1937) and *Man in Revolt* (Eng. trans. 1939), like Karl Barth, greatly influenced the American Reinhold Niebuhr, and D. R. Davies (1889-1958), the Congregational son of a Welsh miner who became an Anglican priest and wrote *On to Orthodoxy* (1939). This 'biblical theology' was in vogue in England for a decade after the World War II, but soon a move towards what has been called 'Christian radicalism' set in.

Letters and Papers from Prison by Pastor Dietrich Bonhoeffer, a victim of Nazi Germany (he was finally hanged on 9 April, 1945) first appeared in English in 1953. The general public was made aware of some of the issues at stake by the publication in March 1963 of *Honest to God* by John A. T. Robinson (Bishop of Woolwich), which became a bestseller. Robinson had imbibed the thoughts of Bultmann, Bonhoeffer and Paul Tillich, whose *The Shaking of the Foundations* (1948) and *Systematic Theology* (1951-63) reflect the thought of the French existentialists, Jean-Paul Sartre and Gabriel Marcel.

There has also been a ferment of new ideas about God and the Christian religion in the Roman Catholic Church, quite apart from the current debates about the question of the seat of authority, which was brought to the fore by the second Vatican Council and subsequent discussions about the 'collegiality' of the episcopate and its relations with the papacy. (On this see Hans Küng, *The Council and Reunion* [Eng. trans. 1961].)

The encyclical *Humani Generis* (12 August, 1950) of Pius XII condemned various intellectual tendencies in the Roman Church, including existentialism, over-emphasis on the Word of God to the detriment of reason, etc. On 1 November, 1950, he defined the doctrine of the Assumption of the Blessed Virgin Mary as a dogma of the Church by an infallible pronouncement. Pope John XXIII (1959–63) was much more in tune with the modern outlook and it was he who inaugurated the second Vatican Council in October 1962. He did not live to see its end, but, despite the encyclical *Humanae Vitae* (29 July, 1968) of Paul VI condemning the use of the contraceptive pill, reaffirmed by John Paul II, some of the developments initiated by Pope John continued. Perhaps the greatest apologist for Christianity in the modern world among Roman Catholic writers has been Teilhard de Chardin (d. 1955), a palaeontologist, anthropologist and philosopher who was also a priest in the Roman Church. His best-known book is *The Phenomenon of Man* (Eng. trans. 1959, revised ed. 1965), but *The Realm of the Divine* (Eng. trans. 1964) is an even more profound work.

The outcome of all this remains in the future. The history of Christianity in the past twenty centuries suggests that, as it overcame the challenge of primitive and of syncretistic beliefs, such as Gnosticism in the early centuries, of barbarian invasions in the Dark Ages, of heresies in the Middle Ages, of the worldliness of the Medici popes of the Renaissance, of Deism and Rationalism in the eighteenth century, of nationalism and liberalism in the nineteenth – so it will overcome the scepticism of the twentieth century and will ultimately return to its roots in the New Testament relevation of Christianity as a historical and yet supernatural religion of the spirit.

Recent Years (Ed.)

Pope Paul VI died in 1978 and his successor John Paul I suffered a fatal heart attack a month after his election. He was followed by Cardinal Karol Wojtyla of Cracow, who took the name of John Paul II. He was the first pope from Poland, a strongly Roman Catholic country, and the first non-Italian pope since 1522. John Paul II became known as the 'travelling Pope', visiting his native Poland the following year, going on to Ireland, North and South America, and later to Asia and Africa. In 1981 the Pope was shot and wounded by a Turkish fanatic in St Peter's Square, Rome, but after a long convalescence he resumed his activities. In 1982 he became the first pope to visit Britain and at Canterbury Cathedral he was embraced by the Anglican Archbishop as 'beloved brother in Christ'.

Illustration page 460

Illustration page 459

John Paul II continued the conservatism of Paul VI, re-affirming his encyclical against birth control and abortion and declaring that the Church would never ordain women to the priesthood. In 1979 Professor Hans Küng of Tübingen, who had questioned some papal attitudes in his book *Infallible?* in 1971, was stripped of his post as a

Above Worship in a modern Baptist Church in London. The Baptist movement maintains that baptism by total immersion should follow a personal confession of faith and hence presupposes adult status.

Above right John Wesley was an Anglican clergyman but with others he set up the Methodist Society which became the Methodist Church and gained widespread support in the industrial regions of the north of England, and Cornwall and Wales. National Portrait Gallery, London.

Opposite above left A religious image is carried through the streets of Cuzco, Peru, at the festival of Corpus Christi.

Opposite above right A Jesuit priest helps mend the road near his dispensary for Untouchables at Tondiarpet, India.

Right Brazilian Indians kill a priest in 1624. Priests were in the van of Europe's drive to colonize Latin America and were often seen as major enemies by the Indians.

Opposite below left Kenya's Cardinal Maurice Otunga, Archbishop of Nairobi, at the Karinga Mission. He was the first black cardinal of the Roman Catholic Church.

Opposite below right Jacqueline Means, first woman pastor of Indianapolis's Episcopalian Church, visits a nursing home.

Right The cardinals and bishops in conclave in St Peter's, Rome, during one of the sessions of the Vatican Council II (1962-65).

Below A historic moment in the history of the Church: Pope John Paul II (right) and Dr Robert Runcie, the Anglican Archbishop of Canterbury, worship side by side in Canterbury Cathedral, England, in 1982.

qualified teacher of Catholic doctrine, though he continued university teaching.

Proposed unions between Churches had uneven progress, though there was a great increase in meeting and co-operation of Churches. Bible translations and liturgies appeared in modern idioms, against some opposition from those who regretted the loss of traditional phrases. Revivalist movements enlightened many Churches and the Catholic Charismatic Renewal in the USA had participants prophesying and healing. 'Liberation theology', especially in Latin America, sought to interpret the gospel as social revolution against political and financial dictatorships. Declining numbers in church attendance in Europe were matched by increases in Africa, where foreign missions were partly replaced by evangelism from 'the younger churches'.

Illustrations pages 459, 511

Chapter Twenty-One

Islam

Early in the seventh century, unnoticed by the rest of the world, a religious movement was born in the interior of Arabia. Within an amazingly short time – little more than twenty years – it gathered momentum and absorbed the unruly tribesmen of the peninsula. Spilling out from Arabia, it rapidly extended political sway over the surrounding regions, consolidated its hold in the years that followed, and in the third century of its existence, developed a most brilliant and creative culture. Its advent changed the course of history and enriched human heritage by the creation of an illustrious civilization. It continues today to be the spiritual anchor and guide of a major portion of humanity.

This religious movement was called 'Islam' by its founder, the prophet Mohammed. Islam is an Arabic word that means 'acceptance', 'surrender', 'submission' or 'commitment', and it expresses the innermost attitude of those who have hearkened to the preaching of Mohammed. Muslims (literally, those who make or do Islam), as followers of the movement are known, indicate by their very name that they have committed themselves into the hands of a sovereign divine ruler, whose will it is their purpose to follow in every aspect of life.

In another sense Islam is also the name of a community, but more profoundly it is a religious word signifying an inner attitude, always renewed in each new situation of life, an attitude of humble recognition of the human obligation to fulfil the purpose of the majestic and all-powerful Creator. A person's proper relation to God is Islam, and it brings in its train both the fulfilment of human life here on earth and reward in the hereafter.

From time to time the word 'Mohammedanism' is also used to designate the faith of Muslims. This custom is unfortunate, for Mohammedanism seems to imply that Muslims worship Mohammed much as Christians worship the Christ, and such is not the case. Islam is Islam to God alone, and it is preferable to use the term by which Muslims themselves describe their faith.

The Extent of Islam

At the present time about 700 million people are Muslim, that is, approximately one sixth of the world's population. Although Muslims are found in small numbers virtually everywhere, the majority are concentrated in a belt of countries on both sides of the equator, stretching from Morocco to the Philippine Islands. These countries occupy territory of great historical and strategic significance, as they lie across the most important lines of trade and communication between the Old World and the New.

The principal Muslim groups are the Arabic, Turkish, and Persian-speaking peoples of the Near East, a large fraction of the inhabitants of the Indian sub-continent, and the majority of the population of the Indonesian archipelago.

The greatest concentration of Muslims occurs in the Indian sub-continent, where the combined Muslim population of Pakistan, Bangladesh and India is more than 240 million people and is increasing every day. Both Indonesia and Pakistan (before Bangladesh became a separate state) laid claim to having the greatest number – each has in excess of 100 million people of Islamic faith – but precise statistics are difficult to obtain. The Islamic centre of gravity thus lies to the east and south of the borders of Pakistan, in spite of the common belief that the Arab countries and Iran are the heartland of Islam.

In Europe, the Muslim population is confined largely to Turkey and the Balkan states, but in medieval times there were also significant numbers of Muslims in Spain, Sicily and Italy. The advent of Communism in the Soviet Union and China has diminished the strength of Islam in those countries, though in Soviet Azerbaijan and Central Asia, both strongholds of Muslim glory in former times, large numbers of Muslims can still be found. They also occur in South China, and among the Chinese immigrants from the mainland to Taiwan. In addition, Africa boasts a large Muslim population south of the Sahara and along the coastal regions, particularly in the east, where there has been much immigration from the Arab countries and the Indian sub-continent. The Muslims of the Americas are mostly immigrants from other regions, or the offspring of immigrants, and their numbers remain quite small in relation to the total population.

Arabia before Mohammed

Islam was born in one of the most desolate regions of the earth's surface – the Arabian peninsula. This area is made up of forbidding deserts, arid steppes and barren mountains, along with a few favoured oases and coastal areas where water is sufficient to permit agriculture and a settled life. Although several advanced cultures with great cities flourished in antiquity in the more blessed provinces around the perimeters of the peninsula, for most of its history it has been the realm of wandering nomadic tribes which alone have had the skill and endurance to survive its rigours. These tribesmen eke out a bare existence by wandering from place to place with their flocks and herds, in search of life-giving water and pasturage. In the spring of each year they venture into the deserts where the rain briefly brings the plants into bloom. Then the nomads return to the high central plateau, and there each group stakes out part of the land for use by its own particular flocks and herds.

The key to this austere life is the presence of the camel, which supplies most of the nomad's need for food, transport and clothing. Flocks of sheep and goats are also kept, and sometimes the famous Arabian horses, but these serve only to enhance their owners' prestige, or for purposes of warfare, and they are often more of a liability than an asset in the conditions of desert life.

Because of the geographical conditions, life in Arabia has followed much the same pattern for many centuries. The untracked deserts and formidable mountains made a barrier which discouraged military adventurers from outside and, to some degree, insulated the people of the interior. Throughout antiquity not one of the great conquerors was able to exert control over the peninsula, nor were the Arabs themselves ever able to unite sufficiently to form a state of their own. Nevertheless, there was always some degree of contact between the Arabs on the northern borders and other civilizations and, as a result, trade flourished. Ideas and influences from the more developed cultures also found their way by such routes into the interior of the peninsula.

Mohammed's Tribe

Like all Arabs, Mohammed was a member of a tribe, the Quraysh, and the conditions of tribal life form one of the important elements in his own background and the rise of Islam. Some time before Mohammed's birth, the Quraysh had come into possession of the barren valley of Mecca, with its shrines and wells, and had settled there. They soon built a thriving community that flourished on commerce, and rapidly rose from their former status of insignificance to become one of the most powerful tribal groups in the peninsula. Although the Quraysh lived in a city, and although Mohammed himself was born in a city, the ties of the Quraysh with their former existence in the desert were still very strong. In order to maintain contact with the desert life, it was their practice to send children to live for a time with a nomad group. Mohammed spent part of his childhood in such a group.

Values of Pre-Islamic Arabia

The Bedouin Arabs were not notably pious, but they did have certain religious practices and ideas. In general they might be described as animists, for they believed in a number of powers, spirits, and demons whom they propitiated. Spirits associated with rocks and springs and trees were of particular importance.

The Bedouin were also influenced by the astral religion of the ancient Semitic peoples, which led them to recognize deities associated with the heavenly bodies. The major figures were goddesses, of whom the most important were al-Lat, al-Uzzah, and al-Manat. A superior deity called Allah was also familiar to them, but his function was vague, and he did not figure strongly in their thinking or practice. Nonetheless, this deity was known to the Arabs, and Mohammed's proclamation of his unique sovereign power did not involve the introduction of a wholly new deity.

The Arabs also made pilgrimages to shrines located at different places in the peninsula. There was a shrine to al-Manat at Ukaz, not far to the north of Mecca, where an annual fair was held in the sacred month (see below). By far the most important centre of pilgrimage, though, was the rectangular stone building in the valley of Mecca, near the well Zam-Zam, known as the Kaaba. In pre-Islamic times the principal god of the Kaaba was Hubal, but there were others associated with the shrine as well. When the Quraysh came into possession of Mecca, each clan erected its own deity in the sacred precincts of the shrine in a position which it claimed as its own. Almost the first act of Mohammed upon the conquest of Mecca was the destruction of these pagan idols and the purification of the Kaaba to free it from pagan symbols.

Illustration page 477

Pilgrimage to the Kaaba and the performance of rites there, including much that is now part of Islamic practice, were made during a certain month of the lunar calendar considered sacred, in which all fighting was forbidden. Renunciation of hostilities allowed tribesmen near and far to assemble, not only for the purpose of trade, but also for poetry competitions and other similar activities which the Arabs enjoyed. The Islamic duty of the pilgrimage built upon this familiar heritage of ancient Arabia, but transformed its meaning by reinterpreting it in a more profoundly religious manner.

There is evidence that there was intense religious dissatisfaction in Arabia shortly before the rise of Islam. A group called the Hanifs, who claimed spiritual descent from Abraham, were known for their virtue and deep religiousness. Mohammed maintained that he was a Hanif and saw the new dispensation which he preached as a continuation of Hanifi teaching. Little is known about the Hanifs, even the meaning of the name is obscure, but their religious thinking was moving towards monotheism and a more reassuring basis for spiritual life.

Further evidence of religious quest in Arabia was the penetration of the two great monotheistic religions, Christianity and Judaism. Settled Christian and Jewish communities existed there. In South Arabia, more than a century before the rise of Islam, there had been a Jewish kingdom which had been destroyed by Ethiopian Christian invaders, who came to avenge the persecution of Christians in the area. There were also widely scattered Arabic-speaking Jewish tribes, particularly in the oasis of Yathrib, where Mohammed was to settle when his position in Mecca had become untenable. Christians were, perhaps, fewer, but there was a well-known Christian community at Najran to the south and east of Mecca. Furthermore, many opportunities were offered to the Arabs to become acquainted with Judaism and Christianity because of their trading connections with the regions to the north. Knowledge of these two religions was important, for it prepared those who came in contact with them to receive the closely related teachings of Mohammed, and thus ultimately contributed to the actual rise and development of Islam.

In addition to the tribal outlook, the conditions prevailing in Mecca were also significant influences on Mohammed and the rise of Islam. Contrary to a commonly held assumption, Islam was born in a city, not in the desert. Some time prior to Mohammed's birth, Mecca had become a thriving commercial centre, and its citizens, the Quraysh, had gained both wealth and prestige. Mecca's growth was the result of contemporary power politics. The long-standing hostility between Sassanian Persia and Roman Byzantine had destroyed trade along the usual overland route from the Mediterranean to the head of the Persian Gulf. A new route was therefore sought for goods which flowed from the East, and this extended along the coastal plain of Arabia, from the seaports of Yemen whence ships plied both to India and Africa. Mecca lay in the coastal plain at a point where the north-south route intersected another major route leading to the east and the markets of Iraq. Mecca was, thus, ideally located to serve as the focus of a rich exchange.

The Prophet

Mohammed, the posthumous son of Abdullah, was born into Bani Hashim, one of the nobler but poorer clans of Quraysh at an unknown date between AD 570 and 580. Shortly after his birth the boy's mother also died, and he was brought up an orphan in circumstances of some hardship by his uncle, Abu Talib.

There are a number of stories and legends about Mohammed's childhood, but it is difficult to place reliance on most of the information concerning his early life. One story, however, can be confirmed, namely Mohammed's marriage to the widow, Khadijah. Prior to the marriage Mohammed had prospered in the service of this lady, who maintained her fortune by commercial dealings. Although Khadijah was allegedly much older than Mohammed, the marriage was happy and produced a number of children. To Mohammed's sorrow none of the boys survived childhood. As long as Khadijah lived Mohammed took no other wives, though he was later to contract a number of marriages.

From an early age Mohammed showed himself a man of religious inclinations and frequently retired alone to Mount Hira, near Mecca, for nocturnal religious vigils and meditation. Some time after his fortieth birthday there occurred the decisive experience of his life, the call to prophethood. According to the traditional account Mohammed was alone in meditation when an angelic being commanded him to *Illustration page 477* 'recite' in the name of God. When Mohammed failed to respond, the angel seized him by the throat and shook him as he repeated the command. Again Mohammed failed to react, so the angel proceeded to choke him until Mohammed was finally compelled to do as he was told. Thus began the series of revelatory experiences that were the chief mark of his prophethood and whose record constitutes the chief work of Muslim scripture, the Koran.

Mohammed was deeply disturbed by the vision and for a long time was uncertain of its significance. He was unable to overcome his doubt easily and he feared that he might be losing his sanity, or that he was possessed by a malignant spirit. Several times the Koran extends reassurance to Mohammed that his doubts are unfounded and that the revelations are, indeed, from a divine source. The crisis of doubt was made worse by a long gap between the revelations. At last, however, they were resumed, and Mohammed won a clear conception of his mission as the agent of a divine message to his generation. Thereupon, he launched into his public career as preacher, reformer, and prophet.

Mohammed in Mecca

Mohammed worked publicly in Mecca for ten years or more. In the beginning there was little to sustain him but his own deep faith, for the majority of Meccans ignored him; but, as he gained some following, they began first to fear, and then to oppose him.

Apart from members of his own family the earliest converts were largely from the lower classes, many of whom were slaves. After some time Mohammed also attracted several leading men of the city, the most important being Abu Bakr and Umar, his first two successors in the leadership of the community. As opposition to Mohammed hardened, the Meccans began to persecute those from the lower classes who had no protection from a clan group. Mohammed himself was ridiculed and threatened, but was spared physical harm because of the support of his clan. This support continued even when the rest of Quraysh enforced a boycott against Bani Hashim in the hope of ensuring the surrender of the prophet. Eventually, one section of Mohammed's followers emigrated to Ethiopia, possibly as a result of the persecutions as Muslim tradition suggests. However, after remaining in exile for some time, most of the emigrants returned to Mecca.

Mohammed found himself in really serious difficulties when first Khadijah, and then his uncle, died. Abu Talib, like most of Bani Hashim, had never become a Muslim himself, but he had been unswerving in his support of Mohammed. Upon Abu Talib's death, another uncle, Abu Lahab, became head of Bani Hashim, and he was among Mohammed's most bitter opponents. Mohammed sought to solve his difficulty by approaching the people of al-Taif, a hill town near Mecca, asking them to accept himself and his community. They refused, but his approach made him more hated in Mecca.

In AD 621, at pilgrimage time, Mohammed entered into negotiations with some citizens of Yathrib and was able to secure an agreement that he and his followers would be accepted and given protection. Thereupon, members of the community drifted away from Mecca to take up their new homes in Yathrib, and they were followed in AD 622 by Mohammed himself. Afterwards Yathrib became known as Medina, the city of the prophet. Mohammed's emigration is called the *Hegira*. Since it marked a decisive turning point in his fortunes and those of his community, it was adopted as the starting point of the Islamic calendar.

Allah

Mohammed's preaching in Mecca centred upon the one sovereign deity, Allah, who controlled the destiny of humankind. In place of the numerous powers recognized by the Arabs, Mohammed proclaimed a unique God who created the universe, established its order, and encompassed its fate in his hand. From all people Allah demands acknowledgment of his sole sovereignty and submission to his ordinance. At first strongest emphasis was laid upon the terrors of the judgment awaiting the recalcitrant ones who were ungrateful to their Lord and refused submission. The Koran paints a vivid picture of the torments of hell. As time passed the revelation turned to other themes. Answers were revealed to criticism which Mohammed faced, and tales of the prophets of former times, together with examples from nature, buttressed the declaration of God's sovereignty.

From the beginning, Mohammed found that his situation at Medina was very different from that at Mecca. Medina was an oasis with well-developed agriculture and a large, settled population. However, for some time, life had been disrupted by fighting between tribal elements over the ownership of land. Some of Medina's citizens, therefore, banded themselves together under the leadership of Mohammed, in the hope that they would be able to restore peace. Arab and Jewish tribes, as well as a considerable number of Mohammed's followers from Mecca, were included in this association. The nature of the new community, or *ummah*, was set out in a famous document between Mohammed and the Medinese, known as the Constitution of Medina.

The first years of Mohammed's stay in Medina were occupied with consolidating his position. He faced difficulties among his own followers because of jealousies between the Medina followers (Ansar) and those who had emigrated from Mecca (Muhajirun). The latter had, for a long time, to depend heavily upon the established people of Medina for assistance, and this burden naturally aroused resentment. More important was the dissatisfaction and covert opposition of a portion of the non-Muslim Medinese whom the Koran condemns as hypocrites. Many in the oasis were threatened or displeased by Mohammed's newly acquired pre-eminence, and such was the strength of their opposition that attempts were made on his life.

There was also trouble with the Jewish tribes, who became increasingly restive as the prophet's understanding of the *ummah* narrowed to include only Muslims. The Jews aroused Mohammed's wrath by their refusal to accept his prophethood, which he had expected them to acknowledge, and by their taunts that he distorted the stories about former prophets contained in the Bible. Eventually the majority of the Jews were removed from the oasis, some by banishment and others, accused of conspiring with Mohammed's enemies at the Battle of the Ditch, by bloody massacre.

Once his position in Medina was secure, the prophet turned to securing a wider support outside the oasis. Several shows of force in the neighbourhood of the city brought alliances with the Bedouin tribesmen. Mohammed's principal method of extending his influence was by forming a complex system of alliances with various tribal groups. Several of the prophet's marriages were probably contracted in the light of this diplomacy; in any event they served to strengthen his relations with specific groups.

Mohammed commenced his campaign against the Meccans by raiding one of their caravans during the sacred month of Rajab when fighting was prohibited. The event scandalized Arabia, but Mohammed persisted in a policy of attacking and harassing the caravans that were the source of Meccan wealth and power. This policy brought him into armed conflict with the Meccans, who saw the very life of their city threatened. The Meccans, however, were inept and half-hearted warriors. Victory went to Mohammed in the first major engagement at the Battle of Badr in AD 624, which is famous for its role in uniting the Muslim community and confirming its sense of mission. In the later engagements the advantage lay with the Meccans, but they were totally inadequate to deal with Mohammed militarily.

In AD 630, as the result of his skilful diplomacy and growing armed might, Mohammed gained possession of Mecca without a fight. Seeking to win over its inhabitants to his side, he dealt with the city leniently, even in the cases of those who had been his bitterest enemies. The result of the Meccan capitulation was an immediate and enormous gain in prestige for Mohammed. Bedouin tribesmen and delegations from all over Arabia came flocking to pledge their allegiance. He was by then easily the most powerful man in Arabia, and before his unexpected death two years later, in AD 632, he was able to bring by far the greater part of the peninsula under his single control, a feat which no man before him had achieved. The concept *Illustration page 477* of his mission was also made firmer by the demand, not only for political submission, but for acceptance of Islam as well.

During his lifetime Mohammed never controlled any territory outside Arabia. It is by no means certain that he thought Islam had any significance except for the Arabs, though later Muslim opinion affirms his universalist purposes. However, toward the end of his life he was responsible for organizing several expeditions against the Christian Arab border states, on the north of the peninsula. These brought Muslims into conflict with the great Byzantine and Sassanian empires and presaged the swift and permanent conquest that followed so closely after the prophet's death.

The Doctrine of Prophecy

Belief in prophecy is one of the very fundamentals of the Islamic religious system. Muslims believe there has never been a people without a prophet who spoke to them in their own language, and some authorities maintain that as many as 240,000 prophets have graced the course of history. The revelations to Mohammed repeat stories of previous prophets, some of whom are well known and occur in the Bible and others not so familiar. Among the biblical

For the Jewish tradition of prophecy, see pages 387–8.

figures mentioned are Moses, Abraham, Joseph, David and Jesus.

The Koran places Mohammed squarely in this tradition of prophecy. His function was to renew and restore the guidance given to others before him, not to found a new religion. Mohammed expected Jews and Christians, who were acquainted with prophecy, to recognize him as a continuation and revivification of their ancient religious heritages. When they did not, he was bitterly disappointed, and his attitude toward both groups hardened as he grew older. There was a difference between Mohammed and previous prophets, however, which set him apart. He was chosen as the Seal of the Prophets, that is, as the end, confirmation and climax of the centuries-old chain of divine messengers. Always before, God had found it necessary to renew guidance for wandering men, but this time the integrity of the revelation would be preserved. There would be no more prophets after Mohammed.

Mohammed's Miracles

The course of Islamic thinking about Mohammed has assigned an ever-increasing importance to his person. By the third Islamic century the prophetic tradition had been erected into a fundamental source of law and theology. Even while the prophet lived, legends were related about him, and his followers collected relics from his possessions, believing them endowed with spiritual power. The generation immediately after the prophet embroidered the story of his life with numerous tales of miracles and wonders.

The classical biographies of Mohammed tell of signs and wondrous events accompanying his birth; of supernatural beings, wise men of other religions, even natural phenomena, making obeisance to him; and of miralces performed by Mohammed himself, or on his behalf. By medieval times the belief was universal that Mohammed had been a perfect and sinless being. This belief was thought necessary to buttress the revelations themselves, otherwise complete confidence in the guidance delivered would have been impossible. In eschatological writings it was taught that Mohammed would act as intercessor for his people on the Day of Judgment, refusing to enter Paradise until all others had done so.

The most profound veneration of Mohammed's person was displayed by the mystics. In their speculations, Mohammed acquired the full dimensions of a supernatural being. One school identified Mohammed with the pre-existent divine light, the first emanation from the unity of the God-head, the power that had created the world and which sustains it. There was no approach to God but through the illumination of the prophetic light; therefore, the mystics copied the prophetic model so that the divine light, or light of Mohammed, might illuminate their souls. This veneration raises the prophet to such a height that some mystic prayer manuals employ the same epithets and attributes about him as they do about God.

From the late nineteenth century, when a new life stirred among Muslims eager to revivify Islam, there has been a sharply increased religious interest in Mohammed. This new concern is exemplified in the large number of prophetic biographies recently published in a variety of languages. Some of them, for example, *The Spirit of Islam* by Sayyid Amir Ali, have attained international reputation. These works are often apologetic, with an avowed purpose of refuting or counteracting what Muslims consider as untrue and unfair attacks on Mohammed. The biographies emphasize the ethical, humanitarian and rational sides of Mohammed's thought and activity, presenting him as a thinker of unparalleled wisdom, as a statesman of great acumen, and as an exemplary character who supremely exhibits the virtues most desirable in human life. The effect of such works has been to endow Mohammed with a direct contemporary relevance, and to make his example particularly meaningful for millions of present-day Muslims.

The Koran

The Koran is the written collection of the revelations which were delivered piecemeal to the prophet by an angelic agent, over a period of more than twenty years. It is, therefore, the basic religious document for Islam and a source of unimpeachable authority for all matters of doctrine, practice, and law.

The name 'Koran' means something to be recited, and each of the separate revelations making up the book we now have is called a Koran. It will be recalled that the angel's command to Mohammed in the very first experience of revelation was 'Recite'. One of the revelations speaks of Mohammed bringing the Arabs a 'Koran' in their own language. Here the implications seems to be that the revelations will serve as recitations in connection with worship, just as Christians and Jews recite their scriptures on religious occasions. In other verses, however, the name 'Koran' seems to point to the Islamic doctrine of prophecy and scripture, for the Koran consists of words recited or read by the angel from an original heavenly book that contains the eternal speech of God.

The Koran is approximately the same length as the New Testament. It is divided into 114 chapters or *surahs,* loosely arranged in the order of their length, with the longest first. A very short *surah* called the *Fatihah* (Opening) is, however, the first of all. It is in the form of a prayer to God for guidance. This little chapter is probably the most frequently recited portion of the Koran, for it is used both in daily prayers and on many different sorts of religious occasions. Each *surah* has a name, a kind of catchword taken from something mentioned in it. Thus, the eighteenth *surah* is called 'The Cave' because it contains the story of some youths who found refuge from persecution in a cave. Every *surah* but one begins with the words '*bismillah al-rahman al-rahim*' (In the Name of God the Compassionate, the Merciful).

The Words of God

Muslim theology considers the Koran to be the very words of God. It is important to emphasize the literal character of the revelation, for many things in both the thought and life of Muslims are explained by it. The revelation to Mohammed consisted of words somehow spoken into his ear (the tradition says that they resembled the ringing of a loud clear bell) by an angelic messenger. Neither the content of the revelation, nor its form, were of Mohammed's devising. Both were given by the angel, and Mohammed's task was only to repeat what he heard. Several statements in the Koran strongly underline the passive role of the prophet. In one verse he is cautioned not to hurry his tongue with the words, that is, to take no initiative in trying to assist the revelation, but to leave all things in the hands of the heavenly agency. The revelations also frequently address the prophet personally to inform him, to encourage him, and even to reprove him. Another indicator of the revelation's character is the word *qul* (say) which occurs frequently at the beginning of a verse. In other words, the angel began his work as an intermediary in the delivery of revelation by the command to Mohammed, 'Say (as follows)'.

Although little is known about Mohammed's mental and physical states during the reception of the revelation, it is clear that his normal consciousness and functioning were suspended. The revelation was accompanied by trance-like states in which he was oblivious to his surroundings. These abnormal circumstances were clearly observable to others. Apparently the revelation was an ecstatic experience, during which Mohammed gave every evidence of being under the influence of a power outside himself that overwhelmed him and bore him down. When he emerged from these unusual states, often severely shaken and weakened, especially in the beginning, he would pass on to his companions what had come to him. The language of the revelations was not his usual manner of expression, but bears the unmistakable marks of its ecstatic source.

The messages 'sent down' to Mohammed were taken from a heavenly book, eternal, uncreated, and co-existent with God. Known as the *Well-Preserved Tablet* or the *Mother of the Book*, this heavenly writing contains the eternal speech of God. The *Mother of the Book* may be looked upon as the expression of God's unchanging truth and will. From time to time portions of its wisdom have been bestowed on prophets as scriptures for the guidance of mankind. Each of the books given to past prophets, the *Injil* (Gospel) of Jesus, the *Zabur* (Psalms) of David, the *Torah* of Moses, etc., was drawn from this heavenly repository of truth, and each in its original form, therefore, was truly a revelation.

The reason for the sending of still another book lay partly in the Arabs' need for a prophet to address them clearly in their own language, and partly in the distortion to which the Christians and the Jews (the Peoples of the Book) had subjected their scriptures. Mohammed did not claim that the revelations making up the Koran had exhausted the content of the heavenly scripture, only that the revelations derived from that divine source. The Koran is that part of the heavenly scripture which God deemed sufficient for the guidance of men and which he 'sent down' to the prophet.

Extraordinary Reverence

Because it is considered to be the *ipsissima verba* of God the Koran is everywhere paid an extraordinary reverence by Muslims. The handling and use of the text are conducted in a way befitting its sacred character. Care is taken never to lay the Koran on the ground and never to allow it to come into contact with an unclean substance. Among the highest acts of piety for Muslims is to memorize the entire Koran and to recite it during the month of Ramadan and on other occasions. One who has mastered the sacred text is called an *hafiz*.

Illustration page 478

Throughout the Islamic world there exist schools to teach the Koran to children, especially boys. So great is the merit of memorizing it that even in non-Arab countries thousands labour to commit the sacred sounds to memory though they may not comprehend the significance of the words at all. Among the superstitious a verse, or even a few words, of the Koran may be employed as an amulet to ward off the evil eye, to cure illness and perform similar acts.

Illustration page 478

The religious value of the Koran is also illustrated by the lavish devotion which is paid to presenting the text in the most beautiful possible form. There exist many thousands of handsomely illuminated and embellished Korans, bound in the finest examples of the Eastern bookmaker's art. Traditionally it has been considered meritorious to write out a copy of the Koran by one's own hand, and many great men of the Islamic tradition, including rulers, have set themselves this pious exercise. Verses from the Koran in elegant and complex calligraphy are the favoured form of decoration for the façades of mosques, religious schools, tombs and other public buildings throughout the Islamic world.

Illustrations pages 478–9

Illustration page 479

Reverence for the Koran appears also in the refusal of traditional Muslim scholars to sanction its translation into other languages. Since the words spoken to Mohammed were Arabic words, their rendering into another language, no matter how skilful, is not the Koran. The best-known English translation, made by a convert to Islam (Marmaduke Pickthall), is, accordingly, called *The Meaning of the Glorious Qur'an*, not simply the Koran. In spite of pious resistance, numbers of translations have been made into the important Muslim languages as well as others. In Islamic countries such translations customarily reproduce the original Arabic text, normally in bold large script with the translation in interlinear fashion. In this way translations become a means for making the text itself better known but they do not replace it.

The Highest Authority

For Muslims the Koran is the highest authority in all matters of faith, theology and law. There is probably no other book in the history of the world, including the Bible, that has been so much read, meditated and commented upon. In one sense the whole corpus of Muslim religious writing may be considered as an extended Koran commentary, but there are also numerous commentaries in a technical sense which give a verse by verse explanation of the sacred text. Such a book is called a *tafsir*. The best-known and most widely used *tafsir* is that by the classical author al-Tabari (died AD 923), a work of great length and enormous erudition that reports the opinions of the prophet and his companions about each phrase of the text. Other respected and often used commentaries are those by al-Baydawi (died AD 1292) and al-Zamakhshari (died AD 1144).

The Koran in its present-day form was assembled and ordered after the death of the prophet by his companions and successors. So long as the prophet lived, he continued to receive revelations and, thus, could not himself have fixed the order of the sacred book. Mohammed, however, did to some degree show concern for the preservation and organization of the text. He employed several different people as amanuenses to record the revelations, and he apparently had worked out the basic scheme of dividing the text into *surahs*. There is, however, no way of knowing the exact state of the Koran upon Mohammed's death, and all authorities are agreed that the major work of collecting the revelations and putting them into order was done in the time of the first three caliphs.

The accounts of the formation of the Koran are conflicting, but they are unanimous in assigning the major role to Zayd ibn Thabit, a young man who had been one of Mohammed's secretaries. Either in the caliphate of Abu Bakr or that of Umar, Zayd is reported to have gathered the records of the revelations that existed among the community. Some he found inscribed on such diverse materials as scraps of leather, pieces of stone, the ribs of palm leaves, and the shoulder blades of animals – the art of paper-making being then unknown to the Arabs. Still other revelations he collected from the hearts of men, that is, from the memories of the prophet's companions.

All this material he brought together into an ordered document which, if the sources are to be believed, passed into the private possession of Hafsah, the daughter of Umar. During the reign of the third caliph, Uthman, a controversy about the Koran threatened the peace of the community. Uthman therefore ordered the same Zayd ibn Thabit to create an official version of the Koran text from the document owned by Hafsah, and this was done. These stories present some difficulties, but the version of the Koran prepared under Uthman's orders has continued to be used in the Islamic community down to our own time.

Previous Religious Writings

A question of much interest about the Koran is its relationship to previous religious writings, especially to Jewish and Christian scriptures. Anyone who reads the Koran must immediately recognize the considerable body of common material among these scriptures. Indeed, the Koran itself acknowledges this similarity by considering itself to be a scripture in the identical tradition of those of the Jews and Christians. There can be no question, however, of literary dependence, for the Koran does not quote the Bible directly, and at many points there are differences between the koranic and the biblical accounts of incidents. Mohammed was accused of having obtained his revelations from a learned Jew, who recited the Jewish scriptures to him, but the content of the Koran shows no such close resemblance to anything in the Bible. In order to underline the genuineness and originality of the Koran's revelation, the Islamic tradition has always insisted that Mohammed was illiterate and, thus, unable to use previous scriptures, even if he had had the inclination to do so.

The attempt to trace the ideas of the Koran back to a source from earlier times is likely to miss the most important thing about the religious experience of the prophet. Although Mohammed lived in an environment that was saturated with knowledge of Christian and Jewish religious ideas, the Koran is an original religious inspiration with a point of view quite different from that of the previous scriptures. Biblical figures and stories do have a place in its pages, but the purpose they serve is to buttress a new and different vision of God, human beings and the world which has a definite integrity of its own. The suggestion, sometimes made, that Mohammed was a mere imitator of those who had gone before is historically inaccurate, as well as offensive to Muslim religious feelings.

Illustration page 480

The Conquests

The unexpected death of Mohammed precipitated a crisis for the Muslims, and their first priority was to find a successor to the prophet to act as community head. Civil war threatened to break out among the jealous and proud tribal factions until, in an act of desperation, some of Mohammed's closest companions succeeded in proclaiming the ageing Abu Bakr as caliph, or successor. Then a number of Bedouin tribes began to fall away from Islam. As the Koran indicates, the Bedouin had never been converted in the ideological sense; rather, they had considered their ties to the Muslim community as personal alliances with its leader. When Mohammed died, they quite naturally considered the bond to have been dissolved. Their defection was expressed in the refusal to pay the *zakat* or alms, one of the basic Muslim religious duties, which had been the symbol of their submission to Islamic control. Abu Bakr fought to bring these recalcitrants back into the fold by a series of campaigns known as the Wars of the *Riddah* (apostasy). However, these wars were not so much counter-rebellions as merely further steps in consolidating a community whose nature the Bedouin had not yet fully understood.

The first expeditions into Syria and Palestine were mainly for purposes of plunder in the time-honoured Arab manner. In AD 634, the most famous of the Arab generals, Khalid ibn al-Walid, plundered Damascus and then disappeared with his troops into the desert again. The decisive engagement which brought Syria under Arab control was the Battle of the Yarmuk, in AD 636, where the Byzantines

Illustration page 489

suffered a crushing defeat and the brother of the emperor was killed. Thereafter, virtually all of Palestine and Syria was in Muslim hands, with the exception of some places which were particularly well fortified, such as Jerusalem. These required a few more years to subdue.

The Muslims had begun raids against Iraq almost simultaneously with their operations in Syria, but there the enemies were the Sassanians, who proved no more a match for the desert fighters than the Byzantines. In AD 637, a small Arab force defeated a Sassanian army in Qadisiyah, took the Sassanian capital of Ctesiphon and brought all of Iraq under Muslim control. Egypt was a Byzantine province, though somewhat disaffected from the empire's rule by religious differences between its Coptic inhabitants and the orthodox doctors of Constantinople. It was invaded in AD 639, and only two years later the whole of the country, except Alexandria, fell to the Muslims. Alexandria was able to hold out for a short time, but soon the last remnant of Byzantine territory in Egypt passed to the Arabs. Thus, in the span of only ten years, the Arabs subdued and permanently controlled the rich provinces on their borders.

Beyond the Oxus

In the east the Zagros Mountains proved an obstacle for a time to the conquest of the Iranian plateau, still held by the remnants of the Sassanian state. However, the great Battle of Nihavand (AD 641), north of present-day Hamadan, brought that vast region within the burgeoning Arab empire. This conquest opened the way not only to Khurasan, which was to become one of the intellectual strongholds of classical Islam under the Abbasid caliphs and their successors, but also to the regions lying still further to the east beyond the Oxus river. Arab armies reached and crossed the Oxus early on, but did not truly subdue the regions beyond until after AD 705.

In the west, Muslim military power slowly expanded across North Africa and in the year AD 711 a mixed Arab-Berber army under a slave named Tariq, from whom the Rock of Gibraltar (Jabal al-Tariq) gets its name, crossed into Spain. Muslim expansion within the Iberian peninsula continued toward the north until the French king, Charles Martel, stopped further Islamic conquest in Europe at the Battle of Tours in AD 732.

Illustration page 480

The unique factor about these conquests, in addition to their rapidity, was their permanence. With the exception of Spain and Sicily, all the territories overrun by Muslims in their first wave of expansion have continued under Muslim dominion until our own time. This statement is perhaps debatable with some of the regions of Central Asia now included in the Soviet Union, but on the whole it may be upheld. None of the many efforts to dislodge the Muslims from these initially conquered territories has been successful.

The further expansion of Islam in Asia and Europe belongs to later phases of Muslim history. In AD 712, during the reign of the Ummayad caliphs of Damascus, there was an invasion of Sind that resulted in the establishment of a Muslim Arab state. However, this

Left The prophet addresses the people on his last pilgrimage, an illustration from *The Book of the Vestiges which Survive of Past Times*. Depictions of any human being were not permitted in most Islamic lands. Edinburgh University Library.

Left Every pilgrim to Mecca tries to touch the black stone at the corner of the Kaaba. The late King Faisal of Saudi Arabia is the worshipper here.

Left The angel appears to Mohammed and commands him to 'recite' in the name of God. Edinburgh University Library.

Above Study of the scriptures at the *madrasah* (theological college) of Ghazanfaraqua, Istanbul, from a seventeenth-century manuscript. Topkapi Sarayi Müzesi, Istanbul.

Above centre Two pages from a Koran by master-calligrapher Ibn Al-Bawwab (died 1022). Chester Beatty Library, Dublin.

Opposite above right An eleventh-century Koran from Islamic Spain or North Africa. Chester Beatty Library, Dublin.

Opposite below right A nineteenth-century prayer rug, from ?Tabriz, Iran. Metropolitan Museum of Art, New York. Mr and Mrs Isaac D. Fletcher Collection, bequest of Isaac D. Fletcher, 1917.

Opposite below left An exquisite *mihrab* in the Imami *madrasah*, Isfahan (1354). Metropolitan Museum of Art, New York. Harris Brisbane Dick Fund, 1939.

Right An Indonesian farmer reads the Koran to his family.

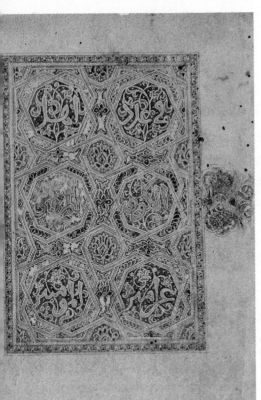

Above Abraham in Nimrod's fiery
furnace, and the sacrifice of Ismail
(Ishmael), showing Muslim
adaptations from Jewish themes.
Zubdat al-Tawarikh by Luqman-i-
Ashuri, Turkey (*c.* 1583). Chester
Beatty Library, Dublin.

Above right The Sultan Ahmet
Mosque, Istanbul.

Right The Muslim invasion of
Spain made a lasting impression on
the art and architecture of the cities
they occupied. The famous mosque
at Cordoba with red and white
arches was later taken over as a
Christian cathedral.

victory was not exploited and the Arabs living in India were gradually isolated from the centres of Islamic power. In the beginning of the eleventh century, the great sultan Mahmud of Ghazni began a series of raids from the mountains of Afghanistan into the rich Indian plains, and eventually annexed a small portion of northern Punjab to his empire. It remained for Mohammed Ghori, though, to carry out the conquest of North India a full century and a half later, and so to bring India within the orbit of Islam.

Islam acquired the other great region of its present-day strength by largely peaceful means. From a very early time, the islands of Indonesia were visited by Arab traders who established colonies along the coasts, and brought their religion with them. The influence of the traders was reinforced by the presence of numerous Sufi saints and preachers, and by the tendency of the Arabs everywhere to intermarry with the local population. By the fifteenth century, there were already Muslim sultanates and kingdoms in the islands which were moving gradually toward the condition of a majority Muslim population which they have today.

Spain Is Lost

Although in the fifteenth century Islam lost the last of the regions of Spain which it had formerly controlled, it gained other territories in eastern Europe. The emerging power of the Ottoman Turks established itself on European soil, took Constantinople in 1453, and began a series of conquests and military campaigns in the Balkan regions. There was a Turkish army before Vienna as late as 1683. During the preceding 250 years it had required the constant efforts of eastern Europe to prevent the Ottomans from overrunning and annexing the entire region. The Muslim populations of the Balkan states, such as Albania, Yugoslavia, and Bulgaria, owe their origin to these years of Turkish greatness.

At present Islam is making significant new gains by peaceful means. In sub-Saharan Africa there has been a growth in the Muslim populations, and a gradual extension of Islamic influence to the south. Some of this growth is due to the activities of missionary groups, and to the conversion of rulers to Islam in sub-Saharan regions. In North Africa much of Islam's expansion was won at the cost of Christianity, but in the tropics both Islam and Christianity have taken advantage of the decline in the traditional religion, aided by modern political and commercial changes.

The Prophetic Tradition

With the death of Mohammed the Muslims lost the living source of guidance that had been so important in the prophet's lifetime. The great conquests brought them into close contact with cultures more sophisticated than their own, and confronted them with all the bewildering responsibilities of governing a vast territory. Although the Koran contains a wide variety of rules to regulate specific areas of life, such a small book could not possibly give definitive guidance for all the new situations which the community now faced. Muslims

victory was not exploited and the Arabs living in India were gradually isolated from the centres of Islamic power. In the beginning of the eleventh century, the great sultan Mahmud of Ghazni began a series of raids from the mountains of Afghanistan into the rich Indian plains, and eventually annexed a small portion of northern Punjab to his empire. It remained for Mohammed Ghori, though, to carry out the conquest of North India a full century and a half later, and so to bring India within the orbit of Islam.

Islam acquired the other great region of its present-day strength by largely peaceful means. From a very early time, the islands of Indonesia were visited by Arab traders who established colonies along the coasts, and brought their religion with them. The influence of the traders was reinforced by the presence of numerous Sufi saints and preachers, and by the tendency of the Arabs everywhere to intermarry with the local population. By the fifteenth century, there were already Muslim sultanates and kingdoms in the islands which were moving gradually toward the condition of a majority Muslim population which they have today.

Spain Is Lost

Although in the fifteenth century Islam lost the last of the regions of Spain which it had formerly controlled, it gained other territories in eastern Europe. The emerging power of the Ottoman Turks established itself on European soil, took Constantinople in 1453, and began a series of conquests and military campaigns in the Balkan regions. There was a Turkish army before Vienna as late as 1683. During the preceding 250 years it had required the constant efforts of eastern Europe to prevent the Ottomans from overrunning and annexing the entire region. The Muslim populations of the Balkan states, such as Albania, Yugoslavia, and Bulgaria, owe their origin to these years of Turkish greatness.

At present Islam is making significant new gains by peaceful means. In sub-Saharan Africa there has been a growth in the Muslim populations, and a gradual extension of Islamic influence to the south. Some of this growth is due to the activities of missionary groups, and to the conversion of rulers to Islam in sub-Saharan regions. In North Africa much of Islam's expansion was won at the cost of Christianity, but in the tropics both Islam and Christianity have taken advantage of the decline in the traditional religion, aided by modern political and commercial changes.

The Prophetic Tradition

With the death of Mohammed the Muslims lost the living source of guidance that had been so important in the prophet's lifetime. The great conquests brought them into close contact with cultures more sophisticated than their own, and confronted them with all the bewildering responsibilities of governing a vast territory. Although the Koran contains a wide variety of rules to regulate specific areas of life, such a small book could not possibly give definitive guidance for all the new situations which the community now faced. Muslims quickly found it necessary to complement the Koran with other authorities in order to answer the questions before them. The most important of these complementary authorities became the *sunnah* of the prophet.

In turning to the *sunnah*, or established practice, of the prophet the early Arab Muslims were showing themselves true to a principle which had been honoured by their forefathers for centuries. Arabs had always held the customs of the past in highest respect, and to the extent that they recognized any standards for human behaviour and morality, these were drawn from the examples of men of former times and from the established custom of the tribal group. The coming of Islam did not necessitate rejecting the principle of traditional authority. Its effect was rather to relocate the source of tradition. For the Muslims, as for the earlier Arabs, the deeds of great men of the past and a time-honoured mode of conduct continued to be normative. In place of Arab heroes and tribal customs, however, the Muslims began to recount tales of the prophet and his companions, and to take the way of life of this earliest Muslim community as their model. In due course, the reliance upon tradition became recognized as a formal principle.

The resort to traditional authority was not without problems. It is obvious that had Muslims always acted or believed strictly as others before them, there could have been no movement or development in the life of the community at all. In fact, the development was rapid in the first two Islamic centuries, and it involved adaptation to circumstances that would have been inconceivable to the Arabs of the prophet's time. There, had, therefore, to be some way of enlarging the scope and relevance of tradition. When the Muslims looked for precedents and failed to find what was needed, they often fabricated traditions to satisfy their need. There was no other effective way to argue a religious or legal point except through citation of tradition.

The Nature of Tradition

Another problem arising from the appeal to tradition was that of determining exactly what tradition was. All were agreed that *sunnah* was the norm, but whose *sunnah*, and how was it to be determined? This question was of utmost importance for jurists, who required to have precise and dependable statements of the obligations and prohibitions of the Islamic religious life. A full two hundred years of the community's existence passed before this question found a definitive answer.

The question of the nature of *sunnah* was solved in the third Islamic century by the famous jurist al-Shafii. In a series of polemic writings scathingly attacking those who held other views, al-Shafii argued for the primacy of the *sunnah* of Mohammed. He held that the tradition of the prophet's sayings, actions and approbations, and it alone, was normative for Muslims. The precedents of all others he rejected as inferior. In course of time, al-Shafii's strict view was accepted by the community at large. Today when it is said that, after the Koran,

Muslims follow the *sunnah*, the *sunnah* of the prophet is meant.

Al-Shafii also established a second important principle by holding that the *sunnah* was known on the basis of oral reports, or *hadith*, about the prophet's words, actions, and tacit approbations. From al-Shafii's time, the Muslim quest for the *sunnah* took the form of the collection and authentication of *hadiths*.

The Hadith Books

In the third Islamic century, scholars made several great systematic collections of *hadiths*, recognized today as second in authority only to the Koran itself. These are known as the *Six Sahih* (Sound) *Books*. Among them the most respected, and most often cited, are the two collections of al-Bukhari (d. AD 870) and Muslim (d. AD 875). Each of these books was assembled after sifting a great number of commonly circulated *hadiths*, the majority of which were rejected as false or weak. The books are organized in chapters according to subject matter, with all the *hadiths* bearing upon a particular point brought together under the appropriate heading. This method of organization demonstrates the close relationship between the *hadith* collections and the needs of the Islamic lawyers, for the categories of organization are drawn from the law. In addition to these six books a number of other lesser known collections are also employed.

The historical significance of the *hadith* collections is controversial. Conservative Muslims accept the *hadith* books as accurate and reliable records of the prophet's sayings, actions, and approbations, arrived at by a careful scientific sifting of the good from the bad. Furthermore, there is an element of faith in their attitude toward the *hadith* which makes any question about its authenticity seem an attack upon Islam. Modern scholars, however, point to contradictions, anachronisms, and tendentious elements even in the *Six Sound Books* themselves and deny that the *hadith* collections give reliable information about the prophet. In their view the *hadith* collections represent the consensus of the Muslim community on the great legal and theological questions of its history, all of which had been settled by the time the *Six Sound Books* were composed. The significance of the *hadith* collections, therefore, lies in what they tell us of the Muslim mentality, especially the learned circles, in the third century, and not in what they relate about Mohammed.

Quite recently, as an aspect of Islamic modernism, some Muslims have attacked the normative role of tradition in the community's past. In order to liberate themselves from medieval attitudes, which they consider to have impeded the progress of their societies, they reject the *hadith* and appeal instead to the exclusive authority of the Koran. Such people, however, represent the extreme of liberal tendencies among present-day Muslims.

Theology

Like followers of other great religions, the Muslims have devoted earnest efforts to stating the meaning of their faith in precise intellectual terms. Although theology has played a lesser role in Muslim religious life than, for instance, in Christianity, it is nevertheless an important division of the Islamic religious sciences. The Arabic word usually translated as 'theolgy' is *kalam*, meaning speech, as in the case of the Speech of God, the Koran. In technical usage *kalam* refers to the presentation of reasoned arguments to support fundamental religious doctrines.

As a series of inspired utterances, springing from Mohammed's ecstatic states, the Koran shows almost no concern for the systematic presentation of religious doctrine. It is notably *not* a book of theology in the usual sense, but a kind of religious rhetoric to warn, admonish and instruct. In a number of matters the Koran is unclear or incomplete, and in others it is contradictory. Koranic teaching about predestination and free will, for example, at times emphasizes the necessity to choose whether to obey God and, at others, underlines God's complete control of human affairs. These conflicting emphases are perhaps explained by the purposes particular revelations were sent to serve, but they pose great difficulty for setting out a clear and definitive koranic doctrine. It was necessary for the words of the Koran to be interpreted so that its guidance might be clear.

The beginnings of Islamic theology date from the efforts to establish the correct koranic text. There were variant readings which involved dogmatic and legal consequences, and it was necessary to be clear about them. Similar motives led to the invention of the vowel points, and other diacritical signs, to permit exact writing and reading in Arabic, and to the construction of grammars and lexicons for Arabic. All of these activities followed the rise of Islam, and sprang directly from the desire to understand the Koran better. More important, however, as stimuli to theological thinking, were the political controversies that followed the murder of the third caliph, Uthman, and the Muslim contacts with the more sophisticated peoples in the conquered territories.

In the confused situation which followed the murder of Uthman by a group of Egyptian dissidents in AD 655, the major personalities were Ali ibn Abi Talib, the cousin and son-in-law of the prophet, and Muawiyah, governor of Syria and member of the great Ummayad family. Ali was elected caliph in Uthman's place, but never fully succeeded in getting his leadership accepted. Muawiyah eventually won in the struggle with Ali and became the founder of the Arab kingdom of Damascus, which endured more than a hundred years, until it fell to the Abbasids in 750.

The Umayyads

Since their rise to power had involved warfare against the prophet's family and some respected companions, the Umayyads were severely criticized. The Umayyad rulers responded by making religious propaganda to legitimize their rule and undercut the religious arguments levelled against them. They adopted the doctrine of predestination as their ideological platform, arguing that all things happen as God wills. It followed, therefore, that the Umayyad rule from their capital

in Damascus was the result of divine intention and not legitimately
to be opposed.

Their opponents took the opposite stand: that human beings have free will and the power to choose their courses of action. Opposition to the Umayyads, in consequence, was nothing more than refusal to accept evil rulers, a duty incumbent upon every right-thinking Muslim. There was, thus, much more at stake in the discussions of free will and predestination than the effort to resolve a persistent, and very difficult religious problem. When a person took a stand with the Qadariyah (from *qadr* or power, 'the advocates of free will') or with the Jabariyah (from *jabr* or force, the proponents of predestination) he was also expressing a practical stand on the political alignments of the day.

In order to govern their vast territories the Umayyads found it necessary to evolve, or adopt from foreign sources, a large number of institutions and practical measures that had been unknown in the prophet's time. There was no escape from such steps, for the Arabs had no previous experience in government. Nevertheless, the Umayyads' policies earned them a renewed measure of condemnation from religious conservatives, who saw these steps as a departure from the *sunnah* and a swing towards worldliness. Islamic historians are unanimous in scorning the Umayyads for having transformed the religiously oriented Muslim community into a secular kingdom, but these accusations do less than justice to an extremely complex situation and are, besides, often coloured by party prejudices.

The most extreme stand toward the Umayyads was taken by a fierce and fanatical sect called the Khawarij. These sectarians held that the innovations of the Umayyads made them sinners and apostates from Islam. Disobedience to such rulers was not only permissible, but their sinfulness subjected them to the penalty of death which the Koran decrees for apostasy. The Khawarij took up arms to enforce their views, and these strict puritans were a source of constant rebellion throughout the first two centuries of Islamic rule.

Faith and Works

Consideration of the questions raised by the Khawarij produced earnest discussions of the relationship between *iman* (faith) and *islams* (works). Some held that there could be no faith without works, since the latter was the proof of the former. Others sought a compromise by distinguishing between big sins (*kabair*) and little sins (*saghair*), teaching that big sins exclude one from Islam, whereas little sins are forgivable and do not affect membership of the community.

The second important stimulus to theology was the Muslim contact with the conquered peoples. The Muslims considered themselves bearers of a new dispensation superior to former religions, but they found difficulty in convincing the conquered peoples who possessed fully developed and sophisticated religious systems. In Damascus, which was an important Christian centre, there were debates, often sponsored by the court and attended by the ruler, between Muslims and Christians over the respective merits of their faiths. In such encounters, the Christians initially enjoyed a great advantage by virtue of the complex theological armoury developed through six centuries of internal discussion in the Church itself. Besides Christians, Muslims also met Zoroastrians, Manichaeans, and, quite probably, Buddhists. In every case the intellectual equipment of the other group had been refined by centuries of thought and controversy. If they were to demonstrate the viability of their own faith, the Muslims had to sharpen their grasp of its essentials, and evolve more effective tools for its expression.

We have, so far, spoken only of the first stages of theological thinking in Islam. The creation of a full-blown theology, or *kalam*, was the by-product of a small but highly important school of thinkers called the Mu'tazilah. The Mu'tazilah appeared in the second and third Islamic centuries, and for a time their doctrines enjoyed the patronage of the Abbasid caliphs as the official theology of the state. The outstanding characteristic of the school was its attempt to give a rational interpretation of Islam. Through their contact with the Hellenized peoples of the conquered territories, the Muslims learned something of Greek philosophy. Already, in the second Islamic century, some Greek writings were translated into Arabic and, in the following century, there was a great movement to appropriate the entire wisdom of the ancient world. Works from every field were rendered into Arabic in centres such as Hawran in ancient Syria and Jundishapur in Persia. This store of knowledge was later to be passed on to the West and became the means by which the medieval world obtained its knowledge of Greek thought. Profiting from their growing knowledge of Greek thought, the Mu'tazilah sought to bring some of its principles to bear upon Islamic religious doctrine.

People of Unity and Justice

The Mu'tazilah called themselves the 'people of unity and justice', and these two emphases embrace the important elements of their thought. Their teaching of unity had to do with the unity of God (*tawhid*), the most fundamental of all Muslim religious assertions. At the simplest level it was a rejection of the dualism characteristic of Zoroastrians and Manichaeans, who taught the existence of two great antagonistic forces in the universe, one of good and one of evil. Such a doctrine was rationally incompatible with the Islamic belief in a single god whose sovereignty was sole and unique.

At a more profound level, the teaching of unity concerned the doctrine of God's nature as it was expounded in the Islamic community itself. The Mu'tazilah would have nothing to do with anthropomorphism of any kind in their theology. All those koranic verses referring to God's having hands, or sitting upon a throne, or otherwise exhibiting human attributes they explained as metaphors for what was otherwise inexpressible. They also denied the possibility of the beatific vision of God, holding that by nature he cannot be perceived by the senses. The doctrine for which they are most famous was their view that the Koran was created, not eternal, as most of the rest of the community believed. To have granted the co-eternity with God of even the Koran would have been, in some subtle way, to compromise divine uniqueness.

Free Will

The Mu'tazilah teaching about divine justice arose out of the controversies on predestination and free will. The Mu'tazilah were firm believers in free will, holding that any other view would be tantamount to accusing God of injustice. Having freedom to choose their actions, people are either rewarded or punished for what they do. God does not create evil, but by his nature must always do what is best (*aslah*) for humankind. Thus, God neither compels people into evil, nor does he punish them for actions over which they have no control. Their position on the free-will controversy also reveals the Mu'tazilah's political stand, for, as we have observed, the doctrine of free will served the cause of the Ummayads' opponents. The alliance of Mu'tazilah thinkers with the Abbasid dynasty was perhaps cemented during the latter's struggle for power, when the Mu'tazilah provided a convenient ideological basis for the movement.

At the height of their influence the Mu'tazilah were never more than a small élite group of advanced thinkers. The majority of Muslims were far more sympathetic to conservative leaders, such as the great traditionalist Ahmad ibn Hanbal (died AD 855). The Mu'tazilah suffered a particularly severe blow when they lost the favour of the Abbasid rulers, and the school eventually passed out of existence. Their ideas, however, have had an enormous influence on the course of Islamic history. They were responsible for introducing the methods of Greek dialectic into Muslim religious discussions, and their theological views have been debated by every important *mutakallim* (practitioner of *kalam* or theologian) to our own day. Their thelogy, to a large degree, has been preserved intact among the Shiah sect of Muslims, who exhibit a much more rational inclination than Sunni Muslims. Quite recently Muslims have shown a reawakened interest in the much maligned Mu'tazilah, whose rationalism accords with the tendencies of modern Islam.

Greek Methods

The man hailed as the great counterbalance to the Mu'tazilah was, in fact, associated with them during his youth. Abu-l-Hasan al-Ashari (died AD 935) had studied with the Mu'tazilah master al-Jubbai, but became dissatisfied with his teacher and began to pursue his own way. Al-Ashari's great contribution was to bring the methods of Greek reasoning and argument which he had learned from al-Jubbai into the service of conservative Islamic opinions. Although the substance of al-Ashari's theological stand was based on the authority of revelation and tradition, he employed Greek terminology and methods to defend, expound, and uphold these conservative views.

The great difference between him and the Mu'tazilah lay in the use which each made of Greek rational philosophy. For the Mu'tazilah, reason became the touchstone of the truth and acceptability of doctrine. They measured and judged religious assertions by the standards of reason. For al-Ashari, the reason played only an instrumental role; it was neither the means to discover the truth, which came through revelation, nor the method of evaluating it. Instead, its rightful function was to provide arguments to buttress the received truth against its possible detractors.

Al-Ashari was a literalist who would make no compromise at all with the words of the revelation. He believed the Koran said exactly what it meant, and sought only to provide the arguments that would convince others of the truth of the revelation. Thus he accepted literally the statements that God has hands and that he sits upon a throne, although God's hands are not like human hands and his sitting is not human sitting. He affirmed also God's real possession of the attributes which the Koran ascribes to him. God possesses knowledge, will, power, sight and other faculties as real and distinct qualities not as mere shadows of his essence. Al-Ashari desired here, as in other matters, to hold two differing things in a kind of paradoxical unity: the manifoldness of the attributes and the essential unity of the divine nature. His final pronouncement on the matter leaves it veiled in mystery.

Perhaps the greatest thinker in the school of al-Ashari was Abu Hamid al-Ghazali (died AD 1111), who is also known as a lawyer, philosopher, and mystic. This man entered the service of the Seljuq rulers and taught in one of the religious schools which they founded to counteract the propaganda of Ismaili revolutionaries. He looked upon the *kalam* as a means of healing souls, but in the final analysis considered it of less value than mysticism. His most important book on the subject is called *al-Iqtisad fi-l-I'tiqad (A Short Treatise on the Creed)*.

Reliance on the Past

After the time of al-Ghazali there was little creative writing in theology. Here, as in all else, the Muslims showed their tendency to traditionalism by relying upon the great authorities from the past. Books on theology took the form of commentaries, manuals, or compendia, but made no attempt at a fresh approach to the great theological issues. Among manuals of this type that by al-Sanusi entitled *al-Aqidat al-Kubra (The Great Creed)* is widely known and used in Muslim religious schools. More recently Muslims have shown very little interest in the discussion of theological questions.

Islamic Law

Islam, it is often said, is a religion of law. Among all the expressions of Islamic piety, law is the most characteristic. The central place of the law in Islamic thought and religious life stems from the fundamental nature of the Islamic experience itself. Perhaps the most important word in the entire religious vocabulary of Muslims is guidance. It was guidance which the Koran brought from on high, and guidance which the prophet's example and the tradition of the

community elaborated and established. Guidance is above all what the Muslim expects from religion, a series of specific directions for the conduct of life so that in no situation will there be doubt about the right way to act.

There are two words for law in use among Muslims. *Shariah*, the first of them, originally meant pathway, the pathway in which people should walk to please God. *Shariah* is, thus, a designation for the eternal pattern that God has ordained for the universe, a kind of cosmic ideal that embodies the divine will. The other word, *fiqh*, comes from a verb meaning to understand, and refers to the human effort to translate the transcendental will of God into specific rules. The *fiqh* means both the science of jurisprudence, that derives rules of law from the source materials, and also the end product of that science as written down in numerous thick volumes. Along with the Arabic language the *fiqh* constitutes the backbone of traditional Muslim religious studies.

Among the *shariah*'s characteristics is its comprehensiveness. It seeks to provide an all-inclusive measure for human conduct. No human action, without exception, falls outside the purview of the law as something belonging to another sphere; rather the entirety of life is judged from the standpoint of the divine pattern. All actions fall into one of five categories: obligatory *(fard)*; meritorious or recommended *(mandub)*; permitted, i.e., neither good nor bad but neutral *(mubah)*; reprehended, but not subject to punishment *(makruh)*; and absolutely forbidden under pain of punishment *(haram)*. The result of this scheme is to bring all of life into a moral order in both its individual and its social aspects.

Moral Duties

The *shariah*, therefore, includes a great deal that for the modern world has nothing to do with law. For instance, it regulates everything respecting religion, both belief and ritual. Theology, thus, is technically a part of the *shariah* though it has developed into a semi-independent religious science. Theology is simply the moral aspect of belief. The law also tells a Muslim when and how to perform their prayers, how to observe the fast of Ramadan, how much to pay in the way of alms, and how to perform other religious duties. In the realm of more mundane affairs, the *shariah* prescribes the food permissible for a Muslim to eat, the manner of acceptable dress, and even the forms of courtesy that lubricate social relations.

There is also a large part of the *shariah* that a modern person would understand as the concern of the law, such as rules governing marriage, divorce, inheritance, contractual relations, commerce, and similar matters. Traditionally, Muslims speak of the content of the law as having two parts: the duties owing to God or *Ibadat* (from *abd*, slave) and the duties owing to people, *Muamalat*. Both derive from the divine decrees, and neither is more or less binding, or important, than the other.

Problems of jurisprudence were among the very earliest concerns

Opposite above A gathering for prayer at the Badshahi Mosque, Lahore.

Opposite below right 'A Dervish dansinge', a Turkish drawing from a book of miniatures representing the Habits of the Grand Signor's Court (*c.* 1620). British Library, London.

Opposite below left The Ashura festival in Srinagar, Kashmir: Shiah Muslims beat their chests in commemoration of the death of Imam Husayn at Karbala.

Illustrations page 499

of the young Islamic community. It was necessary to be precise about the duties incumbent upon a Muslim, but a universally accepted method was lacking for applying, expanding, and detailing the guidance in the Koran and the prophet's life. In the first and second Islamic centuries a number of schools arose, each with a differing point of view, and each locked in dispute with the others. This wide-ranging controversy over the principles to be used in deciding on the specific rules of law was brought to an end by the work of al-Shafii (died AD 820), who won general acceptance for a jurisprudential theory that is still revered by Muslims today.

Al-Shafii worked out the theory of *usul al-fiqh* (roots or sources of the law). He argued that there are four *usul* which stand in a definite order of rank. First is the Koran, the word of God, whose clear commandments take precedence over all else. Second is the authentic *sunnah* of the prophet transmitted in valid *hadith*. *Sunnah* may supplement or modify koranic injunctions but may never set them aside as some thinkers had held. Failing to find what is needed in these two primary sources, the lawyer (*faqih*) may turn to the consensus (*ijma*) of the community in the past. According to the principle expressed in a famous *hadith*, 'my community shall never agree in an error', the agreement of the learned and pious men in the past and the concurrence of the community, especially as expressed in practice, on any point is sufficient guide for an assured basis of judgment. This principle is another indication of Islam's traditionalist outlook, and has been of immense importance to the life of the community. The fourth source, analogical reasoning (*qiyas*), was to be used with great caution, and only when the appeal to the previous three sources had proved fruitless. *Qiyas* was hedged about by very strict rules, and had always to be conducted in subjection to the other three precedent principles. Most emphatically *qiyas* was not a means for introducing mere personal opinion (*ray*), or speculation on legal problems. Al-Shafii, in fact, devoted the major effort of his life to rescuing Islamic law from the arbitrariness of personal preference.

During the first two hundred years of Islamic history there appeared a number of schools of law which flourished for a time, and most of which then disappeared. Four of these schools (*madhahib*), however, attracted a large following and have survived to the present. The formation of the four schools belongs to the third Islamic century, when the great controversies of the early days had lost their heat, and when a broad agreement began to emerge on the community's major problems. This was also the time when the *Six Sound Books* of *hadith* were assembled, and when the structure of the Ashari theology was fixed.

Schools of Law

Each of the four *madhahib* is associated with the name of a prominent jurist whose teachings it has adopted. Al-Shafii, mentioned above, was one of these. His doctrines are observed by the people of Egypt, Indonesia, East Africa and Syria. The largest number of adherents by far belongs to the school of Abu Hanifah (died AD 767), an Iraqi jurist, whose followers are drawn from India, Pakistan, Bangladesh, Turkey, Afghanistan, and Central Asia. Malik ibn Anas, the traditionalist of Medina, was the founder of the third school, and the Maliki law is authoritative for most of the people of North and West Africa. Both the smallest and the strictest of the *madhahib* is that of Ahmad ibn Hanbal, which at present is confined to Arabia where its uncompromising traditionalism has appealed to the puritanical Wahhabi sect.

There is little difference among the schools of law except in matters of detail, and all of them are considered acceptable by Sunni Muslims (see page 497). Individuals, however, are expected to attach themselves to one of the schools and follow its teachings exclusively. It is sometimes permissible also, under special circumstances, for a jurist of one school to adopt a ruling from another, but the practice is generally frowned upon. Muslims of the Shiah sect do not follow one of the four 'orthodox' schools, but have a law of their own. Again, this law differs from that of the Sunni schools only in details.

Recently many Muslim countries have adopted modern codes of law based on French, Swiss, or British examples. As a result, the scope of operation of the *shariah* has been restricted to the realm of personal law. Such matters as marriage, divorce, and inheritance may continue to be governed by its provisions, but the portions that deal with commercial relations, criminal matters, etc., plus the whole realm of Islamic public law are largely in abeyance. Only in the Arabian peninsula is there now an attempt to cling strictly to the *shariah*, and even there the pressure of modern conditions is bringing about changes. The *shariah* remains, however, an ideal for all Muslims everywhere, and is certainly one of the sources of their unity.

Mysticism

In spite of its emphasis on law, Islam has no lack of rich spiritual fervour expressed in a highly developed mystical tradition. Mysticism originated in Islam with the experience of Mohammed himself but did not, at first, affect the lives of ordinary Muslims to a great degree. By the fourth Islamic century, however, there was a mystical movement of the first importance which grew in influence until it dominated religious life. Its success in the medieval period is partially to be explained by the specialized nature of the law and the *kalam*. Both are highly technical and somewhat arid, and neither offers the spiritual nurture and comfort so essential to the common religious life. Mystical leaders provided for religious needs which the canon lawyers and theologians could not meet and, in time, even the learned men of the community were caught up in mystical discipline and devotion.

Islamic mysticism is called Sufism or *tasawwuf*, most probably from the Arabic word for wool *(suf)*. The name comes from the earliest mystics' practice of wearing rough robes of white wool symbolizing both their rejection of the world and their special piety.

It is sometimes argued that Sufism is a foreign import into the

ISLAM Islamic religious system, being the result of Muslim contacts with Christian hermits and holy men, or with mystical forms of Greek thought. It is unnecessary, however, to turn to outside influences to explain the strong Muslim tendency toward mysticism. One has only to read the Koran, or to contemplate the life of Mohammed and his companions, to recognize that all of the materials and stimuli for a more profound and immediate experience of the divine are present there. Numerous verses in the Koran assure the believer of God's nearness, of his ubiquitousness, and of his initiative in seeking men. Other verses urge men to draw nigh to God, to love him, and to remember *(dhikr)* him always. The Koran also recounts Mohammed's night journey *(mi'raj)* to the divine presence where he communed with God face to face *(Surah* XVII). This incident has been an inexhaustible resource for Sufi speculation, leading to a piety focused upon imitation of the prophet who has shown the way to the vision of God's face. The asceticism of the Sufis is also prefigured in the humble and austere life of Mohammed and his immediate successors.

Union with God

The objective of Sufism, as of all mysticism, is to attain union with God. Mysticism seeks for an immediate experience of the divine reality through the suppression of the ego. The method for attaining this most coveted experience, however, demands insight into a special and hidden branch of knowledge. Sufi doctrine teaches that, beside the usual rules for religious life, set out in the revelation and the prophetic *sunnah*, there is another and deeper level of spiritual meaning, which the prophet shared with only a few of his chosen companions. The revelation, thus, wears two faces, one open and obvious, and the other only to be seen by those who have been instructed in its secrets. The relation between the exoteric and esoteric levels of religious knowledge is symbolic, with every command, or rule of *shariah*, pointing to a higher truth that marks one of the stages or stations on the path *(tariqah)* to God.

Knowledge of the *tariqah* has been passed down from the prophet through an unbroken chain *(silsilah)* of saints *(walis)*, each of whom has chosen his successor and instructed him in the secret knowledge of the way to union with God. For the ordinary person, there is no access to the blessing of immediate divine communion except by association with a saint and complete submission to a discipline of asceticism, meditation and spiritual growth, as his preceptor may dictate. Sufis believe that there is always in existence a hierarchy of saints at work in the world, culminating in a principal spiritual power called the *Qutb*, the pole or pivot of the universe. These saints are the continuing means for mediating the divine truth in the universe, the windows through which pours the divine light that invests all things with reality. Without the saints the universe literally could not exist, for it would be bereft of order and reality. The doctrine of the saints is, thus, a cosmology and a metaphysics as well as a pillar of personal mystical piety.

Individual saints are believed to have special powers because of the high degree of their spiritual attainments. There attaches to the saint a kind of holiness or blessedness, known as *barakah*, whose benefits the Sufi devotee may obtain by close association with the holy person. Saints, furthermore, are able to set aside the laws of nature and to perform miracles *(karamat)* and wonders. The saint, however, must not display his miraculous powers but should conceal them and hold them of no account. Belief in these special powers accounts for some of the practices of Sufism in recent centuries of which Muslim modernists have very much complained.

It is the custom among simple people to make visits to the tombs of saints, to take them offerings, to make petitions, and to offer what amounts almost to worship, all in the belief that the saint's power can cure illness or aid in other difficulties of life. Such a cult of the saints can readily degenerate into mere superstition, and modern reformers for this reason have opposed it vigorously. Nevertheless, every year hundreds of thousands of questing souls pay visits *(ziyarat)* to the burial places of the great saints, especially on the occasion of the annual *urs* or commemmorative celebration. The *urs* of Shaykh Muin al-Din Chishti at Ajmer in India, for example, attracts enormous crowds of devotees.

The Search for the Divine

The goal of the Sufi's long journey along the way *(tariqah)* is the achievement of *fana*, or extinction of the individuality in the reality of the divine. *Fana* consists in turning away from the world so that one sees only God. According to al-Hujwiri, 'The Sufi is he who has nothing in his possession nor is he possessed by anything. This denotes the essence of annihilation' (Nicholson's translation). *Fana* is a state of ectasy in which all human attributes have been left aside, and for many it brings the joy of intoxication in the divine love. For others, however, there is a stage beyond even annihilation. In their view the greater value for the Sufi is to achieve subsistence *(baqa)* in God, so subordinating will and humanity to the divine that, passing beyond ecstasy, that person lives continually in and through God. *Fana* may be temporary, a climactic experience to be enjoyed at most a few times in the course of human life, but *baqa* is an enduring condition of complete human in-dwelling in God. These goals are not attained by all who strive in the path, but for those who can attain them they are the *summum bonum* of human life.

In the course of its history Sufism passed through several distinct stages. Its earliest manifestations were an ascetic movement that laid great emphasis upon self-mortification *(zuhd)* as a means of keeping oneself free from worldly corruption. Very soon an element of ecstatic love for the divine was added to the discipline of asceticism, to be followed in turn by the elaboration of Sufi doctrine that produced a great variety of sectarian opinions. The culmination of this development came after the twelfth century with the founding of organized Sufi brotherhoods.

Sufi Orders

At the beginning of each brotherhood stands a great saint who attracted followers by virtue of his piety and spiritual power. The Gilani brotherhood, for example, springs from Shayk Abd al-Qadir Gilani, and the Suhrawardi brotherhood from Abd al-Qadir Suhrawardi and Umar Suhrawardi. The saint is responsible for the peculiar discipline and doctrine of the order, with the continuity of teaching and spiritual life being maintained through a series (*silsilah*) of spiritual successors to the founder. These living heads of the order are known as *shaykhs, pirs, rahbars, muqaddams*, etc.

Associated with the living heads of the orders, and subject to their complete control, is a group of seekers after the truth called *murids* or *shagirds*. The outstanding feature of the brotherhoods was a communal life among their members, often involving the maintenance of a central headquarters *(khanqah, tekke)* where the *shaykh* resided and gathered his disciples about him for instruction. When a *murid* had reached such a point in his development that the *shaykh* deemed him capable of instructing others in the spiritual path, he was often sent to represent the order in some distant place and so to spread its message. Such Sufis, especially wandering mendicants, are sometimes called 'dervishes'. From his disciples the *shaykh* would also choose the one whom he considered most advanced in understanding of the esoteric lore of Sufism to be designated as his *khalifah* or successor. In this way the spiritual heritage of the order was maintained intact. By late medieval times it was the custom for almost every individual to seek initiation into one of the Sufi orders and sometimes into several of them at the same time.

Meditation

Each brotherhood also had its own characteristic ceremonial of worship or spiritual meditation known as the *dhikr*. This was usually a form of words to be repeated over and over again as an aid to the remembrance *(dhikr)* of God. Often it consisted of the divine name or of one or a combination of the divine attributes. Perhaps the best-known Sufi *dhikr* is that of the Mevlevi order of Turkey (founded by the Persian mystical poet Halal al-Din al-Rumi), which consists of a peculiar whirling dance to the accompaniment of instruments. The Mevlevi were also distinguished by a unique costume with

Illustration page 490 wide skirt, flowing sleeves, and a pointed hat.

As late as the nineteenth century Sufism was, to all practical intents and purposes, the real meaning of Islam for the majority of ordinary Muslims. Even today, for millions of people in interior Anatolia and in the villages of the Arab countries, Iran, India, Pakistan and Bangladesh, it continues as a living form of piety centred upon the cult of the saints.

The Shiah and the Sunni

In the course of its history, Islam has been extraordinarily rich in the diversity of its religious belief and practice. Literally thousands of sectarian groups have made their appearance among Muslims: some of them quickly passed away, but others endured and left a lasting mark on history. They are far too numerous and complex to be dealt with fully here.

One important division, however, must be discussed. Broadly speaking, the Islamic community is split into two great groups, the Shiah and the Sunnis, which have been compared with Protestants and Catholics. The comparison, however, is ill-considered, for the Sunnis are not 'orthodox', in any proper sense of the term, nor are the Shiah protesters, for they have not broken away from a long established and universally accepted standard of religious belief and action.

Historically the Shiah belong to the very earliest period of Islamic history, and their peculiar religious characteristics evolved as early, if not earlier, than those of the Sunnis. Furthermore, Islam cannot be truly 'orthodox', for there is no clergy, hierarchy, or other agency which Muslims recognize as having the authority to define correct doctrine and practice.

The origin of both groups lies in the controversies over leadership of the community which followed the death of Mohammed. Abu Bakr was acclaimed caliph, or successor, to the prophet by some of the companions who were eager to avoid civil war. When he died, a little more than two years later, Umar was similarly acclaimed, and after him Uthman. Sunni Islam accepted the validity of the rule of these first three caliphs, along with the principle that the caliphate was an elective office among the Quraysh. However, from the beginning there was also a party which disagreed both with the specific choice of the caliph and with the principle of election. They held, instead, that leadership belonged to the family of the prophet. Their support was given to Ali ibn Abi Talib who, as cousin and son-in-law of Mohammed, was his closest male relative. For this reason they were called Shiah Ali, or the party of Ali. In the view of the Shiah the rule of the first three caliphs was illegitimate and unjust, and therefore there was no true caliph in Islam until Ali came to that position.

The Shiah have many traditions in which Mohammed is reported to have designated Ali as his chosen successor in the clearest terms. They point also to verses in the Koran which, in their view, have the same purpose. All of this material, they allege, was suppressed by their Sunni opponents to aid the unjust cause of Ali's detractors. It has been a custom of many Shiah through the ages to pronounce curses on the first three caliphs for their usurpation of their high office.

When at last Ali became caliph, the realization of his and his supporters' ambitions was only partial. Ali was never fully recognized as leader and soon after the diplomatic defeat by Muawiyah, following the Battle of Siffin, he fell victim to the poisoned sword of a Khawarij fanatic. The hopes of the Shiah Ali then devolved upon Ali's two sons, Hasan and Husayn. The first had no stomach for the struggle and renounced his claims to the caliphate, and the other, in an event of central importance for later Shiah piety, fell a martyr to Ummayad government troops at Karbala in Iraq. The date was the tenth of Muharram in the sixty-first year of the Hegira, corresponding to 10 October, AD 680.

Divine Light

Having been frustrated in the political sphere, the Shiah turned to the religious exaltation of Ali and his family. The result was a peculiar religious doctrine that is the mark of the Shiah. The foundation stone of the doctrine is the belief that Mohammed chose Ali to be the recipient of the esoteric side of Islamic teaching because no one else was capable of understanding it. This profound lore was then passed down from father to son, and all who would have salvation must learn it from them. By a subtle process of transformation this conviction became, in time, a doctrine very like incarnation. In its extreme form the belief held that the divine light was fully incarnate in Ali and transferred, upon his death, to a new *locus* in his descendants. Ali thus came to assume a position even above that of the prophet as a veritable divine being in the world. A more moderate position held that Ali and his offspring were mortal, but that a divine spark was transmitted from one to the other by metempsychosis so that there should continue to be a living source of guidance.

Ali and the line of his descendants were called *imams* (leaders) because of their distinction as the bearers of divine wisdom and guidance. Not only does rule belong properly to the *imam* of the age, but he is the sole source of truth. For the Shiah there is no hope of a proper life or reward hereafter, except through devotion to the *imam*.

Various groups of Shiah differ in the number of *imams* whom they recognize. The largest group acknowledges twelve and for this reason are called the 'Twelver' sect. The last of the *imams* is still alive, though he chose to disappear from human sight (*ghaybah*) to return again in future as the *Imam Mahdi* (the Rightly Guided Imam), who will initiate the events leading to the Last Day. Although he is now hidden, he continues to be the living spring of divine wisdom in the world through the *mujtahids*, or learned men of the Shiah community, by whom he communicates with people. Twelver Shiism has been the official religion of Iran since the rise of the Safawi dynasty in the sixteenth century, and there are also numbers of Twelver Shiahs in Iraq, India, Pakistan and Bangladesh.

The Ismailis

Another group of Shiahs recognize only seven *imams* and for this reason are known as 'Seveners' or Ismailis (after Muhammed ibn Ismail, the last *imam* in the chain). Ismailis have generally been much more radical in their doctrines than other Shiah, and for much of their history they have also been revolutionaries, teaching their doctrines in secret and struggling to overthrow established rulers.

Ismailism found its strongest political expression in the Fatimid

Above An Afghanistani woman prays in the direction of the Kaaba in Mecca as the sun sets in Nangarhar.

Above left Ritual ablutions before prayer in Sarajevo, Yugoslavia. Each mosque has facilities for this mandatory washing.

Left Facing the Kaaba to pray in the al-Azhar Mosque, Cairo, founded in 971 by the Fatimids, a Shiah dynasty from Ifriqa (Tunisia).

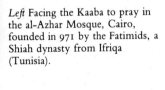

Left Prayer in a mosque at Samarra, Iraq. On the left is the *mihrab*, on the right the *minbar*, a raised platform for preaching and ceremonial announcements.

Right Algerian Muslims gather for the great prayer which concludes the fast during the month of Ramadan.

Opposite The focus of the Muslim world: the Great Mosque of Mecca, the holy city of Islam, and at its centre the Kaaba, the ancient site of a shrine which is said to have been founded by Abraham.

Below Pilgrims at Mecca stone one of the three pillars at Mina, representing the devil. Legend says that he appeared to Ismail to persuade him to disobey Abraham; the pilgrims re-enact Ismail's rejection.

caliphate of Egypt, whose rulers based their claim to power on their being *iman's* and successors to Muhammed ibn Ismail. The reign of the Fatimids (tenth and eleventh centuries) was one of the most brilliant periods in the history of Egypt, and the architectural monuments of the era still adorn Cairo today. The famous sect of the Assassins, who terrorized Muslim lands in the twelfth and thirteenth centuries, were Ismailis, as are the present Druze of Lebanon, Syria, and Israel, and the followers of the Agha Khan.

One of the peculiarities of the Shiah is their emphasis on the passion motif. Its origin lies in the martyrdom of Imam Husayn on the field of Karbala, which is celebrated each year in the great Ashura festival of mourning. On that day and before, the Shiah fly black flags and hold meetings where preachers tell the mournful story of the tragic death to crowds of weeping worshippers. On the tenth of Muharram itself (Ashura) it is the custom to conduct processions that exhibit symbols of the slain hero. Participants in the processions express their grief by beating their chests with clenched fists, cutting themselves with knives, and by other forms of self-inflicted torture.

The passion motif is not restricted to Imam Husayn, however. The Shiah believe that many of the *imams* suffered martyrdom at the hands of their enemies, even though the historical evidence is difficult to discover in some cases. Thus the history of every *imam* has been one of a just and good person suffering for his righteousness at the hands of heartless enemies. This long sequence of heroic self-sacrifice is celebrated in popular religion by lengthy dramas called *taziyahs*.

The Five Pillars

The principal elements that make up the worship of Muslims are called the Five Pillars of Islam. These are duties which Muslims are expected to perform as part of their *Ibadat*, or obligations toward God.

Shahadah, or confession of faith, is the first and basic pillar. The witnessing formula by which the Muslims declare their faith reads: 'There is no God but the one God, and Mohammed is His prophet.' In addition, however, to belief in God and prophecy, Muslims must also affirm their faith in God's books, in angels, and in the Last Day. The *shahadah* is repeated numerous times daily in the life of a pious person, in the call to prayer, in the prayer itself, and often as part of a practice of meditation or a Sufi *dhikr*.

Outwardly the most visible of the pillars is *salat* or ritual prayer. In the *hadith* literature the times of prayer are five daily: at dawn, at noon, in late afternoon, at sunset, and after sunset. Prior to the prayers, the worshipper must prepare by a ritual of purificatory washing (*wadu*). The *salat* proper begins with the worshipper in a standing position, followed by a series of bows from the waist (*ruku*) and prostrations, in which the forehead touches the ground (*sujud*). Each stage of the prayer is accompanied by a quotation from the Koran or some other recitation repeated silently. *Salat* may be performed at any place and often is, but there is special merit to its

Opposite above In many Muslim countries women still go veiled but female emancipation is gradually advancing and the practice is becoming less common in the more westernized countries.

Opposite below left Petro-dollars have initiated great social and religious building programmes throughout the Middle East. This is the Fatima Mosque, Kuwait.

Opposite below right The Ayatollah Khomeini, whose austere interpretation of Shiah Muslim tradition reshaped the political development of Iran.

Illustration page 490

Illustration page 499

performance in a mosque. On Fridays Muslims hold congregational prayers in the mosque (*masjid* or place of prostration) led by an *imam*, and on that day also there is a sermon following the congregational prayers. Five times each day the call to prayer (*adhan*) rings out from the minarets of mosques all over the Islamic world, signalling the faithful to their devotions. This haunting and beautiful summons in the past was always chanted by a *muezzin*, but in recent days the advent of technology has too often replaced it with a recording.

Zakat

In the time of Mohammed *zakat*, the third pillar, was of special importance as one of the outward signs of Islam. *Zakat* is alms paid for the sake of the needy, and calculated on the basis of a percentage of certain specific kinds of property which Muslims own. Although the duty to pay *zakat* is incumbent upon every Muslim of means, the arrangements for its collection have broken down in many modern Muslim states under the pressure of other taxes levied. Additional contributions (*sadaqat*), distinguished from the *zakat* by being voluntary, are also urged on the Muslims as works of special merit. In the early days such contributions were of vital significance since the prophet had no financial resources to further his mission.

The fourth pillar is the fast (*sawm*) during the month of Ramadan, and it is obligatory upon every adult Muslim of sound health, with some special conditions applying to women and exceptions made for travellers, the sick and infirm, etc. Fasting begins at daybreak, from the time a black thread may be distinguished from a white one, and lasts for the entire day until sundown. During this period all food and drink and smoking are forbidden, even the swallowing of one's own saliva. Following the practice of the prophet, Muslims customarily break the fast by consuming a few dates.

Because the Islamic calendar is lunar, the months rotate through the seasons of the year. When Ramadan happens to fall in summer, the fast can be a severe trial for the inhabitants of the hot and arid regions that are characteristic of much of the Islamic world. At the end of the month of fasting there is a great feast which, like the fast itself, is a religious duty. This festival, the Id al-Fitr, is one of the high points of Muslim religious life, with special congregational prayers to mark the occasion.

Illustration page 500

The Pilgrimage

Illustrations pages 500, 501

The pilgrimage (*haji*) to the Kaaba in Mecca is the last of the five pillars. Every adult Muslim possessing the means is expected to go on pilgrimage once in a lifetime. For many people in regions remote from Arabia the *haji* is the climax of years of yearning, and some make it repeatedly. Upon entering the sacred area of Mecca, pilgrims don a special dress (*ihram*) and after completing the ceremonies have their hair shaved. The full ceremony of the *hajj* is quite elaborate and occupies several days, but its principal parts are the circumambulation (*tawaf*) of the Kaaba climaxed by kissing the black stone embedded in one of its corners, and the sacrifice of an animal at Mina. This day

is celebrated through the Muslim world as the Id al-Adha, or Festival
of Sacrifice, in commemoration of Abraham's willingness to sacrifice
his son. This is the second great festival of the Muslim year.

Islam in Modern Times

The outstanding fact of Islam's recent history is a renaissance that has
swept the Muslim world. For several centuries Islamic civilization
had been in the grip of a progressive decline. During the eighteenth
and nineteenth centuries, Muslim political and military fortunes
everywhere suffered a serious setback that was accompanied also by
a loss of cultural and intellectual vitality. The three great Muslim
powers of the seventeenth century, the Ottoman in Turkey, the
Mughal in India, and the Persian in Iran, had by 1850 all fallen under
the domination of Europe.

The great expansion of European influence, wealth and power that
followed the Renaissance, the discovery of the New World and later
the industrial revolution, allowed the Europeans to bring large areas
of the Islamic world under their direct political dominion. The last
Mughal emperor of India was sent into exile in 1857 after the Indian
Mutiny, and India became part of the British Empire.

In Egypt and North Africa the British and French seized vast
territories from the tottering Ottoman sultans; and, though Iran never
became a colonial dependency, she was subjected to relentless Russian
and British pressure and was hard taxed to maintain her independence.
To protect the route to India the British also established themselves
in the south coast of Arabia and the Persian Gulf.

Farther to the east, the Dutch were in firm control of the Indonesian
islands, while Malaysia and Singapore were British. The growth of
European domination over the Muslim world continued even after
World War I, when the mandates system adopted by the Allies
apportioned the Arab provinces of the defeated Turks among the
British, French and Italians. These manifold reversals of fortune created a crisis of thought and faith among Muslims that shook their
civilization to its very roots. The result has been a renewed grasp of
the Islamic heritage that has both a political and a religious side.

Politically, the Muslim renaissance has expressed itself in movements to throw off outside domination and attain national independence. The struggle against the Europeans and toward the present
national states achieved serious proportions in the last quarter of the
nineteenth century. The earliest hero of the rebirth was an energetic
Muslim of disputed origin named Jamal al-Din, sometimes called
al-Afghani. This man travelled throughout the Islamic world urging
Muslims to reject foreign hegemony and seize their own destiny
afresh through revolutionary means. Jamal al-Din made trouble for
the British in India and Egypt. He was a factor in the Tobacco
Concession affair and the assassination of the Persian shah Nasir al-
Din Qajar. He spent some time in Europe publishing revolutionary
journals and he ended his life in Turkey in 1899, where Sultan Abd
al-Hamid, for fear of his influence, kept him in genteel imprisonment.

Revival

A serious effort to stem the internal decay of the community was launched in India by Shah Waliullah of Delhi in the late eighteenth century and carried on by his descendants and disciples through the early decades of the nineteenth. The beginning of a truly modern trend was the work of Sir Sayyid Ahmad Khan (died 1898) who, after the disaster of the Mutiny, organized a movement to rehabilitate Muslims educationally and socially by founding a college at Aligarh in 1875. Sir Sayyid urged his co-religionists to reconcile themselves with their British rulers and to take benefit from Western science and learning. Although his movement never urged a struggle for independence, it awakened Indian Muslims to renewed consciousness of their identity and peculiar interests as a community. Soon Muslims were participating in the Indian National Congress, and in 1906 the Muslim League was founded. By the time of the Khilafat and Non-Co-operation Movements of 1919-21, the Muslims were mounting a full-scale assault on British rule of India.

In the period between the two world wars pressures mounted throughout the Muslim world for the end of foreign domination. The Arab countries, where nationalism had stirred in the nineteenth century, obtained their independence from Ottoman rule as a consequence of World War I only to fall under European mandates. After World War II, however, country after country achieved its independence as a sovereign national state until, today, the colonial system has been erased in the Islamic world. At present the Islamic political revitalization is so complete that a return to foreign control is no longer conceivable.

Religiously, the Muslim awakening is characterized by a conviction of Islam's relevance to the changed circumstances of modern life. Far from abandoning their ancient religious heritage, the Muslims have seen its reaffirmation as the key to their future strength and success. The principal pupil of Jamal al-Din al-Afghani, the Egyptian savant, Mohammed Abduh (d. 1905), for example, advocated a modernizing reform of traditional religious education and put forward an interpretation of Islam by which he hoped to open the door to progress and new life. He attacked the principle of *taqlid* and the pettifogging of medieval lawyers. Abduh held that Islamic teaching is, above all, rational in its essence, that Islam approves, indeed urges, the exercise of the intellectual faculty so that religion and science can never be in conflict. He wished to see Islam reborn of its own strength by a return to its original character. His work was motivated also by the need to defend Islam against both implied and explicit criticisms of the West. Thus, it has an apologetic content.

Determined Action

The present religious revival of Islam is also notable for its dynamism. Modernist thinkers believe Islam, when truly understood, to be an imperative to determined action. This feature of modernism is nowhere more vivid than in the inspired Persian and Urdu poetry of Sir

Mohammed Iqbal (d. 1937), who galvanized an entire generation of Indian Muslim youth to participate in the struggle against the Hindus and the British.

The modern period has also seen the birth of several distinctive sectarian groups among Muslims. In Iran two sects, called Babis and Bahais, separated themselves from the prevailing Shiism. The Bahais, renouncing their specifically Islamic connection, have become a new religion of international importance, professing broad humanitarian ideals. In India a Punjabi Muslim, Mirza Ghulam Ahmad (d. 1908) of Qadian, proclaimed himself the Mahdi (Expected One) and became the centre of a group called the Ahmadiyah. They have their headquarters as a separate community in Pakistan, where they enjoy considerable prosperity and exhibit a great enthusiam for Islam. The community has spread widely in the Islamic world and is notable for its educational and missionary activity.

Islamic Reaction (Ed.)

Contrary to the modernism and westernization advocated by Muslim intellectuals, reaction towards traditional and fundamentalist interpretations of Islam assumed greater importance in the seventies and eighties of the present century. The Shah of Iran had attempted to make his country 'the Japan of the Middle East', but at the cost of repression of dissidents and especially of religious leaders called by their followers *ayatollahs* (signs of God).

Ayatollah Khomeini fled to Paris but returned to Iran in triumph in 1979, hailed by millions of enthusiasts and declaring that 'Islam is the religion of fighters for freedom' who had chosen 'an Islamic republic. All of you must comply or be obliterated.' A more repressive regime than the Shah's was imposed, with countless executions and tortures of opponents. The Bahais in particular suffered, with over a hundred of their leaders executed by 1981, and thousands of others were made homeless or fled the country.

Illustration page 502

Iran and Ayatollah Khomeini were the centre of Shiah Islam, which had always had an element of martyrdom, but similar fundamentalist reactions were to be found in the Sunni world. In Egypt the Muslim Brotherhood opposed reforms and reconciliation with Israel by President Sadat and was held responsible for his assassination in 1981. In Pakistan moves were made towards the establishment of an Islamic republic in accordance with *shariah* law. Islamic studies became compulsory for all students and women were to be veiled, while judges and civil servants were ordered to wear Islamic dress. The traditional Islamic ban on usury led to the introduction of interest-free banking, and the alms tax (*zakat*) was imposed on deposits and savings. Reactionary movements stirred across the Islamic world, while in calmer tones conferences of political and cultural leaders urged the practice of the principles of Islam and abolition of 'all un-Islamic systems, laws and customs, that have permeated Muslim society'.

Illustration page 502

Conclusion

The panorama of the world's religions is fascinating and complex. From the earliest times to the present day religious beliefs have flourished, producing countless rituals and symbols, as men and women have tried to make sense of the world and provide lasting meaning for their lives. Those who have read this book through, from prehistoric and tribal religions down to Islam, may be excused for feeling bewildered at the infinite variety of religious life. Even looking at the illustrations, or selecting a chapter on a special interest, one may receive an impression of confusing legend and rite. At least it is hard to maintain the notion that all religions are the same, and if they have some common goals they have many differences.

The religions described here have all had a history, but for some it was never recorded and they had no scriptures. There are at least eleven historical, scriptural and living religions, from ancient Iran to Islam with two native ones for China. But how active are they and can they survive the pressures of modern life? Is interest in religion merely historical or antiquarian, and will religions be replaced by more rational systems? The traditional faiths of China have suffered severe repression and much may be written about them in the past tense. Judaism and Christianity have been persecuted in Communist Europe and have declined in outward observance even in the more tolerant West. Islam, Hinduism and the rest have been subjected to criticisms, the acids of modernity which erode the faith of intellectuals at least.

To readers educated in Western critical methods it may appear almost incredible that so much mythology has been accepted and still flourishes. Do Hindus really believe in the miraculous or erotic tales of Krishna or Shiva? Millions do, though intellectuals may think the stories as unlikely as those of Isis and Osiris in ancient Egypt. Yet Isis and Osiris retained their appeal until they were replaced by stronger faiths, notably Christianity.

Mythology

Christianity itself has been under fire for the last century. Attack is not new, for the Church was nurtured in persecution for the first three centuries and it has weathered many storms. But modern study has applied a 'higher criticism' even to the sacred foundation text, the Bible, and it has contrasted the pictures of faith with the cosmic views of science. The German theologian Rudolf Bultmann has been a leader in attempts to 'demythologize' Christianity. The old notion, he says, was that the universe is composed of three storeys: heaven, earth, and hell. Into this framework fitted the supernatural powers: miraculous events, men and women guided by angels and tempted by the devil, or spirit possession. 'This conception of the world we call mythological because it is so different from the conception of the world which has been formed and developed by science.'

On the other hand psychologists emphasize the importance of myths or pictorial representations of the universe. C. G. Jung said that symbolical language may be misleading at times and need to be changed, but even when the myth is factually inaccurate 'it is *psychologically true*, because it was and is the bridge to all the greatest achievements of humanity.' The world is dangerous, not a Garden of Eden but a place of terrors. But with faith in divine guidance men and women have faced the most fearful perils. Belief in a universe of law, and trust that truth can be found, are basic to both religion and science and can form the ground for a modern mythology.

Anti-Religion?

Not only have attacks been made upon mythology but upon the very existence of religion. Atheism, agnosticism, humanism, secularism, scientific materialism and Communism have made onslaughts against religion. Doubt of some religious propositions is not new and there have probably always been some individual unbelievers. They can be traced from the cynics and sceptics of ancient Greece, and *charvakas* of India, down to modern secularists.

'Secularism' is a curious term which has undergone changes of meaning. Originally denoting that which lasts for an age or century (Latin *saeculum*, French *siècle*), it came to indicate what is concerned with the affairs of this world, that which is not celestial or sacred and so is temporal or profane. Subsequently the word 'secularism' has been applied to that which opposes religious belief or, more narrowly, is against religious education. Similarly humanism, from being concerned only with human interests, was taken to exclude the divine, and went on to declare that men and women were on their own in the universe, without a god or life after death. Atheists maintain this, though agnostics may not be so dogmatic and prefer to suspend judgement since we cannot know everything.

Religious Communism

More dangerous to religion than science, which in itself is neutral, is atheistic Communism. Communism need not be anti-religious since there have been many religious societies which have practised forms of communistic living, from the Buddhist Sangha to the early Christians. But in most of its modern political forms Communism is not only a system of economics but professedly atheistic, as dialectical or scientific materialism, held almost with the fervour of a religion.

Karl Marx, originator and father-figure of modern Communism, recognized the role and power of religion in the past. He described it as 'the opiate of the masses', a medicine for the sufferings of the proletariat. Religion was 'the cry of the oppressed creature, the heart of a heartless world'. Nevertheless, like other nineteenth-century optimists, Marx thought that religion would disappear with the evils which it sought hopelessly to abolish, and it would be out of place in the new scientific and egalitarian society.

Armed with the dialectic of Marx who, with Darwin and Freud, was among the most influential thinkers of the modern world, the Communist states have put atheism into practice. Using terms of faith or mythology, such as the 'inevitable' march of history with its 'laws', they have tried to accelerate the movement by persecuting religious organizations in the hope that they would disappear.

Religions have been sufficiently deep-rooted not to be suppressed outright and, so far, Albania is the only Communist country which refuses to recognize the existence of any religion. But pressure against churches, synagogues, mosques and temples continues in the Soviet Union, China and other lands and numbers decrease. However, even in the Soviet Union, where persecution of religion has been in effect since 1917, the churches are far from extinct or attended only by the aged, and today's old people were youths when the revolution began.

It has often been remarked that Communism has become almost a religion, whether in minority groups, where it may be a persecuted and fervent sect, or in great mass-organizations. It certainly has many of the trappings of religion. The huge state parades are like religious festivals, and significantly they take place in Russia and China, lands of former great state religions. The early leaders, founding fathers and authoritative teachers are virtually deified. Their pictures are in all public and most private buildings, like icons, and their tombs are places of pilgrimage, at which people queue for hours. The textbooks of Communism are like sacred oracles, treated as infallible and revered like the Bible and Koran elsewhere. The Communist faith in the coming golden age of equality and peace is the direct heir of the eschatology of Judaism and Christianity.

Illustration page 512

Illustration page 512

Both Soviet and Chinese Communism have myths and symbols which resemble those of religion and they provide outlets for emotional and social needs. But when political or economic methods change, and that might take centuries, it will be seen whether they can continue as substitute religions. Communism is too young to be compared with those faiths which have endured thousands of years, and its philosophy provides little or no answer for some of the most profound questions and needs of humanity.

The historic religions have great staying power. Buddhism was harshly persecuted in China in the ninth century, as Christianity was from the first to the third, but they survived and spread. 'The blood of the martyrs is the seed of the church.' Other faiths have revived after centuries of virtual eclipse, and the power of their ideas remains to influence social doctrines or political parties.

Above Members of the Hare Krishna sect at their French headquarters.

Above left A Seventh-Day Adventist baptism in the swimming pool of a Californian motel, USA.

Left Kenya's Holy Spirit Church of Zion holds all its services in the open air. Here believers are summoned to worship.

Right The queue to visit Lenin's mausoleum in Red Square, Moscow. This photograph was taken during his centenary year.

Right Chinese Red Guards refresh themselves with the thoughts of Chairman Mao as they journey through Canton province, spreading his word.

Right Work in progress on the new mosque in London's Regents Park. The star on the facing wall, which was later removed, was sited in the *mihrab*, facing the Kaaba.

New Religious Movements

In many ages there are outbursts of religious feeling and the present is no exception, if a world view is taken. In Africa, not only have Islamic and Christian missions made millions of converts in recent years, but there are about six thousand independent African Christian organizations. They testify to a great concern with religion, studying the Bible closely and seeking to evangelize their continent by African means.

In Europe, America and Asia new forms of religious life may be divided roughly into traditionalist and syncretist or mixed. Traditionalists affirm the authority of old forms of religion, the sacred book and the inspired leader, but they usually have some particular doctrine which they emphasize. So Adventists stress the Second Advent or Coming of Christ and speak of the wars and troubles which should precede it. Such millenarian movements, expecting the millenium or thousand years' reign of Christ, have appeared many times in history. Jehovah's Witnesses are also millenarian, biblical in a fundamentalist manner, and taking an anarchistic attitude to human authority. In the past twenty years Charismatics have stressed the charismata or 'gifts' of the Spirit, often including ecstatic cries called 'speaking in tongues', like the older Pentecostalist Churches. Such phenomena have been common in many parts of the world, among the dervishes of Islam or the shamans of Asia and Africa.

Illustration page 511

Illustration page 511

The Mormons or Latter-Day Saints are different in that they have their own scripture, the *Book of Mormon* (1829), used alongside the Bible. Christian Science, founded by Mary Baker Eddy, also has its own scripture in her *Science and Health* (1875), which is used as well as the Bible to teach the unreality of pain and death.

The impact of world religions upon each another is one of the most significant events of our time. Christianity has sent its missionaries to nearly every country, but the compliment has been returned with Buddhist, Vedantic and Islamic missions to the West. The Theosophical Society from 1875 and the Ramakrishna Mission from 1897 have made Hindu ideas, especially monism or pantheism and reincarnation, known to the Western world. After rather intellectual appeals in the early decades, since the nineteen sixties there have been popular and emotional Hindu missions in Europe and America, such as Transcendental Meditation taught by Maharishi Mahesh Yogi and Hare Krishna from Swami A. C. Bhaktivedanta.

Illustration page 511

Many forms of Yoga, physical, mental and spiritual, have been practised worldwide, often with Hindu or Buddhist interpretations, Zen Buddhism from Japan being especially favoured. Mixtures of East and West appear in Asia in, for instance, many forms of Japanese 'new religions', while the Cao Dai of Vietnam from 1920 unites Taoist, Buddhist and Christian ideas and includes Victor Hugo among its divinities.

Islamic Sufism has appealed to the West among other forms of mystical meditation, but generally the more fundamentalist types of

Islam have been restricted to traditional Muslim centres. Elsewhere movements of population have involved religious mobility, and societies that have become more inter-racial have found that that involves inter-religiosity. Sikhs have taken their religion with them when they migrated and so have followers of other religions, East and West.

Universal Religions

In early times and tribal societies religion was so closely interwoven with particular peoples that it was restricted to them. Then military conquests brought domination over other races and imposition of gods upon them, or acceptance of local gods as the original spirits of the land. Later prophets and reformers looked beyond their own frontiers to a wider spread of religion and eventually to a universal faith.

Few of the historical religions have not had some missionary impulse. It has been said that a Hindu must be a member of a caste, yet in past centuries Hindu religion extended far beyond India and some of its beliefs went to distant places with Buddhism. Japanese Shinto was closely bound up with national tradition but in the days of imperial expansion it was said to be destined to rule all peoples.

There are three major missionary religions in terms of numbers: Buddhism, Christianity and Islam. Buddhism was first in the field, partly due to its appeal to all levels of society but it had greater and more lasting success outside India, the land of its birth, than within. The great emperor Ashoka, in the third century BC, sent missions to Sri Lanka from India, and perhaps to Burma as well as westwards. Buddhist monks carried Indian ideas and culture throughout South-East Asia and then to Tibet, China, Korea and Japan. Despite many setbacks and some persecutions, Buddhists extended their activities peacefully and permeated the life and art of Central and East Asia. In India they finally retreated before renascent Hinduism and militant Islam, after over a thousand years of success, but Buddhism dominated South-East Asia because there was no other literate religion to oppose it. Where there were ancient and national religions, as in China and Japan, Buddhism mingled with them and influenced all national life.

Islam, in the seventh century AD, was the most immediately successful of all religions. Just a hundred years after the death of Mohammed the Arab armies were to be found in the heart of France and Muslim embassies in China. The Near and Middle East became and remained largely Islamic, to the loss of Christianity, and India received its most powerful influence from one of the great monotheistic Semitic faiths. In our day Islam, while long stagnant in some lands, has revived in nationalist and fundamentalist forms, spread its influence abroad in liberal and mystical movements, and made great progress in new areas, such as tropical Africa.

Christianity had a missionary impulse from its origins and extended rapidly throughout the Mediterranean world and into Asia. There were periods of stabilization or decline, and others of revival, activity being intensified in the seventeenth and later centuries. A historian has remarked that this religion has gone farther and increased in numbers more rapidly during the past century than at any previous period in its history. Christianity now claims about twice the numbers of its nearest rivals, some fourteen hundred millions, compared with about seven hundred millions for Islam, two hundred and seventy millions for Buddhism and six hundred millions for Hinduism. Now consolidation is taking place and, in view of internal Christian efforts at unity, it has been asked whether there should not be an inter-religious ecumenical movement. There have been conferences of leaders of all the major religions but little official attempt at a synthesis of their beliefs or membership.

Ways to Truth

It is sometimes said that all religions have the same goal, or are equal ways to the truth, or even that all teach the same doctrines. And if one protests that all religions do not appear to be the same, in belief or practice, this is declared to show prejudice and the inferiority of the protester's religion. Is it that 'all religions are equal, but some are more equal than others'? Yet the ancient Aztecs, who held up the beating hearts of their victims to the sun, surely did not have as good a religion as that of the peaceful Buddha.

Efforts that have been made to create new religions, taking the best from variant traditions, tend to emphasize some distinctive beliefs. The strong Hindu trend in the Theosophical Society has been mentioned. The Bahais proclaim the unity of religions, but they hold that after the prophets of past ages the supreme truth dawned in the Iranian Baha'u'llah, who died in 1892. It seems that a religion must have a dynamic coming from particular teachers and doctrines. The survival of the great historical religions demonstrates this, but while each retains its identity they may influence one another in the many contacts of modern times.

In reaction against artificial amalgamations, there are those who declare that any mingling or influence of one religion upon another is wrong; not only that there is no salvation outside a particular creed but that even to study another faith is dangerous and probably inspired by the devil. Yet influence in some degree is unavoidable. The close communications of our world ensure that, and the knowledge that we have of other religions has increased immensely in the last hundred years. To study different religions need not imply infidelity to one's own faith, but rather it may be enlarged by seeing how other people have sought for reality and have been enriched by their search.

This book has tried to present the facts of religious beliefs and customs. It does not seek to judge or set up any standard but the truth. It attempts to reveal something of the wealth and variety of the age-long quest for reality.

Bibliography

Introduction
Eliade, M. *Patterns in Comparative Religion* 1958; *From Primitives to Zen* 1967
Evans-Pritchard, E. E. *Theories of Primitive Religion* 1965
Finegan, J. *The Archaeology of World Religions* 1952
Frazer, J. G. *The Golden Bough* 1890
Freud, S. *Totem and Taboo* 1919
James, E. O. *The Beginnings of Religion* 1948; *The Ancient Gods* 1960
Lévi-Strauss, C. *Totemism* 1963
Ling, T. O. *A History of Religion East and West* 1968
Moore, A. C. *Iconography of Religions* 1977
Otto, R. *The Idea of the Holy* 1923
Parrinder, E. G. *A Dictionary of Non-Christian Religions* 1981
Steiner, F. *Taboo* 1956

Chapter One – **Prehistoric Religion**
Breuil, H. *Four Hundred Centuries of Cave Art* 1952
Brown, G. Balwin *The Art of the Cave Dweller* 1928
Burkitt, M. C. *The Old Stone Age* 3rd ed., 1955
Coates, A. *A Prelude to History* 1951
James, E. O. *Prehistoric Religion* 1957
Luquet, G. H. *The Art and Religion of Fossil Man* 1930
Maringer, J. *The Gods of Prehistoric Man* 1956
Osborn, H. F. *Men of the Old Stone Age* 3rd ed., 1918
Sollas, W. J. *Ancient Hunters* 3rd ed., 1924

Chapter Two – **Tribal Religions in Asia**
Czaplicka, M. A. *Aboriginal Siberia: A Study in Social Anthropology* 1914
Eliade, Mircea *Shamanism, Archaic Techniques of Ecstasy* 1964
Elwin, Verrier *The Baiga* 1939; *The Muria and their Ghotul* 1947; *The Myths of Middle India* 1947; *The Religion of an Indian Tribe* 1955
Fürer-Haimendorf, C. von *The Chenchus, Jungle Folk of the Deccan* 1943; *The Reddis of the Bison Hills* 1945; *The Rai Gonds of Adilabad* 1948

Chapter Three – **Early Australasia**
Berndt, R. M. & C. H. *The World of the First Australians* 1964
Best, E. *The Maori* 1924
Buck, Peter *The Coming of the Maori* 1950
Eliade, M. *Australian Religions* 1973
Elkin, A. P. *The Australian Aborigines: How to Understand Them* 4th ed., 1964
Grey, Sir George *Polynesian Mythology* 1965
Handy, E. S. C. 'Polynesian Religion' in *Bernice P. Bishop Museum Bulletin*, 34, 1927
Henderson, J. M. *Ratana: The Origins and the Story of the Movement* 1963
Poignant, Roslyn *Oceanic Mythology* 1967
Schwimmer, Erik *The Maori People in the Nineteen-Sixties* 1968
Strehlow, T. G. H. *Aranda Traditions* 1947

Chapter Four – **Traditional Africa**
Davidson, B. *The African Past* 1964
Evans-Pritchard, E. E. *Nuer Religion* 1956
Field, M. J. *Search for Security* 1960
Forde, D. (ed.) *African Worlds* 1954
Griaule, M. *Conversations with Ogotemmêli* 1965
Idowu, E. B. *Olódùmarè, God in Yoruba Belief* 1962
Jahn, J. *Muntu* 1961
Kenyatta, J. *Facing Mount Kenya* 1938
Kuper, H. *An African Aristocracy* 1947
Lienhardt, G. *Divinity and Experience* 1961
Little, K. L. *The Mende of Sierra Leone* 1951
Mbiti, J. S. *African Religions and Philosophy* 1969
Parrinder, E. G. *African Traditional Religion* 1954; *Witchcraft, European and African* 1963; *African Mythology* 2nd ed., 1982
Rattray, R. S. *Ashanti* 1923
Schapera, I. (ed.) *The Bantu-speaking Tribes of South Africa* 1937
Seligman, C. G. *Races of Africa* 1930
Smith, E. W. (ed.) *African Ideas of God* 1950
Taylor, J. V. *The Primal Vision* 1963
Turnbull, C. M. *The Forest People* 1961
Turner, V. W. *The Drums of Affliction* 1968
Wilson, M. *Communal Rituals of the Nyakyusa* 1959

Chapter Five – **Aztecs and Mayas**
Burland, Cottie *The Gods of Mexico* 1967
Caso, Alfonso *The Aztecs, People of the Sun* 1958
Coe, Michael D. *Mexico* 1962
Morley, S. G. *The Ancient Maya* 1946
Nicholson, Irene *Mexican and Central American Mythology* 2nd ed., 1983
Recinos, Adrián *Popol Vuh* (trans. D. Goetz and S. G. Morley) 1951
Redfield, R. *The Folk Culture of Yucatan* 1941
Thompson, J. Eric S. *The Rise and Fall of Maya Civilisation* 1966
Vaillant, G. C. *The Aztecs of Mexico* 1952
Von Hagen, Victor W. *The Ancient Sun Kingdoms* 1962
Zantwijk, R. A. M. *Servants of the Saints: The Social and Cultural Identity of a Tarascan Community in Mexico* 1967

Chapter Six – **Andean Religion**
Avila, Francisco de *A Narrative of the Errors, False Gods, and other Superstitions and Diabolical Rites in which the Indians of Huarochiri lived in Ancient Times* trans. and ed. by Clements R. Markham in 'Rites and Laws of the Yncas' 1873
Bellamy, H. S. and Allen, Peter *The Calendar of Tiahuanaco* 1956
Baumann, Hans *Gold and Gods of Peru* 1963
Bushnell, G. H. S. *The Ancient People of the Andes* 1949
Flornoy, Bertrand *The World of the Inca* 1957
Mason, John Alden *The Ancient Civilisation of Peru* 1957
Molina, Cristóbal de *The Fables and Rites of the Yncas* trans. and ed. by Clements R. Markham in 'Rites and Laws of the Yncas' 1873
Osborne, Harold *South American Mythology* 2nd ed., 1983
Zuidema, R. T. *The Ceque System of Cuzco: The Social Organisation of the Capital of the Inca* 1964

Chapter Seven – **Northern Europe in the Iron Age**
Davidson, H. R. E. *Gods and Myths of Northern Europe* 1964; *Pagan Scandinavia* 1967; *Scandinavian Mythology* 2nd ed., 1982
Filip, J. *Celtic Civilisation and its Heritage* 1962
Gelling, P. and Davidson, H. R. E. *The Chariot of the Sun* 1969
Hagan, A. *Norway* 1967
Klindt-Jensen, O. *Denmark Before the Vikings* 1957
Piggott, S. *The Druids* 1968
Powell, T. E. G. *The Celts* 1958
Ross, A *Pagan Celtic Britain* 1967
Sjoestedt-Jonval, M. *Gods and Heroes of the Celts* 1949
Stenberger, M. *Sweden* 1962
Turville-Petre, E. O. *Myths and Religions of the North* 1964
Wilson, D. *The Anglo-Saxons* 1964

Chapter Eight – **Mesopotamia**

Frankfort, H. *Kingship and the Gods* 1948
Gadd, C. J. *Ideas of Divine Rule in the Ancient East* 1948
Gray, John *Near Eastern Mythology* 1969
Heidel, A. *The Babylonian Genesis* 1957; *The Gilgamesh Epic and Old Testament Parallels* 1949
Hooke, S. H. *Babylonian and Assyrian Religion* 1953
James, E. O. *Myth and Ritual in the Ancient Near East* 1958
Kramer, S. N. *The Sumerians* 1964
Lambert, W. G. *Babylonian Wisdom Literature* 1960
Lambert, W. G. & Millard, A. R. *Atra-hasis: The Babylonian Story of the Flood* 1969
Oppenheim, A. L. *Ancient Mesopotamia* 1964
Parrot, A. *The Tower of Babel* 1956
Pritchard, J. B. (ed.) *Ancient Near Eastern Texts relating to the Old Testament* 1955
Sanders, N. K. *The Epic of Gilgamesh* 1960

Chapter Nine – **Ancient Egypt**

Bell, H. I. *Cults and Creeds in Graeco-Roman Egypt* 1957
Brandon, S. G. F. *Creation Legends of the Ancient Near East* 1963; *Time and Mankind* 1951
Breasted, J. H. *The Development of Religion and Thought in Ancient Egypt* 1912
Budge, E. A. Wallis *From Fetish to God in Ancient Egypt* 1934; *The Gods of the Egyptians* (2 vols) 1904
Cerny, J. *Ancient Egyptian Religion* 1952
Clark, R. T. Rundle *Myth and Symbol in Ancient Egypt* 1959
Edwards, I. E. S. *The Pyramids of Egypt* rev. ed., 1961
Frankfort, Henri *Ancient Egyptian Religion* 1948; *Kingship and the Gods* 1948
Griffiths, J. Gwyn *The Conflict of Horus and Seth* 1960
Ions, Veronica *Egyptian Mythology* 2nd ed., 1982
James, T. G. H. *Introductory Guide to the Egyptian Collection British Museum*, 1961
Mercer, S. A. B. *The Religion of Ancient Egypt* 1949
Sauneron, Serge *The Priests of Ancient Egypt* (trans. A. Morrissett) 1960
Wainwright, G. A. *The Sky-Religion in Egypt* 1938

Chapter Ten – **Ancient Greece**

Cook, A. B. *Zeus* (3 vols.) 1914–40
Cornford, F. M. *Greek Religious Thought* 1923
Festugière, A. J. *Personal Religion among the Greeks* 1954
Graves, Robert *The Greek Myths* 1948
Guthrie, W. K. C. *The Greeks and Their Gods* 1950
Harrison, J. E. *Prolegomena to the Study of Greek Religion* 1961; *Themis* 1912
James, E. O. *The Cult of the Mother-Goddess* 1959
Murray, G. *Five Stages of Greek Religion* 1925
Mylonas, G. E. *Eleusis and the Eleusinian Mysteries* 1961
Neumann, E. *The Great Mother* 1963
Nilsson, M. P. *A History of Greek Religion* 1925; *The Minoan-Mycenean Religion and its Survival in Greek Religion* 1927
Otto, W. F. *The Homeric Gods* 1964
Parke, H. W. *Greek Oracles* 1967
Rose, H. J. *Ancient Greek Religion* 1946; *Primitive Culture in Greece* 1925
Seltman, C. T. *The Twelve Olympians* 1952
Willetts, R. F. *Cretan Cults and Festivals* 1962

Chapter Eleven – **Ancient Rome**

Altheim, F. *A History of Roman Religion* 1938
Angus, S. *The Mystery Religions and Christianity* 1925; *The Religious Quests of the Graeco-Roman World* 1929
Bailey, C. *Phases in the Religion of Ancient Rome* 1932
Cumont, F. *Oriental Religions in Roman Paganism* 1911; *After-Life in Roman Paganism* 1922
Dodds, E. R. *Pagan and Christian in an Age of Anxiety* 1965
Glover, T. R. *The Conflict of Religions in the Early Roman Empire* 1920
Grant, Michael *The Roman World* 1960
Harris, E. & J. R. *The Oriental Cults in Roman Britain* 1965

Perowne, Stewart *Roman Mythology* 2nd ed., 1982
Rose, H. J. *Ancient Roman Religion* 1948; *Primitive Culture in Italy* 1926
Taylor, L. R. *The Divinity of the Roman Emperor* 1931
Vermaseren, M. J. *Mithras, The Secret God* 1963
Willoughby, H. R. *Pagan Regeneration* 1929

Chapter Twelve – **Ancient Iran**

Boyce, M. *Zoroastrians* 1979
Cumont, F. *The Mysteries of Mithra* 1956
Drower, Lady E. *Water into Wine* 1956; *The Mandeans of Iraq and Iran* 1937
Duchesne-Guillemin, J. *The Hymns of Zarathustra* (trans. M. Henning) 1952; *Symbols and Values of Zorastrianism* 1966
Frye, R. N. *The Heritage of Persia* 1962
Gershevitch, I. *The Avestan Hymn to Mithra* 1959
Ghirshman, R. *Iran* 1961; *Persia, From the Origins to Alexander* 1964; *Iran, Parthians and Sasanians*
Henning, W. B. *Zoroaster* 1951
Hinnells, John R. *Persian Mythology* 1971
Jackson, A. V. W. *Zoroastrian Studies* 1965; *Zoraster the Prophet of Ancient Iran* 1966
Modi, J. J. *The Religious Ceremonies and Customs of the Parsis* 1922
Moulton, J. H. *Early Zoroastrianism* 1913; *The Treasure of the Magi* 1917
Vermaseren, M. J. *Mithras, the Secret God* 1963
Widengren, G. *Mani and Manichaeism* 1961
Zaehner, R. C. *The Teachings of the Magi* 1956; *Zurvan, a Zoroastrian Dilemma* 1955; *The Dawn and Twilight of Zoroastrianism* 1961

Chapter Thirteen – **Hinduism**

Allchin, B. and R. *The Birth of Indian Civilisation* 1968
Basham, A. L. (ed.) *A Cultural History of India* 1975
Brent, P. *Godmen of India* 1972
Chaudhuri, N. C. *Hinduism: A Religion to Live By* 1979
Dasgupta, S. N. *A History of Indian Philosophy*, 5 vols. 1951–55
De Bary, W. T. (ed.) *Sources of Indian Tradition* 1958
Fischer, L. *The Life of Mahatma Gandhi* 1951
Gandhi, M. K. *The Story of My Experiments with Truth* 1940
Hume, R. E. *The Thirteen Principal Upanishads* 1921
Ions, V. *Indian Mythology* 2nd. ed., 1983
Klostermaier, K. *Hindu and Christian in Vrindaban* 1970
Michell, G. *The Hindu Temple* 1977
Nikhilananda, S. *The Gospel of Sri Ramakrishna* 1947
O'Flaherty, W. D. *Hindu Myths* 1975; *The Rig Veda* 1981
Singer, M. (ed.) *Krishna: Myths, Rites and Attitudes* 1966
Stutley, M. and J. *A Dictionary of Hinduism* 1977
Tagore, R. *Gitanjali* 1912
Walker, B. *Hindu World* 1968
Zaehner, R. C. *Hinduism* 1962; *Hindu Scriptures* 1966; *The Bhagavad-Gītā* 1969
Zimmer, H. *Philosophies of India* 1951

Chapter Fourteen – **Jainism**

Jaini, J. *Outlines of Jainism* 1916
Stevenson, S. T. *The Heart of Jainism* 1915
Williams, R. *Jaina Yoga* 1963
Zimmer, H. *Philosophies of India* (Jainism: pages 217–262) ed. J. Campbell, 1967

Chapter Fifteen – **Sikhism**

Cole, W. O. and Sambhi, P. S. *The Sikhs* 1978
Khushwant Singh *A History of the Sikhs* vol. 1, 1963, vol. 2, 1966
Macauliffe, M. A. *The Sikh Religions* (6 vols.) 1909
McLeod, W. H. *Guru Nanak and the Sikh Religion* 1968
Trilochan Singh, et.al. (trans.) *Selections from the Sacred Writings of the Sikhs* 1960
Vaudeville, C. *Kabīr* 1974

Chapter Sixteen – **Buddhism**

Conze, E. (trans.) *Buddhist Scriptures* 1959; *Buddhist Thought in India* 1962
Dutt, S. *The Buddha and Five After Centuries,* 1957; *Buddhist Monks and Monasteries of India* 1962
Le May, R. *The Culture of South-East Asia: The Heritage of India,* 3rd imp. 1964
Ling, T. O. *Buddha, Marx and God* 1966; *The Buddha's Philosophy of Man: Early Indian Buddhist Dialogues* 1981
Piyadassi, Thera *The Buddha's Ancient Path* 1964
Pye, M. *The Buddha* 1979
Rahula, Walpola *What the Buddha Taught* 2nd ed., 1967
Seckel, D. *The Art of Buddhism* 1964
Tucci, E. *The Religions of Tibet* 1980
Welch, H. *The Buddhist Revival in China* 1968
Woodward, F. L. *Some Sayings of the Buddha* 1938

Chapter Seventeen – **China**

Ch'an, Wing-sit *Religious Trends in Modern China* 1953
Chang, Carsun *The Development of Neo-Confucian Thought* 1957
Creel, H. G. *Confucius and the Chinese Way* 1960; *The Birth of China* 1936
Dobson, W. A. C. H. *Mencius* 1963
Duyvendak, J. J. L. *The Book of Lord Shang* 1928
Forke, A. *Yang Chu's Garden of Pleasure* 1912
Graham, A. C. *The Book of Lieh-tzu* 1960
Levenson, J. R. *Confucian China and its Modern Fate* 1958
Nivison, D. S. and Wright, A. F. (eds.) *Confucianism in Action* 1962
Shryock, J. K. *The Origin and Development of the State Cult of Confucius* 1932
Smith, D. M. *Chinese Religions* 1968; *Confucius* 1973
Waley, A. *The Analects of Confucius* 1938; *The Book of Songs* 1937; *The Nine Songs: A Study of Shamanism in Ancient China* 1955; *The Way and its Power (The Tao Tê Ching)* 1934; *Three Ways of Thought in Ancient China* 1939
Watson, B. *Hsün Tzu – Basic Writings* 1963
Wright, A. F. *Buddhism in Chinese History* 1959
Wright, A. F. (ed.) *The Confucian Persuasion* 1959
Yang, C. K. *Religion in Chinese Society* 1961
Yu-lan, Fung *History of Chinese Philosophy* 1952

Chapter Eighteen – **Japan**

Aston, W. G. *Nihongi: Chronicles of Japan from the earliest times to A.D. 697* 1956
Bellah, R. N. *Tokugawa Religion: The Values of Pre-Industrial Japan* Glencoe, 1957
Blacker, C. *The Catalpa Bow* 1975
Bunce, W. K. *Religions in Japan* 1973
Eliot, C. *Japanese Buddhism* 1959
Hammer, R. J. *Japan's Religious Ferment* 1961
Herbert, J. *Shinto* 1967
Kitagawa, J. M. *Religion in Japanese History* 1966
McFarland, H. N. *The Rush Hour of the Gods* 1967
Sansom, G. B. *A History of Japan* (3 vols.) 1958–61; *A Cultural History of Japan* 1952
Suzuki, D. T. *Zen Buddhism* 1956
Tsunoda, R. *Sources of Japanese Tradition* 1958

Chapter Nineteen – **Judaism**

Agus, J. B. *The Evolution of Jewish Thought* 1960
Browne, L. (ed.) *The Wisdom of Israel* 1955
Buber, M. *The Legends of the Hasidim* 1962
Epstein, I. *The Talmud* 1935; *Judaism* 1960
Friedlander, M. *The Jewish Religion* 1964
Ginzberg, L. *The Legends of the Jews* 1946; *The Mishnah* (trans. H. Danby) 1933; *The Torah* 1962
Jacobs, L. *Principles of the Jewish Faith* 1957; *Hasidic Prayer* 1972
Joseph, M. *Judaism as Creed and Life* 1958
Levy, I. *The Synagogue* 1963
Parkes, J. *The Foundations of Judaism and Christianity* 1960
Roth, C. *A Short History of the Jewish People* 1953

Roth, L. *God and Man in the Old Testament* 1955
Sandmell, S. *The Hebrew Scriptures* 1963
Scholem, G. G. *Major Trends in Jewish Mysticism* 1955
Singer and Bevan (eds.) *The Legacy of Israel* 1948
Strack, H. L. *Introduction to Talmud and Midrash* 1959
Werblowsly (ed.) *Encyclopedia of the Jewish Religion* 1968

Chapter Twenty – **Christianity**

Atiya, Aziz S. *A History of Eastern Christianity* 1968
Barrett, D. B. *World Christian Encyclopedia* 1982
Barraclough, G. (ed.) *The Christian World* 1981
Bettenson, H. (ed.) *Documents of the Christian Church* 2nd ed., 1967; *The Early Christian Fathers* 1956
Chadwick, Owen (general ed.) *The Pelican History of the Church: The Early Church* by H. Chadwick; *The Medieval Church* by R. W. Southern; *The Reformation* by Owen Chadwick; *The Church and the Age of Reason* by G. R. Cragg; *The Church in an Age of Revolution* by A. R. Vidler; *Christian Missions* by Bishop Stephen Neill
Corbishley, S. J. *Roman Catholicism* 1950
Cross, F. L. *Oxford Dictionary of the Christian Church* 1957
Evans, Joan (ed.) *The Flowering of the Middle Ages* 1967
Every, G. *Christian Mythology* 1970
Moland, Einar *Christendom* 1959
Rouse, Ruth and Neill, Stephen (eds.) *A History of the Ecumenical Movement* 2nd ed. revised, 1967
Sperry, W. L. *Religion in America* 1945
Sweet, W. W. *The American Churches* 1947
Toynbee, Arnold (ed.) *The Crucible of Christianity* 1970
Wiles, Maurice *The Making of Christian Doctrine* 1967

Chapter Twenty-one – **Islam**

Arberry, A. J. *The Koran Interpreted* 1955; *The Seven Odes* 1957
Arnold, T. and Guillaume, A. (eds.) *The Legacy of Islam* 1931
Coulson, N. H. *A History of Islamic Law* 1964
Cragg, K. *Counsels in Contemporary Islam* 1965
Fisher, H. J. *Ahmadiyya* 1963
Gaudefroy-Demombynes M. *Muslim Institutions* 1950
Gibb, H. A. R. *Modern Trends in Islam* 1946; *Mohammedanism* 2nd ed., 1953
Gibb, H. A. R. and Kramers, J. H. (eds.) *Shorter Encyclopedia of Islam* 1961
Guillaume, A. (trans.) *A Life of Muhammad* 1955
Hitti, P. K. *History of the Arabs* 8th ed., 1964
Hourani, A. *Arabic Thought in the Liberal Age* 1962
Lammens, H. *Islam, Beliefs and Institutions* 1930
Levy, R. *The Social Structure of Islam* 1957
Lewis, B. *The Arabs in History* 1960
Nasr, S. H. *Living Sufism* 1972
Rahman, F. *Islam* 1966
Schacht, J. *An Introduction to Islamic Law* 1962
Smith, M. *The Way of the Mystics* 1976
Smith, W. C. *Islam in Modern History* 1957
Trimingham, J. S. *The Sufi Orders in Islam* 1971
Watt, W. M. *Muhammad, Prophet and Statesman* 1961; *Bell's Introduction to the Qur'an* 1970
Wensinck, A. J. *The Muslim Creed* 1932

Conclusion

Barrett, D. B. *Schism and Renewal in Africa* 1968
Bonhoeffer, D. *Letters and Papers from Prison* 1956
Bultmann, R. *Christ and Mythology* 1960
Copleston, F. *Religion and the One* 1982
Davies, H. *Christian Deviations* 1954
Dumoulin, H. *Christianity meets Buddhism* 1974
Jung, C. G. *Psychology of the Unconscious* 1919
Kolarz, W. *Religion in the Soviet Union* 1961
Nasr, S. H. *Knowledge and the Sacred* 1981
Parrinder, G. *Comparative Religion* 1962
Schimmel, A. and Falaturi, A. *We Believe in One God* 1979
Schram, S. *Mao Tse-tung* 1967
Tillich, P. *The Shaking of the Foundations* 1962

Photographic Acknowledgements

A. T. A., Stockholm 109 top right; Aerofilms, Boreham Wood 30 bottom; Alinari, Florence 133 top left, 153 bottom, 171 top left, 171 bottom, 172 bottom, 185 bottom, 186 centre; P. Almasy, Neuilly-sur-Seine 85 bottom, 371 top, 371 bottom left, 478 bottom; Anderson, Florence 17 top, 172 top left; Archaeological Survey of India, New Delhi 207 top left, 217 top right, 229, 267 bottom, 269 bottom; Archives Photographiques, Paris 151 bottom left; Arkeoloji Müzeleri, Istanbul 183 top; Art Centrum, Prague 64 top right; Art Gallery of New South Wales, Sydney 53 top; Editions Arthaud, Paris 332 top; Ashmolean Museum, Oxford 109 bottom; Associated Press, London 290 bottom right, 416 top right; Asuka-en 383 top right; Biblioteca Nazionale "Vittorio Emanuele III", Naples 437 top left; Bibliothèque Nationale, Paris 440 bottom left; J. Bottin, Paris 280 bottom, 289 bottom; M. Boyce 183 bottom, 184 top left, 184 top right; W. Braun, Jerusalem 396 bottom; British Library, London 405 bottom right; British Museum, London 18 top left, 75 bottom, 85 top left, 85 top right, 86, 119 top, 119 centre, 119 bottom, 120 bottom, 121 top, 132 centre, 153, 205 bottom right, 239, 267 top, 310 bottom right, 341 bottom left; Camera Press, London 208 bottom, 258 top, 289 top, 290 bottom left, 291 top, 292 top, 292 bottom, 342 top, 342 bottom, 416 bottom, 418 bottom, 428 top right, 428 bottom, 459 top right, 459 bottom left, 459 bottom right, 460 bottom, 477 centre, 499 top left, 499 top right, 499 centre, 499 bottom, 502 bottom right, 511 top right, 511 bottom, 512 top, 512 centre, 512 bottom; J. Allan Cash, London 195 top; Central Press, London 230 bottom; Chester Beatty Library, Dublin 478-9, 479 top, 480 top left; Cincinnati Art Museum, Ohio 185 top; Cleveland Museum of Art, Ohio 332 bottom; C. M. Daniels 186 bottom, 196 bottom; Dawn Studio, Amritsar 257 top right, 257 bottom left; Department of Archaeology, Government of India, Calcutta 270 top left; Robert Descharmes, Paris 152 top right; Dominion Museum, Wellington 51 top right, 52 top; Dumbarton Oaks, Washington D.C. 75 left; Edinburgh University Library 477 top, 477 bottom; William Fagg, London 63 bottom; Foto Felici, Rome 460 top; Les Films du Château, Paris 96 top; Werner Forman, London 309 bottom; Fototeca Unione, Rome 173 bottom, 395 top; Franceschi – Zodiaque 107 top; Freelance Photographers Guild, New York 417 top; Fujimoto Shihachi 374 top; Gabinetto Fotografico Nazionale, Rome 438 top; Sven Gahlin 18 bottom; Gallery of Fine Arts, Yale University, New Haven, Connecticut 186 top; Editions Gallimard, Paris 133 top right; Thomas Gilcrease Institute of American History and Art, Tulsa, Oklahoma 457 top; Photographie Giraudon, Paris 73 top left, 73 top right, 73 bottom, 76 bottom, 108 top, 205 bottom left, 440 top left, 440 bottom right; Goloubew 227 top; Richard and Sally Greenhill, London 18 top left, 228 bottom, 279 centre, 279 bottom right, 331 top left, 341 top left, 341 top right, 416 top left, 458 top left, 511 top left; Gulbenkian Museum of Oriental Art, Durham 269 top left; C. von Fürer-Haimendorf, London 39 top, 39 centre, 39 bottom, 40 top, 40 bottom, 41 top, 41 bottom left, 41 bottom right, 42 top, 42 bottom left, 42 bottom right; Hamlyn Group Picture Library 17 bottom left, 30 top left, 52 bottom, 54 top, 64 bottom left, 64 bottom right, 74-5, 95 top left, 95 top right, 97 bottom right, 174 top left, 184 bottom, 205 top, 240 top, 257 bottom right, 311 top, 359 bottom left, 373 top left, 383 bottom, 394 bottom, 395 bottom, 396 top left, 396 top right, 405 top, 406 bottom, 417 bottom, 418 top, 427 bottom right, 438 centre, 489, 490 bottom left; M. Hétier, Paris 76 top; High Commission for New Zealand, London 51 top left, 51 bottom; Hirmer Fotoarchiv, Munich 132 top, 132 bottom, 133 bottom, 134 top left, 134 top right, 134 bottom, 151 top right, 151 bottom right, 152 bottom; M. Holford, Loughton 95 bottom, 97 bottom left; Alan Hutchison Library, London 196 top, 217 bottom left, 270 top right, 279 top, 359 bottom right, 373 top right, 437 top right, 459 top left, 500 bottom, 501, 502 top, 502 bottom left; Institut Géographique National, Paris 206 top; Israel Sun, Tel Aviv 406 top, 415 top left, 415 top right; Japanese Information Service, London 374 bottom; Camilla Jessel, Twickenham 98; Jewish Museum, New York 393 top, 405 bottom left; Jewish Theological Seminary of America, New York 394 top left; A. F. Kersting, London 131, 439; Kunstmuseum, Basel 415 bottom, 440 top right; Kupferstichkabinett, Berlin 438 bottom; Library of Congress, Washington D.C. 458 bottom; Bildarchiv Foto Marburg 172 top right, 331 top right; Metropolitan Museum of Art, New York 312 bottom, 330 bottom, 479 bottom left, 479 bottom right; Middle East Archive, London 427 top; Monitor Press Features, London 257 top left; Musée de l'Homme, Paris 27 top, 28 top left, 28 top right, 29, 30 top right, 96 bottom, 97 top; Musée Guimet, Paris 269 top right, 310 bottom left, 311 bottom right; Musées Nationaux, Paris 17 bottom right; Museum für Indische Kunst, Berlin 331 bottom; Museum of Antiquities of the University and Society of Antiquaries, Newcastle-upon-Tyne 108 bottom; Museum of Fine Arts, Boston, Massachusetts 217 top left, 384; National Monuments Branch, Dublin 27 bottom; Nationalmuseet, Copenhagen 107 bottom, 110 bottom; National Museum of Victoria, Melbourne 54 centre, 54 bottom; National Palace Museum, Taipei 310 bottom centre, 329; National Portrait Gallery, London 458 top right; William Rockhill Nelson Gallery of Art, Kansas City, Missouri 312 top; Philadelphia Museum of Art, Pennsylvania 73 top centre; Pontificia Commissione di Archeologia Sacra, Rome 427 bottom left; Josephine Powell, Rome 206 bottom, 207 bottom, 218, 240 top right, 240 bottom, 268 bottom, 270 bottom, 480 top right, 490 top; Press and Information Bureau, Government of India, New Delhi 230 top left, 230 top right; Rapho – D. Brihat 394 top right; Real Academia de la Historia, Madrid 437 bottom; Réalités – J.Ph. Charbonnier 373 bottom; Religious Society of Friends, London 457 bottom; Rijksmuseum voor Volkenkunde, Leiden 63 top right; Royal Academy of Arts, London 217 bottom right; Royal Ontario Museum, Toronto 309 top, 310 top, 311 bottom left, 330 top, 341 bottom right; Sakamoto, Tokyo 359 top, 360, 361 top, 361 bottom right, 362 bottom, 372; Seattle Art Museum, Washington 361 bottom left, 362 top, 383 top left, 383 top centre; Soprintendenza alle Antichità della Campania, Naples 174 top right; Soprintendenza alle Antichità dell'Etruria Meridionale, Rome 171 top right; Soprintendenza alle Antichità di Napoli e Caserta, Naples 151 top left; Staatliche Museen zu Berlin 120 top, 152 top left, 228 top left; H. Stierlin, Geneva 74; Wim Swaan, New York 258 bottom, 280 top; W. Thesiger 122 bottom; Thjodminjasafn Islands, Reykjavik 109 top left; Topkapi Sarayi Müzesi, Istanbul 478 top; United Africa Company International, London 63 top left; Universitetets Oldsaksamling, Oslo 110 top; University of Pennsylvania Museum, Philadelphia 121 bottom; Victoria and Albert Museum, London 207 top right, 218 bottom, 227 bottom, 228 top right, 291 bottom; Roger-Viollet, Paris 122 top, 173 top, 174 bottom, 195 bottom, 208 top, 268 top, 279 bottom left, 371 bottom right, 480 bottom, 490 bottom right, 500 top; Walker Art Center, Minneapolis, Minnesota 64 top left; Yale University Art Gallery, New Haven, Connecticut 393 bottom; Yan, Toulouse 28 centre, 28 bottom; ZEFA (U.K.) – Konrad Helbig 154; Ziolo – Held 428 top left.

The diagram at the top of page 290 is from Benjamin Rowland *The Art and Architecture of India* (Pelican History of Art, Third revised edition, 1967) figure 48 page 263. © 1953, 1967 Penguin Books Ltd. Reprinted by permission of Penguin Books Ltd.

Index

References to the captions to the illustrations are indicated in *italic* type.

521

522

526

527